The Selected Works

of

Eugene V. Debs

THE SELECTED WORKS OF EUGENE V. DEBS

This groundbreaking project by Haymarket Books will republish more than 1,000 of the articles, speeches, press statements, interviews, and open letters of labor leader and socialist activist Eugene Victor Debs. More than 1.5 million words will be reproduced in six thick volumes—the vast majority of which seeing print for the first time since the date of their first publication.

Eugene Victor Debs (1855–1926) was a trade union official, magazine editor, political opinion writer, and public orator widely regarded as one of the most important figures in the history of American socialism. Five times a candidate for president of the United States and twice imprisoned for his role as a strike leader and antiwar agitator, Debs remains today an esteemed and iconic figure of twentieth-century political history.

The Selected Works

of

Eugene V. Debs

Volume 1:
Building Solidarity on the Tracks, 1877–1892

edited by
Tim Davenport
and David Walters

Haymarket Books
Chicago, Illinois

Published in 2019 by
Haymarket Books
P.O. Box 180165
Chicago, IL 60618
773-583-7884
www.haymarketbooks.org
info@haymarketbooks.org

ISBNs: 978-1-60846-548-4 (hard cover)
978-1-60846-972-7 (paperback)

Trade distribution:
In the US, Consortium Book Sales and Distribution, www.cbsd.com
In Canada, Publishers Group Canada, www.pgcbooks.ca
In the UK, Turnaround Publisher Services, www.turnaround-uk.com
All other countries, Ingram Publisher Services International,
IPS_Intlsales@ingramcontent.com

This book was published with the generous support of Lannan Foundation
and Wallace Action Fund.

Cover and text design by Eric Kerl.

Printed in Canada by union labor.

Library of Congress Cataloging-in-Publication data is available.

10 9 8 7 6 5 4 3 2 1

Contents

———

1885

1886

1889

1892

Appendix

Introduction

This is the first of a six-volume series gathering the most important writings of American socialist and union organizer Eugene Victor Debs (1855–1926). As there have been more than twenty dedicated volumes and countless scholarly articles focusing upon the five-time Socialist presidential candidate, it is frankly puzzling that no project of similar scope has been previously attempted.[1] Indeed, so much biographical information has seen print that the lanky orator from Terre Haute—he of the fiery speeches, the incorruptible ideals, and the two prison terms—would seem to be a Lincolnesque figure of American history, one needing no introduction. Debs's personal life has been the foil for a historical novel by Irving Stone;[2] he is the stuff of Kurt Vonnegut's fiction;[3] episodes from his childhood have been imaginatively invented to immortalize him as a paragon and prototype in a hagiographic communist children's book of the 1920s;[4] and the sons of strangers have been named in his honor.[5] A symposium of maudlin poetry has been published to laud him.[6] Claims have been laid on the man's political legacy by liberals,[7] social democrats,[8] Trotskyists,[9] mainline communists,[10] independent radicals,[11] and sundry trade unionists from across the ideological spectrum. Indeed, there has been an "enduring cult of hero worship" of Eugene V. Debs on the part of the American left, a phenomenon described succinctly by University of Pittsburgh professor Richard Oestreicher:

> To his Socialist Party comrades and to political soul mates of the Left ever since, Debs was a secular saint, the center of a modern morality play. A talented man who looked as if he were going to be an all-American success story, Debs gave up personal security to become the voice of the downtrodden and dispossessed. Ignoring his own safety, welfare, and even physical health, he spoke eloquently for victims of capitalism who would otherwise not have been heard. Twice he went to jail for refusing to abandon his principles, the second time, at the age of sixty-two, despite the urging of friends who feared that his unsteady health would not survive the rigors of prison. Indeed, when he left prison after three years, he was sick; and he died only five years later without ever regaining his earlier vigor, a martyr to the cause.[12]

Yet for all the books and articles written *about* Gene Debs, a vanishingly small percentage of his millions of preserved words have been gathered for a modern audience. Over the years a few limited attempts have been made, to be sure, including several worthy of mention. Debs's third run for the presidency under the banner of the Socialist Party of America in 1908 provided inspiration for an initial effort to compile and republish some of his speeches and articles.[13] That volume, *Debs: His Life, Writings and Speeches,* edited by Bruce Rogers, carefully gathered a poem, nine speeches, and thirty articles. Of this material, however, just seven pieces date from the nineteenth century and none of these published before 1894—at which time Debs was 40 years old, well into the second half of his life. The Rogers collection was expanded four decades later in a second major attempt to republish some of the key writings of Debs, a book edited by Joseph M. Bernstein, *Writings and Speeches of Eugene V. Debs.*[14] Bernstein added substantial material produced after the publication of Rogers's 1908 book, doubling the number of republished Debs items.[15] Virtually no effort was made to further explore Debs's nineteenth-century writings, however.

To these important republications of Debs's work may be added three lesser-known compilations from the first half of the twentieth century: a slim tome published in 1916 by St. Louis socialist Phil Wagner, *Labor and Freedom: The Voice and Pen of Eugene V. Debs;*[16] a 1919 pamphlet produced by Frank Harris of *Pearson's Magazine* gathering five biographical articles written by Debs for his publication;[17] and a diminutive volume of excerpts released in 1928 by the publishing house of the Workers (Communist) Party of America, *Speeches of Eugene V. Debs,* edited by Alexander Trachtenberg.[18]

It would be four decades before another effort was made to select and present the articles and speeches of Gene Debs for a new audience. *Eugene V. Debs Speaks,* edited by Jean Y. Tussey, was published in 1970 by Pathfinder Press, publishing house of the Socialist Workers Party.[19] Unfortunately, only one of the thirty-four items selected by Tussey could not be found in a previous collection of Debs's writings. Nor did Ronald Radosh, in his 1971 collection, *Debs: Great Lives Observed,* manage to plow new ground.[20]

The first fifteen years of the twenty-first century have seen the publication of two additional volumes selecting Debs's speeches and articles. The first of these, *The Eugene V. Debs Reader: Socialism and the Class Struggle,* edited by William A. Pelz, merely moves thirty-four items from the 1948 Bernstein volume to new covers,[21] while a more recent effort, Lenny Flank's *Writings of Eugene V. Debs: A Collection of Essays by America's Most Famous Socialist,*[22] published in 2009, does manage to save two "new" Debs works from the mists.

The nine projects mentioned above, published over the course of an entire century, have managed to preserve only about one hundred of an estimated four thousand published Debs items between book covers. Of these, a mere nine pieces date from the first half of Debs's literary activity, the years of the nineteenth century. It is to these early years that we shall turn in the present volume.

The Early Years

The Debs story began during the second half of the 1840s in the ancient town of Colmar, located in the Alsatian region of northeastern France. Jean Daniel Debs, Jr.,[23] known as "Daniel" to differentiate boy from father, seemed to be blindly marching through life to a cadence played by the family patriarch, the prosperous owner of a textile mill and scion of a former delegate to the French National Assembly.[24] It was preordained: Daniel was to be educated well and then learn the textile manufacturing game, managing the factory before ultimately taking the reins of the family business. Alas, *the best laid schemes o' mice an' men gang aft agley*[25]—while apprenticing at the mill to learn the details of the production process, young Daniel made a grave error of the heart, falling in love with a working-class girl employed there. His father forgave neither Marguerite Bettrich's social station nor her Roman Catholic religion,[26] and the relationship between stern father and willful son rapidly deteriorated. Following his father's death in 1848, a bitter fight erupted among the family over disposition of his estate, with Daniel receiving a cash payout equivalent to $6,000 rather than the anticipated factory.[27]

Exhausted with familial narrow-mindedness and parochialism, Daniel boldly cut ties and emigrated for a new life in America.[28] Leaving behind his beloved Marguerite, the twenty-seven-year-old Daniel set sail for the United States, docking in New York City on January 20, 1849. Unfortunately for the young transplant, between departure and arrival a confidence man managed to make Daniel's acquaintance well enough to successfully relieve him of the bulk of his inheritance in exchange for a share of a nonexistent New York City tobacco shop.[29] Alone in the great city, Debs made a frantic search for the phantom business, but it proved fruitless. With his nest egg gone, Daniel found himself cast from his comfortable bourgeois upbringing into the ranks of the working class, forced for the first time to sell his labor for a living. Reality was harsh; plans to establish a comfortable home in America for himself and Marguerite began to seem unreachable. Dark clouds of growing melancholy crept into his letters home to France. Fearing a breaking point was near, Marguerite responded to one of Daniel's particularly desperate letters in the summer of 1849 by resolving to join him in America. The pair were married two days after her arrival in New York City, on September 11, 1849. They would remain partners for life.[30]

After a year in New York and a brief repose in Cincinnati, the émigré Debs family relocated in May 1851 to the midwestern town of Terre Haute, Indiana, a community of approximately five thousand souls. The town's French-Canadian heritage was evident in the very name of the place, meaning "High Ground" in the mother tongue.[31] Terre Haute would be the rich earth into which the Debs family set down roots. Located on the eastern bank of the Wabash River, Terre Haute had emerged as a transportation hub, with the community's providential proximity to riverboat transit helping spur its industrial base—agriculture, grain milling, and pork processing. Between 1850 and 1860 the size of the town doubled, before doubling again in the ensuing ten years. It was an era with bright prospects for material advancement for the young and motivated, although such opportunity did not come without sweat. Upon arriving in Terre Haute in 1851, Daniel Debs took a job in a pork slaughterhouse, enduring long hours and miserable conditions in the stifling summer heat before leaving for less detestable work. A series of brief and arduous jobs followed, intersected by a short-lived return to New York.[32] Back in Indiana, Marguerite and Daniel eventually managed to save $40 by 1855,[33] establishing a tiny grocery store with its limited inventory arrayed in the front downstairs room of the family home.[34] A freestanding market would eventually be launched as the Debs family reinvested its profits in the growing business, with the family relocating to relatively comfortable multiroom living quarters located above the store. Daniel Debs and his family would remain in the grocery trade for more than thirty years.[35]

♻

Eugene Victor Debs was born on November 5, 1855. He was the fifth-born of Daniel and Marguerite, their first son and third surviving child, two daughters having died at birth. His parents would later bring five more children into the world, three of them successfully navigating the perils of infancy. Eugene Victor was named by his father after two literary giants of his parents' French homeland—Eugène Sue (1804–1857) and Victor Hugo (1802–1885). Indeed, the intellectual Debs paterfamilias was such a devoted fan of Sue, the novelist of religious rationality and working-class life,[36] that he and his wife would name a second child in his honor, their next-born daughter, Eugenia. To avoid confusion, the similarly named children adopted the nicknames "Gene" and "Jenny," identities retained throughout their lives. A steady diet of books was provided from early years, with the family gathering each Sunday evening, as though for a religious service, for recitation and discussion of literary themes in the work of such classic writers as Goethe, Schiller, and Molière.[37]

Gene was initially enrolled in the private "Old Seminary School" of Terre

Haute, the family's finances by now sufficient to be able to absorb the substantial tuition of $16 per semester. After the conclusion of the Civil War, state funding of public education in Indiana was increased and the public school system improved commensurately; in 1867 Gene was enrolled in Terre Haute's public high school, where he thrived.[38] A good but not a brilliant student, Gene was ranked in the top 20 percent of his class and was the proud recipient of a prize for one term of spelling perfection—a copy of the Holy Bible, inscribed in ink with a stern mandate from his teacher: "Read and obey."[39] In relating this tale of orthographic prowess and its rewards to friends some decades later, Debs added a memorable punch line, chiming in, "I never did either."

This makes for a pithy witticism—indeed, one that has been repeated endlessly by Debs's biographers[40]—but it is a small joke that twists reality preposterously, as even cursory attention to Debs's early writings will readily indicate. The articles and speeches of Eugene V. Debs are positively saturated with biblical quotations and allusions, moving historian David Burns to discuss Debs's religious philosophy at chapter length in his 2013 study, *The Life and Death of the Radical Historical Jesus.*[41] Burns notes the confluence of religious influences upon Debs, including the unorthodox views of his Protestant father and Catholic mother, neither of whom seem to have attended religious services after Gene's early years; the essence of parochial Terre Haute, called a "God-fearing town where evangelical revivals were commonplace"; his familiarity with the literary output of humanists Voltaire, Sue, and Hugo; and his admiration and personal acquaintance with agnostic orator Robert Ingersoll and later dissident religious thinker George Herron.[42]

Gene apparently learned French in the home, it being his parents' native tongue. One is struck by the fact that he never wrote letters to his parents in that language, nor did he incorporate more than a few French words into his writing or speeches—the recurring phrase *avant courier* being one rare example. Debs studied German in the classroom and was additionally exposed to the language through his father's reading aloud to the family each week from the classics. Gene does not seem to have pursued the reading of the German literature of the international socialist movement in later life, although his copious scrapbooks do include a number of articles from the German-language periodical press. Participating in literary and debating societies from his school years, Gene began at an early age to develop the effective public-speaking skills that would ultimately serve him well.[43]

In May 1870 the fourteen-year-old opted to leave school for the remunerative world of work, thus beginning his short career "working on the railroad"—a brief few years of youthful endeavor elevated by hagiography into heroic proletarian myth. Debs played his own part stoking the smoke generator, telling his official biographer David Karsner in 1922 that he "went to work because I had to, because I knew that my mother and father needed my pennies."[44] This dubious assertion is contradicted by the middle-class prosperity of the family's grocery enterprise. Rather, as Debs's most thorough biographer, Cornell University labor historian Nick Salvatore, has observed,

> Skilled railroad workers . . . were among the most respected and highest paid workers in America during the 1870s and 1880s. Tradition held, and it was borne out by the experience of many, that the opportunities for advancement were impressive, even for a young lad beginning in an unskilled trade."[45]

Working on the railroad offered both adventure and the opportunity for advancement for an ambitious young man exploring a future career. The rival recollection of Gene's sister Emily seems more likely correct: that her brother had gone to work of his own volition despite the fact that their parents had pleaded "time and again" for their strong-willed son to return to school.[46]

Gene found his first employment as a paint scraper in the shops of the Vandalia Railroad, earning the magnificent sum of fifty cents a day. His salary doubled in December 1871 when he advanced to a job firing the switch engines that were used to connect and unhook railcars in the yards of the Terre Haute and Indianapolis Railroad.[47] Firemen performed an arduous and dirty job, loading and breaking coal in a car behind the engine and feeding it into a small opening in the firebox inside the locomotive cab. The fireman also monitored the firebox crown sheet,[48] making sure it was constantly covered with water to prevent an explosion, and assisted the engineer as required. Engineer and fireman worked as a team, albeit in a hierarchical relationship akin to that of master and apprentice, with the engineer receiving approximately double the wages of the fireman, the prospective engineer-to-be.[49] These represented two of the four "running trades" of locomotive operations, crafts that included the all-important conductors—the "captains" of train operations, who were in charge of collecting fares and assisting passengers, maintaining freight manifests, inspecting each car and its couplings, and supervising train personnel. These supervised personnel included particularly the brakemen, the fourth and final craft of the running trades, who manually operated brakes and switches, coupled and uncoupled cars, served as signalmen as necessary, and announced arrivals at incoming stations. In the era before air brakes, some of the brakemen's work was performed on top of a moving train, even in inclement weather, with brute strength employed to manually adjust a number of large brake wheels.[50] It is no exaggeration to say that nineteenth-century locomotive brakemen were employed in the single deadliest occupation in America, with a death toll exceeding the coal and hard-rock mining industries.[51]

Concurrent with his railroad work, Debs managed to return to the classroom, regularly taking courses over three years at a local business college.[52]

Gene was soon promoted from the mundane chores of a switch engine fireman tethered to the rail yard to firing locomotives on the 70-mile run between Terre Haute and Indianapolis.[53] This short-lived joy came to an abrupt end when a layoff during the panic of 1873 put him out of work. Gene was spurred to leave home in September 1874 for greener pastures, traveling to East St. Louis, Illinois, where a lengthy search landed him a job as a substitute night fireman in a railway switch yard. Away from his close-knit family for the first time at the age of nineteen, Debs took a room in a boardinghouse and made the acquaintance of a local French family during his brief sojourn. A speedy return to the secure parental nest was made the very next month, when Gene found himself unable to land a permanent post in the St. Louis area.[54]

౪౨

On the evening of February 27, 1875, Joshua Leach, the founder of a new labor organization, paid a visit to Terre Haute, Indiana, the self-proclaimed "crossroads of America." There he hoped to organize a new lodge of his fledgling fraternal order, a society known as the Brotherhood of Locomotive Firemen (B of LF).[55] It was an organization of and for the workers. The early B of LF was not a trade union in the modern sense, maintaining a staunch position against the use of the strike and professing no aspirations to bargain collectively on behalf of its members. It was, rather, a fraternal lodge and insurance company—a closed society that provided the comradeship of regular personal communication with others in the field; imparted the unifying power of membership, ritual, and ceremony; and organized social activities with the community at large. It gained popularity as a mechanism for railroad workers, men of limited financial means who labored in a frequently deadly profession, to obtain comparatively inexpensive insurance against dismemberment and loss of life.[56] Although he would never fire a locomotive again, Gene Debs nevertheless at that time considered himself to be a coal scooper between jobs; the B of LF seems to have answered an idealistic youthful yearning to participate in a meritorious activity larger than himself. Gene ran for and won election as the first recording secretary of the new Vigo Lodge and would, for three of its first four years, represent his lodge brothers at the annual national convention of the order.[57]

Simultaneous with his activity in the Brotherhood of Locomotive Firemen, Debs embarked upon a new career path—one having nothing to do with the transportation industry. Coming from a family of grocers, Debs was hired in 1875 by Hulman & Company, a large regional wholesale supplier to the grocery trade, purported to be one of the largest such firms west of New York. Daniel Debs was a customer, neighbor, and friend of the firm's proprietor, Herman Hulman, a relationship that paved the way for the employment of his son.[58] Debs would remain with the Hulman firm for five years, gaining stature and authority over time.[59] He would later claim that the move from the dangerous job of railway fireman to mundane work as a wholesale grocery warehouseman had been a conscious decision made to ease his beloved mother's mind.[60] One must treat such a statement with caution, however; Debs's commitment to business school and his subsequent political career as an elected white-collar city employee hints at a different youthful agenda. Similarly, Debs's protestation during his sunset years that he had left the grocery business owing to his being "unable to tolerate" the "grabbing for yourself" implicit in petty commercial enterprise smacks of retrospective self-idealization or false memory.[61]

In his spare time, Debs was active in cofounding and leading a local Terre Haute organization known as the Occidental Literary Club, a debating society and lyceum that hosted lectures by special guest speakers. Under the group's auspices Debs met three personal heroes: abolitionist Wendell Phillips and agnostic orator Robert G. Ingersoll in 1878, and pioneer of the women's movement Susan B. Anthony in 1880.[62]

The young Gene Debs was, in a word, ambitious. Money was never the object; rather, Debs was a young man in a hurry, anxious to exert his independent "manhood," to build reputation and status, to make good in the world. He was aided by a friendly, winning way with strangers and a carefully developed oratorical prowess that allowed his enthusiasm and personal magnetism to shine. This skill set proved a perfect fit for a life in politics; local Democratic Party leaders, noting the youngster's golden tongue and a palpable earnestness that could win a room, were eager to latch on to the blue-eyed Alsatian as a potential future star. And so, just as Debs had abandoned the uncertainties of railroad work for the stability of a job in the wholesale food industry in 1875, he left the grocery business for a career in politics in 1879, still remaining engaged with his beloved Brotherhood of Locomotive Firemen in an ever-growing capacity.

Debs's first venture into electoral politics came in the Terre Haute city election of 1879. During this period of American history, primary elections were largely unknown; rather, parties assembled their slates of nominees in closed conventions of the political faithful. Announcing his candidacy for Terre Haute city clerk in March, the twenty-three-year-old Debs became a part of a field of five local Democrats seeking their party's nomination for the paid government position—a list of prospects that included the incumbent officeholder. Debs positioned himself as an outsider, joining with city attorney candidate Thomas Harper as part of a "reform" slate, running as good-government advocates in opposition to the self-interested. The charismatic Debs quickly gained traction, motivating two regulars to quit the campaign so as not to split the vote against him. Gene triumphed nonetheless, garnering 16 of 30 votes at the city convention to gain the Democratic nomination. Bolstered by support from local business leaders, many of whom were Republicans acquainted with Debs through his employment at Hulman & Company, Debs then swept to victory in the May general election, winning majorities in five of the city's six electoral wards in a three-way race against Republican and Greenback Labor Party candidates. Debs's 2,222 votes proved to be more than those accorded Benjamin Havens, the successful Democratic candidate for mayor.[63]

Although he had run for office under the vague and ill-defined slogan of "reform," Gene's service as an elected city official was ordinary, with the youngster winning plaudits for the effective performance of his duties. The local press noted the efficiency with which he conducted the city's business and his thoroughness in keeping the citizenry apprised of the activities of the Terre Haute city council.[64] Debs did nothing to alienate the local Democratic establishment, campaigned on behalf of the party's ticket in 1880, and was renominated without incident for a second term in 1881—a race that he won easily.[65] Debs would serve the entire four years of his consecutive terms as Terre Haute's city clerk, departing the job only after the election of 1883, by which time he had successfully made the transition to a new position of status and importance, secretary-treasurer of the B of LF and editor of its monthly official organ, *Locomotive Firemen's Magazine*.

Local Democratic worthies remained eager to tap Debs for high office. In 1884 the twenty-nine-year-old was nominated by the Democrats for a place in the Indiana state legislature in the Eighth Assembly District, encompassing Terre Haute and the rural areas of Vigo County. Once again, Debs demonstrated a native aptitude for retail politics, winning majorities in four of the six city wards and garnering sufficient votes from the townships and rural areas of the county to emerge victorious. Debs's crossover appeal to voters other than Democrats was obvious, with his vote tally in Vigo County exceeding the number of votes offered to Democrats Grover Cleveland for president and John Lamb for Congress, both of whom emerged victorious.[66] As a freshman legislator, Debs was afforded the high honor of nominating for reelection Senator Daniel W. Voorhees, a fellow Terre Hautean, who was dutifully returned to Washington by the legislature's Democratic majority.[67] Drawing upon his Brotherhood of Locomotive Firemen experience, Debs self-identified as a reform-minded labor representative rather than a member of the conservative Democratic establishment, introducing bills relating to railway safety and establishment of liability of employers for injuries suffered by employees in on-the-job accidents. Both of these pieces of proposed legislation passed the Democratic-controlled House of Representatives, only to be so badly gutted by amendments in the more conservative Senate that they were finally withdrawn from consideration.[68]

On June 9, 1885, at the zenith of his six-year apprenticeship as an aspiring Democratic politician, Gene Debs married Katherine "Kate" Metzel, stepdaughter of a wealthy Terre Haute druggist. Kate began the couple's life together as a traditional "helpmate," maintaining the home while acting as a secretary and personal assistant for her ambitious husband. Four years after their marriage, by which time Debs had become a well-compensated functionary of the rapidly growing and prosperous Brotherhood of Locomotive Firemen, Gene and Kate Debs would have a large home built in one of Terre Haute's best neighborhoods. The house, with its expansive front porch and costly imported tile in the dining room, remained the family residence for the duration of the couple's lives, although Gene would spend protracted periods away from home as a touring orator and sometime candidate for political office.[69] The couple never had children.

గ౼

Each of the various railway crafts established their own fraternal benefit societies during the years of rapid railway expansion following the Civil War. The first of these was the Brotherhood of the Running Board, founded in 1863, subsequently renamed the Brotherhood of Locomotive Engineers. This organization gradually gained its place in the world, providing a model for other railway crafts, including the Order of Railway Conductors, established in 1868, and the Brotherhood of Locomotive Firemen, organized in 1873. As a member of the B of LF and the leading figure of its Lodge No. 16 from its launch in early 1875, Debs was an active member of the organization from its pioneer years and consequently able to assume a place of national importance and influence in a comparatively short period of time. He regularly attended annual conventions of the B of LF as the delegate of Vigo Lodge, beginning in 1876.[70] He was an enthusiastic reader of the brotherhood's monthly magazine launched in December of that year, penning an adulatory letter of congratulation to editor William N. Sayre.[71] When its chief executive officer, Grand Master W. R. Worth, proved unable to attend the opening of the organization's 1877 annual convention in Indianapolis, it was to the enthusiastic Gene that the other officers turned to deliver a keynote address summarizing the work of the B of LF.[72] Debs was elected to the ceremonial position of grand marshal of the B of LF by the 1877 convention, and at the following year's convention in Buffalo was unanimously elected associate editor of *Locomotive Firemen's Magazine*.[73] Despite his "associate" status, Debs seems to have begun writing immediately, and a portion of the magazine's unsigned editorial content from the next two years can be attributed with confidence to his pen.[74] Debs's written output became more voluminous with his July 1880 promotion to full editorship of *Locomotive Firemen's Magazine*. He would remain in the editorial chair until the fall of 1894, publishing approximately 170 monthly issues of the journal—a total of perhaps 2 million editorial words.

Debs's thinking evolved enormously over time—a transformation paralleled by ideas of the American labor movement in general and the attitudes of society at large as the Gilded Age of corporate authority gave way to the Progressive Era of popular reform. Every serious Debs biographer since the publication of David A. Shannon's influential 1951 article, "Eugene V. Debs: Conservative Labor Editor," has made note of the future socialist's early-1880s commitment to the primacy of self-improvement and the notion of collaboration between railway workers and their employers in common cause for prosperity. Throughout the 1870s and the first half of the 1880s, the Brotherhood of Locomotive Firemen and the sibling orders of engineers and conductors saw their function as one of social service to their memberships and as brokers of reliable labor to their employers. Railwaymen were a notoriously hard-drinking, transient, and ornery lot; the railway brotherhoods attempted to provide a civilizing influence, urging obedience to workplace regulations, disciplining alcohol abuse and sexual impropriety, and attempting to build a sense of neatness, pride of craftsmanship, and loyalty to the employer and the brotherhood alike.[75] Once orderly and faithful behavior was instilled, the brotherhoods believed, then their members would find themselves regarded as desirable employees by intelligently managed modern railroads, and fair and appropriate remuneration would inevitably follow.

Debs's gradual embrace of working-class consciousness, his adoption of anti-corporate politics, and his growing acceptance of the necessity of class struggle for economic improvement is one fundamental thread to be seen in this book.

✑

The second half of the 1880s was a time of realignment for both Debs and the Brotherhood of Locomotive Firemen. Debs set aside personal political aspirations and intensified his commitment to the B of LF as an institution and the organized labor movement as a whole. Working full time as the paid grand secretary-treasurer of the prosperous and growing B of LF, the newly minted labor official Debs began to look at the wageworkers of the United States with a fresh set of eyes. Pushed forward by rank-and-file demands for improved wages, Debs began to move past simple platitudes relating to human perfection through temperance, cleanliness, and thrift toward more mature consideration of such systemic issues as unemployment and poverty and their offspring: hunger, criminality, child labor, and despair. Socialism was never part of Debs's agenda during this interlude. Rather, Debs's grand vision revolved around the achievement of equality of employees with their employers at the bargaining table during the wage negotiation process—a parity that would be possible in the railroad industry only as the result of federation on a broad basis.[76] Through the unified action of the brotherhoods of the railway running trades—engineers, firemen, brakemen, and conductors, together with the switchmen who operated the yards—unfair unilaterally imposed wages dictated by railroad operators would become unthinkable, owing to the likelihood of a financially devastating strike. A new era would be ushered in, featuring the "patient consideration of grievances when presented" though the mechanism of voluntary arbitration.[77]

Debs saw the right of workers to organize as fundamental and inalienable. He asserted with equal force the right of workers to not join a labor association, should they so choose—a perspective regarded today as "open shop."[78] He held an intermediate perspective toward the labor theory of value as advanced by Karl Marx, declaring on the one hand that "only work produces revenues, only work produces wealth," while taking umbrage to the notion that labor itself was a commodity, feeling the equation of human lives with inanimate commodity inputs to be dehumanizing, a relic of slavery, and a severe obstacle to parity between employers and their employees at the negotiating table.[79]

Full employment was a paramount goal for Debs. A strong Protestant work ethic underlay this worldview, with Debs asserting that "the fruit of employment is virtue, that of idleness, vice." The solution of the unemployment problem, to Debs's thinking, was as simple as shortening the hours of labor, with a move from the ten-hour day to the eight-hour day instantly creating massive new opportunities for the jobless to find gainful employment.[80] Debs was deeply committed to the idea that America's fundamental social ailment was a maldistribution of wealth, and he earnestly believed that politics, pulpit, and press were corrupted by this inequality. It would be the effective use of democratic processes, with the working people of the nation making use of the ballot in unison, that would make fundamental change possible, according to Debs. All the working class asked, he naively asserted, was "simple justice" and "honest pay"—an equitable share of the wealth it created. Only then, at last, "labor troubles will cease, the strike, the lockout, the boycott will disappear, and the senseless gabble about the conflict between capital and labor will cease."[81]

❧

The 1888 strike against the Chicago, Burlington & Quincy Railroad Company (CB&Q, known colloquially as the "Burlington," the "Quincy," and the "Q") was a seminal event in American transportation history and put a brutal end to any vague vision that the lion of capitalism would someday congregate blissfully with the labor lamb. The strike began with the grievances of the engineers, including complaints about unpaid work switching cars, unreasonable lengths of time away from home, and demands for pay for time wasted when delayed on the road. The enginemen also sought an appeals process for unjust discharge and institution of a mileage-based system of pay, as was standard with other rail lines of the Midwest.[82] Under the existing pay system, engineers were paid a fixed rate per trip, a figure that varied substantially depending on the route's importance. A fourteen-member grievance committee of the Brotherhood of Locomotive Engineers (B of LE) for the Burlington line had been established early in 1886, which had drawn up a set of rules to be brought before management—provisions that called for adjustment of the rate of pay of locomotive firemen in fixed proportion to the rate of pay of engineers.[83] A parallel grievance committee of fourteen members of the B of LF was subsequently established and the two committees joined into a single bargaining unit for both trades of enginemen in January 1888. A joint set of proposals to the company was compiled.[84]

General manager of the CB&Q Henry B. Stone had defended the current system of rules and compensation and an impasse was reached on February 23, 1888, with conservative head of the B of LE Peter M. Arthur sanctioning a strike unless passenger locomotive engineers were paid at a rate of not less than 3.5 cents per mile.[85] Last-minute negotiations had proved fruitless, and at noon on Sunday, February 26, a strike against the CB&Q was announced to begin at 4:00 a.m. the following day. The suddenness of the strike caught company officials by surprise, with the company seemingly believing that ample time remained for further negotiation. The work stoppage on February 27 was almost universal, with only 22 engineers and 23 firemen out of the 2,137 enginemen employed by the company crossing picket lines.[86]

The scarce human commodity were the locomotive engineers, with the B of LE banking on an assumption that there were fewer than three hundred unemployed locomotive operators in the entire country; this, if true, would make the simultaneous walkout of more than one thousand engineers an insurmountable obstacle. The strikers had believed that the railroad would be forced to shut down owing to the lack of operational personnel, but the railroad successfully raised a motley array of office workers, mechanics, shop workers, conductors, and brakemen to run the engines in the first days after the strike. A hunt for permanent replacements was immediately begun. The company posted notices up and down the Burlington line announcing that all workers who failed to report for duty before noon on February 29 would be considered terminated. Applications for the job of fireman began to accumulate, many from rural men who had never before worked in an engine but for whom the task of breaking coal and stoking a boiler seemed sufficiently simple and adequately remunerative.[87]

Burlington officials retained another powerful card in their hand—the bitter enmity between the B of LE and the Knights of Labor (K of L), an organizational rival for the affections and support of railroad workers. Resentment was deep in K of L circles over the way the B of LE had kept the trains running on the Southwest system during an 1886 strike of K of L shopmen, thereby contributing mightily to the failure of the work action. Adding insult to injury, the collapse of the 1886 Southwest strike was followed by Grand Chief Arthur requiring all B of LE members who held dual membership in the K of L to quit the latter organization or face expulsion.[88] Despite official warnings in the *Journal of the Knights of Labor* that K of L members should respect the B of LE strike, unemployed union members were in no mood to lend support to an organization that had contributed to the defeat of their own interests only recently; hundreds of railroaders, many of whom were unemployed Knights, descended upon Chicago to fill the jobs of brotherhood strikers. Moreover, the two other brotherhoods representing the running trades—the Order of Railway Conductors (ORC) and the Brotherhood of Railroad Brakemen (BRB)—held aloof from the enginemen's strike, continuing to work aboard trains operated by scab crews in the cab. The costly strike faltered. Even the eleventh-hour decision of the Switchmen's Mutual Aid Association (SMAA) to join the ranks of strikers made little difference to the final outcome of the conflict, which was finally called off on January 8, 1889.

Disunity between rival labor organizations spelled catastrophe for the Burlington strike. To Debs the true culprits in labor's own camp were apparent.

cro

The limitations of isolated craft-based railway brotherhoods fighting a united railroad corporation had become amply evident to Debs. A superior form of organization to unite trade-based railway brotherhoods in common cause for just and appropriate wages had become the order of the day. Debs became the most outspoken cheerleader of "federation for mutual support" of the brotherhoods of the railroad running trades, the engineers, firemen, conductors, and brakemen, as well as their closely related brethren of the railway yards, the switchmen. Debs explicitly dismissed the notion of amalgamation of the "separate and distinct organizations" into one conglomerate, instead seeking a new external mechanism to exact solidarity among the brotherhoods when one of its affiliated organizations was "driven to the necessity of making a stand for its rights." Debs's *Locomotive Firemen's Magazine* emerged as a de facto organizing nexus for a new federative railroad labor organization.[89]

Debs was hindered both by the jealous professional bureaucracies of brotherhood functionaries, seeking to hold what was "theirs," as well as a general disdain on the part of the higher-skilled and more highly compensated crafts—the engineers and the conductors—toward joint action with their economic inferiors, the semi-skilled laborers working as firemen, brakemen, and switchmen.[90] Debs argued repeatedly for a general unity of the brotherhoods representing these crafts on the basis of equality regardless of remuneration, but until the summer of 1888 no concrete mechanism for achievement of this principle had emerged.[91]

Still, the federation idea moved forward. In September 1888, the B of LF at its Atlanta convention declared its support for formal alliance of the railroad running trades and the switchmen of the rail yards. Two other brotherhoods rapidly answered the call, each making a stand for federation at their fall annual conventions, with the Switchmen's Mutual Aid Association and the Brotherhood of Railroad Brakemen voting unanimously to join the firemen in a formal alliance. It fell to the powerful Brotherhood of Locomotive Engineers, meeting in Richmond, Virginia, in November, to ultimately decide the matter. Despite their ongoing alliance with the B of LF in the Burlington strike, the B of LE yet again refused federation, delivering a mortal blow to hopes for a monolithic alliance of the running trades. Debs sought to paint this pivotal defeat optimistically, noting it had taken three years for an initial entreaty of the firemen to the engineers for joint action such as that which had been employed against the Chicago, Burlington & Quincy to be acted upon favorably; realistically, more time would be needed for the engineers to come around.[92]

Despite the refusal of the engineers to participate, the efforts of Debs and others to achieve railway federation bore fruit in 1889 with the establishment of the Supreme Council of United Orders of Railway Employees, a small directorate of nine top officials, three each from the three constituent railway brotherhoods—firemen, brakemen, and switchmen. This body included Debs as one of the representatives of the firemen. The centralized group was to meet annually, holding additional sessions to deal with emergencies and critical events as required. The decisions of the Supreme Council regarding strikes were to be binding upon the member organizations. Virtual unanimity of the body was required for action.

The main organization of the conductors, the Order of Railway Conductors, proved to be even more hostile to the notion of federation than the engineers, with its 1888 convention reaffirming the group's anti-strike policy despite growing support among the order's rank and file for use of the work stoppage as a means of "protection." Debs responded to this further setback with the burning of bridges, hailing "with undisguised satisfaction" the November 15, 1888, launch in Los Angeles of a new rival railway brotherhood for conductors, the Brotherhood of Railway Conductors—a group that promised the use of the strike to gain concessions and defend its organizational interests.[93]

The story of the development of the Supreme Council and its subsequent demise in the aftermath of a dirty jurisdictional war between the organized brakemen and switchmen is another important theme of this volume.

~

By the opening of the 1890s, Debs had begun to absorb the ideas of radical populism and was well on the path to activity in working-class politics. In his article "What Can We Do for Working People?" Debs explicitly rejected the paternalistic paradigm, declaring the "whole business of doing something for working people is disgusting and degrading to the last degree." Instead, he called for working people to liberate themselves by combining, federating, cooperating, and acting in concert, making use of their numerical superiority to make "peaceful revolution" by means of the ballot box and thereby achieve "self-management," adequate pay, and true freedom.[94] Not only did Debs advocate adoption of the eight-hour day as a humanitarian and employment-bolstering standard, he was now willing to advocate a general strike to achieve the aim. "If the ring of the anvil, the click of the shuttle, the whir and buzz of spindle and wheel can't be permitted to sing in concert the triumph of justice to labor, let them remain silent," he advised, optimistically predicting that "one day will suffice."[95]

Debs greeted the establishment of the People's Party with sympathy, noting the enthusiasm of the delegates to an organizational convention held in Cincinnati in May 1891, and the timeliness of their program advocating looser money and other reform measures.[96] He touted the "new party" in a syndicated article published in various newspapers the same month, declaring that its orators would "plead the cause of justice to workingmen, the wealth producers of the country" in a coming battle to "overcome the power of organized capital, organized capitalists, [and] the plutocratic class."[97] Change was in the wind as he celebrated Labor Day in 1891, with Debs proclaiming that "the era of robbery and of degradation is drawing to a close" and that the actual "dangerous masses" threatening society's peace and stability were not workers, "but those who use their money power to filch from labor its just rewards."[98] The advocates of labor, regarded by a vast swath of "respectable society" as rabble-rousers and heretics to the gospel of American commerce, suffered a fate akin to that of the abolitionists of yore, Debs averred, working in pursuit of a righteous cause against all the slings and arrows of moneyed society and its press, pulpit, professorate, and politicians.[99]

An early version of a class-conscious and radical Debs had emerged. By 1892, Gene Debs's personal journey from paternalistic careerist to radical agitator was nearly complete.

General Series Notes

The Selected Works of Eugene V. Debs will present his most important writings in six chronological volumes. Each book will include a brief introduction touching upon the major activities of Debs's life during the period of coverage and pointing toward key elements of his evolving thought. Archaic spelling, idiosyncratic punctuation, misspelled names, misquoted sources, and typographical errors appearing in the original published versions have not been treated as sacrosanct, but rather have been silently corrected and standardized for consistency and readability. A few words from defective source documents that had to be guessed from context are provided within square brackets, as are substantive clarifications provided by the editors. The inclusion of full articles rather than excerpts has been given high priority, although a few items have been shortened for reasons of space or clarity. These editorial alterations have been marked by ellipses (. . .) for very short deletions and asterisks (* * *) for longer content removals. Debs himself periodically used a question mark inside parentheses to denote irony about the apparent misapplication of a term or phrase. This editorial oddity has been retained.

Titles of articles and speeches as they appeared in the press varied greatly from publication to publication. Those appearing in *Locomotive Firemen's Magazine* were written by Debs himself and have been generally retained without change unless the same title was used multiple times, as Debs was wont to do, e.g., "Federation," "The Knights of Labor," "The Supreme Council," etc. A few Debs-generated titles that are particularly non-descriptive of actual content have been revised. The titles of articles and speeches appearing in publications edited by others have been either kept or rewritten for clarity as deemed most appropriate; those appearing previously in reprints of Debs's works have been retained to avoid confusion in almost every instance. Whenever titles have been changed, original names are provided at the end of the piece, along with other publication information.

Material has been chosen with a view to illustrating the evolution of Debs's thinking. Mundane contemporary affairs have been accorded low priority; matters touching on the events of the broader labor movement and society at large have been given closest attention. No material has been omitted or deleted for ideological reasons. We emphasize that Gene Debs was neither a saint nor a savant, but rather an evolving human being who was a product of his times, exhibiting at various times crassly individualistic aspirations; ethnic, racial, and gender biases; and ideological inconsistencies. We have attempted to chronicle these foibles and flaws rather than hide them through tendentious selection of content.

Debs never wrote a book in his lifetime, nor did he attempt to compile his memoirs.[100] All of his literary output was of an oratorical or journalistic nature, with the great majority of this material published as newspaper or magazine articles or speeches reproduced in pamphlet form. The editors attempted to review at least cursorily every known article, speech, or pamphlet by Debs for the time period covered by this volume. While this goal was more or less successfully realized, at least one potentially significant item out of more than 1,250 cataloged for the period of this first volume has escaped review: a January 8, 1885, political speech appearing in the Indianapolis press.

While the editors have received no financial support from any individual or institution in the preparation of this volume, they have nevertheless benefited immensely from the activity of others in the world of Debs scholarship, whose work is listed in the footnotes below. The editors additionally wish to thank Cinda May and Kendra McCrea of Cunningham Memorial Library, Indiana State University, and Ben Kite of the Eugene V. Debs Foundation, for their courtesy and assistance. Our friend Martin Goodman of the Riazanov Digital Library Project has aided in the investigation of certain rare publications from New York libraries. Similarly, the importance of radical booksellers to the cause of independent scholarship, especially John Durham and Alexander Akin of Bolerium Books in San Francisco and Lorne Bair of Winchester, Virginia, is worthy of mention. We also thank Nisha Bolsey, Amelia Ayrelan Iuvino, Eric Kerl, and Michael Trudeau, who skillfully handled the manuscript for Haymarket Books, as well as the entire Haymarket editorial board for their unflinching support of the Debs project.

The outstanding contribution to Debs scholarship was made by historian J. Robert Constantine and former Tamiment Library archivist Gail Malmgreen, with their twenty-one-reel microfilm collection and printed guide, *The Papers of Eugene V. Debs, 1834–1945*. The editors note their debt to this pioneering effort to chronicle and collect the speeches, articles, and correspondence of Gene Debs—it is impossible to imagine the successful completion of this project without such an expert plowing of the field having previously been made. This material has already been harvested by Mr. Constantine for his outstanding three-volume collection, *Letters of Eugene V. Debs*, published by University of Illinois Press in 1990. The editors hope that these volumes edited by Mr. Constantine will occupy every shelf next to the volumes of *The Selected Works of Eugene V. Debs* and be viewed as integral parts of the same project.

It is a matter of regret that Bob Constantine, the dean of Debs studies, died in 2017 at the age of ninety-three, before the editors were able to communicate news of this project to him. It is to his memory that this series is dedicated.

Notes

1. A chronological list of the most important biographical sources on Debs in English should include the following: Stephen Marion Reynolds, "Life of Eugene V. Debs," in *Debs: His Life, Writings and Speeches* (Girard, KS: Appeal to Reason, 1908), 1–76; David Karsner, *Debs: His Authorized Life and Letters* (New York: Boni and Liveright, 1919) and *Talks with Debs in Terre Haute* (New York: New York Call, 1922); Floy Ruth Painter, *That Man Debs and His Life Work* (Bloomington, IN: Indiana University, 1929); McAllister Coleman, *Eugene V. Debs: A Man Unafraid* (New York: Greenberg, 1930); Ray Ginger, *The Bending Cross: A Biography of Eugene Victor Debs* (New Brunswick, NJ: Rutgers University Press, 1949; reissued by Haymarket Books); H. Wayne Morgan, *Eugene V. Debs: Socialist for President* (Syracuse, NY: Syracuse University Press, 1962); Bernard J. Brommel, *Eugene V. Debs: Spokesman for Labor and Socialism* (Chicago: Charles H. Kerr, 1978); Nick Salvatore, *Eugene V. Debs: Citizen and Socialist* (Urbana, IL: University of Illinois Press, 1982); J. Robert Constantine, "Biographical Sketch," in Constantine and Gail Malmgreen (eds.), *The Papers of Eugene V. Debs, 1834–1945: A Guide to the Microfilm Edition* (New York: Microfilming Corporation of America, 1983), 4–33 (material which was adapted in the introduction to his three-volume *Letters of Eugene V. Debs*); and Ernest Freeberg, *Democracy's Prisoner: Eugene V. Debs, the Great War, and the Right to Dissent* (Cambridge, MA: Harvard University Press, 2010).

2. Irving Stone, *Adversary in the House* (New York: Doubleday, 1947).

3. Kurt Vonnegut (1922–2007), a native of Indiana who styled himself a latter-day Debsian, if there is such a thing, made Eugene Debs a recurring figure in some of his later work.

4. Henry T. Schnittkind, *The Story of Eugene Debs* (Boston: Independent Workmens Circle, 1929).

5. One of these, Eugene "Debbs" Potts (1908–2003), was a conservative Democratic member of the Oregon State Senate for nearly a quarter century.

6. Ruth Le Prade, ed., *Debs and the Poets* (Pasadena, CA: Upton Sinclair, 1920).

7. Arthur M. Schlesinger, Jr., introduction to *Writings and Speeches of Eugene V. Debs* (New York: Hermitage Press, 1948), v–xiii.

8. The literature is voluminous but see, for example, August Claessens, *Eugene Victor Debs: A Tribute* (New York: Rand School Press, 1946).

9. James P. Cannon, *E. V. Debs: The Socialist Movement of His Time—Its Meaning for Today* (New York: Pioneer Publishers, 1956).

10. Elizabeth Gurley Flynn, *Debs and Dennis: Fighters for Peace* (New York: New Century Publishers, 1950).

11. Howard Zinn, "Eugene V. Debs and the Idea of Socialism," *Progressive*, January 1999.

12. Richard Oestreicher, "Saint Gene: A Review Essay," *Indiana Magazine of History*, vol. 88, no. 1 (March 1992), 49.

13. Reynolds, *Debs: His Life, Writings, and Speeches*. According to David Karsner, this book was compiled by Stephen Marion Reynolds, who contributed the biographical introduction.

14. Joseph M. Bernstein, ed., *Writings and Speeches of Eugene V. Debs.*, introduction by Arthur M. Schlesinger (New York: Hermitage Press, 1948).

15. Despite this expansion, a mere five nineteenth-century Debs articles were selected for publication.

16. Eugene V. Debs, *Labor and Freedom: The Voice and Pen of Eugene V. Debs*, introduction by Henry M. Tichenor (St. Louis: Phil Wagner, 1916).

17. Eugene V. Debs, *Eugene V. Debs, Pastels of Men*, introduction by Frank Harris (New York: *Pearson's Magazine*, 1919).

18. Alexander Trachtenberg, ed., *Voices of Revolt, Volume IX: Speeches of Eugene V. Debs: With a Critical Introduction* (New York: International Publishers, 1928).

19. Jean Y. Tussey, ed., *Eugene V. Debs Speaks*, introduction by James P. Cannon (New York: Pathfinder Press, 1970).

20. Ronald Radosh, ed., *Debs: Great Lives Observed* (Englewood Cliffs, NJ: Prentiss-Hall, 1971).

21. William A. Pelz, ed., *The Eugene V. Debs Reader: Socialism and the Class Struggle*, introduction by Howard Zinn (Chicago: Institute of Working Class History, 2000).

22. Lenny Flank, ed., *Writings of Eugene V. Debs: A Collection of Essays by America's Most Famous Socialist* (St. Petersburg, FL: Red and Black Publishers, 2008).

23. Jean Daniel Debs, Jr. was born December 4, 1820, and died November 27, 1906. He was known as "Dandy" to his children.

24. Salvatore, *Debs: Citizen and Socialist*, 8.

25. From "To a Mouse" (1786), by Robert Burns (1759–1796).

26. Marguerite Marie Bettrich Debs died on April 29, 1906. She was known as "Daisy" to her children.

27. The sum comes from the testimony of Debs's sister Emily in conversation with David Karsner in the early 1920s, confirmed by Gene, and cited in Karsner, *Talks with Debs*, 72.

28. Brommel, *Debs: Spokesman for Labor and Socialism*, 13.

29. Karsner, citing testimony of Emily Debs Mailloux, *Talks with Debs*, 74.

30. Brommel, *Debs: Spokesman for Labor and Socialism*, 13.

31. According to the testimony of Emily Debs Mailloux, Terre Haute's French-Canadian connection was instrumental in its selection by Daniel and Marguerite Debs. See Karsner, *Talks with Debs*, 75.

32. Constantine, *The Papers of Debs*, 9.

33. Testimony of Emily Debs Mailloux in Karsner, *Talks with Debs*, 77. For dates, see Salvatore, *Debs: Citizen and Socialist*, 9.

34. Constantine, *The Papers of Debs*, 4.

35. C. C. Oakey, *Greater Terre Haute and Vigo County: Closing the First Century's History of City and County . . .* (Chicago: Lewis Publishing, 1908), 634.

36. Perhaps the best-known fan of Sue was Daniel DeLeon, who translated two dozen of the French author's books to English for the publishing house of the Socialist Labor Party.

37. Brommel, *Debs: Spokesman for Labor and Socialism*, 15.

38. Constantine, *The Papers of Debs*, 5.

39. Salvatore, *Debs: Citizen and Socialist*, 11.

40. See, for example, Coleman, *Debs: A Man Unafraid*, 11–12; Ginger, *The Bending Cross*, 10; Brommel, *Debs: Spokesman for Labor and Socialism*, 17, etc. Only Nick Salvatore in his *Debs: Citizen and Socialist*, 11, dryly challenges the discrepancy between the quip and the reality of Debs's biblical reading habits.

41. David Burns, *The Life and Death of the Radical Historical Jesus* (New York: Oxford University Press, 2013), 162–197.

42. Burns, *Radical Historical Jesus*, 162–165.

43. Constantine, *The Papers of Debs*, 5.

44. Karsner, *Talks with Debs*, 60–61. Cited in Salvatore, *Debs: Citizen and Socialist*, 17.

45. Salvatore, *Debs: Citizen and Socialist*, 17.

46. Karsner, *Talks with Debs*, 78.

47. Constantine, *The Papers of Debs*, 6.

48. The plate forming the top of an internally fired steam boiler.

49. Paul Michel Taillon, *Good, Reliable, White Men: Railroad Brotherhoods, 1877–1917* (Urbana, IL: University of Illinois Press, 2009), 18–19.

50. Taillon, *Good, Reliable, White Men*.

51. Trainmen on the road had a death rate more than double that of the mining industry during the 1880s, with braking the single most dangerous task. See Mark Aldrich, *Safety First: Technology, Labor, and Business in the Building of American Work Safety, 1870–1939* (Baltimore: Johns Hopkins University Press, 1997).

52. Karsner, *Debs: Life and Letters*, 126; Salvatore, *Debs: Citizen and Socialist*, 17.

53. Coleman, *Debs: A Man Unafraid*, 16–17.

54. Salvatore, *Debs: Citizen and Socialist*, 18–20.

55. The Brotherhood of Locomotive Firemen was organized in December 1873 in Port Jervis, New York, by Joshua A. Leach (1843–1919) and ten other stokers of coal into locomotive boilers. The organization grew slowly and teetered on the verge of financial insolvency for nearly a decade, with grand secretary and treasurer Gene Debs accorded much of the credit for putting the organization onto a more sound fiscal footing.

56. David A. Shannon, "Eugene V. Debs: Conservative Labor Editor," *Indiana Magazine of History*, vol. 47, no. 4 (December 1951), 357.

57. Salvatore, *Debs: Citizen and Socialist*, 27.

58. Coleman, *Debs: A Man Unafraid*, 28.

59. Hulman & Company still exists in the twenty-first century, being best known for its ownership of the Indianapolis Motor Speedway, site of the Indianapolis 500, which it purchased in November 1945.

60. Painter, *That Man Debs*, 10.

61. Interview of Debs by Floy Ruth Painter, Elmhurst, IL, August 28, 1924. Cited in Painter, *That Man Debs*, 10.

62. Karsner, *Debs: Life and Letters*, 124–125. Bowing to public pressure, the Occidental

Literary Club refused to sponsor Anthony's visit, and Debs organized her speaking engagement under his own volition.

63. Salvatore, *Debs: Citizen and Socialist,* 39.

64. Constantine, *The Papers of Debs,* 8.

65. Salvatore, *Debs: Citizen and Socialist,* 41.

66. Salvatore, *Debs: Citizen and Socialist,* 42.

67. It was not until ratification of the Seventeenth Amendment to the US Constitution in 1913 that US senators were directly elected by popular vote, their selection previously having been the purview of the various state legislatures.

68. Constantine, *The Papers of Debs,* 8.

69. Constantine, *The Papers of Debs,* 8–9.

70. Constantine, *The Papers of Debs,* 7.

71. Debs, "Letter to the Editor of *Locomotive Firemen's Monthly Magazine,*" January 1887, this volume, 34.

72. Debs, "Grand Lodge Address to the Fourth Convention of the Brotherhood of Locomotive Firemen," September 11, 1877, this volume, 40.

73. Brotherhood of Locomotive Firemen, *Journal of Proceedings of the first Twelve Annual Conventions of the Brotherhood of Locomotive Firemen, from 1874 to 1885, Inclusive: Fourth Annual Convention, Indianapolis, Ind., September 1877* (Terre Haute, IN: Moore and Langen, 1885), 4–6, 28; *Journal of Proceedings of the first Twelve Annual Conventions of the Brotherhood of Locomotive Firemen, from 1874 to 1885, Inclusive: Fifth Annual Convention, Buffalo, NY, September 1878* (Terre Haute, IN: Moore and Langen, 1885), 28.

74. Seven short pieces from 1879 have been selected by the editors for inclusion in the volume as likely emanating from associate editor Eugene V. Debs.

75. Taillon, *Good, Reliable, White Men,* 79.

76. Debs, "Will Labor Organizations Federate?" February 1887, this volume, 215.

77. Debs, "Federation, the Lesson of the Great Strike," April 1888, this volume, 236.

78. Debs, "Joining Labor Organizations," March 1888, this volume, 234.

79. Debs, "Labor as a 'Commodity,'" March 1889, this volume, 332.

80. Debs, "Opposites," April 1887, this volume, 223.

81. Debs, "Labor Legislation," April 1887, this volume, 220.

82. Donald L. McMurry, *The Great Burlington Strike of 1888: A Case History in Labor Relations,* (Cambridge, MA: Harvard University Press, 1956), 38.

83. McMurry, *Burlington Strike,* 40–41.

84. McMurry, *Burlington Strike,* 46–47.

85. McMurry, *Burlington Strike,* 64.

86. McMurry, *Burlington Strike,* 75.

87. McMurry, *Burlington Strike,* 76–78.

88. McMurry, *Burlington Strike,* 92–93.

89. Debs, "Federation of Labor Organizations for Mutual Protection," June 1888, this volume, 252.

90. Use of the male gender for these occupations in this period is appropriate, as all such railroad workers were male, without exception.
91. Debs, "The Aristocracy of Labor," November 1888, this volume, 293.
92. Debs, "The Progress of Federation," January 1889, this volume, 307.
93. Debs, "The Future of the ORC" and "New Conductors' Order Established," February 1889, this volume, 319, 322.
94. Debs, "What Can We Do for Working People?" April 1890, this volume, 429.
95. Debs, "Eight-Hour Day a Righteous Demand," July 1890, this volume, 452.
96. Debs, "The People's Party," July 1891, this volume, 569.
97. Debs, "Remedies for Wrongs," July 1891, this volume, 573.
98. Debs, "The Lessons Taught by Labor Day," November 1891, this volume, 596.
99. Debs, "William Lloyd Garrison," June 1892, this volume, 655.
100. Debs's friend and biographer David Karsner—brother-in-law of future Trotskyist leader Jim Cannon—helped cobble together a series of ten articles that had been published in the *Washington Times* in the summer of 1922 as a slim posthumous volume under Debs's byline, *Walls and Bars* (Chicago: Socialist Party, 1927).

Portrait of Eugene V. Debs as he appeared on a carte de visite from the early 1890s. With sandy blonde hair and piercing blue eyes, Debs stood 6 feet and 1 inch tall (1.85 m.) and was regarded as having a sturdy build during his prime. Debs's voice was never recorded (sound files purporting to be Debs originate from a *Wilshire's Magazine* phonograph record featuring a voice actor), but is said to have been deep and forceful and his delivery entertaining and earnest.

(Courtesy of Indiana State University Special Collections, Eugene V. Debs Collection.)

Dances and picnics provided ample opportunity for the young, male membership of the B of LF to socialize with young women of the community. The order was not merely a benefit society providing low-cost insurance to its members but also a social institution. This lithographed invitation from 1876 invites the bearer "and ladies" to a ball sponsored by B of LF Lodge No. 22, Urbana, Illinois.

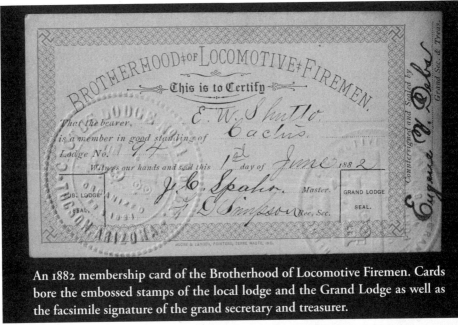

An 1882 membership card of the Brotherhood of Locomotive Firemen. Cards bore the embossed stamps of the local lodge and the Grand Lodge as well as the facsimile signature of the grand secretary and treasurer.

Members transfering to a new lodge presented a "transfer card" upon arrival, a document signed on the reverse by the officers of the former lodge and validated with local and Grand Lodge seals to confirm that dues and assessments had been paid in full.

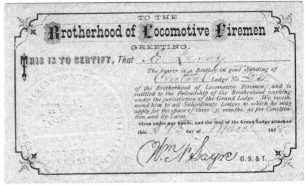

Well-dressed delegates and guests to an early convention of the B of LF, apparently the 1878 Buffalo assembly on a visit to Niagara Falls. Gene Debs was unanimously elected as associate editor of *Locomotive Firemen's Magazine* at the conclave. (Debs is in the middle row, second from the right.)

Their engine decorated in red, white, and blue bunting, these members of the Murphysboro, Illinois Lodge 470 of the Brotherhood of Locomotive Firemen—identified as "McEvilly, Staler, Baskin, and Davis"—appear to be dressed for Fourth of July or Labor Day festivities. Note the full coal car behind the engine, workplace of the scoop-wielding firemen. The image probably dates from the late 1880s.

An annual death rate of more than eight workers per 1,000 made the railroad running trades the most dangerous occupation in America during the 1880s. Badges of the B of LF were reversible with black-and-silver mourning colors on the back so that lodge members could attend funerals and memorial meetings decorated appropriately.

The most dangerous task in the most dangerous industry in the era before the advent of air brakes was performed by brakemen, who worked along the top of the moving train in all weather conditions. The brakemen worked under the authority of the conductor in a master-and-apprentice relationship akin to that of firemen and engineers. This image, from an 1890 *Conductors' Monthly* cover and captioned "A Picnic," was meant to remind conductors of their "bad old days."

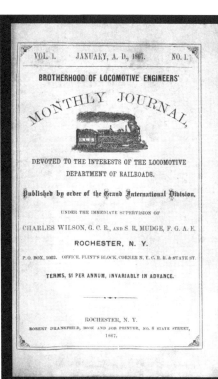

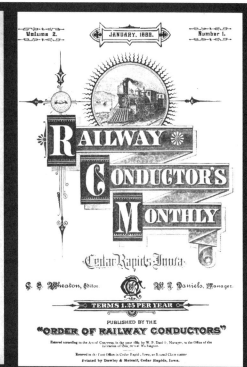

Each railway brotherhood had its own monthly magazine. Below are the 1884 and 1887 iterations of the Debs-edited *Locomotive Firemen's Magazine.*

Top brotherhood officials in 1888
(left to right, from top)

1. Frank P. Sargent (1851–1908)
   Grand Master, B of LF, 1885–1902.

2. Frank W. Arnold (1851–1917)
   Grand Master, B of LF, 1879–1885.

3. Eugene V. Debs (1855–1926)
   Grand Sec. & Treasurer, 1879–1892.

4. Peter M. Arthur (1831–1903)
   Grand Chief, B of LE, 1874–1903.

5. John J. Hannahan (1856–1925)
   Vice Grand Master, B of LF, 1886–1902

Grand Chief Conductor.

Labor Leaders of the 1880s and 1890s
(left to right, from top)

1. Terence V. Powderly (1849–1924)
   Grand Master Workman, Knights of Labor, 1879–1893.

2. Leonora M. Kearney Barry (1849–1923)
   Director of Women's Work, Knights of Labor from 1885.

3. Edgar E. Clark (1859–1930)
   Grand Chief Conductor, Order of Railway Conductors, 1890–1906.

4. Calvin S. Wheaton (1846–1922)
   Grand Chief Conductor, Order of Railway Conductors, 1880–1890.

Take the Great American

SCAB ROUTE

THE

C. B. AND Q.

☠☠ PREPARE TO MEET THY GOD! ☠☠

CLOSE CONNECTIONS with the HEREAFTER

THROUGH TICKETS to POINTS on the STYX!

N. B.---Death Claims Promptly Settled.

PAUL MORTON, G. P. A. M. L.

From the WYMORE DEMOCRAT.   General Prevaricator and Monumental Liar.

The strike is not off, nor will it be until the C. B. & Q. recognizes the fact that it must pay as good wages as its competitors and then sign a treaty with its old engineers and firemen who had worked and been so successful in bringing it up to its former standing and standard of excellence.

The public realize the fact that a railroad like the C. B. & Q., cannot be run with threshing machine engineers and vagrants and drunkards in the places of their old reliable engineers and firemen; and the working men and their friends, or the business public of good judgment, will not patronize a road which is at present a menace to life and property, and a road which seeks to crush out an organization which has done more to make traveling a safety than all the companies on this continent combined, by placing competent and sober men on the engines, and an organization which practices industry, sobriety, truth, justice and morality.

COMMITTEE.

ST. JOSEPH, June 8, 1888.

The 1888 strike of locomotive engineers and firemen against the Chicago, Burlington & Quincy Railroad was one of the seminal events of American labor history during the decade of the 1880s. The strike was long and bitter, with strikebreakers keeping Burlington trains running throughout the strike. This poster by striking railway workers warns potential passengers of the risk of catastrophic accidents in trains piloted by inexperienced enginemen.

1877

Letter to the Editor of
Locomotive Firemen's Monthly Magazine[†]
January 1877

Editor, *B of LF Magazine:*—

I wish to acknowledge the receipt of the first issue of the *Brotherhood of Locomotive Firemen's Magazine*. Its pages were eagerly read, and I can assure you that we are justly proud of having such an intelligent sheet at our command, in which we have the privilege of exchanging thoughts and ideas. We can now truly say that another triumph has been effected, and that success is inscribed upon the banner of our brotherhood. Though our order is not yet fully developed, its cause has established a reputation, which every member is determined to maintain. Each day we are increasing in numbers, and ere long we will claim every dutiful locomotive fireman a member of our beloved order.

In support to this, I might point you to our own lodge. But two years ago, we were organized with 20 charter members, and, for a number of months, found it difficult to follow in the path marked out by our faithful grand officers. Today we can count 45 members *tried* and *true*. Other lodges have increased accordingly, and those who at first frowned upon our efforts are now willing to be one of us. Much credit is due to our grand secretary and treasurer,[1] for the untiring labor which he so willingly bestows in advancing a cause for locomotive firemen, whose motto is Benevolence, Sobriety, and Industry.

Very Respectfully,
E.V.D.
Vigo Lodge, No. 16

---

† Published as "From Terre Haute" in *Locomotive Firemen's Monthly Magazine,* vol. 1, no. 2 (January 1877), 54–55.

Our Brotherhood[†]

March 12, 1877

Brother Sayre, as I've a moment to spare,
I'll devote it unto your editorial chair,
And try and explain as briefly as I can
The love that I feel for our Brotherhood van.

The town of Port Jervis, now so familiarly known,
Is the spot where the first rays of our Brotherhood shone;
There they kindled and nurtured with heed,
By a small band of noble-hearted firemen indeed.

Thus from obscurity all at once did arise,
An object that bound together in brotherly ties,
The locomotive firemen of the Erie Railway,
In a manner that won the admiration of the day.

The effort was welcomed from near and afar
By locomotive firemen as a guiding star,
Whose refulgence revealed to the uncertain sight,
A pathway leading unto inexorable right.

As a greeting to Benevolence, Sobriety, and Industry,
Acclamations burst forth from all parts of the country,
In honor of the advancement of so noble a cause,
That has gained for itself an immortal applause.

From the East to the West in a glorious manner,
Has progress unfurled our Brotherhood banner;
Rearing its insignia in triumph to wave,
Over the land of the free and the home of the brave.

[†] Signed "E.V.D." and published in *Locomotive Firemen's Monthly Magazine,* vol. 1, no. 5 (April 1877), 141.

To the Friend of My Bosom[†]

April 23, 1877

Brother Mullen, I've heard the news this eve,
    That forces a tear from your eye;
You need not explain, I know that you grieve
    For poor Sam, who has whispered good-bye.

He was truly a kind and noble youth,
    Whilst enjoying this frail bit of life;
Always endeavoring others to soothe,
    Who were troubled in this earthly strife.

But his days of sorrow are now at an end,
    For he's gone to the land of the blest,
Where peace and happiness their charms do lend,
    To the weary that are summoned to rest.

Ah, gone forever! So sadly you say,
    When you think of the spirit that's flown,
The sands of life run quickly away,
    And the Giver redeemeth his own.

At the silent churchyard of Effingham,
    'Midst the drooping of willows and roses,
A newly arranged tomb marks the spot where Sam
    In angelic calmness reposes.

—Terre Haute, Ind., April 23, 1877.

[†] Poem signed "E.V.D.," published in *Locomotive Firemen's Monthly Magazine,* vol. 1, no. 7 (June 1877), 201.

Further Suggestions on Insurance[†]

July 18, 1877

Terre Haute, Ind., July 18, 1877

Editors of *B of LF Magazine:*—

In the July number of the *Magazine* there appears an elaborate communication from the pen of Brother Frank B. Alley, of Louisville Lodge No. 23, in which he offers a very wise method of organizing a self-sustaining insurance corporation. I have given this feature of our order a thorough investigation of late, and have observed every suggestion that has been proposed on this subject, and after due consideration must acknowledge that, in my opinion, Brother Alley's idea is at once the production of a conservative mind, and one worthy of being the foundation upon which to base the insurance of our order. In order to make our organization a success and one worthy of the highest merit, we must endeavor to establish a beneficial system that is second to none. It is strictly necessary, therefore, that we should employ every moment of our leisure time in meditating upon this subject and charge our delegates with the necessary instructions so that they will be fully prepared to arrange the matter at the coming convention. I would advise all members to consider this with the greatest care, as there is a tendency at issue which involves the interests of each and every member of the Brotherhood of Locomotive Firemen.

Permit me to depict, in imagination, the benefits which are derived from insurance: It is a cold December night. Unfortunate indeed is he who is left upon the cold mercy of the midnight blast. A small cottage by the roadside marks the spot where resides a locomotive fireman. Without, everything is desolation; within, all is comfort until the dreaded summons of the watchman is announced. His voice is fiercely heard—"Be quick! 'Tis only 15 minutes till leaving time"—and the fireman responds with an "All right," though he feels an inward fear of the task he is about to undertake. There, in a little cradle, with a lovely smile playing over its infantile features, lies a beautiful child—the only gift of heaven which father and mother possess. A parting kiss is hurriedly given, and the fireman hastens to his duty. The ponderous machine, with headlight glaring, is awaiting his coming; a few moments in which to "put in a

---

[†] Published in *Locomotive Firemen's Monthly Magazine,* vol. 1, no. 9 (August 1877), 269–271.

fire," and all is ready for the hazardous trip. Continuous blasts of wind, intermingled with the driven snow, gush into the cab and almost blind the engineer and fireman; however there is no time to ponder. Two shrill screams from the whistle and the magnanimous monster begins to move. Slow and steady are the first strokes of the piston rods. It appears from the moaning of the machinery as though the engine herself were in dread as to what the break of day would bring forth. Revolution after revolution is made, and at each succeeding moment the speed is increased. Fifteen minutes have elapsed since the train has started, and now she is speeding along at a rate of 25 miles an hour. The fireman stoops to "put in another fire," and as he arises observes by looking at the gauge that she is "going back on him;" however this is of no consequence as the summit of a hill has been reached, and now there is a downward course of ten or twelve miles. The engineer looks at his watch and then on the time card; he notes five minutes behind time and therefore does not shut off until the train is halfway down the hill. At this point the engine is rushing along at a frightful speed. The reflection of the headlight is of no avail as the snow is falling fast and thick. "We'll trust to luck, boy," says the engineer, consolingly, as he pulls up the reverse lever and opens the throttle, for the foot of the hill is reached. Scarcely have these words escaped his lips when a deafening crash is heard far above the tumult of the raging storm. Oh, horrors! The train has gone through a trestle and has been precipitated into the stream below. The scene that now follows baffles description. It is useless to describe the fate of the engineer and fireman. Standing at their post of duty, they are hurled into eternity without a moment's warning. Death, in some horrible form, suddenly appears and vanquishes the bloom of life. 'Tis the inoffensive lily, whilst blooming in its most magnificent splendor, that is shattered into fragments by a rude gust of wind. Our fireman lies bleeding and torn under one of the driving-wheels of the engine. The pulsations of the noble heart have ceased, for the soul—all that is immortal of man—has fled. Those pale blue eyes that once sparkled with a heavenly brilliancy, are now sunken and inexpressive. With superhuman efforts he is extricated from the horrible wreck, and his body conveyed to the little cottage by the roadside. Oh, what heartrending scenes a few short hours have wrought. This home of joy has been abruptly transformed into a house of mourning. As we pass down the street which leads into this doleful scene, we encounter throngs of people who are eager to get full particulars of the disaster. We enter in front of the cottage, and as we ascend the steps, light footsteps and low whispers are heard. We are entering the chamber of death. There upon that cushioned couch lies the remains of a locomotive fireman. The loving wife is gazing in abstracted grief upon the pallid countenance of her noble husband who, but a few hours ago, had been in full possession of life and strength, but now lies cold and lifeless within the firm embrace of death. Another day and the body of our hero is deposited in its final resting place, where he "sleeps the sleep that knows no waking."[2]

But wife and child? Now and anon the widowed mother gazes upon the prattling infant, its little hands clapping with joy, heedless of the troubled heart that is beating above. The kind provider and manly protector has been swept from existence, and his family is left prey to the cold mercy of public charity. Their appeal for support is unheard. Through the streets the carriages of the wealthy are dashing by each other in the height of gaiety. On the one hand, we have pleasure to extravagance; on the other, misery to starvation. The pitiful cries of those suffering for the sheer necessities of life are met with a contemptible frown.

Are there no hopes than for these widows and orphans, whose tears fail to awaken even a shadow of sympathy? There is. The Brotherhood of Locomotive Firemen's Insurance Association will throw its mantle of protection over these helpless beings and provide for the wants with which they are surrounded. Of all the virtues which should adorn the personal character of a fireman, none could be more beautiful than a brotherly benevolence and an effort to advance this charitable institution. With this great object accomplished, we could with one voice exclaim, "We have done our duty."

Yours fraternally,
E. V.D.,
Vigo Lodge, No. 16.

Grand Lodge Address to the Fourth Convention of the Brotherhood of Locomotive Firemen, Indianapolis, Indiana[†]

September 11, 1877

Grand Master and Brothers:—

We are again assembled in convention for the purpose of legislating on behalf of our organization.[3] The reception given us by the generous people of Indianapolis is a splendid acknowledgment of their devotion to our cause, and I trust they will never have reason to regret the many favors they have bestowed upon us. In contemplating the past history of our order and determining upon the course to pursue in the future, we should be guided by true motives and a firm determination to do right. Therefore, I would impress upon the minds of this assemblage of firemen the necessity of reflecting with due consideration upon the duties we are about to fulfill.

The past year has been one of unusual interest in connection with our order. Obstacles of every description have been encountered, yet at each test the integrity of the institution has shown forth with a form forcible ray of brilliancy the branch of labor which locomotive firemen represent is of the most vital interest and benefit to the commercial world. What is a railroad, and what means these endless miles of immutable iron?

Indirectly speaking, I might say: A railroad is the architect of progress, and by its magic power the uncultivated inhabitant is lifted from the shades of ignorance and idleness and placed upon an exalted line of equality. The course of a roadbed is the pathway of enlightenment. See with what rapidity our country became populated and developed after having successfully constructed and inaugurated her magnanimous railway system.

The correct guidance and management of a railroad train requires conservative judgment and involves considerable responsibility on the part of the men acting in the capacity of engineer, fireman, conductor, brakeman, etc. It is strictly necessary, therefore, that these men should be thoroughly competent

---

† Published as a section of the article "Fourth Annual Convention of the B of LF: Addresses by Mayor Caven, J. B. Maynard, E. V. Debbs [*sic*], and Others," *Locomotive Firemen's Monthly Magazine* [Dayton, Ohio], vol. 1, no. 11 (October 1877), 345–346.

to fulfill their duties in a faithful manner. Admitting this, is it not equally necessary, on the other hand, that they should in turn receive an equivalent amount of compensation? To this question every fair-minded man will readily answer in the affirmative. Contrary to this, however, the wages of employees have been reduced from time to time, until today these men can scarcely provide themselves and [their] families with the necessities of life. This continual reduction of the price of labor was the direct cause of the recent strikes, which terrified the entire nation. A strike at the present time signifies anarchy and revolution, and the one of but a few days ago will never be blotted from the records of memory.

The question has often been asked: Does the brotherhood encourage strikers? To this question we most emphatically answer: No—brotherhood. To disregard the laws which govern our land? To destroy the last vestige of order? To stain our hands with the crimson blood of our fellow beings? We again say, No, a thousand times No.

Strikes are the last means which are resorted to by men driven to desperation after peaceful efforts to obtain justice have failed. The brotherhood endeavors to qualify its member to become honest and upright citizens, bearing as its motto "Benevolence, Sobriety, and Industry." Benevolence being the principal object, it is obvious that we are organized to protect and not to injure. I trust that we have come together to pursue the same peaceful policy which thus far has crowned our order with success, thanks to the many efforts on the part of our grand secretary and treasurer for the able manner in which he has conducted the affairs of our organization. The name of William N. Sayre will forever be recognized by the locomotive firemen of the United States.

In conclusion, I will hope that the entire proceedings of this convention will be effected with the utmost harmony, and when the day for adjournment arrives we will return to our respective homes confident that all in our power has been done to promote the welfare of our organization.

1878

The Future Prospects of Our Order:
Letter to the Editor of *Locomotive Firemen's Monthly Magazine*[†]
January 12, 1878

Terre Haute, Ind., January 12, 1878

Editor, *B of LF Magazine:*—

I desire to submit a few remarks upon the above subject, as it is quite evident that a great many of our members fail to manifest a willingness to promote the welfare of our organization. It appears as though many of our brothers are impressed with the idea that the order should provide for their every want and secure situations for them, as well as to regulate the price of labor, and if it fail in this, they consider the institution unworthy of support. To the candid mind this is certainly a very wrong impression, as the real merit of the order is entirely ignored, while on the other hand endowments are expected which are not within its power to bestow. We must remember that the brotherhood was not intended to provide for and protect the personal interest of each of its members in all instances. We rather entered into a compact with a view to administer to the wants of the widows, clothe and educate the orphans, who, by the death of a father, husband, or brother, are left comparatively helpless.

'Tis a selfish man indeed who lives for self alone, and one who is not deserving of admittance to any organization whose object is charity. It is a singular fact that the very man who does least toward sustaining his lodge is the first to demand sympathy from its members when in distress. While in a good situation and in the enjoyment of health he neglects to attend his meetings, forgets to pay his dues, and shuns the wants of a needy brother, but the moment he meets with reverses, his first cry is, "Where is your brotherhood?" We have a class of men of this type today who infest our organization, and the quicker we discard them the quicker we establish an order that will meet our every requirement in a prompt manner. We have also members who are prompt in the payment of their dues and willing that the order should flourish,

---

[†] Published in *Locomotive Firemen's Monthly Magazine,* vol. 2, no. 3 (February 1878), 83–85.

yet they always look for others to bear the burden.

Our prospects in the future would be as bright as the glittering rays of sunshine were each member to resolve within himself upon being an example of morality and a promulgator of the prospects which our order embraces. There is not a man living who does not possess, to a certain extent, an influence over his associates. This influence may be for good or evil. The Brotherhood of Locomotive Firemen endeavors to induce its members to exercise an unblemished influence, and thereby stimulate the victims of immorality to enter upon a more righteous course of conduct and emulate its example. This, however, can not be effected until we have banished from our midst all threatening vices, and can point upon our own members, without exception, as being a class of men worthy of confidence and respect. By virtue of the laws which govern us, every member in good standing is entitled to a proportionate endowment in case of sickness or death. We are ever ready to soothe and comfort a sick brother—to sit by his bedside and attend to his wants. A weekly benefit is also allowed during the continuance of such sickness, and when death claims one of our members, we visit the afflicted family, comfort the mourners, join the funeral cortege, and deposit the remains in the silent precincts of the tomb. A donation for funeral expenses is allowed, thereby lessening the burden which otherwise his family have to bear. In addition to all this, we can boast of the most coherent system of insurance in existence, provided it is properly supported. The amount per assessment is but 25 cents, and where is the man who so little cares for his family's interest as to refuse the payment of the small amount for so generous a purpose? Yet here is just where some of our members recognized no benefit. They seem to believe that the amounts paid out for charitable purposes are thrown to the breeze. They forget that they themselves are mortal, and that their own families may be left without a provider at any moment. Then let us cherish the virtues which our order possesses, and not be discontented because it does not embrace more. The organization is an insurance association, is well worthy of future sustenance. It is at our own pleasure whether it shall become a feature of universal recognition in years to come, or whether it shall be permitted to perish for lack of attention and support.

Our grand officers are using every effort at their command to arouse us to a sense of the duty we owe ourselves as well as our families. Then, in considering the vast good they have already done, let it not be said that we are unfit to recognize in their works a struggle for our future welfare. Unless we more vigorously apply ourselves to the performance of this work, a brief season may pass away and find us mourning the loss of the only organization that reared its proud head on our behalf. The realization of this sad prediction would certainly reflect but little credit on its members; therefore let us avoid even the bare possibility of such a termination, and by our own zeal and ambition establish an organization that will forever remain untainted and untarnished.

Fraternally yours,
E. V.D.,
Vigo Lodge, No. 16.

Closing Address to the Fifth Annual Convention of the Brotherhood of Locomotive Firemen[†]
September 14, 1878

Worthy Grand Master and Brothers:—

I desire to claim your attention for a few moments, in order to speak to you briefly upon diverse topics which are entitled to a calm consideration. Through the kind partiality of the people of Buffalo we have met with a welcome of which we have reason to be proud. Upon entering our hall for the purpose of calling the meeting to order, we find that we are greeted by a few of the most eminent citizens of the Queen City of the Lakes. The fervent prayer of the Rev. Mr. Ward on our behalf, the generous reception and cordial welcome of the acting mayor, Mr. Sackett, and the judicious advice given by Mr. Wilder, master mechanic of the New York, Lake Erie & Western Railroad, were bestowed upon us; and I feel it to be a duty incumbent upon every member of the organization to acknowledge the kindness and be grateful to those gentlemen, who on behalf of the people of Buffalo tendered us a welcome which will never be blotted from the records of memory. For all these favors we are not ungrateful, and I venture the assertion that the time will never come when it can be said that we have proven ourselves unworthy to be the recipients of the same.

The impression prevails to a great extent that we, representing a class of

---

[†] Published in *Locomotive Firemen's Monthly Magazine,* vol. 2, no. 11 (October 1878), 341–342.

ordinary laborers, are but the representatives of a rude and uncultivated proportion of the inhabitants of this land. I deny this. Standing as we do beneath the frown of what society is pleased to call respectable, we can give proof that the locomotive firemen of the United States and Canada are entitled to the same respect and consideration that is so lavishly bestowed upon many other classes of laborers. It is true we cannot appear in the gilded laces and gaudy garments necessary to put the polish upon the "gentleman" of our day, yet "beneath many a ragged dress there beats a noble heart,"⁴ and on the same policy, the locomotive firemen of our land are a class of laborers who are not entirely unworthy to receive the respect of society; nor are they destitute of the principles requisite to stamp them as moral and honest citizens.

Five years ago the first rays of the brotherhood were faintly discernible in the distance, but from that time until the present moment the sun of its existence has continued its ascendancy, until today its beams of light and intelligence have penetrated the most remote parts of the nation. As many of our people are somewhat prejudiced regarding the true merit of our brotherhood, it might be well to pause and give those persons an insight into our objects and thereby demonstrate to the satisfaction of all that our institution is one of the most necessary and useful organizations that has ever been established.

First of all I want to prove conclusively that the first object of the association is to provide for the widows and orphans who are daily left penniless and at the mercy of public charity by the death of a brother. Upon looking over our constitution and bylaws and reading the laws contained therein, one half of which have been established for the sole purpose of promoting our insurance system, it is obvious that the benevolent feature of our institution is the basis upon which it is founded. The widows and orphans of our deceased brothers must not suffer for the lack of attention or support. We know that mortality among railroad men is greater than among any other class of laborers, and in view of this fact it should be the duty of everyone to recognize an institution that provides for those who are left bereaved and helpless. Benevolence, then, is the principal object, and with this as a plea, we believe we are entitled to a degree of recognition.

The idea prevails to a great extent that we are banded together for the purpose of conspiring against railway corporations and of resorting to violent means in the event that we cannot exact our demands in a peaceable way. I brand this as an infamous lie. I challenge anyone to show me a single instance where the Brotherhood of Locomotive Firemen has been implicated in an act of violence toward railroad corporations. It is the sheerest folly to suppose that such would be the object of the order, when their interests are so closely allied with those of their employers. But I can tell you, my friends, of the only manner in which our brotherhood intends to take advantage over corporations. It is this. We intend to give them a class of honest and intelligent laborers, men upon whom they can depend, men who are equal in every way to the responsibility under which they are placed, and then I think that we are justified in asking for recompense in accordance with the kind of labor performed. This is our policy and we shall never deviate therefrom.

I now want to speak a few moments upon the proposed consolidation of the two orders of locomotive firemen.[5] For the past year the subject has been handled by both organizations, but it seems that it is impossible to effect a consolidation that would afford terms suitable to both parties. It is deemed expedient by all the members of our order to effect an annexation, as in unity there is strength, but it is apparent that the independent firemen's union is less anxious to consolidate since they were to have a committee present at our convention to hold a conference relative to the matter, but failed to present themselves. Arrangements had been made on our part to meet them with cordiality and courtesy, but their having failed to be present indicates that they were unwilling to meet us. We shall then continue to sail under the colors of the B of LF, and with our past record as a proof of our worth we can safely depend upon the future for a realization of our bright and glorious prospects.

Look at the strength of our order today, and notwithstanding we have experienced panics and a distress in the labor interests of the nation, our organization has steadily increased in numbers. We can point to 84 lodges, all of which are progressing finely, and this goes to show that order is alive and prosperous. Now, my brothers, all that is necessary is that we conduct ourselves in such a manner as to gain the respect of the people, to show them that we are worthy to stand beneath the beautiful motto "Benevolence, Sobriety, and Industry," and then we will soon be recognized as a feature of universal admiration.

I should like to be more elaborate in my remarks, but time at present begs me forbear. We are about to leave one another. Those beloved friends with whom we have become so fondly attached are soon to be separated, and perhaps forever. In leaving you, my brethren, I can only say, God bless and protect you all. My heart is with you in all your endeavors to establish more firmly the pillars of our brotherhood. Remember our mottoes and be determined to be a credit to the order, and then we will be happy and prosperous. Though certain classes may revile against us by calling us communists and stigmatizing us otherwise, the time will never come when it can be said that we have been unfaithful to what we believe to be good and true. In conclusion, allow me to bid you all adieu with hopes that we may meet again in the interest of our order.

Notes

1. William N. Sayre of Indianapolis was elected the first grand secretary and treasurer of the Brotherhood of Locomotive Firemen at its first annual convention, held in Hornellsville, New York, in December 1874. He was also the editor of *Locomotive Firemen's Monthly Magazine* from its establishment in December 1876. During the 1877 railway strikes Sayre was briefly jailed by Circuit Court judge Thomas Drummond for his advocacy of the stoppage. Sayre was replaced as grand secretary and treasurer by Debs in 1880.

2. Fragment from the poem "She Sleeps" (1840), by Mary Emily Jackson (1821–1869).

3. With grand master W. R. Worth absent, the twenty-one-year-old Gene Debs of Vigo Lodge No. 16 was tapped to deliver the keynote report of the Grand Lodge at an opening session of the fourth convention of the B of LF. Debs was not himself an executive officer of the organization at the time; the four executive officers who were present seem to have yielded the task of delivering a largely extemporaneous speech to the enthusiastic youngster. Debs would sit on four of the eight standing committees of the convention and gain unanimous election by that body as the B of LF's "grand marshal," its fifth-ranking official.

4. There were a multitude of similar expressions used during the nineteenth century, although none put precisely as Debs has it here. Debs seems to be adapting the words of the pseudonymous "Grandma B" in the magazine the *Nonconformist*: "Don't be afraid of your sisters, no matter where they live or what they do . . . Many a noble heart beats beneath a ragged dress."

5. The competing firemen's organization was the Grand International Union of Locomotive Firemen (GIULF), which from 1871 published a magazine called *Locomotive Firemen's Monthly Journal* in Schenectady, New York.

1879

Benevolence[†]

February 1879

The word *benevolence,* the headlight of the grand motto of our order, is used and applied by the members in its broadest sense and fullest definition. It means that the members of the order are possessed of a disposition to do good; that they are filled with love for mankind, accompanied with a desire to promote their happiness. Not by wild and reckless charities, whereby the undeserving, the idle, and the profligate are enabled to live without producing by appeals to the active benevolence of our order, but by love and kindness tempered with sense and good judgment. To see that the meritorious do not suffer, and that honest suffering humanity may know that there still lives a sentiment and race of men who have higher aspirations and more lofty conceptions of life and its duties than the mere struggle for sordid gain. To see that the brother disabled in the line of duty is provided for with a weekly stipend sufficient to keep the wolf at bay, the wife and little ones from suffering and want.

Benevolence, as used and understood by this fraternity, means *practical humanity;* that rational application of the laws of right and justice inherent in the heart of *natural* humanity; but too often, alas! educated out of the heart and mind, by too much theorizing and too much theology. We have no patience with that kind of seedy benevolence that starves our next-door neighbor and contributes money to send gospel and food to the benighted heathen. If the heathen needs gospel, the hungry need food, and practical benevolence says: A wise and beneficent father will save in his own good time the untutored mind; let us attend to the demands of suffering, ever-present need.

Benevolence is not a theory full of high-sounding words and platitudes about the elevation and amelioration of the condition of the whole race; it is a living, acting principle that aids the needy and helps the truly deserving to help themselves. If a brother is unfortunate and without blame, aid him until he can aid himself and repay all. If he has lost a position, aid him to another, and thus without squandering recklessly means for the suffering, we only lend a helping hand to the halt, the lame, and the blind, until their lameness is cured and their blindness removed, and they are able to help themselves. We have seen men

---

† Published in *Locomotive Firemen's Monthly Magazine,* vol. 3, no. 2 (February 1879), 47–48. Attributed to Associate Editor Debs by style.

upon the streets respond to a pathetic plea for help and watched the recipient squander his charity for tobacco or whiskey. The world is too full of such sickly sentimentality about true benevolence. Unless your labors for the alleviation of suffering result in some practical good, it is worse than folly to expend either time or money. A false benevolence makes beggars of men and criminals of destitute persons. True benevolence as practiced by our order makes men brave, manly, and self-reliant, and humanity the better for it.

Sobriety[†]

March 1879

This word, forming as it does one of the trio of the motto of our order, means and is intended to mean much. It not only means abstinence from the use of intoxicants, but it means sobriety in language, in judgment, in action, and in thought. "The sobriety of riper years."[1] It is as great an evil to be overheated in imagination, inordinate in the manifestation of passion, and intemperate in the use of language—often leading to the commission of as great crimes, and entailing as much suffering upon humanity as the excessive use of liquors. It is the aim of the order to avoid all these evils, and our motto means just that much—no more, no less. We do not mean that men should become stoics, refuse to smile, or to take pleasure in the things of this life. We mean that they should do all things coolly and deliberately; let judgment ever hold her seat in the court of reason, and mold and guide the head and heart.

Sobriety means more than simply *"don't drink"*—it means do not under any circumstances allow the animal to control the mental; do not subject yourself to the humiliating self-examination that will pronounce you a fool for the want of better judgment. *Think well of yourself; merit* the good opinion you have of your own worth, and the world will not be slow to learn the fact and to give you credit for it. Be sober in all things; intemperate in nothing. With this resolve molding your life and shaping your acts, the world will be the

---

† Published in *Locomotive Firemen's Monthly Magazine,* vol. 3, no. 3 (March 1879), 81.
    Attributed to Associate Editor Debs by style.

better for your having lived in it, and you will reap the reward of a conscience void of offense and that degree of happiness that comes to the lives of very few children of earth.

Industry[†]

April 1879

Benevolence, Sobriety, and Industry, three virtues that ought to be universally practiced, represent the motto of the Brotherhood of Locomotive Firemen. Benevolence and sobriety, the first two links in this moral chain, have already been elucidated and embellished in these columns; it is now incumbent on us to speak of the infinitely good results that emanate from an industrious life, and the pernicious influences and tendencies of an idle one.

Franklin once said, "Laziness travels so slowly that Poverty soon overtakes him."[2] This aphorism will apply perfectly to many of the victims of poverty. The industrious man is invariably the successful man. When we take a glance at those of our businessmen and mechanics who have risen to an elevated plane of prominence, morally and financially, we see the impress of industry stamped upon their very brows. Industry and morality go hand in hand, whilst idleness is the foster parent of all the vice, crime, and licentiousness that have cursed this fair earth in all the stages of its modern advanced civilization. Do you know that an industrious man has not time to spare to acquire bad habits? The man of diligence is constantly thinking of his duties and responsibilities. He is patient and untiring in his labors, and while the sweat stands on his brow, he is devising new means by which he can enhance his own welfare and perpetuate the happiness of his family. Indolence is the great cancer from which all other evils are nourished. It is the fount of crime and immorality. All other vices are subservient to it. Then let us shun laziness, and seek aid and comfort in the realm of industry.

Did it ever occur to you that industry is nearly always well fed and clothed and has a comfortable home? Did you ever notice that the greater part of those

---

† Published in *Locomotive Firemen's Monthly Magazine,* vol. 3, no. 4 (April 1879), 113–114. Attributed to Associate Editor Debs by style.

who cry "No work" and "Hard times" are lazy in the extreme? When a diligent and active man is thrown out of a position, in most instances, he can readily secure another. Men who employ hired help can generally find room for an applicant who bears the reputation of being industrious. Remember, my friends, that all of the pleasures and comforts of this life must be labored for. Would you enjoy your share of them? Then don't stand idly by and steal from the laurels of others. Associate your name with toil and industry, and you yourself will be the source of your happiness.

Our brothers should not only be industrious while out on the road and on duty, but when at home and disengaged, instead of lounging about the roundhouse, let them employ their leisure moments making their homes comfortable. Do you ever stop to think how happy your mother or wife would feel if, in the spring when the verdure begins to peep above the barren soil and the trees begin to bud and blossom, you would clean the rubbish from the yard and make her a little garden spot? Take a few of the dimes that you spend foolishly and invest them in the purchase of plants and shrubberies and in a little while, with the goodwill of your mother, wife, or sister (and they never lack it), you will have an inviting and cheerful homestead. The homes of many men do not blossom with the radiance of happiness; they do not like to spend their leisure time with their families because everything is so cheerless and desolate there. If these very men, instead of helping to build saloons and engaging in the propagation of licentiousness, would spend their time and money, and smiles and stories at home, they would soon have the goodwill and earnest cooperation of their families. The consequence would be a home blessed with joy, from which they would be loath to depart and eager to return. Industry always leads to happiness. In a well-governed family the man earns and the woman saves, and by practicing economy, and being in sympathy with each other, they are certain to prosper.

Brothers, we must be industrious in order to attain the goal for which we are striving. We must be men of exemplary habits, and by laboring zealously for the happiness of our families we will augment our own.

The Labor Problem[†]

May 1879

Whatever politicians may say to the contrary, however much they may attempt to lead the masses away from the truth, the fact remains that the labor question is the great problem of the immediate future. Politicians may howl over the Southern question, so-called statesmen may cry "revolution" at each other, but the thinking man knows that most of it is done for effect; he knows, further, that the future outlook is ominous for peace and prosperity if the wants of the laboring man are not met as they should be. Like the shadow of a great rock in a weary land, the labor issue looms up, prominent, awful, grand; and he only is a true friend to his country, who understands the great difficulty and will use his honest endeavors to solve it. The solution, we hope, will come steadily, peacefully, but come it must, though it be necessary to bring it here on the terrible wings of revolution. Not the revolution of bloodshed, but a revolution that will overwhelm the enemies of the laboring classes beneath ruin unutterable. God hastens the day, say we.

Organization is the great secret of success. A body of men—no matter who they are, or for what purpose they come together—if they are well organized, they will succeed. Our readers will recognize the truth of this by looking at our own grand brotherhood. We are as one man, from Portland, Maine, to Portland, Oregon—East, West, North, South—the same great body of honest, hard-working men. One great body, with one noble heart, beating responsive to the wishes of every member. Let us persevere in our objects, let us organize more fully, and we shall become more of what we are already: a power in the land for good. Brothers, gird on the armor; the whole world is a battlefield, and we must be the heroes in the fight for our rights.

[†] Published in *Locomotive Firemen's Monthly Magazine*, vol. 3, no. 5 (May 1879), 146.
   Attributed to Associate Editor Debs by style.

Temperance[†]

June 1879

Through countless ages gone by, the use of intoxicating liquors has been a bane and curse to humanity. As early as 1639, when our fair land was scarce better than a trackless forest, the people who had settled here to seek a home upon American soil became debauched and depraved from the use of stimulants, to such an extent that it was found necessary by the authorities of Massachusetts and Connecticut to establish laws restraining and prohibiting the use thereof. From that time until the present moment every effort which human ingenuity could devise has been made to suppress intemperance, yet we must confess, much to our humiliation, that but little headway has been made. Wherever we go throughout our country we can see the victims of this dreadful evil. The half-clothed sot, with pale and emaciated countenance, staggering along the street, the most pitiable sight one can imagine, has become an object so common that he does not even excite our attention, much less our compassion. I have often looked at a besotted remnant of mortality whom I had known in earlier years, and then turning from him after a few moments reflection, I could not help but say to myself: "What a respected citizen he might have been had he not fallen a victim to intemperance."

When we think of the families that have been wrecked, the deaths by delirium tremens, the suicides that are recorded, the women and children who have been driven into the streets from homes made desolate by the husbands and fathers of debauchery, and then consider that intemperance is the foster parent of nearly all this misery and wretchedness, we grow impatient for the coming of that day, however far distant it may be, when the human family will have grown sublime enough to firmly withstand all of the temptations that issue from the enticing wine cup. How often do we see a young man starting out upon his journey through life, with prospects as bright as the rays of the morning sun; he is happy and prosperous, has a good business and a large circle of friends. Time passes along, he gets married, has a cheerful little home, and he is soon the husband and father of a magnificent family. Everything goes well for a while, and all is joy about his homestead. It is soon noticed, however,

---

† Published in *Locomotive Firemen's Monthly Magazine,* vol. 3, no. 6 (June 1879), 177.
    Attributed to Associate Editor Debs by style.

that through custom acquired from one of his friends, he steps across the street occasionally and for "companions' sake" takes a social glass. Here now comes the turning point. It soon becomes an established habit with him to take "a little something" when the time comes. In a little while he "nips" a little oftener and is always promptly on hand at the proper time. He is now a "moderate drinker." Dare any man advocate even moderate drinking?

Let us take an imaginary glance at the future. Ten years have elapsed. When we left our good friend he enjoyed and partook of stimulants to a moderate degree only. Let us see what effect it has had. We take a stroll up the street with the intention of calling upon our old associate. We pause at his shop door but find upon inquiry that he has been superseded these five years past. We look at each other amazed for a moment, then ask, "What has become of him?" The answer is, "Gone to a drunkard's grave two years ago. He took to drinking, got worse every day, tried without success to quit, neglected his family shamefully; finally all his property was sold, his wife and children turned into the street, and he, like many of the victims of drunkenness, went down to a grave of shame, wet with the tears of a mourning family of beggars."

My friends, this illustration is not overdrawn. Men equally as firm as yourselves have said: "We can drink moderately without drinking to excess," and then in the course of time became perpetual drunkards.

Have the manhood to say "No" when you are asked to pour a liquid into your stomach that transforms a man into a beast.

Your mission on earth is to cultivate the attributes with which God possessed you, and you should seek to do so rather than degenerate them unto the low and groveling passions of the brute creation.

The Rights of Labor[†]

August 1879

The American people have, within the last two decades, been brought face to face with the greatest of social, political, and economic problems—the problem of the rights of labor. In the presence of this question all others pale into insignificance. Our statesmen may howl about the Negro in politics, the Southern question, presidential frauds, soldiers at the polls, or finances, but they cannot evade the conclusion that there is a deeper current stirring the hearts of the producing classes. It matters very little to the laborer whether he is paid in gold or in paper money, but it does matter much with him whether or not he gets *sufficient* pay for his work, and whether or not he is properly protected by our laws. If the labor problem is solved, all other difficulties, so far as the laborer is concerned, will solve themselves. After all, the great underlying principle of all human justice is simply: give unto every man what is his due. The government that pays most attention to this principle, and that shapes its laws in accordance therewith, will come nearest to doing justice to all of its citizens.

Many great questions have been solved since the dawn of civilization, most of them in tears and bloodshed; nation has warred with nation, fratricidal strife has cursed the earth, all in the name of human progress, but so far human progress has meant only political, social, and economic benefit to the comparatively few, while the many are bound to receive what they can get. A solution of the labor problem means the reverse of this—it means plenty for the many, rights to all. Our organization means to assist in the solution of this problem; not by the means heretofore used—war and rapine—but by a peaceful, honest adjustment of differences. Arbitration, not war; discussion, not the quick, sudden, awful argument of fire and sword. Benevolence, sobriety, industry, organization—these must and will be the great factors in the problem—they are ours and we will use them.

---

† Published as "The Labor Problem" in *Locomotive Firemen's Monthly Magazine*, vol. 3, no. 8 (August 1879), 239. Attributed to Associate Editor Debs by style.

The Misrepresentations of Evil Thinkers[†]
November 1879

There has been a labored effort on the part of evil persons, those we mean who wish no good purpose well, to misrepresent the Brotherhood of Locomotive Firemen by representing it as a conclave of men who encourage the spirit of communism in the companies employing them. We say there *has been* such an element abroad of such evil thinkers and workers, but if the English language means anything, unanimously expressed by a body of men, representing 99 lodges of a fellowship, then the following sentiment should be given its fullest force, for it is significant of the fact that not only does the brotherhood exist on a higher plane of action than that accorded to it, but it stands above the reproach of backbiters and scoffers when in convention it announces:

> We, the Brotherhood of Locomotive Firemen, here assembled in convention, do hereby ignore strikes, and hereafter will settle all differences by arbitration.

This is no doubtful language. It means just what it says, but it is to be regretted that a charitable association, purely and Christianly so, should feel itself called upon to utter such a pronunciamento simply because their employment is of that character that leads to the inference that whatever pertaining to the injury of labor, or the enhancement of its value, they must of all feel it. There never was a greater mistake. It is undoubtedly true there are some hotheads in all charitable bodies whose indiscretions reflect upon the order as a whole, and often give by their acts the belief that their conduct is approved or encouraged by others. This is not the rule by which we must be judged. It is to be hoped that if no other influence can make good our position, as a growing charitable insurance association, that great regulator of all things, time, will bring us a panacea that will soothe the distracted minds of intermeddlers, interlopers, and seekers after fleshpots.

---

† Published in *Locomotive Firemen's Monthly Magazine*, vol. 3, no. 11 (November 1879), 335–336. Attributed to Associate Editor Debs by style.

Notes

1. Probably a common expression of the eighteenth century. The phrase is included in the 1832 dictionary definition of "sobriety" by Noah Webster.
2. From "Preliminary Address to the Pennsylvania Almanac, Entitled, 'Poor Richard's Almanac for the Year 1758,'" by Benjamin Franklin (1706–1790). The original aphorism is "He that riseth late must trot all day, and shall scarce overtake his business at night; while laziness travels so slowly that poverty soon overtakes him."

1880

Letter to the Seventh Convention of the Brotherhood of Locomotive Firemen[†]

September 13, 1880

Terre Haute, Ind., September 13, 1880

Worthy Grand Master and Delegates:—

Today the Brotherhood of Locomotive Firemen of the United States and Canada convenes in its seventh annual session.[1] Regularly for the past seven years these conventions have been held at this season of the year, first at one city and then another, but never in the whole history of our organization did we feel so highly gratified at the work of the past, or look into the future with such sanguine expectations as we do at this very moment. Since our last convention, held in this beautiful and enterprising city, we have made wonderful progress. At that time many of our lodges were only in moderately good condition, while many others were about to totter to their downfall. Only the smaller portion of them were in first-class working order. How different things appear today. We are assembled here with a representation of 80 delegates, coming from the four quarters of the globe to tell each other good tidings relating to the Brotherhood. All our lodges are in active operation, and a spirit of rivalry seems to actuate each to surpass the other in point of good standing. Several new lodges have been organized by Grand Instructor [S. M.] Stevens, while the greater part of them were visited and reconstructed by him.[2] Altogether the closing year has been one of joy and profit to us as an organization. We have seen old prejudices conquered with kindness. Many of those who were once our enemies are now firmly with us in our endeavors to perpetuate the interests of our calling, and we feel like entering upon the coming year with our heads and souls erect, fearlessly battling for the maintenance of an institution that has done so much for us without doing harm to anyone.

If we were only understood, how easy would be our task. The opposition we now have to contend with is precisely the same as it was when we first organized, though, I will admit, not quite so formidable.

Let us see for a moment what it is that eternally seeks our overthrow. Let

---

† Published as part of "Our Seventh Annual Convention" in *Locomotive Firemen's Monthly Magazine*, vol. 4, no. 11 (November 1880), 336–338.

us see who it is that looks upon us with the eyes of suspicion, and with a scorn black as night, forbids our approach.

* * *

In times gone by, laboring men who had been imposed upon formed themselves into a mob and, with a recklessness that makes us shudder, began to burn and plunder the property of the corporations they were working for. These men felt that they were basely mistreated, and being ignorant of the true way of having their grievances adjusted, and being urged on as they were by their so-called leaders, who had nothing at stake and nothing to lose, and with a spirit of revenge, they sought to burn and kill to their satisfaction.

While we always sympathized with these deluded and miserable wretches, we have always felt that they were wrong in acting so violently. There is a different way of adjusting difficulties between the employer and employee. Our organization believes in arbitration. All differences should be settled in this way, for no good has ever or can ever come from resorting to violence and bloodshed. This is our true feeling in the matter, but instead of being recognized as men who desire to avoid trouble, we are very often made identical with those whom I have just mentioned. The prejudice against us is very often deep-rooted and bitter. While many railroad officials through the land treat us with the utmost kindness and consideration, there are many others who look upon us with feelings of dread and aversion. They seem to think that we are banded together to do them injury. This is the key to all the opposition that has ever confronted us. Many railroad superintendents are so much poisoned against us that they will not permit one of our lodges to be organized on their lines. Others punish with dismissal the unfortunate fireman who is discovered as being one of our members, and in this way we meet with a great deal that prevents our institution from spreading as rapidly as it would under more favorable circumstances. It is a fearful thing to be asked to sign away your manhood under penalty of losing your situation if you refuse.

It has frequently occurred that our members were forced to sever their connection with our brotherhood and denounce it as an unholy institution in order that they might hold their situation and provide their families with the wants of life.

How unjust and unreasonable this appears to a fair and right-thinking man. If we were a band of outlaws I would not wonder that we are ostracized in this way, but as our sole aim and object is to do all the good we can without harming anyone, I feel that we ought not to be treated so harshly.

But all of this will finally be overcome. We do not bear ill feelings toward those who seek to crush us, for we know that they misapprehend our motives.

The time will finally come when they will admit that they were wrong, and then peace and harmony will prevail between us firemen. I only wish that those who oppose us could see the good work we have done since we have been organized. If they could see the afflicted widows and sad and suffering orphans to whom we have administered relief, they would not endeavor to check our career. We know that we have accomplished but little, for our capacity has been limited, but in years to come we intend that our institution shall become mighty. We want to be established in every available section of the country and have every worthy engineman in the land to be one of us. We want to be able to protect the widows and orphans of all our members. We want to provide for the widow, clothe and educate the little orphan, and do all the good we can for men of our calling.

In case of the total disability of one of our members, we want to administer to his wants through life. We want to make better men of locomotive firemen. We want them to be honest and upright, sober and industrious. We want to educate them to a standard so that they spend their leisure time with their families instead of gratifying distasteful pleasures. We want them to wear good clothes and be respectable. We want them to treat their families kindly, and with the care of a true husband and father, provide for their every want.

All of this will be accomplished in time to come.

Fraternally yours,
Eugene V. Debs

Organize!†

December 1880

Firemen of the United States, organize! Organize for mutual protection. Not for the purpose of antagonizing our employers, but for the holier, nobler purpose of charity. Charity to our own craftsmen. We must sustain each other in the hour of danger. We must take care of the fatherless and husbandless. When death and disaster have entered the homes of one of our craft, we must fly to

---

† Published in *Locomotive Firemen's Monthly Magazine,* vol. 4, no. 12 (December 1880), 372.

the rescue. Our hands must be the ones to sustain the weak. Firemen cannot afford to pay the high premiums exacted by insurance companies for life policies; therefore, we must insure each other. We are used to danger and hard usage ourselves, but our wives and children, our mothers and sisters must not be left to buffet with fate alone when we are gone. The faster we organize, the larger is the sum we can afford to pay for a death or a total disability.

Fellow craftsmen! You who love your dear ones at home, stop! Consider! Death may overtake you on the rail; the footboard may never again feel your sturdy tramp. What then will become of little Charlie, or Bennie, or little Cora? What then will become of your darling wife or mother? Come and join with us in our holy cause. Humanity says, come. Loved ones say, come. Duty says, come.

Notes

1. The Seventh Annual Convention of the Brotherhood of Locomotive Firemen was held in Chicago from September 13–17, 1880.
2. Samuel M. Stevens, of Lowell, Massachusetts, was organizer and instructor of the B of LF during the first half of the 1880s. Formerly a fireman and engineer on the Boston, Lowell & Nashua Railroad before becoming a brotherhood functionary, Stevens was defeated in a bid for reelection at the September 1885 convention by John J. Hannahan. Stevens went on to play a leading role as a representative of the B of LF in the 1888 Burlington Strike.

1881

The Power of Persistent Effort[†]

January 1881

There is no obstacle in the way of human desire that cannot be overcome by persistent effort. The mighty forces of nature do not act suddenly; they attain their object by persistence. Slowly, grandly, the march goes on, never ceasing, never deviating from the course of success. Through what countless ages the silent drip, drip, of the water drop has gone on which has constructed the cave stalactite. Inch by inch the mud of the Nile built up ancient Egypt, "through the still lapse of ages."[1] Cell by cell, bit by bit, the coral insect lifted to the light of day the mighty islands of the South Pacific; not in a year, not in a hundred years, but in millions of decades. So has it been with human progress. Civilization did not, like Athena, leap full-armed from the brain of Jove. No, civilization is an evolution brought to perfection by centuries of persistent human effort. Sometimes we find breaks in the grand march—stumblings of the giant in his resistless course—but from these apparent failures the needed lesson of persistence was learned, and the onward sweep was the more rapid and sure after the recovery from temporary defeat.

From these examples the individual should learn a grand lesson. Persistence is the secret to all success. Men are not like the night-blooming cereus,[2] bursting into full-blown perfection in a night; they are like the oak of the forest, slow of growth, matchless in strength when grown, if they but meet the storms and trials of life with indifference and defiance.

If we have an object in view, a worthy and noble one, we can only gain it by persistence. The citadel of error and opposition will always surrender if we but lay siege to it. It may take years, it may take a lifetime of struggle, but the object to be gained is worthy of the sacrifice. And what a proud moment it is that we stand upon the ruined ramparts of the enemy's stronghold with the banner of success waving grandly over us. The hero in the battle of life is loved of God and honored of men. Therefore,

> In the world's broad field of battle,
> In the bivouac of Life,
> Be not like dumb, driven cattle!
> Be a hero in the strife.[3]

---

† Published in *Locomotive Firemen's Magazine*, vol. 5, no. 1 (January 1881), 6–7.

As an organization, we have an object in view, the noblest that can actuate humanity—sympathy with the living, charity for the friends of the dead. Not the cold, heartless charity of the world, but the kind, loving charity born of common danger and mutual protection. In order to fully accomplish this object we must organize *all* our working forces. Like the coral insects, we must combine our efforts. Persistently we must labor, through danger, doubt, and opposition.

If we are true to ourselves, true to our loved ones, true to the spirit of manhood, failure can never be our lot. We shall, in time, become the greatest charitable organization in the world. All we need is persistence, unwavering persistence. Slowly have we toiled through the past, slowly must we toil through the future. Has not our toil brought rich rewards? Have we not heard the "God bless you" from the trembling lips of widowhood and the prattling lips of infancy?

> What need have we of greater fame
> Than tears of love on widows' cheeks?[4]

Another year lies before us with its manifold hopes and fears, joys and griefs. The sky looks bright for us. All over the land our craft is awakening to the fact that we must organize for the protection of the loved and loving. Wives must not be left uncared for. Babes must not be left to eat the bread of heartless charity. We must help each other. Death and disaster must be robbed of their terrors.

Firemen of the United States and Canada! Come and join our noble brotherhood. Let us all join our individual efforts as the mountain rivulets join their waters and become at last a resistless river sweeping grandly on, overcoming all opposition, stopping for nothing.

Let us go to work fearlessly, persistently, remembering that

> Work grandly done is always great,
> Though done by men of daily toil.[5]

A Gentleman†

April 1881

There is, probably, no word in the English language more universally misapplied among Americans, than the term *gentleman*. A mistaken sense of politeness employs it to designate any human animal of the masculine gender, and the error is seldom if ever corrected or even discovered by the person of whose character it is a glaring travesty, and of whose manners it is in reality a satire.

The true gentleman is never rude or boisterous; never coarse or vulgar; he never indulges in boastful arrogance or egotistical self-conceit; his language and manner are never patronizingly condescending toward an inferior, nor does he affect undue humility in the presence of those whose station in life is higher than his own. Above all, his deportment is marked by a tender regard for the feeling and reputation of others, never does he (however great the temptation) wound the former, or lend even a momentary sanction to besmirching the other.

United Again‡

June 1881

Through the power usurped by one of our former grand officers, the Brotherhood of Locomotive Firemen was precipitated into the great strike of 1877 and, as a natural consequence, a hatred for the organization was incurred by many railroad officials throughout the land.[6]

As a means of retaliating for the injury sustained, they forced many of our members to withdraw from the institution, and thus succeeded in causing the downfall of some of our best lodges. This was especially the case in the eastern country, where the order was almost entirely swept from existence.

Of course, this was very unjust on the part of the railroad officials, for

---

† Published in *Locomotive Firemen's Monthly Magazine,* vol. 5, no. 4 (April 1881), 108.

‡ Published in *Locomotive Firemen's Monthly Magazine,* vol. 5, no. 6 (June 1881), 169–171.

they were placing the grave responsibilities of the strike and its direful results where they did not properly belong, for as an organization the brotherhood had nothing to do with the origin or development of that strike nor any other. The only manner in which our brotherhood was identified with the strike was that it had an officer at its helm who gave it countenance without power or authority, and thus brought down upon it as much condemnation as though it had plotted and planned to give it life, and then used its power in contributing to its support.

It is a matter of fact that the Brotherhood of Locomotive Firemen has never yet been directly implicated in a strike. They have never destroyed one dollar's worth of property, nor struck one blow at a railroad company. On the contrary they have always counseled moderation and in many instances carefully guarded the property of the corporations. But deep and bitter as was the prejudice entertained against us by many railroad officials, the last vestige of it has been obliterated forever.

We have letters from nearly all the leading managers, presidents, and superintendents of railroads in the United States and Canada, and they speak of us, without exception, in the kindliest terms. We have been furnished with annual passes for our traveling officers over thousands and thousands of miles of road, while many companies who could not, consistently with their rules, grant annual passes have generously offered to furnish us with trip passes whenever we have an opportunity to use their respective lines. The letters we have of them are expressive of the deepest sympathy and warmest friendship for our order, and we feel free to say that we entertain the same cordial feeling toward them, and hope that this unison and harmony of thought and action between us may never be ruffled by any wave of passion or discord.

One of the very highest officials of the Pennsylvania lines writes us that our organization has his warmest personal sympathy, while another of the same standing politely informs us that his road is always at our disposal and that he will grant us, with pleasure, any favor he can within his official capacity. Still another, who until quite recently was bitterly opposed to us, has torn down the barrier that separated us so long and so much to our disadvantage, and tendered our grand officers a hearty welcome, assuring them that he hoped to see the day when all the men in his employ would be working under the banner of our order.

Now that we have the friendship and cooperation of our superior officers, let us preserve them forever. Should any difficulty arise, whereby we should feel ourselves aggrieved, let us go to the heads of our respective departments and respectfully appeal for a restoration of the lost rights. Let us go like men and we will be treated as such. The object of our institution is to make men out of the crude material, and when we have succeeded in that, there will be no occasion for strikes, for when we are fully qualified to receive our rights, they will always be accorded us.

It is no small matter to plant benevolence into the heart of a stone, instill the love of sobriety into the putrid mind of debauchery, and create industry out of idleness. These are our aims and, if the world concedes them to be plausible, we ask that they find an anchoring place in its heart, and that in our humble efforts to carry them out, we will be beckoned onward and upward by those who have the power to assist us.

We wish to be as charitable to our members and their families as our limited means will permit. In the past two months we have sent the proceeds of our bounty into 12 little homes to dispel the darkness and gloom that enshrouded them. Twelve widows have been relieved from the agonies of want, and twice that number of little children have been rescued from the vortex of ignorance and vice, and placed within the sphere of morality, respect, and honor. Without our aid, they would have been reared in idleness and ignorance and thus have added to the shame and dishonor of the world. With it, they have been enabled to secure an education and thus learn the great principles of truth, honor, and justice. The little forms that were covered with the scanty garments of poverty have been made comfortable with warm and decent clothing, and their aching, throbbing hearts have been made light and happy in the knowledge that "Papa" was a member in good standing of the Brotherhood of Locomotive Firemen when he was killed, and that they will see that his little children do not suffer for want of assistance or protection.

Then again we aim to strike, with all the force of which we are capable, at the horrible vice of intemperance. We are well aware that railroad men, as a class, use stimulants more freely than men of most any other calling because of the fact that they are continually exposed to the weather and have been taught to believe, in many instances, that with alcohol in their bodies they could more successfully cope with the wet and the dry, the heat and the cold of the elements. This fallacy we are endeavoring to counteract, and when men have fallen into the habit of soaking themselves with liquor we bring a moral suasion to bear upon them that will reform them if they are capable of reform. If after repeated efforts we fail to bring about the desired end, the man is expelled from our ranks, because we cannot afford to have our good name tarnished by upholding drunkenness, nor hazard the sobriety of others by having them within its contaminating influence.

We regard temperance as the great moral factor that must be the salvation of mankind and we propose, with that portion of it with which we deal, to enforce a regard for it that will ensure sobriety.

The last but nonetheless essential of our principles is industry. We teach every man of our calling that it is honorable to do honest labor and that it is dishonorable to live in idleness, or at the expense of the industry of another.

Industry has no time to seek evil companions, foster bad habits, or commit acts of injustice.

Industry never steals or murders, and never goes to the penitentiary or to the scaffold.

Idleness is the foster parent of every vice.

Idleness is intemperance, dishonor, crime, and death.

Idleness supports every penitentiary and erects every scaffold, for it is the fabric upon which are based all of the vices that curse mankind.

Every member of our order must be industrious if he wishes to have the respect and esteem of his fellow members and be classed as a leader in our noble cause.

These are our aims and everywhere they are being hailed with delight as well as recognition.

With the endorsement of the railroad officials in the East, we have been enabled to reorganize that portion of our order, and thus we are *united again* from shore to shore and coast to coast. New lodges are rapidly being organized and applications for charters are coming in at such a rate as to preclude the possibility of doing all of them justice. The coming convention will represent at least 100 working lodges and the year following that event will open to us an era of prosperity seldom equaled and never excelled by any similar organization.

A word now in regard to our chief officers and we will close. The credit of bringing about a reconciliation between our superior officers and ourselves is due, in a very great measure, to the efforts of our grand master and grand instructor, the former with his pure and unselfish devotion to the order and the latter with his untiring work and matchless abilities. Frank W. Arnold,[7] our grand master, is an honor to our calling and we delight in paying to him a tribute of our esteem and respect. He reflects dignity upon his position, and with the loyalty of a true leader he has discharged every trust with a zeal and fidelity that have enlisted for him the love of all his followers. We can hardly venture to speak in praise of S. M. Stevens, our grand instructor, for we have not the ability to do him justice. Modest, unassuming, earnest, unselfish, and uncompromising in the interest of the order, he is a living monument of the principles it represents. Everywhere he carries with him the dignity of his exalted manhood and sheds about him the benign influences of his generous soul. With such leaders, we have a right to anticipate many glowing triumphs for our order in years to come.

Let every member nerve himself for the contest of the future. The banner under which we are struggling will shed the luster of honor and glory upon all who are enrolled beneath it, and we appeal to every lover of human happiness and progress to contribute by thought, word, or deed, according to opportunity, to the welfare of our brotherhood.

Notes

1. Line from "Thanatopsis" (1811) by William Cullen Bryant (1794–1878).
2. A family of nocturnally blooming cacti.
3. Stanza from "A Psalm of Life" (1838) by Henry Wadsworth Longfellow (1807–1882).
4. The origin of this literary snippet is uncertain.
5. Snippet from the poem "Our Brotherhood Chart," written for *Locomotive Firemen's Monthly Magazine* in February 1880 by young Indianapolis attorney H. N. Spaan.
6. The target of Debs's criticism is not completely clear, as the 1877 railway strike movement was widespread and spontaneous. According to the account of B of LF secretary-treasurer William N. Sayre, who was briefly jailed during the conflict and would logically be the object of Debs's ire, "firemen, brakemen, and laborers" were principals in the stoppage over back wages and a proposed wage reduction. See: "The Strike," *Locomotive Firemen's Monthly Magazine*, vol. 1, no. 9 (September 1877), 274–276.
7. Frank W. Arnold (1851–1917), a native of Columbus, Ohio, entered the railway service in 1866 as a "starter" for the Louisville City Railway Co. He became a brakeman in 1869 on another line and worked in that capacity until 1871, when he quit to open up a tobacco shop in Columbus, before moving on the next year to take a position with a dry-goods wholesaler. When the Panic of 1873 hit, Arnold found himself unemployed, so he returned to the railroad, taking a job as a fireman on the Chicago, St. Louis & Pittsburgh. He joined the fledgling B of LF in 1876, shortly before quitting the railroad again, this time to study law; he passed the Ohio State bar exam in February 1879. Arnold was elected grand master of the B of LF by the Chicago convention of 1879, and he remained in that position until 1885. Arnold was elected grand secretary and treasurer of the B of LF to succeed Gene Debs. He would remain in that position until his resignation in January 1904.

1882

The Square Man[†]

January 1882

While there is nothing meaner among men than the sneak, there is none grander or better than the square man. The sneak no one respects. The square man everybody honors. Riches and social position may belong to the former, but they will not bring him that mead of self-respect, that full measure of love from his fellow, which the square man enjoys as a result of his grandeur of character. Poverty and toil may be the lot in life of the latter, but he walks with his head amidst the stars. He is a king among his fellows.

The square man sympathizes with his friends in distress. His is the kind heart to devise means of help for the downtrodden and the lowly, and his is the hand to do the kindly bidding of his heart. The widow and the fatherless have a sure friend in the square man; nor does he wait till they come to him for his ready succor. He goes to them quickly when the heart is bleeding and trouble is lurking about the path of life, and by his earnest, hearty, helpful sympathy soon drives sorrow and trouble away. Everybody respects the square man. He may not wear good clothes; he may be a little ungrammatical in speech; he may even swear a little and look rough and uncouth, but the good, honest, square man is there.

If the square man grasps the throttle of an engine there will be no sleeping at that post. Lives are entrusted to him; all his faculties are on the alert for danger. No drink touches his lips while he is making his run. Clear-brained, keen-eyed, strong-armed he stands at his post, and if the hour of danger overtakes him while there, he will never desert it. Duty does not call him in vain. All the time while his engine is skimming along the rail like a thing of life under the sun's light, while it thunders into the darkness of night, while it crashes into the storm and out again into the morning light, he stands there silent, watchful, fearless. All who know him feel safe, for a square man is at the post of duty. So it is with the square man in all the walks of life. It makes no difference where you find him—on an engine or in a palace; homely, uncouth, and poor or rich, elegant, and handsome—he is always the same undaunted, honorable, square man.

---

† Published in *Firemen's Magazine*, vol. 6, no. 1 (January 1882), 16.

United Efforts[†]

February 1882

No one can estimate the vast amount that can be accomplished in all enterprises with united efforts. Nowhere is this fact made more manifest than in our organization.

In the whole history of its existence not a single lodge has gone down from any other cause except a lack of cooperation. Neither has one ever prospered without it.

Members may have their personal feelings for or against each other but they should never allow them to predominate in the lodge room. When the good of the order is at stake the bitterest enemies should work together in unison and harmony—remembering that only with united effort can the purposes in view be accomplished. It is very unfortunate that members should fall out with each other at all and doubly so when it interferes with their duties of membership. The aim of every ambitious member should be to harmonize all factions of dissenters. Without harmony there can be no success in any enterprise.

Great armies upon the field of battle depend upon a harmony of action, as much as anything else, to carry them on to victory. Political parties, in antagonizing each other for supremacy, must be united to succeed. The most powerful are beaten if there is a division and a lack of cooperation while the weakest are triumphant if harmony prevails.

This fact should be borne in mind by our members. Whatever your relations may be with your fellow members, let them not interfere with your aiding them when they are engaged in enhancing the welfare of the order. We want only good lodges and we will have no other kind if our members will pursue a straightforward, consistent, and manly course and blend their efforts harmoniously while discharging the solemn duties of membership.

---

† Published in *Firemen's Magazine*, vol. 6, no. 2 (February 1882), 80.

Masterful Men[†]

April 1882

Men confide in leaders. The bold man, the man of action, the man who grasps situations and masters them—he is the man whom his fellows love to honor; he is the man who becomes the standard-bearer in any great moral or political movement; he is the man who brings succor in the hour of danger, and upon him all hearts rely. Few men in moments of personal danger or in days of national turmoil act intelligently if left to their own resources. Some leader always springs to the front and assumes a command questioned by none. Such men are self-poised, heroic, calm. The swirl and clash of contending intellects, the mighty shock of arms, the hour fraught with fear and destruction have no power to disturb the masterful balance of mind possessed by these leaders of men.

Alexander crossing the river of Granicus in the face of the mighty hosts of Porus[1] is an example. The calm, self-assured, indomitable Greek intellect mastered a million foes simply by the power of leadership. Every Greek soldier became an unconquerable hero when fighting under the influence of the mastermind.

Caesar at Pharsalus became the master of Rome,[2] not because his army was stronger than Pompey's, for it was much less, not because he was a better general, but because his was the master intellect. Under his leadership his legions became as one man with but a single purpose. Fearlessly, blindly, they moved upon Pompey's ranks and won. From the beginning the result was inevitable; the leader of men was there.

There is something grand about the heroism of great warriors who, on the battlefield, amid smoke and carnage, remain the same stern, relentless, unstampedable leaders. Marshal MacDonald,[3] at the battle of Austerlitz, when commanded to storm a certain point, massed his forces and carried out his great emperor's command. The terrible fire of the enemy for hours mowed down rank after rank of his soldiery, but MacDonald sat upon his horse, cold, impassionate, pale, but as relentless as death; the only command he gave during those terrible hours of blood was "close on the center, forward." Even Napoleon turned away with a shudder, saying: "My God, what slaughter." MacDonald carried out his commands. Such leaders never fail.

These are examples of great leaders, men whose names are upon the lips of

---

† Published in *Firemen's Magazine,* vol. 6, no. 4 (April 1882), 170–171.

all; there are others who deserve no less of the world's honor. Men who risked life in the service of others. Men who saw the needs of the moment and grasped the golden opportunity. The engineman who stands by his engine in the hour of danger, going down with her in order that the lives entrusted to his care may be saved, is no less a hero, is no less a masterful man, than is the hero who dies for his country. To stand grandly at the post of duty, knowing the danger but flinching not, calm, alert, and active to avert destruction, is a picture of heroism as great, if not as tragic, as MacDonald at Austerlitz.

Sand[†]

June 1882

There is no quality in human nature more admirable than "sand." The man who has lots of "sand" is the successful man. No obstacles daunt him, no allurements turn him aside from the path he has marked. Grant's declaration—"We will fight it out on this line if it takes all summer"—has become a proverb because back of the statement stood the man of "sand."[4]

Sand means grit; it means the power to hold on. When an engine is called upon to exert its greatest strength it needs sand to give it a better grip on the track. When men are called upon to exert their greatest mental and physical strength, sand is necessary. Men who have plenty of sand in their boxes never slip on the path of duty. Wet weather and greasy tracks do not affect them, their sand will not let them fail.

The man of sand is a moral hero; no wavering on his part when duty commands his action. Be it at the bedside of the suffering or in the wild rush of the midnight train, the man of sand does what he is called upon to do, quickly, calmly, boldly—no quiver in his iron nerve. Death alone can conquer the man of sand.

† Published in *Firemen's Magazine,* vol. 6, no. 5 (June 1882), 268.

Labor's Reward[†]

August 1882

Skilled labor of all kinds is the great demand of the age. In these later days it is a practical, universal principle that every man must depend upon his own efforts for subsistence. The skilled labor of railroad employees is rendered, by this fact, more necessary and important than in any other case. The greatest interests of humanity are continually centered in their hands. There is no man who so often as the railroad employee has complete charge and control of the lives and fortunes of so large a part of humanity. Every impulse of nature and reason unite in loudly demanding that the railroad employee be preeminently a man of the very best good principle and good habits. This is as plain as the noonday sun, and the man who does not know and recognize it must be asleep or dead.

Labor, thanks to progress and common sense, is the good, broad, highway of this latter day and generation that leads to honor and greatness. This, at least, must ever remain the fact in this country. Industrious, skilled labor, with confirmed good habits of sobriety, order, and industry, is the grand free road that will lead all railroad employees to all that is desirable, or to be desired in this life, for any man in any station and at any time. The road for a railroad employee is as good to rise by as any other. It is certain and safe, and those who travel it are sure to reach the summit of their ambition. It becomes every man of good sense to travel it. The road to wealth and fortune, said our own great philosopher Franklin, is as plain as the nose on a man's face, if you desire to travel it.

Besides the other great advantages offered by this route, it is more pleasant than any other. The truth of it is that waste of time, drunkenness, and all those things that are usually called bad habits, do not *pay*, in a business sense. There is not enough fun in them to commend them to our consideration. The best enjoyment of life is to be of some account, and no man can get the best out of life and have the best it has in store for him unless he is of some account and does the best he knows. We all have sense enough to know what is best for us, and no man is bound to take second-class passage, and no man should do it.

[†] Published in *Firemen's Magazine*, vol. 6, no. 8 (August 1882), 365–366.

It is, by far, more pleasant to be honest, honorable, sober, and industrious than it is to be otherwise. We believe in getting the good out of life. That is what we are here for. All these great facts being so plain, it becomes important that every railroad employee should ally himself with those associations and relations that will more effectually recommend him to the great and common interests of all the people. No man lives or can live to himself in this world. Our interests are all common, and we all have an interest in each other. The base of all our great interests rests on industry, and what helps one laborer will help another. If one laborer, of whatever kind, is prosperous, we are all benefited by it. The managers of all our great corporations know this as well as anybody. The mission of the railroad employee is one of peace. He goes to his employers with an olive branch in his hand. Their interests are his interest, and his interests are theirs. There is every reason why they should work together in unison and harmony. By that means each can the most effectually advance his own interest.

The field of free and open business competition is *wide*. There is many an empire of wealth and honor to be conquered in it, and no matter what a man can accomplish with law and honor on his side, he has a *right to do;* nay! he *should* do—it is his *duty.* There is no end, no limit to what the employees of railroads accomplish for their own good, if they will only combine, and organize, and *stick together.* All other interests are organized to advance their welfare, and why should not *they?* There is no better organization for furthering the interests of railroad employees and putting them on the way to success in its best sense than the Brotherhood of Locomotive Firemen. It embraces every interest that is theirs and inculcates by its principles and laws all that will lead them to success and prosperity. This same brotherhood is certain to be the leading power in advancing and securing the interests of all laborers, more especially of its own members.

A Feeling of Success†

September 1882

Success is labor's prize,
Work is the mother of fame,
And who on a "boom" shall rise
To the height of an honest name?
[*Harper's* for August.]

The meeting of our Ninth Annual Convention brings with it a feeling of success that is encouraging beyond an ordinary degree.⁵ It is the success of a teaching that is noble and elevating. Our calling in life is a humble one, but we have brought it far above the degraded condition that it occupied a few years ago. At that time we struggled beneath a false education that received an impetus from a popularity that should have given its frown where it smiled. This degradation came from the baseness of the animal of our humanity, by drowning our finer instincts in liquor and dissipation. A drunkard is a murderer of the vilest order; he kills all the divine of his nature and leaves but the ungovernable baser passions to ruin his health, his intellect, and his soul. We have supplanted those vices and in their stead we have implanted aspirations for a higher and nobler ambition. We have persistently kept before the eyes of our members the dignity of self-respect—and we need not enlarge on the requirements to support this. We have removed from the minds of our members the false light that has heretofore existed in which they looked on the relation of employer and employee, and showed them clearly how closely one was identified with the other.

We wish it understood by these few, whose narrow minds seem to hold a contrary opinion, that we are men as other men, with the feelings and affections of other men, and holding a right to a consideration when our interest and welfare are at stake, which we are determined never to relinquish while Christianity and civilization exist or a free people hear a grievance and announce a judgment. This has been and shall continue to be the teaching of this order, and the success that has crowned our efforts breathes upon us a refreshing smile. But our duty, our undertaking does not end here: We attend

---

† Untitled editorial published in *Firemen's Magazine,* vol. 6, no. 9 (September 1882), 407–408.

the sick, we bury the dead, and we give to the widows and orphans a proof of our heartfelt sympathy in dollars and cents, the requirements of this world's demands upon us.

Railroad corporations and railroad managers, superintendents, and master mechanics all over the country have given us most flattering proofs of their appreciation of our good work, not only by their many acts of courtesy extended to our organizer and instructor [S. M. Stevens], but also to our traveling delegates, and in many instances they have displayed a personal interest in the welfare of our subordinate lodges. We shall simply say here that such acts of kindness are not lost upon us.

Now, as to our standing today. Entering on our tenth year, we shall briefly state that we number 115 lodges, with a membership of about 5,000. We have paid in the past year $20,000 on insurance claims to the widow and orphan fund, and have a balance of $10,000 in the treasury. Our organizer and instructor has traveled about 50,000 miles in the interest of the order, pushing on far into the territories, organizing lodges at Mandan, Dakota; Chama, New Mexico; Eagle Rock, Idaho; and Cheyenne, Wyoming, leaving a most substantial proof of his work behind him.

Our list of subscribers to the *Magazine* has increased to nearly 8,000, scattered all over the United States and Canada, giving us a direct and unbroken chain of communication every month.

Prosperity looks upon us at every hand and invites us onward and upward in our noble mission.

The convention will be an occasion of pride and satisfaction, for the members will receive an ovation at Terre Haute that will never be forgotten. The people will receive them with a warmness that will strongly indicate the standing that the brotherhood has where it is best known.

Let us then join hands and hearts anew in this commendable work, and while congratulating ourselves upon triumphs of the past let us nerve ourselves for the grand achievements yet in store for us.

The Last Ride†

October 1882

The man who earns his bread upon a locomotive risks his life and limb every moment he occupies in the discharge of his hazardous duties. Almost every hour brings the report of a wreck on the rail—of a train loaded with humanity gone down—of an engineer and fireman who "took their last ride."

Every precaution is taken against these dreadful calamities, but without avail. They seem to be inevitable as fate itself. The dangers give no warning of their approach. Silently they lie in ambush until their prey is certain, when they spring upon the unsuspecting victims with an insatiate fury. Their havoc is sad indeed to contemplate and the scenes that ensue are frightful to behold. Here and there, midst the shattered wreck of iron and timber and hissing steam are strewn the dead and dying. The king of terrors made no discrimination for we see the most sacred relations torn asunder with a merciless hand. Father, dead and mangled beyond recognition; mother, cruelly maimed; and little children imploring their aid. The coldness of death, the intense agonies of suffering, and the wailings of grief combine to make this scene heartrending in the extreme. Words can never express the depth of its horrors.

But thank fortune such calamities do not always follow a wreck. Between the train of living, throbbing, freight and approaching danger there stands the man in front: "the man of sand—the moral hero." No matter what element of destruction may reveal itself, he is there to avert it if he can; and if he cannot, to offer the first victim to appease its wrath. He may stop the train in time to save the precious lives committed to his keeping; but his own, he has to sacrifice as the price of his heroism. In almost every instance he is first to encounter the shock— first to hear the death knell sounded. How often we hear it said: "The train was saved without the loss of a single life, but the engineer and fireman were killed."

The passengers may, and often do, escape unharmed; the men in front, scarcely ever. They are found under their engines, shapeless, ghastly, frightful. No thought of home and loved ones light their last solemn moments on earth. A crash; a stifled cry of agony and despair; night without a star, and all is over.

> 'Tis the wink of an eye, the draught of a breath,
> From the blossom of health to the paleness of death.[6]

---

† Published in *Firemen's Magazine*, vol. 6, no. 10 (October 1882), 448–449.

Then begins the work of raising the ponderous mass of machinery to recover the remains. He who was first to breast the elements of destruction is last to be rescued from its terrible grasp. In the mass of debris is found his fallen form. The nameless hero has taken his last ride. He was faithful to the end.

Now comes the deepest and blackest shadows of this gloomy picture. We see two households in mourning—two wives brokenhearted and their fatherless children in abject despair. Again we look and see their cottages surrounded by mourning relatives and friends. The slow tolling of the bells indicates that the funeral day has arrived. Next come the sad and pathetic sermon, the funeral cortege, and the grave. All is over now. The men who were in front a few days ago have glided into the vast unknown.

Thus the engineman lives and thus he dies. In the midst of life and health and plenty he is cut down never to rise again. To contemplate their situation, it seems to us, should impress them with the necessity of being at all times prepared to "take their last ride."

They should never mount their engines without being in readiness to answer the call. If they have loving ones who depend upon them for support, they should make every provision for them in time. They should have a moral standing in the community in which they live so that the public sympathy will not be withheld from them in the hour of their emergency. They should have a clear and consistent record as men. They should be prepared to leave this world with a spotless character—one they need not fear to answer for in the world to come. To impress these principles upon the minds of men is the object of the Brotherhood of Locomotive Firemen, and upon the merits of its aims and purposes it will rise to the high sphere of usefulness it is destined to occupy. The grateful widows and orphans it has relieved, the maimed sufferers it has comforted, and the erring and infirm it has reclaimed from the world of vice are willing witnesses to its eternal progress.

Notes

1. Porus was a local king from the Punjab region of northern India. His forces engaged Alexander the Great (356–323 BC) at the Battle of the Hydaspes in 326 BC.
2. The Battle of Pharsalus, fought in Greece in August 48 BC, was the decisive battle in the Great Roman Civil War of 49 to 45 BC, in which the forces of Julius Caesar (100 BC–44 BC) emerged victorious over those of Pompey the Great (106 BC–48 BC).
3. Marshal Étienne Jacques Joseph Alexandre MacDonald (1765–1840) was a French-born military leader of Scottish extraction who was one of Napoleon Bonaparte's top field commanders.
4. Slight misquotation of a famous May 11, 1864, battlefield dispatch to Washington by Lieutenant General Ulysses S. Grant (1822–1885) following the first days of the Battle of Spotsylvania Court House, the bloodiest battle of the 1864 Overland Campaign.
5. The Ninth Annual Convention of the Brotherhood of Locomotive Firemen met in Terre Haute from September 11–15, 1882. Debs delivered a detailed report to the gathering detailing the financial and editorial progress of the organization over the previous year.
6. Couplet from the poem "Mortality" (1824), by William Knox (1779–1825).

1883

Labor, the Genius of Civilization[†]

January 1883

If all the money in the world were heaped together in one vast pile, it would be as powerless to do good for man as is the nerveless hand of death. Labor is the power that moves the world. Labor has brought us out of the darkness of the past into the noonday light of the nineteenth century. To labor, our country is indebted for its magical development of the past hundred years.

Labor has built our cities, scooped out our canals, bound ocean to ocean with bands of iron over which rush the commerce of millions, wiped out time and space by girdling the earth with electric wires, and she has made it possible to send not only the messages, but the very tones of love, across continents by means of the wonderful telephone.

Labor brings to the feet of man the minerals of every zone. Ships come home to him laden with the fruits of every climate. The diamond of Brazil reflects the beauty of woman and the gold of the Urals and Sierra Nevada form her ornaments. The wool of cashmere is woven into the beautiful textures of the Orient, while the iron of the Occident is welded into locomotives and steamships. The wheat of Dakota feeds the hungry millions of Europe, while the trained laborers of Europe manufacture the cloth which clothes the Western farmer. Over all this the genius of labor presides. Her magic wand touches the rough, unhewn things of earth and shapes them into forms of beauty and use.

The deft hand of the sculptor turns the forbidding block of marble into shapes of historic beauty. The Apollo Belvedere slept for ages a shapeless mass in the quarries of Carrara. Labor forced it from its dark and damp resting place and formed it into lines of beauty that have been wondrous for centuries. The genius of the painter shapes itself into immortal images on canvas out of the common clay and pigments of the earth.

Art, science, religion, government cannot exist without labor; she makes all these things possible. The king cannot wear his crown till labor gives him the power to do so. The pampered beauty cannot array herself in jewels and silks till labor has fitted them for things of adornment.

The world recognizes the value of the laborer more as the years go by. The days of lords and ladies, the days of feudal barons and kings, by right divine,

---

† Published in *Firemen's Magazine*, vol. 7, no. 1 (January 1883), 24.

are surely passing away. The lines which have been so cruelly drawn between the rich and titled on one side and the laboring classes on the other are being rapidly obliterated. The newer, brighter day is dawning; the day wherein the laborers of all kinds, from the skilled artisan down to the shoveler upon the streets, will be justly rewarded. Civilization has placed her hand trustingly in the hand of her mother, Labor, and together they walk with majestic step along the highway of progress, drawing after them all the honored laborers of earth and trampling to death the drones and the worthless.

Man's Power and God's Power[†]

March 1883

Man gathers the beautiful stones from the quarry; the iron, the silver, the gold, and the precious jewels from the mine; the many costly woods from the forest; and builds a palace. He decorates it with the genius of the painter and the sculptor and with the deft work of the artisan. He surrounds it with groves of beautiful trees and beds of many-colored flowers. Deer wander amidst the sylvan shades, and birds sing in the leafy bowers. The palace is complete; it stands proudly in the sunlight.

God scoops out great hollow places in the solid earth and fills them with the rushings of many waters. He heaps up mountains of rock and between them places the fruitful valleys. With His finger He traces the courses of mighty rivers, and above and around all places the storm-riven atmosphere. Millions of ages ago He sent it whirling into space around its central luminary, and there it still swings, swiftly, silently, grandly, held by nothing but the eternal will of its creator.

One is the work of a finite, the other of an infinite mind.

Man consults with his genius and produces the engine. In one of its many forms he sees it rushing like a thing of life from ocean to ocean. Whirling along dangerous precipices, skimming over vast prairies, panting through the hearts of great cities, creeping through dark tunnels, unloading its burden at last where the waves forbid its farther progress. The engine is man's emblem of power.

---

† Published in *Firemen's Magazine*, vol. 7, no. 3 (March 1883), 122–123.

God gathers the forces of the universe and makes a sun. He sends it upon its grand march into the starry depths, drawing after it a mighty train of planets, moons, comets, and meteors. It sends its rays millions of miles into space, heating with burning heat the mountains and plains of Mercury, and giving to the earth its seasons of ice and verdure. Great storms sweep over its surface whose effects are felt to the outmost bounds of Uranus. Jets of flame shoot from its surface a hundred thousand miles high and fall back into the eternal sea of fire. Around it lie other suns. Together they sweep through the awful abysses of space, answering obediently to the will of their creator.

The engine is the type of man's highest power, the sun is the type of God's.

Man calls into activity his ingenuity and makes a watch. It is a marvel of skill and beauty. In the day and through the silent night it keeps up its ceaseless time beat, measuring the seconds as they run.

God takes the wheat of the field and places it in a human stomach; there it is changed by a wondrous chemistry into blood. From the blood a mechanism equally wonderful extracts bone, sinew, muscle, nerve, and skin, and a living, breathing man walks forth. Most wonderful of all, a part of the wheat passes into that mysterious alembic, the brain, and a thought is born. It may be a poem of love and hope or a tragedy of fear and death. It may whisper of green fields and pleasant homes or it may dream of prison cells and the hangman's rope. It may breathe anthems of praise to its creator or it may revel in the orgies of the debauched and the ruined. It may dwell in the mind of the sordid miser or it may prompt the smile upon the face of sleeping beauty dreaming of love and heaven.

The watch is the mechanism of man. Man is the mechanism of God.

Honesty[†]

April 1883

What is grander than an honest man? Who is nobler than the man who pays his debts? "Pay as you go" is a very common proverb, but it means more than men usually imagine. To run in debt with no hope of paying is as bad as highway robbery. The only difference between the man who borrows, not intending to repay, and the man who picks a pocket is that the latter goes to the penitentiary, while the former ought to.

Owe no man anything longer than it is possible to repay! The man who pays his debts stands a better chance for heaven than the man who shouts at revivals while his washwoman is starving to death, because the devout Christian has taken the bankrupt law. Plank down the cash every time; don't say, "Send in the bill." Pay your board bills, your wash bills; pay your dues at the lodge; don't be a deadbeat, always behind and always asking your creditors to call again.

There is more genuine Christianity in one man who pays up than in a hundred professed Christians who subscribe to foreign missions with no intent to pay the subscription. Don't sail under false colors! It is better to be poor and not have much enjoyment than to be rich at the expense of your creditors. The man who beats a boardinghouse will steal the first chance he gets. A deadbeat is a thief.

Meet every obligation in life! It is better to die poor with your debts paid than to leave your heirs a fortune in your wife's name. Don't let your wife and children lose the benefits of our brotherhood simply because you failed to pay your way! The proudest legacy you can leave your children is an honest name. Don't allow any man to say to your children, "Your father owes me money."

The world will forgive a man many shortcomings if he will only pay his debts. If you can't afford an expense, don't indulge in it; it is better to do without than to make some creditor do without. If you make only $50 a month, don't spend $70—the $20 belong to some other man. Pay as you go, be honest, and you will gain men's respect; run in debt and you will have to make friends with the constable.

[†] Published in *Firemen's Magazine,* vol. 7, no. 4 (April 1883), 162.

The Rights of Labor[†]
April 1883

Great questions, relating more especially to the rights of laboring men but touching in their relations all the interests of humanity, are forcing themselves more urgently every year on the attention of the people. It is impossible to avoid these great problems; they must be solved. Bound together as all humanity is in an eternal union, mutually and equally beneficial, there can be but one judgment, that the universal interest is that they be solved justly. Success and the security of justice can only come by seeking the greatest good of the greatest number. This is the first, the greatest fundamental principle. It is the primer of our government. Our members, their wives, and their children are all deeply interested in the success of our order. To them our attention is especially directed. Our cause is of national importance. It is a part of justice and humanity, all who are interested in these are interested in our success.

The rights of labor have been the subject of agitation for centuries. The more we contemplate them the more certain it is that nothing but good can come of them and the justice done them. In advocating the rights of labor we have an eye single to justice and universal good. Labor is the grand builder of all to be desired; it builds up the world and is the source of all good. It opens up the floodgates of prosperity. No encomium of labor can be too great. To it we owe our blessings. It is the salvation of humanity, our great fortune, the source of unlimited bounty.

When we contemplate the vast fields of labor of all kinds open in our country we are filled with wonder and admiration. Truly here is a scene to inspire the soul of the greatest genius. How gloriously we shall gather in the sheaves of our greatness. Let us possess the goodly land before us. Labor is civilization, and civilization is labor. By supporting the interests of labor we secure to ourselves all the great benefits of civilization. Pampered idleness and snobbish dandyism is barbarity. Who has a better right to the fruits of labor than the laborer himself?

Our labors are the result of our sweat and toil, of brain and muscle, by virtue of which we have made them our own. We have identified ourselves with them; they are a part of us; they and their fruits belong to us; they have our brand upon

---

† Published in *Firemen's Magazine*, vol. 7, no. 4 (April 1883), 162–163.

them; and we will own, reclaim, and acknowledge them wherever we find them. It is an individual work, essential in every way. No one will be found to perform it for us and no one so well qualified as ourselves to do our own duty. We are the best informed on the subject, and we hold it to be self-evident that we are the best and, indeed, the sole judges of our own interests. The interests of labor have been too long neglected for the good of us all. Let them be supported and all will be happy, successful, and prosperous.

In forwarding the interests of labor we make no war on capital. Capital's best interests are in a well-rewarded and fostered system of labor. What could capital ever hope for from impoverished labor? When labor becomes impoverished and beggarly paid, capital must become the prey of robbers and plunderers. Labor is the prop that supports capital, and when the prop is gone, what depends upon it must fall. Our great capitalists know this. They will heed it. We will not meet with any opposition from them. Their salvation depends upon us. They understand our grand object, the general good of us all, and will assist us. We seek not to overturn, but to improve.

As the military power is subject to the civil, so should the interests of capital be subject to the interests of labor. We propose to represent, protect, and secure the best interests of all our members in the fullest manner possible, in order that justice be done. We must have a voice in the decision of our affairs.

Self-Respect[†]

May 1883

The man that respects himself will meet with the respect of others. As we measure ourselves, so do others measure us. This is exemplified every day. The loafer, the bully, and the deadbeat are despised by all. Why? Because they have drawn their own measure and men accord it to them. The diligent, sober, honest citizen meets with the applause of his fellows. Why? Because he too has measured himself, and men accord him the measurement. If one desires to be respected, that one must respect himself. Be proud! Pride yourself on your

---

† Published in *Firemen's Magazine,* vol. 7, no. 5 (May 1883), 213.

integrity, on your sobriety, on your industry, and self-respect and the respect of others will follow.

The man who slouches through life, who evades his duty, who deadbeats his friends never attains anyone's respect, not even his own. A sneak can't respect himself; how then can he, in reason, expect others to do so? The manly man, the man of broad views, of liberal action, of fearless conduct, the world hastens to honor, while the coward, the dishonest man, and the lazy meet with swift condemnation.

Self-respect does not belong to the rich. Many a man who wears fine clothes is a dog at heart. The engineman, with the stain of smoke and grease on his face, is just as capable of commanding respect as is the man in broadcloth and fine linen; it is a question of conduct and not of clothes.

We desire to enforce upon our members the necessity of self-respect. Respect yourselves too much to get drunk, too much to neglect your duties, too much to play the deadbeat. Ours is an honorable calling, and we can make it more so by acting honorably. Scorn littleness! Turn from dishonesty as you would from a snake. Pay your way. Help the needy. Be true to your friends. These things, well done, will make you honorable, self-respecting citizens.

Old Time Prejudice†

June 1883

When our railroad system was in its infancy, it was exceedingly loose-jointed in many ways. The very best minds in the management were often vexed and bewildered beyond measure. Railroads at first were chiefly built on local subsidies. Extravagant promises were made to counties and individuals to secure stock subscriptions, and when obtained, the builders generally finished with money negotiated by trust companies and secured by bonds. Then came default in payment of interest, foreclosure, sale, and purchase by parties who knew little and cared less for local interest. In this way the friendship of the people was changed to bitterest prejudice. The lawmaking power was evoked

---

† Published in *Firemen's Magazine,* vol. 7, no. 6 (June 1883), 254–255.

to hamper railroad property in every conceivable way. Railroad commissioners were created and every method of hounding the railroads fully inaugurated. And so railroad investments, especially all local investments, were regarded with suspicion. It brought on a war between capitalists and organized counties, and in some instances whole states became involved. Such were some of the embarrassments in our early railroad development.

In addition to these, the operation of the roads themselves, even after their construction, was but poorly understood. It was a long time before a complete accounting system could be provided. There seemed, at first, to be no way to stop the leaks. The smaller roads, one after another, soon perished, and consolidations followed. This unsettled state of things pervaded every department. The train men, engineers, and firemen, among others, did pretty much as they pleased. There was no such thing, in many instances, as telegraphic orders, so the movement of trains was governed almost entirely by the arbitrary rules furnished in the timetables. Once behind, they must wait for time. There were none to tell them how they could make it up when lost. Accidents were multiplied, and the destruction of property was very great. General superintendents and their men were constantly at war with each other. The whole system seemed to rest on bad faith, and insubordination took the place of authority.

This state of things held sway for many years. After numerous experiments and as many failures, the management of the most competent men in the country was brought into requisition. At first these movements were cautious and slow, but always forward. Organization soon began to take the place of anarchy. Comptrollers were put into position and auditing departments organized. This enabled the management every day to see just where they stood. Superintendents took heart, the men began to feel the force of discipline, and railroads generally reared their structures on stable foundations.

Prosperity once inaugurated, the managers began to contrive for larger profits and more extended power. No one of the roads could accomplish this thing alone—competition was in the way of it. Associations were accordingly formed and pools established. The excuse assigned was self-protection. This all seemed well enough. There was no law against it, and being inside its limits, the legal justification of their conduct was freely conceded. But some of these managers wanted the thing to stop here. They desired to make a monopoly of self-protection. They entered into the bonds of organized cooperation. The Brotherhood of Locomotive Firemen, among others, was instituted. There were many reasons for it. Locomotive firemen are chiefly young men, away from the endearments of home, and need care and sympathy. The courts had held, quite generally, that employees could not recover against corporations for personal injuries. The risk of their work was great, and accidents were certain. The brotherhood provided for this. Nothing could have been more humane. The organization guarded them against the arbitrary sway of greed. Its members well understood they were a necessary part of the railroad system, and that the value of their labor should go hand in hand with the prosperity of their employers. That was right, and based upon the soundest principles of political economy.

Strikes have sometimes taken place, and there is still a fossilized class of railroad managers who say they are the certain adjuncts of brotherhood. Some of them will not employ our members. This is very shortsighted. Our brotherhood prevents strikes. It inculcates sobriety and obedience. No railroad management can stand on any other foundation. A sober, just man is not likely to strike if justice is meted out to him. All strikes are easily explained and just as easily adjusted. Let common justice be done all along the line, and strikes will be unknown.

Backbiting a Calamity[†]

July 1883

There is nothing more baleful in our order than personal unfriendliness. A vicious rumor flies like the winds—the truth is rarely able to overtake it. There is nothing more to be dreaded than the forked tongue of slander—slander spoken and slander published. He who retails a deliberate slander, knowing it to be such, at once becomes as vicious as its author. What is life without a good name? It costs years of sober, steady care. Slander cannot destroy it, but it may place burdens upon it. It is so much better to help than discourage mankind.

Life is a great struggle—a hard struggle. It is all uphill. The slanderer on the way is more to be dreaded than the robber. The robber seeks our money; the slanderer would crush every precious hope.

Slander sometimes creeps into the sacred precincts of our brotherhood. There can be no excuse for it. If any brother has been aggrieved, our laws give him a rational remedy. Every injury can thus be entirely repaired. Ours is not

---

† Published in *Firemen's Magazine,* vol. 7, no. 7 (July 1883), 306.

only a tribunal of justice, but of affection. If any man is unworthy of a seat in our order, and the fact is made manifest in the plain way provided, he is summarily sent away to return no more. Misapprehension is an ever-present source of mischief. Inquiry, moderation, and forbearance will go far beyond the reach of slander in the redress of personal grievances.

Railway Officials†

October 1883

We have had opportunities recently to be brought in contract with some of our superior officers. The results in all cases have been mutually pleasant and gratifying. The fact was made manifest that they are interested in our work and that they are willing to assist us in performing it. In all cases they received and treated us with cordiality, consideration, and respect. They were not so busy that they could not listen to what we had to say on behalf of our order. In fact, many of them were anxious to learn all about its condition and then generously proffered their assistance to the cause. The railroad official who is alive to the interests of the corporation he represents is bound to be our friend. In helping us, he is helping himself, for surely the efforts we are making to give him faithful and reliable men are in his interest as well as our own. Railroad officials generally are aware of this fact. They understand that in proportion as we succeed in carrying out our objects, their engineers and firemen will become sober, reliable, and faithful men.

Of course, all railroad officials are not so considerate, and even if they knew that we were toiling to advance their interests, they would not have the candor to admit it. Their hearts are calloused with prejudice and their souls narrowed with selfishness, arrogance, and conceit. But they do not represent the ideal railroad official of today. In fact, they are only fossils and are looked upon as the relic of a past generation. We neither crave nor care for their friendship, for the reason that it is not worth having. We want to deal only with men of warm hearts, broad views, and liberal ideas, and there is no question but that they are

† Published in *Firemen's Magazine,* vol. 7, no. 10 (October 1883), 456.

rapidly supplanting the fossil element. The time is coming when the employer and employee will stand upon basis of equality so far as their common rights are concerned. There will be kind treatment on the one side and obedience to duty on the other, and the result will be a mutual bond of sympathy and support.

1884

The Mission of Our Brotherhood[†]

May 1884

Since the organization of the Brotherhood of Locomotive Firemen the question has been often asked, "What is its mission?" Questions are more easily asked than answered, and yet we propose to answer this interrogatory with becoming frankness.

The reader will at once perceive the necessity for prefatory remarks. We shall approach the main question with considerate caution. Locomotive firemen are preeminently practical. They are not distinguished as devotees of panegyric or pyrotechnic displays of impractical theories. Locomotive firemen are remarkable for common sense. They are bronze-browed, hard-fisted, noble-natured men. They are forever dealing with problems which demand and command serious thought. A locomotive fireman cannot, in the nature of things, be a dude. He is forever facing danger. Every faculty is on the alert. There is not a bit of the ideal or of fiction in his chosen calling. He deals with fire, steam, speed, danger—responsibilities which, when on duty, demand ceaseless vigilance. In all the avocations known to modern civilization, the locomotive fireman has chosen the most perilous. When he mounts his engine, he takes his life in his hand. His partings with his loved ones are always in the nature of adieus. He has no assurance that he will see them again until the day when "the sea shall give up its dead."[1] Say what we will, there is a mournful grandeur in the calling of a locomotive fireman. He lives a year sometimes in an hour, in a minute. His iron horse, fed on fire, dashes on over bridges, around curves, through tunnels and cuts 25, 40, or 60 miles an hour, in the light, in the twilight, in the darkness. Behind him a train with precious lives, his own life at stake; home, wife, children are in his thoughts; wakeful, watchful, he plunges on. Hopefully he peers into the darkness, and when the route is run and the steed stands still, we opine—indeed, we know—the locomotive fireman thanks God.

There are at least 22,000 of these men in the United States and the Canadas—10,000 of whom are enrolled as members of the Brotherhood of Locomotive Firemen. All hail comrades! Let us reason together. The *Magazine* is your friend. It speaks for you. Its high ambition is to promote your welfare. What is the mission of our order? Let us be in earnest. Locomotive firemen

† Published in *Firemen's Magazine,* vol. 8, no. 5 (May 1884), 277–282.

are not fanatics. They are not vagarists, utopians. They seek the attainable. It is within reach. It is not a myth, a fantasy, an illusion, a hallucination, a phantom, or a dream. We state the case boldly. The best for locomotive firemen is not to be found within the domain of *strikes*.

A strike means war. The shibboleth motto of locomotive firemen is peace. But, for the nonce, dismissing these propositions we repeat, "What is the mission of the Brotherhood of Locomotive Firemen?" As we write, the glory of our order is unfolded to our vision. We see its citadel lodges embracing the continent from rock-ribbed Maine, from the Thousand Islands of the Saint Lawrence, to the Golden Gate, to where the Oregon pours its mighty flood, a continental brotherhood. We indulge our fancy and surmise that every scream of the locomotive whistle tells us that a locomotive fireman is on duty and doing his duty. We survey the map of our country. We note the intermingling of railroad systems, embracing cities, towns, districts, and including a continent, and then we say, on all these highways of travel are scores of locomotive firemen. We fancy the day is near at hand when every locomotive fireman will be a member of our beneficent brotherhood. Why? Because it is organized to promote the welfare of men of his calling. Still, the question recurs, "What is the mission of our brotherhood?" Is it understood? Is it fully comprehended? Do we individually and collectively appreciate the majesty of our mission? The Brotherhood of Locomotive Firemen has certain high ambitions in view of certain purposes, certain aims. What are they? Its ambition is that every locomotive fireman shall be in the highest and best sense of the term a gentleman; self-poised, self-assured, true to every trust, every obligation; a *chevalier sans peur et sans reproche;*[2] a man who knows his duty and performs it with unwavering fidelity; sober, industrious, self-respectful; the peer of any man who walks God's green earth. The purpose of the order is to have such men, and only such men, within its charmed circle—men who pay their dues, who are ambitious to maintain the morale of the order, who appreciate the obligations of membership, and who recognized the sacredness of their responsibilities. Ours is a benevolent organization. We propose to *stand* by the living—that we may *stand* by the dead. It is more than benevolent. It is an organization designed to build character, perfect and adorn it, give it symmetrical and substantial proportions, the foundation stones of which are sobriety, industry, and fidelity. What more can we say in regard to the mission of our brotherhood? Much. It is designed to make a home a type of heaven—a snug harbor for "poor wanderers of a stormy day"—where wooing wives and prattling childhood give every cloud a silver lining, and attune every chord of the human heart to melody. We could pursue these felicitous thoughts indefinitely, for our faith of the future of our order knows no boundaries.

But negatively, rather than affirmatively, the Brotherhood of Locomotive Firemen was not, we are bold to say, organized to inaugurate strikes nor to favor strikes. We assume, and do not hesitate, to proclaim our convictions that labor strikes are not, and in the nature of things cannot be, in the interest of labor. We assume that labor is capital. We ignore technical distinctions. Capital to be profitable must be employed. We are not unmindful that we are upon the threshold of controverted propositions. We enter the arena of debate with confidence. We invite criticism. We have the courage of our convictions. The mission of the Brotherhood of Locomotive Firemen is not to antagonize capital. Strikes do that; hence, we oppose strikes as a remedy for the ills of which labor complains. Our purpose is to do away with misapprehensions. We cannot afford to be misunderstood. Locomotive firemen are employees— their employers are the owners and managers of railroads. In the very nature of things we should understand each other. The Brotherhood of Locomotive Firemen was not organized to dictate prices. It is no part of its mission. It will not deviate one hair's breadth from its course.

Our brotherhood proposes to offer to railroad officials sober, industrious, moral, competent men, tried and true. We propose that the time shall come when a brotherhood fireman shall be preferred to an outsider. It is the purpose of the Brotherhood of Locomotive Firemen to banish from the order every unfaithful man. Deadbeats, men of crooked ways are to be ostracized, banished. Ours is to be a brotherhood of gentlemen—honest, faithful, sober men. Railroad officials want that class of men. They cannot do without them. Their character, their reputation, their money, their profits all combine to make honest, sober, industrious, faithful firemen a desideratum. We take it for granted that when such men are employed, railroad officials will pay them all they can afford. There may be exceptions. We are discussing the rule. Be this as it may, if locomotive firemen engage in strikes, they do it outside of the Brotherhood of Locomotive Firemen. The order has no striking machinery. It was not founded for strikes. We have a better theory for disagreements between employer and employee. Strikes never settled any labor question. Strikes have invariably inflicted incalculable evils upon the strikers.

We desire to make ourselves distinctly understood. Let us introduce a few illustrations: A man at $2 per day, $60 per month, earns $720 a year, which is equal to an investment of $18,000 in government bonds bearing 4 percent interest. The proposition illustrates the idea of labor capital. It is a trite saying that "capital is sensitive"—timid. Approach a money capitalist, propose to him an investment, and his first inquiry will be: "Will it pay?" In discussing the subject with him, in answering his inquiries, there will be no time to introduce poetry or sentiment. He wants facts and figures. He balances probabilities. If the favorable predominate he will invest, otherwise he will withhold his money. The proposition is of universal application. There is absolutely no exception. We hold that labor capital is as sensitive as money capital, and there are many and cogent reasons why it should be the more sensitive and cautious. Money capitalists seldom invest their all in any enterprise, but the labor capitalist, the workingman, the wage earner does, for the time being, invest his all—his time, his skill, his health, his life; hence, we assume that labor capital is more vitally involved than money capital in all matters pertaining to strikes.

We have said we are opposed to strikes as a means of settling controverted labor questions. We are opposed to strikes primarily because we are satisfied they do not promote the welfare of laboring men. We are persuaded from our readings, observation, and experience that there is a better way out of labor disagreements with employers than to "strike" out. If there is anything in fact and logic, if there is anything worth considering in figures and common sense, we are persuaded that our proposition can be satisfactorily demonstrated, and we invite the attention of the brotherhood to an honest solution of the problem. It is stated by the highest authority that the average cost of 100 miles of railroad is $3,074,474; for our purpose we take the round sum $3,000,000. The average number of locomotives on each 100 miles of railroad is given at 20. We will assume that these 20 locomotives require 30 locomotive firemen. Here, then, we have the situation clearly defined. The road is built and equipped. The locomotives are on the track. The train is made up and ready to start. But there is no locomotive fireman on the engine. Now comes into bold prominence a fact which must forever be recognized, that money capital is useless without the assistance of labor capital, skill capital, muscle capital, and this fact ought to, and must eventually, bring money capital and labor capital into harmonious existence. They are necessary to each other. It is an indissoluble connection and cannot be revoked, and we plead guilty to the charge of a desire to make this association profitable and agreeable to both parties. We believe we see the dawning of a new era, and every word of ours shall be a harbinger note of peace and goodwill.

Again: We have said the 100 miles of railroad cost $3,000,000, and that the train was on the track ready to move, awaiting only the presence of the locomotive fireman. At this juncture we are told that the locomotive firemen have *struck* and that the train cannot move. We have the picture fully outlined— vivid as lightning. We are in a position to contemplate it in its immediate and remote consequences. We shall endeavor to be frank. We have no sinister ambitions to subserve. Invested money in the amount of $3,000,000 stands still. It is doomed to inertness. Authorities say that for the year 1882 there were in operation 107,158 miles of railroads; that the capital and funded debt of these roads amounted to $3,456,078,196, and that the total dividends paid amounted to $102,031,434, or about 3 percent. Our authority for these figures is *Poor's Manual*[3]—hence we assume that the 100 miles of road which we have introduced to illustrate our argument, if there had been no strike, would have earned dividends for its owners during the year amounting to $90,000, but which, owing to the strike, earned nothing.

We have shown in this article that a locomotive fireman, earning $720 a year, is equal to the man who has $18,000 invested in government securities bearing 4 percent interest. We have assumed that every 100 miles of railroad require 30 locomotive firemen. If we are correct (and whether exact or not, the figures illustrate our argument), then the 100 miles of railroad represent an investment of firemen capital of $540,000 at 4 percent, yielding dividends amounting to $21,600 a year. Now, be it remembered, the strike not only compels $3,000,000 money capital to earn no dividends, but it also compels $540,000 of locomotive firemen capital to earn no dividends. The money capital and the labor capital stand still—do nothing and earn nothing. We protest that such a state of affairs is not founded in wisdom.

But this is not all, nor the worst of the situation. We have assumed, for the sake of the argument, that the strike continues one year. Even numbers are better than fractions for our purpose, while ratios remain the same. At the end of the year, we will assume, the strike is ended. There is always a limit to human endurance. How stands the account? The owners of the $3,000,000 invested in the road have lost $90,000, and the locomotive firemen, who represented $540,000 labor capital, have lost $21,600. The aggregate loss has been $111,600. The $3,000,000 money capital has lost what it failed to earn— $90,000. How about the firemen? They have not only lost what they failed to earn, $21,600, but, assuming that it has cost them the same to live while idle as it cost when employed, they are out of pocket at the end of the year $43,200. We here discuss the money problem. We omit the demoralizing consequences of idleness—tramping, abandonment of family, and home topics of admitted seriousness. With such facts in full view, we are bold to assert that strikes have no compensations equal to the losses they entail.

We believe there is a better way out of such disagreements as occasionally arise between locomotive firemen and railroad officials, between money capital

and labor capital, and it is the purpose of the Brotherhood of Locomotive Firemen to find that way and the high ambition of the *Firemen's Magazine* to place
the facts relating to such subjects in such a light as to bring about a perfect
understanding between railroad managers and our brotherhood. The mission
of the Brotherhood of Locomotive Firemen is to build—not tear down. It is
to enthrone confidence rather than distrust. We detest sycophancy. We abhor
arrogance. We admire manhood. The Brotherhood of Locomotive Firemen has
for its foundation principles which dignify and glorify human nature. It champions the cause of labor not by antagonizing money, but rather by showing that
between money and labor capital there is and must forever remain an intimate
alliance, which, when the terms of the federation are honestly and honorably
adjusted, will be productive of untold benefits. But, again, referring to our order: Its growth and prosperity are in all regards phenomenal. There is nothing
to parallel its progress. There are now in operation 210 lodges. Our membership
exceeds 10,000. We have stated that in 1882 there were in operation in the United
States 107,158 miles of railroad, and the entire North American system in 1882
amounted to 127,830 miles. If there are 20 locomotives to every 100 miles of
road, then, we assume, there are in the country 22,560 locomotive firemen. Of
these more than 10,000 keep step to the music of our brotherhood. It is a music
which glorifies benevolence. Every wheel, and every wheel within a wheel, of
our order is set in motion by the inspiring, heaven-born spirit of benevolence.

Intoxication[†]

August 1884

We have frequently heard it said, by engineers and firemen, that they never
get drunk on duty, leaving it to be inferred that they are free to indulge to an
unlimited extent when not on their engine. This is a false idea, and the brotherhood emphatically denies that any locomotive engineman has the right to
allow himself to become intoxicated under any circumstances, or at any time.
If he does so, he forfeits his membership in our order. If at one time or place

---

† Published in *Firemen's Magazine,* vol. 8, no. 8 (August 1884), 472.

he gives to his passion such an unbridled sway, what guarantee has he that he will not do so at another?

It is said with truth: "Play with the fool at home, and he will play with you abroad." We cannot too severely condemn the criminality of drunkenness in men of our calling, and we urge on every lodge in our organization to punish it as it deserves.

Truth[†]

August 1884

It is always better to tell the truth than a falsehood. No matter what the circumstances may be, candid and truthful statement of the facts will always prove beneficial in the end.

We cannot afford to indulge in misrepresentation for, sooner or later, the fact comes to light and then even the truth will awaken doubt and suspicion. We must be absolutely honest. We must represent our aims and purposes fairly and we must practice what we preach. It will not do for us to declare war on drunkenness simply for effect. If we establish laws in opposition to intemperance and fail to enforce them, we are guilty of misrepresentation. We must not pretend to be what we are not. If our principles are good, and we believe they are, we should strictly adhere to them. Every member should be the embodiment of our teachings.

As applied to our relations with our employers, the matter of being truthful is a very important one. They will respect us in proportion as we deal honestly with them. It sometimes occurs that engineers and firemen get into trouble on the road, through negligence or a similar cause, and in order to avert the blame they misrepresent the facts to their master mechanic or superintendent. In other words, they indulge in falsehood to screen their guilt. This policy will not do. As a general thing, the truth eventually comes to the surface, and he who told the lie can never hope to be trusted again. It is certainly better to tell the truth and manfully bear the consequences. No matter what the result may be, we will at least preserve our honor and manhood.

---

† Published in *Firemen's Magazine,* vol. 8, no. 8 (August 1884), 471.

Railroad Managers and the B of LF[†]

September 1884

In the discussion of any subject, social, scientific, or moral, religious, educational, or financial—it matters not what—a very large margin should always be allowed for ignorance, stupidity, and bigotry. There are always to be found in every community an element composed of those who wear the "human face divine"[4] for no other purpose, seemingly, than to disgrace and degrade it, and these creatures, when "dressed in a little brief authority, play such fantastic tricks before high heaven as make the angels weep."[5]

The Brotherhood of Locomotive Firemen was organized, primarily, for the social, moral, and intellectual advancement of its members. Its aim is to inculcate sobriety and frugality, self-respect and independence—in a word, the highest type of manhood and citizenship. We unhesitatingly challenge the severest scrutiny of the fundamental principles of our noble order by friend or foe, and demand of them to point out in the constitution and bylaws of our brotherhood, or in its record, from first to last, any measure or practice which bears testimony in conflict with the declarations we have made.

It must be admitted, therefore, that our purposes are strictly in accord with all things of good report. Our aims are high, our ambitions praiseworthy. Locomotive firemen are not theorists, visionaries laboring to give hallucinations the force and value of verities. They are, on the contrary, preeminently practical men—necessarily so, for their vocation compels them to deal with problems demanding caution, vigilance, courage, and risks of life and limb. Inebriety, carelessness, or neglect invite such terrible penalties that locomotive firemen cannot fail to observe that however lightly such defects may be regarded by others, for themselves, they cannot be tolerated without increasing in a terrible ratio the damages which forever accompany them in their perilous rides on the rail.

The Brotherhood of Locomotive Firemen, as an organization, seeks to intensify the abhorrence of its members of all things calculated to imperil life, character, or employment. It seeks to create and to foster those ideas of manhood and citizenship which, if carried into practice, must of necessity make a brotherhood fireman the peer of his fellow citizens in any and every walk of life—sober, industrious, frugal, intelligent, and self-respectful.

---

† Published in *Firemen's Magazine*, vol. 8, no. 9 (September 1884), 539–541.

The Brotherhood of Locomotive Firemen, as an order, has reasoned thus: "If our members are temperate men, intelligent men, cautious and watchful, men of integrity and high social standing, they will be in demand by all railroad managers throughout the land." In this we conclude they have reasoned intelligently. The logic is sound. The proposition cannot be successfully controverted, and yet it must be written that there are railroad managers who will not employ firemen who are members of our brotherhood. We confess it is difficult to believe that, at this high noon of intelligence, the country is disgraced by such railroad managers. They are not men of common sense. They are victims of vulgar prejudices. Their judgment is warped and distorted. They are the enemies of the roads they control and the foes of society. They are public nuisances. They refuse to employ men who are honest, sober, capable, and industrious, qualities of head and heart which should be a passport to employment everywhere, and in which the public is profoundly interested, because such locomotive firemen belong to an organization designed to inculcate such virtues. These bull-headed burlesques of humanity by their acts, and acts speak louder than words, inform the public that a drunken, dishonest, negligent fireman, who does not belong to our brotherhood, is preferable to a sober, honest, watchful fireman who does belong to our brotherhood.

In pursuing a course so manifestly in conflict with the interests of railroads, and which is well calculated to fill the public mind with alarm, it becomes important to ascertain, if possible, the reasons which prompt such action. It is at war with prudence. It is a protest against virtue. It is in open revolt against sobriety, intelligence, and manhood. It is a bid for ignorance, drunkenness, and incapacity, and railroad managers who discard Brotherhood firemen say to the owners of their roads, "As between a sober, industrious, vigilant fireman and a drunken, profligate, incapable fireman, we prefer the latter." And in view of the stupendous infamy of the choice, the people ask, "Why?"

We answer the question without hesitancy. It is because railroad managers who pursue such a course belong to that class of despicable creatures who a few years ago throughout the South were known as Negro whippers, a class of brutalized creatures whose vocation, in the eyes of those who employed them, sunk them by irrevocable laws to a level infinitely below that occupied by the helpless victims of their lash. These railroad managers, who make war upon the Brotherhood of Locomotive Firemen, would have their employees destitute of intelligence and independence, cringing, fawning slaves, devoid of manhood and ready to do their bidding, as if they were chattels. If a locomotive fireman spends his earnings like a profligate, if his associations are low and vulgar, if he cares little or nothing at all for character, if he is devoid of noble ambitions and neglects his wife and children and makes no provision for them, if death or sickness overtakes him, he is the man who is wanted by the class of railroad managers who refuse to employ brotherhood firemen.

It is difficult to understand why it is that great interests are committed to the keeping of such men as the railroad managers we have referred to, whose inherent meanness defies description. They are the advocates of all that is groveling, abject, and contemptible in life and character, because when a locomotive fireman descends to such a level, the arrogant, mercenary, and narrow-minded manager can dictate his destiny and keep him forever in the despicable position of a serf.

But it is to us a source of extreme gratification to say that such railroad managers as we have referred to and who arouse our ineffable contempt are not numerous, nor is their influence such as to stay in any degree the gigantic step and upward march of the Brotherhood of Locomotive Firemen. Their vulgar antipathies, their arrogant, dictatorial policy, their patronage of drunken thriftlessness and opposition to intelligence, industry, integrity, and capability, will in due time arouse such unutterable loathing and universal denunciation that they will be compelled to abandon their policy or get out of the way. The time is at hand—indeed, it has already come—when railroad managers will recognize in the Brotherhood of Locomotive Firemen an organization which is putting forth its mighty energies to produce a class of workmen worthy of the confidence, the respect, and the esteem of all men, and the great traveling public, quick to appreciate faithfulness to trusts involving life and property, will join us in anathematizing such railroad managers as seek to place upon our noble order the brand of persecution, or subject its members to penalties for their devotion to manly and virtuous lives.

Employer and Employed[†]
October 1884

When rightly considered, the interests of employer and employed are identical. In the first place, both make their living out of the same business or undertaking. The railway company furnishes the track, roadbed, engine, cars, machine shops, etc.; the employees furnish the labor by which this system or business is operated. All are interested in the profits. The employee gets his wages from this source and the employer, or the railway company, gets the balance.

In fact, any business is a partnership to a certain extent. The employer puts in the capital; the employee furnishes the labor. Out of the result of this combination both are paid. From this reasoning it necessarily follows that any harm done to capital injures labor, and any harm done to labor injures capital.

As society is now constituted, capital is largely in the hands of one class and labor in the hands of another. In some instances these classes may disagree, or the one may attempt to coerce the other to certain obnoxious measures, but in either case injury results to both.

Take a strike for an instance. Capital and labor cannot agree upon the amount of wages to be paid for certain work. Capital offers so much, labor wants more. Production ceases. Whose loss is this? It is the loss of both capital and labor. Capital loses its profits, interest on its investment, and the useless deterioration of its machinery. Labor loses its wages. Nay, more than all this, the whole world loses because there is less wealth produced.

One of the great objects of our organization is to prevent unnecessary clashes between employer and employed. One of our fundamental doctrines is that labor and capital are brothers. With hand in hand they march along the highway of progress, and it is wrong and suicidal to put them at enmity. Demagogues, who expect to ride into political power on the waves of disturbance, are continually attempting to make a breach between labor and capital. These men are not the friends of those who toil. Their motives are entirely selfish. They should be ignored.

With our intricate system of civilization it is next to impossible to prevent some differences to creep in between labor and capital; if, however, these differences are honest, they should be adjusted peaceably and honorably. Both

---

† Published in *Firemen's Magazine*, vol. 8, no. 10 (October 1884), 616–618.

sides ought to give and take. Capital should extend its hand to labor and labor should grasp it in a friendly manner. There should be no insulting demand on one side nor insulting difference on the other. This truth should be bound upon the foreheads of all men. Capital depends upon labor; labor depends upon capital.

Very few people stop to think about the real relations of employer and employed. Many have the conception that employers ought to pay as little as possible for labor, and labor perform as little as possible for its wages. This is all wrong. The successful outcome of the business engaged in is the interest of all.

Some have gone so far as to say that there is a natural, a necessary conflict between labor and capital. These are very shallow thinkers, or else very great demagogues. Argument is of no use against these people; either they cannot or will not see the falsity of their statement.

To see the proper relation between labor and capital and to teach that relation is one of our objects. The fact that this is our object has given as much of our influence as a brotherhood and added much to the respect in which we are held in railway circles. We desire our employers to fully understand that we are organized for no purpose harmful to their interests, but on the contrary we seek to make the relations between us and them pleasant, profitable, and mutually beneficial in all respects.

Railway officials should second our efforts and show to their employers that their welfare and that of the men who labor for them are identical. A harsh, unsympathetic employer obtains only half-hearted service. An employer with a heart gets good service with respect thrown in. If differences arise, as they often will, both sides should be above all other things manly. No cringing on the one side, nor arrogance on the other. In the first place, the difference should be real or cease to exist; in the next place, both sides ought to be willing to compromise. An employer should bear in mind that to make arbitrary rules or to cut down wages without cause is as much of a "strike" as one indulged in by laborers who "strike" for higher wages. To "strike" is simply to demand something that is not given willingly. When, as an organization, we say to our members "do not strike," we say at the same time to our employers, "treat us fairly." If the difference is great, let us confer about the matter, let us both understand the situation fully. All are men and should be treated as such. If this feeling is carried out faithfully, no great disturbances need arise. Wisdom is our best counsel always, and to compromise is wisdom.

Again, we repeat, capital and labor should not antagonize each other. There is no natural conflict between them. Together they make a noble combination, capable of subduing the world to the full use of man. All the enginery, all the cities, all the great highways, all the inventions of this century have their life and progress as the result of combined capital and labor. From the tiny toy manufactured for the baby to the Corliss engine that drives a thousand wheels,[6] all things result from the combined effort of labor and capital. Why then should these brothers quarrel? False friends and bitter foes may cause differences, but they should be forever united.

One of the great drawbacks to a complete understanding of the true relations between capital and labor springs from ignorance. Men will not or cannot think. They are led astray by the designing or by the equally ignorant. It is our duty, as an organization, to educate our members to a correct understanding of their relations to their employers. This duty we are striving to perform. This ignorance of the proper relations between capital and labor is not confined to the ranks of the employed. Some of our employers are woefully ignorant on the subject. They have learned to look only at immediate results and have failed to see the situation from a high point of view. An employer who has many men under him and who has great results to obtain should be a man of great grasp of mind. Not a little, narrow fellow who sees in every demand for higher wages an attempt to coerce capital, but a broad-gauged man who tries to remedy the evil that makes the wages too low. The little fellow, as soon as a laborer approaches him with a demand for higher pay, cries "socialist," "communist," "revolutionist," and wants the military called out to suppress these dangerous laboring men. The man of brains, the man who understands the relation of employer and employed, listens with respect to the demand and affords relief if he can or a reason why if he cannot.

We are in the midst of great financial and commercial disturbances, and we know not what a day may bring forth, but we desire it to be known that we deprecate violent differences between employer and employed; that we encourage honorable settlement in all cases; and if our employers will meet us halfway, they will always find us ready to agree to anything that is fair and honorable. We believe in capital *and* labor, not in capital *against* labor.

Tramps and Tramping[†]

October 1884

About ten years ago the "tramp," as a recognized element of society, made his appearance in the United States. He was the outgrowth of circumstances which he did not create and which he was powerless to modify or control. The tramp was the legitimate product of the panic which began in 1873, a panic which swept over the country like a tornado. To understand its terrible effects, it is only required to say that from 1872 to 1878, both inclusive, seven years, there were 51,264 failures, involving a loss of $1,321,964,132, an average of 7,323 failures a year, and an average annual loss of $187,423,476. These failures and losses touched every interest and every industry in the land. It was a period of indescribable gloom. Consternation and dismay were everywhere enthroned. The wheels of industry stood still; silence reigned in factory, shop, and forge. Work and wages went down together. The sheriff's hammer beat funeral marches everywhere. Then came idleness, poverty, crime, and the tramp. From out of the gloom, from all directions came the cry for bread, and thousands of men started out to find work. To remain at home was to starve; to go away in search of work involved consequences often worse than death. Men said goodbye to wife and children to return no more. They were called "tramps."

Here is an inviting field for graphic pens. Fact takes on all the glamour of fiction. The truth, unadorned by fancy and free from the embellishment of imagination, rivals the creations of Victor Hugo, or any other genius whose weird conceptions of man's misfortunes have ever startled society. We have read, since the time of which we write, of floods, of earthquakes, and of cyclones. Here and there cities and towns and districts have fallen victims to fearful scourges, but none of them, nor all of them combined, compare with the direful consequences produced by the panic of 1873, which inaugurated the "tramp curse" in this country, a calamity the effects of which are still too apparent and which all good people deplore.

What we have written is simply preliminary, to make way for the declaration that while tramps and tramping were unavoidable in the past, and are still unavoidable to a certain extent, there are those among the number who have no righteous excuse for their wanderings.

[†] Published in *Firemen's Magazine,* vol. 8, no. 10 (October 1884), 613–614.

We have all sympathy for the man who is compelled to leave home and friends in search of employment, and we would cheerfully exert our influence on his behalf as often as the opportunity arises, but for the restless, roving, unsettled man who places himself in the ranks of the tramp because he is too lazy to work and goes from place to place, ostensibly in the search of work, but whose real mission is to live without work, we have only feelings of inexpressible contempt.

The cry of "hard times" is music to his ear, for under that plea he assumes the distressed look of an actual sufferer and enlists the substantial sympathy of his hardworking fellow men.

When the pall of business and financial depression settles upon our land, when the fires in the shops, mills, and factories go out, and men are driven out into the world in search of employment, they are entitled to our sympathy and our protection, and it is no part of our mission to decry their misfortune. But while espousing the cause of such men we make positive discrimination against the class above referred to, who are out of work the year around as a matter of choice and who take advantage of business depressions to urge upon honest men their pretended claims for charitable consideration.

To us it is a source of profound regret to know that our noble brotherhood is afflicted with these impostors, for they serve to weaken our faith in honest poverty, lest our aid be given to encourage idleness and profligacy instead of alleviating unavoidable distress. A moment's reflection will give these views commanding importance in every lodge of our continental brotherhood. Our pride and our glory centers on the fact that locomotive firemen are gentlemen, by which we mean men of integrity, true to duty and every obligation of the order, peers of the best, self-reliant, high in purpose, and ambitious—men who, in seeking their own welfare, are striving for the good of all.

This being true, we cannot tolerate impostors, nor will we make the lodges of our order their hiding places. On the contrary, we will expose their nefarious schemes, denounce their corrupting practices, and scourge them from our ranks. Our 240 lodges, dotting all the hills and valleys from ocean to ocean, are to be known of all men as the citadels of honor and of all things of good report, where congregate men to devise ways and means to advance the general welfare of the brotherhood and make it the admiration of the world.

What Is Success?[†]

October 1884

What is a successful life? A few moments' thought will convince us that the question is by no means an easy one to answer. We say this, that, or the other man is successful, but what do we mean by it? One man has houses and lands, has a large bank account, drives fast horses, and has many apparent friends; such a man is accounted successful. Yet all of these things that minister to his pleasure have been acquired by unremitting labor, by hard, avaricious dealings with his fellow men, by trampling upon the hearts and affections of thousands; in the face of these facts, is the man a successful one?

The question will be answered differently according to the views of life of the one answering it. Some think wealth is the only measure of success, no matter how attained. Such people have tuned their psalm of life very low. Such people will read the grand tragedies of Shakespeare and remember only this line: "Put money in thy purse."[7] The horizon of their lives is bounded with dollars and the chink of silver is more melodious to them than the symphonies of Mozart.

The man who becomes wealthy is in a measure successful, but only so far as the acquirement sharpens his intellect, broadens his powers, and develops him into a self-reliant, powerful member of society for its good. Selfish wealth is never good. One may be a millionaire, but if with it comes greed, avarice, oppression of others, the success is small indeed. Scattered along the path of life we find examples of men whose success brought them fame and glory and proved an unqualified blessing to all mankind. Baron von Humboldt, born to nobility and riches, left behind him the pleasures of wealth and the luxury of ease and climbed the distant Andes in search of facts for his immortal work, *Cosmos.* The winter's storm and the summer's fervid heat could not stay this grand man in his enthusiastic pursuit of knowledge. He did not spend his life in acquiring wealth; he lived but to commune with nature and wrest from her the secrets of physical life. Was not this man successful? This is what another great genius said of Humboldt:

> I have seen a picture of the old man sitting upon a mountainside; above him the eternal snow, below the smiling valley of the tropics, filled with

---

† Published in *Firemen's Magazine,* vol. 8, no. 10 (October 1884), 615–616.

vine and palm; his chin upon his breast, his eyes deep, thoughtful, and calm, his forehead majestic—grander than the mountain upon which he sat—crowned with the snow of his whitened hair, he looked the intellectual autocrat of this world.[8]

Agassiz was at one time importuned to go upon the lecture platform and make money out of his vast knowledge as a naturalist. His reply will be ever memorable: "I have no time to make money." Such a man would be hooted at on Wall Street by the men who speculate in the earnings of others and imagine themselves the great businessmen of this age. Yet whose success is greatest, that of Louis Agassiz standing among his pupils upon the sea shore of Penakese, teaching them the secrets of nature,[9] or that of Jay Gould heaping together millions wrung from the failure of thousands of his fellows? One rests secure in a pure fame, the other is hated and feared by his neighbors and at the last will have been simply notorious.

There is one criterion by which success can be fairly measured: that is the estimate placed upon us by our fellows. If a man is hated, is feared and shunned, if he is looked upon as small, avaricious, greedy, he is not a successful man, though he be worth millions. On the other hand, if a man's praises are upon the lips of all, if his reputation is that of an honest, sincere, and sympathetic gentleman, his success is assured, although he has not a dollar of his own.

Labor and Law[†]

November 1884

The records show that statisticians, statesmen, political economists, and politicians are forever heralding to the world the triumphs of labor. From year to year, and from decade to decade, the capacity of figures is taxed to demonstrate the wealth-producing power of labor, until sum totals bewilder the imagination. It is a self-evident fact which needs only to be stated to find universal acceptance that the men who produce this wealth—the wage men, the breadwinners—outnumber all other classes combined, but whoever heard of a labor

---

† Published in *Firemen's Magazine*, vol. 8, no. 11 (November 1884), 661–662.

party that controlled legislation in any land?

Why is it so? The inquiry at once opens to laboring men a vast field for thought and investigation. It may be said in explanation that laboring men have never perfected an organization, in power and influence, in any sense, commensurate with the vast and vital interests at stake. Local organizations there are, and national organizations are spoken of, but, as factors and forces in shaping political affairs, they have exerted little influence, if any at all.

Tersely stated, politics is the science of government. Government relates to the enactment and to the administration of laws. Laws are enacted to protect the rights and promote the welfare of the people. The people are not required to consider any questions bearing upon their well-being more important than those which relate to property. These propositions bring to the front the question of the relationship existing between property and labor. And here we have it stated, by eminent authorities, that "all value is born of labor and is composed essentially of wages; in other words, that *no* wealth has its origin in privilege or acquires any value except through *work;* and that consequently labor alone is the source of revenue among men."[10]

The proposition is irrefutable and, therefore, forms an indestructible foundation upon which to build labor organizations having for their supreme purpose a direct influence upon legislation and government.

It would be natural to suppose that since labor is alone the source of revenue among men, since all value is born of labor and that wealth has its origin in work, that political economists, social scientists, statesmen, and philanthropists would urge, in their writings and public addresses, the importance of advancing the interests of laboring men in every way practicable and consistent with good government. But, unfortunately, such is not the record. Nowhere on God's green earth have the men whose work creates the revenues of nations been permitted to enjoy more than a pittance of the values they have created.

The serious question that such facts force upon the attention of thinking men is to what extent law in the past, or laws as they exist at present, are responsible for the situation? There is no law inherent in human nature which decrees one man poor and another man rich—one man a servant and another man master. There is no natural law, like that which moves the stars in their orbits, which distributes the wealth that labor creates inequitably.

We assume, therefore, that the laws that have been enacted from time immemorial relating to the distribution of the wealth that labor creates have been unjust laws administered by unjust judges. If we appeal to the records, the testimony is overwhelming. But we care little for the unjust laws of the past.

Our inquiries relate to the present and to the future. How stands the case now? Are the laws enacted designed to lift the burdens which former laws imposed from the bowed form of labor? In the United States of America laboring men have the ballot. If the laws are unjust, they can command their modification or repeal. We are not advocating now the enactment of laws specially, or rather directly, designed to promote labor interests, that is to say laws which shall fix the price of labor or the price of the products of labor, but we do mean that laws shall not be enacted designed to make the rich richer and laboring men poorer, laws which permit the inequitable distribution of wealth, laws which take care of the palace and neglect the cottage, laws which permit money capital and water capital to exact dividends from labor capital and leave it to starve in sight of the wealth it creates.

We are by no means forgetful of the fact that it has been the purpose of writers to mystify rather than elucidate questions relating to the honest adjustment of profit and loss in matters where capital and labor combine, for the purpose of solving the problems of progress. We are aware that it has been said that "machinery causes not only cheapness, but obstruction of the market and stoppage of business;" that "competition ends in oppression;" that "taxation, the material bond of society, is generally a scourge, dreaded equally with fire and hail;" that "credit is necessarily accompanied by bankruptcy;" that "property is a swarm of abuses;" that "commerce degenerates into a game of chance;" and, in short, that disorder exists everywhere; but, true or false, such things do not now enter into our argument.[11] What labor wants to ascertain is whether laws, as they stand on the statute books, operate to its disadvantage or are promotive of its interests. The investigation so far leads to the conclusion that the wealth that labor creates is unjustly distributed and that the laws are not only not in the interest of labor but prejudicial to its welfare.

In this connection, we hazard the prediction that a new era is to dawn, at no distant day, upon the country. Labor is organizing for its protection and will not long tolerate the wrongs under which it has labored, insofar as the enactment of just laws can apply a remedy. The ballot is the weapon of labor in the United States, and when thorough organization is secured, results will give it a power and a dignity which, while it will secure for labor simple justice, will confer lasting blessings upon society at large.

Notes

1. From the order for the burial of dead at sea in the Anglican Book of Common Prayer (1662).
2. A knight without fear and without reproach.
3. Henry V. Poor, *Manual of Railroads of the United States* (New York: H. V. and H. W. Poor, issued annually).
4. A phrase from *Paradise Lost,* (1667), book 3, by John Milton (1608–1674).
5. One of Debs's favorite expressions, lifted from *The Merchant of Venice* (1604), act 2, scene 2, by William Shakespeare (1564–1616). The original lines are "but man, proud man, / Drest in a little brief authority, / Most ignorant of what he's most assured, / His glassy essence, like an angry ape, / Plays such fantastic tricks before high heaven / As make the angels weep; who, with our spleens, / Would all themselves laugh mortal."
6. Patented in 1849 by George Henry Corliss (1817–1888), the Corliss engine was a stationary steam power device that enabled the construction of factories in places without a ready source of water power. It is regarded as one of the most important inventions of the nineteenth century.
7. From *Othello* (1603), by William Shakespeare.
8. From "Law, Not God; or, The Message of Humboldt" (1883) by Robert Ingersoll (1833–1899).
9. Biologist Louis Agassiz (1807–1873) was given the tiny Massachusetts island of Penakese, one of the Elizabeth Islands, by a wealthy patron as the site for a school of natural history.
10. Pierre-Joseph Proudhon, *System of Economical Contradictions; or, The Philosophy of Poverty* (1846).
11. All of these quotations are from Proudhon's 1846 book, *The Philosophy of Poverty*, which was famously polemicized against by Karl Marx with his 1847 work, *The Poverty of Philosophy*. Debs either read Proudhon's book in the original French or in an unknown translation that preceded the 1888 English translation by Benjamin R. Tucker.

1885

Speech to the Indiana Legislature Nominating Daniel W. Voorhees for the US Senate[†]

January 20, 1885

Mr. Speaker:—

A privilege in connection with my duties as a member of the House, which I esteem an honor of high consequence, has fallen to my lot, and I shall ask the generous indulgence of the chair and of my fellow representatives while to the best of my ability I respond to a request well calculated to embarrass men of more years and experience than I can boast. I need not state to this House, as a matter of information, that the important duty of electing a United States senator to be the successor of Hon. Daniel W. Voorhees devolves upon this general assembly.[1] I could not hope, did the agreeable task I have assumed require it at my hands, to enlighten this house in regard to the superior abilities necessary to enable a senator of the United States to meet all the high requirements of his office and worthily discharge its serious duties. The merest reference to such subjects is suggestive of qualities of head and heart that should command the reverence of the people.

I am aware that there have been, in the common acceptance of the terms, good men who were not great and great men who were not good, but I have learned from the lessons of history, notwithstanding the frailties of human nature and the imperfections of the methods of government, that in the lottery of politics do very often become the favorites of fortune, and in taking the chances secure for their servants the right men, and in all matters pertaining to the welfare of the state, such men may be properly designated as the highest prizes, since there can be nothing better, nothing of greater value in government, than the right man in the right place. It cannot be expected that the people, however intelligent and sincere, will always secure for places of great responsibility men distinguished for talent, energy, courage, and virtue, but such great and good fortune is often bestowed, and when obtained the people, if qualified to appreciate the blessing, will unite in a patriotic determination to perpetuate it.

The man who in public life has been proved and tested, who again and again has passed through the ordeal of temptation without scar or blemish,

---

[†] Published in *Indiana Daily Sentinel,* vol. 34, no. 21 (January 21, 1885), 5.

becomes a public benefactor, defying the ordinary methods of computation whereby to estimate his value to the state; and wisdom and patriotism win universal applause when the people retain such men in official positions.

Mr. Speaker, I shall not detain the house by an extended reference to the lives, the characters, and the deeds of the distinguished men who have represented Indiana in the Senate of the United States. We frequently hear men who, in speaking of the past, deplore in comparison the degeneracy of the present. I shall stop no longer than to say I am not in sympathy with their vagaries.

In the month of November 1877, James D. Williams, then governor of Indiana, appointed Daniel W. Voorhees as the successor of Oliver P. Morton, deceased, to represent Indiana in the United States Senate. The name and fame of Morton had filled the land. His great abilities had made him the leader of his party in the Senate. It was thought to be no ordinary responsibility to occupy the place made vacant by the death of Morton. It was deemed a herculean task to maintain the advanced position of the state that the admirers of Mr. Morton claimed was due to his masterly powers, but, sir, I do but repeat the truth of history when I say that as soon as opportunity offered, Mr. Voorhees came to the front in a speech that triumphantly vindicated the prescience of Governor Williams, a speech that electrified the nation by the profundity of its statesmanship, the majesty of its grasp, and the overwhelming power of its arguments and eloquence, and whatever else may be said of the sad event, the fame of Indiana did not wane by the death of Morton. Voorhees caught the standard as it fell from Morton's hands, and the whole country, as he bore it aloft in the fierce contest between monopolies and the people, with a united voice gave him an ovation of gratitude.

In 1878, a Democratic legislature ratified the wisdom of Governor Williams' appointment by electing Daniel W. Voorhees to a seat in the United States Senate, and for nearly six years he has, in a manner worthy of the highest commendation, maintained his own and Indiana's renown in that august body. His term expires on the fourth day of March next, and now, Mr. Speaker, I nominate Daniel W. Voorhees to be his own successor in the Senate of the United States for the ensuing term.

Mr. Speaker, the fact that I am one of the representatives of Vigo County, the home of Mr. Voorhees, is doubtless the reason why the honor has been given me to nominate him for senator, and though I am among the youngest members of this house, with legislative experience as limited as that of any other member, I am neither so juvenile nor unschooled as not to be familiar with the scholastic attainments, the erudition, the statesmanship and patriotic devotion to the state of Indiana and the whole country, that have preeminently distinguished the official career of the citizen and senator whom I have the honor to place in nomination today.

Coming here as a workingman, with whatever duties attach to my position as the representative of workingmen, I feel just pride in placing in nomination for the exalted office a man who has availed himself of every opportunity to champion the cause of toiling people of the state and nation. In every emergency Mr. Voorhees has been the friend of labor, the foe of monopoly, and the defender of the eternal right. And fully appreciating the patriotism, the privations, and the heroic service of his fellow citizens, who went forth at the call of their country to battle for the Union and preserve it "one and indivisible," he has on all occasions demonstrated by prompt action and eloquent words his unerring devotion to the interest of the Union soldier. In the campaign just closed, which has placed the Democratic Party of the state and the Democratic Party of the republic in power, a splendid array of great men has been in the van of the Democratic hosts, and of them all not one has rendered more effective service than the eloquent orator and distinguished statesman whom I now nominate to be his own successor in the United States Senate, and whom the people of Indiana delight to honor—Daniel W. Voorhees.[2]

Capital and Labor[†]

February 1885

The Brotherhood of Locomotive Firemen has taught from its inception to the present time, and shall continue to teach and demonstrate the truth of this teaching, the identity of the interests of capital and labor, believing that all their business relations conducted with this fact in view will be harmonious and friendly, and avoid what might otherwise result in discord and strife. When this school of education is abandoned by our brotherhood, then indeed we will not know the seasons from each other nor the day from the night.

That the results following the establishment of this truth on the side of labor may be full and complete, it is necessary that capital should manifest a

---

† Published in *Firemen's Magazine*, vol. 9, no. 2 (February 1885), 95–96.

disposition to meet labor a generous halfway, thereby showing its appreciation of our efforts in that direction. Nor do we know of any more intelligible or comprehensive plan of displaying its sincerity in advancing the teaching of this doctrine than by paying to its employee a fair and just compensation for their labor and conceding to them those considerations for their feelings that they claim for themselves, and that all men shall receive from each other, particularly the humble from the exalted.

Looking at this matter from the standpoint of modern civilization and seeing the advantageous position that the employer naturally occupies, it seems to us that the very polish of our highly lauded politeness, requiring those of higher rank or station in life to be a little more condescending in their manner and bearing toward those who are beneath them in the social scale than to their equals, has been entirely ignored, if it ever existed, much less the alleged chivalry that pretends to throw its shielding and protecting arm over the weak as against the strong. While these things are eminently true in our organization, they are sadly wanting in the body politic. Much of the success of business ventures and enterprises depends upon the faithful discharge of the duties of employees, and we may add that the honest fulfillment of these duties proceeds in a great measure from the just remuneration given to the labor employed. The lower animals receive for their labor a sufficient quantity of food and the necessary care to insure health. Man, the masterpiece of God's creation, and bearing the impress of the Creator on his soul, needs more than this; yet there are thousands, nay, hundreds of thousands in our very midst whose reward for their toil of ten hours a day does not reach that of the horse.

There never lived a king, emperor, or potentate, no matter how wealthy or powerful, whose family affections were stronger, whose sympathies were deeper or wider, whose sense of justice was keener, or whose love of the beautiful was more tender than the humblest peasant in his kingdom, or laborer in the workshop; and if there is or has been such, it is not owing to his exalted position or amassed wealth.

We say this in reference to the arrogance and petty tyranny that certain railroad managers and their subordinates practice upon the employees under their charge. A mark of respect or consideration never comes from them to the wageworker.

Such are the tools, debased and narrow-minded, that some of our capitalists and railroad corporations employ, who, with the concrete soul of a Shylock, wrench every particle of energy from their employee, leaving him in return for a faithful service of perhaps ten or twenty years, a broken and shattered health, a premature old age, and a family in poverty. Death ends his misery and adds to that of his wife and children. When such crimes are permitted to continue, let not the student of history look aghast at the record.

The school of the brotherhood has given to railroad corporations (and we appeal to the annals of the organization to prove the assertion) a body of men not only efficient in their work, but honest in its performance, displaying an individual interest in the care and protection of property directly or indirectly under their charge. Then, in view of this fact, we ask in all reason that these men receive a just compensation for their labor. True, the great bulk of our enginemen receive fair wages, but there are many who do not, and for these do we plead. Some of our Eastern railroads barely pay their men sufficient to keep body and soul together. These men have tasted of every danger within the compass of their hazardous calling; they have felt the severity of every storm that swept their course, but the existing circumstances make their contemplation of the future their bitterest cup of suffering.

The Lessons of Elections[†]

February 1885

On the fourth day of November last [1884], by the fiat of the American people, the machinery of the federal government was transferred to new hands, as provided by the laws of the Republic. It is no part of our purpose to write of the incidents of the partisan struggle which resulted in a change of public servants. We shall indulge in neither eulogistic nor denunciatory comments upon parties or party leaders. The *Magazine* is not partisan, but the patrons of the *Magazine* are profoundly interested in the lessons of elections, that it is say, that class of elections which can be said to have any appreciable effect upon the general welfare. In this connection, it may be prudently said that elections, particularly those which relate to state and federal affairs, have a profounder significance than in any other country, where the ballot is used to settle any questions relating to the public weal.

---

† Published in *Firemen's Magazine,* vol. 9, no. 2 (February 1885), 89–91.

Here, with a few exceptions, the sovereignty of citizenship is acknowledged. Manhood sovereignty is supreme. It is secured to the humblest toiler
as certainly as to the millionaire. In the presence of the ballot box all men are
equal, and this lesson of elections is one that can be studied with profit by
those who entertain misgivings, touching the capabilities of men for self-government. There is no grander spectacle presented for the contemplation of
mankind than when 55 million free people quietly, in a day, designate at the
ballot box who shall be their rulers, their lawmakers, their public servants, and
what shall be the policy of their government.

It would be profitable in this article to refer particularly to all the lessons
which elections teach, and which invite serious reflection, insofar as such lessons relate to policy and measures rather than to men. The students of events
will not fail to notice that one of the lessons taught by the recent presidential
election had special reference to labor interests. The speeches, the documents,
the press discussed, with more or less directness, labor topics. The industries of
the country and the industrial classes came in for a larger share of attention than
was ever before awarded to them, and it is therefore prudent to assume that the
most important lessons of the election relate to the labor interests of the country. If this proposition is true, if all the facts warrant the conclusion, then it may
be said that labor has advanced in the direction of influence to a plane upon
which it may achieve triumphs in the future fraught with inestimable blessings.

The lesson of the election which may be studied by laboring men with special profit teaches that by national unification, legislation can be so shaped that
the wealth, which labor creates, shall be equitably distributed. That means not
only honest pay for an honest day's work, but that the government shall not tax
labor to any extent beyond its absolute need when economically administered.
There can be no equitable distribution of the wealth which labor creates (and
labor creates all wealth) if labor is taxed to any extent to maintain monopolies,
and the lesson of the late election teaches the fact, beyond controversy, not because Cleveland was elected or Blaine defeated, but because the labor interests
of the country were brought into such commanding prominence as to teach
laboring men that, united and harmonious, they can dictate the policy of the
government without reference to which party triumphs.

In discussing the lesson of the election, insofar as the labor interests of the
country are concerned, we remark that the laws should be so framed as to prevent men or corporations from collecting dividends upon what is known as "watered stock." One illustration will suffice: It is known that the Western Union
Telegraph Company collects dividends on $80 million when the investments of

the corporation do not exceed $40 million. If, as is now universally conceded, labor creates all the wealth of the country, it also pays all the debts, all the dividends; hence, laws which permit such gross injustice as the collection of dividends on "water" must be, in the nature of things, vicious. Such laws strike labor a staggering blow. And the lesson of the late election demonstrates that the united protest of laboring men against such monstrous injustice will hasten the era of reform. Labor has the ballot and can wield it intelligently, and when it strikes at wrongs, the result of legislation, or the want of legislation, it may hope to achieve results fraught with incalculable blessings to society.

In the August number of the *North American Review,* a writer upon "The Encroachments of Capital" begins by saying: "It is one of the maxims of Machiavelli that in order to preserve soundness and health, all nations should often go back to first principles,"[3] and the reason given is that each form of government is usually framed in the outset on principles which belong to its best conditions, and that all departures, to any serious extent, are unnatural and therefore dangerous. As a general proposition, Machiavelli, in the light of events, must be regarded as a false theorist. In times gone by, when it was assumed that the few had a "divine right" to rule over the many, it may have been true that "governments were framed in the outset on principles which belonged to their best condition," but such a theory has long since been exploded and finds few advocates in lands where the ballot, in the hands of the masses, dictates rulers and measures. In the United States, however, it is true that the government in the outset was framed upon principles which belonged to its best condition and, therefore, it is the part of wisdom for the people to often go back to first principles if they would escape "unnatural and dangerous" departures.

If capital is making encroachments in the United States, upon whom does the invasion bear most heavily? Certainly not upon the rich. Whose rights are dangerously infringed? Whose interests are the most seriously imperiled? The few do not complain. Capitalists are content. Just here the question arises. If capital is making encroachments, as is claimed, is the wrong perpetrated under cover of law, or is the injustice in violation of the statutes? In either case, the lesson of election teaches the remedy. It should be understood that labor is self-reliant. Labor demands to be let severely alone. It does not demand that wages shall be determined by statute, but it does demand that the statutes shall not embarrass labor, place obstacles in its way, impoverish and degrade it, and, if elections teach anything, they voice the declaration that labor with the ballot in its hands can remedy the glaring evils which environ it. It can deprive monopoly of its power for much of the evil it inflicts.

It is well known that capitalists combine to "corner" the essentials of life, bread and meat, by which prices are made to advance and labor made to suffer. If the laws shield such nefarious transactions, they are vicious and should be repealed, and others enacted in consonance with the sentiments of all honest men, and labor has the power to apply the remedy. The subject suggests a broader field of thought, but our space forbids elaboration. We may refer to it again. For the present, it must suffice to say that the lesson of elections teaches working men that their duty to themselves and to the state is to protest at the ballot box against legislation which in its operation compels labor to bear an undue proportion of burdens and receive too small a share of the wealth it creates.

Progress and Poverty[†]

February 1885

Recently Henry George[4] has written a work with the above title.[5] Every laborer in the land should read and study it well. There is much thought in it and much melancholy truth. Some of the pictures drawn by this mastermind are very dark indeed, but before he quits his task he points out a remedy. He says:

> From all parts of the civilized world come complaints of industrial depression; of labor condemned to involuntary idleness; of capital massed and wasting; of pecuniary distress among businessmen; of want and suffering and anxiety among working classes. All the dull, deadening pain, all the keen, maddening anguish that to great masses of men are involved in the words "hard times" afflict the world today.

* * *

> Where population is densest, wealth greatest, and the machinery of production and exchange most highly developed, we find the deepest poverty, the sharpest struggle for existence, and the most enforced idleness.

* * *

---

† Published in *Firemen's Magazine,* vol. 9, no. 2 (February 1885), 96–97.

And, unpleasant as it may be to admit it, it is at last becoming evident that the enormous increase in productive power which has marked the present century and is still going on with accelerating ratio has no tendency to extirpate poverty or to lighten the burden of those compelled to toil. It simply widens the gulf between Dives and Lazarus, and makes the struggle for existence more intense. The march of invention has clothed mankind with powers of which a century ago the boldest imagination could not have dreamed. But in factories where labor-saving machinery has reached its most wonderful development, little children are at work; wherever the new forces are anything like fully utilized, large classes are maintained by charity or live on the verge of recourse to it; amid the greatest accumulations of wealth, men die of starvation and puny infants suckle dry breasts while everywhere the greed of gain, the worship of wealth, shows the force of the fear of want. The promised land dies before us like the mirage. The fruits of the tree of knowledge turn as we grasp them to apples of Sodom that crumble at the touch.

This is the picture Mr. George draws of civilized countries under our present progress. He concludes after a careful survey of the field of human effort that poverty is the associate of what has been called modern progress. Why this is so Mr. George undertakes to answer in his work. He shows why it is that the rich are growing richer and the poor poorer; why it is that the laboring man finds it such hard work to live in a land where a few men grow enormously wealthy.

Mr. George is earnest in his efforts to get at the bottom of our social difficulties and he says in his opening chapter:

I propose to beg no question, to shrink from no conclusion, but to follow the truth wherever it may lead. Upon us is the responsibility of seeking the law, for in the very heart of our civilization today women faint and little children moan. But what that law may be is not our affair. If the conclusions that we reach run counter to our prejudices, let us not flinch; if they challenge institutions that have long been deemed wise and natural, let us not turn back.

These words breathe the spirit of the enthusiast and the fearless reformer, and Mr. George has fully maintained himself in both characters. His recent visit to England, Ireland, and Scotland and his lectures there have done more to awaken interest in the laboring men of those countries and their condition than anything that has occurred this century. We will present to our readers from time to time some of Mr. George's ideas on current labor topics, knowing that profit will come from their study.

The Attempted Blacklist Degradation of Employees[†]
March 1885

In a recent debate in the United States Senate on interstate commerce, Senator Vance of North Carolina[6] said: "Now, our laws forbid absolutely the tyranny of one man over another, or of any kind of restraint whatever by one man over the personal freedom of another." The proposition is so self-evident that discussion would obscure rather than add luster to the truth it embodies. It may be said, indeed, the proclamation cannot be too frequently or too emphatically made that when one seizes an opportunity to tyrannize over another, he becomes a monster of such hideous mien, is so corrupted by vile propensities, and so hardened by the cultivation of detestable purposes, that whatever may be his position or surroundings, he has only to be known to be at once consigned by all honorable men to a class of miscreants whose existence can be accounted for upon no rational hypothesis. He is a human reptile, and only an inscrutable creator could tell why he exists. To this class belong those railway superintendents who have evolved what are widely known as "blacklisting" methods, whereby employees, who from any cause may be discharged, are blacklisted—that is to say, branded as unworthy of employment and confidence, and followed up in their search for work and made to realize that these sleuth hounds of persecution, as relentless as death, are following them through every lane and avenue of life, ready and prepared to deprive them of employment and make their lives an intolerable burden. This movement, the gods be praised, is said to be confined to about 30 "down east" superintendents, and manifestly has for its object the degradation of employees, freemen, men robed in the sovereignty of American citizenship, to the condition of serfs, creatures who belong to certain railways and wear the collar of certain superintendents.

Honestly analyzed, the blacklisting infamy is designed to bring about that condition among American laborers. To illustrate: *A* is in the employment of *B*, an Eastern railway superintendent, with whom he disagrees, as he has a perfect right to do, receives his discharge, and is therefore required to seek employment elsewhere and under some other "boss." What is the result? Simply this: *B* enters his name upon the blacklist, and forthwith it is sent to every other blacklisting superintendent. *A* goes forth with a blacklisting mark upon

[†] Published in *Firemen's Magazine*, vol. 9, no. 3 (March 1885), 157–159.

him. He goes the rounds; everywhere *B* has preceded him. If he finds work at all it must be outside of his chosen vocation. He must apply elsewhere and for employment in which he has little or no experience. The blacklisting curse may even follow him there. He is doomed to idleness and to all the ills which idleness entails—poverty, tramping, ostracism, degradation, and possibly crime. These blacklisting scoundrels doubtless reason among themselves, "Our men know the penalty of a discharge, of abandoning our employment, and rather than take its risks will submit to our degrading demands, and be silent and submissive to our rules." By such processes, it is understood that about 30 Eastern railway superintendents anticipate lordly control over their employees.

We learn from *The Railroader,* published in Toledo, Ohio, that there is a widespread protest throughout the West against this blacklisting program. It cannot be too extended, too unanimous, nor too emphatic. Blacklisting is a move in the wrong direction. It will not be tolerated. It is opposed to law, justice, and common decency. The superintendents who practice the execrable outrage upon workingmen should be everywhere held up to public scorn and contempt. They are enemies of public order. They dethrone law. They invite anarchy. They are the assassins of character. They inaugurate deep-seated enmities and are the deadly foes of free institutions. We hear much nowadays about the murderous designs of dynamiters, of the vagaries of socialists, of "red-handed" communists, to the end of the chapter, but here we have it stated that some 30 railway superintendents have organized a blacklisting Ku Klux Klan, whose mission it is to follow up certain blacklisted mechanics and workingmen for the purpose of robbing them of the means of subsistence, dogging their steps for the purpose of keeping them in idleness till gaunt hunger gnaws at their vitals, until rags bespeak their degradation and blank despair shrouds their lives.

This is certainly a new departure in railroading. It demands the widest possible notoriety. It means mischief. It cannot survive light. It is dirty in its very conception and damnable in every feature. It is anti-American. It is an exhibition of arrogance and turpitude deserving crushing resentment. American workingmen are not serfs—they will not wear the collar of railway superintendents, East or West. They are not cringing, fawning lickspittles, to approach railway superintendents on their bellies in the dust. The blacklisting gang, by the fiat of justice, will be required to change their policy. This should be the motto not only of all the railway papers in the land, but the press generally should demand that the blacklisting railway superintendents should at once change their program.

War Clouds†

June 1885

About 760 years before Christ, Isaiah, who is styled "prince of all the prophets," in prophesying the coming of the Messiah and his reign on the earth, said,

> He shall judge among the nations, and shall rebuke many people: and they shall beat their swords into ploughshares, and their spears into pruning hooks: nation shall not lift up sword against nation, neither shall they learn war anymore.[7]

That sublime declaration of the "prince of all the prophets" was made more than 26 centuries ago. In the meantime the Messiah has come, established his kingdom, delivered his message of peace, and departed, but swords are not beaten into plowshares, nor spears into pruning hooks. Nations continue to lift up the sword against nation, and the study of war receives more attention than at any period since the "prince of prophets" proclaimed his prophetic visions to the Jews. Manifestly the "Prince of Peace" does not direct the affairs of nations, particularly Christian nations. It is doubtless true that the sword and the spear are less used now than in the days of Isaiah, but they were laid aside because their death-dealing qualities were not up to the standard required by Christian nations. We would not be irreverent, we would not discredit prophecy, we would not, if we could, detract from the majesty and sublimity of Isaiah's prophecies, but, if he had been blessed with powers of vision to see Christian nations of the present time preparing for war; if he could have seen the standing armies, the ironclad fleets; if he could have seen the numerous modern inventions constructed with special reference to the greatest possible slaughter, and for the destruction of the monuments of labor, it occurs to us that all his God-like faculties would have been aroused and that thunderbolts of denunciation would have been hurled at the nations which, professing Christianity, excel savages in devising methods of slaughter and destruction; and yet, these Christian nations, with an impudence which defies hyperbole, mutually implore the Prince of Peace, the Son of God, the Messiah of whom Isaiah prophesied, to bestow upon them heaven's choicest benedictions, assuming forsooth that their prayers are answered most fully when their instruments of death have done the largest possible execution.

---

† Published in *Firemen's Magazine,* vol. 9, no. 6 (June 1885), 343–346.

Notwithstanding such reflections, and paradoxical as it may appear, we are of the opinion there have been and will continue to be Christian wars, wars which heaven has approved and will continue to approve. When a crushed, enslaved, and cruelly treated people go to war for their liberty, then it may be said that:

> Oh! If there be on this earthly sphere
> A boon, an offering Heaven holds dear,
> 'Tis the last libation Liberty draws
> From the hearts that bleed and breaks in her cause![8]

And he who would like to determine approximately when such wars will cease on the earth may survey the map of the world, find its dark spots, where despots rule, and say, "Until these are made light and bright by the effulgent sun of liberty, wars will not cease."[9] When the downtrodden are emancipated, when kings and potentates admit that "all men are created equal, and are endowed by their Creator with certain unalienable rights; that among these are life, liberty, and the pursuit of happiness,"[10] then the world may prudently anticipate an era of peace, then it may be that the swords will be beaten into plowshares and spears into pruning hooks; but not till then.

The student of current events finds all Europe preparing for war. England and Italy and Germany are fighting Arabs and Negroes in Africa. France proposes to bombard Alexandria while conducting a war in China. England and Russia are preparing for war in Afghanistan, which, if finally declared, will be felt throughout the civilized world. Chile has not yet relaxed her grasp upon Peru. The relations between Brazil and the Argentine Republic are warlike, Central America is convulsed, and in the far Northwest of the Dominion of Canada, the Indians and half-breeds are on the warpath. "Men may cry, peace, peace," but there is no assured peace on earth.[11] It is war, or preparation for war. There can be heard no harbinger voice proclaiming universal peace; no ray of light glows along the horizon, betokening the dawn of an era when nations shall learn war no more. Why these war clouds, and what are to be the results of the conflicts they portend? If a laconic reply could be tolerated we might say manifest destiny accounts for the clouds, and final results will demonstrate that the world has been improved by the convulsions of war. In every quarter of the globe civilization confronts savagery, barbarism, and semi-barbarism. A higher type of civilization bears down upon the lower type. Intelligence is in conflict with ignorance; power treads upon weakness. The question is the "survival of the fittest," and the fittest in war is the strongest. The right in every conflict does not prevail; the truth is often cloven down; but ultimately, truth and right and liberty are to be enthroned. When this high noon of civilization and progress is reached, when all men are citizens—crowned sovereigns by constitution and law—when education is universal and savagery and barbarism disappear, when the boundary lines of nations are clearly defined and made inviolate by the consent of all, then it may be that swords will be transformed into plowshares and the nations will be at peace. To accomplish such results may require ten thousand years or ten times ten thousand years. The question of time is of little consequence, but if with all the light before us we are able to determine that the drift of events is in that direction, generations, as they come and go, can afford to be satisfied if they can in any way expedite the grand consummation. Taking human nature in the aggregate, as it is, wars are inevitable. To determine with any degree of accuracy the causes which provoke war is of less importance than to contemplate the results. No one except the parties engaged cares particularly why English soldiers are in the Sudan or the French in Tonquin,[12] but the world looks on with ever-increasing solicitude to note results. If El Mahdi is vanquished,[13] then a vast region is redeemed from the thralldom of barbarism; otherwise darkness will continue to overshadow the land. It is difficult to understand why the French are at war with the Chinese, but upon general principles, all Christendom hopes for a triumph of French arms, because the exclusiveness of the Chinese is not in consonance with the civilization of the age and will not be tolerated. But such struggles are dwarfed to comparative insignificance when contemplating the impending conflict between England and Russia; causes are lost sight of and only results are discussed. Treating the question negatively, it cannot be said that the resort to arms between the two nations will be in the interest of others than those who are ambitious of power and dominion.

It will not be unprofitable in this connection to state, with some degree of definiteness, facts relating to the extent and power of the two mighty empires whose belligerent attitude startles Christendom. The British Empire embraces with its colonies and dependencies about one-third of the terrestrial surface of the globe, and nearly one-fourth of its population. Such a vast extent of territory naturally suggested Daniel Webster's figure of speech, "drumbeat" and "martial airs" "following the sun and keeping company with the hours."[14] In Europe the British Empire includes: Great Britain and Ireland, Gibraltar, Malta, and Heligoland;[15] area, 121,000 square miles and 32 million population.

In Asia: British and Farther India, Hong Kong, Aden, Straits Settlements, Labuan, Ceylon, etc.; area, 1,600,000 square miles and 200 million population.

In Africa: Cape of Good Hope, Natal, Gold Coast, Gambia, Sierra Leone, Mauritius, and St. Helena; area, 250,000 square miles and 1.5 million population.

In North America: The British possessions from Newfoundland to Vancouver's Island; area, 3,800,000 square miles and 4 million population.

In the West Indies and Central America: Honduras and 15 islands and groups of islands; area, 28,000 square miles and 900,000 population.

In South America: British Guinea and Falkland Islands; area, 80,000 square miles and 150,000 population.

Australia: New South Wales, Victoria, South Australia, West Australia, Tasmania, Queensland, and New Zealand; area, 2,550,000 square miles and 2 million population.

Making a grand total of 8,427,000 square miles and 240,550,000 population.

The Russian Empire includes 8,088,331 square miles, having a population of 78,732,000. Of this territory, 2,226,982 square miles are in Europe, with 70,880,000 population, and 5,861,348 square miles in Asia, with a population of 7,924,000. It will be observed that the Russian possessions are in Europe and Asia, while the possessions of England are scattered over the whole earth. A glance at the map of Asia will help materially in revealing the cause of the war cloud which now portends a terrific struggle. British India extends northward until it touches the southern boundary of Afghanistan, while the Russian possessions extend southward until they touch the northern limits of Afghanistan. If Russia invades and conquers Afghanistan, then Russia comes down to the British India boundary. To prevent this occasions England's hostile attitude. Russia is looking for a pathway to the sea. She has maritime ambitions. With such facts in full view the intelligent reader will be able to form conclusions more or less satisfactory until the war begins or the threatening cloud is dispersed by the triumph of reason over pride and passion. The nations to be engaged have staying qualities and vast resources. Both are Christian nations, boasting of established churches. They civilize with catechisms and cutlasses, bombard with bibles and bombs, reform with rituals and rifles, and canonize with cannon. The missionaries in Asia are making poor headway. In all of its 15 million square miles there is not now an inch of "holy land" left, unless Siberia and India may lay claim to the title. There is idolatry, ignorance, and idleness, requiring the gospel of gunpowder and the baptism of fire. Such, at least, is the view that Russia and England take of the situation. As we write, the war cloud hanging about Afghanistan grows darker. What the outcome will be the Infinite Disposer of Events only knows, but it may be gratifying to believe Asia cannot be injured.

When a Hundred Years Are Gone[†]

July 1885

When a hundred years from the date of this number of the *Magazine* have joined the innumerable host of centuries gone, and 1985 makes its debut, what will be the condition of affairs in this great American Republic? Such an inquiry may not be usual, and yet, we opine, there are readers of the *Magazine* who do often, in moments of reverie, interrogate themselves upon the subject.

The estimate is that there are now in the United States 55 million souls. When a hundred years are gone an infirm and tottering remnant of the vast multitude, possibly a score, will remain, to recite to reporters their feeble recollections of events; the great majority, the millions, will have moved on and taken their places in the "silent halls," where death is master of ceremonies.[16]

There may be those who, in contemplation of this grim phase of the subject, will feel disposed to indulge themselves in the luxury of sentimental reflections, in which the lachrymal machinery will bear tearful testimony to the intensity of feeling aroused by freaks of the imagination.

In fancy they will behold on the streets and highways of the country 55 million funeral processions, the plumed hearse, the casket, the veiled mourners—possibly the brass band—all, even the horses, keeping step to the doleful dirge of death. Manifestly, death, instead of being a curse, is a great blessing. It makes room for the newcomers, and sentimentalists can afford to take a thought of the births while deploring the ravages of death. When a hundred years are gone, the republic will have, in spite of all that death can do, at least 275 million inhabitants.[17] Marriage bells will make merry music while funeral knells are telling what death has done—and as there will be more births than deaths, there will be more rejoicing than mourning in the land, while the next hundred years go marching on.

This reference to population suggests the topic of food. We are now producing, say, 500 million bushels of wheat annually, of which we have a surplus, after supplying the home demand, of about 225 million bushels, estimating the consumption for bread and seed at five bushels per capita. If, therefore, in

---

† Published as "When a Hundred Years Gone" in *Firemen's Magazine*, vol. 9, no. 7 (July 1885), 409–412.

1985 we maintain the average of five bushels per capita, 1.275 billion bushels of wheat will be required as the annual crop.[18] Such figures may be startling, but they are not necessarily depressing. When a hundred years are gone it is safe to assume that the arable, the food-producing, land of the world will be occupied, and made to contribute by scientific cultivation, abundant harvests for the sustenance of man; at any rate the present generation can do little for posterity except to set an example of pluck and industry.

Speaking of population, suggests the area of the field when the multiplied millions are to operate, and the inquiry leads directly to consideration of race peculiarities. With 55 million people it is found difficult to restrain aggressiveness. The Anglo-Saxon element predominating, the acquisition of territory will distinguish the future as it has the past, and when a hundred years are gone, it is prudent to assume that the Republic will embrace the North American continent. The pressure westward being arrested by the Pacific Ocean, it must be northward and southward. Already thousands, citizens of the Dominion of Canada, discuss with steadily increasing favor the annexation of that country to the United States, and those who are capable of understanding the logic of events, of self-interest, of population and wealth, do not hesitate to predict the absorption of Mexico and the Central American States by the United States before a hundred years are gone.

There may be those who will say that such intimations of progress are huge hallucinations, the vaguest of vagaries, the result of mental infirmity. They will be forced to admit, however, that we have outlined possibilities. Probabilities admit of wider discussion. It might be well to state the proposition as follows: If 3 million people, in a hundred years, from 1783 to 1884, gained 52 million and acquired territory embracing an area of 2,765,640 square miles, what may be expected of 55 million people during the next hundred years in the way of acquiring territory, provided the land is in sight and approachable? We submit that the probabilities are abreast of the possibilities, and that we do not overestimate the greed and aggressiveness of the American people—indeed, we doubt if these characteristics admit of overestimates.

But in the further prognostication of the situation, when a hundred years are gone, the possible acquisition of territory need not be regarded as the most cheering branch of the subject. In the year 1985 we shall be the richest nation on the globe. In this connection it may be said that the accumulation of wealth in the United States means more, when development and wealth are considered, than in any other country.

When a hundred years are gone, who, of all the seers of the present, can estimate the magnitude of the industrial enterprises which will then command the attention of statisticians?

When a hundred years are gone, it may be profitable to inquire if New England or the South will be the center of the cotton manufacturing industry of the republic. Indeed, we might extend the inquiry and ask if the probabilities give assurance of England's control of the manufacturing industries of the world when a hundred years are gone. Manifestly, New England will yield her supremacy to the South, and England, no longer the money center of the world, will be required to succumb to the inevitable. Cheaper food and cheaper materials and greater wealth will rule in the realm of industries, and when a hundred years are gone the United States will control the markets of the world.

Those who take pleasure in contemplating the possibilities of progress would find little difficulty in giving their fancies the coloring of fact were they to read the history of events during the past hundred years. Who, of all sages and soothsayers living a hundred years ago, so much as dreamed that a day was coming, near or remote, when steam, on the sea and on the land, would stand crowned by the genius of man, a moving power, compared with which science can find no equal—a power which defies winds and waves, which has revolutionized commerce, peopled waste places, and made deserts fruitful as Edens. Harnessed to the locomotive continents are traversed in a few hours, while millions of men and women in palace cars are transported as if the solid earth had been transformed into dreamland.

Who, of all the poets and prophets since the days when Joseph interpreted the dreams of Pharaoh,[19] intimated that a time would come when man, by the fiat of his inscrutable genius, should command the lightnings to do his bidding, that time and distance should be annihilated, and the remotest places on the face of the earth should be brought into instantaneous communication? In the presence of the telephone and the telegraph, who, of all the doubters and croakers, has a right to intimate that still more and far more astounding revelations are not to bless the world, when a hundred years are gone?

Today, those who predict that the time will come when men will fly— cleave the air with artificial wings—are regarded as vagarists, fanciful cranks, whose whims serve only to amuse philosophers, and who play the role of "court fool" to embellish the leisure of thinkers when relaxation takes the place of work. But it may be said in reply that those who now predict astounding achievements of mind, who map out new highways for thought and invention, who believe, with all the accumulation of knowledge which the past has conferred upon the present, the foremost of discoverers have but entered the vestibule of the unknown, but not the unknowable, are not treated with greater rudeness than others in the faraway days who, like Galileo, were persecuted for asserting that the earth moves.

It would be interesting, in view of the gigantic strides man has made during the last century, in exploring the mysteries of nature, to outline still further the victories that will challenge the admiration of the world when a hundred years are gone, but space forbids, and yet our readers have a right to anticipate the inquiry: What of the railroad system when a hundred years are gone? Such an inquiry suggests another, which comes still nearer to the great body of the patrons of the *Magazine*. It is, what of the Brotherhood of Locomotive Firemen of North America when a hundred years are gone? We confess that the possibilities of the brotherhood warrant estimates which task the imagination to the utmost limits of rational conjecture. We know that the railroad interests of America are in their infancy, and that our beloved order is still more juvenile. The growth of the former means the expansion of the latter. An increase of the mileage of railroads means an increase in the grand army of locomotive firemen—more lodges and more benevolence. It is a sublime idea. We are building lodges not only for the present, but for the future, not only for ourselves, but for posterity. We are laying the foundations deep and strong. Our theory is in consonance with the principles of truth, justice, and benevolence, fraternity and the dignity of labor. We are builders, and our work is to go on forever. Our order is to renew its youth as the years speed on. Broad-based as the continent and as enduring as the everlasting hills, it is designed to resist antagonistic influences from without, and can be overthrown only on the treason of its professed friends. But we indulge no misgivings, preferring to predict for the brotherhood imperial sway and worldwide renown when a hundred years are gone.

Standing Armies[†]

August 1885

Among the governmental ideas, peculiarly American, there is not one more distinctly defined than the deep-seated opposition to large standing armies. It is a fact universally accepted that large standing armies are flagrantly inimical to the liberties of the people, and no more judicious protests were ever made against the encroachments of centralized power in the United States than those which relate to the maintenance of a large military force. Of 35 countries, officially reported, the number of men constituting their standing or regular armies is given at 4,938,080. Of these countries there are 13 of which have standing armies, numbering 3,810,643 men, out of a population of 345,431,003,[20] and costing annually $609,422,316, as follows:

Country	Population	Standing Army	
Austro-Hungary	37,759,407	289,100	$53,386,915
Belgium	5,476,668	46,383	8,776,429
Denmark	1,969,454	35,727	2,359,027
France	36,905,788	502,764	114,279,761
Germany	45,194,172	445,402	98,330,429
Great Britain	35,246,562	131,636	74,901,500
Italy	28,209,620	736,502	42,947,263
Netherlands	3,981,88/	65,113	8,397,000
Russia	72,520,000	974,771	137,812,202
Spain	16,333,293	90,000	24,802,930
Switzerland	2,831,787	117,500	2,352,100
Turkey	8,866,582	350,000	610,300
United States	50,135,783	25,745	40,466,460
TOTAL	345,431,003	3,810,643	$609,422,316

It should be understood that the foregoing figures relate to armies on a peace footing. When war is declared, armies are indefinitely increased. So far as

---

† Published in *Firemen's Magazine,* vol. 9, no. 8 (August 1885), 471–473.

our figures relate to European countries, little need be said about the purpose for which standing armies are created and maintained. They are a necessity of despotism, and the figures relating to the armies of France and Switzerland in no wise modify the conclusion, since if they do not sustain home despotisms, they are required to repel invasions in the interest of despots. Remove the standing armies of Europe, and the people would be free in a day. European wars are, as a general proposition, for the wrong—a conflict of evils. Sometimes a great wrong has been overthrown or shorn of some of its power and the right advanced to a stronger position, but the chief business of standing armies in Europe is to support thrones and keep the people in subjection to royalty and aristocracy.

Referring to our figures, it will be observed that 12 European countries keep constantly equipped in time of peace 3,784,893 men, and pay annually for their support $568,955,850. This vast number of men earn nothing, they produce nothing, they simply consume. Europe is full of paupers—half-fed, half-clothed wretches—who enjoy few more rights and privileges than beasts of burden, and to keep them in subjection, to kill them if they demand "life, liberty, and the pursuit of happiness" is the chief business of standing armies. A standing army has always been regarded in the United States as a standing danger, to be reduced to the lowest practicable number. The figures relating to the regular or standing army of the United States, from 1789 to 1879, are instructive. They are for officers and men as follows:

Year		Strength of Army
1789	One regiment army, one battery artillery	840
1792	Indian border wars	5,120
1794	Peace establishment	3,629
1801	....	5,144
1807	....	3,278
1810	....	7,154
1812	War with Great Britain	11,331
1815	....	9,433
1817–1821	Peace establishment	9,980
1822–1832	....	6,184
1833–1837	....	7,198
1838–1842	Florida war	12,439
1843–1846	Peace establishment	8,613
1817	Mexican war	17,812
1848	....	30,890
1849–1855	Peace establishment	10,320
1856–1861	....	12,931
1862	Civil war	39,273
1863–1866	....	43,332
1867	Peace establishment	51,641
1868–1869	....	52,922
1870	....	37,313
1871	....	35,353
1872–1874	....	32,264
1875–1879	....	27,480

A glance at the foregoing figures fully establishes our proposition that a large standing army is anti-American and in conflict with the genius of our institutions. In this country wars have been for the right, forced by circumstances and inevitables, and on all occasions the people have responded with alacrity to the call, and the right has been vindicated, and when the war was past, the policy has been to reduce at once the army. It was not wanted and was dangerous. The only requirement for an army is to fight and oversee a few straggling, half-starved Indians who, if they were not shamefully cheated and oppressed, would be quiet and peaceable—such is the testimony of the best-informed soldiers of the army.

In view of all the facts, the widespread demand for organizing the militia of the various states is worthy of profound thought. There is neither war nor a probability of war. No foreign nation is anxious to challenge the United States. Canada is much more inclined to annexation than war, and Mexico makes overtures of lasting peace by proposing a commercial treaty upon the most liberal terms. Such facts are well calculated to arouse interest when a demand is made to equip about 4 million soldiers in the various states. The question is asked with ever increasing interest: Why so much military ardor and enthusiasm? It begins to leak out that in certain quarters labor troubles are likely to take place in the near future, and that soldiers will he handy to shoot down strikers, who are usually denounced as communists, socialists, and dynamiters.

We have heard much of late, but not too much of the encroachments of monopolists upon the rights of laborers, the wage men and the wealth creators of the land. In various localities the piteous appeals of suffering men and women for work have made the days and the nights hideous. Wages are reduced or entirely suspended. When such things occur, labor troubles sometimes supervene. At such times, as in the case of the Hocking Valley troubles, soldiers are wanted that blood may mingle with the tears of the famine-afflicted unfortunates.[21] Powder does sometimes produce peace, and bullets, like bread, have a quieting influence. Autocrats, despots, kings, and sultans cannot govern at all without such appliances, but prudent and thoughtful Americans cannot be too earnest in their investigation in regard to the purpose of those who are asking for a large military force in all the states of the Union.

It has long been known that the influence of West Point upon society has been vicious in the extreme. As a general proposition, the graduates of that institution are insufferable snobs. They have the idea drilled into them that they constitute a ruling class. They are supported off of the earnings of the people and acquire a strut and swagger indicative of feelings of superiority, at once disgusting and humiliating, and the knowledge that they are life pensioners upon the government adds indefinitely to their offensive superciliousness. West Point annually inflicts upon the country a horde of these gold-lace parasites, public crib-loungers, who toil not and for whose services there is neither a present or a remote necessity. And now, with this useless burden upon their necks, there is a set of people demanding a military establishment larger than that which obeys the nod of any European despot, and when it is asked what is the necessity for the existence of such a monstrous military machine in the United States, the answer is, "There may be labor troubles in the near future." Laboring men everywhere throughout the broad land may well regard the movement with deep concern. It means their ultimate subjugation. It is to bring on a conflict between bread and bullets, pay and powder.

It is shown by official figures that the people are now taxed more than $40 million a year to support a standing army, and though it numbers less than 28,000 men, thousands of these are mere loungers who might as well be dead as alive, so far as any benefits arising from their existence is concerned. Why, then, seek to increase the burdens of taxation by the creation of more military establishments?

The time has come for workingmen to give this military craze serious attention. It means mischief.

Dynamite and Legitimate Warfare[†]
October 1885

The average man—that is to say, the man with the average amount of common sense, intelligence, and conscience accepting the dictum of rulers, at once perceives that "legitimate warfare" is that kind of warfare which they choose to engage in. The term "legitimate" is at once robbed of its relations to right and justice, and is made to do duty in the interest of those who decree war, without the slightest regard for the motives which influence their decisions. The warfare is legitimate because the supreme governing power so determines. "Legitimate" means lawful, according to law. Hence, if a powerful country or government decides to make war upon a country or people unable in men and materials to cope with it, for the purpose of subduing it, it is denominated "legitimate warfare" though the purpose is to rob the weaker people of their lands, their homes, their rights, liberties, and privileges. It does not require a labored effort to comprehend, under such circumstances, the fact that the term "legitimate" is made to signify wrongs and curses, for the proper characterization of which, the English language is totally inadequate.

We are not unmindful of the fact that war is generally regarded as a calamity, a scourge, and by not a few, as an exhibition of divine wrath, sent as a punishment for the sins of those who are the victims of its devastations. We

---

† Published in *Firemen's Magazine,* vol. 9, no. 10 (October 1885), 615–617.

have no inclination to explore for testimony for or against such fanciful propositions. We are inclined to the belief that there is such a thing as "legitimate
warfare," and our convictions are equally firm that wars, generally, have been
waged in the interest of oppression, to perpetuate wrong, to crush liberty, to
degrade humanity and strengthen despotism in the world.

No more interesting question engages the attention of thoughtful people than the triumph of liberty in the world. The emancipation of the oppressed from the tyranny of despots is the question of questions. It means
ceaseless agitation—it means war, legitimate warfare. The question arises: Is
liberty worth what it costs? Is it better to die free or live in bondage? Is it better to live the crawling, abject, manacled, degraded helot, or die robed and
crowned with all the rights and prerogatives of citizenship? He who does not
know that such questions are being asked throughout the civilized world,
and that they are to be answered if necessary by political convulsions for
which the past furnishes no parallels, is totally disqualified to comprehend
the logic of events.

It should be noticed that in conducting what is termed "legitimate warfare" nations are anxious to discover the most terrible death-dealing forces,
and never, from the beginning till the present, have sticklers for "legitimate
warfare" cared a farthing who of the enemy they killed or made homeless, and
the records demonstrate conclusively that as science has developed new and
more destructive agents, those in favor of "legitimate warfare" are quick to avail
themselves of the discovery that human slaughter might be more expeditious
and the banquet of death more imposing. To assume that these advocates of legitimate warfare have hesitated because their death-dealing agents killed innocent people or subjected them to the horrors of destitution is so astoundingly
preposterous that an ebony statue of a Goth or Vandal would blush crimson
in the presence of such hypocrisy. Those who doubt may read in sacked and
burning cities, fruitful fields laid waste, and happy homes wrecked and desolate
confirmations strong as holy writ.

The idea of "legitimate warfare" is to conquer, regardless of consequences—to
weaken the enemy, and "enemy" includes all within the boundaries of the enemy's
country. Women and children, old and infirm—and these are subject to the horrors of war in a majority of instances, that men, who, by the latest revision of the
Bible, were created "a little lower than God," shall never know the joy of liberty.

Hitherto the triumphs of science in the discovery of death-dealing agents
have been such as only nations could appropriate—iron-clad ships, torpedoes,
Krupp and Gatling guns, etc., but the discovery of dynamite is working a

revolution. It is easily, cheaply, and expeditiously made, and in the matter of power it astonishes by the majesty of its performances. It has set the world to thinking. It is giving despots untold anxiety. Their sleep is disturbed and, even in their palaces and strongest fortresses, they realize insecurity. At the mention of dynamite, the tsar calls all Russia to order and demands of his slaves extra vigilance. His countenance is changed and the joints of his loins are loosed and his knees knock against each other. He sees the skeleton hand writing his doom on his palace walls. Dynamite is forever saying to despots, "Let the people have freedom. Let the people rise from their prostrate condition." It is the old demand made by Moses to Pharaoh, "Let my people go," and Pharaoh's stubbornness should teach despots of the present age a lesson of prudence.[22]

Legitimate warfare should be warfare for the right, warfare against oppression, warfare for liberty and equality. Such warfares stand the test of criticism. The more they are examined the better men like them. But it is noticeable that those who prate of "legitimate warfare" most are opposed to the use of dynamite except by themselves. Kings and potentates demand a monopoly of dynamite. They do not propose that the plebeian shall expand to the proportions of the patrician. Power, if they can have their way, is to forever remain in the palace on the hill, never to be known in the hovel at its foot. The children of slaves are to be slaves through all succeeding generations. Such are not the signs of the times. The world is invited to contemplate a far different picture. Legitimate warfare in the future is to be in the interest of the weak, the oppressed, those who aspire to be free. Dynamite is to be a potent factor in the contest, and the world is to recognize the truth of Peter's declaration that "God is no respecter of persons,"[23] and that other self-evident truth that "all men are born equal." When despots, from the little tyrant who lords it over the few to the autocrat who counts his slaves by millions, are willing to break their scepters and fling away their crowns and titles, dynamite will have accomplished its supreme mission in the world. Till then no decree, no combination of forces, will be able to retire dynamite from the conflict.

It is the friend of the slave, nor is there on the face of the earth a victim of oppression who deplores its advent. For:

> When a deed is done for Freedom, through the broad earth's aching breast,
> Runs a thrill of joy prophetic, trembling on from east to west;
> And the slave, where'er he cowers, feels the soul within him climb
> To the awful verge of manhood, as the energy sublime
> Of a century bursts full-blossomed on the thorny stem of Time.[24]

Railroad Kings[†]

December 1885

It is not presumed that the term "railroad kings" when coined was intended for anything more than a compliment to such men as had acquired large railroad interests or were at the head of what are termed "railroad systems," but of late the title is made to signify something more and a "railroad king" has come to mean power, often equal and sometimes superior to any power known to the legislative bodies of the country—that is to say railroad kings, by virtue of influences which they can command and of circumstances which they can create, can often shape legislation to suit their interests and defeat opposition.

It is not to be assumed that the average citizen is familiar with the vast power which railroads exert in public affairs, nor is it surprising that such should be the case. The growth of the railroad interests of the United States and of North America has been phenomenal to an extent that defies exaggeration. There are now about 125,000 miles of railroad in the United States, and men are living, in the prime of their mental faculties, whose recollection goes back to the period when the first mile of the entire system was built.

Year	Miles in Operation	Annual Increase
1830	23	-----
1831	95	72
1832	229	134
1833	380	151
1834	633	253
1835	1,098	465
1836	1,273	175
1837	1,497	224
1838	1,913	416
1839	2,302	389
1840	2,818	516
1841	3,535	717
1842	4,026	491
1843	4,185	159
1844	4,377	192
1845	4,633	256

† Published in *Firemen's Magazine,* vol. 9, no. 12 (December 1885), 723–726.

Year	Miles in Operation	Annual Increase
1846	4,930	297
1847	5,598	668
1848	5,996	398
1849	7,365	1,369
1850	9,021	1,656
1851	10,982	1,961
1852	12,908	1,926
1853	15,360	2,452
1854	16,720	1,360
1855	18,374	1,654
1856	22,016	3,642
1857	24,503	2,487
1858	26,968	2,465
1859	28,780	1,812
1860	30,635	1,855
1861	31,286	651
1862	32,120	834
1863	33,170	1,050
1864	33,908	738
1865	35,085	1,177
1866	36,801	1,716
1867	39,250	2,449
1868	42,229	2,979
1869	46,844	4,615
1870	52,914	6,070
1871	60,293	7,379
1872	66,171	5,878
1873	70,278	4,107
1874	72,383	2,105
1875	74,096	1,713
1876	76,808	2,712
1877	79,089	2,281
1878	81,776	2,687
1879	86,497	4,721
1880	93,671	7,174
1881	104,813	11,142
1882	113,329	8,516
1883	117,580	4,251
1884	124,317	6,737

Such figures are eloquent of enterprise such as embellishes the history of no other land under the sun, for it should be stated that the railroad history of the country is one of marvels. It is the romance of fact, and to build and equip these roads has required an expenditure of more than $6 billion—a sum so vast that no ordinary mind can grasp it.

It might be interesting to show the quantities of the various materials that have entered into the construction and equipment of railroads in the United States and the number of men required to build them, but such statistics would be foreign to our purpose at this writing, but it is pertinent to say that these roads employed, in 1880, 236,058 men, other than clerks; they employed 2,069 officials and 12,331 clerks and bookkeepers—a grand total of 250,458. If it be assumed that 200,000 of these employees are married men with families averaging five members—then we would have a population dependent upon railroads of 1,050,248.

In view of such facts, it is not surprising that when individuals control systems of railroads which embrace a large number of miles that they should receive the title of "king." There is more in the title than appears on the surface, as we shall endeavor to show.

As we have intimated, the title "railroad king," whether applied to the owner of railroad property or the president of railroad corporations, means that the man bearing the title possesses great power, that he is chief ruler—having the power to enforce his views and, if antagonized, can remove those who have the temerity to oppose him.

We shall not attempt to tell how many railroad kings there are in the United States. There are, doubtless, a large number who have not yet been crowned and whose coronation day may never come, but who exercise kingly powers nevertheless. The powers of railroad kings are numerous, extending all the way from granting a railroad pass to the purchase of a judge or a legislature. They have the power to "water stocks." It is an extraordinary power and takes on some of the peculiarities attending the working of miracles. The miracle of changing water into wine is familiar to our readers, but railroad kings have been known, in numerous instances, to transform water into stocks and money. When railroad kings combine their power they can make the products of the soil cheap or dear, as they may choose. They can put up or put down rates of transportation, and if complaints are made, they ask with frigid nonchalance: "What are you going to do about it?"

When legislatures meet, the first thing in order is to see that every member has a railroad pass. The kings see to it that their decrees in this regard are obeyed to the letter, the theory being that a legislator with a railroad free pass in the pocket is going to vote the way he rides. From the moment he accepts the pass he is secure. It is what is called strategy. If there are those in the legislature who have refused passes, then the kings adopt other means to accomplish their purpose. Lobbies are organized, and money directly or indirectly is used in a way to do it most good (?). What has been said to legislatures applies with equal force to Congress.

Railroad kings, it should be said, are without exception men of brains, men of large intellectual caliber. They are not only practical businessmen but are shrewd politicians and farseeing statesmen, and whether reasoning from cause to effect or vice versa are acutely logical. They understand the maxim that politics is the science of government, and they assume that government ought to be of the railroads, by the railroads, and for the railroads, and to a man railroad kings have the courage of conviction.

Instances are rare in which railroad kings have taken their titles by inheritance. As a general proposition, railroad kings are of the Napoleonic school, men who have fought their way into prominence and power and have earned the right to rule. We have selected for the embellishment of this article a few names known to fame, who are recognized as railroad kings in this and in other lands, giving the number of miles of railroad systems which constitute their realm. They are as follows:

King	System	Miles
William H. Vanderbilt	Vanderbilt	2,800
Jay Gould	Wabash	6,000
Alex Mitchell	Chicago, Milwaukee & St. Paul	5,000
C. P. Huntington	Huntington	9,000
Leland Stanford	Huntington	(above)
Charles Clark	Illinois Central	2,000
Robert Garrett	Baltimore & Ohio	1,700
Milton H. Smith	Louisville & Nashville	2,366
Frank S. Bar	Cincinnati Southern	1,200
W. B. Shay	Santa Fe	2,000
Thomas F. Oakes	Northern Pacific	2,000
James J. Hill	St. Paul, Minneapolis & Manitoba	1,700
David H. Moffat	Denver & Rio Grande	1,700
Charles F. Adams	Union Pacific	4,700
Albert Keep	Chicago & Northwestern	5,600
John P. Roberts	Pennsylvania	2,200

Here are 16 railroad kings who control 50,666 miles of the railroads of the country, an average of 3,000 miles each, or about one-third of all the railroads in operation.

We have shown that the 125,000 miles of railroads employ, all told, 250,458 persons or, say, two to the mile. This would give the railroad kings named control of 101,333 men who, with families averaging five persons each, would give a grand aggregate of 506,665 persons dependent upon them for support; omitting officials, and for the sake of round numbers, we will say 500,000 persons are directly within control of the railroad kings we have named.

To what extent railroad kings can exert their power over employees, and the methods employed in that direction, are regarded as questions of great importance. They can, at their pleasure, increase or decrease wages. They are not required to consult their employees on the subject, nor do they. This is a tremendous power. If the railroad king is just, noble, and humane, and history gives accounts of such potentates, then employees are comfortable, happy, and contented; their homes are bright and cheerful, their wives wear smiling faces, and their children are blithe. But when the railroad king is mercenary, cold, and callous, a man who, to dress in purple and fine linen and to fare sumptuously every day, reduces wages, then the condition of employees is changed; then discontent prevails, then is gloom in the homes of the employees, and content takes its departure. And it may be said, as a further illustration of the power of railroad kings, that they may at their pleasure dismiss the discontented employees, exile them from work entirely and absolutely, and reduce them to tramps and vagrants.

Are we asked for a remedy for such exhibitions of the power as we have pointed out? We answer, we did not start out to discuss remedies, but rather to show the vastness of the railroad systems of the country, in the management of which men have developed into what has been significantly styled "kings," possessed of vast powers which are yearly becoming more formidable. What the result will be, time only can determine, but the close observers of the signs of the times are of the opinion that labor is organizing for the purpose of discussing with employers propositions looking to a more perfect agreement relating to the subject of wages, and a more equitable distribution of the wealth which labor creates. And as railroads are, in every instance, the creations of legislation, and partake quite as much of public as of private enterprise, it is not surprising that the people have their attention particularly directed to their management.

Notes

1. Daniel Wolsey Voorhees (1827–1897) of Terre Haute first won election to Congress in November 1860 and was returned to office several times before moving to the Senate in 1877. A staunch states' rights Jacksonian and white supremacist, Voorhees was an advocate of the preservation of slavery in the South and a bitter opponent of the Abraham Lincoln administration.

2. Following Debs's nomination of Senator Voorhees, the Republicans placed the name of A. G. Porter, with Voorhees winning election to the Senate by a tally of 64–35.

3. James V. Campbell, "The Encroachments of Capital," *North American Review*, vol. 139, no. 333 (August 1884), 101–108.

4. Henry George (1839–1897) was one of the most influential American economic theorists of the nineteenth century. An opponent of plutocracy and the poverty which it left in its wake, George proposed a simple (and simplistic) "single tax" on the unimproved value of land as the ideal mechanism to eliminate the extraction of value by the wealthy in the form of rent by virtue of mere ownership rather than productive enterprise. Individuals would be incentivized to use as little land as possible and to make it as productive as possible, making land reform and greater economic equality possible. The single tax on land values was believed sufficient to cover all costs of government, thereby allowing the elimination of all other forms of taxation. In addition to authoring a best-selling book on his economic ideas, *Progress and Poverty*, George was himself a political aspirant, running an independent campaign for mayor of New York against the Tammany Hall Democrats in 1897.

5. Henry George, *Progress and Poverty: An Inquiry into the Cause of Industrial Depressions and of Increase of Want with Increase of Wealth: The Remedy* (San Francisco: W. M. Hinton, 1879).

6. Zebulon Baird Vance (1830–1894) was a conservative US senator from North Carolina who served from 1879 until the time of his death. He was one of the leading political voices of the American South in the years after the American Civil War.

7. Isaiah 2:4.

8. From *Lalla Rookh* (1817) by Thomas Moore (1779–1852).

9. This poetic fragment could not be traced.

10. From the Declaration of Independence (1776).

11. From "Speech to the Virginia Provincial Convention" (1775) by Patrick Henry (1736–1799). The original lines are "Gentlemen may cry, peace, peace! but there is no peace. The war has actually begun!"

12. Today's Vietnam.

13. The Mahdi, literally the "enlightened one," is a prophesied Islamic redeemer who it is believed will arrive to rid earth of evil in anticipation of the final day of judgment.

14. From a speech to the United States Senate, "The Presidential Protest" (1834), by Daniel Webster (1782–1852). Webster called Great Britain "a power which has dotted over the surface of the whole globe with her possessions and military posts, whose

morning drum-beat, following the sun, and keeping company with the hours, circles the earth with one continuous and unbroken strain of the martial airs of England."

15. Heligoland is a small chain of islands in the North Sea, currently held by Germany.

16. "Silent halls of death" is a turn of phrase used in the poem "Thanatopsis" (1811) by William Cullen Bryant (1794–1878).

17. According to US Census Bureau statistics, the population of the United States in 1985 was approximately 237.9 million.

18. According to the US Agriculture Department, American wheat production was 2.42 billion bushels in 1985, of which 909 million bushels were exported. Statistical Abstract of the United States (1991), 661.

19. Allusion to Genesis 41.

20. Debs gives two different tallies for total population of the countries that he surveys, neither of which match the actual sum. The total population figure has been corrected here.

21. The Hocking Valley, located in southeastern Ohio, was the scene of a bitter coal strike during the second half of 1884 and the first months of 1885. The strike collapsed in defeat after nearly eight months.

22. Reference is to Exodus 9:1–6.

23. Reference is to Acts 10:34–35: "Then Peter opened his mouth, and said, Of a truth I perceive that God is no respecter of persons: But in every nation he that feareth him, and worketh righteousness, is accepted with him."

24. From "The Present Crisis" (1845) by James Russell Lowell (1819–1891).

1886

William H. Vanderbilt[†]
March 1886

William H. Vanderbilt, before his death, gave one of his boys a million dollars. His grandfather [Cornelius Vanderbilt] gave him a million, and now the young man starts in business with $2 million. If he attends strictly to business, waters his stock, sands his sugar, etc., he may manage to make a living. If he should fail, however, his father can set him up again.

If a locomotive fireman could work 4,444 years, 300 days each year, at $1.50 per day, he would be in a position to bet Mr. Vanderbilt $2.50 that all men are born equal.

Employees the Wards of Employers[‡]
April 1886

Before the Sumter gun sounded the death knell of chattel slavery in the United States there were a great many owners of slaves who were anxious to provide well for the comfort of their human chattels. In such cases, the slaves were provided with comfortable shelter, wholesome food in abundance, and with clothing suitable to their degraded condition. In numerous instances the best medical talent was employed when the slaves were sick, and in matters of religion the poor creatures could go as they pleased, and it often pleased them to be exceedingly devout. The masters were in the habit of saying, "I must do what I can for these people, whom divine providence has committed to my care. It is a great responsibility, but I must bear it and be resigned."[1]

Workingmen, who are inclined to listen to the sayings of a certain class of employers and to certain writers of the day, will hear remarks not specially different to those which in slavery times were made by owners who felt the

---

† Published in *Locomotive Firemen's Magazine,* vol. 10, no. 3 (March 1886), 131.

‡ Published in *Locomotive Firemen's Magazine,* vol. 10, no. 4 (April 1886), 206–207.

weight of their obligations to be merciful to their slaves. As we write, we have before us a clipping from a newspaper published in Indiana. The writer is hopeful that workingmen will be successful in the formation of societies for their protection from "improper treatment and inadequate compensation which they claim to be subjected to by capitalists." The writer concludes that the employer "should be taught that there is something due those who are employed besides the prompt payment of wages, and the latter should learn that his whole duty is not performed when the shriek of the whistle or the tolling of a bell informs him that he may at that instant drop his tools or promptly resume them by the same signal." As a matter of fact, aside from gentlemanly deportment, the employer owes his employee his wages, and when the employee has performed his day's work, obligation ceases then and there. The obligation of neighborly kindness exists independent of employment and need not be discussed. The employee owns himself, is a man, a citizen, independent. He is not the ward of the employer. The employer is not his guardian, and that sort of stuff is out of place when discussing the relations of employer and employee. But the writer proceeds to say that "in the old country many a large employer provides his laborers with good comfortable homes at moderate rentals, with his food and clothing at a small advance above cost, with his medicines, books, papers, and almost everything he needs at prices far below those of cooperative stores." In this, we have a fair sample of the old slave times literature. Employers, as the guardians of their laborers, provide them with homes, etc. In America laboring men are citizens and when properly recognized will provide themselves with homes, food, and clothing, without the oversight of employers, and it should be understood and will be eventually that laboring men provide their employers with homes, clothing, food, and all their luxuries. But again, the writer says, "I am informed that an iron company in the state of Delaware largely carry out this mode of procedure. A large number of snug, comfortable dwellings for their operatives were erected by them at the incipiency of their works, to which additions are made as circumstances require. These houses are rendered attractive by yards and gardens attached, which are enclosed by neat picket fences. They are sufficiently commodious and present an inviting appearance." The time is at hand when workingmen, whatever has been true in the past, and whatever is true in the present, will see to it themselves that they and their families are properly sheltered, fed, and clothed, not because their employers provide for their necessities, but because it is incumbent upon them to attend to such things quite independent of their employers.

The patronizing talk of a certain class of employers and writers upon labor topics is degrading to workingmen. It robs them of their independence and sinks them to the humiliating level of dependence. It is virtually saying they require an overseer, props, and supports, that they are incapable of taking care of themselves and need a warden, a keeper, protector, and defender; and it must be said, however mortifying may be the confession, that thousands of workingmen have consented to the degrading bondage.

That there should exist mutual respect between employee and employer goes without saying, but there can be no such sentiment while the employer assumes to be the guardian of the employee, or while the employee consents to any personal oversight by his employer. Such a condition, on the one hand, is certain to beget arrogance, and on the other hand, servility as debasing as it is vile. What is wanted now is a leveling-up policy, and everywhere the indications are that the good work is progressing. Workingmen are not only looking up, but they are standing up with their hats on. They do not cower in the presence of millionaires. They know

> A prince can mak a belted knight,
>   A marquis, duke and a' that.
> But an honest man's abon his might,
>   Guid faith, he maunna fa' that.[2]

Workingmen are growing in thought, education, intellectual power, and influence. They are learning their rights, comprehending their duties, and are preparing to assert their claims to recognition in public affairs. Employers are to be relieved of their self-imposed guardianship, and workingmen, emancipated from even the appearance of bondage, will receive the long-delayed recognition which the majesty of their triumph will secure.

Overproduction[†]
April 1886

The term "overproduction" has a significance which, when analyzed, is anything but gratifying. It is difficult to associate privation, haggard poverty, with overproduction. The mind does not readily conceive of plenty and destitution going hand in hand. But overproduction is, nevertheless, a calamity which becomes the prolific parent of misery. To the laboring man "overproduction" is the synonym of idleness and a long list of ills, the contemplation of which fills the mind with horror.

To illustrate our meaning we will take the industry of mining coal, insofar as that fuel is used by manufacturing establishments to create steam for driving engines and machinery. The result of overproduction operates to the disadvantage of the miner in two ways. He is required to remain idle a portion of his time or he loses work entirely. He finds when working full time that he is barely able to support his family, to work half time is to endure privation, while to be thrown out of work entirely means crushing destitution. He will doubtless inquire the reason why the manufactures do not purchase the coal as usual, and is told they have shut down their works owing to an overproduction of wares, or that they are working half time or less, and hence thousands of their employees are working on starvation wages or are not working at all. Need we particularize? The ironworkers find there is an overproduction of pig iron, bar iron, nails, steel, etc. Weavers and spinners of wool and cotton hear the same complaint, and thus we might proceed throughout the entire list of industries always hearing the same ominous cry, "overproduction."

It would appear to be the mission of a crank to complain of labor-saving machinery. The present is an era of invention, and how to construct a machine that can perform the work of two or a thousand men is the high ambition of men of an inventive genius. This is quite natural, since such a machine is certain to sell. Every manufacturer wants one or a dozen. He reasons thus, "Here is a labor-saving machine. I can run it by steam; one man can tend it. It will save the work of 20 men; cost of machine, $5,000; 6 percent, on investment, $300; wear and tear 10 percent, $500; cost of one man to run it at $1.50 per day, 300 days, $450; total, $1,250. Cost of 19 men which it displaced at $1.50

---

† Published in *Locomotive Firemen's Magazine,* vol. 10, no. 4 (April 1886), 203–205.

per day, 300 days, $8,550, saving first year $7,300."[3]

The 19 men thrown out of employment must look elsewhere. They often look in vain. They start out to find work. They everywhere find the same labor-saving machinery in operation. They become tramps. Many of them find their way to the penitentiary. These prisons are becoming great manufacturing establishments. The state takes this criminal muscle and operates it at a small cost; floods the market with an "overproduction" of prison, crime-produced wares; sells them cheap, as it can afford to do; and thus makes it impossible for honest men to compete with it, and then they are forced into idleness that the state may have a revenue from its criminals.

The questions that naturally arise in the discussion of overproduction are: first, is it practicable to do away with labor-saving machinery? Manifestly, it is not. Second, is there any way to remedy the curse of overproduction? We think there is. What? Sell the wares. That is just what everybody is trying to do, but there is no market. We are at the point sought. The real question of statesmanship before the country is to supply a market for our surplus manufactured products. Is it possible? There is little doubt in the minds of practical men upon the subject. The *New Orleans Exposition Gazette* of November [1885] furnishes authoritative figures which are convincing. It refers to the trade relations between the Spanish and Portuguese American countries and asks, "What shall we do with our surplus manufactured products?" In answering the question the *Gazette* says "that every commercial interest of the United States is closely identified with a hemispherical policy by which Americans shall be induced to trade with Americans, and by which $710 million of South and Central American commerce now carried on with England, France, and Germany shall be diverted to the United States, where it rightfully and geographically belongs; and to develop more intimate trade relations between the 55 million producers and consumers of the United States and the 48 million producers and consumers of Mexico, South America, Central America, and the West India Islands; in other words, to stimulate an exchange of our surplus raw materials." There are 22 of these countries, and it is shown by recent reports to the Department of State that these countries annually import products to the amount of $475,061,000, of which the United States supplies $77,141,000, while Europe supplies $397,920,000. These countries annually export $479,912,000, of which the United States receives $168 million, while Europe gets $307,912,000.

Manifestly there is a great wrong existing somewhere, and if the people will investigate the subject it will be found that the wrong rests almost entirely with Congress. These Central and South American countries do not dislike to deal with the people of the United States. They entertain no hostile feelings against us; the probabilities, on the contrary, are that they would prefer to trade with the United States, but the government of the United States, or rather the legislative branch of the government, places obstacles in the way of the trade instead of seeking to encourage it, and this policy is shown in the hostility of Congress to the Mexican treaty.

The point we wish to make is that the wage-men of the country have vital interests at stake in this "overproduction" question. It is a question which they ought to study, and upon which they ought to bring their votes to bear in the election of men to represent them in Congress and in state legislatures. What manufacturers want is cheap raw materials. With these as low as the foreign manufacturer obtains them, the American manufacturer could favorably compete with foreigners in the markets of the world, and if the wage-men of the country can be induced to federate for the purpose of influencing legislation calculated to promote their interests, they may do much to hush the cry of "overproduction" and thereby help themselves to obtain employment, notwithstanding the constant increase of labor-saving machinery and the stupendous wrong perpetrated by states which, to increase their revenues, operate their crime-stained convicts to embarrass their law-abiding citizens.

Reformations[†]

April 1886

———————

In individual reformation, a change for the better in thought, life, habits, and practices is sometimes thought to be sudden, without premeditation, the result of impulse, of immediate rather than remote influences. There may be such well-authenticated instances. There may be those who have witnessed them. We do not recall them in our experience or in our readings. We regard them altogether mythical. At best, if the world has witnessed such reformations, we do not believe they were permanent. They did not last long, and the persons so reformed were doubtless like the Scriptural female swine, which speedily returned

———————

† Published in *Locomotive Firemen's Magazine,* vol. 10, no. 4 (April 1886), 201–202.

to her wallowings in the mire. Any reformation worthy of the name is the result of causes which, whether recognized or not, were remote rather than immediate. At any rate such is the history of all great and permanent reformations. Take for instance the cause of slavery. It would be interesting to know when it did not in some form, more or less aggravating and revolting, "blacken the page of history." There are even now slave-catchers plying their vocation, and in many lands where all men are nominally free, there exists a vassalage, the contemplation of which by freemen arouses deep indignation and indicates conclusively that the task which emancipating philanthropists have undertaken is not yet accomplished. But the world is hopeful and work proceeds.

It would be interesting to inquire when all the rulers of European countries, by whatever title known, exercised despotic sway. It would be found that the time is not vastly remote, and now but two of such despots remain. Full emancipation has not come, but it is coming. It is destiny, and if men are permitted to have any rational conception of God it is safe to say He is pledged to break the scepters of tsars and sultans and place the governments of the earth in the hands of the people.

It will be conceded that reformations, if permanent, move forward slowly, but it should be remembered that they never move backward; halting there may be, at least apparently to the superficial investigator, but retrogression never occurs. Despotism is on the wane; bigotry is almost universally condemned. Ignorance is disappearing. Truth and right are coming into closer alliance. The wrong is vigorously entrenching, always on the defensive, but its citadels are crumbling while the armies of the right are ceaselessly moving on his works. The conflict is to last not only all summer, but all the centuries until victory is won.

Who does not know that the world has always been wrong on the labor question? Who dare aver that labor has ever had even justice awarded it in all the march of civilization, let the starting point be where it may? Who is so blind as not to see that the work of reformation has begun and is making headway? Who is so imbecile as not to know that the wage-men of the world are not in the minority. We know that it will require time to accomplish this great labor reformation. We know that it will require the great masculine virtues of courage, endurance, fortitude, and patience. We know that the young men of today will grow old and die before the day of labor's jubilee, but we know that as one dies ten will stand ready to take his place and that the reformation will move on, and we know that it will gather power, force, and momentum, and will yearly become more formidable.

Is it asked what we mean by labor reformation? We answer, a change for the better. We mean the ushering in of an era when thought and law and custom shall be in accord to deal justly by labor. We mean the coming of the long delayed period when the badge of labor shall dignify rather than degrade labor in the eyes of the pampered few who live by exacting tribute from labor.

Those who believe that this reformation is destined to reach full-orbed meridian glory are not utopians, they are not dreamers, they are not crackbrained visionaries. They are not anticipating miracles. The men who champion the labor reformation are preeminently practical. They believe in educating men up to the full appreciation of their unalienable rights. They believe in mental manliness. They believe in union and federation. They know that labor has suffered through all the centuries since God said that by the sweat of his face man should eat bread. They know that time is required to place labor on its feet and give it an erect and a defiant attitude and demand justice. They know that when one great emancipating word a century ago was spoken for justice, ten thousand are uttered now. They know that men are learning the lesson of their rights and are getting ready to act their parts. They know that drill, not charging, makes soldiers. They know that struggle, not shouting, builds character and advances the army of progress and reform. They know that to make oaks of acorns time is required, and they are willing to bide their time, but they know the sturdy oaks do come from acorns and they know the seed they are planting will, in due time, furnish an abundant crop of success. Here, in America, they are preparing to demonstrate the majesty of the ballot. If laws are vicious they will see that they are repealed. The days of wheedling demagogism are numbered. Land stealing will cease and land thieves will be made to disgorge. Hours of labor will be regulated, and in the presence of "overproduction" the lamentations of the hungry will not be heard. This millennium may be some distance away, but it is coming, and when it comes "the morning and the evening" will record the first day of the reign of justice on the earth, and then the righteous may tune their harps and throats and sing:

> Sound the loud timbrel o'er every dark sea,
> Labor has triumphed, her people are free.[4]

Current Disagreements Between
Employers and Employees[†]

May 1886

There never was a time in the history of the country when the disagreements between employers and employees were as numerous and as varied as at present. Thoughtful men are diligently seeking for the cause—for the reasons why. Scarcely any locality is exempt. Complaints come from every trade and occupation. Strikes are numerous, some of them extensive and exceedingly embarrassing, and each involves complications which require consummate ability to unravel.

In this connection we esteem it pertinent to introduce the thoughtful conclusion of Mr. Arthur T. Hadley, Commissioner of Labor Statistics of Connecticut.[5] In his report to the governor, Mr. Hadley says:

> The relations between labor and capital cannot be treated as a mere matter of private business, but involve social and political questions. The fact is becoming clearer every day, whether we like it or not. The state of things is this: *The men who do the most physical work, as a class, seem to have the least to show for it.* Their wages are often barely sufficient to meet the expenses of living. They sometimes cannot get work at all. At best, they are working for others, with little independence of action, and often with little hope of anything better. In their life, their work and their relations to their employers, evils and abuses have arisen, which it seems impossible for any individual to prevent, while the attempt to remedy them by organized action often proves worse than useless. In this difficulty there is a demand for public investigation, and *for legislative action.*

The fact that men who perform the most physical labor have less than anyone else to show for it might not of itself create disturbances, as in all the ages past no one has ever been able to determine how much an honest day's work is worth; but when an honest day's work does not secure a sufficient supply of the absolute necessaries of life, then everybody knows and everybody possessed of a soul is willing to admit that a cruel, flagrant, stupendous wrong has been done the workingman or woman. To reach that conclusion, political economists, mathematicians, persons learned in logic and law are not required.

---

† Published in *Locomotive Firemen's Magazine,* vol. 10, no. 5 (May 1886), 262–264.

"The wayfaring man though a fool," will not err in his conclusion.[6] Hunger with its gnawing agonies bears testimony to the fact. Homes destitute of comforts denounce trumpet-tongued the wrong. Shivering mothers and children pronounce that a curse, cancer-like, is upon them, and is sending, deep down into their vitals, its poisonous and destroying roots.

If, then, the question is asked, why this widespread unrest in labor circles throughout the land? The answer comes quick, emphatic and conclusive: workingmen are not receiving fair wages—by which we mean, here, sufficient wages to supply themselves and those who are dependent upon them a respectable support.

There may be—indeed there are—other causes assigned for the labor infelicities which now exist. We shall not attempt to enumerate them, nor is it required. Locomotive firemen are keeping abreast of the times and are familiar with the causes which are creating the widespread unrest. But it may be well to say that hours, working time, enters largely into the deliberations of workingmen. They declare that not only are wages too low, but that they are required to work too many hours to secure even such wages as they do receive. They contend that they are placed between two wrongs, between the upper and the nether millstones, *overwork* and *underpay*, and that they are simply trying to escape from the grinding, crushing curse.

Now, it should be understood that there never was a time in the history of the country when workingmen were asking themselves so many questions as now. We doubt if average citizens, however intelligent and thoughtful, have prudently estimated the lifting, expanding, invigorating, and disenthralling power of intelligence, or, if they have stopped to inquire to what extent this growth of intelligence is responsible for the present perplexities and embarrassments which now surround the labor interests of the country?

We boast of our schools and libraries, and the disappearance of illiteracy—and well we may—and it is this universal diffusion of knowledge which is bringing workingmen to the front and emboldening them to assert their claims to a larger share of the products of their toil. And it is vastly material to say in this connection that American workingmen are resolving to live like American citizens, not like the heathen Chinese. If this is done, better wages must be secured and will be secured, and a reasonable advance in wages will, in no respect whatever, prove detrimental to employers.

We have said that workingmen are now everywhere engaged in asking themselves questions—and this done, they are extending the area of the field of interrogatories until the great public stops to listen and to answer.

We have what is called a Christian civilization. We refer to the present as the high noon of the Christian era. We boast of our schools and our churches, we talk of the nation's wealth and power, we discuss and tabulate the fabulous productions of our soil and of our ability to supply other nations with food. We get bewildered with the sum totals of our foreign and interstate commerce, and yet we are today confronted on all sides by harrowing conditions, and hear the declarations of men, women, and children that hunger is gnawing at their vitals, that they are cold for the want of comfortable clothing, and that their homes in thousands of instances are little better than hovels. There is idleness and destitution because, with all our boasted civilization, wealth, culture, progress, and Christianity, we are unable to do simple justice by those who create the wealth and carry forward the great enterprises of the period.

It is not strange, therefore, that working people are asking questions, not strange that they have grievances and that they are seeking for a remedy for the evils which have befallen their lot.

We are not unmindful of the fact that some people complain because it is their nature to be dissatisfied—they belong to the croaking-frog family of humanity—on dry land or in the water, they croak; hot or cold, sick or well, "in poverty's vail or abounding in wealth"[7] it matters not, they are discontented; but such people are the exception. The great body of men, we refer to workingmen, desire contentment and would suffer inconveniences rather than create derangements and commotion. The history of labor is preeminently distinguished by conservatism, and hence when there is widespread unrest, there is popular conviction that underlying the disquietude there are potent reasons—any other conclusion antagonizes commonsense views of human affairs. It goes for nothing to say that workingmen make mistakes, or that their methods to redress their grievances embody errors. Such things are inseparable from human nature, and when such accusations are made, who is there among accusers to throw the first stone? Employers? Nay, verily. In the presence of facts they should remain speechless.

The demand is for an honest analysis of the situation; this accomplished, the discussion of remedies will be in order.

First, are the statutes just? Take for instance the well-established fact that if the law permitted certain foreign commodities, raw materials to be imported free of duty, certain classes of goods could be so manufactured as to compete with foreign countries in the markets of the world. This would stimulate profitable manufacturing and increase the demand for labor. Hence, labor is deeply interested in such legislation.

Again, it is believed that to make 8 hours a legal day's work would indefinitely benefit the laboring class. We refer simply to the financial aspect of the case. The problem worked out discloses the fact that if 100 men working 10 hours a day were to work only 8 hours, the change would make room for 25 more men; hence if 1 million men are working 10 hours a day, by reducing the hours to 8, room is made for 250,000 idle men who need work. The change from 10 hours to 8 more widely distributes earnings, and if wages paid for 10 hours are paid for 8 hours, then labor comes nearer than at present to receiving its fair share of its products. There is profound economical philosophy in the 8-hour proposition, and once inaugurated and honestly carried out, it would exert a beneficial influence. Labor contends that the state pursues a vicious and demoralizing policy by seeking to derive revenue from its felons, in which case honesty and good citizenship is required to compete with crime for sustenance. We have not the space now at our command to elaborate these propositions, but they enter into the present labor troubles and should command consideration. To correct such errors, whether of legislation or practice, demands neither strikes nor boycotts. They simply require thought and study and an honest purpose to find a remedy and apply it.

Dismissing such questions and taking a wider survey of the field, complaints multiply, but those the most frequent relate to wages. There are localities and enterprises where harmony between employer and employee exists, but as a general proposition, labor complains of inability to obtain fair wages. In some instances, there is a crusade against labor organizations, and again complaints are heard in regard to the flagrant wrong of "blacklisting." Each of these complaints present many and different phases, often trivial, but more frequently of such gravity as to place in peril the security of capital, the employment of workingmen, and the peace of society. But we are clearly of the opinion that for their adjustment there are better methods than strikes or boycotting, and we still have faith that peaceful remedies will be found.

The present agitation of labor questions will, we are convinced, inure to the benefit of the wage-men of America. Facts hidden from the public eye have been laid bare and their importance is now up for discussion, and workingmen in thousands of instances have qualified themselves to present their rights and interests with such cogency and force that there need be little solicitude as to the final verdict. There have been mistakes, errors in judgment and methods; there has been headlong precipitancy, when great caution was required; there has been a resort to extreme measures where moderation was demanded by every consideration of justice and propriety; and yet we are confident when the normal condition of business is again established, every labor problem that has demanded investigation will be nearer a rational and a just solution than ever before. Having boundless faith in American workingmen and in American institutions, appreciating the power of intelligence, books, and ballots, we anticipate at no distant day when logic and law, faith in man and fealty to justice and right, will place employer and employee in harmonious relations, and that the trials through which they have passed, since they led to peace and concord, will be remembered as benedictions instead of afflictions.

T. V. Powderly and the Knights of Labor[†]
May 1886

The exigencies of labor in the United States have brought to the front a number of men who are now exerting an influence of such power for weal or for woe that their words are watched with extreme solicitude by the entire country—of these men, it is probable that T. V. Powderly, grand master workman of the Knights of Labor,[8] is at this time, by a combination of circumstances, the most conspicuous and powerful.

The history of the Knights of Labor, until recently, has not been sufficiently eventful to attract special attention.

It was organized in the year 1869, and its founder was Uriah S. Stephens.[9] The growth of the order has been phenomenal and its membership is now variously estimated at from 300,000 to 650,000 and reports have it that the membership is increasing at the rate of 175,000 a year. How true, or how approximately true, these statements are we have no means of knowing, and give them, as we find them, for what they are worth. It is stated that "any person who stands well in his trade, above the age of 18, whether male or female, without distinction of creed or color, whether tradesman or manufacturer, employer or employee, may become a member; the order excludes lawyers, bankers, brokers, professional gamblers, or any person who derives a profit from the sale of intoxicating liquors."

The executive committee is composed as follows: T. V. Powderly, grand

---

† Published as "T. V. Powderly, Grand Master Workman, His Executive Associates, and His Official Declarations" in *Locomotive Firemen's Magazine,* vol. 10, no. 5 (May 1886), 257–261.

master workman; Frederick Turner, secretary and treasurer; and John W. Hayes, W. H. Bailey, and T. B. Barry. This executive committee is clothed with extraordinary powers. Its orders are of tremendous import. It can "order strikes, continue, or terminate them. It can investigate grievances, and its decisions are final. It can order, continue, and 'lift' boycotts. It is empowered to confer with corporations, capitalists, and employers, and may investigate charges against the character and acts of local and district officials and assemblies." T. V. Powderly is at the head of this committee and at the head of this great organization. Mr. Powderly is a native of Carbondale, Pennsylvania, and is now 37 years of age. In starting in life, he learned the trade of a machinist. Subsequently he educated himself for the profession of civil engineer. He joined the Knights of Labor at the age of 28 years and became an active worker, and to his efforts was mainly due the meeting of the first grand assembly which occurred eight years ago. It is stated that "the order of the Knights of Labor was founded to prevent the encroachment of capital on labor. The local assemblies govern themselves. They have the power to boycott whenever they please in their own district. Boycotting is the most effective weapon of the order. Striking is less frequently resorted to, but strikes can also be ordered by the local assemblies; if they hope, however, to obtain aid from the General Assembly, the strike must be *legalized*. To do this, the local assembly must notify the District Assembly, whose officers must investigate the reasons for discontent. Two weeks notice is given and if in that time the district officers cannot bring about harmony between the employer and the employed, the strike is legalized, after which the financial support of the entire district may be secured. If the strike extends to other branches of trade or other assemblies, and the district is unable to sustain it, then an assessment may be laid on the entire organization throughout the country and throughout the world."

Such is a brief outline of the powers of the grand officials and of the local authorities of the Knights of Labor as they have been made public.

It will be observed that as the order was founded in 1869, it is now 17 years old—a period sufficiently extended to develop the value of the methods adopted to accomplish the purposes of its founders, and those who have had, and now have, control of its operations. What are the results? We shall not pretend to enumerate the instances where either failure or success has attended the strikes and boycotts ordered by the Knights of Labor; we are without the necessary data for such statements. We simply know there have been strikes and boycotts and that they have been, according to public rumor, ordered by the Knights of Labor. Fortunately we have before us the official declarations of T. V. Powderly, grand master workman. The authenticity of the important document is un-questioned—in fact, is *in toto* admitted by all Knights of Labor. This official paper was issued to all the assemblies of the Knights of Labor at Philadelphia, March 13, 1886. The document is in many regards most extraordinary, and that the grand master workman regards it of supreme importance we infer from the fact that the "recording secretary" of every assembly of the Knights was required "to issue a red-letter call for a full meeting" for the purpose of hearing it read.

It will be observed by those who read Mr. Powderly's communication or "circular" that he refers to an order "recently issued to suspend the organi-zation of new assemblies for 40 days." Such an order from the grand master workman of the Knights of Labor demands more than a mere mention. It is a signal of danger. It is an intimation from the captain that the ship is becoming unmanageable and is on a lee shore, drifting amidst rocks and reefs. We have quoted current talk in the press showing that the order of Knights of Labor was organized "to prevent the encroachment of capital on labor." It was orga-nized to initiate "any person who stands well in his trade, above the age of 18, whether male or female, without distinction of creed or color" and for 17 years the order has progressed, grown in numerical strength. Those in charge have had 17 years to eliminate errors, readjust machinery, note consequences, and prepare for emergencies—and now, an order is issued to arrest for 40 days the organization of assemblies of Knights of Labor. Why? Let Mr. Powderly speak. In his "circular" of March 13 he says:

> If the order is to perform its mission as intended by its founders and those who have worked with it from the beginning, a radical change must be effected. A stop must be called, and the ship brought back to her moor-ings. It has always been, and is at the present time, my policy to advocate conciliation and arbitration in the settlement of disputes between em-ployer and employee. The law of knighthood demands at the hands of our members an adherence to that policy. Thousands of men who had become disgusted with the ruinous policy of the strike as the only remedy for the ills we complain of were drawn to us because we had proclaimed to mankind that we had discarded the strike until all else had failed. The men and women who flocked to our standard have a knowledge of their wrongs. They have endured these wrongs for years; and in reason are in duty bound to learn how to right these wrongs by the least expensive and satisfactory, as well as lasting, remedy.
>
> Six months will not teach men our principles and proper methods, yet men are impressed with the idea that they can learn them in six weeks

or six days, and before the ground work for a proper education is laid we find our assemblies on a strike or lockout; and in too many cases the provocation comes from their own hasty and inconsiderate action. No matter what advantage we gain by the strike, it is only medicating the symptom; it does not penetrate the system, and therefore fails in effecting a cure. The only natural sequence is a relapse, and a relapse always means more medicine and a weaker patient than before. You must bear with me and read this letter to the end, for it may be the last one I will ever write to you.

In reading the foregoing there can be but one rational conclusion and that is that the order of the Knights of Labor have totally misconceived the objects of the organization, or that the methods devised by the order to correct evils were originally and fundamentally wrong. Mr. Powderly's view of the situation is that the order has gone wrong and is pursuing a career of error and injustice which demands a "stop," and these wrongs have grown to such proportions that Mr. Powderly demands their prompt correction or he must be permitted to resign.

Just here our readers should be reminded that the public has been told that "local assemblies govern themselves, and that they have the power to boycott and strike whenever they please." If this is true, and current events demonstrate that it is absolutely true, the fact will occur to a great many people that the mistake, if it be a mistake of the order, a misapprehension of power and prerogative, ought to have been corrected long ago. Seventeen years is a long time for an error to exist in an organization, for in that time it will become so embedded, so interwoven into the fiber and muscle and thought of men, that it will be accounted a vital virtue rather than a wrong, fruitful of untold ills and crushing disasters. In this connection Mr. Powderly says:

> While I, as the chosen mouthpiece of the order, am proclaiming to the world that the Knights of Labor do not advocate or countenance strikes until every other remedy has failed, the wires from a thousand cities and towns are bearing the news of as many strikes by Knights of Labor, in which arbitration and conciliation were never hinted at. Not that alone, but they were in many cases scorned and rejected by our own members. In some cases these strikes were entered upon against the advice of the General Executive Board.

The declarations of Mr. Powderly rivet the conviction that the great mass of the Knights of Labor have totally misunderstood the mission of the order—strikes and boycotts have multiplied in all directions. The authority of the executive board has been ignored and local assemblies and district assemblies, believing they had the power, have ordered strikes and boycotts *ad libitum*.[10] Mr. Powderly sees in the growth of the Knights of Labor as an order multiplied dangers, elements, and forces which alarm him—a blind Samson, preparing to shake down the superstructure,[11] and he does not disguise his fears. He says, "Five hundred assemblies of Knights were organized in February last—as many as were organized in the first eight years of the order's existence," and just here appears another source of danger. The men and women, "men and women without distinction of creed or color," "new recruits," undisciplined and un-educated, join the order because they believe it can protect them against the "encroachments of capital on labor," and hence strikes and boycotts which local assemblies have the right to order, but says Mr. Powderly, "To attempt to win concessions or gains with our present raw, undisciplined membership would be like hurling an unorganized mob against a well-drilled regular army." Nor is this all. Mr. Powderly intimates that strikes have increased because of the fact, which we have stated, of pecuniary assistance from other Knights who continue at work. He says, "It is not fair to the older assemblies to bring in new members, pick up their quarrels as soon as organized, and have them expect pecuniary aid from those who helped build the order up for a noble purpose. It is not wise to give men and women a premium for joining us. It is wrong to encourage them in the idea that they have nothing to do themselves, that they are to lean upon others; they must depend upon themselves, and in any case cannot receive assistance inside of six months, and I will hold out no induce- ments that will encourage them in the belief that they will receive assistance even then." Manifestly it operates as an inducement to strike when the strikers know all other Knights within a certain territory are to be assessed to support them, but unfortunately, many Knights of Labor regard this as a fundamental principle of the order, and if they have entertained erroneous opinions upon the subject, Mr. Powderly ought long since to have corrected the grave mistake.

In reading the circular of Mr. Powderly, we confess to sensations such as hitherto we have not experienced. Mr. Powderly, we believe, has been elected four times to the position he now holds in the order of Knights of Labor, and how it happens that he has not long since discovered the tendencies in the order which he now deplores is a mystery which we find quite impossible to explain—organized to arrest the "encroachments of capital on labor," the order has become unwieldy, and by its growth defeats the purpose of its existence. Local and district assemblies, empowered to order strikes and boycotts, are doing the cause of labor immense damage by doing the very things they were organized to do. Starting out with the proposition that manufacturers and the employers of labor might join the Knights, we are now told that it was "not intended that the order should harbor unjust employers" and now, the advice is to "take in as few employers as possible." Mr. Powderly says that "the name of this order and its principles are published everywhere and men who stood openly arrayed against us two years ago are now our friends. Beware of them. Take them in if you will, but watch them." Mr. Powderly warns the assemblies against men who, studying the purposes of the order for two years, have been converted from enemies to "friends," and advises that such friends should be "watched." Mr. Powderly further observes that "the politician is planning night and day how to catch the Knights of Labor for the advantages of himself and party, and rest assured he has his emissaries in our ranks."

If this be a danger, then by Mr. Powderly's admission, the blood of the order is already poisoned with it.

The circular abounds with statements well calculated to discourage the friends of the Knights, and we are not surprised that Mr. Powderly is willing to retire to private life if the outlook does not at once become more assuring. He says that "nearly every State Assembly that has been formed since the General Assembly met has been organized amid discord and contention. I fear that the struggle is not to serve the order so much as to serve personal ends. Nearly every assembly in the states of Kansas and Michigan has complained to me about the attempts being made to organize State assemblies. Such official declarations are an indication of anarchy and dissolution." The grand master workman tells the Knights of Labor in an official circular that men who organize assemblies are prompted by selfish motives, and not to serve the order—and now surveying the entire field the grand master workman tells the Knights of Labor that "these words of mine must be heeded or this order goes down as surely as night follows day."

What are his words? Stop striking, stop boycotting, stop doing the very things you have been doing, else the order goes down "as surely as night follows day." The order of Knights of Labor started out with the motto, "An injury to one is the concern of all." These were ordained the shibboleth words of the order, and the Knights have for 17 years proclaimed it as their battle cry. Mr. Powderly now sets down with great vigor on this motto. He shows the converse of the motto which most effectually upsets it. In his circular Mr. Powderly says: "While I write, a dispatch is handed me in which I read these words: 'They discharged our brother, and we struck, for you know our motto is, "An injury to one is the concern of all."' Yes, 'an injury to one is the concern of all,' but it is not wise to injure all for the concern of one." This is *striking strikes and strikers,* and the grand master workman adds: "It would have been better to continue at work and properly investigate the matter." Manifestly that is true, but for 17 long years, the Knights of Labor have been educated in the other direction, they have struck and boycotted, and now their grand master workman tells them there must be a change or their order "goes down as surely as night follows day"—and he tells them his words must be heeded or he will resign—and in conclusion Mr. Powderly announces his ultimatums. He says:

> Strikes must be avoided; boycotts must be avoided.
> Those who boast must be checked by their assemblies. No move must be made until the court of last resort has been appealed to.
> Threats of violence must not be made.
> Politicians must be hushed up or driven out.
> Obedience to the laws of knighthood must have preference over those of any other order.

In reading Mr. Powderly's "circular" we fail to find in it one solitary word commendatory of the operations of the order during the past year. According to Mr. Powderly's view, everything has gone wrong, and wrong to such a degree as to threaten the existence of the order, wrong to such an extent that he can no longer bear up against the swelling tide of error, and therefore, plainly tells the Knights of Labor they must change their course or he will retire. Such is the order of Knights of Labor as told officially by their chief, and it must be confessed that the account is anything but assuring. If Mr. Powderly can speak in such terms of the severest censure of the Knights of Labor, what must necessarily be the estimate of the public of the order? If Mr. Powderly is alarmed, is it strange that the entire community entertains doubts and fears? It is to be hoped that Mr. Powderly's authority and personal influence will be equal to the requirements, but he is likely to find that errors in methods of long standing are seldom if ever suddenly corrected.

Boycotting[†]

June 1886

In writing of boycotting, it is required that the readers of this magazine should be somewhat informed of its history. The public generally comprehend its meaning—particularly where it has been practiced.

In common parlance, boycotting, is an importation. It is not an outgrowth of American institutions. It could not have been born in the United States, simply because the conditions which made it a necessity in a foreign land never existed in this heaven-favored and freedom-favored republic.

We do not say that boycotting is to be condemned because it is an importation, or because it had its origin in a foreign land—such a position could not be logically sustained. It would be as unwise as to contend that because a workingman in any foreign land is required to work for 25 cents a day, therefore, American laborers should be content with such degrading wages.

Boycotting had its origin in Ireland and was the product of conditions of the most harrowing infernalism, such as cannot be inaugurated in America while its rivers flow to the sea.

As we write, a native-born Irishman of large information and culture gives us the following brief résumé of the origin of boycotting. He says:

> During the famine period in Ireland eight or nine years ago, just after the formation of the Irish National Land League, a Captain Boycott, a retired military officer and an Englishman, who had some years previously become the owner of a landed estate in one of the interior counties, Kings, I believe, made himself very obnoxious to the people in his vicinity by his arbitrary methods of dealing with his tenants and others over whom he had any power. He was a "resident magistrate" besides, and this gave him additional facilities for exercising his "sweet will" over the people. They resolved to put him and his belongings in "coventry," an old term long in use in Ireland, to which country it had come from England, and which meant to let Captain Boycott and all his belongings, his interests, severely alone—to neither buy of him, sell to him, work for him, nor in any way, directly or indirectly, have anything to do with him.[12]

---

† Published in *Locomotive Firemen's Magazine,* vol. 10, no. 6 (June 1886), 326–329.

Our informant further says:

> The plan worked successfully, notwithstanding that Captain Boycott resorted to every means the law afforded to break the resolve of the people. Finally he left the country, partly in disgust and partly for fear of violence.

This Captain Boycott was a heartless despot who had for his victims men, women, and children, who by the failure of crops were reduced to the direst conditions, and who were unable, therefore, to pay their "rack-rents." Subsequently, other landlords who pursued Captain Boycott's methods of cruelty and oppression were treated in the same way, and hence the term "boycotting."

It will be readily observed that the boycott is a terrible weapon, to be used only when a terrible wrong exists.

Unfortunately, we think, boycotting has been introduced into the United States—unfortunate, because no such conditions and no such flagrant wrongs as existed in Ireland in the days of Captain Boycott, and still exist in that unfortunate and oppressed country, exist in the United States, and hence the weapon which Irish tenants wielded so effectively against Captain Boycott and others of his type cannot be justly used against people in the United States, unless it should so happen that men or corporations should adopt Captain Boycott's methods of cruelty and oppression toward those who might be in some measure under their control.

Just here we inquire, what has been the history of boycotting in the United States? We shall not assert that in no instance it has been justifiable, because we do not pretend to a knowledge of every instance where it has been employed, but, as a general proposition, we contend that boycotting in the United States has been from the first and continuously a mistake, a stupid error, a total misapprehension of conditions, situations, institutions, and rights. In this connection we do not hesitate to say that there exist circumstances of a palliative character. We are familiar with instances of hardships endured by workingmen which were well calculated to test their patience to the uttermost limits. In such cases, rashness finds reasons of an extenuating character. But we are not commenting upon isolated incidents. We are discussing a principle in human affairs as they exist around us, and of which we are required to take cognizance, and our conclusion is that boycotting is a wrong of such magnitude, of such wide-spreading and far-reaching injustice, that it never can have popular approval and in fact never ought to have such approval.

Furthermore, we are of the opinion that the average man—we like the term "average," because it does not include cranks, visionaries, utopians, but takes in men of common sense, which is, after all, the best sense the world possesses—such men oppose boycotting, if for no other reason than that it does more harm than good, often striking with disastrous force the very men it assumes to benefit.

There must be no misunderstanding in regard to the position which the *Firemen's Magazine* occupies in the discussion of labor problems. It is first, last, and all the time the champion of the wage-men of America.

Is it the question of organizing brotherhoods, trade unions, or Knights of Labor? We do not stop to discuss names—we are in favor of all organizations of workingmen. It is their right, their inalienable right, and we bid them God-speed. It means elevation, dignity, better comprehension of rights and duties.

Is it a question of wages? Then by every agency known to honesty, fair dealing, justice, and equity, we would have the scale of wages elevated every-where, upon the broad principle that where labor is well paid prosperity and peace prevail.

Is it a question of a less number of hours for toil, and more time for rest and mental culture? Then we are the ceaseless advocates of such a modification of existing rules and regulations as shall conduce to the moral, intellectual, and physical improvement of workingmen throughout the country. With these dec-larations we proceed to point out that boycotting, whatever may be the purpose of those who employ it, ought to be dismissed as a regulating force or weapon in the industrial affairs of this country. It must be admitted by all workingmen as a fundamental right, that they may or may not, just as they may elect, join a labor union, by whatever name it may be called. Strike down that right, and the idea of personal liberty disappears and exists no more in the United States of America than it does in Russia or Turkey, or in any other despot cursed land. Admitting this fact, it follows that a man who does not belong to a labor union has as much right to work as the man who is a member of such an organization—upon the principle that a man exercising one right cannot by any conception of justice surrender any other right—hence a man exercising the right to stand aloof from a labor organization does not surrender his right to seek employment and accept employment when and where he pleases, and at such prices as he chooses to take, being, in this respect, independent, and any interference is a low aimed at inde-pendence, at fundamental and inalienable rights, which cannot and will not be tolerated. Reasoning further, if a man has a right to seek employment where he pleases and accept employment at such prices as he pleases, then it follows that the man at whose hands he seeks employment may employ him if he pleases and at such prices as the two independent men may agree upon.

These principles, in our conception, are bedrock, fundamental, primal, and to attack them is to attack the superstructure of liberty, freedom, personal rights, and all that American citizens hold dear.

The question arises, does boycotting as it is practiced in the United States attack these principles? In our opinion it does, and is therefore a grievous error and ought to be everywhere discouraged and discontinued. Manifestly, we have placed ourselves under obligations to our readers to state such reasons as we can command to justify our conclusions. We have not the space to multiply illustrations and a few must suffice, our purpose being to exhibit the injustice of boycotting to workingmen and totally innocent parties.

We will take a cigar factory which employs, we will say, 100 men. The proprietor, as we have shown, has the right to employ men without reference to membership in the Cigarmakers' Union, hence, the employees may or may not be members of that organization, as is their right. The men demand various prices for their labor, as they have a right to do, and the proprietor pays such prices as he and his employees agree upon. In all of this, personal rights have been exercised—every one of which to a free man is as dear as life itself and cannot be surrendered without humiliation. The union at this juncture, we suppose, demands that all the non-union men shall be discharged. This is a blow aimed not only at personal rights but at laboring men who have committed no offense under heaven. Exercising their rights, they declined to join the union; exercising their rights, they accepted such wages as their employer agreed to pay and were at work peaceably. At this juncture, how stands the case? One class of workingmen exercising a right, which no one questions, joined the union. Another class, exercising the same right, decline to join the union, and for exercising this right the union workingmen make war upon them and demand their discharge. This is despotism, a wrong of such proportions that when its inherent injustice is exposed, honorable men cry out, "Shame." But if the employer concludes to continue the employment of the non-union men, what is the next step? If there are union men employed, they leave the factory, and if that does not sufficiently cripple the business of the establishment, then a boycott is ordered. When the boycott is established no union man is to purchase cigars made at the boycotted factory. Again, if any customer of the factory continues his purchases, he too is boycotted—as for instance, all stores, no matter what may be their line of business, if the boycotted cigars are found on their shelves, they too are boycotted, drug stores and grocery stores, etc., and the order is that this boycotting business is to continue until the non-union men are discharged, or until they join the union. Then the boycott, to use a phrase, is lifted, and the embargo is revoked.

And just here appears another phase of the boycotting business, which cannot be discussed without feelings akin to anger. The men out of work, because they were at work, now find themselves idle; without means to support themselves and those dependent upon them, they become mendicants and drift into crime, and when it is asked who drove them from employment to idleness? The answer must be not employers, not monopolists, but workingmen, members of the union. It is said that the way out of their difficulties is to join the union, but there can be no certainty of success when voting is conducted with black-and-white balls, and in case of failure, a poor fellow finds that he is the victim of a double calamity—the loss of his rights, his personal liberty, and of opportunities to work. Again we will suppose the case of a newspaper, the proprietor of which employs printers without regard to membership in the printers' union. He simply exercises his right as an American citizen, and every man in his employ does but maintain the same inestimable prerogative. For doing this, a boycott is ordered, and the decree is that to take the paper, to buy it, or to advertise in its columns is to be visited with the penalty of boycotting. A merchant has a stock of goods, he desires to reach the public by advertising, but if he does advertise his wares in the boycotted paper, he too is boycotted, and thus the wrong proceeds and spreads, involving in its crushing influence men, women, and children who have committed no wrong against anyone. It may be supposed that a contractor wants to employ a dozen men, but should he seek to acquaint the public with his necessities, he becomes a victim of the boycott, though the advertisement was clearly in the interest of labor. We have no purpose, other than to illustrate the operations of the boycott, in selecting a cigar factory and a newspaper establishment; they simply stand for any and for every other case of boycotting in the country, and those who feel inclined may at their leisure select any other case and, with certain modifications, one boycott answers for the entire list.

The American motto is "fair play." Boycotting is not fair play—it is not in consonance with American ideas of justice, it is fruitful of injustice, it does not recognize personal liberty and personal rights. It is violent, and if ever resorted to should only be adopted when all else has failed and the wrongs complained of touch the very marrow of existence. It originated to punish a man who was cold and heartless, a petty tyrant who took advantage of misfortune to multiply the sorrows of his victims, and not because he hired Irishmen to work at such prices as were fixed by mutual agreement. We write with the hope that the time will never come when boycotting in the United States will be justifiable.

We write with a certain conviction that that direful period has not yet arrived, and we write in the hope that throughout the country, workingmen will discountenance boycotting as a means of redress for any troubles which may environ them.

The Locomotive Engineers
and the Locomotive Firemen[†]
[excerpt]
July 1886

This article is written in the interest of harmony; it is also written in the interest of truth, and since harmony cannot permanently exist where truth is exiled, ignored, or crushed, it will be our purpose to state the truth. This done, we shall leave consequences to take care of themselves.

Let it be distinctly understood that we write in a spirit neither vaunting nor apologetic. We shall, however, in the language of the sturdy old carpenter, "hew to the line," regardless of where the chips fly. Our statements will be verities, and those who may choose to assail them shall be welcome to all the trophies they may secure.

In 1863 the Brotherhood of Locomotive Engineers was organized; Division No. 1, in the city of Detroit, took its place at the head of the column, which now numbers 317 divisions. The brotherhood has grown in 23 years from one division to 317 divisions, from a membership of 12 to a membership of 18,000. This growth, this success, demonstrates the necessity for such an organization which defies rational contradiction.

We assume, pretending to no positive knowledge upon the subject, that each of the 12 engineers who formed Division No. 1 in 1863, in the city of Detroit, had been locomotive firemen, that they had graduated from the "scoop," and by their education and experience as firemen had become capable of assuming all the weighty responsibilities of engineers.

It is held to be a most reprehensible trait of character for a man who has gone forth from a humble home and achieved success in the world's broad field of battle

---

† Published as "The Brotherhood of Locomotive Engineers and the Brotherhood of Locomotive Firemen" in *Locomotive Firemen's Magazine*, vol. 10, no. 7 (July 1886), 385–393.

to treat his brothers who are struggling up the same steep and rugged declivities with supercilious disdain—to assume an arrogant demeanor, to put on offensive style—in a word, to act the damphool[13] generally. The verdict of the world in such cases is always that the man so deporting himself has more brass than brains, that he has bartered probity for position, conscience for cash, and that the conspicuousness secured by such a course is yielding a harvest of contempt.

The organization of the Brotherhood of Locomotive Engineers manifestly marked an important era in the history of railway wage-men. It was a move in the right direction. It was an organization for noble purposes. It had in view not only individual rectitude but the improvement in character and qualifications of engineers as a class. It started out with the declarations that to become a member of the Brotherhood, "an engineer must be of good moral character, of temperate habits," and the motto of the Brotherhood was, "Sobriety, Truth, Justice, and Morality."

We shall feel obliged to our readers if, in following us through this article, they will keep the foregoing in mind.

In the year 1873, 13 years ago, in the town of Port Jervis, in the state of New York, about a dozen locomotive firemen met and founded the Brotherhood of Locomotive Firemen. We assume without hesitancy that there exists an urgent necessity for the organization of the Brotherhood of Locomotive Firemen—a necessity as pressing and as importunate as that which demanded the organization of the Brotherhood of Locomotive Engineers, indeed, more decided in its character. We choose to dwell upon this phase of our subject. We propose to try this case fairly. We propose to call witnesses and make them speak. This case has been long enough on the docket. The Brotherhood of Locomotive Firemen was organized for noble purposes. It contemplates the moral, intellectual, social, and financial improvement of its membership. It had in view better citizens and better workmen and its motto—its shibboleth words from the beginning were, "Benevolence, Sobriety, and Industry."

Now what we desire is that the Brotherhood of Locomotive Engineers shall call the roll of its 18,000 members belonging to its 317 divisions, and as each member answers to his name, let him state if he was at one period in his life a locomotive fireman, if he was at one time a member of the Brotherhood of Locomotive Firemen? Let us have the ayes and noes. Let the record go to the world. Let it be seen and read of all men that they may know the incalculable weight of obligation the Brotherhood of Locomotive Engineers is under to the Brotherhood of Locomotive Firemen for supplying it with its membership as it stands today. What says the grand chief of the Brotherhood of Locomotive

Engineers [Peter M. Arthur]? This: "To become members of the Brotherhood of Engineers an engineer must be of good moral character, of temperate habits." Now then what says the organic law of the Brotherhood of Firemen? This: "That a man qualified for membership shall be of good moral character, industrious, sober, and sound in body and limb."

Here we ask in what regard has the Brotherhood of Locomotive Engineers mapped out a line of march more desirable than that which the Brotherhood of Locomotive Firemen has designated for its membership? Is the question of benevolence brought into the controversy? It was stated by the grand master of the Locomotive Firemen in his public address at Philadelphia that the Brotherhood of Locomotive Firemen, since its organization in 1873, had paid out for benevolent purposes the sum of $315,764. It was recently stated by the grand chief of the Brotherhood of Locomotive Engineers that during the past 16 years the Brotherhood had paid $1,850,000 on account of deaths and injuries. Now then, if the dates of organization of the two great Brotherhoods are considered, as also the great disparity in wages paid engineers and firemen, it will be seen that upon the score of benevolence the Brotherhood of Locomotive Firemen have been true to every obligation.

The goal of the average fireman's ambition is the throttle, and just here comes into the boldest possible relief the inquiry: Has the Brotherhood of Locomotive Firemen been true to its high mission in preparing its membership for the responsibilities of engineers? If not, in what regard, in what particular, in what instance has the Brotherhood of Locomotive Firemen been derelict? We put the question with special and commanding emphasis. Here and now we challenge investigation. We know that the Brotherhood of Locomotive Firemen began its career in weakness—with less than a dozen members 13 years ago. We know through what ordeals it has passed. We know how intense has been the heat of the furnace. We know "what masters laid the keel" of our good ship:

> What anvils rang, what hammers beat,
> In what a forge and what a heat
> Were shaped the anchors of thy hope![14]

We know that courage more self-sacrificing, ambition more exalted, fidelity worthy of higher commendation never animated a body of men to execute a mission born of devotion to private and public welfare.

Again the grand chief of the Brotherhood of Locomotive Engineers justly boasts of the *Journal* of the Brotherhood, which he says "has a circulation of 16,000 copies per month." We applaud the undertaking and the success of the *Engineers' Journal*. It speaks well for the Brotherhood. It means literary and intellectual culture. It means the improvement of the mind forces of the membership. It is in consonance with the spirit of the age, and beneficent results must follow.

The Brotherhood of Locomotive Firemen early appreciated the importance of issuing a publication under its auspices that should monthly give information of the progress of the Brotherhood and discuss questions relating to the welfare not only of the membership, but of the workingmen of the country. How well it has met expectations let the figures tell. We now issue monthly 23,000 copies of the *Firemen's Magazine* and its popularity is a source of ceaseless satisfaction.

We record such facts because they place the Brotherhood of Locomotive Firemen on a plane calculated to inspire respect and confidence in all circles where honest endeavor is appreciated.

Such is the Brotherhood of Locomotive Firemen, such its bedrock principles, such its growth and grandeur, such its work and success. It is large enough to be seen. Its boundaries are the horizons of the continent. Its lodge fires across the continent, and from the Dominion of Canada to the Republic of Mexico are the beacon lights of progress. Its principles are enduring, its purpose exalted, its influence commendable, its motto universally accepted as praiseworthy. What more? It has been congratulated by men enthroned in public esteem. Statesmen, governors, legislators, divines, writers of renown, men profoundly learned in law, literature, logic, and divinity, men who have studied all the labor problems of the day and whose opinions pass current where thinkers debate. This Brotherhood of Locomotive Firemen, having been for 13 years sedulously engaged in preparing men for locomotive engineers "of good moral character, industrious, sober, and sound in body and limb," now and here asks what recognition it has received and is still receiving from the Brotherhood of Locomotive Engineers? And here we repeat the challenge contained in the May number of this magazine for anyone interested, "to point out one word, one line ever published in the *Engineers' Journal,* in which even a reference is made to the Brotherhood of Locomotive Firemen, one word, one line in recognition of the organization; one word, one line in favor of harmony; one word, just one that would indicate, or even intimate that such an institution as the Brotherhood of Locomotive Firemen ever existed."

We beg not to be misunderstood. The Brotherhood of Locomotive Firemen is not languishing because of the assumed superiority of the Brotherhood of Locomotive Engineers. There are laws regulating the amenities of life, its civilities and manners, as irrevocable as the laws of the Medes and Persians—and the penalties for their infraction are as certain as death. Haughtiness, pride, presumption, self-conceit, big headedness win, inevitably, pity from all manly, right-thinking men—and yet such majestical imperiousness, swelling importance, is a public calamity, since society is benefited by common sense, and is the loser when any considerable number of its members become enamored of ideas which subject them to ridicule.

We repeat that for 13 years the Brotherhood of Locomotive Firemen has sought to prepare men for the position of Locomotive Engineers. This it has done by methods recognized as eminently prudent and praiseworthy. That the Brotherhood of Locomotive Engineers should fail to recognize such a brotherhood is anomalous to an extent which defies prudent characterization. It is fundamentally erroneous. It taboos the commonest courtesies of life. It is a vulgar thrusting aside of those urbanities which distinguish the gentleman from the boor. It degrades rather than elevates those who practice it. It is an exhibition of that vanity which distinguished the Pennsylvanian who "struck ile"[15] and thereafter couldn't see a poor relation though he was seven foot high. But the Brotherhood of Locomotive Firemen care little for such things; nevertheless the position taken by the Brotherhood of Locomotive Engineers has developed in an attack upon the Brotherhood of Locomotive Firemen fruitful of indignation rather than contempt. It brings into view a purpose of such flagrant injustice as will in our opinion defeat itself. Do we hear the inquiry, what is this injustice? It is this, that no locomotive engineer who is a member of the Brotherhood of Locomotive Firemen shall ever become a member of the Brotherhood of Locomotive Engineers, and that no member of the Brotherhood of Engineers who is a member of the Brotherhood of Firemen is allowed to represent his division in annual convention. Why? In the name of all things decent, prudent, and honorable, why? The question goes resounding through all the lodge rooms of the order, and the echoing reply is, why? Why this blacklisting, this boycotting rule of the Brotherhood of Locomotive Engineers? Why this gratuitous stigma? What stain has the Brotherhood of Locomotive Firemen placed upon the escutcheon—the life and character of its members? It has demanded good character, sobriety, industry, soundness of limb and body. The fireman has been for years a member of the Brotherhood of Firemen. Every noble ambition has been cultivated. He has broadened in intelligence, habits of sobriety and industry have been fixed—fidelity to obligation has been developed into a principle of life and action. He numbers his brotherhood comrades by hundreds. He is deeply attached to the history, the traditions, the associations of the brotherhood. It has warmed him into a noble life—prepared him for the duties and responsibilities of engineer—and now, what? This, by the fiat of the Brotherhood of Engineers, he shall never pass the threshold of a division door, never wear the badge of the Brotherhood of Locomotive Engineers until he has renounced allegiance to the Brotherhood of Locomotive Firemen. Gods! If that is not blacklisting, what is? If that is not boycotting, what is? If that is not imperialism, what is? It is asking a man to disrobe himself of his manhood, of his self-respect, of his independence, of his personal liberty, for what? That he may enter the charmed circle of a division of the Brotherhood of Locomotive Engineers without the smell of a locomotive fireman upon his garments—and that is the lofty commendation locomotive firemen receive from the Brotherhood of Locomotive Engineers. Look at it— turn it around, turn it inside out, view it from any possible standpoint—and the more you contemplate the astounding insult, the more you discover the purpose of the Brotherhood of Locomotive Engineers to be the humiliation of Locomotive Firemen.

At a recent union meeting of Locomotive Engineers at Hartford, Conn., the grand chief of the Brotherhood of Locomotive Engineers is reported to have said:

> I say to you, ladies and gentlemen, that men who will not stand up in defense of their own rights, but who bend to the wishes of the officers, and withdraw from an organization which no man who is honest can possibly object to, *lack the essential qualities of manhood.* No man has the right to say to another, "thou shalt" or "thou shalt not." * * * A man has the right to belong to any organization, provided it is not contrary to law. We have had railroad managers tell our men, "If you belong to that Brotherhood we don't want you." * * * We do not believe in *dictation* in any form, but we do believe in justice, in equity, and in truth.

Such are the recent declarations of Grand Chief Arthur of the Brotherhood of Locomotive Engineers.[16] How do they tally with the decrees of that Brotherhood relating to members of the Brotherhood of Locomotive Firemen? If an engineer, a member of the Brotherhood of Locomotive Firemen, asks admittance into the Brotherhood of Locomotive Engineers, what is he told? This: to gain admittance you must abandon your membership in the Brotherhood of Locomotive Firemen, and yet he says to the Hartford meeting, "that a man who withdraws from an organization which no man who is honest can possibly object to," because officers demand that he should withdraw, "lacks the essential qualities of manhood," but that is just what the B of LE demands of a member of the B of LF who seeks admittance into a division of the B of LE. The very thing denounced is practiced. The order is that no member of the B of LF shall ever enter the Order of B of LE. The demand is that such applicants shall first renounce all allegiance to the B of LF. The grand chief says no man has a right to say, "thou shalt or thou shalt not," and yet when a member of the B of LF desires membership in the B of LE the order is, "thou shalt" withdraw from the B of LF, and if the demand is not complied with then the order is "thou shalt not" become a member of the B of LE. The railroad official says, "If you want work, renounce the B of LE," and the B of LE says, "If you want to join this order, renounce the B of LF." Grand Chief Arthur says, "We do not believe in dictation in any form," still, when the B of LE says to a member of the B of LF you shall not join this Brotherhood unless you withdraw from the B of LF, it practices the most odious and repulsive form of dictation, a form of dictation to which, if a man yields, "he lacks," in the language of Grand Chief Arthur, "the essential qualities of manhood."

We unequivocally endorse the grand chief's opinion and declaration. We heartily second the motion. We vote aye every time. And we frankly tell the Brotherhood of Locomotive Engineers that their grand chief has sounded a keynote which will find a hearty response throughout the entire Brotherhood of Locomotive Firemen.

The membership of the brotherhood are not wanting "in the essential qualities of manhood." They will not be forced to abandon their parent brotherhood to become members of any other brotherhood. They will not permit humiliating dictation. In all things that go to make up manliness, good character, probity, sobriety, industry, a brotherhood fireman is the peer of a brotherhood engineer. As a citizen he possesses the same rights and prerogatives, his aspirations are as high, his purposes as pure and as unselfish, and he will never consent to cause the burning blush of shame to mantle the cheek of parents, wife, or children because of his recreancy to obligation.

We are not seeking to underestimate the character or influence of Grand Chief Arthur of the B of LE. Hitherto, in a manner both frank and kind, we have referred to some of his public utterances, some of his infelicities of speech, but never offensively—always courteously. In this we fearlessly challenge the record. But now we have this to say, in all seriousness, that while his policy—and we refer to the treatment of the B of LF—may meet with the approval of a majority of the B of LE as it now exists, he will be required to change his methods if he is ambitious to be the grand chief of engineers now preparing for graduation. A grand army of brotherhood firemen are pressing toward and are reaching for the throttle, their feet will soon stand upon the "footboard," they will be found loyal to their alma mater, nor will they enter the B of LE upon any terms which require them to sacrifice their self-respect to the extent of a thousandth of a milligram. If it were otherwise, if the mission of the Brotherhood of Locomotive Firemen was to prepare men for engineers who, when they had reached the goal of their ambition, would disown their comrades, assume arrogant airs, and point to them with disdain, then by all the sacred memories of struggle and triumph, by all the heroic dead and heroes living, it were better to disband, better to fold our banners in silence, put out the lodge fires and make the humiliating confession that the children of the brotherhood trained and educated for responsible duties, in the hour of their triumph, turned traitor to every manly and ennobling sentiment, and for the consideration of membership in the B of LE, exhibited to the world a degree of apostasy and ingratitude, for which there can be neither condonement nor atonement. But we are not afflicted with such misgivings. We know whereof we write, when we say that a more self-reliant body of men than the members of the Brotherhood of Locomotive Firemen does not exist upon the face of the earth; and if the Brotherhood of Locomotive Engineers is equally generous in its pride of membership, it may to its heart's content indulge in congratulatory phrases, but it should remember a large proportion of its membership graduated from the Brotherhood of Locomotive Firemen; that is where they were trained for their positions on the "footboard," and it should remember that when the B of LE demands that a member of the B of LF shall withdraw to become a member of the B of LE, it practices a dictation as odious as ever characterized a railroad official, a dictation embodying insult and ingratitude, dictation humiliating and degrading, dictation which no manly man will tolerate and which all honorable men will condemn.

* * *

In our strictures upon the policy of the B of LE we have sought to influence its action in the line of justice and those proprieties which should distinguish an organization made up largely of men who have graduated from the B of LF. In this we have been animated by purposes which we do not blush to own. They will stand the test of criticism—and in the future, as now, afford us satisfaction in their contemplation.

The B of LF has not sought to control the personal action of its members. It builds no Chinese walls for its protection. The intelligence of its membership would brook no dictation from any source whatever, and what we say for members of our brotherhood is equally true of a vast number of the members of the Brotherhood of Locomotive Engineers. They are not and never will be in sympathy with a policy which seeks to degrade an engineer who retains his membership in the B of LF, of whom there are now at least 2,000, as noble and as true as ever stood upon a footboard or held a throttle. We could bank on their fidelity, though the temptation was as great as the devil offered the Master on the Mount. They would say, "Get thee behind me, Satan."[17] They will never wear the badge of apostates. They will never barter their manhood, their independence, for position. They will never withdraw from our order, unless it be of their own free will. And thousands more are coming up in our ranks whose loyalty will never waver, and when they learn, as they are now learning, that no engineer can belong to the B of LE who is a member of the B of LF, then their loyalty to their parent fraternity takes on a higher significance, then the password has a new meaning, and the die is irrevocably cast.

We can live apart. If the B of LE assumes that engineers belonging to the B of LF would make the control of that organization impossible—as Mr. Phelan[18] says would be the case—they can be of service to the B of LE by remaining on the outside, where at no distant day, a vast number of Locomotive Engineers will be found, preferring to maintain their manhood, their integrity, than to accept any position in any organization which requires their degradation. This action will not be because the B of LF imposes restraints or pledges, or assumes to dictate, but because it will be in consonance with those principles of honor and rectitude which it has been the ambition of the B of LF to inculcate.

We have always voiced the sentiment and voice it again that we are not opposed to engineers withdrawing from our order. When they leave us and cast their lot with the B of LE we bid them Godspeed—all we plead for is their right to leave us when they will instead of being driven out under the lash without regard to their personal feelings or rights.

* * *

Why Eight Hours for a Day's Work?†

July 1886

The inquiry we have selected as a caption for this article supplies abundant food for reflection.

Say what we will about the dignity of labor, of work—and too much has not been said—human nature is so constituted that work, if it could be avoided, would not be sought after as a means of increasing the sum of human felicity. By the term "work," we do not mean employment, mental or physical. We have reference to a condition which involves toil, drudgery, weariness, physical and mental bondage from which there is no escape, and which ceaselessly confronts the worker, demanding of him, like a Shylock, the fulfillment of the letter of the bond.[19] We have reference to the worker at wages, which in multiplied instances barely supplies the unremittable necessities of life, the man who is the daily legatee of the same hard fortune.

In the school of experience, he is taught lessons of economy which render the term obnoxious, for it is economy which means privation. It is the schooling of the stomach to a scarce supply of coarse food; it is the education of the body to resistance of pinching cold in the winter and the torture of summer heat; it is the training of the eye to scenes of squalor, unrelieved by a single redeeming ray of beauty in the house where he has his dwelling place.

Work, under such conditions, is not attractive. The worker enters upon the struggle early in life, and seldom lays down his burden except at the grave. See him anywhere, and the battle is raging. He is contending, against formidable odds, for life. Early and late, often into the darkness, he toils on to keep his soul within its clay tenement, and if there are others, wife and children, dependent upon him for subsistence, then the situation puts to a test which defies exaggeration the strength of every obligation that binds the worker to his task.

We know that the great mass of mankind have employment, which in a certain sense means work, the rich as well as the poor, but we know, also, that the difference between the work of a Gould, in his palatial office at a thousand dollars a day, and that of a fireman on one of his engines, is as the difference between a diamond and a lump of coal. It is said sometimes that men of great wealth are hard workers. We are quite willing to admit that with

† Published in *Locomotive Firemen's Magazine,* vol. 10, no. 7 (July 1886), 394–397.

the management of large estates comes great responsibilities, involving mental tension and physical exhaustion, but to intimate that such employment bears the remotest resemblance to the ceaseless drudgery of the man whose daily meals depend upon his daily toil is to remand the most expressive words of our language to the limbo of the obsolete, and decree in the interest of idiocy that words shall no longer be the signs of ideas.

The Malthusian idea is that pauperism means the overproduction of children; that the moment a child is born for whom there is no plate laid at the banqueting table of nature, it becomes a surplus production, and that nature decrees its death—necessarily by starvation—and will see to it that it is removed. But in the face of this Malthusian philosophy, the world is required to contemplate the astounding fact that there is in certain countries an overproduction of food products, that nature does lay the plate in the banqueting hall for the child, but that some heartless wretch removes the plate. Illustrations abound. Facts as broad-based as the eternal hills loom up on all sides. Why is there famine in Ireland? Is it because nature has laid no plate for Irish children in the banqueting halls of Ireland? Ireland left to herself could feed the millions of people, but Ireland, the victim of rapacity, sits in the gloom of starvation because land pirates not only remove the plates but confiscate the food.

But we are not in Ireland, nor in continental Europe. We are in America, and are dealing with labor problems as they are presented here; and here, where there is ceaseless talk about the overproduction of food; here, where the people tear down their barns to build larger, wherein to store their goods; here, where one man with the help of machinery can produce food sufficient for a hundred men; here, where Jehovah's beneficence must be the admiration of angels, there are thousands multiplied who go hungry, who are without sufficient food or clothing and who suffer for decent shelter. They look in vain for their plate at the banqueting table of nature. Why? Because there is an overproduction of children? No—but because work is not fairly distributed and wages rule below the subsisting line, and because there are those who are so demonized that they seek for their own gain to advance the price of food and reduce the buying power of the pittance a workingman receives for his toil.

But it may be asked what bearing such facts have upon eight hours for a day's work. From one side may come the reply, nothing at all. But, from another direction comes the declaration that they bear more or less directly upon the eight-hour question and are vital and of commanding importance.

We have read much of late of debates in and out of Congress relating to the dangers of illiteracy. We are told that the ballot, in the hands of ignorant, illiterate men, place our liberties in ceaseless peril—and that safety to our institutions lies in the education of the masses. There need be little controversy on this point. The Blair bill would appropriate many millions of the nation's money to overcome the illiteracy of the people, and the chief argument in support of the measure is that by such appropriation, the bulwarks of liberty are strengthened and our boasted institutions are made more secure.[20]

As a substitute for the Blair bill, a proposition is before Congress to appropriate for educational purposes the revenues derived from the sales of public lands. We refer to such facts simply to prove that the public mind is profoundly impressed with the idea that one of the greatest hazards which now confronts the institutions of the country has its existence in illiteracy, the ignorance of the masses, and that this great peril can be removed only by education. We freely admit that, to an extent which it is difficult to express, there is wisdom in such educational propositions. We believe they are fundamental. We do not, however, give our assent to the proposition that education is a panacea, a universal remedy for all the ills which afflict society, by which we mean that education which comes from training in the schools, as now conducted. But, be this as it may, the educational influences abroad in the United States of America are working a revolution in the popular mind.

We are not particular about terms. There is an education, a mental training, a thought, discipline, a depth, breadth, and height of knowledge, comprehension of conditions and rights, a perception of wrong and injustice which men obtain, though they can neither read nor write. The illiterate man may not be as capable as the educated man to analyze problems relating to his welfare, or that of the public, but while far less thorough in his investigations, his conclusions are scarcely less exact. He employs no sophisms, he is incapable of making figures lie, he is not trained in the legerdemain of logic, he finds a fact and adheres to it. As he wends his way to and from his comfortless home, he cogitates, not about systems of government, not about parties and policies, kings or cabinets, tariff and finance. He has found one fundamental fact which occupies his mind— which is that his wages are not sufficient to supply himself and his family with the absolute necessities of life. He knows that his breakfast was scanty, that the dinner prepared for him is not sufficient to keep him strong. He knows that his wife and children are not properly clothed and fed. He broods over the subject, he finds another workingman in the same condition. They talk it over and their discussions are the crude elementary propositions of what, in cultured circles, is called political economy. Others in the same, or similar, circumstances are consulted and finally they conclude to make an effort to better their condition.

This is education—not taught in the schools, not learned from books, but in the school of experience—and the lessons are committed to memory. They are interwoven with every fiber of their thought, and the men thus educated are demanding of employers an advance in wages that they may surround themselves with conditions more in consonance with the dignity of American citizens. If men are learning such lessons without going to school, what is to be expected of them and of their children when they are privileged to drink at the fountain of knowledge, forever flowing from the free schools of this country, where men have the ballot? It should be understood that every blow aimed at illiteracy is also a blow aimed at arrogance, at the disgusting superciliousness of men who affect a proud disdain of workingmen.

In the process of education in this country, in and out of school, it is beginning to be understood that workingmen are not machines, or, if employers will still contend that they are machines, then they are to be taught they are thinking machines—machines with heart and soul and brain, machines endowed with willpower, with noble ambitions and with unalienable rights which they will not surrender.

Education, without reference to when or how acquired, has taught workingmen in America certain great truths, which are now and will continue with ever-increasing power to influence their action and their lives. The workingmen, being in the majority, the destinies of this country rest in a large degree upon their shoulders. They are responsible; they cast the most votes; they create the wealth; they push forward the car of progress; they make constitutions and laws. Education lifts and expands them. They are now saying that by lessening the hours of labor, more laborers are required. If all the workingmen in the country were employed, there would be less poverty, less crime, more happiness, contentment, and prosperity. They say, and they speak truly, that such things are in the interest of society. Hitherto, the wealth which labor has created has concentrated largely in the hands of the few—hence, if eight hours commands the wages paid for ten hours, there will result a more equitable distribution of the wealth which labor creates. It may be well to demonstrate the proposition: We will suppose there are 5 million workingmen in the country; of these, that 4 million are employed at ten hours per day; one day is therefore equal to 40 million hours. If the time is reduced to eight hours per day, what is the result? This: you at once make room for the idle 1 million men. If that would not be a blessing to society then figures lie, words have lost their meaning. The proverb that "idleness is the parent of crime" becomes a stupid vagary, and a stubborn fact is of no more consequence in the practical affairs of life than a Gulliver tale.

But there is no trouble about eight hours a day; if workingmen will accept in wages the difference as eight is to ten, that is a reduction of one-fifth. That is to say, if workingmen feel sufficient solicitude in the welfare of their fellow workmen to surrender one-fifth of their wages to improve the condition of the unemployed, well and good; otherwise, say the opponents of the eight-hour movement, "things must remain as they are." Stated in figures the proposition is as follows; we like round numbers:

If 4 million men working 10 hours a day at $1 a day receive $4 million and they are willing to take 80 cents a day, they may have the privilege of letting the 1 million unemployed go to work—since 5 million men working 8 hours a day at 80 cents receive $4 million. In that case, as we have said, society takes no stock in the movement. It doesn't care a fig whether there is one or 1 million idle men in the country. If the 5 million men were employed at the 10-hour price, say $1 a day, there would be distributed $5 million instead of $4 million daily, an increase of $1 million a day, say for a year an increase of $300 million. Just here, we ask, what becomes of the additional $300 million? Well, it goes for food, clothing, and shelter. It circulates in all the channels of trade. It swells the tide of prosperity. It gives peace, contentment, social order. It reduces idleness and necessarily crime to the minimum, and carries virtue and all things of good report up to the maximum. We cannot do better here than to introduce the words of Col. R. G. Ingersoll, today the most eloquent man in the world, and than whom none love their fellow man better. He says:

> Why should labor fill the world with wealth and live in want? Every labor-saving machine should help the whole world. Everyone should tend to shorten the hours of labor.
>
> Reasonable labor is a source of joy. To work for wife and child, to toil for those you love, is happiness, provided you can make them happy. But to work like a slave, to see your wife and children in rags, to sit at a table where food is coarse and scarce, to rise at four in the morning, to work all day and throw your tired bones upon a miserable bed at night, to live without leisure, without rest, without making those you love comfortable and happy—this is not living, it is dying—a slow, lingering crucifixion.
>
> The hours of labor should be shortened. With the vast and wonderful improvements of the nineteenth century there should be not only the necessaries of life for those who toil, but comforts and luxuries as well.[21]

Of all the unprovoked slanders upon workingmen there are none more aggravating, none more heartless than the intimation that with fewer hours of toil they would squander their leisure instead of devoting it to mental culture and rational recreation. Workingmen love their homes as ardently as their more favored fellow citizens—love their wives and children with a devotion as sacred. They are animated by ambitions as fruitful of fruitions, and are as mindful of the interests of society. They are being educated. They are mastering the most abstruse problems relating to labor, production, finance, and trade. They are asking for nothing that is not in the interests of right and justice. The eight-hour movement is to take no backward step. The federal government has pronounced in its favor. States will follow the example. The public mind is being convinced and victory is in sight. With less work for the same pay we are to have less idleness, less crime, more peace, and greater plenty—brighter homes, better fed and better clothed children and wives, a more intense devotion to our institutions, and the ballot, so often referred to as a danger, is to be exercised with a higher regard for the public weal.

More Soldiers[†]

August 1886

Hon. Charles F. Manderson, representing the state of Nebraska in the United States Senate, is seriously alarmed, because the regular or standing army of the United States, in numbers, is so small and its organization so imperfect.[22] Mr. Manderson, of Nebraska, as his vision sweeps around the horizon, sees war clouds in various quarters; in fact, at almost every point of the compass, he is able to discern portents of war. He wants to be prepared. The distinguished senator, almost the first time he addressed the Senate, fired off a war speech. He quotes the Constitution, that Congress has power "to raise and support armies, provide and maintain a navy, provide for organizing, arming, and disciplining the militia, and for calling them forth to execute the laws of the Union, suppress insurrection, and repel invasion." And having all these powers, the Nebraska statesman wants Congress to exercise them fully and forthwith. And he maintains that if Congress, in the past, had exercised its powers to raise and support armies, provide and maintain a navy, etc., "many

---

† Published in *Locomotive Firemen's Magazine*, vol. 10, no. 8 (August 1886), 453–454.

of the darkest pages of our history would never have been written."

The Manderson idea appears to be that where large standing armies are kept in readiness to fight, no fighting occurs. He would have the country believe that if the Colonies had had a large standing army, England would never have provoked the Revolutionary War; that if the United States, in 1812, had had a large standing army, England would not have insulted our flag on the high seas; that if we had had a large standing army, the war with Mexico would never have occurred; and that a large standing army would have prevented the war of the rebellion.

It will occur to a good many people that the Nebraska statesman has forgotten much that he should have remembered. European countries maintain large standing armies, but they do not prevent war, and this fact makes Manderson's rhetoric appear rickety. He owed it to the Senate to have stated that European nations maintain standing armies in times of peace amounting to about 4 million men, and he should have told the Senate that notwithstanding these standing armies, wars in Europe are of almost yearly occurrence. But the Nebraska Senator proceeds to point out why the land of the free and the home of the brave needs a larger standing army at an increased expenditure of $1 million a year. In the first place it will create a demand for the product of the West Point officer manufacturing establishment, and since these gold-buttoned lilies who toil not, but draw their pay all the same, from money earned by workingmen, it will be proper to give them soldiers to command.

But, as we have remarked, the Nebraska warhorse smells war in various directions. In that section where a few strolling bands of murderous Apaches dwell, more soldiers are required. The Navajos are to be squelched in New Mexico, and in the great Northwest, Indians remain who paint their faces and engage in the war dance. Then, again, the Mormons require more soldiers, to put a stop to polygamy. The Nebraska man sees in New York, Pittsburgh, Cincinnati, socialists and nihilists whose pranks suggest the importance of a standing army of increased shooting abilities. Then, again, the Isthmian canal calls for more soldiers, and a larger standing army is also required to keep Cuba in the possession of Spain, and American railroad investments in Mexico require a standing army to see that our sister republic does not confiscate the property of American speculators in that country. But the Nebraska senator, who is so terribly alarmed about Apaches, Navajos, Sioux, Mormons, the Isthmian canal, Cuba, and railroad investments in Mexico, is still more alarmed, lest by the neglect of Congress to increase the standing army of the country, laboring men may rise someday and overthrow constitutions, institutions, law, and order, and introduce anarchy, rapine, and savagery generally.

Hear him:

> There are other elements threatening disturbance, but we can only glance at them. The riots in New York, Pittsburgh, Cincinnati, and other places within the last few years are the simple mutterings of a discontented condition liable to break out in widespread destruction and anarchy.

In this statement the Nebraska man gives himself clean away. In a nutshell, Mr. Manderson's anxiety for a larger standing army is to quiet laborers with cold lead instead of cold victuals. It is the European idea—the policy of every despotic government on the face of the earth, tsar, sultan, shah, mikado, et al. Mr. Manderson is an implacable foe of the workingmen of the United States. Labor is conservative. Labor builds, it does not tear down. Laboring men represent all that is solid and substantial in the empire of right. They demand only a respectable living in the United States. They produce everything, and their opposers and oppressors produce nothing. There never was a strike in America, when the demands of laboring men were in excess of absolute necessities, and there ought never to have been a strike, because there ought never to have been a refusal of the just demands of laboring men. And discontent among laboring men has always been the result of injustice and oppression.

Standing armies always and everywhere are the foes of liberty. They are terrible machines operated by despots to crush out the aspirations of the masses for liberty, and when Mr. Manderson pleads for a larger and a better-equipped standing army in the United States to shoot down laboring men when they show signs of discontent, he becomes a foe of hideous proportions. Laboring men have the ballot, and they are federating for the purpose of using it intelligently, and when once in a condition to make themselves felt, men of the Manderson stripe will not be permitted in legislatures or senates to advocate standing armies for the purpose of keeping laboring men in subjection to taskmasters who require them to live lives of want and degradation.

Notes

1. If this is a direct quotation, its origin has not been determined.
2. From "A Man's a Man for A' That" (1795) by Robert Burns (1759–1796).
3. Debs's calculations were off slightly in the original, silently fixed here.
4. Adapted from the refrain of the Biblically inspired "Miriam's Song" by Thomas Moore (1779–1852). The original reads, "Sound the loud timbrel o'er Egypt's dark sea: / Jehovah has triumphed—her people are free!"
5. Economist Arthur Twining Hadley (1856–1930) is best remembered as the president of Yale University from 1899 to 1921.
6. Adapted from Isaiah 35:8: "And an highway shall be there, and a way, and it shall be called The way of holiness; the unclean shall not pass over it; but it shall be for those: the wayfaring men, though fools, shall not err therein."
7. Line from an old Christian hymn, "Believers' Sufferings," traced back as far as an 1822 songbook, *Social and Camp-Meeting Songs for the Pious*, fourth edition (Baltimore: Armstrong and Plaskitt, 1822), 205. The original verse reads, "In every condition, in sickness, in health, / In poverty's vail, or abounding in wealth; / At home and abroad, in the land, on the sea, / As thy days may demand, shall thy strength ever be.
8. Terence Vincent Powderly (1849–1924) began his working career as a young railway switchman, later becoming a machinist. He joined the Knights of Labor in 1874, was elected secretary of his district assembly in 1877, and was elected grand master workman to succeed Uriah S. Stephens following his resignation in 1879. Powderly was an opponent of use of the strike and was ousted as head of the union in 1893. He served as commissioner general of immigration during the administration of Republican president William McKinley.
9. Uriah Smith Stephens (1821–1882), a Mason and union organizer of Philadelphia garment cutters from 1862, was the first head of the Knights of Labor. He resigned as grand master workman, to be replaced by Terence Powderly, in 1879.
10. The Latin phrase is the full form of the Anglicized abbreviation "ad lib."
11. Allusion to the story of Samson in Judges 14–16.
12. The original source of this quotation has not been located.
13. Damn fool.
14. From "The Building of the Ship" (1870), by Henry Wadsworth Longfellow (1807–1882). Checked to the original.
15. Struck oil.
16. Peter M. Arthur (1831–1903), née Peter McArthur, was the Scottish-born head of the Brotherhood of Locomotive Firemen from 1874 until his death. A railroad employee beginning in 1849, Arthur was an early member of the B of LF and an outspoken advocate of the brotherhood as a fraternal benefit society rather than a striking organization. Arthur was a staunch opponent of combining B of LF activity with the activity of other railway crafts and favored collaborative negotiation with employers to solve wage disputes. Under his leadership the B of LE stood opposed

to the more aggressive activities of the Knights of Labor, Supreme Council of United Orders of Railroad Employees, and the American Railway Union. Arthur became a wealthy landowner in Cleveland in his later years.

17. Words attributed to Jesus in Luke 4:8 and Matthew 16:23.

18. J. E. Phelan, a machinist from Brainerd, Minnesota, was the "Traveling Engineer" (organizer) of the Brotherhood of Locomotive Engineers.

19. Allusion to *The Merchant of Venice* (c. 1599) by William Shakespeare.

20. The Blair Act of 1886 provided for $79 million in federal funding of common schools to be distributed by the states over an eight-year period. Extra funds were to be dedicated to states with high rates of illiteracy. The bill was defeated in the senate due to the opposition of southern reactionaries, who feared additional funding of black schools throughout the region would lead to racial unrest.

21. From the speech "Labor, Capital, Etc." (1878), by Robert G. Ingersoll (1833–1899).

22. Charles F. Manderson (1837–1911) was a Nebraska Republican who was elected to two terms in the US Senate. He was an officer during the American Civil War, mustering out as a brevetted brigadier general of Union volunteers. After his second term in the Senate ended in 1895, Manderson was named general solicitor for the Burlington railroad system for its roads west of the Mississippi River.

1887

Politics[†]

January 1887

The *Locomotive Firemen's Magazine,* be it remembered, is not a political publication in the common acceptation of the term. But in the United States, politics should never be degraded as the synonym of anything opprobrious. Politics, be it understood, is the "science of government," and government, in the United States, is established and maintained by the consent of the governed.

This much preliminary to saying that in the late elections, Labor came to the front as a force in politics that has astonished the country, made men open their eyes and exclaim, "What next?"

The pages of this magazine will bear ample testimony that what has happened did not take us by surprise. We have said labor is organizing to better its condition by practicable and lawful means. We have said labor has the ballot and we have sought, as best we could, to magnify its power. We have said that the educational forces abroad in the land were lifting, by their more than Archimedean power, the workingmen of the country to a peership with those who have in the past controlled governmental affairs. Results confirm our predictions, and now labor stands ready to be crowned as the coming king, whose mission it is to eliminate wrong from statutes and courts, correct antiquated abuses, and to see that right and justice have a respectful hearing when the interests of the great body of the people are involved.

In recalling what labor has demanded in the past, men of prudent thought confess astonishment that its moderate requests have not been granted, but refusal following neglect, and neglect taking on all the offensiveness of ostracism, labor at last grasped the idea of unification and, in turn, discarding parties, or, for the nonce, selecting men from the various parties known to be in sympathy with the great body of wage-men, at the first onset won a victory and in the ranks of those whose policy had been in flagrant antagonism to the interests of the workingmen inaugurated confusion and changed in a large degree the current of political thought.

As we have predicted, the workingmen of America will seek assiduously for means of bettering their condition, apart from strikes and the boycott. They will discard anarchy and anarchists, violence by whatever name it is known or

---

† Published in *Locomotive Firemen's Magazine,* vol. 11, no. 1 (January 1887), 3.

by whatever method it may seek to gain its ends. The stupendous falsehood, whether insinuated or independently announced, that *workingmen are not law abiding* is to be throttled or choked to death, or indignantly crushed under the feet of the triumphant hosts of men who, knowing their rights and daring to maintain them, appeal to the ballot, to the law and the testimony.

We are to hear less in future about the war between labor and capital, because such a war is the creation of diseased brains. Such a war does not exist, and in the nature of things cannot and never did have an existence. But there has been a war waged in public sentiment, grasping monopolists seeking by statutes and precedents, established usages, to maintain a crushing ascendency over the wealth-producing millions of men the maintenance of a policy of injustice by which the few sacrificed the rights of the many, and in justification of their course, have been able to plead the statutes and the decisions of courts.

Under the new regime, inaugurated by the wage-men of the country, such forms of injustice are to disappear, and the blessings to flow therefrom are, like the rain, to fall upon the unjust as certainly as the just, by which we mean that the reign of right is to be a national benediction.

It is most gratifying to observe that the great body of the people hail with evident satisfaction this new departure in politics, the "science of government." It is a case in which politics is being rescued from the mere partisan, the boss, and the bummer, and made to honestly represent the will and best interests of the governed. It bears glowing testimony to the power of the ballot for good, when wielded with an honest purpose to secure the largest practicable good to the largest number of people.

Pullman[†]

January 1887

The term "Pullman" has become at last the synonym of almost anything odious that heartless, crushing, degrading monopoly suggests to the minds of honorable men. "Pullman" means "purple and fine linen, sumptuous living—silks, satins, diamonds, palaces, and a herd of cringing, fawning lickspittles who do the bidding of King Pullman, submit to kicks, cuffs, and such other degradations as are known and practiced in dominions of tsar, sultan, shah, or khedive. In Pullman's realm, there is no independence for workingmen. The decrees of the ruler are as autocratic as are known in benighted lands where men prostrate themselves, then heralds shout, "The King is coming!"

King Pullman owns towns, he owns houses, highways, parks, ponds, churches, schoolhouses, rinks; he has under his sway morals, education, religion, and amusements: he is all powerful in his little seven by nine territory up in Illinois, the land of Lincoln and Douglas.[1] Talk about dukedoms and earldoms and principalities, Pullman, the car-builder, whose real name is as wide as sleep, and whose palace cars outnumber all the equipages of all the potentates of Europe and Asia combined, to say nothing of American codfish, coal oil, and bucket shop snobs, whose appearance excite ineffable contempt. We say Pullman, the palace car nabob, enjoys a dictatorial power, which lays them all in the shade.

But it is not so much of Pullman in his little principality in northern Illinois that we write or care as it is of Pullman on all the iron highways of the country. Highways chartered by states and built with money of the people, and supported by the money of the people, and protected by the laws enacted by the people. It is on these public highways where Pullmanism reaches the extreme limit of all that is infamous in the industrial enterprises of the country.

The Pullman "sleepers" have conductors and porters. These men, half-paid, are subjected to ceaseless surveillance. Spotters are forever on their track, and it is charged that porters and conductors combine to filch in some way from passengers, enough to make up the difference between fair wages and starvation pay which Pullman allows his overworked men.

The *New York Times,* in a recent issue, exposes the unspeakable infamy of the

---

Pullman policy by which he increases his wealth, regardless of right and justice, and in a way the legitimate fruits of which are fraud and widespread demoralization.

The article referred to, based upon information from one who knows, bristles all through and all over with such atrocities as must excite universal indignation. Men are overworked and underpaid. Pullman, the conscienceless employer, by his policy, says in effect, "I know I am an unjust man; I am pursuing a course well calculated to make my employees thieves; and to guard my coffers I will put spotters, always scoundrels upon their track. I will employ men innately villains to watch men who, in my employment and by virtue of their meanness, are liable to become thieves."

The public has a right to know all about the Pullman iniquities practiced on men who attend to the "sleepers." A conductor on a Pullman car receives $70 a month and pays 75 cents a day for his meals when on the road. He is requested to purchase not less than two full uniform suits a year at a cost of $44. On each train the conductor is held responsible for the three cars on his train and the porters under him. If the porters divide their "tips" with the conductors as waiters do with headwaiters in several New York restaurants, the company is presumed to know nothing of it. A conductor's salary is supposed to be sufficient for all his personal needs and his expenses in the service of the company. Allowing $20 a month for meals bought on the road, and $4 a month for his uniform, a conductor does well if he can get $50 a month for his family out of his salary. But owing to the system of inspection and fines to which the Pullman men must submit, the chances are that the conductor will not get anything like that sum.

The conductors and porters are under the constant surveillance of "spotters," as the train hands call them, or "special agents," as they call themselves and are called on the company's payroll, who report at division headquarters the slightest infringement on the rules of the company. As a general thing, the Pullman conductor can no more tell a spotter from an ordinary passenger than the horsecar conductors in the city can single out the company spies who are sent around to see that they do not knock down on registered fares. Is it possible to conceive of a more humiliating position than that of a conductor or porter on a Pullman car? Everything is in the line of degradation. Suspicions of scoundrelism begin with the beginning and are never relaxed. To make matters still worse, to reduce pay and increase temptations to steal, Pullman instructs his spotters to be ceaselessly on the alert for mistakes, called in all cases "misdemeanors." These can be multiplied at the will of the spotter, being himself a villain and ready and willing to lie to maintain his place since the more he can reduce the pay of conductors and porters, the better it is for him. "A conductor," says the *Times* article, "considers himself lucky if he gets off with $6 in fines in ten months out of twelve. This makes a big hole in his salary. He has no chance to explain or to contradict the charges. The spotter is believed, and the conductor must submit or leave the service.

In addition to this, says the *Times,* "on nearly any full train with three or more Pullman cars that run over the trunk lines between New York and Chicago a special detective is employed to watch for graver misdemeanors, which may be considered outside the bailiwick of spotters." Conductors handle some money and the detectives are on the alert to see that stealing does not occur, and if there is no theft perpetrated, a mistake answers the purpose, as, "if a conductor makes an error in his diagram, a thing likely to occur at any time when passengers are dissatisfied with berths selected and desire transfers, he is fined for it, and if the offense becomes too frequent he is liable to suspension."

Such is the history of the Pullman reign on the road, and if anything can be brought to light more detestable, it has yet to occur. It is such detestable practices that breed the unrest and vindictive spirit abroad in the lands that furnish anarchists and socialists with the raw material for their diatribes against law and social order and keep alive the cry that there is an irrepressible conflict between capital and labor, when the conflict is between right and wrong. The press of the country, if true to its high privileges, will follow the lead of the *New York Times* and expose such hateful practices as are expressed by Pullman.

Trial of the Chicago Anarchists[†]
January 1887

The trial of the Chicago anarchists created throughout the country the most profound attention. Chicago, more than New York or any other great American city, had been for a number of years the converging center for a set of restless and reckless spirits under various names—"anarchists," "socialists," etc.—and their immunity from arrest or interference of any kind had emboldened them in the

---

† Published as "The Chicago Anarchists" in *Locomotive Firemen's Magazine,* vol. 11, no. 1 (January 1887), 11–13.

use of language in their papers and public harangues, which indicated a disregard for law and order, and America, with her boasted liberty, free schools, manhood suffrage, freedom of speech, and freedom of press, became as odious in the eyes of anarchists as Russia, Turkey, or any other despot-cursed country under heaven.

These anarchists saw nothing, or little, in American institutions worthy of favorable consideration; saturated with ideas born of European methods of government, they assumed that every wrong perpetrated by individuals or corporations against the rights and interests of workingmen was fundamental, rather than superficial; that is to say that such wrongs are inherent in the principles upon which the government was founded, rather than innovations, at war with its spirit, and hence they sought to inculcate by speech and press opposition to institutions which, by their liberality, permitted them to openly and defiantly antagonize them.

It is by no means surprising that men holding such views of government should attract to themselves an exceedingly dangerous element, men whose passions, the outgrowth of ignorance, make them mad and blind, and who, with or without provocation, resort to murderous methods to accomplish their own, and the ruin of their associates.

It must be remembered, in this connection, that *free speech* and *free press* are the twin glories of the American government. Strike them down, throttle them, murder them in court or on the battlefield, and no matter by what captivating name the government is known, it is a despotism nevertheless, as odious and as infamous as was ever known on the earth, since the devil, serpent, or Satan transformed Eden into a thorn-bearing wilderness.

But free speech and a free press do not mean unlicensed devilishness, and on very many occasions the courts have been required to draw the line between license and licentiousness. Such cases, however, in this country, have related to the rights of individuals, communities, and states; the federal government has seldom been involved, and never, we think, in time of peace.

The Chicago trial of the anarchists forms an exception, though in that trial there was a blending of charges of actual felony with the menace of social safety, and the condemnation to death is the first instance in the criminal records of the country when a jury adjudged that free speech could be carried to such excess as to make the death penalty a requirement and justifiable by the laws of the land.

Judge Gary, in his sentence condemning the anarchists to be hung, said: *"It is nowhere asserted or claimed that these prisoners threw the bomb, but that their doctrines, ideas, opinions, and teachings prepared the way and led to the throwing of the bomb."*

We have italicized the extraordinary words of Judge Gary because, since the prisoners did not throw the bomb which did the killing, they are to be hung for the expression of opinions which led to the murder. These prisoners did inveigh against the government, against the laws, against the policy and practice of corporations and monopolists and the loose and often shameful administration of the laws. They saw, or thought they saw, monstrous wrongs which enslaved some while they enriched others. They saw rich criminals go unwhipped of justice because they could, by the use of money or social influence, transform courts into tribunals, in which technicalities had the consideration and force of letter and spirit of the law, and under cover of which they escaped the penalties due their crimes while the poor wretch, without money or friends, was made to suffer.

The righteous denunciations of such things has not been confined to Chicago anarchists; the stump, the rostrum, the forum, and the press has ceaselessly arraigned legislatures, congresses, and political parties as being parties to such flagitious practices as being venal and corrupt to the core. The press, and men of high repute, have declared that cities where the people's representatives meet to enact laws are little less than Sodoms, and that the institutions of the country were in peril of being overthrown by corruption in high places.

Anarchists, whether foreigners or native born, have had ten thousand texts glowing with denunciations of parties and the government, of "doctrines, ideas, opinions, and teachings" well calculated to breed anarchists, but whoever thought of arresting the authors of such opinions, ideas, and teachings, of trying them and condemning them to be imprisoned or hung because of their insane and incendiary litterings?

The language of Judge Gary in sentencing the Chicago anarchists is startling. It rings like an alarm bell. He said it was "nowhere asserted or claimed" that the anarchists "threw the bombs." They were not on trial for killing. They had committed no murderous act, but had proclaimed "doctrines, ideas, opinions, and teachings" which "prepared the way and led to the throwing of the bombs," and for this exercise of free speech, carried to dangerous courts, they are condemned as worthy of death.

With such a decision, unrevoked, what is the situation? What is the status of free men? What are the privileges of the press? A moment's reflection leaves the mind overwhelmed in confusion.

The verdict of the Chicago jury and the language of Judge Gary effectually obliterates the line separating language and overt acts; that is to say, a word is equal to a blow or a bomb, not a word in itself felonious, but a word, an opinion, an idea, a doctrine, a teaching, which "prepares the way" for the overt act.

There have been strikes which were the direct outgrowth of "doctrines, ideas, opinions, and teachings," and in numerous instances these strikes have resulted in various grades of felony. The Chicago verdict and the language of Judge Gary does not distinguish between the men who committed the felony and those who harangued the people against chronic and flagrant wrongs. On the contrary, for the first time in American jurisprudence the astounding declaration is made that a difference does not exist. "It is nowhere claimed," said Judge Gary, "that these prisoners threw the bomb." It was not claimed, it was not asserted, it was not proven that they threw the bomb, but that they had expressed doctrines, opinions, and ideas which led to the throwing of the bomb. Let this verdict stand, let it become the practice of the courts, let it have popular approval, let it go unrevoked, and free speech is as dead in America as it is in Russia, and a free press becomes a haggard aggravating misnomer, as treacherous as a mirage or an *ignia fatuas*—Dead Sea fruit—which tempts but to deceive, and once endorsed, the pillars of our boasted temple of liberty disappear as if by a decree of Jehovah.

In this age it will not do to hang men for their doctrines, ideas, opinions, and teachings, however dangerous they may be or may appear to be, and a moment's reflection will, we think, convince rational men that the proposition is impregnable against attack, no matter from what quarter it may come.

We are by no means opposed to laws which punish men for the abuse of free speech. We are not in favor of mobs, mob rule, or mob law. We are unalterably opposed to the teachings of anarchists—the bomb, the torch, the using of the weapons of assassins—but we would guard with ceaseless vigilance free speech and a free press, and could we speak with the tongue of an angel, we would not condemn a man to death for inveighing the wrongs which have crept into American methods of government. In other words, if there is no law for hanging men for holding opinions, ideas, doctrines, and for teachings, we would not hang them for such things; and if an attempt were made to enact such a law we would oppose it with all the power of mind we could command. With such a law upon the statute books, the world would begin a retrograde movement, and despotism worse than anarchy would be reinstated.

If anarchists threaten the peace of society, we would restrain them; if they commit murder, we would hang them. But the bare mention that teaching certain doctrines or holding to certain opinions of government, we care not how monstrous, are worthy of the death penalty—if it does not thrill the American mind with alarm, then it must be confessed that the American mind has reached a point on the road to despotism far more alarming than any of the insane harangues made by the Chicago cranks.

Nothing was ever gained in the way of suppressing ideas and opinions by hanging or burning men for ideas and opinions. Ideas and opinions escape the death penalty, the halter, the faggot, and the wheel.

Abolitionists[†]

February 1887

In days not so far away as to be forgotten by millions of men and women, the term "abolitionists" was one of crushing reproach, and he who dared plead guilty to the charge of being an abolitionist was everywhere ostracized, and over a vast extent of territory the charge ranked with crimes which could be expiated only by imprisonment or death. Notwithstanding all this, abolition thrived, abolitionists accepted all the penalties, dared every peril, gloried in chains, prisons, exile, and death. Their motto was no truce, no compromise. They saw the wrong, the curse, the crime of slavery, and they attacked it resolutely, continually, ceaselessly. They shaped events, they created circumstances, they grasped fate and destiny, and wrung from them decrees that slavery in the United States should cease. For all this they were maligned, persecuted, and killed. William Lloyd Garrison, whose name was once the synonym for all things infamous, said in Philadelphia on one occasion:

> There is too much quietude in this city. Your cause (the abolition cause) will not prosper here. The philosophy of reform forbids you to expect it, until it excites popular tumult, and brings down upon it a shower of brickbats and rotten eggs, and is threatened with a coat of tar and feathers.[2]

The tumult came, it increased until the tramp of more than three million armed men shook the continent, and when the tumult ceased, more than six million slaves stood erect, free, emancipated by the power of agitation, tumult, discussion, led on from small beginnings through fire and smoke and blood to results which constitute an epoch in history such as men and angels never before witnessed since time began.

† Published in *Locomotive Firemen's Magazine,* vol. 11, no. 2 (February 1887), 67–68.

It is in order to say that revolutions never go backward. They may meet with enemy and be arrested for a while in their march, but they never abandon an inch of ground once gained. The idea holds the fort and succeeding efforts always begin where the preceding ones halted. Tyrants can't kill ideas; opinions, they live on, proof against faggot and wheel and halter. Indeed when an eloquent voice is *silenced* it is only heard the more *distinctly,* and by a thousand times larger audience it echoes, reverberates around the world.

There are abolitionists now, not those who demand that chattel slavery shall cease where the stars and the stripes wave, an emblem of authority, because the slave pen and the slave block and the slave lash have disappeared, but there are those who behold every day other wrongs which they have set out to abolish, wrongs of a character which will admit of neither truce nor compromise, nothing will answer the requirement but their abolition. They are wrongs which take on some of the forms of slavery, wrongs which work the degradation of men, which sap the foundations of citizenship and imperil the stability of American institutions. The conflict is not between capital and labor, between money and misery, cash and credit; it is between man and man, the man who works and the man who pays, the man who employs and the man employed. It is between the man who holds the office and the man who holds the ballot. It is a conflict between right and wrong, truth and error, justice and injustice, a conflict between citizens who make everything, build everything, and the men who simply supervise and manage.

Tumult has followed tumult. There has been and there is still agitation, unrest. The courts have been invoked and the military power has been exerted, but the revolution does not move backward, nor yet stand still. To those who are willing to study the situation, it is easily understood. The men who do the work demand fair pay for their labor, decent food, decent clothing, decent shelter, homes such as become American sovereigns, clothed with the high responsibilities of shaping the destinies of the great American Republic. They are not peons, they are not helots, but freemen who have the ballot, and they will accept neither truce nor compromise, they will have their inalienable rights, and it is of the first importance for those who assume to manage affairs not to forget it.

As the case now stands, if the laws are right, they are criminally administered. If the laws are defective they will be repealed. If justice has been cloven down, it is to be re-enthroned. If in the olden times, by God's decree, it was a sin to "muzzle the ox when he treadeth out the corn,"[3] what must be the damnable nature of laws and politics that make a supply of bread doubtful to those whose toil feeds the world, and worse still, subjects them to the pangs of hunger and starvation?

The revolution now in progress is not to change the form of government, it is not to abolish courts, overthrow institutions, but rather to make government, courts, and institutions subserve the happiness of the American people. We have sovereignty of the people, we have equality of conditions and responsibilities. We have made the ballot the standard; the majority must rule. The wage-worker is not demanding a palace, he is not coveting the property of his more fortunate fellow citizen, but he is demanding in the distribution of the profits of labor, so much as shall redeem him and those dependent upon him from the curse of hunger and rags, and protect him and his family from beastly shelters.

It is worthwhile to say that this revolution may be peaceable. The tumult may be only the clash of contending opinions within the limits prescribed by law, but violent opposition to the reign of right may be productive of a state of affairs, the contemplation of which sends a shudder through all ranks and conditions. Let it be understood that wage-men are everywhere organizing for the conflict. It is supreme folly for people to close their eyes to the fact; far better will it be for the country to enact wholesome laws and fearlessly administer them. It is not a question for purse-proud arrogant corporations with Pinkerton's hired assassins to settle. The military can be better employed than in shooting down half-fed and half-starved citizens. Such things only change the character of the tumult without settling any question in controversy. Courts are often bribed by a thing so insufferably contemptible as a railroad pass. Banks, the creatures of law, supply the funds to enable bucket-shop brokers to corner food, and thus we might enumerate curses which ceaselessly create social, political, and industrial tumults. Manifestly such wrongs cannot continue. They will be swept away, abolished.

Abolitionists are not only increasing in number but in power. It will be the part of wisdom to take the load off the backs of toilers, better for the lawmakers to arrest stupendous villainies, better for the courts to cease making distinctions, better at once to inaugurate a reign of justice and right. It can be done; it must be done; it will be done. The signs of the times declare that a revolution has begun, is on the march. The masses demand fair play. The Constitution guarantees it; the laws must enforce it. Abolitionists point to the wrongs and say they must disappear, and as certain as tides ebb and flow they will disappear.

Will Labor Organizations Federate?[†]

February 1887

We do not mean to be understood by the interrogatory, which forms the caption of this article, as propounding an inquiry which, however answered, would indicate a wish on our part that all labor organizations should abandon their distinctive features and form one grand central organization. On the contrary, we ask the question that we may put upon record such reflections *pro et con* as the subject suggests.

We do not regard as a probable result that labor organizations will federate in any sense that will require the abandonment of names, distinctive purposes of their membership, their constitutions, laws, rituals, etc. Nor do we believe that such a federation is desirable. It would require the abandonment of "home rule," and would, we think, result in confusion instead of order and harmony.

But we fail to discover any good reason why labor organizations of certain trades could not federate with decided and great advantages. To some extent this has already been accomplished.

Printers' unions have federated. There is a national printers' union.[4] There may be other national unions which, in their annual conventions, legislate for all subordinate lodges. The idea is eminently practical, and only good results follow.

The organization of the Knights of Labor seeks to embody all trades and to draw into its embrace all workingmen without reference to trade or employment. It is not a federation of labor organizations, but a union of all classes of laboring men and women. It seeks to combine in one fold the workingmen of the country, to formulate policies and enact laws and regulations by which men of trades and without trades shall be governed. And this being the case, the task must of necessity be herculean.

It is by no means a difficult matter to name all the trades (we refer to mechanics) known to the country. They are numerous and include a vast army of wage-men. Thousands and tens of thousands of these wage-men are now members of unions peculiar to their trade. These unions, lodges, or by whatever name their organizations are known could have state and national organizations, and delegates from state organizations could form a national organization, like the state and federal governments, exercising so much and no more power than

† Published in *Locomotive Firemen's Magazine*, vol. 11, no. 2 (February 1887), 71–72.

is delegated to them. This done, there could be organizations of laboring men who are not known as mechanics, but who are profoundly interested in labor questions, and these could be and should be organized and represented in the state and national organizations.

Do these propositions appear utopian? Visionary? Impracticable? If so, then the federation of labor, or labor organizations, is an idea to be classified with other vagaries, and should be remanded to the limbo of hallucinations.

But federation is not impracticable. On the contrary, federation is feasible, and if labor is ever to reach the goal of equality with capital in shaping policies, in the assertion of prerogatives, it will have to federate.

In contemplating the subject it is quite probable, if there are those who are doubtful, that their distrust arises from the fact that the number of wage-men of America is so great that hesitancy in accepting the practicability of federation is in the line of prudence. To this we reply by using the old aphorism "Rome was not built in a day." We recognize that time will be required, and when courage, perseverance, and intelligence are in alliance with time, there is no obstacle in the pathway of human advancement which may not be removed.

The present generation may not see the glad day of the complete emancipation of labor from its enthrallments. It may not see the hand of oppression lifted from labor, but it may lay the foundation upon which other generations can build. It may send circling around the world those ideas and words which, taking root in the minds and hearts of men, shall eventually produce results to the glory of God and the emancipation of men from oppression.

We are well aware that the federation of American workingmen is not a problem to be solved in a day, and we are quite as confident that an oak whose mighty arms defy the storm is not produced in a day. We are not required to discuss time. Time, like space, defies calculation. We are only interested in the purposes, the ambitions, the determinations of workingmen. The subject of "Capital and Labor" has been discussed ad nauseam. Be assured capital will federate, combine, organize, and will be heard. Nobody antagonizes capital, and no more apologies from labor in that direction are required.

To assume that labor has no other object in view than to fix prices, maintain prices, and determine the hours of a day's work, is a driveling estimate of the ambitions of workingmen. They demand to be heard on the subjects we have named, but there are other aspirations which animate workingmen. They demand absolute freedom from social and political ostracism. They demand a public opinion in which the badge of labor shall no longer be a badge of degradation. Hitherto the so-called learned professions—law, medicine, theology—have had a monopoly of social and political dainties. In legislative assemblies there must be 90 percent law and of the remaining 10 percent, labor has been content with a fraction of 1 percent, or no percent at all. And as labor is the great interest of the country, it proposes to increase its percentage of importance and influence in the politics of the country, in the science of government, and this can be accomplished in its fullest measure by federation, and only federation.

No greater service could be done for society, for the welfare of all, than for thoughtful men to devise plans whereby labor organization could be brought into a grand national federation. This done, there would be something more and better than a Labor Bureau in Washington city, there would be a Labor Department of the government, and when the president called his counselors together, there would be found at the board a man able and ready to speak for men, without whom there would be no government. Therefore, adopting the poetical and practical philosophy of Longfellow, we say:

> Let us, then, be up and doing,
> With a heart for any fate;
> Still achieving, still pursuing,
> Learn to labor and to wait.[5]

The Situation in Europe[†]

March 1887

The news from Europe is warlike, and it is said if hostilities begin, the Lord only knows how many nations will be involved or when peace would be declared. On this side of the ocean it is believed that a European war would increase indefinitely the demand for wheat and other cereals, and make times livelier.

There is high authority for saying that the standing armies of Europe consist of 12.6 million men. The men are drawn from peaceful pursuits, mostly the industrial classes—mechanics, laborers, farm hands, etc. As a result, in time of war Europe is dependent upon other countries for food, and that is what the United States can supply. Europe, with about 300 million population, expends annually

† Published in *Locomotive Firemen's Magazine*, vol. 11, no. 3 (March 1887), 141.

$850 million to supply her standing armies, and with the interest on her national debts, together with her annual expenditures to maintain her armies, is required to pay annually $1.965 billion. When it is understood that this enormous sum comes out of the earnings of labor, it is not surprising that workingmen want to emigrate.

Labor and Station in Life[†]
April 1887

A writer in a journal of wide circulation writes of "labor" in a way which in many regards is wholesome; as for instance the following:

> There is always hope in a man that actually and earnestly works. In idleness alone is there perpetual despair. Work is the law of our being—the living principle that carries men and nations onward. The greater number of men have to work with their hands, as a matter of necessity, in order to live; but all must work in one way or another, if they would enjoy life as it ought to be enjoyed.[6]

We unequivocally endorse the foregoing statements of the writer, but when he adds that labor "may he a burden or a chastisement" we think he upsets his premises, and taking the whole sentence, "Labor may be a burden and a chastisement, but it is also an honor and a glory," we think the climax of nonsense is reached. Work being "the law of our being," it is only a "burden and a chastisement" when some fundamental law, not of our being, but of right and justice, has been violated. As a matter of course, we do not include convict labor, which may be imposed as a punishment, and is intended to be "a burden and a chastisement." We are in full accord with the declaration that without labor "nothing can be accomplished. All that is great in man comes through work, and civilization is its product. It is idleness that is the curse of man—not labor. Idleness eats the heart out of men as of nations, and consumes them as rust does iron. Happiness, prosperity, and safety in any attained position depend upon

---

† First published as "Labor" in *Locomotive Firemen's Magazine*, vol. 11, no. 4 (April 1887), 207–208.

work, which, of some sort or other, may be pursued by every member of the race." Such ideas we have sought, from time to time, to place on record in these pages, and we have sought to show that the labor capital of the world is the only capital that should the most seriously engage the attention of philanthropists and statesmen. But, says the writer, "to do our duty in that station of life into which it has pleased God to call us, is the infinite thing to live for; which is full of blessed realities in the present, and prophetic of an ever-brightening future." To all such propositions, we enter our protest. We do not believe God assigns anyone a station in life or "calls" anyone to a particular "station in life." The theory is preposterous, repulsive, and degrading to God and man.

The dominating theory of government in the past, and one that still prevails in many countries is that certain persons have a "divine right," a God-given right to rule, and out of this theory has sprung every other God-dishonoring and man-degrading theory in regard to "station of life." Kings and lords, autocrats and aristocrats, by inheritance or fortune, love to prate about "the stations in life it has pleased God to call us." They survey the field and note the station of ruler and the station of subject; the station of master and the station of slave; the station of wealth and the station of poverty, and complacently say, "Behold what God has done." Accept the theory and civilization goes back to the Hindu idea of caste.

Our idea is, insofar as God is concerned, that He creates all men equal. It is the shibboleth declaration that is to redeem mankind from the thralldom of degradation, if man is ever redeemed, that is to lift him to the glory-crowned highlands of independence, if he ever reaches the elevation.

The world has had enough and more than enough of the drivel about God assigning men their stations in life. At the mere mention of such an ironclad law, ambition and self-respect, manhood and independence revolt, and intuitively men know it to be a monstrous perversion of every principle of human action.

The power which the strong have exercised over the weak, the injustice of governments, the venality of the rich, all combined, have filled the world with lamentations until the fact is universally admitted that

> Man's inhumanity to man,
> Makes countless millions mourn.[7]

And yet, those who have been guilty of the wrongs have sought to reconcile the nations to the theory that it is God who calls them to stations in life, too often stations of misery.

The mission of work is not only to obtain bread and meat, clothing and shelter, but to secure for the mind wider fields for enjoyment, intellectual as well as material luxuries. Work may be the law of our being, but to rise by virtue of work into other and better conditions is also a law of our being, and the present is an age, we are glad to believe, when the laws of our being are to have full sway. Labor is not degrading; it never was degrading. The law of work is to work up, not down; it is to enlighten, not to darken. It develops the good, not the bad in human nature, and when human laws which obstruct the way are annulled, as they will be, man, who according to the late revision of the Bible "was made but little lower than God,"[8] will ascend to his rightful position and hold the fort against the devil, or what is worse, the aristocratic enemies of man's advancement.

Labor Legislation[†]

April 1887

During the month of January the legislatures of 21 states were in session, and we surmise that in each of these lawmaking bodies bills were presented and acted upon more or less directly affecting labor. The supposition is probable because, in all of the states, without an exception, there have been what is called in common parlance "labor troubles."

It is quite out of the question to catalog these labor troubles or to assign the real cause for each one of them. Legislators know that they exist, and that it is their duty to ascertain the cause, find a remedy, and apply it.

Preliminary to the discussion, we will state that it is the boast of this country that its free school system emancipates men from the thralldom of ignorance and the degradation which ignorance entails. It is accepted as a self-evident truth that education, intelligence, is the eternal foe of servitude, enslavement, hence, in this God-favored land, a schoolhouse is freedom's citadel, and the spelling book, the reader, the arithmetic, the pen, ink, and paper, put into the hands of American youth are the weapons which are designed to beat down all opposition to the triumphant emancipation of American workingmen. The process is going steadily forward, and he who does not see it is as blind as a bat, and he who does not hear the harbinger notes of the new dispensation is

---

† Published in *Locomotive Firemen's Magazine*, vol. 11, no. 4 (April 1887), 201–203.

as deaf as an oyster. And this fact, which glows and burns like a star of the first magnitude in the firmament of our political system, like Bethlehem's star, foretells the coming of a time, now near at hand, when the ballot in the hands of workingmen, redeemed from ignorance by the genius of universal education, shall inaugurate an era of equality before the law, in fact as well as in theory. This done, gilded villainy, "robed in purple and fine linen,"[9] will be sent "over the road," in a line as direct to the prison as he of less cash, less hypocrisy, and a lower (?) position in the social scale.

But, to our subject. What is labor demanding at the hands of legislators? If one measure is proposed not in the interest of society at large, some organ or advocate of monopoly ought to point it out.

It has passed into a maxim worthy of high commendation that ours is "a government of the people, by the people, and for the people." It is not, at least it was never intended to be, a government of capital, by capital, and for capital. It was never designed that this government should be of monopoly, by monopoly, and for monopoly. If for the people, the government should protect the weak against the strong, the poor against the rich, the employee against the employer. The working people, the wage earners, the breadwinners, the wealth creators, are in the majority. These people, the most vitally concerned in good government, simply demand at the hands of legislators justice. Take, for instance, the proposition recently up for debate in the legislature of Indiana. In that state it has been the practice of employers, in numerous instances, to pay their men in scrip receivable for goods at the employer's store, but when this scrip was offered, the employee found that he was charged 10, 15, or 25 percent more than was charged others who paid cash.

Since the day when Jehovah, amidst the thunders of Sinai, said "Thou shalt not steal,"[10] was there ever a proposition submitted to legislators bearing more distinctly the impress of justice? To charge more when the employee offered the scrip than when cash was offered would be ironclad, conscienceless scoundrelism, and the difference between the scrip and the cash would be nothing less than robbery, taking the advantage of conditions to perpetrate piracy—not capital antagonizing labor, but a venal, heartless capitalist or employer taking advantage of poverty, of necessity, of conditions, to increase the inconveniences, the embarrassments which environ labor, to degrade labor and humiliate the workingmen. It is such gold-plated knaves, such mercenary miscreants, such sleek, plausible scoundrels who have, in a thousand ways, brought about labor troubles in every section of the land, and hitherto they have had legislatures and courts at their command to do their bidding, and even yet, there are men in legislative halls who boastingly and impudently oppose measures designed to make employers take their claws from the throats of workingmen and their vulture beaks from out of their hearts, and in the pursuit of their damnable designs have the effrontery to claim they are serving the best interests of the state. No more pitiable exhibition of the wreck of integrity, of mental debasement, of corruption and rottenness was ever made, or ever will be made in legislative halls.

In the name of all that is of good report, what is the chief, the highest, the most imperative demand of society? Is it not that justice shall be enthroned? Is it not that truth shall be exalted and a lie stamped into its native hell? Is it not that virtue shall be extolled and vice overthrown? We have said that in January 1887, 21 legislatures were in session; Congress was also in session, all at a cost of not less than $1 million a day. Why this vast expenditure, to be paid out of the earnings of labor, if labor is to be thrust aside when it demands exemption from wrongs as flagrant as ever cursed the world since Egyptian slaves built the pyramids? And what in God's name is labor demanding? Protection in the mines, protection on the rail, and when labor has earned its dollar, that no man, nor combination of men, under cover of law, precedent, custom, or any subterfuge whatever, shall cheat him out of a fraction of a mill.[11]

Look abroad, survey the field, note the toilers, the dinner bucket brigade, in mine, factory, mill, shop, carrying forward all the great industries of this wonderfully active, progressive age. They are earning the revenues of the state and of the republic; only work produces revenues, only work produces wealth. Work builds, repairs, sustains, and yet there are blatherskites, the paid attorneys of monopolies, the beneficiaries of pools and lobbies, who assert that were it not for the capitalist, labor would starve. The fact is that were it not for work, the advancing armies on all the highways of progress would stand still. No anvil would ring, no forge would blaze, no shuttle would fly, no wheel would revolve, no plow would turn a furrow, from valley to mountaintop no locomotive whistle would be heard. Such self-evident truths the wage-men of America are comprehending in all their lifting, humanizing power, and when they ask of legislators that simple justice be done them, it will be the part of wisdom to heed the demand. If labor is honestly paid, if it receives an equitable share of the wealth it creates, if it is honestly dealt with by legislatures, laws, and courts, society, as its high reward, will receive a baptism of peace and prosperity. Then labor troubles will cease, the strike, the lockout, the boycott will disappear, and the senseless gabble about the conflict between capital and labor will cease. The occupation of the spotter, more infamous than that of hangman, will be gone, and that unspeakable atrocity, the "blacklist," the weapon of the assassin, will live only in history, a relic of civilized savagery, worse, if possible, than thumbscrew, wheel, or faggot.

We congratulate and felicitate the wage-men of America upon the advanced position of their cause, which is the cause of good government, at once a revolution and a revelation. Federation will win. Education is doing its work. Intelligence, a comprehension of the situation, is bringing about the unification of the wage-men of America, and the great republic is to be in a nobler sense than ever, since the declaration of independence was read, the land of the free. The aristocracy of codfish, coal oil, bank, bucket shop, and corporation are to find that laws and prisons are made for them as well as for those whose skill and muscle have redeemed the continent from a wilderness, planted Edens of beauty and fruitfulness from ocean to ocean, and from the land of the orange and cotton to the land of apples and corn, who have built the cities, laid the iron rail, bridged the rivers, tunneled the mountains, plowed and sowed and reaped, until all may sing with the spirit and the understanding in loftier and more animating strains than ever made free men rejoice or tyrants tremble:

> Workingmen united, workingmen are free.
> With ballot in their hands, they will issue their decree.
> And he who refuses aid, Justice to enthrone,
> Invites for this Republic the decline and fall of Rome.[12]

Opposites[†]
April 1887

Mr. Ralph Waldo Emerson once wrote what has since been called a "prose masterpiece" entitled "Compensation," in which, among many other things that embellish his essay, he holds that in nature everything has its opposite as, for instance, heat and cold, male and female, ebb and flow of waters, day and night.[13] Every sweet has its sour, every evil its good. For every grain of wit there is a grain of folly. For everything you have missed, you have gained something else, and for everything you gained you lost something. The writer proceeds in this line and impresses the reader with the idea that this odd and even arrangement is fixed and

† Published in *Locomotive Firemen's Magazine,* vol. 11, no. 4 (April 1887), 205–206.

immutable, and it requires an effort of the mind to disengage it from the thrall of conviction. Opposites there are, but the question is, are they required, are they inevitable? Must there of necessity be a lie for every truth? A vice for every virtue? A bad man for every good man? And, to explode the whole theory, must there be ten thousand poor men for every rich man? The theory upon which a very large class of men are now operating is to readjust such things as have confessedly gone wrong in the past. If there can be no good without attending evil, then the demand is to increase the good to the maximum and reduce the evil to the minimum.

Now, the opposite of riches is poverty, and the trouble is not that the rich are rich, but too rich; the few, by methods which have only to be mentioned to excite universal rebuke, have not only made the poor poorer, but have, to an extent hideously monstrous, increased their number. There is a theory abroad in the world that poverty is a removable evil, that it is not a condition willed by the Creator, but that it has been brought about by causes which, though of long duration and deep-seated, may be eradicated, not immediately, but eventually. It is not required that for every elevation there shall be a corresponding depression. On the contrary, nature would not revolt if the dry land were a tableland, a plane. It is not to be supposed that heaven would be displeased if every man in the universe were possessed of so much land, of so much of the treasure of the land, whether mineral or vegetable, as would suffice to make him comfortable and happy, nor is it to be surmised that the infinite ruler would object if poverty should disappear from among men. Admit that injustice is the opposite of justice, that sin is the opposite of righteousness; it does not follow that these opposites are fixed fast in fate, that they exist by virtue of irrevocable decrees. To assert that such is the case is simple madness, and totally destructive of hope, of ambition, and of faith in God. Admitting that the Master said, "For the poor ye have always with you,"[14] but he also said, "Woe unto you, scribes and Pharisees, hypocrites! for ye devour widows' houses."[15] Possibly Agur, the son of Jakeh, had about the right idea when he prayed, "Remove far from me vanity and lies; give me neither poverty nor riches; feed me with food convenient for me."[16] Agur hit upon an idea eminently distinguished for common sense. He did not want to be rich and proud, nor destitute and miserable; he wanted simply his equitable share of needful things, and these obtained he would be neither rich nor poor—he would be independent. This is the modern idea. It is sensible, just, righteous. This is attainable. It is within the reach of human endeavor. There is nothing utopian, visionary, about it. The task may be herculean, but when the great majority bend all their energies to its accomplishment, success will crown their efforts. There is land enough for all if each is to have so much and no more than he can till. There is food enough for all, if it is righteously distributed, and there is work enough for all, if each is permitted to share in the time required to perform it. Does someone contend that such propositions are hallucinations, because the time will never arrive when there will be no rich men and no poor men? The position is indicative of a misapprehension, since the time may come when all may be rich, in the sense we use the term "rich"—that is, as Agur would put it, neither rich nor poor, but having enough, in which case, rationally understood, opposites would disappear. Some might have more than others, but since all would have enough no cause of complaint would exist.

If there are those who, to make a case, would fly to the extreme and discuss misfortunes, the infirm, the lame, the halt, and the blind, we protest that such a course is a tacit admission for all for which we contend, and we dismiss the controversy. We contend that it is within reach of human endeavor to establish justice. This done, the most difficult feature of the problem is solved. We adhere to the oft-repeated declaration that the great mass of the people are honest, but have been overreached and made poor by conditions largely artificial, and that these conditions can be changed. Unjust laws can be repealed, and just laws can be enacted. The misfortune of ignorance, the opposite of intelligence, or education, can be removed, that all men can be taught their rights and the proper methods by which to enforce and maintain them, and this intelligence, this education, will regenerate the whole man, intellectually, morally, and physically. This done, the man becomes a new being. In his case he has advanced from the mere animal into an intellectual existence, he has overcome the opposites of vice and ignorance. Being able to comprehend justice, he beats down its opposite, injustice. Knowing when a law operates to the detriment of the human family and what laws will best subserve the welfare of the state, he enthrones the good, and with iconoclastic sway compels its opposite, the bad, to disappear. The opposite of employment is idleness. The fruit of employment is virtue, that of idleness, vice. The question of the times is, Can all have employment? The solution of the problem is found in reducing the hours of labor. Now, suppose there are 5 million working men in the country, and 1 million are idle, the question arises, how can the 1 million idle men obtain employment? We say by reducing the hours of work. We will suppose that the 4 million work ten hours a day, that is, 40 million hours a day. Reduce the hours to eight hours a day, and 5 million men working eight hours a day is 40 million hours. Tabulated thus:

> 4 million men, 10 hours a day, equals 40 million hours.
> 5 million men, 8 hours a day, equals 40 million hours.

In this we see the solution of the problem, and if the opposite of employ-ment is idleness, we thereby destroy idleness, the opposite of employment, and if idleness is promotive of vice, the opposite of virtue, insofar as idleness is concerned we destroy vice, which is the opposite of virtue. In this matter soci-ety, communities, the state, and the nation are vitally concerned, and no more important question is now up for debate. Certain propositions are in the line of common sense and justice, the good of society and the welfare of the state. To devise means for the employment of idle men requires the best thoughts of the wisest statesmen, and when all the resources of mind have been exhausted it will be found that to destroy the opposite of idleness the reduction of the hours of labor is the *ultima Thule*[17] of the prudent possibilities of the case. It will be found that the problem is solved without violence and injustice, and upon the basis of absolute equity.

Land, Labor, and Liberty[†]

August 1887

Population is steadily increasing, but the quantity of arable acres of land in the world is fixed; there can be no increase of land. The land question, whether rec-ognized or not, has from the first been the supreme question. It is not worth-while to burden our columns with argument showing that labor has created the wealth of the world, that capital is the child of labor, that without labor there would be no capital, without labor there would be no revenues, not a dollar would ever find its way into exchequers of governments. All writers capable of comprehending the simplest proposition in political economy give to labor this supreme prominence, that labor creates all revenues, pays all debts and taxes, and yet these same writers with rare exceptions, if indeed an exception can be found, in classifying population, place laboring men at the bottom, and those who have been the most successful in robbing labor of its rights at the top of the social system, made them the governing class always and invari-ably, seeking by various methods to impoverish and degrade labor. A writer, in

---

† Published in *Locomotive Firemen's Magazine,* vol. 11, no. 8 (August 1887), 454–456.

describing the workingmen's program of the times, goes back to the Middle Ages and finds the same social grades existing as at present, and that

> one grade and one element—the landed interest—dominated all the others. The reason is a simple one—the economic conditions of the time. Agricultural produce was the staple wealth. Trade was but slightly developed, manufacturing still less, and movable possessions were so little thought of in comparison with possession of the soil that chattels were alienable without the consent of the heirs, while property in land was not. Four highly important social consequences resulted from this predominance of the landed interest. First, the feudal system with its obligations of service in the field; second, the limitation of the right of representation to the owners of real estate; third, the exemption of landed proprietors from taxation on the principle that a ruling, privileged class invariably seeks to throw the burden of maintaining the existence of the state on the oppressed classes that have no property; fourth, the contempt with which every labor and profession not connected with the land was socially regarded.[18]

To obtain possession of the land enabled the landowner to rule all other classes. The landed aristocrats were despots, their rule was "blood and iron," and if it be asked, has this rule come down to our times, to our day and generation, it is only required to study affairs as they exist in Ireland and to note the tendency of land monopoly in the United States. The shibboleth of the workingmen of America is not only the equitable distribution of the capital which labor creates, but the equitable division of land, and eternal hostility to land monopoly. It is true that land monopoly in the United States has not met with the stubborn hostility the enormity of the crime against the welfare of the country demands, and this is all the more inexplicable since in the United States the workingmen have the ballot, and by federation could put an end to the monstrous iniquity. Such action is postponed, we assume, for various reasons. In the first place, we are lulled into security because it seems impossible that the vast area of our country admits of anything approximating land monopoly as it exists in European countries. The vastness of our domain seemingly precludes the possibility of land monopoly to an extent that shall at any future time embarrass the people. Such conclusions indicate stupidity, a total ignorance of the growth of population, of the tendencies of the times and of the grasping designs of men who have it in their power under the laws as they exist to obtain possession of the land of the republic. With 60 million people land is already scarce, and when another hundred years are gone, unless laws are enacted against land monopoly, a condition of things will exist in the United States in many regards not dissimilar to those which constituted the colossal curse of the Middle Ages. There is but one thing which can prevent it, and that is the intelligence and the independent action of the workingmen of America. If they fail to comprehend the situation, if they can be hoodwinked by the monopoly press of the country, if they can be debauched by the money power, if they cannot be influenced by considerations as vital as were ever set forth in any campaign for life, liberty, and the pursuit of happiness, then results may be foreshadowed as certainly as if a skeleton hand were to write our doom on the blue vault of the sky. But there are encouraging signs of the times. The government is taking hold of the subject and millions of acres of arable lands are taken from the grasp of monopolists and given back to the people. Apostles of right are coming to the front and the work of agitation is going forward. Public opinion is assuming a more healthful tone and workingmen are federating and "Land, Labor, and Liberty" are becoming battle cries all along the line, and though victory may be delayed,

> Still from the sire the son shall hear
> Of the stern strife,[19]

Until the battle is won and the victor's shout shall be heard, "There is land for the landless."

Child Labor[†]

September 1887

The command to "multiply and replenish the earth"[20] is one that bears about even date with the introduction of the fig leaf costume improvised by Adam and his beautiful spouse. And it may be said, we think, without fear of successful contradiction, that poor men and their wives are exceptionally loyal in their obedience to the heavenly mandate, for in all lands they multiply with astonishing rapidity, and we doubt if many of them will be shut out of Paradise because of disobedience of the command. But dismissing all speculative views upon the subject, what are the facts? Poor men will marry. They usually marry healthy women. The result is a numerous progeny. It so happens that in

---

† Published in *Locomotive Firemen's Magazine*, vol. 11, no. 9 (September 1887), 521–522.

many cases, in the rural districts, where food is abundant and cheap, no special embarrassment is experienced by the parents in rearing their flock. Food is plentiful and, though common, is healthy. The expense of clothing is reduced to the minimum, and as a consequence, the work of multiplying and replenishing the earth goes bravely on. Children are not overworked; they live much of their time in the open air and physically develop into splendid specimens of men and women.

But an entirely different state of affairs exists in towns and cities—except in the matter of multiplying. It does not seem to matter particularly where poor people live or how they live. The multiplying business is always kept up. Under certain conditions the fact would be one of the most agreeable that political economists and statisticians could comment upon, for where children are numerous, well clothed, fed, and sheltered, the three great essentials of prosperity and happiness are supposed to exist, and ordinarily do exist. But where child labor exists as a necessity of living, then the whole aspect of affairs is changed. Under such circumstances it will be found difficult to exaggerate the deplorable surroundings and conditions.

Mr. Arthur T. Hadley of the Connecticut Bureau of Labor Statistics says:

> That the prevalence of child labor indicates a bad state of things hardly needs proof. If a man sends his children to the mills at an early age, it means either that he cannot support his family himself, or that he cares more for a slight increase in his present earnings than for the future welfare of his family. It means that these children are growing up without the advantages of regular education. It means that there is great danger of physical deterioration, and little chance of intellectual improvement. It means an addition to the ranks of unskilled labor at present, at the expense of the higher development of those laborers in the future. It means that the community is more anxious to increase the quantity of its products than the quality of its citizens.[21]

Such a picture. Turn it in any direction, view it from any point, presents to the minds of thoughtful people a state of affairs essentially repulsive. There is not one redeeming feature in it. It is fraught with danger to society and to the state. It must be remembered that it is an American picture, not an English nor a continental European picture. Children of tender years compelled to work to keep themselves in food, to supply clothing and shelter, to keep gaunt hunger from their miserable homes. What are the causes which underlie such terrible effects? Who is responsible for the situation? What is the remedy? The cause is readily found. It is that the father cannot support his family at current wages.

He cannot earn, or, more properly, cannot obtain enough for his work to supply his family with food, clothing, and shelter. But, Mr. Hadley says:

> If a man sends his children to the mills at an early age, it means either that he cannot support his family himself, or that he cares more for a slight increase in his present earnings than for the future welfare of his family.

We think it quite probable there are human monsters who would, for mercenary considerations, compel their children to work when able to support them and send them to school, but we hold that such creatures are exceptions, and yet, were it otherwise, the wretched proceeding might be traced to the experience of the father, which had taught him that no enemy is so relentless as hunger and no friend so good as money, and to secure the friend and circumvent the enemy the sacrifice of the welfare of his children is defensible. After all, the cause of child labor, with all its deplorable consequences, is traceable directly to the fact that the father's wages are below the supporting point, and down to the starvation level. To gloss over the facts, to remove in some measure its hideous aspects, or to shift the responsibility from where it properly belongs, statistics are furnished demonstrating that in Europe, people live on less wages than are paid in the United States, and this is done, presumably, upon the principle that "misery loves company," and that A, because he is starving, will be reconciled to his situation if he knows that others are in like condition.

Legislatures are endeavoring to remedy the evil of child labor by enacting laws with severe penalties attached, forbidding the employment of children under a certain age. Such laws are believed to be philanthropic, and in strict accord with the best interests of society. Nor is this all, but laws are enacted requiring parents to send their children to school. Who is there to question the wisdom of such legislation? But the question arises, if a father cannot support his children by his wages, how can he send them to school, or what benefit is a law which forbids their employment, whereby they are able to live outside of a poorhouse? Manifestly, under such conditions legislation only aggravates the evils it seeks to remove. It might have the effect of sending the mother to the mill and thus with the responsibilities of maternity and physical labor send her to the graveyard some years sooner than would otherwise be the case. Such things may be remedies, but if seriously analyzed they will be found little, if indeed any, better than the disease they are expected to cure.

The wrong, the curse, is that labor is not honestly rewarded. Capital, capitalists, and the pets of capitalists receive more than their just portion of the wealth which labor creates. Labor ought to receive so much as will decently clothe and shelter it. Labor should be able to keep the children out of factories and shops and at school. Children should be so situated as to have full mental and physical development, and this they would have if simple justice was meted out to workingmen.

But the skies are brightening. The night of wrong is disappearing. The sun of justice is rising. The full orbed moon is to come. A baptism of joy is in store for the children of workingmen. The school is doing its work. The newspaper and the magazine, the pulpit and the rostrum are coming to the rescue, and more than all, the ballot will inaugurate a peaceful revolution, and the truth and the right are to prevail.

The work of multiplying and replenishing the earth is to proceed, and the children are to have an abundance of food and clothing in this free and heaven-favored land.

Notes

1. Stephen A. Douglas (1813–1861) was a pro-Union Democratic senator who ran against Abraham Lincoln in the election of 1860.
2. Speech at Pennsylvania Hall, Philadelphia, May 15, 1838. The hall was destroyed by a mob two days later.
3. Deuteronomy 26:4.
4. The National Typographical Union was formally established in 1852.
5. Concluding stanza of "A Psalm of Life" (1838) by Henry Wadsworth Longfellow (1807–1882).
6. The quotation is from the book *Character* (1871), by Samuel Smiles (1812–1904), and was excerpted in *The Canadian Monthly and National Review*, vol. 3, no. 1 (January 1873), 64–75. The line "In idleness alone is there perpetual despair" was extracted without credit by *Smiles from Past and Present* (1843), by Thomas Carlyle (1795–1881).
7. From "Man Was Made to Mourn: A Dirge" (1784), by Robert Burns (1759–1796).
8. Apparently a reference to Henry Darling, *The Use and Abuse of the Greatness of Man: A Baccalaureate Sermon* (June 18, 1885), which adapts Psalm 8:5. The original King James version reads: "For thou hast made him a little lower than the angels, and hast crowned him with glory and honour."
9. Allusion to the rich man in the story of Lazarus from Luke 16:19–31.
10. Exodus 20:15.
11. A mill is the smallest unit of American currency, defined as one-tenth of one cent.
12. The source of this poem is unknown.
13. "Compensation," by Ralph Waldo Emerson (1803–1882), first appeared in the volume *Essays* in 1841.
14. Slight variation of Matthew 26:11, John 12:8, and Mark 14:7. The rendition in Matthew is "For ye have the poor always with you; but me ye have not always."
15. From Matthew 23:14.
16. Proverbs 30:8.
17. One of Debs's favorite Latin expressions, meaning "final outpost." Thule was a far northern location that was part of ancient mapmaking, frequently rendered as an island on the borders of the known world.
18. Although presented as a direct quotation, this is actually an extract from the pamphlet *The Working Man's Programme* (1884), by Ferdinand Lassalle (1825–1864), 6–9.
19. Snippet from *Marmion: A Tale of Flodden Field* (1808) by Walter Scott (1771–1832).
20. From Genesis 1:28.
21. Arthur T. Hadley, Second Annual Report of the Bureau of Labor Statistics of the State of Connecticut for the Year Ending November 30, 1886 (Hartford, CT: Case, Lockwood, and Barnard, 1886), xvi.

1888

Joining Labor Organizations[†]
March 1888

The population of the United States and the Dominion of Canada may be set down at 65 million. Of this vast number we will suppose 10 million are wage-men, men dependent upon their muscle and skill for support. In this estimate we make no pretensions to accuracy: we state a round number for convenience, though possibly not far from the fact. The present is prominently distinguished for labor organizations. There are brotherhoods and unions, guilds, associations, etc., indefinitely.

The *Locomotive Firemen's Magazine* is an advocate of labor organizations. It is the official organ of one of the great and prosperous labor organizations of the times. The Brotherhood of Locomotive Firemen has demonstrated, beyond cavil, that it has a mission, and that it comprehends fully its sphere and its duties. During all the years of its existence it has been a student of events. It has learned in the school of experience, and with miserly care has garnered and guarded the treasures of wisdom which experience always secures, and the conclusion we have arrived at is that locomotive firemen act wisely by becoming members of the brotherhood and remaining true to the obligations they voluntarily and solemnly entered into. Were the task required and had we time and space, we could easily show in many hundreds of instances the benefits that have accrued to firemen and their families, by virtue of faithful membership to the brotherhood. And we assume, indeed we know, that in labor organizations, when wisdom and prudence hold sway in their government, benefits of incalculable value are the certain and legitimate fruits of the association.

But it must be remembered that all the workingmen of the United States and Canada are not members of labor organizations; not a majority of them are on the rolls of brotherhoods or organizations of any name. Why? Simply because they do not so choose, so elect. They prefer to remain outside. In referring to this fact, we have neither the right nor the inclination to be censorious. In fact, that they so choose is nobody's business but their own. The right to choose is our individual right, as sacred as the right to think or speak. It is a right every man exercises when he joins a labor organization or any other organization. To seek to impose any penalty whatsoever upon men who choose

---

† Published in *Locomotive Firemen's Magazine,* vol. 12, no. 3 (March 1888), 164–165.

to become members of such organizations or who decide not to join them is an outrage of monstrous proportions, which cannot be, will not be, and ought not to be tolerated. And yet such penalties are imposed and are creating denunciatory comment, far and wide. The subject is well worthy of the most careful consideration—indeed, it is up for debate, and will not down at any man's bidding, nor ought it to be tabooed. It is one of the important questions of the age. It should be subjected to the severest analysis.

The question is, has a man the right to choose for himself whether he will or will not join a labor organization? With one voice, then, comes the answer, "Yes." No man, no set of men, no government has a right to say no. The right is inherent and unalienable. It is a primal right, and can be cloven down only by despots, and only despots will impose any penalty whatever for the full, free exercise of that right. If a man desires to join a labor organization, who shall say "nay?" Who has a right to say "nay?" Who shall impose a penalty for this exercise of free will, his unalienable right to choose? What is the penalty, too often imposed? Not prisons and stripes. No, but loss of work, all too often. On the other hand, what has been the penalties imposed, when a man, exercising his unalienable right to choose, to decide for himself declines to become a member of a labor organization? Again, the penalty has been the loss of work. Ostracized and exiled, he has found himself an idler and a tramp. Manifestly, there is no right side of such things. There is nothing to be said in their justification. There is no element of justice or fair dealing in such a condition of things, and hence there is but one course left for those who would deal justly with men, and that is to expose such wrongs and seek to do away with them.

We would keep no honest man from obtaining a day's work; such an act is a crime against life and health. It is a crime that breeds idleness, hunger pangs, starvation—a crime that denies a man shelter and a bed. It may not be a crime known to the statutes, but it nevertheless is a crime. It touches the most sacred of individual rights and is a crime against society, peace, and order. When a man wants work, when he offers his strength and skill for the necessities of life, in the name of all that is sacred in life, liberty, and the pursuit of happiness, let him have it without hindrance and without penalty.

If workingmen who join unions and brotherhoods can persuade others to join, well and good, but there should be no coercion, enmity, or penalty if men choose to remain independent of such organizations; it is a matter of choice and no penalty should attach. And, on the other hand, if men choose to join labor organizations, seek to improve their condition and advance their interests, they should be encouraged, rather than have obstacles placed in their way or be made to pay any penalty whatever. In all such matters there is a commonsense view to be taken of them, but above all things, let it be the universal sentiment that no penalty shall attach for the exercise of an unquestioned right.

Federation, the Lesson of the Great Strike[†]
April 1888

A railroad strike creates intense and widespread excitement and alarm. It is not surprising. The railroads of the country, now estimated at 148,000 miles of track, and costing $8 billion (or are capitalized at that amount—practically the same thing), constitute the highways of traffic and transportation, and any serious disturbance in their operation produces at once incalculable calamities. It dwarfs the subject to discuss the various systems, since all roads, by their connection, constitute one great system, and any serious disturbance anywhere is more or less disastrous everywhere. Governor Martin of Kansas[1] is credited with saying

> All the commercial and industrial pursuits of the people have been adjusted to the carrying trade of the railways. Block the wheels of the Kansas railways for one week, and nine-tenths of all the mills and factories of the state would lie compelled to close. Block them for three weeks, and every commercial and agricultural pursuit in Kansas would be paralyzed.

What is true of Kansas is equally true of every other state in the Union. Such self-evident truths do not demand discussion. As a consequence, the first lesson taught by the great strike is that the whole people are profoundly interested in all that pertains to its inception and progress as they will be in the final results of the disturbance.

It may be assumed, we think, that the great body of the people, being aroused by the great strike, will insist upon knowing definitely the causes which led up to it and, since their interests are jeopardized, will, as they have a right to do, discuss remedies that shall in the future act as guarantees against disagreements which in their effect are fatal to the prosperity of the country. And we do

---

† Published in *Locomotive Firemen's Magazine,* vol. 12, no. 4 (April 1888), 246–248.

not hesitate to assert our belief that the people will favor such remedies only as will do full justice to the parties immediately involved in the controversy, viz.: employer and employee. But the faith of the people must, of necessity, be largely dependent upon the information which the people have relating to matters in dispute. Hence, the great strike emphasizes the importance of furnishing the people with the facts, clear-cut and bedrock. But the great strike has taught the strikers the lesson that the press cannot be relied upon to furnish such information. It is always found in alliance with corporate interests and opposed to strikers. We speak of the rule, and not of the exceptions, and this fact brings into bold prominence another lesson taught by the great strike. It is this: if corporations and the press confederate to overwhelm workingmen when they demand redress for grievances, they too must federate to enforce their rights, which corporations deny them when demands are made in a becoming manner.

It goes without saying that there exists a strong bond of union between railroad corporations when the demands of their employees are for an equitable share of the wealth they create, the theory being that in the matter of wages corporations shall always determine the rate, regardless of the rights and interests of the wageworker, and instances are rare in which, as a right, employees have been consulted. And if a case can be found in which wages are even approximately fair, it will be discovered upon investigation to be the result, if not of a stoke, of latent forces which could have been called into operation if the demand had been ignored.

Another lesson taught by the great strike, and one which should be profoundly studied by railroad employees, is that since railroad corporations federate, coalesce, when any effort is made to advance wages on the part of any one of the brotherhoods of railroad workers, a similar federation is indispensable on the part of all the brotherhoods when, as a last resort, a strike is ordered. As in the one case it is found that the corporations federate against the workers, it becomes supreme folly to expect success if one brotherhood is left to fight the battle singlehanded. And the contest invites federation from the fact that the question of fair equitable pay is alike vital to all. It is the question of labor vs. corporate power and injustice, and in this every worker is equally interested. It is a question in which the interest of one is the interest of all. If wage-men doubt the proposition, so far as they are concerned, they have only to contemplate the fact that corporations act upon that principle, which has been given special emphasis since the CB&Q strike, which we denominate the great strike, was inaugurated.

If strength is found in unity, it needs no argument to prove that weakness is in alliance with division, and this fact being fully comprehended by corporations, it will be well for all the brotherhoods of railroad workers to give it due consideration, and if, upon reflection, it is found, as it surely will be found, that success lies in federation, no time should be lost in forming an alliance, offensive and defensive, by virtue of which justice would be secured and strikes would at once and forever disappear.

We deem it prudent to suggest that preliminary to such a federation of brotherhood railroad workers there must be a recognition of mutual interest—all brotherhoods must stand on the same plane. The idea of superiority and inferiority must be dismissed. The motto must be "United we stand; divided we fall." For purposes of protection the throttle and the scoop, the switch and the brake must be in close alliance and equally firm and defiant, and when corporations see this federation accomplished no strike will occur, because a strike under such circumstances would mean an immediate cessation of railroad transportation on the line or system where it occurred. Instead of a strike there would be arbitration, a patient consideration of grievances when presented, and a prompt application of remedies when found.

Of all the lessons taught by the great strike, not one, as we view the situation, is of more importance than the one which emphasizes the wisdom of a compact federation of engineers, firemen, switchmen, and brakemen for mutual protection when their rights and interests are involved, because the question of honest pay for honest work is a supreme question in which all are involved, and here we repeat that the wisdom of such a federation cannot be questioned by railroad corporations, since they federate for mutual protection against labor when it complains of unjust treatment at their hands.

We are not unmindful of the fact that strikes of railroad employees are disastrous. We need not to be reminded of their cost in sum totals of dollars, nor the sufferings they entail upon those who, to secure justice at the hands of corporations, accept the sacrifice with heroic devotion to right. We would have a settlement of every dispute without a resort to extreme measures. We would have employer and employee meet amicably and in a spirit of fairness adjust every grievance. We would have employers recognize their employees as men upon whom vast and exacting responsibilities devolve, and without whose services railroad operations would cease as certainly as if by a decree of Jehovah. Nor would we have employees demand more than their rights, tested by any standard which might be accepted as embodying approximate justice, but we would have employees consulted in all such matters and their consent obtained because, while recognizing to the fullest extent the power and value of capital in carrying forward the enterprises of the day, we know that it is inert and powerless until vitalized and set in motion by labor.

Viewing the subject from such standpoints, we venture the prediction that the day is near at hand when the brotherhoods of railroad employees will federate for mutual protection, and we further predict that when such a federation is perfected, railroad strikes will be numbered among things of the past. It will not be a federation against capital, but, on the contrary, a federation seeking a closer alliance with capital—an alliance which will be just to all parties concerned, an alliance in which arbitration, mutual concessions, shall take the place of strikes, a federation for the purpose of investigating for justice, of enthroning the right, which may be found if the seekers are in earnest, and which when found and established exiles jealousy and distrust and inaugurates peace, contentment, and prosperity. Federation means victory for the right, and the great strike on the CB&Q has brought its necessity into such bold relief that its advocacy becomes a duty and its consummation will be fraught with incalculable blessings, not only to employees, but to employers, to society, and to the whole country.

The Policy of the Order of Railway Conductors[†]
May 1888

In writing of the policy of the Order of Railway Conductors, we are animated by a desire to place prominently before the readers of the *Magazine* such reflections based upon facts as will result in a broader comprehension of the relations existing between railroad employers and railroad employees. That we write of the policy of the ORC, is because papers of late date contain extracts from reports purporting to be the official utterances of Mr. Calvin S. Wheaton,[2] grand chief conductor, and Mr. William P. Daniels,[3] grand secretary and treasurer of the order.

These official documents contain declarations and expressions the objectionable character of which we are not required to magnify to obtain for them a careful perusal by railroad employees who are not members of the ORC, and this perusal will, we think, be accorded all the more certainly because the documents referred to indicate a total lack of sympathy on the part of the writers

† Published as "The Policy of the ORC" in *Locomotive Firemen's Magazine,* vol. 12, no. 5 (May 1888), 325–328.

for all railroad employees who are not members of the ORC.

In our readings, associations, and experience, we fail to recall any fact in the history of conductors in any wise calculated to lift them to such sublime altitudes that they cannot, without soiling their clothes, fraternize and sympathize with other railroad employees. We have failed to discover any good reason why Messrs. Wheaton and Daniels should, in making their official reports to the order, secretly forward them to railroad managers in advance, unless it be, as has been suggested, to gain some consideration in the eyes of railroad managers by playing the role of abject sycophants, than which there is nothing more repulsive in the estimation of all honorable men. We reproduce from a paper at hand the following extracts from Grand Chief Conductor Wheaton's utterances that our readers may at their leisure bestow upon them merited comment, and that we may have unquestioned foundation for such criticisms as we shall deem prudent. Grand Chief Conductor Wheaton, in referring to the strike on the CB&Q system, says:

> The "Q" Company have all the engineers they want, and they are all old, experienced men. They are doing good work, and as soon as they learn the road they will do as good work as those who have just left the service. There has not been an engine burned by these men, nor an accident happened, although the press is full of such reports. They are nearly all men with families and have come here to stay, and are now looking around for houses to rent so as to be able to move their families here. They cannot be bought off; the CB&Q officers are satisfied with and intend to keep them. Any engineers formerly in the service who report for work, should the company see fit to reemploy them, must take places behind all those now in the employ of the company and be considered new or extra men, no concession will be granted them, and few, if any, will ever be taken back.[4]

It is notorious that the statements volunteered by Mr. Wheaton in the interest of the "Q" are without foundation in fact, and this must have been known to Mr. Wheaton when he made them. The "Q" has not all the engineers it wants, nor are those it has in any sense competent or reliable. On the contrary, they are known to be incompetent, deficient in every quality of head and heart required for the responsible position of engineers. They have been hunted up from the degraded haunts of idleness and vagabondage, and put in charge of locomotives in flagrant disregard of every consideration of propriety, and it is such facts that make the "circular," or report, of Mr. Wheaton a calculatingly devised mass of untruths, and the managers of the "Q" system, unless irredeemably depraved, cannot but regard such statements as a fawning overture on the part of Chief Wheaton for recognition which hitherto has been denied.

The real animus of Mr. Wheaton's "circular," or report, is found in the following extract, in which will be discovered in combination an exhibition of selfishness and jealousy, characteristic only of men who are born parasites, ready at any time to disrobe themselves of the prerogatives of manhood if thereby they can advance in any degree their own selfish ends. Chief Wheaton says:

> We can assure you that the Order of Railway Conductors have made a great record for faithfulness and loyalty to principle by its members among railway officers. To say that we are surprised at the feelings expressed by some members of the order in other parts of the country who appear to sympathize with the engineers in this trouble is but placing it mildly. This is not a fight between capital and labor, but one between right and wrong, as all know that the engineers are the best paid class of men on the railroad, and they are today receiving pay that is justly due the conductor. The public have been educated that they were the responsible person on the train, and the conductor merely a figurehead, while we know that modern appliances are being placed upon our engines that greatly reduce the need of unusual skill that may have been required in days gone by to handle this machine, while the conductor's duties are continually growing more arduous and complicated. The engineer has no interests that are identical with ours. They court our friendship to enable them to secure the transportation of their members with us, and to show their feelings, as a class, we insert a portion of a resolution adopted by them at a union meeting held in Kansas City recently, and which we believe fully expresses their sentiments that "the difference between a scab engineer and a conductor who pilots him over the road is so small that a microscope is not strong enough to find it, and after this matter is settled we will refuse to pull a train that is handled by an ORC conductor."

In the foregoing is seen a purpose to promote the interests of conductors by assailing the character, skill, and responsibilities of engineers, and the strange announcement is made that engineers are overpaid, and that the excess of payments over earnings is taken from the pay of conductors, the idea being that the pay of engineers should be reduced and that of conductors advanced.

Now it may be, and doubtless is true, that conductors are not paid as much as they are entitled to, and the reason for this injustice is, we think, easily found. In every effort made on the part of railroad employees to secure fair wages, the Order of Railway Conductors take the side of the railroad officials and antagonize the employees, which Mr. Wheaton calls "faithfulness and loyalty to principle," but according to Mr. Wheaton's statement, so far this "loyalty to principle" has not resulted satisfactorily in the way of pay, and it is not surprising, as Mr.

Wheaton states, that "some members of the order appear to sympathize with the engineers," an intimation that there are conductors who believe that the way to obtain justice at the hands of railroad corporations is not that which is pursued by Mr. Wheaton. When engineers, firemen, switchmen, or brakemen demand higher wages, it is supremely unbecoming on the part of conductors to take their places for the purpose of aiding the roads in their efforts to defeat the demands of their underpaid employees, and as a general proposition officials, while willing and eager to accept such services, regard those who perform them as men quite incapable of that sort of self-assertion, without which, in this age, a man becomes a mere appendage, and wanting in those traits of character which are conspicuous in other men who know their rights and dare demand and defend them.

The purpose of Mr. Daniels, the grand secretary of the ORC, in his report sent out to managers of railroads in advance, was to inform these magnates "in order that the position of the order in regard to labor troubles and strikes in general, and the strikes of engineers in particular, shall be fully understood." It was scarcely necessary. Railroad managers and railroad employees are fully posted in regard to the position occupied by the ORC.

Mr. Daniels tells the railroad managers that the position taken by the ORC is not owing to any "love for railway companies." He tells the managers that conductors realize that injustice has been done them, and that this is all the more grievous considering the "loyalty of conductors to corporations in time of trouble." This loyalty is not the result of any "philanthropic feeling" toward railway companies, but to keep other railway employees from obtaining fair wages, because such a course would place it out of the power of railway companies to give to "conductors the recognition and remuneration they believe they are entitled to." There may be a lower plane of selfishness than that which Mr. Daniels outlines and sends to railway managers for their approval, but it will be difficult to find, and it is not surprising that there are a large number of members of the ORC who have discovered the inherent viciousness of a policy which, while it does not secure justice for those who practice it, is well calculated to injure others who are striving to obtain fair wages. Mr. Daniels says a majority of the membership of the ORC favor the policy of fealty to the corporations and the resistance of all other employees who seek to improve their condition by obtaining fair wages, but, he says, a minority that has been steadily increasing for the past five years are weary of waiting and in favor of changing the entire plan of the association in the hope of present gain and regardless of ultimate results, and he adds, with a threat to railway managers, if certain things are not done, that within the next five years this *minority* of the membership will have control of the ORC and change its policy. In that event the ORC would at once be entitled to the respect of all classes of railway employees. It would cease to be a fawning, cringing, abject organization at the feet of railway managers. It would dismiss its real or fancied causes of complaint against locomotive engineers, and dismissing its present fawning chief and bringing a man of broad and liberal views to the front, would be accorded its rightful place in the family of railroad fraternities. The "minority" of whom Mr. Daniels speaks are even now in full accord with the spirit of the times. They are evidently bold and aggressive men who believe that all classes of railroad employees are underpaid, and that the right way to proceed is to demand justice at the hands of railway corporations and manfully contend for the right.

Mr. Daniels intimates to the railway managers that a suggestion has recently been made relating to a federation of all the railroad fraternities. He tells the managers that "such an alliance is being widely advocated by all other classes of men employed in their service and by some conductors; the more intelligent of the conductors look to the future and wish no such an alliance with other organizations," but if conductors are made to feel that the opinion given to them in so many words by one railway officer, that "the engineers, firemen, and brakemen must be taken care of or they will strike, but we are not afraid of you because you can't strike," is general, such alliance will come as certain as death despite the present majority. Mr. Daniels's idea, evidently, is that the railway managers, to keep the ORC out of the alliance, will at once advance the wages of conductors. Such childish confidence may be beautiful, but it will not pan out to the advantage of the conductors. But such a federation as Mr. Daniels speaks of is one of the certainties of the near future, and the sooner it comes the better.

It is no part of our business to defend locomotive engineers from the attacks made by the conductors; the engineers are eminently able to take care of themselves, and according to Grand Chief [Peter M.] Arthur, the charges made by Messrs. Wheaton and Daniels are beneath contempt.

In writing this article we have no desire, even were it within our power, to dwarf the ORC, and we are glad to know that there is a large minority of its membership whose views manifestly coincide with ours upon labor questions, and we hail with special pleasure the probability that the minority will at no distant day expand to the majority, and this done we are satisfied that when switchmen or brakemen strike, conductors will not as in the past on two notable occasions take their places for the purpose of defeating just demands. According to our view of such matters, when a conductor takes the place of another man who is seeking to obtain fair pay, he is wanting in those essentials of manhood universally recognized among honorable men.

In every instance when a strike occurs there is a reason for it, and when it is found that the reason is sound and that the cause of the employee is just, the men are entitled to the support of society and, above all things, they should have the support of workingmen who are dependent upon their daily wages for support.

The CB&Q strike will end in the victory or the defeat of the engineers and firemen, but whatever may be the result, the lesson learned will not be forgotten—and as he who laughs last laughs best, if defeat should be the verdict, there will come a time when strike and victory will be synonymous terms.

The Great Strike[†]

May 1888

In the April [1888] *Magazine* we had an article captioned "The CB&Q Strike," which we designated as "the great strike."[5] In closing the article we said:

> As we write the strike is still on, and no one can predict final results, but we deem it prudent to say that the loyalty of the men to honest conviction demands the highest praise. Prudent, conservative, and anxious to work, they realized that the officials of the CB&Q were studiously and steadfastly denying them honest pay for honest work—belittling them as compared with employees on other roads and denying them consideration when their grievances were set forth in a way demanding prompt and patient consideration. Under such circumstances the men behaved like veterans under fire. Their rights and their manhood were at stake, and they would yield nothing that could, by any possible construction, be regarded as conceding what was justly their due—and whatever may be the final result, the men will have maintained their integrity and will have demonstrated that their courage was equal to their convictions.

More than a month has elapsed since the strike was inaugurated. It is still on, nor are there any indications of its immediate termination. On the

† Published in *Locomotive Firemen's Magazine,* vol. 12, no. 5 (May 1888), 322–324.

contrary, the strike is daily developing new phases and is steadily extending to other roads.

Manifestly, we were not mistaken in referring to the strike as "the great strike"; such is to be its position in the history of the labor troubles of the times, and it is eminently becoming and important that working men shall fully understand the strike from inception to triumph or defeat. And here let it be said that the locomotive engineers and firemen originally involved in the strike have at no time underestimated the gravity of the situation. They knew their grievances were just and upon general principles they had a right to believe that the officials of the CB&Q would deal justly by them. In a manly way they presented their grievances. They had patiently borne the wrongs complained of for years. They were competent and faithful men. They had proven themselves worthy of the confidence of their employer. They believed their grievances well founded in fact and their demands just. In presenting their grievances, and in demanding remedies, there was no precipitation. Every move was the result of calculating deliberation. Repulse did not dishearten them. They made concessions and exhausted expedients, and struck only when every consideration of right, justice, honor, and manhood impelled them to take the step.

Such reflections may be deemed unnecessary, but they are bedrock facts in the history of the strike and should be vivid in the mind of every engineer and fireman in the country. There must be no question relating to the absolute justice of the strike. If the men who went out were wrong, if their grievances were unworthy of consideration, equivalent to no grievance at all, no amount of writing can make the strike anything but a stupendous mistake, but if the grievances were well founded, if the demands of the men were just and equitable, then the strike dignifies the men who are engaged in it, and the more stubborn their resistance of wrong, the more defiant their attitude, and the greater their sacrifices in the cause of right, the more they expand to the full stature of men and citizens, and the more they are entitled to the sympathy and support of the brotherhoods whose principles they maintain.

It is a fact worthy of note and reflection that the press, as a general proposition, has antagonized the rights and interests of the engineers and firemen, while it has championed the course pursued by the officials of the CB&Q. This is not a surprise, since on all occasions the press takes the side of the corporation when labor complains of injustice. There are honorable exceptions, but the rule is as we have stated it, and hence we have heard through the press from the very first that the CB&Q had won the fight, and that business on their system was proceeding smoothly, that trains were running regularly, and that the places of the strikers had been filled, and thus on to the end of the chapter of statements totally devoid of truth, sent broadcast over the country to poison the public mind against the men and to aid the corporation to perfect its nefarious policy of injustice to men, the length and breadth, the height and depth of whose offending was the demand for a fair day's wages for a fair day's work.

But there is a phase of this press championship of the corporation and this disgraceful antagonism of workingmen which defies exaggeration. The position taken by the press is scarcely less than criminal. It would have the public believe that the men who have taken the places of the strikers on the CB&Q are competent and trustworthy, when the statement is known to be notoriously false—the CB&Q having been driven to the direst extremity to obtain men at all, and having accepted the services of engineers notoriously unqualified, have placed the traveling public in peril by the employment of such characters.

It is well known that the CB&Q system has paid already a terrible penalty in the loss of business and the wreckage of rolling stock for its flagrant injustice to its former employees. Its interests in every department have suffered. Its stock is without market value and its earnings are not sufficient to pay expenses. It is today a financial wreck, and its chief officials have been placed upon record in court proceedings showing them to be capable of business methods characteristic of freebooters.

The arraignment of the CB&Q by the general manager of the Rock Island road, Mr. E. St. John, has exposed the knavish schemes of its officials and placed upon record the fact that they favored a strike to obscure a conspiracy, the purpose of which was not only to injure competing lines but to oppress and defraud their employees.

Nothing could be more preposterous than to assert the triumph of the CB&Q. It has not been at any time, since the engineers and firemen left its service, more demoralized than at present. It is losing money by the millions. Its officials are losing character and credit. In their frantic efforts to maintain a semblance of business, they are forced to resort to deception and falsehood. Their engines are being wrecked, their traffic has fallen off, their cars are sidetracked, and ruin stares them in the face.

To add to the embarrassments of the CB&Q, the switchmen, whose labors, always arduous and dangerous, are made indefinitely more perilous by incompetent engineers, refused to continue in its employment. They refused to work for a corporation which had less regard for the safety of its men than it exhibited for the security of mules, and they demanded that competent men should be employed, thereby reducing the chances of death and mutilation.

The officials of the CB&Q, in refusing the reasonable request of their switchmen, evinced a heartless brutality strictly in consonance with their treatment of engineers and firemen.

As we write the strike is still on. It is as vigorous and as defiant as on the 27th day of February [1888], when it began, notwithstanding the vaporing declarations of a subsidized press that the engineers and firemen have been vanquished.

We are not unmindful of the strength of corporations, nor of the fact that the wrong has all too often triumphed over the right, and it may be that in the struggle with the CB&Q, in alliance with other powerful corporations and aided by the influence of a venal press, workingmen will be required to retire from the contest, to nurse their misfortunes with such philosophical composure as they can command; but that time has not yet come—nor is it, we conjecture, in the near future. In the desperate game the CB&Q has chosen to play, it does not hold all the winning cards. In the battle now being waged, it does not command all the strategic positions. The edict has gone forth that CB&Q cars must be isolated. The system is to be hedged about by a power which, when fully exerted, will leave it alone in its moral and financial ruin. Even now, the system so strong and arrogant that was unmindful of the penalties which sooner or later overtake prosperity based upon perfidy is reading the handwriting of the skeleton finger of fate on the walls of its depots and the dead walls along its lines. It is now, like the boy passing the graveyard, whistling to keep up its courage. Its language is that of bravado, and while a parasitic press proclaims victory for the road, the facts show that decay and demoralization have seized upon its business and property and that death is inevitable if it does not speedily change its policy.

On the other hand, the engineers and firemen, convinced of the righteousness of their cause, were never more confident. From Canada to Mexico, from the Pine Tree state to the Golden Gate, from the inland seas to the gulf, from ocean to ocean, 50,000 brotherhood men are pledged by considerations radiant with love and truth, honor and manhood, to stand by their brethren, comrades of their mystic fraternities, to work for them and to make sacrifices for them, because by so doing they are dignifying labor and magnifying justice.

It may be—indeed, it is probable—that the strike will spread. Who will be responsible? The engineers and firemen stand before the world saying to an arrogant corporation, "Pay us fair wages—and to determine what is fair wages, let there be arbitration, and we will abide the issue." Such is self-evidently fair, honorable, and just to all parties. Heaven could offer nothing more in consonance with uprightness. Why is it that the press does not see the righteousness of such a demand? Why is it that other corporations whose interests are involved do not say to the CB&Q, "Be just"? To do an act of simple justice to men, citizens, not serfs, would settle the trouble in an hour. To withhold this act of justice is replete with peril—and the responsibility, by a decree which will be irrevocable, will rest upon those who prefer ruin to the reign of right.

Other brotherhoods of workingmen besides engineers and firemen are coming to the rescue. They see that the strike involves a principle vital to their own welfare as men and brotherhoods—and in this voluntary federation for the good of all, there is moral grandeur that defies hyperbole.

We profess no powers of prophecy; we are not the student of vagaries, but we have a right to discuss the signs of the times; we have a right to anticipate coming events, and exercising this right, we indulge the conviction that the strikers will win the fight, and at any rate, whatever may be the outcome, we realize that the brotherhoods, whatever may be lost or won, will never have cause for reproach that they put forth their strength in a cause which not only involved their own welfare, but the best interests of society.

The Scab[†]

May 1888

Philosophers, particularly those who have sought to solve the simpler mysteries of creation, have always been greatly perplexed when endeavoring to find any plausible reason for the existence of certain insects and reptiles which curse the earth, the air, and the water. They have never succeeded. The mystery is unexplained and unexplainable. But while it is impossible to explain the whys and the wherefores of repulsive, pestiferous, and poisonous creatures, we may study their habits and guard against contact with them.

It becomes our duty at this writing to discuss the "scab." Generally, people quickly comprehend what is meant when a creature, in the form of a man, is referred to as a "scab." Shakespeare says a scab is a "low fellow"[6]—how low, the great bard does not intimate, but he doubtless believed that a scab was the

† Published in *Locomotive Firemen's Magazine*, vol. 12, no. 5 (May 1888), 335.

lowest in the list of bipeds. The term "scab" has a significance wholly repulsive. It is suggestive of filth, disease, and corruption. There is nothing in the term "scab" to redeem it from loathing. When a creature, in the form of a man, rightfully receives the sobriquet of "scab," he is known to be a mass of moral putrescence. He sinks to the level of a loathsome reptile. Honorable men shun him as they would a pestilence. A scabby sheep, a mangy dog, outrank him. He becomes a walking, breathing stench. He is as destitute of soul as a dungeon toad. He is as heartless as a man-eating tiger. He has no more conscience than a tarantula. To call him a dog would be an insult to the whole canine race.

The average scab is a moral leper, unclean through and through, so vulgar and beastly in his instincts that he is as destitute of all sense of obligation, of what is due to others, as a hungry hog with its snout in a swill tub. The scab is a sneak—analyze him, resolve him to his original elements, and all the subtle arts of the chemist would never discover the millionth part of a milligram of manhood. A scab is as totally deficient of ability to comprehend the right as a piratical wolf. Being depraved by nature and association, he has no more ambition than a buzzard. When he sees a manly endeavor on the part of others to better their condition, the incident simply suggests to his mind that there is a chance for him, and with his hat under his arm and with bowed form he asks, like a menial, to work for wages that an honorable man refuses. The scab always comes to the front when honest workingmen strike against oppression and injustice. On such occasions employers fish for scabs in the stinking pools of idleness and depravity, and they are ready to do their duty for such considerations as their masters may offer. The scab is a filthy wretch who, though the Mississippi ran bank-full of soapsuds, could not wash him clean in a thousand years.

The scab is the natural-born foe of labor in its efforts to advance from the condition of servitude to independence, and such he has been found to be in the struggle of the engineers and firemen with the CB&Q, and he is destined to play the same degenerate role in the future. The scab merits universal reprobation, and that will be the verdict of all honorable men.

The Record of the CB&Q Strike[†]

June 1888

History must be made before it is written. In this age of lightning and steam, it is about all the daily press can do to record incidents as they occur. From the *Firemen's Magazine,* published monthly, all that can be expected is that important events having a bearing upon the interests of the brotherhood it represents shall be recorded as a matter of history, and especially is it required that every important feature of the CB&Q strike shall have due prominence. So far, the *Magazine* bears testimony to the fact that nothing important has been overlooked, and at this writing our purpose is to show that while the engineers and firemen have not won the battle, they have not sustained a defeat, and that if the soulless corporation has gained any advantage over them, it has been at such a fearful cost of money, such a loss of business, as to amount to a notable defeat, and as nearly as we can approximate the facts, we propose to demonstrate the absolute truth of our propositions.

It goes without the saying that on the 27th of February, 1888, the CB&Q system was rich, powerful, and prospering. True it was mercenary and unjust towards its employees and managed by a system of classification and other adroit schemes, in the concocting of which its officials are experts, to rob its engineers and firemen of at least $200,000 annually, money they had honestly earned.

On the 27th of February, when the strike was inaugurated, the fortunes of the system began to wane—nor have they ceased to decline from that day to the present. Demoralization, disaster, wreck, and ruin are everywhere observable throughout the entire system. The latest authoritative advices show a fearful wreckage of engines, and in but one locality is the road doing 50 percent of the business it had previous to the strike, and elsewhere 30 percent is the highest estimate made. The traveling public, as far as practicable, avoid its trains, and shippers seek other channels of transportation, and in the open market its stock has been hammered down until the decline represents millions. Those in a position to know aggregate the losses of the CB&Q system since the strike at $5 million, and this amount, it is contended, is below rather than above the amount the strike, so far, has cost the road. If it be accepted as approximately true that to have acceded to the demands of the engineers and firemen it would have cost the

---

† Published in *Locomotive Firemen's Magazine,* vol. 12, no. 6 (June 1888), 402–403.

corporation $200,000 a year more than it was paying them, then it follows that the losses already sustained by the corporation would have been sufficient to pay the additional wages demanded for 25 years. That we do not exaggerate the situation it is only required to consult any prudent railroad manager in the country and the reply will be heard that upon any system of the magnitude of the CB&Q, a bonus of $5 million would be no temptation to pass through such an ordeal.

Not only has the CB&Q lost money and lost business, but it has lost character, lost standing, lost prestige. The traveling public is aware that its engineers and firemen are characterless and incompetent—men raked up from the slums—and people will not, when they can avoid it, take the unusual risks of traveling on its trains; and as shippers have no guarantee that their goods will reach their destination, shipments, when it is possible, are made by other routes. Everywhere on the system engines are smashed and dead, roundhouses are full of wrecks, passengers are few, and freight is scarce, and as a consequence trains are discontinued, even when scabs stand ready to run them. Under such circumstances, losses already sustained, though alarming to every stockholder, are not all they will be required to face, for it is true that when a railroad has earned a reputation as infamous as that which the CB&Q has secured, it requires years to regain its standing, and it is to be doubted if the CB&Q, under the management that has wrecked it, can ever be reinstated in public confidence.

The investigation conducted by the Warehouse and Railway Commission of Illinois found its engineers and firemen incompetent, and now the Interstate Commerce Commissioners propose to unearth some of its shameful methods and expose the mismanagement of its officials.

In grouping all these facts, what is the conclusion? It is this: the two great brotherhoods of engineers and firemen have established beyond controversy the justice and righteousness of their demands, and the word has gone forth that they are men who have the courage of conviction and who are willing to make sacrifices to maintain their cause before the world.

As we write, the strike is still on—the men are firm. What the final result will be we do not know, but this: whatever may ensue, we can say, every page of the record is luminous with the facts that engineers and firemen who were the victims of the unequal struggle have no cause for blushing. Their honor is unstained. Their manhood, their fealty to obligations and to every demand of citizenship, redeems them from obloquy, and their brethren who have stood by them have added dignity and imperishable glory to the principles of brotherhood. The word may not have a new meaning, but it means more than ever before in the history of the two brotherhoods.

It has a wider sweep, a loftier significance. They are not vanquished, nor jostled, nor deflected from their upward and onward course, and whatever may be the result of the strike, the brotherhood banners are not trailing in the dust.

Federation of Labor Organizations for Mutual Protection[†]
June 1888

In advocating the federation of labor organizations for mutual protection, we shall state as definitely as possible our reasons and shall seek to state propositions which we believe will stand the test of the severest scrutiny. The wealth of nations is created by work—without work there is no wealth. As all workingmen are engaged in producing this wealth, it follows logically that there is an identity of interest. There are many departments of work—workers have a diversity of tastes and ambitions. Their modes of living may be widely different, their habits dissimilar, their thoughts and education unlike, and yet upon one point there ought to be and ultimately and inevitably there must be perfect agreement, and that point is fair, equitable wages. Upon this proposition there is no room for debate. But when the question arises, "What are fair, equitable wages?" disputations begin and are endless. The employer insists that he shall be permitted to fix the rate—that the wageworker, the breadwinner, the wealth creator shall have no voice in a matter of supreme importance to him, and equally important to the welfare of society. The long prevailing policy has been that the worker shall take what he can get and be content.

Of late years the workingmen of the United States, having grown in intelligence, comprehend more fully than ever before the injustice of which they have been the victims, and with an independence born of intelligence have organized themselves into unions bearing various names, for the purpose of securing fair wages, a more equitable share of the wealth they create. What is the significance of this movement? It means simply that workingmen shall live in better houses, shall have better shelter, better homes, better clothing, better

---

† Published in *Locomotive Firemen's Magazine*, vol. 12, no. 6 (June 1888), 410–411.

and more abundant food, all of which signifies better citizenship, more influence in human affairs, in all of which every workingman has the same identical interest, and to secure which is the chief end of labor organizations. As a consequence, in the advocacy of the federation of labor organizations for mutual support, we are doing that which, if consummated, must result in securing for wageworkers their rights, a just recognition of the value of work in carrying forward the great industrial enterprises of the times.

During the year 1888 the various labor organizations will hold their annual conventions. Labor questions are to be discussed with a zeal and an intelligence hitherto unknown. There are some special reasons for this growing out of the fact that important elections are pending. The interests of labor are to have a hearing on the rostrum, but as it is said, "God helps those who help themselves," the question of federation for mutual support becomes more than ever before vital. It is not what can a party, or a politician, do for them, but what can they do for themselves?

It must not be understood that in advocating federation we favor the abandonment of separate and distinct organizations. We do not favor amalgamation. We do not desire to blend, fuse the various labor organizations into one conglomerate whole, but regarding the supreme purpose of each to better the conditions of its members, we would have such an understanding, such a federation, that when one is driven to the necessity of making a stand for its rights, for justice, honest wages, it shall have the sympathy, and at least the moral support of all, that in no instance should the enemy of workingmen have the support of any labor organization, but on the contrary, all should, within prescribed limits, do all things proper to enable the organization in the struggle to win a victory. The plan is feasible, prudent, and patriotic. It contemplates no wrong to anyone or to any interest. It signifies unity in case of emergency, and victory for the right against oppression. The *Magazine* in its advocacy of federation for mutual protection includes all labor organizations. It is broad enough to take them all in. It is the organ of a brotherhood of workers whose high aim is to achieve better conditions and advanced positions, and in the spirit of fraternity we address all the labor organizations in the land, believing the emancipation of workingmen depends upon their working together when the rights of any organization are invaded and imperiled, and we earnestly invite all labor organizations to give the matter we have briefly stated their consideration. United for mutual protection, workingmen of America would be invincible. Once federated in the interest of right and justice, they would exert a moral power which would bear down all opposition. In that event, strikes would disappear and peace and prosperity would reign supreme.

Invincible Men[†]

July 1888

True courage has in all ages challenged the admiration of manly men and womanly women. Courage is not bravado, bluster, and brag. Such things are characteristic of cowards, chicken-hearted creatures who simply have the form of men. They are fair-weather sailors, parade-drill soldiers. In times of storm they want to get into the forecastle, between decks. The surging billows and the howling wind frighten them. Their influence is demoralizing. In time of battle, such creatures skulk. Their hearts get down into their boots. They are the first to run and hide. The storm of battle, the whir of bullets, the scream of shells, the sulfurous smoke, and the sight of blood suddenly reduced them to a limp condition. All too often, they can't help being cowards; they were built that way, but the fact seldom lessens the contempt they receive from all brave men. This thing we call physical courage may be cultivated, developed sometimes, until the weak-kneed raw recruit may be made an unflinching veteran; but as a general proposition, courage is an inherent quality and is certain to make itself visible the instant danger appears.

We hear much of "moral courage," which, stated tersely, means that a man has the courage of conviction. Men who when persuaded that they are right stand forth, and stand firm, in the defense of the right as they understand it. For this right they will make sacrifices. They will endure privations. They will look poverty square in the face and defy its blighting power—such men are the salt of the earth, they are the glory of our much-abused human nation. Remove them from the active participation in human affairs, and Jehovah would again repent that He made man at all. The man of physical courage has won all the battles of the world since the ark rested on the summit of Ararat,[7] and the men of moral courage have gained every victory for principle since the day that Jehovah wrote upon tables of stone the moral law of the world.[8] The men of moral courage are invincible men. They will, if need be, stand alone. They will say, we know we are right, and though all the world deserts us, we will stand by the right. Look at them, moral heroes. They loom up like mountains in the midst of molehills. They are the hundred-armed oaks in a forest of weeping willows. Have we such men nowadays?

---

† Published in *Locomotive Firemen's Magazine,* vol. 12, no. 7 (July 1888), 487–488.

Behold the invincible engineers, firemen, and switchmen on the lines of the CB&Q system of railroads. They have the moral courage to stand. They asked only for the right, not for themselves alone, but for every locomotive engineer and fireman and switchman on all the 140,000 miles of railways in the United States and Canada. Nor do the rights for which these invincible men contend end with engineers, firemen, and switchmen, but include every other railway employee and every bronze-browed workingman who depends upon his toil for his daily bread. All hail the strikers on the CB&Q. Oratory never had a nobler theme. No pomp and circumstance surround them, no ovations attend them, and yet they stand determined and hopeful. They present a magnificent spectacle for workingmen to contemplate, for they are fighting, against tremendous odds, the battle of labor. The opulent CB&Q corporation could rob them, but it could not degrade them, and now the striking engineers, switchmen, and firemen, as true to principle as the needle to the pole, are inviting the world to look on and see men of more than Spartan courage stand by principles which once cloven down in America signifies the enslavement of workingmen.

The fight is the fight of organized labor against soulless corporations, and labor organizations now have an opportunity to contemplate an exhibition of moral courage which redeems human nature from the curse of degradation, which, without the united resistance of workingmen, is as certain to come as that rivers flow to the sea. The example the engineers, firemen, and switchmen on the CB&Q are now engaged in setting for workingmen, will not, we are confident, go unheeded. They are defending a principle which must be maintained if workingmen are ever to have their rightful share of the wealth they create.

The Common Laborer Is Essential[†]

July 1888

We notice that a writer is of the opinion that one of the serious embarrassments of the times is owing to the fact that there are too many "common laborers." He says, "in every industry the common laborers are the frequent applicants." The "common laborers" are men without trades, "unskilled" laborers, the idea being, if all laborers were skilled mechanics, all capable of taking *first* positions instead of being "helpers," the labor question would at once assume a more cheering and cheerful aspect. Such views are seen to be vagaries at a glance. The trouble is that there has grown up in the United States an aristocracy in the ranks of labor. The "common laborer" has occupied the position of *plebeian,* while his skilled fellow citizen has assumed the airs of *patrician.* The importance of the "common laborer" can be made to appear about as conspicuously as that of his skilled coworker. In the great business of architecture the hod carrier has occupied the lowest level.[9] No special skill is required to be a hod carrier. He needs be strong and sure-footed, able to climb a ladder with a hod on his shoulder. He need not be educated. It matters to his employer very little how he lives or where he lives. He occupies, ordinarily, the bottom strata of social life.

Well, recently, the hod carriers in several cities concluded to demand an advance in wages. In some instances, no more attention was paid to their demand than if they had been so many blind paupers. But hod carriers, however humble their calling, however common their labor, had learned that hod carriers are as necessary as bricklayers, and they concluded to quit work unless wages were advanced. This done, work *stopped.* Not a brick could be laid. Then bosses ascertained that "common labor" is as essential as skilled labor—and common laborers, being American citizens, are coming to the conclusion that they ought to live in a way in some measure becoming their prerogatives.

We view the situation as eminently cheering. It betokens more than an advance in wages. It voices a spirit of independence which society should value above price. It is a move upward. It is indicative of dissatisfaction with squalor, poverty, and degradation. It is significant of better homes, happier wives and children, more education for the children, a larger attendance upon church and Sunday

---

† Published as "The Common Laborer" in *Locomotive Firemen's Magazine,* vol. 12, no. 7 (July 1888), 486.

schools, and a higher appreciation of the inestimable blessings of free government.

Why this ceaseless depreciation of the common laborer? All cannot be skilled mechanics, or if such a thing were possible, then skilled mechanics would be required to perform what is called "common labor." Common labor must be done by someone. As well might the head complain of the feet, or the heart make degrading reference to the kidney. A man who would grind the common laborer, who would rob him of just compensation for his toil, becomes a detestable monster, a highway robber. What is common labor? It digs the canals, it makes the bed of railroads, it hews down forests, it prepares the clay for brickmaking; in a word it performs the beginning work of all enterprises requiring labor. It is essential, a supreme necessity, and was never properly recognized nor half paid. In the United States the common laborer holds the ballot, and it will never be surrendered, and if the "common laborer" is beginning to realize his responsibilities, and is anxious to qualify himself for their intelligent performance, the fact, instead of creating alarm, should be hailed as a glowing tribute to the vitalizing influence of our institutions, which level up, elevate, and dignify all who come within the boundaries of their operations.

The Situation in the Great Strike[†]
July 1888

We are still required to write of the great strike on the CB&Q. It is not a pleasant task. We had hoped ere this date to have had the satisfaction of recording the triumph of justice over flagrant, long-continued injustice. We know that it is written that

> Truth crushed to earth shall rise again;
> The eternal years of God are hers;[10]

But it seems that eternal years will be required to enthrone truth and dethrone and crush error. But, thank God, "hope springs eternal in the human breast,"[11] and it is a matter for ceaseless felicitation that the brotherhoods of engineers, firemen, and switchmen contain men who know their rights, and knowing

† Published in *Locomotive Firemen's Magazine,* vol. 12, no. 7 (July 1888), 482–483.

dare maintain them, dare contend for them, and are equal to all the sacrifices which a contest to secure them demands.

We are well aware that the present is a practical age, a money-making and a money-getting age. An age of greed and grab, an age of monopolies, trusts, syndicates, and combinations, in which the opulent few, by processes of chicane and legerdemain, seek to make the toiling many pay them tribute money. This fact was conspicuously and notoriously true of the CB&Q corporation. Rich rascality was constantly devising schemes to defraud honest labor. It was successful. The device was an amalgamation of fraud and falsehood, cash and cussedness, deceit and depravity, vulgarity and venality. Every element of baseness was injected into the plot to defraud workingmen of a portion of their honest earnings. For years the plot was successful—successful to an extent that staggers credulity. Not less than $200,000 a year was the sum total of the steal taken from the pockets of the engineers and firemen. Every five years a million dollars pocketed by pirates as heartless as any freebooter that ever sailed the seas, floating a black flag at the masthead. It was robbing not only men, but wives and children. It was a piracy that attacked every employee's home. It filched bread from the mouths of women and children. It clothed them in rags. It denied them books and schools. It compelled them to take the pauper's bench in the sanctuary or never near the glad tidings of salvation, and this was done by the CB&Q that its stockholders might roll in luxuries, dress in purple and fine linen, and strut through the world as millionaires. The infamous policy was endured until patience and forbearance were no longer virtues, and resistance became a duty as binding as ever challenged men to do and dare, fight and pray for the right. To have longer suffered under the stinging degradation was to have willingly accepted the condition of helots and pariahs, the degradation of serfs. It involved the sacrifices of citizenship—American citizenship with all its prerogatives, the abdication of American sovereignty with all its inviting possibilities, and the acceptance of humiliations which defy exaggeration.

The *Magazine* in previous issues has given its readers a faithful record of the strike on the CB&Q, from its inception up to the time when the engineers, firemen, and switchmen looking forward to the meeting of the stockholders in May, hoping these men would see the justice of their cause and afford them relief. They were doomed to disappointment. The stockholders, like their creatures, the officers, favored the bloodhound pursuit of the employees. It is said of man-eating lions and tigers that once having a taste of human flesh, they never cease hankering for it, and the CB&Q stockholders, having pocketed $200,000 a year from the earnings of their engineers and firemen, determined not to let go of the delicious morsel, and they voted unanimously to continue the robbery.

The action of the stockholders of the CB&Q created an emergency which the strikers were required to face. The brotherhoods had exhausted all the power conferred by their constitutions—and now, for the action of the men in their individual capacity. The joint committee consulted with the men and found them immovable as mountains. The question was: Will you continue the strike? A vote was taken and almost to a man the response was, "We will stand by our colors—the strike is still on." United, appealing to the world, appealing to all labor organizations for the rectitude of their conduct from the beginning, these men—engineers, firemen, and switchmen—declare the strike will be continued.

In writing of the chivalric courage of these striking engineers, firemen, and switchmen, we confess to an inability to do the subject justice. With limited resources; idle, with a frowning future in full view; these men, without fear and without reproach, trustful and defiant, willing to work if they can be men, but preferring obloquy to serfish conditions, realizing that they are American citizens, with all the responsibilities resting upon them that the condition imposes—fathers who love their wives and children, sons who love their mothers and sisters, men whose manhood revolts at injustice and degradation, have resolved to maintain their attitude of defiance and independence rather than yield to the dictation of men who have robbed them, and would rob them again and continually, were it in their power.

We invite workingmen everywhere to note the attitude of the men, engineers, firemen, and switchmen, late employees of the CB&Q corporation. It may be asked, why should these men immolate themselves? Why should they seek martyrdom? Why not yield and accept such terms as their oppressors may see fit to give?

Those who propound such questions have been in all time the camp followers of the armies of progress and independence; the Esaus, selling their birthrights for pottage;[12] the scavengers and scabs, who have no higher ideal of life than is embodied in rations, who live without knowing or caring what life is worth. If only such men had lived in the ranks of labor, every workingman would today be wearing an iron collar with his master's name engraved upon it.

The men who are maintaining the strike on the CB&Q with unyielding tenacity are confronted by statutes which from the first have been embarrassing. Statutes made in the interest of corporations, and under which they have been and are still enabled to play the role of oppressors.

It matters not under what outrages employees of corporations may labor, no officer, chairman, or leader of any labor organization can so much as advise resistance without being held liable to prosecution for conspiracy, the penalty being fine and imprisonment. Shielded by such a law, the oppressors and robbers of labor take courage and give the screws as many turns as they may deem advisable, and if resistance follows, an army of detectives, human hounds, are put on the track for the purpose of arrest and intimidation. And yet, notwithstanding such things, the striking engineers, firemen, and switchmen present a bold front to the enemy and fearlessly await developments.

Such is the situation as we write for the July *Magazine*. Before we go to press, before this article meets the eyes of the thousands of readers of the *Magazine*, there may be new developments, but now, the engineers, firemen, and switchmen, standing together as one man, are presenting the old-time attitude of defiance and are hopeful of results which will demonstrate that courage and endurance are still forces and factors in securing justice, when truth confronts error.

Home Rule in Ireland[†]
August 1888

We can readily imagine that someone of our readers will ask, why write of home rule in Ireland? We hope to answer the question as we proceed.

The estimate is current that of the 60 million inhabitants of the United States, at least 10 million are Irish-born and the immediate descendants of Irish-born citizens. As a consequence, there are more Irishmen (we refer to blood rather than birth) in the United States than in Ireland. This fact of itself might be urged as a sufficient reason for writing of home rule in Ireland.

American statesmen and orators have vied with each other in pleading the claims of Greece to independence. To write and speak of home rule in Greece, to champion the cause of Grecian liberty, at one time challenged the brightest intellects of America. The theme stirred the great American heart to its profoundest depths. Said one,

---

† Published in *Locomotive Firemen's Magazine,* vol. 12, no. 8 (August 1888), 566–568.

Confident that I never appeared as the advocate of a more worthy cause than that of the afflicted Greeks, I shall address you on this occasion with earnestness, and as my object is not to gratify the feelings of the ambitious, the appetites of the voluptuous, or the cravings of the avaricious; but to raise up the bowed down, to alleviate the sufferings of a whole people, to exalt in the estimation of mankind the character of our country, and, above all, to please God, I entertain no apprehension of disappointment.[13]

If more than half a century ago, an American could thus discourse upon unhappy Greece and plead for home rule for that Turk-cursed country, why should it be regarded singular for Americans in these later days to plead for home rule in Ireland? We quote still further from the oration of the American in the cause of Greece, and we ask the reader to substitute Ireland where "Greece" occurs, and note how eloquently the orator pleads for Ireland:

The calamities of unhappy Greece [Ireland] are not only great but without a parallel. The history of the world, from that awful moment in which God cursed this guilty globe, down to the present time, does not exhibit a more wretched people than the inhabitants of Greece [Ireland]. Agitated by hope and apprehension; by momentary triumphs and numerous discomfitures; by the cheering prospects of foreign aid, and the mockery of their hopes; by internal enemies and outward foes, they present an assemblage of disasters unequalled in the annals of time.

We submit that every word uttered by the orator more than fifty years ago in the interest of home rule in Greece is today, and a thousandfold more emphatic, a plea for home rule in Ireland, and the American native-born, regardless of ancestry, glorifies American institutions and the American character when he pleads for home rule in Ireland.

We have no desire to unduly eulogize the Irish nation, nor the Irish character, but if the one trait, that of love of liberty, be selected, then in the face of authentic history we do not hesitate to declare that Irishmen occupy a proud eminence above the Greeks. Unlike Greece, Ireland was never the home of art. In Ireland, the "rugged rock may not have taken on the forms of beauty under the hand of Irish genius."[14] Ireland was a wilderness when Greece was in the zenith of her glory. When Grecian philosophers, poets, statesmen, and warriors were educating, enrapturing, and conquering the world, Ireland, the emerald gem of the sea, was in the grasp of savagery; but from the dawn of her redemption to the present, Irishmen have loved liberty, and amidst disasters and defeat, subjected to woes unutterable—exile, prisons, poverty, and famine, the fires of liberty were never quenched, nor were the days ever so dark, or the crushing curse of foreign invasion and domination ever so heavy, that Irishmen were not ready to make another effort for liberty, independence, and home rule.

If it were our purpose to write of Ireland's woes we could "a tale unfold" which would add tremendous force to the argument why Ireland should have home rule, and awaken every slumbering energy of civilization and make it cry out for justice to Ireland. Robbed of her land, robbed of her independence and nationality, her temples and shrines desecrated, and her people's devotion to their baptismal vows treated as a crime, the world stands aghast as it contemplates the worse-than-vandal ruin to be seen on all sides, and yet amidst this unspeakable desolation, which defies hyperbole, to see a people still contending for independence and home rule presents a picture of courage that sends a thrill of joy throughout all Christendom, and which must challenge the approval of heaven.

A writer says, "Ireland is a part of the United Kingdom of Great Britain and Ireland. The other part is Great Britain." And it should be added that Great Britain holds Ireland in subjection and denies to the people home rule, that is the right to regulate their domestic affairs. As a result, Ireland is governed by foreigners. Home rule in Ireland does not mean the separation of Ireland from the British Empire any more than home rule in any of the American states means a withdrawal from the Republic. It does not mean the disruption of the kingdom; it simply means that Irishmen shall have a parliament the same as Canada, and that all laws made for the regulation of Irish domestic affairs shall be made by Irishmen in Ireland, rather than by Englishmen in England.

There are those who write for the American eye and ear in the interest of English rule in Ireland, who declare that when Irishmen take upon themselves the obligations of American citizenship, it is their duty to "discard the national sentiments in which they were nurtured." The proposition is preposterous on its face. An Irishman nurtured in the sentiment of liberty, independence, and home rule, emigrating to America, instead of discarding the "national sentiment" finds it indefinitely strengthened, because the sentiment is preeminently American. He becomes a good American but retains, naturally, his abhorrence of despotism in Ireland, and just here we introduce again an allusion to America's sympathy for Turk-cursed Greece. If it were wise and patriotic for Americans to exhibit a profound sympathy for the Greeks and contribute aid for their emancipation, why should it be thought improper for Americans, and especially Irish-Americans, to urge the emancipation of Ireland from British domination to the extent of introducing home rule in Ireland? Greek and Turk were never more unlike and antagonistic than Irishmen and Englishmen. Nor did Greece ever suffer more from the invasion of the Turk than Irishmen from the invasion of the English.

Nothing is more frequent than to hear it said that Irishmen are incapable of self-government. Fortunately, Americans do not have to go to Ireland to learn the Irish character. From the foundation of the government, Irishmen, native-born and the descendants of Irishmen, have participated in American affairs. They have been in school, college, university, and on the battlefields, and everywhere have demonstrated their capabilities for self-government, for home rule, and in England as well as America, history bears irrefragable proof of the towering talents of Irishmen, of their ability to stand in the van of the armies of progress and high civilization. Ireland's orators, statesmen, poets, and warriors have commanded the admiration of the world, and the intimation that such qualifications of head and heart can flourish and benefit the world only under foreign banners, and cannot be utilized for the elevation of Irishmen at home, is to assert that which no honest man believes, and stands refuted by truth as luminous as the sun and as resistless as a tidal wave.

Americans can well afford to plead for home rule in Ireland because it is a fundamental idea in American government. It means justice to all. An American, we care not who he is, nor how lowly his condition, who stands forth with the ballot in his hand becomes a figure of surpassing grandeur. Starting from the least important of all the lawmaking bodies to the august Senate, he has a voice and participates in home rule—and this divine right, if cloven down, reduces him to a vassal. It is a right which the poor man should hold as sacred, because it creates an equality of conditions which nothing else can bestow. To demand this for Irishmen in Ireland, for Poles in Poland, and Greeks in Greece is worthy of Americans, and when Americans no longer feel an interest in the struggles of the oppressed for freedom, from that day will date the decline of the American idea, a calamity more direful than pestilence or war.

It would be supreme folly as well as base injustice to oppose home rule in Ireland, because Englishmen contend that the conferring of such a right would be antagonistic to England's interests. To enthrone the right can only antagonize the wrong, and such is the view of Gladstone,[15] than whom England has produced no greater statesman, and the fact that Gladstone has joined his mighty power with Parnell's,[16] to secure for Ireland the inalienable right of home rule, should carry conviction to every wavering mind that home rule in Ireland means the strengthening of the United Kingdom of Great Britain and Ireland.

It would not be difficult to strengthen our advocacy of home rule in Ireland by particular reference to the land laws of Ireland by virtue of which the tenant farmers of that unhappy country are often reduced to the verge of famine, and to depict, as the result of such legislation, the horrors of eviction, but any discussion of such topics would extend this article beyond prudent length; our purpose is accomplished if we have demonstrated that it is patriotic for Americans to feel a profound sympathy for Irishmen in their struggle for home rule, a right which Americans regard as sacred, and which would be surrendered only amidst such convulsions as would demonstrate to the world that the last hope of freedom had perished.

The CB&Q and Pinkerton Conspiracy[†]
August 1888

Conspirators, in all ages, have been detestable creatures. Webster defines conspiracy as "a combination of men for evil purposes; an agreement between two or more persons to commit some crime in concert, as treason, sedition, or insurrection."[17] Conspirators always have the commission of some crime in view. Conspirators are criminals in the most odious sense of the term. Their methods are the most villainous that can be conceived. They adopt unhesitatingly any means, no matter how vile, to accomplish their ends. A conspirator is always a coward, always a sneak, without one redeeming quality of head or heart.

A conspirator is always a liar. In carrying out his plots, truth is never considered. He does not hesitate to commit perjury, and, if to consummate his devilish designs murder is required, he is readily demonized for the bloody deed. It is impossible to exaggerate their hellish characteristics. They excite universal abhorrence. Judas Iscariot and the high priests, bent on the death of Christ, can always be contemplated with profit when the purpose is to arrive at a correct estimate of the depravity of conspirators, and in the case which we shall discuss, Judas fitly represents a Pinkerton detective, while the officials of the CB&Q may stand for the high priests who urge him forward in his damnable work.

It is not required that we should rewrite the history of the strike of the engineers, firemen, and switchmen on the CB&Q. The readers of this magazine, all

† Published in *Locomotive Firemen's Magazine,* vol. 12, no. 8 (August 1888), 642–645.

brotherhood firemen, know it by heart. And yet, it seems prudent in discussing the CB&Q and Pinkerton conspiracy to refer again to some of the more prominent facts connected with the strike. In the first place, it is the most notable strike of railroad employees that ever occurred in the United States. One of the greatest, richest, and most prosperous railroad corporations in the country, under the control of despicable officials, arrogant and venal, systematically pursued a course of injustice toward its employees. They would neither arbitrate nor make concessions. They preferred a policy of injustice and defiantly challenged the oppressed employees to strike. As a last resort this was done. The weeks and the months sped by. What was the result to the CB&Q? Demoralization on every mile of its tracks, daily disasters, wreck and ruin everywhere. The splendid property passed into the hands of scabs, incompetent men, a large percent of whom were vagabonds, the filth and scum, discarded and discredited men known to be characterless. What was the further result? The downfall of the property, the loss of millions of money. Travelers and shippers shunned the tracks of the CB&Q. Receipts went down while expenses increased. In the markets, where CB&Q stock once stood high, there were no buyers and values went down, steadily down. Capitalists looked on in amazement. A thousand times a day the strike was declared "off," but it would not go, it would not down. There stood the sturdy engineers, firemen, and switchmen, appealing to the world to bear testimony to the rectitude of their conduct and the righteousness of their cause, and declaring, "Sink or swim, survive or perish, we stand and plead for justice." There was moral grandeur in the spectacle. Poor but not purchasable, idle but willing to work, they had made demands becoming American skilled workingmen, and they would not retreat. Manifestly, the attitude of the heroic men was exasperating to the officials of the CB&Q. They had played their game of arrogance, injustice, and falsehood. They had lied to the public, lied to each other, and lied to the stockholders of the property, but their policy had panned out in disaster.

The question then arose in the minds of these depraved and irritated officials, if a conspiracy could not be inaugurated which would crush the strikers and put the CB&Q on its feet again. The idea was regarded as fortunate. True, it involved perjury and forgery, crimes against God and man, society, and the state, but the officials were desperate. Every other device had failed. The case demanded heroic treatment. The strike was not off, wrecks multiplied. The scab was not a success, profits had gone glimmering. The last resort was to form a conspiracy with the Pinkertons.

We have written of the Pinkertons. The pages of the *Magazine* bear testimony of our estimate of the Pinkerton detectives. We regard them with unspeakable loathing. By inheritance and association they are the foulest blots and blotches upon our civilization. They are distorted, deformed, hideous, mentally and morally. Their trade is treason, their breath pollution, and yet the officials of the CB&Q formed a conspiracy with these professional liars, perjurers, forgers, cutthroats, and murderers to overcome a strike, the result of a policy of flagrant injustice.

The people of Chicago and the country generally had become justly alarmed upon the subject of dynamite. If, therefore, any plausible lie could be concocted whereby the strikers on the CB&Q could be shown to favor the use of dynamite, a tidal wave of indignation could be set in motion which would inure to the benefit of the CB&Q and forever wreck the brotherhoods whose members were engaged in the strike. The idea took deep root in the minds of the CB&Q officials and the conspiracy was at once formed between them and the Pinkertons.

The first step taken in the program was to select a number of the Pinkerton thugs to play the role of locomotive engineers or firemen, become members of the lodges of these brotherhoods, gain the confidence of the strikers, then report proceedings to the CB&Q officials.

To carry out the plot, the Pinkerton detective becomes at once the most blatant, the fiercest, and the most unscrupulous man to be found. His indignation knows no bounds. He is from the first in favor of extreme measures. He denounces the CB&Q officials and their heartless policy. He glows and burns with resentment, and finally, at the proper time, suggests the use of dynamite. He knows where it can be obtained. He volunteers to go and procure it. Thus the professional scoundrel in the employment of the officials schemes and plots for the downfall of men, workingmen, who are simply demanding fair pay for honest work and in whose minds the thought of crime against life and property never entered until it was injected by these paid villains of a great railroad corporation.

We invite our readers to contemplate the picture. In the sacred precincts of friendship, fraternity, and confidence, a hired apostate, a traitor, a creature whom it would be a compliment to call a villain, ingratiates himself, selected for his smooth-tongued hypocrisy, with a cheek of brass and a tongue trained to treason, on the one hand with fiery invectives he denounces the CB&Q officials, and on the other hand deplores the injustice to which the workingmen have been subjected—watches with eager eye and bated breath the influence of his scheme and reports to his co-conspirators how things stand. Day and night, in storm and shine, he follows his victims through every lane and avenue, until at last, rejoicing in the prospects, he reports that the plot is a success and that some thoughtless, misguided man has been won over to the dynamite scheme. This done the CB&Q officials, with a grand flourish of trumpets for the purpose of obscuring the cruel wrongs they had perpetrated, seek to secure popular approval and cast obloquy upon men who, in their struggle for their rights, had never so much as dreamed of perpetrating a crime against life or property, and against whose integrity no such charge could be made or sustained, except as shown to be the result of a conspiracy entered into between the CB&Q officials and the vile creatures known as the Pinkertons.

If it can be shown—if it is ever shown in a court of justice that any engineer, fireman, or switchman on the CB&Q favored the use of dynamite, it will be shown that a Pinkerton detective, in the employ of the CB&Q, a member of the CB&Q and Pinkerton conspiracy, suggested the use of the explosive, and that prior to the concoction of the plot by the CB&Q and the Pinkertons to inveigle railroad employees to do wrong, no thought or purpose of criminal acts ever had an existence in their minds.

In discussing the personnel of the conspiracy, no epithet within the entire range of the language need be omitted out of any regard for the proprieties of language, but it would seem that in the entire sweep of villainy, the creatures known as Kelly and McGilvery have earned a weight of infamy rarely obtained by a Pinkerton.[18] The warts on the repulsive backs of dungeon toads are a thing of beauty in comparison. When Pinkertonism can produce adepts in crime and railroad officials can employ them, it is safe to say that society is corrupt and that law is a sham—and yet such creatures, such scoundrels, are employed to plot crimes, and are brought into court to swear away the characters and liberties of men as much superior to them as an archangel is superior to a cobra. A sadder or a more humiliating spectacle cannot be exhibited. It brings all courts where such abominable specimens of humanity are permitted to have any standing into everlasting odium—in fact, it makes the courts where the facts are known a party to the conspiracy, and in making the testimony of such abnormally developed apostates, traitors, and liars, the measure of any penalty at all upon their victims brings law, courts, judges, and juries into contempt, and buries them beneath an eternal weight of ignominy.

The two miserable wretches, Bowles and Wilson, played their part in the conspiracy as its managers had prepared for them,[19] and with Kelly and McGilvery must take their places in the pillory to be spit upon by all men who have the remotest conceptions of honor or self-respect, or who are not inoculated with the Pinkerton virus, more deadly in its influence than the fabled Upas.[20]

The country is called upon to witness the denouement of a conspiracy which in its inception and in its progress discloses a sum total of infamy rarely if ever recorded. A corporation, once honored and respected, controlled once by men of honor, character, and probity, deliberately bargains with thugs, sneaks, perjurers, villains of the lowest order, that men whose only crime was a righteous demand for honest pay might be robbed of reputation and of liberty. What the final result will be no one can tell nor foresee. It may be that someone of the victims of the CB&Q's injustice may have his liberty sworn away by a Pinkerton perjurer. It will not be the first time in the history of the world that traitors and conspirators have won. But the case will not be without its compensations. The convicted men, should the conspiracy triumph by the aid of the perjuries of the Pinkerton scamps, will not be disgraced—they will only swell the list of martyrs who have suffered for a righteous cause and exalted it by their fidelity. But Pinkertonism will have arrayed against it, and all its devilish devices, every workingman in America who is worthy of the right to wield a ballot.

Another compensation will be the federation of certain brotherhoods of railway employees for protecting their rights against the oppressions of employers. Under the various necessities brought into prominence by the CB&Q strike, the brotherhoods have gained rather than lost strength.

Already public sentiment is reacting. The infamy of the conspiracy is being fully comprehended, and the indications are that when the trial comes and all the interior facts are known, and the conspiracy exposed, the management of the CB&Q will harvest sufficient odium to sink it in the estimation of honorable men to the fathomless depths of infamy, where Pinkertonism has its abode.

The Pinkertons[†]

August 1888

We do not expect by writing of the Pinkertons to extend the area of their notoriety. If we can in any degree aid our readers in forming even an approximately just conception of them, we shall feel amply compensated for the task.

---

† Published in *Locomotive Firemen's Magazine*, vol. 12, no. 8 (August 1888), 563–565.

As we understand it, there are two departments of Pinkertonism—the "detective" and the "protective," so called. Under the influence of our much-vaunted civilization, crime, in what is known as the "upper crust," the "upper tendom" of society, has, during the last few decades, alarmingly increased. There are a vast number of honest-minded men who never tire of telling the world that the sublimation of human nature must come through the influences exerted by the school and the church, and certainly there ought to be no objection to the proposition. Education and religion ought to exert an elevating influence, and such is doubtless the case, but the fact remains nevertheless that in circles distinguished for intellectual culture and devotion to religious teachings are found the Napoleons of crime. Take the army of boodlers in all of our great cities, and they will be found to average well in matters of education and literary standing, but when we are required to contemplate the multitude of bank and railroad wreckers, insurance plunderers, the defaulters, embezzlers, and thieves whose operations are upon a large scale, they will be found, in almost every instance, to be men of large educational attainments, often graduates of colleges, and in a majority of cases, "pillars" in some one of the orthodox churches. When any of these gilded, colossal scoundrels engage in crime, they go for all that is in sight. The stake is always immense. They shake down fortunes as earthquakes do buildings, and being educated, they are able to cover up their tracks, necessitating the work of expert detectives. Under such circumstances, Pinkerton, the father of the Pinkertons, was carried into business life and prominence.[21] He had a nose for detective work. To put him or his trained men on the track of a thief, a defaulter, an embezzler, or a boodler promised good results, and as educated criminals multiplied, Pinkertonism thrived. It fed and grew fat on crime, and as in every great American city crime of the character we have named increased, Pinkertons multiplied.

Those who take the time to study and analyze social problems, whether of virtue or vice, will discover many startling facts well calculated to create anxiety if not alarm. They will find society in all the large cities corrupt to an extent as almost to defy exaggeration. Mr. James Parton, the historian,[22] in a paper published not long since, in speaking of matters moral and criminal in the city of New York, says:

> For forty years past the aldermen have been little but a gang of thieves. As a body they have done scarcely anything but steal. As a rule they were elected for nothing else, sought their seats for nothing else, and nearly every act done by them has had in it some taint of iniquity.[23]

Here we have the statement that the very foundation of the government of the great American metropolis is contaminated by crime, a festering mass of pollution, an aggregation of infamy. Not in the ranks of the poor, the working people, but of the officials, the government itself. In such a Sodomized community Pinkertonism decks itself in purple and fine linen. The government is the dog, and the Pinkertons are the fleas in the hair of the dog. In such a community as Parton describes, is it a matter of surprise that the knights of the jimmy are on the alert to secure their share of the boodle, that sneak thieves and footpads increase in number and boldness? And what is true of New York is equally true, measured by population and opportunity, in all of the great centers of population in the country, and hence, as a consequence, we hear of the Pinkerton detective agencies in all of the great cities.

While some of the educated and pious scoundrels engage in robbing banks and insurance companies, in wrecking railroads and watering stocks, cornering the food products of the country to make it more difficult for poor men to get bread and meat, another set of scoundrels engage in concocting schemes whereby they can impose additional burdens upon workingmen. The detective agencies of the Pinkertons may be well enough for aught we know, or care. The old aphorism, "set a thief to catch a thief," doubtless holds good in the present as in the past, but we come now to speak of another department of Pinkertonism, a later development, and one which merits and receives from workingmen universal detestation. We refer to what is known as the "protective department."

We have referred to the fact that taking their cue from that numerous class of high-toned criminals who rob and wreck by wholesale, certain corporations, like the CB&Q, seek to increase their dividends by robbing their employees, a system of robbery in all regards more odious and atrocious than that of robbing a bank. The men who rob workingmen of their honest wages, who seek to deprive them of the necessities and comforts of life, are men whom it were a compliment to call villains. They are the enemies of humanity, the creators of hunger pangs, the promoters of poverty, the distributors of rags, and the disturbers of the peace of society. It has so happened in the past that their cruel injustice to workingmen has been productive of labor troubles, ultimating in strikes. American workingmen have said, "We can no longer endure your injustice. Your piracy upon our lives is a wickedness to which we shall not longer submit," and they as a last resort strike. This done, what happens? A call is made upon the "Pinkerton Protective Agency," and as if by magic, the city swarms with Pinkertons, armed with Winchester rifles and pistols, clothed with authority to shoot down workingmen with or without provocation.

Who are these bloodthirsty, murderous Pinkertons? What of their character? What of their antecedents? Only God and the Pinkerton agency know. They come as carrion crows come to a carcass. They go as bloodhounds go into the chase. They are gangs of mercenaries who are suddenly clothed with power to kill workingmen. They are beetle-browed ruffians who have no more regard for the welfare of society than would be accorded to the same number of vagabond dogs. They are the skimmings of the filth of the slums, and yet these miscreants, uniformed and armed by the "agency," are sent forth to kill, as to their brutal natures may seem proper. The list of cold-blooded murders these wretches have perpetrated horrifies all right-thinking men, and has earned for them an eternal night of ignominy.

But, after all, where rests the supreme burden of blame, of censure and infamy for armed Pinkertons, when workingmen in the grasp of corporative cussedness demand justice? When in slave times the bloodhounds were put in pursuit of the slave fleeing for liberty, who thought of denouncing the hounds? The men who put the hounds on the track of the fugitive were responsible for the bloodcurdling horrors of the chase and the capture. The Pinkertons who go forth with shotted rifles and pistols to kill workingmen have in a large degree the instinct and nature of hounds, but behind these human monsters are other monsters still more inhuman, who are responsible for the damnable business. Who are they? Well, they are creatures put into power largely by the votes of workingmen, and when workingmen federate for the purpose of electing honest men to office the Pinkertons will disappear, and not till then. The workingmen of the great cities, once united, they can have humane officials and humane laws. When may the world anticipate the dawn of the new era? When shall the sleck, rotund scoundrels who plot the degradation of labor, and commission cutthroats to slay workingmen for protesting against savagery and slavery combined, have the power wrested from their unholy grasp? It will be when workingmen, comprehending their rights and prerogatives and using the ballot for their weapon, transform city governments from Augean stables into seats of cleanliness, represented by justice and righteousness.

Equality of Conditions†

September 1888

The American idea is that all men are born equal, and are endowed by the Creator with certain unalienable rights. Grand old St. Peter ascertained, very much against his inclination, that God is no respecter of persons. Hence the propriety of the caption of this article, "Equality of Conditions." Equality before the law is often a topic in the discussion of which the genius of American institution is extolled. So far as the state is concerned there is an equality of rights, privileges, and opportunities. We have no titled nobility, no recognized aristocracy; class and caste are unknown. Class legislation is unconstitutional. One American citizen has just as much sovereignty as another. The sovereignty is lodged in the ballot.

In writing of the equality of conditions we have one purpose in view, and that is, if possible, to exalt the declaration that "an honest man is the noblest work of God."[24] An honest man may be poor, but that does not diminish his nobility, and a dishonest man, though rich as a Gould, a Vanderbilt, or a Rothschild, is his inferior.

In writing of the equality of conditions, we mean natural conditions, and conditions recognized by the laws of the land, insofar as they pertain to the rights and privileges of the people. We do not overlook the fact that there are artificial conditions, adventitious conditions, none of which, nor all of which combined, could affect the proposition that all the people in the United States, excepting criminals, insane persons, and idiots, insofar as laws are concerned, occupy absolutely the same level, the same plane.

Now, it is true that while the people of the United States recognize the fundamental facts which we have stated, as constitution and statutes bear ample testimony, there are a great many people who from the first (and the number, we regret to think, is increasing), who now believe that mere adventitious in equalities should be regarded as primal, fundamental, and should exert a more potent influence in affairs generally.

The man who happens to be rich looks with proud disdain upon the man who is poor. The man who is educated regards the unlearned man with aversion. The major general revolts at associating with the man who carries the knapsack and the gun. The skipper who commands a steamship, an ocean

---

† Published in *Locomotive Firemen's Magazine*, vol. 12, no. 9 (September 1888), 653–654.

greyhound, has a contempt for the captain of the little craft. The architect who plans the palace or the monument groups all who work by his plans and rear the edifice very much after the style that Pharaoh contemplated the slaves who built the pyramids and hewed out the Sphinx.

We could multiply illustrations indefinitely. But we have said enough to enable the reader to "catch on," if he desires. Still, it may be added that this tendency of thought and action has not escaped workingmen and organizations of wage earners. This may seem strange, but it is not more strange than true, and the facts crop out now and then in a way that cannot fail to excite comment, if not derision.

To such of the great fraternity of workingmen who assume superiority over the more humble toilers the idea does not seem to occur that they, too, wear the badge of labor, that they live by work, and that when they curl their lips or elevate their noses in the presence of their less fortunate comrades, they demonstrate a desire for an alliance with those who treat all laboring men with supercilious disdain. They are at heart autocrats and aristocrats, and on all occasions, when opportunity offers, do not hesitate to air their arrogance and authority.

From individuals this peculiar weakness not infrequently passes to labor organizations, and that, too, chiefly, because one class of workers receives more pay than another class of workers. And here, again, the bedrock of the ostracism is money—not brains, not character, not probity, not fidelity to obligation, but money—as if money were the test of nobility. If that were the touchstone, who could vie with a Vanderbilt or a Gould, a Huntington[25] or a Sage?[26] If that be the test, then the CB&Q corporation could justify its arrogance when it treated engineers, firemen, and switchmen as of no more account than so many mules.

There is just now talk of federation: the federation of engineers, firemen, switchmen, and brakemen. The CB&Q strike has taught workingmen on the rail a lesson, never to be forgotten—it is the equality of conditions when a strike is on hand and must be lost or won. A strike levels down and levels up, and if there is to be a federation of the orders we have named, the equality of conditions must be recognized. The man who throws the switch, the man who handles the scoop, the man who holds the throttle, and the man who handles the brake must stand absolutely equal without regard to wages. In the grand federation of states which makes our ocean-girt republic, little Rhode Island stands equal to Texas, out of which a hundred Rhode Islands could be carved.

If there are those who indulge the vagary that anything less then a recognition of equality can or will be tolerated, they should dismiss it. The interdependence of the orders must be recognized, and this done, the work of federation will go forward, and will accomplish its beneficent mission.

Federation[†]

September 1888

The motto of the United States is "e pluribus unum," which means "one from many," or " one out of many," or "one composed of many." It brings into prominence the maxim, "In union there is strength."

The term "federation" has numerous synonyms, such as "league," "alliance," "coalition," "union," "combination," "compact," etc., but the term "federation," as we shall use it, embodies in the fullest sense our idea of a union of brotherhoods of certain railroad employees for purposes of strength when union is required to secure a righteous settlement of controversies which relate to their welfare.

Just here we desire to place upon record for the hundredth time, more or less, the fact that the *Locomotive Firemen's Magazine,* since it has been under our editorial management, has advocated such fraternization, such harmony and unity of organizations of railroad employees as would lead ultimately to federation.

To our mind, federation has not been a dream, a vague, undefined, or ill-defined theory. It has not been a whim, a mere vagary, but rather a necessity which would ultimately come to the front and demand action. We are fully of the opinion that organization leads to federation by laws in human affairs as certain in their operation as the laws of attraction and gravitation. The tendency is always and steadily in that direction. This, we think, will be admitted even by those who have not been able or willing hitherto to comprehend the logic of events.

Organization has its origin in the idea of the strength of united effort. Single-handed, little can be accomplished, while united effort bears down opposition, removes obstacles, and achieves victories.

† Published in *Locomotive Firemen's Magazine,* vol. 12, no. 9 (September 1888), 648–649.

The tendency in the United States among workingmen is to organize, and the reason for this is easily found. Here the workingman is a citizen, clothed with sovereignty and with all the rights and privileges that belong to other men without regard to condition, profession, or calling. Notwithstanding these things, for years past the condition of workingmen in the aggregate has steadily grown worse. We speak of the rule, not of the exception, and of the exceptions it should be said, their better condition with little effort can be traced to compact organization.

As a general proposition, organizations of workingmen begin with trades, that is, particular trades organize—form unions, or leagues, or orders, or brotherhoods. These organizations have in view not only the maintenance of fair wages but include social and benevolent features of great value to society and to the state. By exacting small dues they provide against many ills and sorrows incident to human life. They care for the sick, bury the dead, and provide for widows and orphans—in doing which, they illustrate many of the divinest precepts of Christianity, and to the extent that such things are done, our civilization is richly adorned.

One of the great benefits which such organizations have secured has been the education of their members in matters pertaining to financial and economic questions. They have investigated the question of the relations between capital and labor, taxation and revenue, earnings on the one hand and profits on the other hand. Nor have they been unmindful of the fact that they have been the victims of unrighteous and oppressive laws and of the decisions of corrupt and venal judges. They have seen men pleading with uplifted hands for so much of their honest earnings, as would enable them live, as become American citizens, to provide for themselves and their dependent wives and children the simple necessaries of life, thrust aside by arrogant and soulless corporations and made to suffer the penalties of death and imprisonment for their temerity.

Such things have indefinitely expedited the organization of workingmen in the United States, and with organization has come boldness of speech and considerate investigation as to what other steps could be taken to still further improve their condition.

It so happens—fortunately, we think—that when men are hesitating to take an advanced step, those of all others most opposed to a new departure do the very thing which makes it inevitable. It brings into prominence the fact that "behind a frowning providence" a "shining face" is often hidden,[27] to beam forth upon the men of courage who dare to stand for their rights when fortune and fate seem to have combined against them, and who are ready to lead a forlorn hope and make one more effort to wrest victory from the jaws of defeat. In the CB&Q strike the soulless corporation had, as they thought, prepared for every emergency. They knew the strength of the engineers and firemen, they counted noses, and believed after a little delay they could supply their places. We speak of what the corporation thought, not of the fact; and it is true that to a certain extent the corporation did supply the places of the engineers and firemen and switchmen. There was an alliance from the first between the engineers and firemen, and subsequently the switchmen came in. The strike and all of its attendant circumstances as one of its compensations has brought into the boldest possible prominence the unqualified importance of federation, because now it is seen if from the first there had been federation between engineer and firemen, switchmen and brakemen on the CB&Q, victory for the right would have been achieved in a day.

It is not our purpose in this article to suggest the methods by which federation is to be accomplished; these will require deliberation, consultation, and legislation. That the question will come up at the Atlanta convention is a foregone conclusion,[28] and we hail with undisguised approval the advent of the question in the deliberations of our brotherhood. We see in it the harbinger of a new era, fraught with untold blessings to workingmen. It is at once a fortress and a lighthouse. It is the olive branch of peace. It voices arbitration, concession, and compromise on the one hand, and if this will not win, then it means such a federation of forces as will secure victory and command approval.

Nor will federation end with the brotherhoods we have named. It is as the voice of one crying in the wilderness, to prepare the way for the triumphant march of labor to its rightful place in the affairs of men and of governments. To the toiling masses, federation is to be like the shadow of a great rock in a weary land, and it will be to us ever a source of inexpressible satisfaction that in our day and generation we had an opportunity to bear some humble part in advocating its establishment in the industrial affairs of the country.

Night and Morning[†]

September 1888

The heroic strikers on the CB&Q, the engineers, firemen, and switchmen, since February 27, 1888, have been, to use a figure of speech, marching and struggling for their rights under circumstances suggestive of nighttime. It has been a winter of discontent, of contending hopes and fears, but never of weakness or cowardice.

This magazine, argus-eyed, awake, and vigilant, has watched with ceaseless solicitude the progress of the combat from its inception, and, from the first, has believed the wronged strikers would win, if their courage and tenacity were equal to the righteousness of their cause.

Here, the *Magazine* puts upon record the declaration that the strike should never have been ordered if at any time or under any circumstances a surrender was contemplated, before endurance and sacrifice had ceased to be virtues in the estimation of all honorable men.

As the case now stands, we are required to contemplate the attitude of the belligerents and estimate with the facts before us, the possible results. Let it be understood that the strike was ordered as a last resort, to secure justice and to maintain a principle. Up to this date, justice has not been secured, but the principle, which cannot be surrendered without dishonor, has been maintained. The strikers, with Spartan courage, have maintained their defiant attitude. It may be, it is doubtless true, that here and there a striker has weakened, but the great body of the men have neither faltered nor wavered; and here, it should be said, to the everlasting credit of the men who are battling for justice and for principle, that they are fighting for the brotherhoods of which they are members; more, they are championing the rights of every wageworker and breadwinner in all the broad land, as certainly as that this CB&Q corporation is massing all its resources to crush and degrade labor.

This magazine here and now puts it upon record that the struggle on the CB&Q must pass into history, as demonstrating the measure of importance attached to a struggle in which the central, pivotal purposes were the securing of justice and the maintenance of principle, without which the very term "brotherhood" is shorn of its dignity and becomes a delusion.

---

† Published in *Locomotive Firemen's Magazine,* vol. 12, no. 9 (September 1888), 659–661.

It must not be forgotten that the brotherhoods of engineers, firemen, and switchmen struck for justice and for principle—not the individuals employed on the CB&Q—and the great brotherhoods, having decided to go to war, the question arises, when should they retreat or surrender? When should they ask of the enemy for terms of capitulation? When should they fall upon their faces and crawl upon their bellies in the dust to the feet of the CB&Q, beg for pardon, and accept such terms as the corporation might deem proper to bestow? Such interrogatories would arouse a sleeping devil in a Rip Van Winkle.

And here the *Magazine* asks, why entertain a remote idea of surrender? Has the CB&Q made any concessions? Not one. Has the CB&Q indicated any purpose whatever of doing justice to its engineers, firemen, and switchmen? None whatever. Has the CB&Q, when its fortunes were waning, and demoralization, wreck, and ruin came as a penalty for its vicious policy, maintained an honorable attitude toward the strikers and the brotherhoods? No, a thousand times, no. On the contrary, it formed an alliance with an organization of spies, forgers, and perjurers, and forever damned itself in the estimation of the brotherhoods and all honorable men by a resort to means and measures as villainous as blackens the records of crime in any age, civilized or savage. And this is the infamous corporation, this is the enemy of labor, this is the foe of the strikers and of the brotherhoods to whom the brotherhoods must surrender, if they surrender at all.

The record, so far as the public is permitted to know the facts, shows that the CB&Q has suffered financially to an extent that challenge credulity. Its losses are counted by millions. The *Chicago Tribune,* in a late issue, says that the decreased earnings of the Burlington Company for the month of May, as compared with May 1887, amounts to $808,000 and for the first five months of 1888, as compared with the corresponding period last year, the decrease of earnings reached the astounding sum total of $4,194,172. The *Tribune* searchingly analyzes the financial condition of the CB&Q, and the showing is simply startling. Its stock amounts to $77 million. Previous to the strike it paid dividends of 8 percent; this has gone down to 4 percent, but even at 4 percent, the dividends have not been earned by the road. The interest requirements amount to $6 million a year, or $500,000 a month, but the net earnings for five months are only a little over $1 million—or less than half of the sum required for interest, and the statements show for the first five months of the year a deficit amounting to $1.4 million, or, as the *Tribune* puts it: "The Burlington Company lacks $4 million of being able to pay its debts." At the end of 1887, the Burlington had a surplus of $1 million. This has been wiped out, and its floating indebtedness now approximates $3 million, and the corporation is now in the market trying to borrow money to keep its machinery in operation. Chicago refuses to loan it the money, and its securities are being hawked about in eastern markets.

But the evil days of the Burlington are not ended; on the contrary, the night of its darkness and demoralization has but just set in. The season is at hand for the movement of the products of the field and farm to the markets of the country and of the world. In its present condition these products will not go over its tracks manned by scabs, aided by Pinkerton mercenary thugs and thieves. The traveling public avoids its cars, and shippers seek when it is possible other avenues of transportation, and the losses of the past five months are vivid reminders of what the immediate future has in store.

The *Magazine* has no hesitancy in declaring that the brotherhoods can and will win the CB&Q fight, provided they are equal to all the responsibilities they assumed when they ordered the strike. Why should they surrender when after five months of night, of struggle, the morning of victory is dawning? True, sacrifices have been made. They were inevitable, they were expected, but they have not exceeded probabilities, and are far within the realm of possibilities. The strikers are determined, courageous, heroic to an extent demanding applause and eulogy. The brotherhoods are strong. As yet they have not put forth their mightiest energies. Their reserve power is incalculable. It is the reserve power of 60,000 men in a struggle for justice and for the maintenance of a principle which they cannot abandon without the loss of reputation and character, as dear to brotherhoods as to men.

In all such struggles there should be the coolest deliberations when the question is, shall they be ordered? But when the subject has been discussed from every standpoint, and the judgment is arrived at to "let slip the dogs of war," then surrender is not to be thought of until the last stronghold has been captured, until munitions and provisions are gone and every avenue of retreat is closed.

Such is not the condition of the brotherhoods which engaged in the strike with the CB&Q. It challenged the corporation to combat, and the men who were to feel the crushing weight of the corporation's forces are as defiant as they were on the 27th of February, when the battle was inaugurated. What do they expect? What have they a right to expect? This: that the brotherhoods whose battles they are fighting, that the brotherhoods which ordered the strike, shall not only stand by them, but by the declaration of war which they made.

This magazine, comprehending as best it can the magnitude of the interests at stake, maintains that a surrender would be attended with the most humiliating consequences, unjust to the strikers and disastrous to the brotherhoods. Besides, so far, not one prudent reason can be urged for surrendering, by declaring the strike off—which, of all things, the CB&Q most devoutly desires, for it sees in its tremendous losses the handwriting on the wall, which means its total wreck, if the present status of affairs is maintained.

Nor should the fact be overlooked, and to this the *Magazine* calls special attention, that the conventions of the brotherhoods are near at hand, and the strike, with all its attendant circumstances, is a proper subject to come before the representatives of the brotherhoods for final action. It touches their honor at many points, and it is a matter demanding the united wisdom of the orders. Let no final action be taken until the brotherhoods, in convention assembled, shall have had an opportunity to speak.

This magazine is confident that the brotherhoods, by putting forth their energies, can win the fight. The day is dawning. Already the CB&Q is defeated. The strike has touched its pocket—and therefore its soul. It is growing weaker every day. Its resources are crippled, its surplus is gone, and its dividends are diminished. Victory is coming to the brotherhoods. To surrender now would be a folly scarcely less than a crime. The demand is for the brotherhoods to mass their energies and stand firm. This done, the day is not far away when the CB&Q will make overtures of peace. That corporation, like all other corporations, will be influenced by the logic of cash. The stockholders will not long tolerate a policy by which an investment of $77 million not only earns no money for dividends but earns less than expenses.

The *Locomotive Firemen's Magazine* puts the foregoing facts and reflections upon record as the reason why the strike should be continued and maintained with renewed energy.

General Benjamin Harrison— Relentless Foe of Labor: Speech in Terre Haute, Indiana[†]

October 27, 1888

Mr. Chairman, Ladies and Gentlemen:—

The presidential campaign of 1888 is rapidly drawing to a close. There have been discussions upon the most important topics of far-reaching consequences. Great truths have confronted great errors, but we have every right to believe that after all the right will prevail because truth crushed to earth shall rise again. Now, my friends, you have heard the subjects that interest you discussed from both sides. You have heard the Republican orator, you have heard the Democratic orator, and if ever there was an election day in the history of the great American Republic when workingmen can vote intelligently, that election day will be on the sixth day of next month.

I am before you tonight to discuss but one issue in this campaign, and that I regard as a very important issue. It has been charged that from the time that General Ben Harrison was nominated until this day that he was the everlasting friend of monopoly and the foe of the workingmen, and I propose to prove tonight, if fact and argument can prove anything, that the candidate of the Republican Party for the presidency never in all his life had one sympathetic heartthrob for the working people of the country.[29] *[Applause.]* I proposed tonight to speak by the record, the record that he has made, the record that he must stand by. His record is there, black as a raven's wing, and there is no more escape from it for him than there is from monopoly taxes while the Republican Party remains in power.[30] *[Applause.]*

The Strike of 1877

The charges that I propose to make tonight are not made as a Democrat, but as a citizen, as a workingman. From 1873 until 1878 was a period of universal gloom in this country. Wages, under the high protective tariff, mind you, had gone down and down and down until workingmen were getting, in many

† Published as "Debs on Harrison" in *Terre Haute Weekly Gazette,* November 1, 1888, section 2, 1–4.

departments of industry, but a dollar a day for their work. You remember the year 1873, you workingmen. You remember all of the troubles in the East. You all remember that there was a continual reduction of wages. The men submitted to the utmost point of endurance. There was no disposition to protest, to make trouble, to create strife or discord. Upon the other hand, the men accepted the situation rather than to create trouble. When in July 1877 the great strikes reached the city of Indianapolis, the men were in a condition to need a friend. They had been wronged; they had been outraged; they had been oppressed by the corporations of the country until forbearance ceased to be a virtue. And then what? They struck. Struck for what? They struck for just simply enough wages to keep soul and body together. They struck for enough of their earnings to decently clothe themselves and their families. They struck against what? They struck against monopoly, they struck against oppression, they struck against hunger, they struck against hovels, they struck against rags. That is what they struck against. They needed sympathy. They were in trouble.

In order that you may fully understand the cause of their grievances I want to give you a little statement of the reduction in their wages that actually took place. In 1873 engineers were getting an average of $70 a month, firemen $45, brakemen $45, and switchmen $45. In 1877, when the strike originated, engineers were getting $58, or a reduction of $12 a month; firemen $32 a month, or a reduction of $13 a month; brakemen were getting $35 a month, or a reduction of $10 a month; switchmen were getting $35, or a reduction of $10 a month. There is no reasonable man within the sound of my voice who will dispute the fact that the time had come to protest against any further reduction of wages. A man's first duty is to his family, and when a man toils honestly and faithfully, especially in an occupation that involves ceaseless peril, and he cannot make a living for his family, he owes it to his family and to himself to protest because somebody is drawing at least a portion of his wages. *[Applause.]*

Who Were the Strikers?

Now then, who was it that struck? Railroad men—engineers, switchmen, firemen, brakemen. Some people in the city of Indianapolis took it for granted that because a strike had been inaugurated the city would be thrown into the hands of a mob and anarchy would reign supreme. Now I admit, my fellow citizens, that the term "strike" has been brought into disrepute, into odium, but I want to tell you that while, as an original proposition, I do not favor strikes, I believe there are times when every expedient to obtain justice has failed that the strike is absolutely justifiable. I have said before, and I say tonight, that there is not a star, there is not a stripe in the American flag that does not tell of a strike for liberty and for independence. *[Applause.]* From Lexington to Concord, all along that track of gloom and glory was one continuous succession of strikes against British oppression in the interest of the flag that enriches the heaven in which it floats.

Now I have said that these men were forced to the extreme limit of endurance and they struck simply to obtain a reasonable day's pay for an honest day's work. Through the petition of some of the citizens of Indianapolis, the governor issued a proclamation, to which the striking employees responded, and, if you will be patient a moment, I just want to read you what they said:

> Your proclamation issued this day has been read by the employees of the railroads entering in the city and we wish to make known that our purpose is to preserve the peace and use such caution as is necessary to follow the dictates and commands of your proclamation.

Was It a Mob?

Does that sound as if it emanated from a mob? They continue as follows:

> We desire peace and prosperity and ask in the name of our city and our citizens that the proposition for the adjustment of our wages presented to the committee of citizens be immediately acted upon by the officers of the railroad and the same can be accomplished to the satisfaction of employers and employees. We do not ask for riches. We desire to be law-abiding citizens. We appeal to you to further the plan of settlement through the committee to whom we have left our grievances for consideration.

Now here was the proposition: The striking employees were willing to submit their grievances to a committee of citizens, impartial judges, and abide by their decision. Isn't that a fair proposition? Is there anything unreasonable, anything unjust about it? Now then, here were the two propositions—the first was to settle all these difficulties by arbitration, mutual concession, conciliation, and compromise. The other was the shotgun policy, and at the head of the shotgun policy we find our friend, the Republican candidate for president, General Benjamin Harrison. *[Applause.]* John Caven, a Republican for whom I have the highest possible regard personally and officially, was mayor of the city of Indianapolis at that time.[31] He had so much confidence in the striking employees of these roads that he immediately clothed 300 of them with police authority to protect the property of the railroad and preserve the peace, while

General Ben Harrison organized Company O—the largest company organized in that city during that trying period—to shoot them down. *[Applause.]*

Mayor Caven vs. Ben Harrison

I want to say to this audience tonight that I have always been opposed to strikes. I have always been opposed to troubles of any kind between capital and labor. I prefer peace and harmony and goodwill. Mayor Caven understood these men. He knew that they were not lawbreakers, that they were not criminals, that they did not intend to destroy the property of the company they were working for. He knew that all they asked and all they expected was just simply to get a decent remuneration for their services. He did not find it necessary to suppress them with the approved Springfield rifles. He did not find it necessary to shoot them down. Not a bit of it. In a personal conversation with me regarding the trouble, Mayor Caven said: "I had faith in these men. I knew the men that I was dealing with. I knew that they were honest workingmen. I knew that their demands were reasonable and just. I had no fear of them, not the slightest, but if prudent counsels had not prevailed, there would have been bloodshed in the city of Indianapolis and plenty of it."

That is what Mayor Caven said to me. Now whom did he refer to in speaking of the opposite counsels? He referred to the men who, when the strike broke out, felt as a duty upon them to suppress the men with the aid of the militia. Now, my friends, I have said, and I say again, that from the beginning of that trouble that General Ben Harrison was against the men. If he ever spoke a kindly word to them—just one—there is no record of it anywhere that I know of. *[Applause.]* Had he gone out among them, as Mayor Caven did, and said, "Men, this is a trying, troublesome period, be patient just a little while. We will investigate your grievances and we will do you justice," there never would have been the cry raised against him in this campaign of a dollar a day, but he never did it. He was against them from inclination; he was against them by nature because he is built that way. *[Applause.]*

No Better Than the Tin Bucket Brigade

So far as General Harrison is personally concerned I have not a word to say against him, not one. He is said to be an excellent citizen. I have no doubt of it. He is said to have a pure and happy home. I have no doubt of it, but no better than thousands and thousands and thousands who keep step to the music of the dinner bucket brigades of this country. *[Applause.]* He is just as good, no doubt, but no better than thousands and thousands of workingmen who toil hard and honestly and faithfully all day long for a dollar a day. But against General Harrison as a United States senator, as a paid attorney of the Ohio & Mississippi Railroad, against him I have everything. I give you my word and honor tonight that I would not support Benjamin Harrison for president of the United States if he were the nominee of the Democratic Party. *[Applause.]* I give you my word and honor that I would not support him if I were a Republican, and my only regret is that multiplied thousands of workingmen, honest in their convictions, no doubt, will shout for him, vote for him, and help to elevate him to an office that he does not deserve at your hands because he has been your relentless foe as long as he has had any influence. *[Applause.]*

Harrison's Persecution of the Strikers

But I want to go back to the strike. I want to show that during the trying period that he persecuted and prosecuted workingmen to the exact extent of his influence and his power—and if there was one escaped, I will guarantee that it was not by virtue of his charity or his mercy. The strikers, as I have said, appointed their committee to arbitrate and settle these difficulties. The committee met. There was a meeting at the old council chamber. The purpose of it was to hear the grievances of those men. Now, common courtesy would dictate that these men should have been patiently heard. They were in trouble. They were in distress; they wanted a fair and impartial hearing. That is all. At that meeting a number of addresses were delivered. Among others, Governor Porter spoke, and I want to say in justice to Governor Porter that he was a friend of the workingmen at that time and is to this day, so far as I know.[32] Governor Porter addressed those men. He spoke to them in the kindly spirit of humanity, and he said, among other things: "We are here to listen patiently to your grievances and we are going to do you justice." The men all felt kindly toward him. After he got through General Harrison took the floor, and what did he give those men in the line of encouragement? From the time he took the floor until he was driven from it, he insulted them. He told them in the first place that they were lawbreakers, that they had no rights that the people of Indianapolis were bound to respect. Now, there is no report of that speech. There never will be, and I will guarantee to you that General Harrison will never give you the full text of it. *[Laughter and applause.]* But here is what the *Indianapolis News* said about it. It was very brief and to the point. The *Indianapolis News* was General Harrison's supporter then and it is his supporter now. Here is what it said:

> When the reports were all in, General Harrison took the floor and began to present the aspect of the strike from the other side.

Now that is suggestive. Here is what he said:

> "Have you a right while you are breaking the law to appear before a committee of law-abiding citizens with an appeal to redress the wrongs you claim to be suffering from?"

Just think of that as a sentiment of consolation to a few half-starved workingmen.

> At this point (the report continued) the railroad portion of the audience rose en masse and made a break for the door.

That is the *News* account, coming not from a Democratic standpoint, but it is the report of his own organ. In that meeting he is charged, among other things, with having said that a dollar a day is enough for a workingman. He is charged also with having said that if he were in authority, he would put the men back to work if he had to do it at the point of the bayonet. That is what he is charged with having said. Now I have here the testimony of 14 men who were in the meeting—railroad men, every one of them—and while they all differ, as they naturally would, as to the exact language, they say in substance that he *did* say that a dollar a day was enough for the workingmen, that he could live on that and they ought to be able to do the same. They said that he did say that if he were in authority he would suppress them at the point of the bayonet. Now I know that the testimony of some of these men has been impeached—at least the Republican press of the state has undertaken to say that because these men are workingmen, because they are not backed by any corporation, that their word is not entitled to consideration.

Circumstantial Evidence

Now I am not here tonight to do, knowingly, General Harrison the slightest injustice, but after seeing this testimony, after meeting and talking to the men personally who were in that meeting, I have concluded—I believe, in fact, I *know*—that that was the substance of his utterances, and if he did not say it in so many words he acted it from the very beginning of that trouble.

The circumstantial testimony is all against him. He knew just as well as I know that many of the men who were striking were getting even less than a dollar a day. He never denied that he said that the men were lawbreakers and that they had no rights that the people of Indianapolis were bound to respect. He has never denied that and he never can deny it. He knew, as I know, that many of the men who were represented in that meeting were getting 90 cents a day. Now just think about it! And yet he said they had no right to break the law of the land; they ought to be forced back to work because it was against the law to obstruct transportation and to interfere with it on any of the lines of the railway in the land.

Governor Porter Makes No Defense of Him

Now here is another point that I want to impress on my hearers tonight. Governor Porter was at that notable meeting. He heard the speech of General Harrison. He is in a position to know what he said. Now Governor Porter was here not long ago and delivered a speech under the auspices of the Railroad Club of this city. I fully expected that Governor Porter would say something in the line of defense of his candidate for the presidency. Now Governor Porter is a man of character, a man of standing, a man who is respected by the workingmen. By one statement he could have dismissed this charge that has been made against General Harrison. Now then, I ask you whether in his address, there or elsewhere, he has ever undertaken to say one word in defense of General Harrison. Now, why not? He was there and he is in a position to make this defense. Why is he silent upon the question? Simply because he is a truthful man and he could not say one word in defense of General Harrison without telling an untruth, and he is too honorable a man to do that. *[Applause.]*

The Springfield Rifle Brigade

I have said that General Harrison voluntarily organized a company of III men—the largest that was organized at that time—to suppress the workingmen. The plea of his friends is at this time that he merely intended to scare them. Now just think about it, will you? He merely intended to scare them! If that is true why did he organize, equip, and drill his soldiers? Why did he equip them with the latest approved Springfield rifle and teach them how to shoot? I will tell you. It was just simply because he was willing at the word of command to send the naked souls of workingmen to the bar of God for simply striking for their rights. *[Applause.]*

That was his position, and he maintained that position from beginning to end, but he did not stop there. He was not satisfied with threatening to kill these men; he was not satisfied with lying around in the dog fennel during all this time waiting for a chance to pull the trigger. After he was foiled in that the trouble was finally settled, and that without the loss of a single life or the destruction of a cent's worth of property, after that was all over, what did he do then? We find him acting the role of the persecutor. He was not satisfied with having done all that he could to defeat those men in their effort to secure simple justice, but when the matter had all been settled he singled out his victims and pursued them until he had them landed behind prison bars. Just listen to this. The following is the title of a cause as appears by the record in the federal court at Indianapolis:

> See evidence in cause No. 4785 in the United States Circuit Court for the District of Indiana. The O&M Railroad Company vs. J. H. Wentworth, George Lovejoy, H. H. Barnaby, John Reeves. Appearance: For plaintiff, the Hon. Ben Harrison.

Harrison Prosecutes Them

These men were arrested and put upon trial. They were as innocent of crime as you and I. There was not a single charge against a single one of them, yet they were put upon trial. Uncle Sam had his great big paw upon every one of them. And yet Ben Harrison was not satisfied. He felt there was still a duty for him to perform. And what did he do? He volunteered his services to prosecute those four helpless men, and he succeeded, and I hope his ambition was gratified in putting all four of them behind prison bars. He succeeded in labeling every one of them as lawbreakers and criminals. Lovejoy, that I have spoken of, one of these defendants, is now a conductor on the Evansville & Terre Haute Railroad running into this city. He is a Republican in politics. Ask him what he thinks of General Harrison. *[Laughter and applause.]* Another of these defendants is a man by the name of John Reeves, now located at Clay City, Indiana. He had no more to do with the strike at that time than I had, and the testimony of record will prove the fact.

A Striker's Testimony

Now I would like to read you the statement made by John Reeves, the man that General Harrison sent to prison. This statement is dated August 10, 1888.

> I have been disgusted with the efforts put forth to show that Ben Harrison occupied a friendly attitude toward the railroad strikers. I was in a position to know whereof I speak, and I feel it my duty to speak right out in meeting and refute the statement, notably that of D. E. Crawford, circulated in campaign documents, that Ben Harrison was a friend of the strikers. I am now in the employ of the E&I Railroad at Clay City, Ind., having charge as watchman of engine No. 73, which runs between Clay City and Brazil. I have been in the employ of railroads for 34 years as

brakeman, fireman, engineer, conductor, section foreman, etc., and am a member of the Brotherhood of Locomotive Firemen, the Brotherhood of Railroad Brakemen, and the Masonic and Odd Fellows fraternities.

Previous to the general strike of 1877 I had been in the employ of the Ohio & Mississippi at Vincennes, but some months before the general strike, I, with other employees of the road, struck for back pay, and I had not returned to work when the general strike for an increase of wages was inaugurated in 1877. When the strike did come on I was working in the country near Vincennes as a threshing machine hand, and had been guilty of no offense whatever, unless it is an offense for a laborer to want his pay, but I had incurred the ill will of the Ohio & Mississippi. They wanted my scalp. I was an old offender because I had hitherto refused to work unless I was paid for it.

On Friday, in the latter part of July 1877, it being rainy weather, it was decided to do no more threshing until the following Monday.

I suppose Harrison would take care of the rest of the threshing. *[Laughter.]*

I went to town on Friday afternoon, expecting to return to my work on Monday. On the following Sunday I was standing on the platform at the Union depot when General Spooner stepped up to me and stated that he wanted me, at the same time pushing me back into the hands of the soldiers. They closed in around me and I was placed on board a train and at once taken to Terre Haute, the entire detachment of fully 200 United States soldiers guarding me on the way. *[Laughter.]* I was placed in jail and on Tuesday the United States Marshal brought to jail three other Ohio and Mississippi strikers named Barnaby, Wentworth, and Lovejoy, who had been arrested at Flora, 54 miles west of Vincennes. I was the only man arrested at Vincennes during the strike. On Wednesday we were all taken into court for trial on the charge of interfering with trains. Judge Drummond of Chicago presided, Judge Gresham, as I understand, refusing to act in our cases.

In the courtroom were many spectators. Harrison was sitting down at the time, but at once arose to his feet and saluted the court with a slight bow and a broad, bland smile. The O&M men whom Mr. Crawford says he saw in a restaurant near the post office handcuffed were the three Flora men and myself, making four instead of five, and instead of us all being acquitted through the influence of General Harrison, as is alleged in campaign documents on the authority of Mr. Crawford, the three Flora men entered pleas of guilty within an hour after it was announced that General Harrison had volunteered to prosecute us, while I myself, knowing my innocence, entered a plea of not guilty.

Harrison's course during the trial which followed shows that he was entirely void of any feeling or respect for the strikers. Surrounded as he was by high officials of a wealthy corporation, at the bar of one of the highest and most powerful courts in the land, entirely at home, because versed in the laws and rules and usages of the court, and standing as he did at the very head of the bar, he displayed a spirit of the greatest contempt for us poor beings who sat before him, fresh from our prison cells, three already convicted on their own plea of guilty and another unfortunately at his mercy.

We needed a friend at this particular time; we needed a strong friend and a powerful friend. We needed a friend with influence at the bar of the court and in high places; in fact, we needed precisely the same kind of friend Mr. Crawford and certain campaign documents claim Ben Harrison was to the striker. But we did not find that friend in Ben Harrison; on the contrary, this same Ben Harrison was bitter, vindictive, unjust, and unfair in the fight he volunteered to make against me as well as the others and, notwithstanding the fact that there was not one word of testimony that showed I was guilty of any wrong, yet he secured my conviction and had me placed under bond of $1,000 to keep the peace. This talk about Harrison being friendly to the strikers makes me tired.

—John Reeves.

A Deaf Ear to Distress

If Senator Voorhees had occupied the position that General Ben Harrison occupied at that time, do you suppose for one moment that he would have turned a deaf ear to the appeals of those men in their distress? He would have been with them body and soul, as he has always been on every occasion when there was a laboring man concerned. *[Applause.]* Instead of that, General Harrison took it upon himself to persecute and prosecute this man against whom there was not a single charge, nor was he satisfied until he had landed him in a prison cell. Now, for these reasons, I am against the election of General Ben Harrison for the presidency of the country. *[Applause and cries from the audience of "We, too; we, too!"]*

Not only that—he has used his official position, his high power in the counsels of this nation, to oppress the workingmen of this country. It is a matter of record that cannot be disputed or denied that he cast 14 votes in the Senate of the United States to place the workingmen of this country upon a level with the five-cent Chinaman, with the man who comes from abroad and carries a five-cent god in his pocket. *[Applause.]* He says at this time that he did it because of the doubt that he had of the legality of casting a vote against unrestricted Chinese labor. Now then, if he had a doubt about that subject, why in heaven's name didn't he give the workingmen of this country the benefit of that doubt? *[Applause.]*

Harrison's Pay as Railroad Attorney

Now then, there is just another phase to this question. When he told the men at Indianapolis that they were getting enough pay and that they ought to be satisfied and go back to their work, it so happened that he was in the employ of the railroad company himself. He was not on strike because I don't think he had any cause. I don't think he had any occasion to strike. I don't think I would strike myself if I were on a payroll at the rate of $1,000 a day. He made an affidavit to the fact in the United States Court at Indianapolis that he had been engaged in the cause the greater part of almost six days, that he was familiar with the fees and charges usually made by attorneys. He made an affidavit to the fact that his services, which consumed the greater part of six days, were reasonably worth $1,000. Now that explains the situation. The men on the Ohio & Mississippi Railroad, many of them, were getting a dollar a day. He told them they ought to be satisfied with that and go back to work, that it was all the company could afford to pay. If they had many attorneys like Harrison, I don't wonder that it is all the Ohio & Mississippi road could afford to pay their employees. *[Laughter and applause.]*

While they were being underpaid, while they were working night and day and day and night for just simply enough money to clothe and feed and shelter themselves and their families, there were those at the head of the corporation, among whom Harrison is a prominent representative, that were scooping in all the proceeds. Not only that, but in what they call the final record, he got for his services as the attorney of that road the princely sum of $21,000. I don't wonder that the Ohio & Mississippi Railroad Company was not able to pay its employees and that they went out on a strike. That explains the whole situation. Now just think of a man getting $1,000 a day according to his own bill, backed by his own affidavit; just think of that man telling those workingmen that they were being well paid and they ought to go back to their work because they were getting all the company could afford to pay them. Now tell me, if you will, if a man with that kind of a record is a real friend of the workingman? *[From the crowd: "No, no, never, of course not!"]*

Refuse Him Your Vote

Tell me if you can afford by your votes to elevate that kind of a man to the presidency? *[From the crowd: "No, no, no, no!"]* He has been guilty of those things that are an outrage to every propriety and an outrage to justice, but we cannot punish him. We can do this though: When a man of his kind poses for office and asks for votes, you can withhold them. You can refuse to vote for him, as I believe the workingmen of this country will do on the sixth day of next month. *[Applause.]*

A Word About the Tariff

I will pass to just another question. We have been told again and again by the Democratic Party that the tariff is a tax. Now, the Republican Party says that the tariff is wages to the extent that you increase the [rate], you increase the wages of the workingmen. The Republican leaders, at least those who are prominent among them, have from time to time advocated the reduction of the war taxes. They were considered by the Republican Party as being wise and eminent leaders and advanced thinkers, but when some Democratic statesman advocate the same thing he is called a free trader. The Democratic Party is no more in favor of free trade than the Republican Party is. It simply demands that taxation shall be limited to the actual needs and wants of the government economically, prudently, and carefully administered. They demand that the tariff—the taxes—shall be so levied and distributed as to fall upon the luxuries in place of the necessaries of life.

Now you workingmen have been told again and again that if you undertake to tamper with the tariff it is not good for workingmen. I recollect very distinctly that from 1873 to 1877 during the high tariff reign was a period of universal gloom. Factories, mills, and shops shut up and shut down, and the sheriff's hammer beat funeral marches everywhere. During that period the tramp era was inaugurated. There never was a tramp in the United States previous to 1873. A high tariff was not good for workingmen then. It is not good for him now. It is good for one purpose, and for one purpose only, and that is to multiply millionaires and mendicants. *[Applause.]* To create in the same breath both monopolists and paupers. If you want to centralize the wealth of the country in the hands of a few, if you want to see poverty-creating trusts everywhere, keep up the high tariff, vote the Republican ticket, and you will get there in due time. *[Applause.]*

Closing Words

I have already taken up much of your time, and you have with you here tonight a distinguished gentleman whom I know you are eager to hear talk. I want to say just simply this before I close—that this campaign, more than any other campaign that has ever preceded it, has been of interest to the workingmen.

The question of labor has expanded to continental proportions. The immortal words of Grover Cleveland, "Tell the truth," have been inscribed upon the banners of the Democratic Party, and I believe that when this campaign will have closed the workingmen throughout the country will have dignified and glorified themselves and their cause by having shown to the people of the country that the man who volunteers to organize a company of soldiers to shoot down the workingmen when they are striking for their rights never can become president of this country. *[Long and continued applause.]*

I now have the pleasure of presenting to you Senator Voorhees.

[At the conclusion of Mr. Debs's speech Senator Voorhees made some brief remarks, after which the meeting adjourned.]

The Aristocracy of Labor[†]
November 1888

The term "aristocracy" signifies a condition of things totally anti-American in government—and therefore in government affairs is unknown in this country. We have no titles of nobility—and officials are simply the *servants* of the people; the people make them and unmake them at will. Notwithstanding this, it so happens with a large number of officials that the moment they are inaugurated, they play such fantastic tricks as to make not only angels but all sensible people weep.[33] Nevertheless it is true that anyone at all observant cannot fail to note on all sides a tendency to exclusiveness which is the bane of our social structure, and an essential ingredient of aristocracy.

We have in this country a variety of aristocracies, each one of which, when subjected to analysis, is fruitful of derision and contempt.

In the North we used to have what was known as the "codfish" aristocracy— an exclusiveness based upon the catch of cod and mackerel, crabs and clams. True, there was in all New England an aristocracy or aristocracies which, while owing their dignity to cod and clams, were confronted with instances of exclusiveness,

† Published in *Locomotive Firemen's Magazine*, vol. 12, no. 11 (November 1888), 804–806.

based upon a superior religion which whipped Quakers, banished Baptists, and hung witches; but as cod and clams were abundant the codfish aristocracy gradually gained an ascendancy and maintained it. Some laid the foundation of their superiority in bartering rum and trinkets for African savages, while others boasted of blue blood, but to a greater or less extent, the smell of cod permeated the entire mass.

More recently the brood of American aristocracies has multiplied. Beginning with "striking ile,"[34] we now count our aristocracies by the score in banks and bucket shops, land and cattle, trusts and monopolies, until every town, village, and station, as well as the large centers of population have their aristocrats and exclusiveness, plumed and diamond, the aristocrat swaggers and struts on all the highways. Every village aspires to have its Gould, its Vanderbilt, or Astor, its aristocratic pimple, and in all communities are found a degenerate gang who have no higher ambition than to play the role of parasite; and now, heaven save the mark, we have what may be called an "aristocracy of labor"—an aristocracy in which one department of labor looks with proud disdain upon another department of labor—and if the subject of federation is mooted, then the aristocratic idea flames out like a blast of a volcano. Our attention has been called to a communication in the *Engineers' Journal* for October [1888], signed F. D. Toms, in which he says:

> That the engineers and firemen should always act as one man, and if a satisfactory constitution can be adopted, should hereafter be known as one order, all who have the welfare of both organizations at heart will agree.

So far, no proposition has been made to make the two brotherhoods, engineers and firemen, one brotherhood. It is not proposed to fuse, blend, amalgamate the brotherhoods but to form an alliance, which in time of trouble will result in concert of action. But Mr. Toms proceeds as follows:

> But are we willing to place our skilled labor on a level with the unskilled labor of switchmen and brakemen?

In this interrogatory we have the outcroppings of what may be styled the aristocracy of labor. It is the idea of exclusiveness. It is an idea of caste in embryo. In the various departments of labor no one underrates skill. The skilled laborer always receives higher wages than the unskilled laborer, but the unskilled laborer is "a man for a' that."[35] He may live in a humble home, "wear hodden gray and a' that," but he may be as intelligent as the skilled laborer, as well read, have as high ambitions, and be as good a citizen. More, he is an absolute necessity to the skilled laborer; indeed, it is not difficult to prove that the skilled laborer is positively dependent upon the unskilled laborer. We ask with commendable emphasis, what would become of the master bricklayer, the skilled mechanic, were it not for the humble, unskilled hod-carrier?

But without further divergence from the text, what would become of the skilled engineer but for the switchman and brakeman? No train would run, and the engineer's occupation, like that of Othello,[36] would be gone. When, we ask Mr. F. D. Toms, was it conceded that locomotive firemen were skilled laborers? When did the fact find lodgment in the mind of Mr. Toms? The idea of federation is not based upon skill or wages, or the superiority of one department of labor in comparison with another. The proposition of federation of railway employees is based upon the irrevocable necessity of one department to another in case a wrong exists which demands redress. It matters not how exclusive, how boastful, how aristocratic one department may be when its members are off of duty; the moment one takes his place on the rail all must be at their posts of duty. If the train can't move without an engineer, no more can it move without a firemen, a switchman, a brakeman, and a conductor. Here we have, federation or no federation, cooperation, interdependence—a necessity of one to the other, absolute and irrevocable—and any proposition looking to federation which docs not include all, or at least four of the departments named, is futile and preposterous.

We have no comments to make upon Mr. Toms's estimate of the Brotherhood of Locomotive Engineers, commendations in that direction are worthily bestowed, but says Mr. Toms:

> If we place ourselves in the power of other orders so they can call upon us to strike whenever they see fit, we will at once lose all the advantages we have gained by twenty years of conservative action.

Federation does not contemplate strikes. On the contrary, federation proposes the avoidance of strikes. There is no purpose to forego arbitration and concession. Corporations will be invited to adjust grievances as before; expedients to secure justice will be exhausted, as with the CB&Q, but when all fail and a strike is ordered, all train men will go together. It is then that men, skilled or unskilled laborers exert their power, and the fact that they would act as a unit, it is believed would prevent a strike and secure justice by the exhibition of federated force.

Mr. Toms, in speaking of the "Q" strike, expresses the opinion that the engineers and firemen could not have been "more successful had every brakeman and switchman on the road gone out with us," and immediately calls in question the declaration that "the conductors are the ones who have beaten us," and adds, "they would beat the engineers and firemen out of their jobs at any opportunity, but not many conductors would be anxious to take the positions vacated by the switchmen and brakemen." We italicize for the purpose of emphasizing Mr. Toms's inconsistency. The conductors would play engineers and firemen, but not switchmen and brakemen. Necessarily, therefore, if the switchmen and brakemen had "gone out" with the engineers and firemen, they would have helped to gain the victory over the "Q."

As for the conductors, it is even now believed that a majority of the members of the ORC are in active sympathy with other railroad employees who propose federation for protection and who, though not skilled workmen, are able, according to Mr. Toms, to defeat the engineers and firemen.

Mr. Toms further says:

> The switchmen have struck because a railroad company employed non-union men. Would we endorse any such actions? That would be contrary to all our principles. We never have, and I hope we never will so far forget our principles of American freedom, as to dictate to anyone who they may or may not employ.

This is simply chaff. It gives away everything. The strike on the "Q" is continued because the "Q" employs scabs and refuses to reinstate the old employees. If it be an American principle that anyone may employ whom they please, no one should kick if they employ Chinamen. And if it be an American principle that anyone can employ whom they please, it is certainly an American principle that they may pay them, if not such prices as they please, at least such prices as the parties may agree upon, and this being true, the question of wages is thrown out of court, remanded to the limbo of things obsolete.

Not so. The American idea is justice, the enthronement of the right, and that, too, by federation—"one in many"—not to defend the wrong, but to extirpate it and establish the right. Federation does not mean war, but more properly resistance of wrongs and injustice. In the American colonial federation, and in forming the union, little Rhode Island was crowned with all the dignity that attached to New York, Pennsylvania, and Virginia. There was no aristocracy of colonies, no feeling of exclusiveness when Rhode Island and Delaware entered the council chamber, and Mr. F. D. Toms can well afford to regard the importance of switchmen and brakemen when discussing the federation of railroad employees for mutual protection when they have wrongs to redress. Let us be done with everything that smacks of aristocracy in labor. The man who quarries the marble is a necessity to the artist, whose skilled hand and eye produce a statue, and the man who throws a switch, sets a brake, or shovels the coal, is as important to running a train as the engineer—and in discussing federation, where necessity forces cooperation and interdependence, exclusiveness regardless of real or supposed superiority is not to be tolerated.

Necessary Strikes[†]

December 1888

In a recent issue of the Brookfield, Missouri, *Argus* appears an editorial article on strikes, in which the writer bemoans the fate of workingmen who, faithful to their allegiance, sometimes strike because an injustice has been done one or more of the men who are associated with them in a union or a brotherhood.

The editor of the *Argus* wails like a north wind around the corner of a pigpen, and sobs like a squeezed sponge over the fate of workingmen's wives and children, whose husbands and fathers strike rather than submit to degradation and crawl in the dust on their bellies at the feet of those who insult and oppress them.

The Brookfield paper is not an *Argus*. It has not a hundred eyes.[37] It doesn't seem to have even one good eye. Its vision is defective. It should be called the *Bat* or the *Owl,* though such titles would be doing injustice to the leather-winged and hooting curiosities which subsist on beetles and mice, for they have the good sense, possibly instinct, not to make themselves offensive during daylight, not even to birds of better feather.

The editor of the *Argus,* alias the *Bat,* reminds one of a poll parrot or a split-tongued crow, taught to repeat words and expressions, and which, regardless of occasions and proprieties, let slip their acquirements. Listen to the Brookfield *Argus*. It says:

> Strikes have entailed more suffering upon our working classes than any other visitation not sent direct from heaven.

---

† Published as "Strikes" in *Locomotive Firemen's Magazine,* vol. 12, no. 12 (December 1888), 885–887.

What are the "visitations sent direct from heaven" that have entailed as much or more suffering upon "our working classes" than strikes? The *Argus* doesn't name the heavenly visitations. "Our working classes," we guess, would like to have the heavenly visitations that cause them suffering enumerated. Are they earthquakes, cyclones, tornados, fires, famines, overflows, droughts, pestilences, panics, embezzlements, cornering food products, robbing savings banks, watering stocks, forming trusts and monopolies, cutting down wages, and importing cheap labor, etc., to the end of the chapter? We suppose the *Argus*, if it has a hundred eyes, or one eye or the half of an eye, could tell the "working classes," what are the visitations sent "direct from heaven" that cause them as much or more suffering than strikes.

The idiotic gabble of the Brookfield *Argus*, alias *Owl*, would be totally unworthy of notice, were it not for the fact that in a great majority of cases, the press, from motives which bear the stamp of subsidy, studiously ignores the devilish wrongs which underlie strikes—wrongs which, if not antagonized or extirpated, are as certain to lead to squalid poverty and the enslavement which is born of degradation as that light is the opposite of darkness.

Admitting that strikes are calamitous, the same is true of wars. Indeed, a strike is war—and just here arises the question, should a nation go to war for a wrong done one of its citizens? If it would not put forth all its power to redress such a wrong, it deserves and is certain to receive the contempt of nations and the execrations of its own citizens. Its flag symbolizes cowardice, a pusillanimity, a poltroonery, which defies exaggeration.

Let any nation worthy of recognition learn that one of the humblest of its citizens has been wronged by another nation, and redress is speedily demanded. A correspondence is at once begun. The history of the case is obtained; every fact is brought out. This done, and the facts being established that a wrong has been perpetrated, redress is demanded. Preceding extreme measures, there will be negotiations, offers of concessions and compromises to secure a just settlement, and finally offers will be made to arbitrate—but, failing in their efforts, there will be a declaration of war, and such wars are righteous wars. They are avoidable only by debasement, degradation, and enslavement, than which annihilation is preferable. They bring calamities, famine and pestilence, death and desolation, widows and orphans; but, while wrongs are perpetrated and the right has a champion, there will be wars. It is then, when strikes are inevitable if degradation would be avoided, that labor unions and brotherhoods are lampooned and all the resources of vituperative malice is heaped upon them.

What is wanted is not lamentations over strikes, but that a righteous indignation should everywhere be aroused, on account of the cursed causes which
lead inevitably to strikes. Defend the wrong, apologize for it, perpetuate it,
and as certain as rivers flow to the sea, there will be ceaseless disturbances.
The men who denounce strikes and are silent about the wrongs that produce
strikes would, in time of pestilence, denounce a sanitary committee who would
compel the removal of nuisances that originated and continued the scourge;
they would lament the effects of malaria but remain silent when its victims demanded the draining of the bog in which the poison was germinated and from
which it went forth on its death-dealing mission.

Labor unions and brotherhoods are not organized for strikes any more than
governments are instituted for war. But labor unions have striking powers just
as governments have war powers, and it requires no argument to demonstrate,
if such powers are surrendered, the result will be degradation and enslavement.
Labor unions, like governments, ought not to tolerate wrongs inflicted upon
their members—nor will they remain supine when injustice is perpetrated,
unless they are willing to accept degradation and enslavement, and this is just
what the editor of the Brookfield, Missouri, *Argus* would have labor unions and
brotherhoods accept, and in doing this he but echoes the hootings of a press
found in almost every community, which howls like paid mourners at a funeral
over the sacrifices strikers heroically endure, but has never a word denouncing
the wrongs and crimes which occasion strikes.

Notes

1. John Alexander Martin (1839–1889), a Republican, was elected the tenth governor of Kansas in November 1884. He served from January 1885 to January 1889.
2. Calvin S. Wheaton (1846–1922) of Elmira, New York, was elected the tenth grand chief conductor of the Order of Railway Conductors in October 1880. He served in that capacity until resigning in September 1890 over the organization's decision to end its no-strike policy. He briefly founded a dissident organization, the Independent Order of Railway Conductors, serving for a time as the group's president. After his time as a brotherhood functionary ended, Wheaton returned to train conducting, finishing his career in Columbia, South Carolina, running a regular passenger train route during the years of World War I to Augusta, Georgia, on the Southern Railway.
3. William P. Daniels (1851–1921) of Cedar Rapids, Iowa, was elected grand secretary and treasurer of the Order of Railway Conductors in October 1878. He remained in that position until 1895.
4. From *Railway Age*, vol. 13, no. 1 (January 1888), 225.
5. "The CB&Q Strike," *Locomotive Firemen's Magazine*, vol. 12, no. 4 (April 1888), 242–246.
6. There does not seem to be an instance in which Shakespeare described a "scab" using these exact words, although he does use the term as an epithet in *Much Ado About Nothing* (1598), act 3, scene 3; *Twelfth Night* (1599) act 2, scene 5; *Troilus and Cressida* (1601), act 2, scene 1; and *Coriolanus* (c. 1607), act 1, scene 1.
7. Allusion to Genesis 8:4.
8. Allusion to Exodus 20.
9. Hod-carriers are assistants to bricklayers or stonemasons who transport heavy supplies to the craftworker via a metal trough called a hod, generally mounted on a shaft and carried over the shoulder.
10. From "The Battle-Field" (1839), by William Cullen Bryant (1794–1878).
11. From *An Essay on Man* (1734), by Alexander Pope (1688–1744).
12. Allusion to Genesis 25:29–34.
13. William Brittingham Lacey, "Discourse at St. Peter's Church, Albany, New York, April 20, 1828," in *Lacey, An Illustration of the Principles of Elocution: Designed for the Use of Schools*. Albany (Websters and Skinners, 1828), 179. Lacey's work was frequently reprinted in nineteenth-century elocution textbooks.
14. The source of this quotation has not been identified.
15. William Ewart Gladstone (1809–1898), leader of the Liberal Party, was four times the prime minister of Great Britain. He was in the parliamentary opposition at the time this article was written.
16. Charles Stewart Parnell (1846–1891) was the leader of the Irish Parliamentary Party and former head of its predecessor, the Home Rule League. A member of parliament from 1882 until his death in October 1891, Parnell was regarded as one of the preeminent forces in British politics.

17. Noah Webster, *An American Dictionary of the English Language*, vol. 2, (New York: S. Converse, 1828).
18. John J. Kelly and John H. McGilvery were undercover operatives of the Pinkerton Detective Agency who had gained employment as secretaries of S. E. Hoge, chairman of the Burlington strike committee of the Brotherhood of Locomotive Engineers, and J. H. Murphy, his counterpart with the Brotherhood of Locomotive Firemen. The secret testimony of these agents is said to have led to the July 1888 arrest of Hoge and Murphy for production of a circular advising striking engineers to engage in the sabotage of locomotives before walking out on strike—a circular that union leaders claimed was a provocative fabrication intended to discredit the walkout.
19. J. A. Bowles was a Burlington striker implicated in a conspiracy to dynamite CB&Q tracks. Wilson was the Pinkerton agent provocateur whose activity led to his arrest.
20. A deciduous tree native to tropical Africa, Indonesia, and the Philippines, the sap of which is used for poison darts. It was believed at one time that the fragrance of the tree was itself toxic.
21. Allan J. Pinkerton (1819–1884) was a Scottish-born detective who rose to prominence as the head of the Union Intelligence Service during the American Civil War. Pinkerton's organization, the Pinkerton National Detective Agency, established in 1850, became actively involved in anti-labor intelligence and the armed intimidation of striking workers during the postwar years.
22. James Parton (1822–1891) was a prolific biographer, writing on such leading figures of American history as Horace Greeley, Aaron Burr, Andrew Jackson, Benjamin Franklin, and Thomas Jefferson.
23. James Parton, "Outgrown City Government," *Forum*, vol. 2, no. 6 (February 1887), 544.
24. Line from "The Cotter's Saturday Night" (1785), by Robert Burns (1759–1796).
25. Collis Potter Huntington (1821–1900) was one of the so-called Big Four railway financiers who jointly sponsored the Central Pacific's intercontinental line. He was named president of the Southern Pacific–Central Pacific system in 1890.
26. Russell Sage (1816–1906), a close business associate of Jay Gould, maintained a number of railroad investments. He was a major investor in the Union Pacific Railroad.
27. Extracted from the lyrics of the Christian hymn "God Moves in a Mysterious Way" (1774), by William Cowper (1731–1800).
28. The upcoming 1888 national convention of the Brotherhood of Locomotive Firemen.
29. Benjamin Harrison (1833–1901) was elected the twenty-third president of the United States in November 1888. A grandson of President William Henry Harrison (1773–1841), a Whig, the younger Harrison was an early convert to the Republican Party, working for the election of the new party's ticket in the election of 1856. The lawyer Harrison raised a regiment of Indiana volunteers during the Civil War and was afterward commissioned as a captain and company commander. He saw

action in a number of battles and was brevetted to brigadier general a few months before the end of the conflict. Harrison raised a citizen militia to support the railway companies during the Great Strike of 1877 and was tapped by the Republican Party as its nominee for US Senate in 1878, losing to Democrat Daniel W. Voorhees in the legislative vote. In 1880, Harrison was finally elected to the Senate in his second attempt, winning a second term in 1886.

30. Reference is to the protective tariff, a benchmark of Republican policy, which had the effect of raising the price of consumer goods.

31. John Caven (1824–1905) was elected mayor of Indianapolis five times, interrupted by two terms in the Indiana State Senate.

32. Albert Gallatin Porter (1824–1897) was a Democrat who left the party for the Republican Party in 1856 over the issue of slavery. A member of Congress during the Civil War, Porter was elected the nineteenth governor of Indiana in November 1880 and served a single four-year term of office.

33. From *The Merchant of Venice*, by William Shakespeare.

34. Allusion to "Striking Ile [Oil]" (1865), a popular song by Daniel Decatur Emmett (1815–1904) that dealt with the gold rush–like quality of early petroleum prospecting.

35. From "A Man's a Man," by Robert Burns.

36. Allusion to *Othello* (1603), by William Shakespeare. Othello was a former military commander.

37. Argus Panoptes was a one-hundred-eyed giant of Greek mythology.

1889

The Knights of Labor[†]

January 1889

For a number of years past the organization known as the Knights of Labor has been conspicuously before the country. Its rapid growth, its vast membership, its commanding influence in the industrial affairs of the country constituted the order an arbiter in matters of supreme importance to its members and their employers.

The membership at one time approximated a million. All men contemplated its colossal proportions with amazement, some with alarm. Its membership was composed of men and women, white and black, learned and ignorant, skilled and unskilled, working people. It aimed high. Its purposes were the amelioration of the condition of the working people of the country. It started out with the motto that "an injury to one was the concern of all." It was organized to *strike*. It believed in the *boycott*. It is not surprising that grievances were numerous. They existed in every department of labor. Wrongs, more or less flagrant, were brought to the attention of the assemblies of the order. The course of procedure was sharply defined by law. Assemblies were clothed with extraordinary powers—designed, ostensibly, to correct abuses and improve the condition of the membership. If employers were stubborn, a strike was ordered and a boycott inaugurated.

The order is modern—and it is American. It sounded a keynote. It recognized certain great fundamental facts—the independence and the sovereignty of the American citizen. It grasped the vital idea that, if American wageworkers were prosperous and content, the welfare of society was secure. If, on the contrary, the people, whose moral, intellectual, social, and physical well-being depended upon their wages, were underpaid, poverty and degradation would inevitably result, and that social disorder would follow with unerring certainty.

There is not a statesman, a political economist, or a philanthropist on the continent worthy of the name who will controvert such propositions. They are self-evident; they have the force of axioms—and yet, society as a whole antagonizes the Knights of Labor. Not only Knights of Labor but every other organization of workingmen whose purpose it is to better their condition pecuniarily.

If working people are content to accept such wages as are offered, and out of their scanty revenues provide assistance for the sick, bury the dead, and pay

---

† Published in *Locomotive Firemen's Magazine*, vol. 13, no. 1 (January 1889), 11–12.

widows and orphans a few hundred dollars, when husbands and fathers are beneath the sod, society applauds. But the instant these wage-men complain of low wages, of poverty, of inability to provide the comforts and necessities of life for themselves and those dependent upon them, millionaires, monopolists, members of syndicates and trusts, bankers, speculators, food cornerers, and brokers—the entire brood of those who receive tribute from labor—set up the cry that workingmen constitute a dangerous element; the press is subsidized, the untold blessings which labor confers upon society are ignored, and there are wild denunciations of labor organizations.

During the convention of the Knights of Labor in Indianapolis in November,[1] some startling facts were made public, facts which all well-wishers of this great organization must deplore. In the first place it was shown that the membership had astonishingly decreased—that at least 500,000 members had withdrawn. It was shown that there were internal dissensions and, worse still, that the order was virtually bankrupt—that its liabilities exceeded its revenues, and that financially the order had reached the point of danger. To the superficial observer the conclusion is natural that under such circumstances the organization had ended its mission, and nothing was left but to die as gracefully and as philosophically as circumstances would permit. We prefer to look upon a less gloomy side of such pictures. In the first place, an organization with 300,000 loyal members ought not to be financially embarrassed, nor can it be for any extended period, provided a policy of wise economy prevails. The danger that confronts the Knights of Labor is not finance, but faction. The moment faction is eliminated, harmony is enthroned, and with harmony comes health and strength.

Faction may reduce membership, but it cannot destroy principle. That there was a necessity for the order of Knights of Labor is not to be questioned. That it has made mistakes need not be asserted nor denied. That its mission is ended we do not believe. Its birth was not premature. Its phenomenal growth is convincing proof that the best interests of society demand its appearance. That it has waned is not a mystery. The reason why is easily understood, and the remedy is within reach. The head of the order, Grand Master Workman [Terence] Powderly, has discovered the causes of decline, and in his address points them out with such vividness that retrievement need not be delayed. That the Knights of Labor are sailing in dangerous seas just now is patent to the most superficial observer. Mr. Powderly said in his address that the deliberations and final conclusions of the late convention would seal the fate of the order: rescue it from death, or give to it new vitality. Most devoutly do we wish the order freedom from every entanglement that has reduced its membership, impeded its progress, and threatened its dissolution. But whatever may be the fate of the Knights of Labor, it will not arrest the determination of the wageworkers of America to improve their condition.

> For Freedom's battle, oft begun,
> Bequeath'd from bleeding sire to son,
> Tho' baffled oft, is ever won.[2]

In the Indianapolis convention, the fact was discovered that the Knights have an abundance of funds, and the prompt offer of financial assistance indicated a strong faith in the future of the organization. We are not disposed to criticize, *pro et con,* the amazing features of the meeting. It is enough to say that the organization remains intact, with Powderly at its head, and that we wish it the largest possible measure of prosperity.

The decree for the emancipation of labor has gone forth. It will not be modified nor revoked. Workingmen, like other men, will learn wisdom in the school of experience. If there are those who oppose and condemn labor organizations, and surmise that the disintegration of the Knights of Labor or any other union or brotherhood of workingmen means the triumph of those who antagonize such unions, they are doomed to disappointment. A Waterloo may have sealed the fate of Napoleon, but not of France. A Bull Run did not decide the fate of the Union. Revolutions may be arrested in their march, but they do not move backward. The world may deprecate strikes, but they will come in some form until the cause for strikes is removed.

> Go, wing your flight from pole to pole,
> Nor cease till all the zones are seen
> That belt the earth, where oceans roll
> Where hills and vales are decked in green;
> Find all the lands beneath the sun,
> Where mountains rise and rivers run;
> Where man for man has toiled and died;
> Where tyrants have been defied;
> Then tell me where the men are free,
> Who have not struck for Liberty.[3]

The Progress of Federation†

January 1889

This magazine makes no apology for advocating with such ability as it can command the policy of federation. We have no wish to disguise or dwarf any of the obstacles in the way of progress and of ultimate triumph. We are not disheartened because here and there some subsidized organ declaims in opposition to the movement. Such things are to be expected. There is not a movement on record designed to liberalize the mind, to crush the wrong, to enthrone, dignify, and glorify the right, that has not been required to fight for every inch of advancement. Viewing matters from such a standpoint, we arrive at the conclusion that opposition helps on a good cause. It invites discussion. It keeps alive agitation. It sets men to thinking. It brings the truth to the front. The danger lies in listlessness, not in alertness. The demand for labor organizations is conceded. The strength of unity is not doubted. Federation carries organization to its extreme limit of usefulness. The Brotherhood of Locomotive Firemen is unanimous in favor of federation. At the Atlanta convention it placed itself on record. Circumstances enabled it to be the first labor organization to make the declaration. For this, the brotherhood takes only so much credit as attaches to doing its duty fearlessly. It had the courage of conviction. It would emancipate labor from degrading conditions. It is not shackled by aristocratic exclusiveness. It believes that an "honest man is the noblest work of God,"[4] that

> His words are bonds, his oaths are oracles;
> His love sincere, his thoughts immaculate;
> His tears, pure messengers sent from his heart;
> His heart as far from fraud as heaven from earth.[5]

Believing such things, the B of LF is in a situation to federate with other labor organizations engaged in the railway service. And here, let it be said, if honest men are to be found anywhere it will be among the membership of organized labor. This is not panegyric, not fulsome eulogy. It is simple truth, known and read of all men who are not blinded by bigotry. The B of LF in advocating federation does not stop to inquire the amount of pay a man receives, or whether he handles switch, brake, punch, throttle, or scoop, but rather, is

---

† Published in *Locomotive Firemen's Magazine,* vol. 13, no. 1 (January 1889), 3–5.

he an honorable member of an honorable organization, struggling against adverse surroundings to secure honest pay for honest work that he may have the necessities of life and some of its luxuries, and that he may live as becomes an American citizen; to clothe, educate, and train his children to act well their part in a God-favored land, where the government is of, for, and by the people? Laboring men know that they are denied such wages and hence they organize that if possible they may improve their condition. Federation of labor organization contemplates aid, mutual assistance in such an honorable endeavor.

The idea of federation is not modern, but its application to organizations of workingmen engaged in the railway service is of recent date. What progress has been made? We reply that it is eminently creditable and encouraging. Immediately following the action of the B of LF at Atlanta, the Switchmen's Mutual Aid Association unanimously declared for federation. Switchmen are courageous men. A coward can't be a switchman. Only clearheaded, steady-nerved, and keen-eyed men can be switchmen. Their vocation is perilous in the extreme, and of all the orders of men engaged in the railway service, not one has given more attention to the rights and wrongs of railroad employees. Here, then, we have two organizations in line at the earliest practicable period. In October, when the great Brotherhood of Railroad Brakemen assembled in convention at Columbus, the question of federation was up for debate. This brotherhood, coming third, had ample opportunity to investigate the subject. It had as large interests at stake as any other brotherhood engaged in the railway service. The delegates to the convention were competent men. They knew what they wanted, and they decided unanimously to federate with the firemen and the switchmen. As a result, we find that in two months, three brotherhoods of railway employees decide to federate. We regard the record as eminently satisfactory. And now comes the Brotherhood of Locomotive Engineers. At the annual convention of the order held in Richmond, Virginia, in November, the engineers decided not to federate. The reason for this action, or rather non-action, we shall not attempt to explain except upon a hypothesis warranted by circumstances.

We do the engineers no injustice by saying that up to the time of the CB&Q strike, they regarded their brotherhood invincible, and not in a condition to need the assistance of any other labor organization. The CB&Q strike, in its inception, was an affair of the engineers. It is a well-known fact that the firemen on the CB&Q could have run the engines which the engineers abandoned. They were competent. The officers of the road recognized the fact. But in this supreme moment, the firemen made the cause of the engineers their own and sacrificed everything to a spirit of loyalty, of federation.

Nor was this all of their service to the engineers. That brotherhood, by its previous course, had engendered many animosities in the minds of Knights of Labor, the justice of such hostility we are not required to discuss, we simply state the fact, but the firemen discarded all such considerations and placed themselves between the engineers and those who sought to antagonize their interests. In attempting to explain the hostility of other organizations toward the B of LE, it may be said, we think, that it grew out of the policy of exclusiveness which had characterized it. It had been wanting in sympathy for all other labor organizations when in trouble. Toward the B of LF this spirit of exclusiveness had been decided to the last degree of endurance, but the firemen on the

did not enact the role of neutrality, they promptly took sides. They resolved to share the fate of the engineers. Now what of all this! It is told in a few words. The engineers refuse to federate with the switchmen and brakemen, but declare in favor of cooperation with the firemen. Toward all other brotherhoods in the railway service, a "strict neutrality is to be maintained." What is neutrality? Is it not a total disregard of the rights and the wrongs involved in any controversy? Is it not a mental and moral condition, in which all the finer perceptions of right and justice are blunted or kept in abeyance, not permitted to act? It simply amounts to this, that no matter what grievance a switchman or brakeman may have—no matter to what extent their rights may be outraged, no matter how flagrant may be the wrongs to which they are subjected—the engineers propose to maintain a "strict neutrality," strict indifference, totally regardless whether the right or wrong triumphs. But with the firemen, the engineers propose to "cooperate." To cooperate involves the idea of coordinate, coequal, of the same rank. But the B of LE declares that a member of the B of LF, who is a member of the B of LE, shall not represent his division in a convention of the B of LE. In such a case, what becomes of the coequal, the coordinate idea? Is it not exploded? Does it not vanish?

Notwithstanding such considerations, it may be said that the B of LE is making some progress toward federation. Three years ago, the B of LF, at its convention held in Philadelphia, passed the following resolutions:

> *Resolved,* That it is the sense of this body that we do all in our power to create and maintain a harmonious feeling between the Brotherhood of Locomotive Engineers and the Brotherhood of Locomotive Firemen.

> *Resolved,* That we place ourselves on record with the Brotherhood of Locomotive Engineers and that the secretary of the Grand Lodge [Debs] be authorized and directed to make a statement to the said organization under real

of the Grand Lodge, to the effect that our order is now a labor organization, made such by the action of this convention, and that we are desirous of cooperating with them in all their grievances, and that we shall expect the same from them in our troubles; knowing the fact that in union there is strength we are ready to meet them halfway.

Resolved, That these resolutions be presented to the Annual Convention of the Brotherhood of Locomotive Engineers, at New Orleans, October 21, by a committee of one, who shall endeavor to bring about a proper recognition of this body, in order that we may be enabled to carry out the purposes of these resolutions by a friendly understanding during times of trouble.

A delegate was commissioned to present the foregoing resolutions to the B of LE, in convention assembled, in the city of New Orleans. The resolutions were presented to the grand chief of the brotherhood, P. M. Arthur, who stated to the delegate that "the B of LE never had and never would cooperate with any other labor organization; that it was amply able to take care of itself, and that other organizations must do the same." That the convention was heartily in sympathy with Grand Chief Arthur is evident from the fact that no action was taken upon the resolutions passed by the B of LF and presented by its appointed delegate to the convention of the B of LE. That the resolutions were treated with the utmost indifference, it is only necessary to state that at the New Orleans Convention was enacted the law that no member of the B of LF should be eligible to membership in the B of LE.

This was three years ago. Then the B of LF wanted to cooperate with the B of LE and were ignored. Its resolutions were treated as trivial, unimportant, and evidently excited neither concern nor attention. Now we are informed that the B of LE is willing to cooperate, and we predict that when another period of three years has elapsed, the B of LE will be willing to federate. We recognize the fact that great bodies move slowly, and we congratulate the B of LE that it is willing now to cooperate. We leave it to the conquering logic of events and of progress.

It is safe to say that every engineer on the CB&Q was, and is, in favor of federation. These men understood the situation, they were in a position to appreciate the unwavering loyalty of firemen, and had the entire membership of the B of LE been similarly situated, there would have been no difficulty about federation in the Richmond convention.

In conclusion, let it be said that the firemen, the brakemen, and the switchmen have determined to federate, form an alliance, offensive and defensive, for the general welfare. These brotherhoods are students of the signs of the times.

They understand their mission. They are conservatively progressive. If there are those whose pretentiousness, vanity, or conceit keeps them to themselves—out of the broad current of human sympathy—their cynical views and practices will not deflect the firemen, brakemen, and switchmen from federating, and as for final results there is neither doubt nor fear.

Triumph Through Federation[†]
January 1889

The *Locomotive Firemen's Magazine* has in the past advocated the of locomotive engineers, locomotive firemen, railroad brakemen, and switchmen, nor have we been disinclined to include railroad conductors. We have discussed the subject entirely free from passion. We have assumed throughout in the discussion of wages, the improvement of the condition of workingmen, that society at large, as certainly as the individual workingman, would derive large benefits by the enthronement of a policy which would insure to workingmen fair, honest, living wages.

This magazine, while it is the recognized organ of a great brotherhood, and on all occasions champions the interests of the Brotherhood of Locomotive Firemen, has done what it could to arrest the growth of the pernicious idea that there is an aristocracy in labor—the India-pagan idea of caste, than which nothing could be introduced into the discussion of topics designed for the welfare of the workingmen of the country more detrimental to their well being.

Let us say just here and now that the aristocratic, the caste idea is not only repugnant to American institutions, but is rebuked by God Himself. The apostle Peter, and a braver man never drew a sword or offered up a prayer, declared that he had learned that "God is no respecter of persons"—and our own immortal Declaration of Independence declares that "all men are created equal." It would be blind, impudent folly, after quoting such authorities, to favor aristocracy or caste in society, and it is an insult of colossal proportions for one wageworker to

† Published as "Federation" in *Locomotive Firemen's Magazine,* vol. 13, no. 1 (January 1889), 8–11.

assume a haughty, disdainful, and overbearing air towards another wageworker because, forsooth, his pay is more remunerative. In pursuing such a course, he does what God Almighty never did since He created Adam, and he does that which the genius of American institutions condemns. In the discussion of federation of railroad brotherhoods we dismiss sentiment, though we fully recognize a sentimental side to the subject. We favor federation because we believe it capable of producing beneficial results, financially. If this is admitted, if this is true, other benefits relating to moral, social, and educational conditions are certain to follow.

Those who favor federation are, we conceive, in duty bound to state their reasons for the position they have taken. To win, their reasons must be cogent and convincing. They must be free from sophistry. Every proposition should be sharply stated. Conclusions should be based upon facts. In such discussions the tricks and arts of the demagogue should have neither place nor consideration. This done, men will be able to determine the course of action which ought to be pursued.

In the first place take the four orders of railroad employees, engineers, firemen, brakemen, and switchmen. They are especially identified in running railroad trains; they are absolute necessities. Without them trains could not move. In the very nature of things, as employees, these men must cooperate; they are interdependent, the one cannot operate without the other. In their employment for one to assume any superiority over the other is sheer nonsense. There can be no rivalry. These different classes of railroad employees organized brotherhoods. Why? It may be said in reply, to improve their condition, morally and socially. But this is not all—the fundamental, bedrock fact in forming the organizations was the bettering of conditions financially. Wages was the supreme question. There is not an organization of workingmen in the country which was not prompted by the belief that it would be the means, directly and indirectly, immediately and remotely, of advancing wages, or at any rate, preventing a decline in wages.

It is scarcely required to say in this connection that labor creates the wealth of nations. Workingmen after many years of education grasped the fact, and the conclusion followed that they were not receiving their equitable share of this wealth. They saw distinctly that their environments were such as were calculated to keep them forever in a condition of subjection, to prevent their advancement—to blast their hopes and defeat their aspirations. They created the wealth and remained poor. They tilled all the fields and harvested all the crops, but were hungry. They manufactured all the clothing, the hats and the shoes, but had to be content with scanty raiment. They built all the houses for the people and the barns for the cattle and were compelled to inhabit shelters unfit for human beings. Their country conferred upon them sovereignty and they had the ballot, but the laws were so framed that their rights and interests were ignored. In a word, labor was degraded.

Under such circumstances, workingmen concluded to organize themselves into unions and brotherhoods. Nothing could be more natural. The causes were numerous, of long standing, deep-rooted and powerful. They created a necessity for organization—compact, determined, and persevering organization. It is only needed to look around to comprehend to what extent labor has organized during the last 25 years. Almost every trade that can be named has an organization, and the purpose of which primarily is to secure fair and honest wages.

We are not unmindful of the fact that many of these organizations have what are termed benevolent features, that the sick and afflicted are cared for, and that certain pecuniary benefits accrue to relatives in case of death, but at the bottom of this benevolent policy lies the question of wages—fair pay for fair work. With this question settled all others are easily managed. With fair wages we have the bright and cheerful home, good food, good clothes, books and papers and refinement such as should adorn the American home.

It will be admitted, we think without controversy, that organization has accomplished vast good for the American workingman. It has taught him his power in the body politic, social, and commercial. He has found that organization educates and elevates, that it gives power and consequence, and exerts an influence which statesmen recognize as potent. But the workingmen have learned that while they have been organized for bettering their condition by advancing and maintaining wages, the employers have been busy in devising ways and means whereby they might hope to maintain their ascendancy, nor have they been disappointed.

We readily comprehend how that in this connection we could devote some space to the discussion of certain facts upon which employers rely for ultimate success in defeating labor organizations—chiefly, that what is termed the "labor market" is oversupplied with men, and that if one man quits work, no matter what the cause may be, two men stand ready to take the place at the wages offered. It is this fact that brings into the boldest possible prominence the benefits of federation—the inauguration of an alliance between organizations whose members are identified with carrying forward an industrial enterprise, in which each one is absolutely necessary to the other.

And here, coming down to business, we take for an illustration a railroad. Necessarily, it employs engineers, firemen, switchmen, and brakemen. In case of a grievance on the part of one class of these employees, the road might be slightly embarrassed by a strike, but if the other three classes remain loyal to the corporation, the places of those who had quit work could be readily supplied, and things would move forward without serious embarrassment. In this case it is readily seen that the purpose of organization would be defeated. This sort of a victory has often been achieved by railroad corporations. It matters not how serious and exasperating may have been the grievances of the employees, the more indefensible the wrongs, the greater the triumph of the corporation, and, emboldened by success, it gives other employees to understand that the same fate awaits them for any similar assertion of manly independence.

What is the logic of such a case as we have cited? It is this: that the corporation is stronger than any one organization of its employees, and can defeat it in any contest without regard to justice or the rights of the employees. This has been done in the past, and will be done in the future more frequently if occasion requires, because corporations are combining for defense. Quick to comprehend situations, watchful of the signs of the times, they see the day of battle approaching. American workingmen, at least the more intelligent and progressive of them, have determined to enjoy their rightful share of the wealth they create. They have organized for the struggle. In the contests that have taken place, organized labor, though "baffled oft," has compelled corporations to show their hand. Their purposes, strategy, and policy are understood and the knowledge gained is not, like the talent we read about, to be hid away in a napkin. With railroad employees it is to be used for their benefit. It may be that the corporation can defeat one or even two labor organizations, but it will find it difficult to strike down three or four when federated to secure justice and acting as a unit. Organized labor has accomplished much—how much can never be told. It has been an educating force of transcendent power. It has brought into play the mind-forces of millions which before were dormant. It has aroused energies and ambitions in consonance with American rights and privileges that cannot be lulled to repose. The maxim that "in union there is strength," trite but true, has been clothed with new significance. Organization has prepared the way for federation. Organization is federation's *avant courier.* It is as one crying in the wilderness of doubt; in the wake of defeat, prepare the way for federation and the triumph of labor.

Are there those who doubt? Probably. Are there those who hesitate? Certainly. When, we ask, in the history of the world's advancement was there ever a movement made to emancipate men from oppression that there were not men who doubted and hesitated? When was there an army organized that did not have its cowards? Where in the world's history has truth confronted error that there was not to be found a Judas Iscariot to betray with a kiss for a consideration? Men who take counsel of their fears stand still or recede. It is not required to particularize. History supplies multiplied instances. Workingmen who organize are courageous. Men who stand by their colors in the storm of battle, in the hours of darkness, men whom defeat cannot dishearten, clear-visioned, clear-headed, and trustful, are now, as in the past, the hope of the world. Workingmen see distinctly that final triumph is to be secured by federation.

Locomotive firemen, railroad brakemen, and switchmen have declared for federation. These organizations are pledged to an alliance that cooperation, however liberally construed, does not create. Federation is a compact, a treaty. It has a significance, a power and influence that cooperation does not and cannot possess.

It is not our purpose at this writing to discuss fine distinctions in the meaning of words. That may come later. Our chief purpose now is to say that this magazine is unalterably committed to the federation of the organizations of railroad employees engaged in moving trains. As we have said, three of these organizations have voted in favor of federation, and they will federate.

The important preliminary steps have been taken. There are no insuperable obstacles in the way, and final results are no longer matters of discouragement or special anxiety. The question may be asked, will other organizations come into line under the federation banner? We might answer by asking, why not? What have they to gain by remaining isolated? The men who federate are the peers of those who may decline to fly the federation banner—their equals in moral excellence, in mental grasp, in the comprehension of the problems to be solved, in manly independence and in all things that go to make up good citizenship, and since trains cannot move without their assistance, the necessity of discussing any phase of the subject which does not directly relate to the settlement of such grievances as are common to railroad employees does not appear.

In closing this article we desire to say that we have undiminished faith in the conquering power of education. It levels up, and it levels down. Aristocratic ignorance and superstitions are certain to disappear. The brotherhood idea is sweeping along with resistless power, and the time is not distant, as we read the signs of the times, when the throttle, the pick, the brake, and the switch, arrayed in artistic style, will symbolize the federation of the men who wield them, not only in their own interests but for the interests of society, and we do not hesitate to believe that the festive punch sooner or later will have its allotted place on the shield of the federated brotherhoods.

Termination of the Burlington Strike[†]
February 1889

On January 7, 1889, the strike on the CB&Q railway system was declared off by the joint action of the Brotherhood of Locomotive Engineers and the Brotherhood of Locomotive Firemen. The strike began on the 27th day of February, 1888, and being declared off January 7, 1889, it follows that it continued ten months and nine days. The readers of the *Magazine* are well informed regarding the origin of the notable and now historic struggle, and still, it may be worthwhile to briefly recapitulate the more important facts which led to it. The real grievance, or that which bore the most heavily upon the engineers and firemen, related to wages. The CB&Q paid their men less for the same work than was paid by other railways which centered at Chicago, and upon which the work was not more arduous or the responsibility greater than fell to the lot of the men who were in the employ of the CB&Q. In addition to this, the CB&Q had established a system of classification which, it was contended, was unjust to the engineers, and the full significance of which was that it enriched the corporation at the expense of the men from whom fair pay was withheld.

To arrive at a settlement without a resort to a strike, strenuous efforts were made by the engineers and firemen; their grievances were presented in an elaborate schedule and the corporation was most respectfully asked to consider each specification, but such solicitations were without avail. The corporation determined at last to make no concessions that in any wise satisfied the just demands of the men, and its defiant ultimatum was without concession or compromise, to stand by its peremptory refusal to arbitrate the grievances of the engineers. As a result, the engineers and firemen, on the 27th of February, quit work. The question was then, did they do right? Did they act wisely? The same questions are still up for debate.

We do not hesitate to say that the general conclusion is that the CB&Q has won a victory, or, in other words, that the engineers and firemen have been defeated—in common parlance, "whipped." The strike has been declared off and the conditions under which the men who quit the service of the CB&Q will again enter the employment of the corporation are practically unchanged. Necessarily, on the face of such facts, the conclusion is inevitable that the men,

† Published in *Locomotive Firemen's Magazine,* vol. 13, no. 2 (February 1889), 99–101.

after a struggle of nearly one year, are defeated. But this is not all that can be said, or that ought to be said, upon the subject. There are instances on record in which the word "victory" is but another term for "defeat," as was the case of the British at Bunker Hill, and of Xerxes at Thermopylae.[6] In discussing wars and battles, for the purpose of arriving at conclusions relating to combatants and issues, it is well to be precise. In the CB&Q struggle we find arrayed upon one side a corporation thoroughly organized and equipped, and of immense financial resources—one of the great corporations of the times—and on the other side two brotherhoods of wageworkers, two organizations whose only financial resources were their daily wages.

It will be well to note, with some care, the parties to the contest. There they stand on the 27th day of February, 1888. The corporation, proud, arrogant, defiant, with splendid property, money by the millions, and confident. It had determined to grant no concessions, and it must be said that it was plucky. As a foeman it had immense proportions as well as resources. But it was not so colossal as to frighten the two great brotherhoods who had challenged it to combat in defense of right and justice—the principle of fair dealing between employer and employee, a principle that must be asserted and defended if truth and justice are to prevail in the earth. We do not doubt, indeed we know it to be true, that there are those who deemed the strike unwise and ill advised at the start, and who now say, "I told you so." In this there is nothing strange. It has been so from the beginning. The timid, the hesitating, those who predict defeat and are content with supineness, never did nor never will help to rescue their fellow men from the enthrallments of oppression and degradation. The engineers and firemen who went into the struggle were inspired by sentiments such as have animated all men since the world began who have had the courage of conviction and have sought as best they could, when opportunity offered, to emancipate themselves and their fellow men from oppression. That in far too many cases defeat has been the result will not be gainsaid, but that ultimate victory is to come is as certain as that God and Heaven and true and good men are in alliance to enthrone, crown, and scepter justice and give it universal dominion in the world.

Whatever may be said of man's stolidity and mental obtuseness, he can be taught in the school of experience. Such lessons are ineffaceably engraved upon his mind, and if any one lesson has been taught by the CB&Q strike, more important than another, it is that in "unity there is strength," and that for the purpose of securing and maintaining the right, federation is the supreme requirement, the desideratum, and that with federation of all employees, victory, with all the desired trophies, is assured.

In the CB&Q strike we have an example of moral heroism that it will be found difficult to parallel in these degenerate times, where men, as never before in the history of the world, worship with more than pagan idolatry at the shrine of Mammon. The man who prayed for

> A scourging tongue, a scorpion's lash,
> To flay the backs of fools who worship cash,[7]

would now have ample opportunities to gratify his ambition, but his victims would not be found in the ranks of the brotherhoods of engineers and firemen. These men, in the struggle with the CB&Q, sought diligently for the right, and believing they had found it, demonstrated their loyalty to conviction by deducting from their hard-earned wages the magnificent sum of $1.2 million and giving it freely to the cause they had espoused; they set an example of devotion which cannot fail to challenge the admiration of honorable men everywhere. And be it remembered, to the everlasting credit of locomotive engineers and firemen, the giving of this great sum of money did not demoralize them; on the contrary, to their glory, be it said, it solidified the membership, and in a sense of transcendent significance, at the close of the struggle, the brotherhoods are stronger than ever before in their history. The storm has been fierce, and though the brotherhood ships have battled long against adverse winds and tide, they came into port without the loss of a sail, a rope, or a mast.

It affords us no satisfaction to state the disasters that have, during the struggle, overtaken the CB&Q. The victory achieved by that corporation has been the dearest in the history of the labor struggles of the century. The corporation has lost on every hand. There is no necessity, nor is there any desire, to magnify the sum total of its financial disasters. It is modest to place it at $10 million, and there are experts in such matters who place the sum vastly above the figures given. But, more or less, the corporation will not again place itself in a position to duplicate its embarrassments.

In closing this article, which virtually closes the discussion of the CB&Q strike in this magazine, we are persuaded that it will prove in many ways beneficial to railway employees. It supplies an example of courage and endurance which will not be forgotten in a hundred years. It demonstrates that workingmen with a just grievance, and satisfied that they are right, will contend for the right regardless of sacrifices and yield only when further resistance would be folly, and it furthermore serves to impress upon organizations of railway employees the demand for and absolute necessity of federation, that strikes in the future may not occur, or if they must come in spite of friendly overtures, that they shall be so quick and decisive in their work that whether victory or defeat attends the effort, results shall be speedily attained.

In declaring the strike off it is generally believed that ultimately three-fourths of the old employees will regain their positions on the CB&Q. Many of those who will go in search of employment elsewhere will be bearers of letters of introduction from the officers of the corporation. And just here we desire to say that all the brotherhoods of railway employees should make it their special concern to help the men who so valiantly stood by their colors on the CB&Q during the memorable struggle to obtain employment, and that this help should be extended engineers, firemen, brakemen, and switchmen. To overlook or to neglect this duty would be cruel to the last degree. The CB&Q has pledged itself to treat the men who left its employment honorably and the same treatment is due from the men to the corporation. The war is ended. The bugle no more calls to arms. Let the battle flags be furled.

The Future of the ORC[†]

February 1889

In the January issue of the *ORC Monthly* the question is editorially asked, "What has the future in store for the conductor?" If the future knows, it won't tell. The future is closemouthed: it don't blab, don't "shoot off its mouth." Still it is gratifying to see it stated that "during this last year" the question has been "thought upon more than ever before in the history of railroads." Manifestly, it is a momentous question. The railroads having "thought upon" it during the "last year," have concluded, in numerous instances, to put "spotters"[8] on the track of the conductor, and about 1800 of these trained "ferrets" are following the brass-buttoned and nickel-punch brigade on thousands of miles of railways in the United States. In that way the railroads are giving conductors a "recognition" of wonderful significance, which, to some extent, answers the query relating to what the future has in store for the conductors. The activity in the "spotter" business is a sort of recognition not well calculated to bring "about

† Published in *Locomotive Firemen's Magazine,* vol. 13, no. 2 (February 1889), 101–102.

a better feeling between employer or employee." It may be true that employer and employee "have been benefited" by the spotter. At any rate the "employer" must be benefited or he would not employ the sharp-nosed and keen-eyed hounds to dog the conductor and place his reputation and character, all that is dear to a man of honor, in the hands of men who have earned the detestation of decent men throughout the world.

The *Monthly* says "the conductor is of a naturally retiring disposition" who "has been, from his first step in railroading, trained to obey without question the orders given him." And still, the employer finds that the conductor is not sufficiently *retiring,* and so he puts spotters on his track, and upon the report of the trained hound, *retires* conductors by the score.

The *Monthly* facetiously remarks that the conductors, during the past year, have moved up and are now "a little nearer the throne than they have ever been before." That is certainly encouraging. To stand near the throne is a great honor. To wear throne toggery, to receive the smiles of the king and his courtiers, to mingle in the aristocratic throng; gods! that is fine! What next? Gold buttons and a gold punch, an exchange of blue for royal purple. And still, the complaint is, why don't the railroad companies manifest their appreciation of conductors by taking them "into their confidence?" Manifestly the conductors are not sufficiently near the throne. Spotters will have to be dismissed before the conductor will be taken into the confidence of the companies. And yet, says the *Monthly,* the future "is full of hope, and the prize, a fair recognition of services and just compensation for labor performed, hangs ready." But the prize is too "altitudilum"[9] for the conductor, it is the one persimmon that the conductor's pole can't quite reach; when he gets a "little nearer the throne" he may grasp the prize.

Now comes the robust declaration that the article to which we have made reference was not written for the benefit of railway managers, but for conductors. Such a declaration will not push the ORC a "little nearer the throne" and it may result in the employment of more spotters to note the movements of the punch and where the nickels go.

Now comes the climax. "The conductor of the future will be a man of large experience, well versed in all things pertaining to his calling, an honored citizen, a man without reproach, enjoying the confidence of his employer and respected everywhere." But what of the conductor of the present? Thousands of them are honorable men who are in alliance with their co-employees on the railways of the country. They will not remain in the ORC under its present policy. The edict has gone forth; the revolution is already inaugurated.

The manifesto recently issued by the new Brotherhood of Railway Conductors, which will be found elsewhere in our columns, vividly foreshadows the future of the ORC. It is a declaration of independence. It is an arraignment of the old ORC upon the charge that it is not in sympathy with other organizations of railway employees, and that its influence has been exerted to establish and perpetuate wrongs and injustice; that it has been the willing tool of corporations and has lent itself to the abominable business of scabbing to defeat the just demands of workingmen, and such facts being established beyond all controversy, its existence ought to terminate.

We have anticipated such a movement. It is in consonance with the logic of events. It is in the right direction. Its influence will be of the very best. The conductors who have gone into the movement are men of moral courage. The *Monthly* says of conductors that they are "trained from their first step in railroading to obey without question the orders given them," and that this obedience "becomes a second nature," and that conductors "often suffer in mind, body, and pocket because of this trait of character." There was never a more humiliating confession made. If it is true, it accounts for the degeneracy of conductors when they obey the orders to scab, to commit a flagrant wrong against their co-employees, and tells in trumpet tones that the new order of ORC was demanded to rescue railway conductors from further degradation. The *Monthly,* in closing the article to which we have referred, charges that railway officials have treated conductors "as a part of the machinery to carry out certain schemes of their own." That is doubtless true, indeed it is undeniably true, and the treatment will be continued unless the conductors protest, and cease to obey orders that sink them to the most abject condition of serfs. The new Order of Railway Conductors proposes to inaugurate reforms, to assert their manhood, and to rescue the old ORC, if possible, from being "a part of the machinery" of railroad corporations to perpetuate injustice upon their employees. If this cannot be done, then the new order will include, at no distant day, the conductors who have the courage of manly convictions, and will take its place in the front rank of the labor organizations of the age.

New Conductors' Order Established[†]

February 1889

Considering the policy of the ORC, it has required no soothsayer to arrive at the conclusion that it must either change its policy or make up its mind to lose power and prestige. We have time and again, in the columns of the *Magazine,* and in the most friendly spirit, warned the order and its organ, the *Conductor's Monthly,* of coming events, of the inevitable, but as none are so blind as those who won't see. The old policy, in defiance of common sense and sound judgment, was seized with a firmer grasp, and as a result, consequences predicted have followed, and another Order of Railway Conductors has been organized. We have before us the prospectus of the new organization bearing date of November 15, 1888, and quote so much of the document as will afford our readers an idea of its purposes:

Los Angeles, Cal.,
November 15, 1888

Gentlemen:—

It being generally understood by the railway conductors of the United States, Canada, and Mexico, that the present status of the ORC wholly falls to inert the requirements of organized labor, and in promoting that harmony which should exist between railway conductors and other organizations of railway employees, especially that of the Brotherhood of Locomotive Engineers, and it has been deemed expedient and a move has been entered into by the conductors of the western country, especially those on the Pacific coast, whereby an organization has been effected to be known as the Brotherhood of Railway Conductors of the United States, Mexico, and Canada, whose object is to promote and protect the interests of railway conductors generally.

The foregoing tells the whole story. The old ORC, having totally failed "to meet the requirements of organized labor," the new order, the Brotherhood of Railway Conductors of the United States, Mexico, and Canada, has been

---

† Published as "The Brotherhood of Railway Conductors" in *Locomotive Firemen's Magazine,* vol. 13, no. 2 (February 1889), 106–107.

formed, and at the latest advices, December 26, 69 applications for charters of subordinate divisions had been applied for. That this should have been accomplished in the short space of 40 days demonstrates, beyond all controversy, the absolute necessity for the new order.

That labor should organize for the benefit of labor is a proposition too self-evident to require argument, and when labor organizes to injure labor, to defeat labor in its efforts to secure simple justice, such an organization, whatever may be its fate, cannot retain in its membership the friends of labor. Such friends of labor in the old ORC will naturally and inevitably drift to the new Brotherhood of Railway Conductors.

It is not required for us to state that this magazine hails with undisguised satisfaction the organization of the Brotherhood of Railway Conductors of the United States, Mexico, and Canada. Coming as it does, when federation is demanded for the elevation and prosperity of railway employees, it becomes cheeringly significant. It voices sentiments of harmony and unity, and strengthens faith that the day is not distant when all the organizations of railway employees will be united in the bonds of federation to promote the welfare of each and of all.

We suggest to locomotive firemen, members of our brotherhood, that they can do much to promote the interests of the Brotherhood of Railway Conductors in many ways and certainly by seeking opportunities of calling the attention of conductors to the position occupied by their brotherhood toward the new order and upon the subject of federation, as also to the fact that the *Magazine,* the organ of the Brotherhood, is zealously endeavoring to aid in promoting the success of the Brotherhood of Railway Conductors, whose grand lodge is located at Los Angeles, Cal., and whose grand officers are as follows:

W. A. Osgood, Grand Chief Conductor; W. O. Mohler, Assistant Grand Chief Conductor; A. W. McLean, Grand Secretary and Treasurer; W. J. Bigelow, Grand Senior Conductor; G. H. O'Dell, Grand Junior Conductor; T. B. Whiteside, Grand Inside Sentinel; J. E. Hartell, Grand Outside Sentinel; and W. M. Usher, Grand Chaplain. These officers are gentlemen of the highest repute, and their names guarantee that every movement made will evince unwavering devotion to the interests of organized labor. Should any of our readers desire to correspond with the Grand Lodge B of RC, the address of the grand secretary and treasurer, A. W. McLean, is Los Angeles, Cal., P.O. Box 935.

The Strength of All for the Good of All[†]

February 1889

We have no hesitancy in declaring that the stability of American institutions depends upon the enactment of such laws and in the adoption of such a policy as will secure justice to labor.

The affirmation that labor creates all the wealth, and that from labor all the revenues of nations are derived, requires neither qualification nor apology.

To withhold any rights which in the nature of things belong to labor is a wrong for which there is no palliation. It is in itself a crime. It is more prolific of ills than the fabled box presented to Pandora by Jupiter. It is a crime in whose infernal womb there are forever quickening into life ills, compared with which nature's forces, whether above or below the crust of the earth, in their most destructive displays become almost meaningless. Nor do we exaggerate if to these are added all the scourges which from time to time create woe and lamentation, and fill the mind with horror.

It is a fact, disguise it as we may, that "an injury to one is the concern of all." It is made so by the "brotherhood of man" and the "fatherhood of God." Treat it as fable or fact, it matters not; Cain's crime has concerned all people, tongues, tribes, and kindred since the date of that fratricide. It stands for an example—nor has the blood of Abel ceased crying from the ground.[10] It is so ordered. It is the law. No mortal stab of man was ever feloniously made which did not open a "poor, poor dumb mouth" into which fate put a tongue, that it might harangue the world forever against the crime of murder. But there are crimes compared with which murder is a benediction and deserving all the wealth of rhetoric. Take an eviction in Ireland, made by the sanction of law and executed by creatures of the law—old men and old women, bending beneath the weight of years, innocent youth, and helpless infancy, mothers in the pangs of parturition, thrust into the road to suffer and to perish. Such crimes are worse than murder, and are the concern of all, though all may not feel concerned, but when such infamies are perpetrated humanity receives a shock; they touch the nerve centers of nations. The human family is one. There is a bond of sympathy between all nations. The man who steals a man and sells him into slavery commits

---

† Published as "Federation" in *Locomotive Firemen's Magazine,* vol. 13, no. 2 (February 1889), 102–104.

a crime against all men. If a wrong is done to the humblest American citizen by any foreign power, it becomes the concern of every other American citizen, and the resources of the Republic are pledged to redress the wrong.

In discussing federation, we presuppose the independence of the federating parties, but which, nevertheless, have certain interests in common, and that the supreme purpose of federation is to protect such common interests. The original thirteen American colonies were absolutely independent of each other. They existed by virtue of distinct charters, but they had certain interests in common, and when these interests were menaced and attacked, they federated for mutual protection, and with federation they won a victory and secured blessings, in the presence of which hyperbole sits dumb—and yet every colony retained in its autonomy, its power and rights of self-government.

Labor organizations—we refer specially to those connected with the railway service—have found in the past, find now, and are likely to find in the future certain interests, alike common to all, in jeopardy. The menace is perpetual, and attacks upon their rights, frequent and often exasperating. In the maintenance of their rights, labor organizations have found that separate action was, as a general thing, a delusion and fruitful only of disaster. The lessons of experience have convinced those capable of analyzing the situation that security lies in federation.

But the fact need not be disguised that there are obstacles in the way of immediate success, and it is in the line of prudence to name them and estimate their obstructive, their hindering power. In this discussion, it will be well to inquire what motive prompted railway employees to organize. Or, rather, was the obtaining and the maintaining of just wages one of the inciting purposes? If it is found that any of the organizations of railway employees ignores the question of wages, or is content with such wages as employers may see proper to pay, such an organization cannot be expected to federate with another organization which makes honest wages and just treatment bedrock propositions. If there is an organization of railway employees whose members, at the behest of corporation officials, will "scab"—divest themselves of manliness, of self-respect, of independence, and voluntarily become the cringing, fawning tools of the enemies of workingmen, in their honorable efforts to secure and to maintain their rights—we say, if there is such an organization of railway employees, it is not expected that it will federate with any other organization for any honorable purpose whatever. It will be found wanting in brains, in spine, in *sand*. Its predominating characteristic is that which distinguishes the serf—it is serfdom. It permits others to create conditions to which it yields as uncomplainingly as an ass to its burdens and blows. Only such organizations will federate, as will not "scab," as will not abdicate any right, human or divine—unalienable, constitutional, or statutory—whose members know they are sovereign citizens, and feel ennobling, vitalizing thrills of independence, who organize, federate, and work, not only for their own good but for the welfare of others. Such organizations of railway employees as favor federation take an eminently wise view of situations and surroundings. They have self-respect without vanity, courage without false pretense, and in advocating federation, make no surrender of allegiance to the parent organization. They do not arrogate to themselves any superiority over other organizations; they recognize the fact that as employees in the railway service, while engaged in promoting their own welfare, have certain interests in common with other organizations which can be fully protected only by federation, a fact, so clearly demonstrated by experience, as to render argument unnecessary.

The ultimate triumph of federation hinges upon the final result of the conflict between truth and error, right and wrong, education and ignorance. So far, no valid objections have been brought forward. The wrongs which environ railway employees are numerous, often flagrant and degrading. Insufficient wages when earnings are large confront employees in every direction. None are overpaid, while thousands are underpaid. Men are discharged to gratify the malice of some official, whose arrogance can be placated only by a serf-like submission and degradation, and the blacklist has been introduced to compel men to choose between humiliation and idleness. To correct, or at least to mitigate, such evils, railway employees organize. That good has resulted in many instances is not to be questioned. But the evils have not disappeared. The right has not triumphed. Labor has not utilized all its resources. Peace has not been declared, and the battle is still on. There is hope in federation—in combining the strength of all for the good of all. It is rational. The more it is discussed, the more the facts are brought out, the more convincing becomes the argument. Time and truth are in alliance. Only the right was born to live. Let the work of agitation and education go forward. Nothing is so fatal as stagnation. The Brotherhood of Locomotive Firemen stands pledged for federation, and this magazine, as its organ, will not misrepresent its noble purpose. The truth is iconoclastic. Neither idols nor images, nor shams of any class or character can expect exemption from its eternal hostility.

The sun of labor is rising grandly to the zenith. The boys of today have advantages which their fathers did not possess. The educating forces have multiplied in a ratio that defies exaggeration. Organization is progressing, and federation is coming, and it is coming to stay. It will establish arbitration and enthrone justice, and finally relegate strikes to the limbo of extinct measures of redress.

Allegiance to Principle[†]

March 1889

To men of well-developed, healthy, vigorous minds in which noble ambitions take root and thrive, where generous feelings and kindly sympathies hold sway, there is always to be found the tenderest regard for home, for youthful scenes, and memory treasures nothing so fruitful of felicity as

> The orchard, the meadow, the deep-tangled wildwood,
> And every loved spot which my infancy knew![11]

It does not matter that they have traveled in their own and in foreign lands. It does not matter that fortune has smiled and that they have become rich and exchanged the cottage for the palatial residence; it does not matter that they have formed new associations and have changed surroundings, they still cherish "with fond recollection" "the old oaken bucket that hung in the well,"[12] and "the old family Bible that laid on the stand," they still recall with delight the old schoolhouse on the hill or in the valley, and often early associates pass in review, and especially is it true that their comrades, those with whom they were associated in their early struggles to advance, whose companionship and friendship they enjoyed and upon which they leaned, are never forgotten. There is no nobler trait in man's character than this keeping fresh and green throughout all the vicissitudes of life, fond memories of home, of kindred and comrades. To forget them, to turn from them, to neglect or disown them, is universally regarded as apostasy in its darkest and most repulsive form. It takes the form of ingratitude, and Shakespeare says:

> I hate ingratitude more in a man
> Than lying, vainness, babbling, drunkenness,
> Or any taint of vice whose strong corruption
> Inhabits our frail blood.[13]

This fealty to early friendships and associations, this unflagging and unchanging attachment to comrades, is universally regarded among all honorable men as convincing testimony of a noble, generous, courageous nature, and the absence of it becomes equally convincing that the victim, whatever may be his surroundings, is to be numbered among the world's unfortunates.

It should be understood that our remarks are not intended to apply to

---

† Published in *Locomotive Firemen's Magazine,* vol. 13, no. 3 (March 1889), 193–195.

a class of men whose childhood and young manhood was bereft of examples and associations such as inspire noble ambitions, in whose memories there are few if any pictures, the contemplation of which are fruitful of felicities, and who in mature manhood remember only scenes and associations calculated to deflect them from pathways of rectitude and usefulness. Of such men it is not to be expected that they will supply the world with examples of unwavering devotion to things of good report, and yet it may be said that instances are numerous in which noble examples of courage and fidelity to obligation have won from the ranks of men whose early life was clouded by the misfortune of neglect and examples of vice, and given them worldwide fame as the champions of principles which are admitted to be the bulwarks of society.

As a general proposition, and in the highest degree commendatory, men are inclined to regard their own country, their own homes, the school, the college where they were educated, the church where they worship, and so on to the end of the chapter, as the best, and on all proper occasions they do not hesitate to give their reasons for their preferences. No man ever lost character or prestige by championing such convictions—on the contrary, in the estimation of men of correct sensibility, the man who asserts his allegiance to home, country, church, school, and friends, to all institutions that have helped him to advance or held him from retrograding, is esteemed virtuous and courageous. He at once takes a position as one who, however fiercely the storm may beat, however sanguinary may be the battle, can be trusted. He will not flinch. He will not tamely surrender. He will not abandon his cause nor his comrades. He can neither be bribed nor intimidated. He will never sacrifice his independence nor his self-respect. He admires friendship but detests the schemes of the flatterer. He knows his duty and dares perform it. He will not apostatize. He is neither traitor, deserter, nor bounty jumper, and he has unmitigated scorn for the man or set of men who by any mean artifice seek to humiliate him in his own estimation or in the estimation of others by "going back on his friends and associates."

To illustrate, there was established in the year 1873 a Brotherhood of Locomotive Firemen. What of it? What of its foundation, its growth, its prosperity and present position? Why was it organized? To answer such questions would require more space than we have at our command, nor is it required that we should enter into details. Go back fifteen years, start with Lodge No. 1, and then march with the brotherhood in its continental journeyings until you are the guest of Lodge No. 400, and you can answer our interrogatives. It will be seen why the brotherhood was organized, and the measure of its growth and prosperity will be comprehended. Has it made mistakes? Certainly, and as certainly there are dark spots on the shining disk of the sun. Has it had defeats? Often. Vanquished? Never. Victorious? In the history of brotherhoods, nothing more resplendent can be found. Its career is one splendid victory. Has it met every obligation? The records show that it has not only met every obligation, but that in the spirit of fraternal forgiveness it has exceeded its obligations. It has taken delinquents by the hand and lifted them into fellowship, and poured its treasures by thousands to make joyous disconsolate widows and orphans. We could write in eulogistic phrase for hours, and tell the truth of the Brotherhood of Locomotive Firemen. But our purpose is to ask the membership of our powerful and prosperous brotherhood if there is any other brotherhood in existence that has a more resplendent record, of duty done, good work performed, of obligations met? If so, what brotherhood can make the boast?

To be more direct, is there a brotherhood of railroad employees that has a better record than the Brotherhood of Locomotive Firemen? If so, name it. We are not aware of its existence. We have no adverse criticisms to offer on any brotherhood of railroad employees. This magazine has demonstrated in the past that it is the friend of them all. It seeks to bind them in the closer bonds of federation, for the good of all. We simply assert that the Brotherhood of Locomotive Firemen is the peer of the best and abreast of the most advanced. Is it a question of brains? Is it a question of courage? Is it a question of fidelity to obligation? Let the questions multiply until they include all things for which manly men should strive, and the Brotherhood of Locomotive Firemen, it will be found, is not required to take a back seat—and yet it is found that the Brotherhood of Locomotive Engineers assumes to be the superior brotherhood, and that there may be no mistake upon the subject, places two laws upon its statute books, at once an insult and a menace to the Brotherhood of Locomotive Firemen, and then with an effrontery that defies exaggeration, solicits members of the Brotherhood of Locomotive Firemen, men who for years have had locomotive firemen for their associates, for their comrades, with whom they have associated in the lodge room and around the counsel boards of the order—to apostatize, to strip themselves naked of independence, of self-respect, disown their brothers and trample upon oath and obligation that they may be eligible to membership in the

. Why? Wherefore? What is to be gained by this apostasy? No man answers the questions. The Brotherhood of Locomotive Engineers is as silent as a tombstone. Its grand chief has never ventured a reason or an explanation. The organ of the order wisely remains silent.

Are the engineers better men than the firemen? Have they more brains, more courage, more character, more of anything that entitles them to respect?

To answer such questions, let it be said that the entire membership were but yesterday locomotive firemen—the knights of the pick and scoop. The Brotherhood of Locomotive Firemen made them engineers. They are bone of its bone and flesh of its flesh—and yet this Brotherhood of Locomotive Engineers, grasping its bootstraps, and with haughty, disdainful, consequential airs, seeks to lift itself into such prominence that no engineer in its charmed circle who is a member of the Brotherhood of Locomotive Firemen can represent his division in the grand councils of the order, and as if that was not the climax of insult and unmitigated insolence, it further enacts that no engineer, a member of the Brotherhood of Locomotive Firemen, shall ever become a member of the Brotherhood of Locomotive Engineers until he has renounced his parent brotherhood, cleansed himself of the odium of being a brotherhood fireman. Having done this, having thus committed moral suicide, having apostatized and gone forth like Cain with a mark upon his brow, the Brotherhood of Locomotive Engineers, if they choose, may take him in. And suppose he is taken into that brotherhood, what does he gain? In what way is he benefited? No one knows and no one attempts to explain. Nor is there any superior advantage to be secured, or if it can be shown an advantage does accrue, how will it appear contrasted with the sacrifices made to secure it?

It is not surprising that the Brotherhood of Locomotive Engineers seek to make the Brotherhood of Locomotive Firemen its recruiting camp, its breeding pen, but it would be surprising if Locomotive Firemen, members of the brotherhood, did not at once, and in manly emphasis, rebuke the spirit which prompted the enactment of laws by the Brotherhood of Locomotive Engineers, than which no greater indignity could be offered them. And just here it should be said that there are thousands of engineers who view the subject as does the *Locomotive Firemen's Magazine*. That ultimately the odious laws to which we have referred will be repealed we do not doubt, but while they stain the statute books of the B of LE, no engineer, a member of the B of LF, should seek to enter the engineers' brotherhood. He should not permit himself to be cajoled nor intimidated, and any attempt of that character should be met with a firmness and sternness that would be so convincing that the party trying it on would realize that the Brotherhood of Locomotive Firemen, and each member of the order, proposes in the future not to yield to arrogance nor to retreat one inch from the high ground it has taken, that when reciprocity is disdainfully declined, dignified non-intercourse will be maintained.

The Brotherhood of Railway Conductors[†]

March 1889

We have informed the readers of this magazine that in November last the Brotherhood of Railway Conductors was organized in the city of Los Angeles, California. The movement was consequent upon the fact that the Order of Railway Conductors, long established, had developed into a standing menace of the rights and interests of every other organization of railway employees. The ORC was everywhere recognized as the pliant tool of corporations, without manliness, without courage, without ability to appreciation conditions, as ready and willing to submit to any command, however humiliating, making its bread and butter, or bread and water, or its bread without butter, the standard, and the only standard of action.

Thousands of its members realized that the policy of the ORC was vicious and venal and they tried to change it, but being defeated by a majority of *two,* or some other insignificant number of votes, and recognizing the abomination of scabbing, their indignation triumphed over their patience, and as a result, the Brotherhood of Railway Conductors was organized at Los Angeles in November 1888. The new brotherhood has had, so far, unexampled prosperity, and already has a membership of over 600. Why this success? The question is easily answered. There are thousands of railway conductors who in principle and interest are in hearty alliance with other railway employees. They are champions of the right and abhor the wrong, and in every struggle they want to see the right prevail. Such men organized the Brotherhood of Railway Conductors at Los Angeles and placed at its head George W. Howard, than whom no better man could have been found on the continent.[14]

The Brotherhood of Railway Conductors gave special prominence to "protection" in their declaration of principles, and the word, in the sweep of its significance, includes the dearest rights of workingmen, and this being true, every organization of railway employees will wish it the largest possible measure of success, and will labor to disseminate its principles and promote its welfare.

---

† Published in *Locomotive Firemen's Magazine,* vol. 13, no. 3 (March 1889), 255.

Labor as a "Commodity"†
March 1889

For some months past the subject of "tariff reform" or tax reform has been going forward in and out of Congress, and the agitation is likely to continue indefinitely. In this discussion we hear much about the importance of admitting "free of duty" or tax certain commodities, raw materials, because such a policy would lessen the cost of manufactured goods and enable the United States to compete with other nations in the markets of the world. Such a policy, it is boldly stated, would be of incalculable benefit to the workingmen of the country because by opening new markets for the products of American factories the demand for labor would be increased and wages would advance, and as new markets would be found for our surplus products, overproduction would disappear and workingmen would have continual employment.

Those who are watching the debates in Congress and the discussions going forward in the press of the country have noticed that labor comes in for special notice, and that great prominence is given the interests of wageworkers. This, to say the least of it, is a cheering indication. It is the recognition of fundamental facts, which advanced thinkers believe will result, ultimately, to the great advantage of workingmen and necessarily to the welfare of the country.

But our purpose at this writing is not to discuss "tariff reform," nor the importance of extending the free list of imported articles. Such topics may engage our attention at another time. For the present we desire to call the attention of our readers to the fact that in the Congress of the United States, "labor" is designated as a "commodity," and this is done by a statesman who professes to be the champion of the interests of laboring men. A member of Congress in a speech said:

> What is labor? Why is it that capitalists construct mills, purchase materials, and employ laborers to work the same up? It is because by combining the materials and the labor, he produces something for which there is a market and which he can sell at a profit. When he sells the product, he sells the *materials and the labor that he has purchased* and sells both at a profit. By combining the materials and labor he has a product for which there is a demand. If there is no demand for his product, if the market has been supplied, he

† Published in *Locomotive Firemen's Magazine,* vol. 13, no. 3 (March 1889), 196–198.

at once closes his factory, stops the purchase of materials, and discharges his employees. *Labor is as much a commodity, selling in the market, as the materials to be worked up.* If there is a great demand for the product, there is a great demand for the materials and for the labor necessary to manufacture it. If the price of materials goes up, wages go up. *If labor is but a commodity selling in the market, its price is regulated solely by supply and demand.* If the demand is great, wages will go up; if it is small, wages will go down. It requires no argument to convince laboring men that in a community where a large number are out of work and seeking employment, wages will be low and work hard to obtain. Competition will force them down to the lowest standard of living in spite of organization. But when there is work for all, when two employers are after one laborer instead of two laborers being after one employer, wages will be high. *[Italics are ours. —EVD.]*

The distinguished gentleman asked, "What is labor?" and he answered his interrogatory by saying, "Labor is as much a commodity, selling in the market, as the materials to be worked up." We confess our inability to fitly characterize such a declaration. It is a sentence in which words are not the signs of correct ideas— or ideas of any sort. It is jargon. Nations have commodities. The United States boasts of an extended list—iron, coal, cotton, lumber, tar, and turpentine— commodities of forest, field, and mine. We import commodities, raw materials, wool, jute, hair, and hides. And now we have the announcement made in Congress that "labor is a commodity," as much a commodity as the "materials" workingmen are required to "work up." If so, manifestly, labor must take its chances with other materials, pig iron and wool, rawhides, and so on to the end of the list. The labor market is like any other market. Has it come to this? The subject is worthy of the severest analysis. The distinguished congressman asks, "What is labor?" and says, "It is as much a commodity as the materials to be worked up." Is that true? A manufacturer purchases 500 bales of cotton. It is a commodity. He concludes to store it for a time till the price of goods advance. He insures his "commodity" and closes his factory. His cotton commodity "rests." It is sheltered and watched. It neither gets sick nor hungry, it simply waits a favorable change in the market, and then the owner reaps his profits.

Just outside of the factory is "labor," which the distinguished congressman, the professed friend of the wageworker, says, "is as much a commodity" as the cotton; the "material" and the labor occupy, in the opinion of the congressman, precisely the same position, and in legislation, are to be treated as identical; and this vaunting statesman, this champion of labor says: "I am willing to answer to that great body of intelligent wageworkers that I have the honor to represent, as to whether I have been true to their interests." Is it to the interests of wageworkers to be degraded to the level of raw materials? "What is labor?" asks this "representative" of a great "body of intelligent wageworkers," and he tells them they are as much "commodities" as the "materials they work up." We ask, what is labor? And we tell this half-fledged, illy-informed congressman, this pseudo-statesman, that labor is not a commodity. We tell him that it is not bought and sold in the markets of the United States like the raw materials of commerce. It was so once. In a large section of the United States there was a time when labor was bought and sold. There were labor blocks and labor pens. There were millions invested in labor. But to own labor, to make it a "material," a chattel, to offer it in the market to be bought and sold as a "commodity," is in the United States of America a thing of the past, and it is not in the power of Congress to degrade labor to a commodity.

It has been the monstrous curse of the world, of all ages, to degrade labor to the level of a commodity, a material, a chattel, to be bought and sold, and the price of it regulated in the market as any "materials to be worked up." It has been thought, it has been affirmed, that in the United States of America, the time had come when labor had been redeemed—emancipated from the dishonor, the disgrace and humiliation of a "commodity," to be bought at private sale or at auction as commodities are disposed of, but according to the declarations of a latter-day statesman, a man who puts himself forward as a student of political economy, who under all circumstances is to secure the workingman's vote, labor occupies the same level as "any commodity selling in the market," as much a material as anything to be "worked up." If this is true, if it has in it one element of truth, then labor has not moved a step in advance since the slaves of the Pharaohs built the pyramids. Labor is still a chattel, a "commodity," a raw material to be "worked up." It is an article of commerce. It belongs to the nations that produce it. It may be shipped and consigned, imported and exported, and that this is the idea of certain corporations is easily demonstrated. But it is not the American idea. It is not the conception of men who are capable of comprehending the logic of events, of facts, of reason, or of righteousness. To class men who announce as a fact that labor is a "commodity," as much so as guano, as hair and hides, is to do violence to common sense. It makes the term "commodity" everlastingly odious.

What is a commodity? It is something tangible, palpable, and substantial. It can be handled—analyzed—resolved into component parts. It can be put into barrels or bales, or it can be shipped in bulk. Is labor the same; is it "as much a commodity as the materials to be worked up." Can the distinguished congressman, who degrades labor to a "commodity," analyze it? Can he analyze fire or light? If the distinguished congressman whose remarks we discuss should call upon the head chemist and request him to analyze any commodity known to commerce, he would be listened to respectfully, and the task would be performed, but if he were to ask the chemist to analyze labor, he would be regarded as a person who ought to be in an insane asylum rather than in Congress. If the chemist were disposed to test the hallucination which had taken possession of the congressman, he might tell him to bring on his "labor commodity," and the congressman would doubtless introduce one of the "great body of intelligent wageworkers" he has the "honor to represent." There stands the congressman and beside him the "commodity," "as much a commodity selling in the market" as pig iron or any other "material to be worked up." The chemist possibly tells the congressman that he "is a crank." If the congressman insists upon having his labor commodity analyzed, it is not difficult to guess what would be the result. In the first place, it is rational to conjecture that the "commodity" itself (or himself or herself) would object. It might result in a warm discussion. The "intelligent wageworker" might say, "To analyze labor you analyze me. Here I am, body, life, soul, spirit, skill, thought, ambition, aspiration, and imagination. Here I am, created a little lower than God Himself, the original worker, laborer, and creator," and addressing the congressman, says, "do you rank me with a commodity?" "That is just what he does," says the chemist. "I am to extract the labor from you, cut you up into chunks, pound them and grind them, subject them to intense heat to find 'labor,' the 'commodity,' that is like any other commodity that sells in the market, that must go up or down, according to 'supply and demand.' If the supply is small, then labor, wageworkers, will be fat, well fed, well clothed, happy, and contented, the 'commodity' will be in demand; otherwise the 'commodity' will be idle, it will be clothed in rags, it will be hungry and starve and die, or it will commit crime and go to prison, or have its neck broken with a halter. I confess, I cannot get the labor out of the laborer—out of the 'intelligent wageworker,' and the congressman must dispose of his 'commodity' elsewhere. My apparatus is not constructed to analyze labor, it is a commodity unknown to modern chemistry or ancient alchemy."

According to this modern statesman, this American servant of the people, this would-be savant, this *avant-courier* of the wageworkers' millennium, labor is a commodity like any raw material known to commerce or to manufacturers, and its doom is irrevocably fixed. Labor means the laborer, and we are told that labor must take its chances with other commodities, and that in spite of organization, wages will be high or low as supply and demand may determine. If this is true, God pity the laborer in the United States of America. There is no help for him, reduced to a "commodity," degraded to a chattel. Wageworkers, with bowed heads, may contemplate the inevitable. Their condition is worse, far worse than that of the beasts of the field.

Does the congressman whose words we have quoted represent the American idea? Do wageworkers say amen? The American idea is that in organization and federation legislation can be had that will promote the interests of wageworkers. It is not the American idea that labor is a commodity. It is rapidly becoming the American idea that, to give all employment, the hours for labor shall be reduced. The wageworkers of the United States are the strength and glory of the nation, and when anyone in Congress of the United States degrades labor to a "commodity," classes it with raw materials, a blunder of the most vicious character is committed, and it behooves workingmen in casting their ballots to guard against elevating men to positions of power and influence who regard labor as much of a commodity as any raw material, and who proclaim that the organization of workingmen for their protection is in vain.

The Labor Movement[†]
March 1889

There was a time, not remote, when it was held that the only weapon of the wageworkers in America was the strike. But a change has come. Wageworkers have advanced in intelligence. They have become readers and thinkers, and they have become close observers. They have devoted their leisure to the study of conditions, surroundings, circumstances, and have advanced to positions which enable them to arrive at just and wise conclusions. We refer to the many, not to the few. There are still those who believe that "our varied industries and heterogeneous population necessitate all phases of warfare, from the guerilla system, incident to isolation, to the arbitration of differences consequent upon the higher civilization of congregated citizenship." But the great mass of wageworkers in the United States believe that the ballot is the weapon which is ultimately to secure them justice and equal privileges before the law. It is an old aphorism: "Like people, like the king," or vice versa, and it may be said, "Like people like law,"

---

† Published in *Locomotive Firemen's Magazine*, vol. 13, no. 3 (March 1889), 206–207.

and certainly this may be said when the ballot is in the hands of all the people.

In the United States the wage-men are in the majority; they have the ballot; majorities rule. Now, then, if lawmakers are corrupt, if laws are vicious, if injustice is practiced, if rights are cloven down, if courts are venal—who is to blame? Manifestly those in the majority, who, having the ballot, can, if they choose, remedy the evils complained of.

Does someone ask, if the wageworkers have this power, why do they not use it? It is an easy matter to ask questions, but not always as easy to answer them. We shall attempt a reply. In the first place, wage-men have been allied to some one of the political parties of the country, and have permitted their fealty to party to obscure the fact that legislation has been to their detriment rather than to their advantage. To use a phrase, they have "run with the machine" regardless of consequences. They have been the victims of false professions, of pledges made to be broken. It has required time to educate workingmen out of the old rut and up to a higher plane of purpose. What is the spectacle now? Workingmen are federating. Not for the purpose of "guerrilla" warfare, not for the adoption of the policy of anarchists, not to revolutionize society and government by bludgeons and bombs, dynamite and kindred explosives, but by the ballot. They realize that they are American citizens, that they create the wealth of the country, that revenues are derived from their labor, that in peace they pay the taxes and in war fight the battles, and rising to the dignity of their rights under the Constitution they are saying, "We will elect just men to office. We will have just laws administered by honest men, and this we will do by the use of the all-powerful weapon—the ballot," and this they can do by the ballot, and they can achieve such victories as will astonish the world.

Does someone ask, When will these wonderful things transpire? When will this full-orbed day occupy its place in the calendar? When will this millennial era dawn? Such queries have a taint of querulousness. It is sufficient to say that the labor movement is a growth. To emancipate labor from the thralldom of injustice is not a task of a day or a year. Labor confronts an antiquity of injustice. It bends beneath wrongs which began before the pyramids were built. It has been prostrate for 40 centuries, and in all lands beneath the sun it is prostrate today, save in this God-favored land, and here, after a century of freedom wage-men have, by processes of political and judicial chicane, been kept under the ban. We say "political and judicial" because by law and by decisions of courts, grasping and conscienceless men have been able to so shape business affairs as to make *work* all too often the synonym for poverty and degradation. In this connection we desire to be understood as saying that a new departure has been inaugurated, that a new revolution has been begun which means the emancipation of labor from many forms of injustice and wrongs. Not by the mob, not by incendiary harangues, not by arousing and firing the passions of men, not by disturbing the peace and security of society, but by means ordained by the Constitution and in harmony with order.

What, we ask, is more fashionable than to quote wages in king-cursed European lands? As if to tell workingmen of America that citizenship and all of its privileges, responsibilities, and high aspirations is to be measured by wages. We have a rational conception of the power of money, but let it be understood that wage-men of America are not to be silenced by any per diem. The high resolve is to change unjust laws and place men in the legislative, executive, and judiciary departments who will see that just laws are righteously administered. We admit that the task is herculean, but not more formidable than to successfully redeem a continent from a wilderness and make fruitful Edens as numerous as the stars. This labor has done for America, and if wage-men are true to themselves, true to their noble heritage, the time is not distant when they will behold their banner waving in triumph where legislators deliberate and where judges proclaim the law.

The Church and the Workingman[†]
April 1889

A word fitly spoken is like apples of gold in pictures of silver.
—Proverbs[15]

In the February number of *The Forum*, Rev. C. M. Morse[16] has a paper captioned "The Church and the Workingman."[17] The paper contains many words fitly spoken and bravely spoken. The Rev. Mr. Morse (may his tribe increase), like Abou Ben Adhem, loves his fellow man, and therefore loves God.[18] Those who do not love their fellow man, but profess to love God, are the most despicable hypocrites that the devil ever entertained with distinguished consideration.

---

† Published in *Locomotive Firemen's Magazine,* vol. 13, no. 4 (April 1889), 289–291.

Mr. Morse is one of the cloth that he has been "called" to preach, will be admitted by those who read his courageous words without debate. He talks as if his lips have been "touched with live coals from off the altar."[19] "Fifty years ago," says Mr. Morse, "aristocratic pretensions were looked upon as vagaries and treated with contempt. In the churches, people felt nothing of the chill of caste." This is all changed. Everywhere there is "rivalry in the erection of splendid edifices." "The poverty of the workingman is accentuated by comparison with the richness of the sanctuary." "The chief seats are lined with purple and fine linen." The church is full of pomp, pride, and arrogance. "With the vast aggregation of wealth in the possession of the few and the increasing pressure of poverty in the homes of the many, the time is at hand," says Mr. Morse, "when there will exist between classes gulfs as impassible as between Dives and Lazarus."[20] According to Rev. Mr. Morse's theory, the church, whose mission it is to bring Dives and Lazarus into sympathetic alliance, exerts an influence to deepen and broaden the gulf of separation. "Intensifying social struggles," says Mr. Morse, "are working a transformation in the character of the church, as is manifest from the new terminology coming into general use, such as 'star preachers,' 'first-class churches,' 'wealthy congregations,' and 'our poor charges.' The adverse of this is found in the expressions of the workingmen: 'We can't dress well enough to go to church;' 'your leading members don't notice us on the street;' 'your preachers run after the rich;' 'the preachers side against us in the matter of strikes.'" Evidently Rev. Mr. Morse knows what he is talking about. He sees clearly and speaks honestly. The church is aristocratic. With more pride than piety, the influence of the church is to repel not only workingmen, but all men who abhor shams. "The great human heart of the people," says Mr. Morse, "comprehends in some measure the fact that Christianity is not a cement to hold a rich veneer to a body of inferior materials, but a furnace to fuse all elements into one homogeneous mass."

But the church is not a furnace, it does not fuse; it is more like a refrigerator, it freezes. The "star preacher" is like the "star actor." The "first-class church," from a religious point of view, is a first-class fraud. "Under present conditions," says Mr. Morse, "it is sheer folly to talk about the rich and the poor meeting together in the house of God; the poor decline the invitation." Why? Because the poor discover that the rich Christians do not regard religion as a pledge of equality in the church nor "outside of the church." Mr. Morse says, "The two great classes of our population, capitalists and workingmen, are separated by an irreconcilable antagonism in assault and defense of a system which, in the thought of the masses, is founded on injustice and denounced by God's word."

The church arrays itself on the side of the capitalist. "The churches," says Mr. Morse, "maintain, at least by implication, that the great fortunes of the day are the fruit of legitimate industrial enterprise, and belong to their possessors as against the world," and that "poverty is due to laziness and inefficiency, waste, mismanagement, extravagance, injurious indulgence, and absence of a definite and resolute purpose to escape from poverty."

Admitting that Mr. Morse states the facts in the case, what inducement does the church hold out for workingmen to look upon it with favor? It is in alliance with those who oppress them. In the sanctuary (?), which in numerous cases are merely clubhouses surrounded by every luxury wealth can procure—with a "star preacher" paid a bank president's salary—the monstrous iniquities practiced by the rich to grow richer and to make the poor poorer receive no rebuke from the church. On the contrary, the church accounts for the wrongs by repeating the phrase "the will of God." But, says Mr. Morse: "The working-man does not believe it. Looking around upon the apparent disorder he replies, 'God would have done a better job.'" Says Mr. Morse, "Christ teaches the fatherhood of God and the brotherhood of man; why does His doctrine show so little income?" "To all these inquiries there is but one answer, the providence of God." "Providence, then," asserts the workingman, has been overlooked, "and he turns to his labor organization for relief and sympathy." "In all his difficulties, and to all his better pleadings, the church returns decrepit generalities, and is earnest and definite only in defense of vested rights when threatened by labor agitation."

It is well for society that occasionally a man like Rev. C. M. Morse is found who has the courage to point out the mistakes of the church, and who has the capacity to comprehend the character, capabilities, and services of workingmen. Society is never more deeply wronged than when injustice is done any one of its component parts, and though it should be asserted that the blow is aimed at the foot rather than at the head of the body social, the injury inflicted may not prove the less fatal; society has a right to appeal to the press, to the courts, and to the church for justice in all matters affecting its welfare. If the influence of these acknowledged factors in the progress of enlightenment become debauched, if, by any means whatever they are deflected from the shining pathways of truth, probity and high endeavor for the good of all, and are made to pander to base designs of cliques, society feels the wrong and realizes that there is treason in her camp and that calamities are to come. It may be said in extenuation for the press and the courts that they are simply human, but the church, with its divine commission, the church with robed priests and sacred symbols, the church pleading its soul-saving mission in the earth, the church with its altars and shrines—the church, claiming the eternal God as its founder and Christ Jesus, the son of God, as its head; the church with its sermons, prayers, and communions; if the church goes wrong, who is to set it right? The Rev. Mr. Morse does not hesitate to say the church has gone wrong. It has planted itself on the side of the rich, and in opposition to the poor—and as a result, workingmen turn away from the church, from its pride and pomp, and seek for religious teaching elsewhere, turn to their "labor organizations for relief and sympathy."

"The workingman," says Rev. Mr. Morse, "believes that in the estimation of the church, gold, stocks, and bonds must be protected, while bodies, hearts, and homes are left at the mercy of erratic economic principles. And when we remember Christ's example and words, can we censure the workingman for the stand he has taken?" The idea that "star preachers" of "first-class churches" and "wealthy congregations" can be of any religious advantage to men, who say, "Such preachers run after the rich," is too preposterous to be entertained for an instant. They do not believe it. There are to be no second-class seats in God's house, no second-class religious prescriptions to cure the sins of workingmen, while the members of "wealthy congregations" are to have their pills sugar-coated. The moment the church insults Jehovah by being a "respecter of persons," its glory departs. The church edifice may be built of diamonds—pulpits may be overlaid with gold. The theological seminary may turn out "star preachers" whose eloquent periods may ring like thunder peals—and the rich and the proud, the exclusive, may go in and worship, but under their influence hollow-heartedness will increase, rottenness and corruption will prevail in high places, and the church will stand forth as a whitened sepulcher. The Rev. Mr. Morse thinks that a "crisis has come—and that the church must continue to support the present order of things," or "champion the cause of the poor and oppressed." But workingmen are not going to wait to see what the church will do. They are able to take care of themselves, religiously and pecuniarily. If they want a preacher they can call a fisherman and the master will commission him.

The real significance of the paper of Rev. C. M. Morse is found in the fact that there are men in the church who have courage, and who dare tell the church that in its treatment of workingmen, its course is neither honorable nor politic. Rev. Mr. Morse is clearly of the opinion that the churches need reforming, as at present managed they are accomplishing little good.

In view of all the facts, workingmen must have their own press—and this they have, and the number of papers devoted to their interests is increasing.

There is to be no miraculous intervention on their behalf. With the ballot, and an intelligent comprehension of its power, the laws of the land are in the near future to map out vivid lines by which courts are to be guided. The church will be the last to swing into line, but should it maintain its present attitude, as pointed out by Mr. Morse, it will be powerless to arrest the onward and upward march of workingmen. The age in which we live is iconoclastic. Images and shams must go. The votaries of jugglery are decreasing in number and power. If the churches are to fake a position in the van of the advancing armies of progress, they must read and remember such wholesome advice as is found in the paper by Rev. C. M. Morse published in the February *Forum*.

Unmasking Hypocrisy[†]
April 1889

Dishonesty takes on many forms, among which hypocrisy is probably the most common. It is always the guise chosen by the cunning knave. The hypocrite is a conscienceless creature. He is the Pharisee, who to be seen of men, and for a pretense, makes long prayers while engaged in "devouring widows' houses."[21] Like "the devil, he can cite scripture for his purpose."[22] He appears like "a goodly apple," but is "rotten at the core."[23] His forte is dissimulation; in false professions he is always loud. The modern hypocrite, the better to make duplicity service-able, is very apt to put on pious airs. He gracefully wears the cloak of religion and, in his private intercourse and public addresses, takes great interest in the souls of men, and quite likely at such times he is pondering in what way he can make his deceit most profitable in the way of gaining someone's confidence and of improving his financial condition. But abandoning such reflections for the nonce, we turn our attention to one E. H. Belknap, who in February 1888 was a conductor on the CB&Q. Paul Morton,[24] who won imperishable notoriety as a champion of mendacity, was just the sort of a fellow to appreciate the talents of E. H. Belknap. The CB&Q, when it concluded to resist every demand for fair, honorable treatment of its engineers and firemen, had a pressing necessity

---

† Published in *Locomotive Firemen's Magazine,* vol. 13, no. 4 (April 1889), 342–344.

for scabs, and E. H. Belknap, a member of the ORC, filled the bill. Be this as it may, E. H. Belknap, in association with one W. C. Cross, signed a circular dated Burlington, Iowa, March 10, 1888, captioned, "Position of the ORCs" and addressed "To all members of the Order of Railway Conductors." Mr. Belknap, in addressing "all members of the Order of Railway Conductors," says:

> We can assure you that the ORC has made a great record for faithfulness and loyalty to principle by its members among railway officials.

Manifestly, Belknap, like Wheaton, don't care a continental for grammar; his purpose is accomplished if he can make "all the members of the Order of Railway Conductors" understand that the conductors on the CB&Q scabbed, as if they had been under a solemn obligation to crawl in the dirt like worms, rather than hold up their heads and walk erect like men. But not being content with his own degradation, he exhorts "all railway conductors" to emulate his own abject selfishness, and says:

> Now, brothers, in conclusion, let me say to you as conductors, as employees, as members of the ORC that, in case this strike spreads and your road becomes involved, "Go thou and do likewise."
> The circular from which we have quoted has the following endorsement:
> I have given permission to Brothers Belknap and Cross to issue the above circular.
>
> *C. S. Wheaton, GCC*[25]

Now then, we submit that the quotation we have given from E. H. Belknap's circular has the ring of honest convictions—the robust utterances of a man who entertains the highest possible respect for railway officials. We submit that 999 men out of every thousand would conclude, Belknap is a man who intimates that he never saw even one fly on any railway official, and that members of the ORC never had and never expect to have anything approximating a complaint or a grievance against their employers. Belknap's circular, apparently, affords the most positive assurance. Belknap's circular was evidently intended for the eyes of railway officials. His purpose was to ingratiate himself in their favor. He understood that in these degenerate times thrift often follows fawning. He was playing the game of Machiavellianism. Is this true? Was his policy one of duplicity? Did his anxiety to retain his position obscure all sense of manliness? In a word, while glorifying the members of the ORC on the CB&Q for scabbing, was he honest? And when he exhorted "all members of the Order of

Railway Conductors" to scab, did he not indulge in dissimulation? Such questions E. H. Belknap may answer before the tribunal of the public.

For some reason, which we shall not attempt to divine, E. H. Belknap was called upon to deliver the annual address before the representatives of the Railway Passenger and Freight Conductor's Mutual Aid and Benefit Association, held in Chicago in November last. *The Railway Conductor's Monthly,* of which Calvin S. Wheaton, GCC, is editor, in referring to Belknap's address on the occasion, says: "The address of Bro. E. H. Belknap, delivered on the above occasion, is, we think, one of the very best ever delivered before that body." Here we have an unqualified endorsement of Belknap's address by the highest authority of the order.

Let it be understood that whether it be Belknap or Wheaton, or the *Conductor's Monthly,* or any other person authorized to speak for the order, their public utterances are always designed to impress railway officials and the public generally with the idea that railway conductors, members of the order, have no grievances against railway officials, but in private, hypocrisy lays aside its mask—then Belknap ceases to crawl and stands up. Belknap issuing a circular "To all members of the Order of Railway Conductors," and Belknap making an address before the delegates to the Mutual Aid and Benefit Association of the order, judged by utterances, are as unlike as a spaniel and a royal Bengal tiger. In his circular Belknap whines; in his address he growls and roars. In his circular he is as destitute of spine as a tapeworm; in his address he has the backbone of a grizzly bear. In his circular he is as meek as a muley cow;[26] in his address he is an untamed bull, with horns ready for attack, and with tail erect he spurns the earth and bellows like a thunderstorm.

We have before us the full text of his address, delivered on the 21st of November, 1888, before the Mutual Aid and Benefit Association. It is official. It appears in the proceedings of the convention of that association, on pages 15 and 23, inclusive. For the information of the public, for the delectation of the readers of the *Magazine,* and for the purpose of unmasking hypocrisy, we give a few extracts from the address, which the *Conductor's Monthly* for February 1888, page 55, pronounced "one of the very best ever delivered before that body." Belknap, in his address, deplores the fact that conductors are "made the scapegoats of every passenger's fancied wrongs," and then asks, "Wherein lies the remedy and the cure?" And he answers, "Cast your frown and stamp with the seal of infamy everything, yes everything, that is false and unworthy; show by you life and your character, to all mankind, that you stand at the top of the ladder." In this strain Belknap soars and coruscates; he is a pyrotechnic display all the way from a shooting cracker to a ten-pound rocket. After pointing out how conductors can mount up the ladder of fame and "reach the top," he says: "And you ask again, will this ever be?" He answers, "it must be," and adds, "I have looked far enough in the future to tell you what most is needed for your welfare, for your permanent success." Steadily Belknap approaches the climax. He has been looking into "the future." He has seen the ladder; the conductors climbing steadily. He urges them to climb faster and get higher. He wants them to "reach the standard which all business men must reach to be considered first in the list of honorable businessmen." Belknap sees conductors skulking, biding, obscuring their light, and he goes for them as follows: "Let me say to you in all kindness, that the sooner you emerge from this hiding place and believe the opposite to be the truth, the better it will be for you."

At this juncture, Belknap inquires of the conductors, "Have you gained one step each day of your life?"—that is to say, have you gone up one round in the ladder every day of your life? Have you scabbed when ordered to scab? Have you exhorted, in a circular or otherwise, your fellow conductors to scab when ordered to do so by a railway official? Have you learned the arts of duplicity? Can you play the role of lickspittle, that you may be blessed with a smile from your boss, while in your heart of hearts you loathe yourselves for your degeneracy? Such interrogatories would seem to be in the line of Belknap's public expression. But we are now dealing with him as a spokesman in war paint, feathers, and eagle claws—in the council chamber of braves. The great medicine man of the tribe, the man with two faces and a double tongue, and we want to quote him verbatim. He is the man the *Conductor's Monthly* delights to honor but dares not quote in full. Belknap says in his address:

> Have you gained one step each day of your life? Others have, have you? If not, then sit no longer idle and repining, but rather awake, as awaken you must, if you too would be successful.
>
> "Ah," but says one, "we do *not receive pay enough* to do all this for any company on earth." Nothing more true than this have you ever uttered and no one more *to blame than the one who utters* it. None to blame but the conductors of America that this is, alas, so true; some isolated cases have been known where here and there one has gone and asked for more pay; *as well breathe his breath on the frosted pane of your window in hopes to warm the world; as well that General Grant had approached, alone, the battlements of Lee and Johnson, and said, "Kind sirs, please lay down your arms and surrender."* Would they have done so? Ah, no; but when he approached them with 60,000 Union soldiers, the bands playing "My Country, 'Tis of Thee," and the shot, shells, and *bullets singing,* "Down

with the Traitor, Up with the Stars," they *sang another tune* and learned the greatest lesson of their life, that right is might.

Then act as men; *go to them sixty thousand strong.* Not with dynamite, nor bearing the red flag of anarchy (thank God, it is not a native of America), but en masse and *state* your *grievances* as becometh men. Show to them in a *solid phalanx* what *someone has tried to do unaided and alone,* and then come to me and tell me the result. And finally, *what you owe your employer is only the same which is expected and exacted from the servants* of all practical, substantial, and prosperous business firms in the world.

In the foregoing the italics are ours (the grammar is Belknap's), our desire being to aid our readers in their analysis of Belknap. We have quoted the *Conductor's Monthly* as saying Belknap's address was "one of the very best ever delivered" before the Mutual Aid and Benefit Association. The *Monthly* reproduces portions of the address, but it is careful to omit the paragraph we have reproduced. Why? It dared not. They are an overwhelming exposé of the perfidy, the hypocrisy, of the policy of the men who have controlled the affairs of the ORC. Never in the history of any labor organization have declarations of hostility to corporate injustice been more emphatic than those made by Belknap. They sting like a scorpion's lash, like whips of fire. Belknap, in the presence of railway officials, tells his fellow conductors that railway officials are so heartless, so mercenary, so unjust, that a conductor going to them alone, asking for the redress of a grievance, might as well "breathe his breath on a frosted windowpane in hopes of warming the world." That is to say, railway officials are never generous, never just, never honest, never noble, but always venal, always arrogant, always contemptible. There never was a more terrible arraignment. Belknap makes no exceptions; he bandies all railway officials together, including the CB&Q, and flays them. But to still further impress upon his hearers the stolid, soulless indifference of railway officials to any honest appeal of conductors for justice, Belknap exerts himself to exhaust metaphor and says Grant might as well have approached the battlements of Lee and Johnson and said, "Kind sirs, please surrender," as for a conductor to approach a railway official alone and ask for simple justice. What does Belknap recommend? He tells conductors to emulate Grant—never to go to railway officials alone pleading for justice, but to go "sixty thousand strong," "en masse," "in a solid phalanx"—in a word, to strike for their rights. The language admits of no other construction, and this conjecture is the reason why the *Conductor's Monthly* declined to publish Belknap's utterances.[27] It hadn't the courage of conviction.

It is this cowardice, this vulgar duplicity that has made it necessary to organize the Brotherhood of Railway Conductors. Hypocrisy is not popular. Honest men will not tolerate it. The time has come for workingmen to be manly, to have the courage of conviction—to demand their rights with dignified independence, and this Belknap advocates in private, but when he issues a circular with the permission of Wheaton, his utterances are hypocritical and deceptive. Such duplicity, endorsed by the grand chief of the ORC, when known, must of necessity lead to disintegration. No order can live long that so outrages the decencies and proprieties of life. The conclusion must be, from what Belknap says, that railway officials have a supreme contempt for the ORC. They pay no attention whatever to the grievances of its members. When they want a member of the order to scab, or to perform any menial duty, the member obeys, and when the member has a grievance he might as well expect to "warm the world" by breathing on a "frosted" windowpane, as to expect that a railway official will grant his request.

The circular and address illustrate the disgusting methods to which a certain class of men will resort to win approval, and the address points to the circular with merited scorn, and to compare the two documents extorts the verdict that such tactics merit universal contempt.

Jay Gould†

May 1889

It is no part of our mission in the world, insofar as we are capable of comprehending the somewhat occult question of missions, to write panegyrics of Jay Gould. He belongs to a family or a tribe of millionaires whose history is never referred to by divines to illustrate prophecy relating to the millennium, when the devil is to be chained a thousand years, and when, if the world can credit apocalyptic scripture, monopolists, stock-waterers, food-cornerers, and bucket-shop gamblers generally will be required to take back seats. But the question arises: Is Jay Gould the chief of sinners in his line? Is he a victim of total depravity? Is he without a parallel? Is he sui generis? Is he, like vice—

> A monster of so frightful mien,
> As, to be hated, needs but to be seen?[28]

---

† Published in *Locomotive Firemen's Magazine,* vol. 13, no. 5 (May 1889), 390–391.

Manifestly, the drift of public sentiment is in the direction which answers all such interrogatories affirmatively. Jay Gould does not enter the arena in self-defense. With him, silence is golden. His mission in the world is to make money. The more mysterious his methods, the better he is pleased. He likes to be regarded as inscrutable, unfathomable, dark. He is not particular what people say. He is a student of character, disposition, deeds. He believes that men, like railroads, stocks, and bonds, are purchasable. When he wants a man, a judge, a legislature, he bids and buys. There is no foolishness about Jay Gould. There are no flies on him. In his line of endeavor, high or low, as people may choose to regard it, Jay Gould has been a financial success. He has large assets. As a youth, we see him with a trap, and now in his mature years, bordering upon the sere arid yellow leaf, the November of life, we see him with lots of game. His philosophy teaches that—

> Gold is the strength, the sinews of the world;
> The health, the soul, the beauty most divine;
> A mask of gold hides all deformities;
> Gold is heaven's physic, life's restorative.[29]

But the question arises, why single out Jay Gould for censorious criticism? Has he amassed a colossal fortune by ways that are dark? It is equally true of others. Has he the power to change water into wealth? Others possess the miraculous faculty, and do not hesitate to use it when opportunities are presented. Jay Gould is only one of a thousand of the same type who pursue the same methods in different enterprises—the difference being simply in ability to concoct schemes and use money to carry them out. As they accumulate cash they become more potent, as it was said of the "Young Napoleon," Ives,[30] keeping well within the law, they manage to make the world pay tribute and defy the courts.

The strange feature about the business is that Jay Gould comes in for by far the largest share of denunciation. "As the savages of Africa," says one, "make for themselves an idol to be beaten when the weather does not suit them, as the boys of England prepare an effigy of Guy Fawkes to be gibbeted and burned,[31] so our politicians, from the ragged anarchist to the well-fed Congressman, dress up an image constructed of the odds and ends of their own worthlessness, and label it Jay Gould."

This is very pretty, and is chiefly objectionable because Jay Gould alone is selected for condemnation. It is a great mistake to suppose that "ragged anarchists" and "well-fed Congressmen" are the only persons who censure Jay Gould. Occasionally this fault-finding becomes epidemic and defies all quarantine barriers, and then Jay Gould becomes the object of universal wrath, and yet it is difficult to discern wherein he is worse than others of his type, except that he has more money than some of them and more ability as a schemer.

It is well known that Jay Gould dabbles largely in railroads. His connection with the Union Pacific has brought him before the country in a way which seemingly justified the charge of general malversation; but says a writer in a paper devoted to railroad interests:

> Now, the fact is that when in 1873 he (Gould) bought a controlling interest in its stock he found it so poor that there were none to do it reverence. Even its projectors and constructors had no faith that a profitable business could ever be created in the sterile plains through which it ran, or built up upon the Pacific coast against the competition of water routes. It was chiefly constructed with iron rails laid upon pine ties and with numerous wooden bridges and culverts; it had efficient protection against snow blockades; it was poorly equipped with rolling stock. It had neither a branch of any nature nor an ally upon whose friendliness it could rely. It was attacked by would-be rivals with pro-rata schemes which if successful would instantly have bankrupted it. It had never earned nor paid a dividend, and there were but few, if any, besides Mr. Gould who had faith that it ever would be able to pay one.

Now, we submit that, accepting the foregoing as true, Jay Gould stands out conspicuously as a benefactor of his country. To take an old, decaying bankrupt railroad and make it an efficient highway for commerce and travel is equal to making two blades of grass grow where but one had previously flourished, and Jay Gould, being credited with having accomplished such a work, ought to receive proper credit. It is further said:

> Immediately he commenced a system of utilization of its resources to the utmost. By his influence with other lines in which he was interested, he secured for the Union Pacific the power to make through rates over other lines upon as favorable terms as were enjoyed by any of its competitors; moreover, these rates were divided between it and its connections, not upon the pro-rata basis which was customary throughout the country, but upon a basis much more favorable to it, a basis which the commissioners report to be still in force, and by which the Union Pacific is even now earning at least half a million dollars per annum in excess of the amount which it would receive if this arrangement had not been enforced by the power and favor of the man whom they abuse. Every natural resource of the line was by him steadily encouraged and rapidly developed; the tracks

were raised above the plains by embankments three or four feet in height, so that the winds, instead of blowing snow upon the track and thus blockading it, would blow the snow off and thus keep it clear. Steel rails were substituted for iron, oak ties for pine, masonry and earthwork and iron bridges for wooden bridges and culverts. No rates were increased, but such reductions were made as would lead to an increase of business and of revenue. The result was that the line commenced almost immediately to earn dividends, and having earned them the company actually distributed them to their stockholders instead of laying up the money to pay a debt that did not become due for nearly 20 years, and for the ultimate payment of which they were engaged in making another provision.

In such matters the readers of the *Firemen's Magazine* are as good judges as can be found. They are practical railroaders. They know a good road from a bad one, and can quickly distinguish between an efficient and an inefficient management.

It is in the interest of society, when it can be honestly done, to rescue the names of men from obloquy. At least the truth should be spoken, and always due credit given. We do not believe that Jay Gould is a sinner above all the rest of his class. As a matador he has slain a good many bulls and bears and taken their hides. As a trapper he has been a success. He spreads out amazingly, but is nowhere very thin. He may lack conscience and soul because he can't buy such things nor trap them. He has gold, brass, water, and steam, an iron will and a sharply defined purpose. In such things he is neither worse nor better than the Vanderbilts, the Sages, Scotts, Garretts, Corbins, et al., to the end of the list. He is credited with a clean home. He is said to be an affectionate husband and a doting father. In such things he is human, if not a Christian. If he prefers gold to God as an object of worship he can play pagan to his heart's content, and if he wants a monument when he dies to perpetuate his name and deeds he can build it while he lives, or direct how it shall be done when he is dead. But he is entitled to credit if he keeps his railroads in good order, and if he pays fair wages to his employees and deals justly with men who earn their bread in the sweat of their faces, he may find favor with St. Peter and step in through the "pearly gates."

Labor Organizations[†]

April 1889

We are not required to offer tabulated statistics to prove that labor organizations have during the past 25 years rapidly multiplied. And, on the other hand, the proof is equally conclusive that the great majority of workingmen refuse to enroll their names in any of the guilds, unions, or brotherhoods designed to improve the condition of men dependent upon their labor for existence. The fact that a majority of workingmen are not members of labor organizations has often provoked the inquiry, "Why do they stand aloof from such organizations?" No one, so far as we are informed, attempts to answer the interrogatory. That it is one of supreme importance no man credited with common sense will gainsay. In the line of elucidating what may appear to many as a difficult proposition, we inquire why it is that within the past 25 years, workingmen, more than ever before in the world's history, have instituted unions designed to promote their welfare? We unhesitatingly assert that during the period named workingmen have possessed more intelligence in the aggregate than at any previous time known to authentic history. We refer to the United States of America, but the declaration holds good in England, and in some countries on the continent of Europe.

In the United States, where the declaration that "all men are created equal" stands forth as a political fact of powerful and conquering significance, there are special reasons not found in other countries why American workingmen should organize to protect themselves from injustice at the hands of employers, because here a workingman is a sovereign in his own right, with all the privileges and prerogatives that belong to any other man, and because any injustice to him is a blow aimed at the fundamental principles upon which the government rests. But there is another reason why American workingmen have been actively engaged in organizing during the past 25 years. They have seen on the part of employers a purpose to reduce their wages to a point totally insufficient to maintain them and their families as should become American citizens. The charge is fully substantiated by the facts, and the alarm has extended from the center to the circumference of the country. On the one side statistics have shown fabulous prosperity and the accumulation of untold wealth, while on

---

† Published in *Locomotive Firemen's Magazine*, vol. 13, no. 4 (April 1889), 342–344.

the other hand there have been such exhibitions of poverty and wretchedness as to defy exaggeration. The workingmen who produced the wealth have been the victims of continuous calamities, the result of policies as vicious as were ever put in practice in any land.

Workingmen have believed that by organization, by united action, many of the ills to which they have been subjected could be modified, and in time extirpated. This being an eminently rational and practical view of the subject, the question recurs, why do so many workingmen remain outside of labor organizations? There are, we conceive, many reasons, the chief of them all, we assume, being the inability to comprehend the logic of facts, circumstances, and conditions—in a word, a lack of intelligence and a disinclination to study those problems which relate to their own welfare, and upon the proper solution of which depends their emancipation from degradation. Such persons constitute the great bulk of that degraded and labor-degrading army known as "scabs." They are men who never had an aspiration above those counterfeit men who crawl on their bellies in the dust and lick the boots of bosses, creatures of the parasitical type, who would rather be a flea in the hair of a rich man's dog, or a louse in the hair of a king, than one of nature's noblemen, with the independence and courage of a free man who dare hold up his head and assert his rights. The scab, in practice and purpose, is the enemy of labor organizations. He may not be absolutely beyond the reach of the educating and elevating influence abroad in the world, and as a consequence here and there one of the tribe may be converted, but as a general proposition we should deem it quite as probable that a tree toad could be transformed into an archangel as that a confirmed scab could be made a loyal, intelligent member of a labor organization.

But fortunately all the workingmen outside of labor organizations are not scabs. Thousands of them are thoughtful men who act upon convictions, and of their ultimate action there need be little anxiety. They are in sympathy with truth and justice, and desire to see labor emancipated from every degrading thralldom. They do not antagonize labor organizations, but in many ways evince their approval. It is to be assumed, and we doubt if any intelligent man will controvert the proposition, that the educating influences abroad in the country are on the whole advancing the cause of labor organizations. In saying this we are not unmindful of the power of a subsidized press. We do not underestimate the impelling, controlling, and directing power of money, and yet facts satisfy us that in spite of every adverse circumstance, labor organizations are moving forward in the direction of ultimate triumph. Labor has a press. It has a literature. It has knowledge. It has not only the wisdom of experience, but it has men capable of solving the most abstruse problems relating to the growth and permanency of organization. Labor organizations have succeeded in getting labor into politics. In saying this we have no reference to partisan squabbles over the loaves and fishes. We refer to that higher plane of politics which relates to the enactment of just laws for the protection of society, in which labor has vital interests. If it is said that little has been accomplished in that direction, we unhesitatingly admit the impeachment, but it must be remembered that workingmen so far have done but little in that direction to modify or to repeal vicious laws, or to enact laws calculated to improve their condition.

Labor has not federated for this wise purpose to any applaudable extent. Still, much has been done, enough to show workingmen that when they decide to federate for their own emancipation, and for the welfare of society, a great victory will be achieved. It is simply required to be patient and to work. Labor organizations have nothing to lose, but everything to gain by having their purposes searchingly investigated. Their aims are few and easily understood. They are totally exempt from deceit—no art of dissimulation is practiced. Labor organizations seek first to obtain fair wages, and then to maintain fair wages. The wage question is the supreme question. With fair wages obtained and maintained, labor organizations are in a position to inaugurate and carry forward enterprises the benefits of which inure to society as well as to those who are identified with such organizations. We could indefinitely elaborate upon this feature of labor organizations. Having secured fair wages, they are in a position to adopt plans for the benefit of their membership, and be it remembered that these benefits are in proportion to the wages received.

With such data as we have at hand, we assume that since their organization, the brotherhoods of engineers, firemen, brakemen, switchmen, and conductors have paid out a sum of money closely approximating $5 million as benefits to disabled members and to widows and orphans who, in numerous instances, would have been absolutely destitute without such aid. In doing this, the brotherhoods named have assumed such burdens as have relieved society, the state, the taxpayers of all responsibility in providing for the welfare of their poor. Widows and orphans have not been required to go from the grave, where husbands and fathers were buried, to a pauper asylum, but the brotherhoods have come to their rescue, and out of the earnings of their membership, too often far below the demands of justice, have rescued them from want and the degradation of mendicancy. And this the brotherhoods have done while contributing their full share to the revenues of the state and to the maintenance of those unfortunates who, failing to become members of labor organizations, are thrown upon the cold charity of the world and compelled to endure hunger and nakedness, or accept such comforts as a "poorhouse" affords.

We have referred to certain labor organizations because we happen to be more familiar with their operation than with other labor organizations, but if it were possible for us to tabulate the payments made by all the labor organizations of the country for purely benevolent purposes the sum total would be of such magnitude as to excite surprise and admiration. The facts would demonstrate beyond cavil that labor organizations are the staunch friends of society, the promoters of peace, order, and prosperity, and are therefore deserving of encouragement. To antagonize labor organizations is scarcely less than a crime, and those who seek to disrupt them are the enemies of society. The objections urged against labor organizations relate chiefly to their efforts to secure honest pay for honest work, and of their scanty earnings they give back millions to redeem men, women, and children from pauperism. As we have stated, the benefactions of five of these organizations amount to millions taken from their earnings, and it would be interesting to place beside the sum total of the benefactions of labor organizations in the United States the sum total of gifts for charitable purposes made by their enemies. Fortunately for society, labor organizations are increasing in number and in power. They are doing good. Their purposes are honorable and their high ambition attainable. They are all young in years. Taught in the school of experience, they are displaying capabilities of the highest order. Under the influence of educating forces they will learn to appreciate more fully the strength of unity, and then will come federation. With this, obstacles to success will disappear, and labor, emancipated from every form of oppression, will receive its just reward.

Meeting to Perfect Federation†

May 1889

On June 3 [1889], the first Monday in the month, a meeting will be held in the city of Chicago for the purpose of perfecting a federative compact between the Brotherhood of Railroad Brakemen, the Switchmen's Mutual Aid Association, and the Brotherhood of Locomotive Firemen, in accordance with the directions of the last conventions of these orders. Each order will be represented by its three chief grand officers, to whom full power has been delegated to formulate the principles upon which the compact shall be established and put into practical operation. Since the date of the conventions of the orders, conferring authority upon their grand officers to establish federation, the subject has been widely and pretty thoroughly discussed, and while much has been said in favor of federation, not one rational objection to the contemplated alliance has been urged from any quarter whatever.

This silence is easily explained. No objection can be urged against federation, while a thousand convincing reasons can be assigned in its favor. Federation contemplates no wrong. It is simply a compact between orders having certain interests in common, for the purpose of repressing wrongs and of maintaining the right—a compact, the influence of which extends far beyond the parties immediately concerned, and which touches society at large. Indeed, it would not be difficult to prove that federation contemplates, in a preeminent degree, the prosperity of the railroad enterprises of the country. So high an authority as Charles Francis Adams[32] sees in the frequent disturbances between railroad companies and their employees the great necessity for doing away with all unnecessary frictions so that strikes may be avoided. Federation, it is believed, will prove "the prevention" for which Mr. Adams has industriously sought. It will bring about arbitration—regarded by all thinking men as a panacea for strikes. In this spirit the grand officers of the orders we have named will meet in Chicago on the first Monday in June to establish federation, and that success will attend the effort, we feel a degree of confidence amounting to assurance.

---

† Published in *Locomotive Firemen's Magazine*, vol. 13, no. 5 (May 1889), 448.

Pin and Principle†

June 1889

In the faraway southwestern Pacific Ocean lies a group of islands known as Samoa, or the Samoan group. These islands are situated on the line of commerce between the United States and Australia. Some years since, the government of the United States deemed it prudent to enter into negotiations with the government of Samoa for the establishment of a "coaling station" on one of the islands. Permission was granted and the United States obtained certain rights which, by the action of German authorities at Samoa, have been placed in peril, and the circumstance has led to much talk about the possibility of war between the United States and Germany.[33]

We have stated the case in a nutshell for the purpose of referring to an interview with Admiral Porter[34] of the United States Navy upon the subject. The views of Admiral Porter are entitled to great weight. He knows all about war, its costs and sacrifices. He does not talk at random. He weighs his words. A war with Germany would require, he thinks, the immediate outlay of at least $250 million for ships and guns and other munitions of war. As a preliminary step he would have the government purchase all the big guns England and France may have for sale. After all, he thinks, for a time, that Germany, as she has the best navy, would have the best of the fight, but that ultimately the United States would destroy her commerce and sink her navy. Admiral Porter does not think that it would be child's play to have a war with Germany. This much is said to introduce an expression of Admiral Porter worthy of all commendation. After discussing the possible losses and gains of war, he said; "A pin is worth fighting for if a principle is involved."[35]

In that declaration we find the keynote of every song of liberty and independence that was ever sung since God said, "Let us make man." There is no slobbering about cost and sacrifice. The question is, is there a principle involved? A principle of right, of justice, of truth, of independence. In that case, "a pin is worth fighting for." Is war to be declared at once? Not necessarily. What should precede war? Manifestly, negotiation, discussion, arbitration. If failure follows, then war. If not war, degradation. But says some weak-kneed, spineless, white-livered croaker, "You might get defeated, then what?" Simply

---

† Published in *Locomotive Firemen's Magazine,* vol. 13, no. 6 (June 1889), 491–492.

submit to the inevitable and "pick your flint" and try it again at the first opportunity. The difference between courage and cowardice is as the difference between the truth and a lie. A coward is no more like a courageous man than a Digger Indian[36] is like an archangel. The courageous man fights, the coward runs or hides.

See you those two houses around which crowds of men, women, and children are assembled? Do you ask the reason for such motley gatherings? It is easily told. In the night burglars assailed them. At No. 1, the husband and father, hearing the midnight marauder and murderer, rushed to the rescue of his home with such weapons as were at his command, and having saved his home, fell dead on his doorsill, with a bullet in his head.

At No. 2, the dwelling was robbed of its treasures, and at the sound of danger the husband and father took shelter under the bed, and from his covert was dragged forth limp as a dishrag, a poor driveling wretch, whom it would be a compliment to call a cur.

The man of home No. 1, dead, lives, by virtue of courage, in the affectionate memory of wife and children for whom he died, and his heroic devotion to his family becomes the subject for ceaseless laudation, and a monument is built to perpetuate his memory and his courage. His example is inspiring. Old men and young men, matrons and maidens fair, love to recite the story of his devotion and his deeds. The verdict is, "Well done."

The man of home No. 2 is universally scorned. He lives, but it would have been better for him if his cowardice had killed him. His name becomes a synonym of all things pusillanimous, dastardly, and poltroonish. The mastiff, the rat terrier, even the vagrant hound that bays the moon is of more value in the world than such a degenerate specimen of humanity.

The question of strikes is constantly up for discussion. Strikes are subjects for statisticians. We are treated to the number in a year, the number of persons engaged in them is given. We are told how many succeed and how many fail, losses in dollars and cents are stated, but those who supply the statistics never refer to any principle involved. They magnify money and advise workingmen not to strike. They advise workingmen to work and submit, take what they can get, and be silent. They would have workingmen see the shadows of gloom gather around their homes without protest; they would have workingmen see their pay reduced until every comfort in life is relinquished and destitution sits gaunt and haggard upon their doorsteps and hearthstones, without a murmur; the immortal words of Admiral Porter, that "a pin is worth fighting for if a principle is involved," they would regard as rank treason to the soulless corporations which amass millions by their inhumanities to man.

It is not to be assumed that every strike involves a principle any more than it is to be assumed that every war involves a principle. There have been unwise wars and unnecessary strikes. In such matters it is not difficult to discover the principle if a principle exists, and when found, a courageous man will fight for the principle. A coaling station on a Samoan island is an exceedingly small matter, in itself considered, and thousands have said, "Who would go to war for such a trifle? What nation with a modicum of common sense would spend millions and sacrifice life for what at most is worth but a few thousand dollars?" But that is not the question. Is there a principle involved? If so, a pin is worth fighting for.

In a vast majority of strikes, a principle is as sharply defined as that involved in the rights of the United States to a coaling station in the Samoan Islands. It was so in the fight on the CB&Q, and every man that did battle in that strike, and every man who helped to sustain that strike won imperishable renown. Did the CB&Q win that battle? Yes, just as the British won the battle of Bunker Hill, but they didn't want any more such victories, nor does the CB&Q. What was the influence of the Bunker Hill defeat? It taught the colonists that they were equal to British regulars, and this England learned to her sorrow in the long run; and though Warren[37] and hundreds of his compatriots fell on Bunker Hill, fighting for a principle, their example was a ceaseless inspiration to the handful of colonists, and Bunker Hill, where the colonial militia was defeated, has become one of the sacred mountains of the world. And as certainly as that tides ebb and flow, the wrecked condition of the CB&Q will deter other corporations from engaging in a similar folly, and in this fact the strikers on the CB&Q, and all who, with heroic devotion, sustained them, may see, if they will, their defeat expand to a continental victory, and learn to admire the immortal words of Admiral Porter, that "a pin is worth fighting for if a principle is involved."

Truth and Fiction†

June 1889

Mr. George W. Childs, editor of the *Philadelphia Public Ledger,* in a recent issue, has an editorial article captioned "Equality and Sympathy," which contains about equal parts of fact and fiction. The fiction is prominent, undisguised, while the facts are obscured by sophisms and special pleadings totally out of place, and which are made to subserve a purpose at war with common-sense ideas of American equality. Mr. Childs starts out as follows:

> Many excellent people, in their zeal for equality among men, and in their haste to abolish all class distinctions, overlook the laws of natural attraction and repulsion, which are as immutable in the sphere of humanity as they are in the domain of physical science. These reformers see with righteous indignation the false distinctions made by shallow and scornful people to separate the rich from the poor, the fashionable from the unfashionable, the stylish and expensive household from the plain and unpretending. But they would not only break down these barriers, but all others, and compel men and women to mingle together familiarly in social and domestic life, without regard to congeniality of thought or life, taste, or temperament. It is as useless to antagonize a natural law as it is to fight the air. There must be some bond of sympathy, some mutual interest, something in each that awakens a responsive chord in the other in order that any two persons shall take pleasure in each other's society.

There may be such "reformers" as the *Ledger* designates, but we are not acquainted with them, nor with their written or oral utterances. The fundamental American idea is expressed in the declaration that "all men are created equal," that they have "certain unalienable rights," such as "life, liberty, and the pursuit of happiness." The American idea of equality, the real idea, has no reference to what mere flunkeys call "equality." If there are those whom the *Ledger* styles "reformers," who are trying to bring about a condition of things in which A, the workingman, shall demand that B, the millionaire, shall exchange visits, dine, dance, and drink together, then such "reformers" are cranks, really idiots. The workingmen of America have a lofty contempt, unmitigated scorn for American codfish aristocracy. They do not belong to

† Published in *Locomotive Firemen's Magazine,* vol. 13, no. 6 (June 1889), 489–490.

the growing army of fashion's fools. The true reformer is a man who demands that "class distinctions shall not be supported by statute; that there shall be no "class legislation," that there shall be absolute equality before the law, and if the law anywhere under the American flag makes "class distinction" that that law shall be repealed. The workingmen of America need not be told that a Vanderbilt can dress in "purple and fine linen," that he can have a $10,000 cook and fare sumptuously every day; he need not be told that when the millionaire travels it is in a palace car decorated with oriental magnificence. He knows that in the gatherings of such peacocks of society, such diamond-decorated dudes and dunces, there is arrogance, pomp, and pride, but such things only excite his derision, and he simply demands that such degenerate creatures shall not use their money power, nor any other power, to place laws upon the statute books which in any degree shall detract from their rights and privileges as American citizens.

The true reformers of the times, coming down to specialties, do not demand that the families of railway employees, men, women, and children, shall "mingle together familiarly in social and domestic life," with the families of railway presidents, bondholders, etc. The reformation demanded is that such dignitaries shall not use their position and power to degrade employees, that before the law, in every business relation, in every tribunal, the employed shall be recognized as the equal, the peer, of the employer. It is well known that notwithstanding the genius of our government and all of its institutions recognize this sort of equality, that laws have been enacted utterly subversive of it. Infamous laws have been enacted, well calculated to feed the arrogance of wealth, and courts have been debauched to an extent well calculated to create universal alarm. This apprehension of danger is not premature. The reform is not demanded a day too soon, and fortunately for the country, the workingmen of America have taken the matter in hand. They are intensely aroused and are everywhere massing their forces. The workingmen of America are the true reformers of the period. Caring nothing for what millionaires and their satellites call "class distinction," the workingmen of America have determined that such distinction shall not have the sanction of law nor of judicial decisions, and they are massing their strength and their intelligence to inaugurate permanent reforms.

In what we have said there is no appeal to sympathy or sentiment. The day has gone by for workingmen to prostrate themselves in the presence of those who seek to make the law subserve class distinctions. The workingmen are in the majority. The question is, will they unify for their own welfare? Those who are capable of reading the signs of the times will answer in the affirmative. Says the *Ledger:*

The real equality for which we should work is the equality of *opportunity*, the spread of the most favorable conditions of life, the extension of a fair chance to everyone who comes into the world. Certainly this is a large work, involving many long and complicated processes, and demanding all the thoughtful wisdom and forceful energy that can be brought to bear upon it; but just as fast as it goes on so fast may we expect to see realized that complete brotherhood of man which we all long for. Whatever tends to promote intelligence, to spread education, to foster habits of industry and economy, to instill principles of justice and integrity, to turn the currents of passionate desire from channels of self-indulgence and vice into those of purity, love, and goodwill, will also tend to ensure an increasing sympathy and congeniality among our people and to draw them together by the only bonds which can never be broken. Every noble effort of philanthropy and reform, every public measure carried for the public benefit, every private attempt to teach the ignorant, to raise the fallen, to help the unfortunate, to comfort the distressed, to lift men and women to a higher level, is in fact working in the direct line of human brotherhood and true equality.

The fundamental idea of government in the United States, as we have said, is "equality of opportunity," equality in the matter of "life, liberty, and the pursuit of happiness." We started right. We made an announcement that thrilled the world. But the declaration, as the nation has advanced, has become like "Dead Sea fruit." It tempts the eyes, it delights the ear, but practically, in thousands of instances, life is a burden till it is not worth the living. We are required to contemplate it under the most revolting conditions. Men work and starve because the laws are vicious, because one class is permitted to prey upon another class. In such a condition of things the term "liberty" is one of cruel irony, and the "pursuit of happiness," as fruitless as to seek for a cooling, life-giving spring amidst the sands of Sahara. We are not of those who believe in reforming the world by statute, but obstacles in the way of a fair race for life, liberty, and the pursuit of happiness, placed there by law, can be removed by law. Indeed, it does not matter how or why they obstruct the highways of progress. Eads, by a simple contrivance, removed the bars at the mouth of the Mississippi,[38] and dynamite annihilated the rocks of Hell Gate,[39] and the united votes of workingmen in the United States can and will at no distant day expunge from the statute books of the states and of the nation every unjust law that tends to degrade life, that abridges liberty, and that makes the "pursuit of happiness" a delusion.

The fight is on. It is not a psalm-singing crusade. It is the massing of a mighty force demanding fair play. It is the voice of sovereignty demanding that laws shall be just and courts undebauched. The reformation is on. The reformers are millions against the millionaires. The "fatherhood of God" is a fact; the "brotherhood of man" is a fact. They require no statute to establish them. The time may come when all men will recognize and be governed by their sublime teachings. Be this as it may, the demand of the present is to enact righteous laws, beat down idols and shams, monopolies, and trusts, set limits to aristocratic insolence and rapacity, and enthrone justice. The signs are auspicious. True reformers are federating. Victories have been achieved, and more are coming. Labor, in all the centuries gone, was never so exalted as in these closing years of the nineteenth century. It has its champions in every forum. Its literature is making its way to the front and is holding its own grandly. Labor is learning its power and is wielding it for the general good.

Federation Inaugurated[†]

July 1889

A new era has dawned. Federation is an accomplished fact. The *Firemen's Magazine,* animated by a fraternal spirit, sends cheerful greetings to all railroad employees. The *Firemen's Magazine* long ago placed itself on record in favor of the federation of the various organizations of railway employees. Since the first article appeared in its columns, the subject has been widely and searchingly discussed. The proposition did not escape criticism, nor was exemption from the severest analysis desired. The friends of federation had nothing to fear from honest opposition, nothing to fear from the logic of history, of events, of facts, conditions, or worthy ambitions. The grand old maxim, "In unity there is strength," embodying a truth that develops vitality as time speeds on, blooming and fruiting as centuries come and go, is the central truth of all federations. To make headway against federation, as a principle of action, finds its parallel in antagonizing an axiom in mathematics, in science, and philosophy. Federation is "e pluribus unum," one composed of many. Without federation, the great American Republic would not exist today. Its foundations were laid in federation.

† Published in *Locomotive Firemen's Magazine,* vol. 13, no. 7 (July 1889), 585–586.

Federation, whatever it has done for others, is preeminently American, and the motto, "United we stand, divided we fall," hackneyed though it be, embodies the principles and the truth which holds all the states, like stars of a constellation, in their rightful places, and when Sumter's gun obscured the skies by its smoke, and its roar awakened a nation from a lethargy born of fancied security, the one terrible truth confronted millions of patriots that division would produce a downfall, compared with which the fall of Rome is but an idle tale. As a result, the "more perfect union" born of federation stands today, and more than ever before, the "land of the free and the home of the brave"—and what is more, new states are constantly entering the confederacy adding to its strength and glory, and wherever its coins are seen, and wherever its flag waves, they speak more eloquently than words of the strength and influence of federation.

Federation, wherever found, means an effort to increase in power. True, it may be said for the purpose of doing wrong, or of perpetuating the wrong, bad men federate. We make no estimate of the wickedness of men. We need not be told of schemes concocted by bad men to multiply and intensify human ills. Nor are we required to read history, ancient or modern, sacred or profane, to arrive at rational conclusions upon such matters. The present is prolific of schemes productive of woe to men, women, and children, for which the past furnishes no parallels, and it is such facts that have prompted workingmen to organize and to federate in the holy hope that to some extent, at least, artificial wrongs may be reduced in number and virulence. And here let it be said—here it must be said—if organization and federation on the part of workingmen cannot mitigate the wrongs under which they suffer—cannot ameliorate conditions which, like the mills of the gods, grind exceedingly small, then within the entire realm of vagary, no such colossal sham as our "boasted civilization" ever lured men on to destruction. No such Dead Sea fruit ever tempted the eye, to turn to ashes on the lips.[40]

But we do not take such a view of the subject. If there are bad men in the world, there are also good men in the world, and we believe the good are in the majority—and in that majority we believe are included the great body of workingmen—and included in the body of workingmen are the organizations, known as the Brotherhood of Locomotive Firemen, the Brotherhood of Railroad Brakemen, and the Switchmen's Mutual Aid Association. We believe there are other organizations of railroad employees included in the majority, but we name those which on the sixth day of June, AD 1889, federated in the city of Chicago for the high and honorable purpose of "mutual justice."

What of these federated orders? How do they stand in the full glare of the noonday sun of the centuries? What do they demand? What is the measure of their federated ambition? These are pertinent questions and demand answers. They are workingmen whose extreme demands are fair pay for honest work, and fair treatment at the hands of their employees. With fair pay they can rear their families in respectability, to lives of usefulness and honor. With fair treatment they can maintain their independence and maintain the dignity of American citizenship. If such rights are denied, they believe, and have a right to believe, that federation will help them to secure their rights. Not necessarily by resorting to strikes, but because united for mutual justice, they will be more potent than by acting singly. But should arbitration be denied, and concession and compromise set aside, and a strike result from a stubborn resistance to all reasonable demands, in that case it is held—and the logic is invulnerable—that a strike by all the federated orders would introduce a convincing logic well calculated to secure victory.

We believe that federation is based upon an immutable principle, and in the case under consideration only good can result, because only good is intended; and no law enacted by virtue of which a wrong can be perpetrated can escape detection. The federation consummated at Chicago by the three orders we have named contemplates, ultimately, the federation of all orders of railway employees. The laws of the federated body are framed with a view to that desirable end. No overestimates of the consequence of the federated body are made, nor are misgivings to result from underestimates of its power and influence. It is not an organization of Utopians. No idle dreaming forms the basis of action. It deals with practical problems in a practical manner, and the good anticipated in its utmost reach is embodied in "fair dealing." We bespeak for the new departure a fair trial. Attacks may come, but we are not apprehensive of danger. That defects may be found, we do not doubt, but we do not believe they will be pronounced fatal. At any rate, there is no exclusiveness. The door for admission is broad, and the invitation to other organizations of railroad employees is generous and manly. To them the latchstring is within reach, and when they come they will be received with a true brotherhood welcome, and should they come, then as certain, as that "truth crushed to earth shall rise again,"[41] the era of strikes will have disappeared. We believe that reason will in due time triumph over prejudice, and that, fortified by the practical workings of federation as inaugurated at Chicago, the victory will come at a much earlier day than the most sanguine now anticipate.

Supreme Council of the United Orders of Railway Employees Established[†] [excerpt]

July 1889

In furnishing the readers of the *Magazine* with a summary of the proceedings of the meeting of delegates representing three orders of railway employees, held in the city of Chicago, Illinois, commencing June 3, 1889, we deem it appropriate to refer to the fact that as early as February 1887, the *Firemen's Magazine* referred to "federation" as the hope of workingmen of the country.[42] We refer to the fact here and now because we desire to have it understood that while the CB&Q strike brought into the boldest possible prominence the importance and necessity of federation, it did not suggest such action on the part of workingmen to the *Magazine*. We said:

> Federation is not impracticable. On the contrary, federation is feasible, and if labor is ever to reach the goal of equality with capital in shaping policies, in the assertion of prerogatives, it will have to federate.
>
> * * *
>
> No greater service could be done for society, for the welfare of all, than for thoughtful men to devise plans whereby labor organizations could be brought into a grand national federation.

At the time these expressions were printed, the CB&Q strike was not thought of, but when it did come, "as waves come when navies are stranded," it served as a convincing argument in favor of federation, and the logic of facts and the logic of events finally, and at a much earlier date than was anticipated, culminated in the federation of the three orders of railroad employees, viz.:

The Brotherhood of Locomotive Firemen,
The Brotherhood of Railroad Brakemen,
and the Switchmen's Mutual Aid Association

---

† Published as "Federation" in *Locomotive Firemen's Magazine,* vol. 13, no. 7 (July 1889), 627–629.

The great strike on the CB&Q had but just begun to develop the staying qualities of the strikers and the corporation when this magazine put upon
record its views relating to "federation, the lesson of the great strike"[43] and,
among other things, said:

> Viewing the subject from such standpoints, we venture the prediction
> that the day is near at hand when the brotherhoods of railroad employees
> will federate for mutual protection . . . Federation means victory for the
> right, and the great strike on the CB&Q has brought its necessity into
> such bold relief that its advocacy becomes a duty, and its consummation
> will be fraught with incalculable blessings, not only to employees, but to
> employers, to society, and to the whole country.

During all the dreary days and months of the strike on the CB&Q, days of
hopes, and doubts, and fears, when money flowed in from a thousand sources and
the hearts of all brotherhood workingmen beat responsive to duty, and sacrifices
were endured with a heroism as sublime as ever embellished the pages of fiction or
fact, thoughtful men saw the weak link in the chain of circumstances which was
the want of federation on the part of all the brotherhoods of railroad employees on
the system. As a consequence, federation became the theme of the one important
subject of discussion in the lodges of railroad employees. It reached beyond the
boundaries of the organizations and was discussed in the press of the country, and
the more it was discussed, the more convincing became the conclusion that federation was the one thing needful to achieve victory for the right.

In the month of September 1888, the Brotherhood of Locomotive Firemen,
at its first biennial session, held at Atlanta, Georgia, took action upon the subject and decided to federate with such other organizations of railroad employees
as should arrive at the conclusion that federation was required to emancipate
them from oppression and secure to them their rights as men and citizens.

Fortunately the Switchmen's Mutual Aid Association was then in session
in the city of St. Louis, and was at once informed of the action of the Brotherhood of Locomotive Firemen. Promptly, without delay, the Switchmen's Association came into line under the banner of federation. Its bugle blast was
grand. Doubts and fears were given to the winds. Reason triumphed. There was
conviction and the courage of conviction. Misgivings went down before the
conquering power of facts, and the outlook was such as to dispel despondency.

In the month of October 1888, the Brotherhood of Railroad Brakemen
held its annual convention in the city of Columbus, Ohio. It is needless to say
that all eyes were turned toward that city, and the question was everywhere
asked, what will the brakemen do? The country did not have long to wait. In

fact, it never had been a debatable question, and soon the wires flashed the tidings. "The brakemen have declared in favor of federation." Then there were three great orders in line, shoulder to shoulder, knee to knee, hand in hand, they had decided to form a national and an international alliance, the fruits of which they hoped and had a right to believe would be fruitious. This done, the discussion went forward, and the agitation strengthened conviction that federation was in the line of emancipation.

The subject having been thoroughly analyzed, the Brotherhood of Locomotive Firemen issued [a] letter to the organizations of Switchmen and Brakemen . . .

* * *

The response to the letter was favorable. The time and place were agreed upon, and as a consequence the official representatives of the federating orders assembled in the city of Chicago on the first Monday in June, 1889, to formulate a plan of federation.

The representatives of the Brotherhood of Locomotive Firemen were: F. P. Sargent,[44] grand master; J. J. Hannahan,[45] vice grand master; E. V. Debs, grand secretary and treasurer.

The representatives of the Switchmen's Mutual Aid Association were: Frank Sweeney, grand master; John Downey, vice grand master; John A. Hall, grand organizer and instructor.

The representatives of the Brotherhood of Railroad Brakemen were: S. E. Wilkinson, grand master; W. G. Edens, vice grand master; Edward F. O'Shea, grand secretary and treasurer.

Organization

The representatives of the orders having assembled, they were called to order by S. E. Wilkinson, whereupon an organization was effected by the election of F. P. Sargent, permanent president; E. V. Debs, permanent secretary, and J. A. Hall and Edward F. O'Shea, associate secretaries.

The organization having been effected, a committee of three was appointed, representing the three federating orders, to formulate a plan of federation. The committee was constituted as follows: S. E Wilkinson, J. A. Hall, and E. V. Debs. J. A. Hall was made chairman of the committee, and E. V. Debs, secretary. The committee promptly entered upon the task of formulating a constitution for the government of the orders in their federated capacity. After two days of exhaustive work, the delegates were reconvened and the constitution prepared by the committee was submitted for final action. Every section and paragraph was critically considered, and when a vote was taken the constitution, as submitted, with a few unimportant alterations, was unanimously adopted and subscribed to on Thursday, June 6, 1889 . . .

* * *

Immediately following the adoption of the constitution, the representatives of the federating orders proceeded to the election of officers for the Supreme Council, resulting as follows: F. P. Sargent, president; Frank Sweeney, vice president; Edward F. O'Shea, secretary and treasurer, who are to hold office one year, or until their successors are elected and qualified. The Supreme Council meets annually at Chicago, on the third Monday in June, and the constitution makes provisions for special meetings as exigencies may arise.

The constitution makes provisions for admitting other organizations of railway employees, which the Supreme Council will welcome when application is made, and it is believed that other organizations will, at no distant day, see the reasonableness of the movement and unite their power and influence with the federated orders.

At present, and as it has ever been, the weak are at the mercy of the strong. Power is only overcome by power. In theory, the wrong is always weak, the right always strong. The saying is as old as the hills that "truth is mighty and will prevail," but the history of the world shows conclusively that error has stubbornly resisted truth, and by federating its forces has scored innumerable victories.

The time has come for truth to federate its forces and stay the onward march of error. The firemen, the switchmen, and the brakemen have federated to secure and to maintain the right. The right wrongs no man. Its triumph is alike a benediction to all—to the employee, to the employers, to society, to the state, to humanity.

The Supreme Council of the federated orders of railway employees sets up no claim to infallibility. It believes its constitution fairly meets demands, but it may be amended as time and circumstances make known requirements.

With this, for the present, it must be content. Every provision hears the impress of an earnest desire for the betterment of conditions, the elevation of labor, in which, say what we will, the hopes of humanity (croakings to the contrary) center.

The Johnstown Horror[†]

July 1889

In writing of the indescribable horrors that befell the people residing in Johnstown and other villages situated in the Conemaugh Valley,[46] no effort will be made to introduce pen pictures of the awful scenes that transpired. In due time, the camera, the photographic art, will supply in some measure the demand for pictures of death, destruction, and desolation brought about by the deluge of water, but when the most in that line has been done, the half will not be presented to the eye or to the mind. Graphic pens have been at work from the first. Men of fervid imaginations, having at their command the wealth of all languages, will find their descriptive powers totally inadequate for the task of portraying incidents of the mountain tide of desolation as it rolled in awful majesty down the valley of death.

The Johnstown catastrophe, for such it is to be known, is to be monumental. It is to pass into history and will be referred to when centuries are gone. There is nothing to compare with it in modern times. Nor does fancy conjure up anything more horrifying, in the contemplation of the overthrow of Pompey, Herculaneum, or Sodom. The rain of ashes and the storm of fire could not have been more sudden or overwhelming, and had an earthquake lent its earth-splitting force to the mad wave of the mountain reservoir, the horrors of the hour could scarcely have been more appalling.

Occasionally someone refers to the awful visitations of providence; to the mysterious ways of providence; to Jehovah's inscrutable will. When such things can be saddled upon an omniscient God, the convenient verdict, "nobody to blame," is natural, and always in order.

The Conemaugh River was subject, like all mountain streams, to sudden floods. The people living along its banks were familiar with its eccentricities and, though frequently giving them trouble and inconvenience, it was not regarded as specially dangerous, but in the mountains, a few miles distant, was a reservoir, originally constructed as a feeder to a canal. Its elevation above the bed of the Conemaugh was at least 175 feet. When the canal was abandoned a number of rich persons obtained possession of this reservoir, extended its area until it became a lake three miles long, one and a half miles wide, and of

---

† Published in *Locomotive Firemen's Magazine,* vol. 13, no. 7 (July 1889), 583–584.

a depth of from 40 to 100 feet. It was for private sport, fishing, duck shooting, and sailing; elegant residences and clubhouses adorned its banks. It was a place for elegant, luxurious leisure. It was known to be dangerous, and the millionaires who owned it had been required to give bond in the sum of $3 million to make the banks of the lake safe and keep them in that condition, but the bond was never executed. Millionaires have a happy way of avoiding responsibilities; it is so much easier and less expensive to make providence responsible. The cry had often been heard, "The dam has broken!" or some similar warning, but as the dam did not give way, the people were lulled into security.

The storms of the week preceding the fatal Friday, May 31, created alarm. The pleasure lake was often referred to, but men had heard such things before and went about their business. But the rains had swollen all the mountain streams, and they poured their floods into the lake far above the doomed valley. The Conemaugh had risen rapidly, but the people were familiar with its tantrums. It would rush and roar for awhile and then subside, and they pursued their avocations. The mountain streams continued to pour their floods into the lake. The pressure increased, until finally its banks collapsed. Then the desolating tide began its march. One man mounted his steed and sped down the valley, crying, "The dam has broken, fly to the mountains!" A few heard the alarm and fled for their lives—only a few. A bank of water 40 feet high, descending from an altitude of 175 feet, gathering momentum as it flowed, swept down the valley of the Conemaugh. Its roar was the "voice of many waters."[47] In its pathway were villages, hamlets, towns, cottage homes, palatial homes, massive public buildings, churches, schoolhouses and factories, shops, stores and warehouses, depots, and industries too numerous to mention: splendid triumphs of labor and capital were on every hand. It was the abode of enlightened civilization, of education, art, and culture. There was wealth and luxury. It was a busy valley—one company, the Cambria, employed from 5,000 to 6,000 workingmen. Other industries employed hundreds of men. It was a highly favored locality. There was iron and coal in the surrounding mountains. It is not difficult to fancy such a valley—such a hive of industry. It requires no effort of the imagination to picture the towns or villages of Conemaugh, Woodvale, Kernville, Ninevah, and the thriving city of Johnstown.

The mind readily grasps the picture. The Conemaugh is rising, but the swelling river gives wild beauty to the scene. It whirls and foams and roars, but it sounds no death notes. Occasionally, someone refers to the reservoir in the mountains, but no special solicitude is aroused. Now, suddenly, like thunder from an unclouded sky, comes the cry, "The dam has given way! Fly for your lives!" In the near distance, the moving mountain of waters is seen, and in 20 minutes—hamlet, village, and town have disappeared, and in the track of the flood there is desolation and death, and thousands of men, women, and children are dead. The millionaire pleasure lake has done its work.

We could fill the *Magazine* from cover to cover with harrowing details of the flood. This is not required; our readers are familiar with the story, as it has been flashed over the country and under the ocean. Referring to the force of the wave we note its effects upon the railway tracks. A special from Johnstown, June 5, says:

> Everyone has seen the light iron beam shafts and rods in a factory lying in twisted, broken, and criss-cross shape after a fire has destroyed the factory. In the gap above Johnstown the water has picked up a four-track railroad covered with trains, freight, and passenger, and with machine shops, a roundhouse, and other heavy buildings with heavy contents, and has torn the track to pieces, twisted, turned, and crossed it as fire never could. It has tossed huge freight locomotives like barrels, and cars like packing boxes, torn them to pieces, and scattered them over miles of territory.

Railroad men will readily comprehend that only incomprehensible power could do such things. The dispatch adds that

> thirty-three locomotives were in and around the roundhouse and the repair shops near. Of these 26 have been found or, at least, traced, part of them being found scattered down into Johnstown, and one tender was found in Stony Creek. The other seven locomotives are gone; not a trace of them has been found up to this time. It is supposed that some of them are in the 60 acres of debris at Johnstown, above the bridge. All the locomotives that remain anywhere within sight of the roundhouse, all except those attached to the trains, are thrown about in every direction, smashed, broken, and useless, but for old iron. The tenders are all gone. Being lighter than the locomotives they floated more easily and were quickly carried away. The engines were apparently rolled over and over in whichever direction ran the current which had hold of them, and occasionally were picked up bodily and slammed down again, wheels up or whichever way chanced to be most convenient to the flood. Most of them lie in five feet of sand and gravel, with only a part showing above the surface; some are out in the bed of the river.

Such a catastrophe staggers credulity, and fiction sits dumb in the face of the horrifying facts. As we write, thousands are engaged in exploring the miles of debris to rescue and bury the dead. The great heart of the nation is touched, and contributions are flowing in from all directions. The estimated loss in money is placed at $25 million—and another estimate is that the flood made hundreds orphans. As we have said, the loss of life reaches thousands; some of the survivors have gone insane, and finally comes the fears of the physicians that a scourge will set in, the ravages of which must be a matter of conjecture.

After a time inquiries as to the cause of the unparalleled catastrophe will be in order. It need not be protracted. The final conclusion will be that a select number of rich men wanted a pleasure lake in the mountains—they wanted a place to fish and shoot and sail their pleasure yachts. Their ambition was gratified and the world knows the result.

Prize Fighting[†]

August 1889

Prize fighting as an American industry is making rapid strides, and if matters progress in the future as they have in the near past, we see no reason why the United States should not be the most advanced prize-ring nation in the world. We have an abundance of the required raw material—bone, spine, muscle, courage, staying qualities. We have young men of the various weights and of the proper build, ready to enter the ring at any price named, from $50 to $5,000. If a man needs newspaper notoriety, the prize ring offers every inducement that the most exacting could demand. The wires are at his command. From the day the "forfeit" is put up and the bully begins "training," the press keeps him before the public. His diet, his running, walking, sleeping, bathing, his rubbings—everything is noted by the press, the great educating power of the country. The trainer comes in for a fair share of fame. The backers, stakeholders, bottle holders, and referees are not overlooked.

As the time approaches for the fight, interest increases. The out-of-the-way locality where the fight is to take place excites the public mind. As the talk proceeds, the fighters grow in importance. They obscure statesmen, philanthropists, educators, explorers, warriors, and divines, and when the battle is over, then great newspapers view with each other in describing incidents. Every "round" is

---

† Published in *Locomotive Firemen's Magazine,* vol. 13, no. 8 (August 1889), 720.

described with graphic accuracy. "First blood," "first knock down," condition of "peepers," "smellers," "hash holes," etc., are particularly noticed. "Left handers" and "right handers" are given special prominence, and thus column after column heralds to the world the incidents of a prizefight. The great public devours the literature with eagerness. It is never surfeited, and yet the same papers will deplore the civilization of the Spaniards, who delight in witnessing bullfights and aid in raising money to send missionaries to convert savages.

Funny, isn't it?

Nationalism[†]

September 1889

Boston, the Athens of America and the Hub of the Universe, has gone all to pieces over what is called "nationalism." It is interesting to read the Yankee Doodleisms of the Boston savants on the newfangled theory. Fortunately for the baked-bean enthusiasts, it is claimed that many distinguished literary men are taking stock in the discovery: such men for instance as Edward Everett Hale,[48] Laurence Gronlund,[49] Col. T. W. Higginson,[50] Edward Bellamy,[51] and others of note in the literary world. It is interesting to know that the plan of the nationalists is to nationalize all industries and solve industrial problems. They say that "the increasing labor strikes and lockouts, the clamor for higher wages and shorter hours, the mighty organizations of laborers for mutual protection, the hue and cry raised against monopolies and trusts, the abuses of capital and the legislation seeking to destroy them, the misery and wretchedness of the poor, and the increasing numbers of the unemployed all go to prove to the nationalists that the times are ripe for a change in the industrial world." It is only a question of time, they say, when, unless anticipated by wise measures, this change must come, and with a suddenness which may engulf the nation into a bloody revolution.

The nationalists propose to down brakes in time to avoid such a calamity, and they should be praised for their good intentions. The nationalists propose to make the people "their own rulers, producers, and employers, to abolish money,

---

† Published in *Locomotive Firemen's Magazine,* vol. 13, no. 9 (September 1889), 780.

interest, wages, rent, and taxes, and confiscate, by popular vote and peaceful means, all the lands, public works, railroads, telegraphs, telephones, electric and gas lights, and all other branches of industry now conducted by private enterprise, and operate them all for the people and by the people." They would form a gigantic industrial army from service in which no able-bodied man or woman should be exempt. Every worker should have free play in the choosing of that particular line of work he may wish to engage in, with the sanction of government, of course. If a man wanted to be a farmer, and if the state demanded his services on the railroad as being more valuable to the welfare of his fellow men, he could not appeal; or if a man thought himself fitted to be a musician, and the state decided he could do better work as a clerk in a dry goods store, the state would have its way. Likewise if a woman chose to be a seamstress, and the state decided that she was competent to be a professional nurse, she would have to acquiesce. Physicians, statesmen, engineers, editors, artists, authors, historians, all should be chosen upon the same general plan, and as this would result in the choosing of only the very best men for those particular vocations, the public would never, or at least rarely, be imposed upon as it is now.

The schemes of the Boston nationalists may not be vagaries of the most pronounced type, but if they are not, it will puzzle the most astute Philadelphia lawyer to tell what they are. If the only chance to protect the country from dire calamities is found in the hallucinations of the nationalists, then Gabriel might as well blow his horn now as to postpone the interesting ceremony to a later date.

The Dignity of Labor†
September 1889

A Chicago paper bearing the title of the *Industrial World and Iron Worker,* in a recent issue, prints an editorial article with the caption, "So-called Dignity of Labor." The editor starts out by saying:

> A vast deal of nonsense has been written and spoken about the dignity of

---

† Published as "'The So-Called Dignity of Labor'" in *Locomotive Firemen's Magazine,* vol. 13, no. 9 (September 1889), 775–776.

labor, mostly by men whose daily lives were a perpetual protest against the sincerity and correctness of their laudatory utterances. We insist, on the contrary, that there is no such real thing as the dignity of labor. What dignity is there in tasked muscles and a smirched face? What dignity is there in dropping sweat and a posture of merely physical exertion? What dignity is there in nagging strength and a tired frame? Let us not be deceived. Hardship is the most conspicuous attribute of labor. It is the outcome of the primal curse: "In the sweat of thy face shalt thou eat bread." It is degradation from a higher and nobler sphere of existence. Every adult member of society must work for his support, if he be not in independent circumstances; the many are obliged to labor for their daily subsistence; some are compelled to toil incessantly for the pittance which they earn; drudgery fails to the lot of these who are lowest in the community. A man wishes to complete his work; he is desirous of resting from his labor; he seeks a respite from his toil; he submits reluctantly to drudgery. Labor is hard work; toil is grievous labor; drudgery is debasing toil.

At the first glance, men may be disposed to fall in with the conclusions of the editor of the *Industrial World and Iron Worker,* and render a verdict against labor. Manifestly the editor of *Industrial World* draws his inspiration from the dictionary. He glues himself, so to speak, to the word "dignity," as an oyster attaches itself to a rock. He is as conservative as an oyster. His range of vision is limited. He does not see how he can make the term "dignity" play any part in the labor questions of the times. In this he does Mr. Webster,[32] the great lexicographer, serious injustice. Mr. Webster defines "dignity" as "the state of being worthy or honorable; elevation of mind or character; honorableness, nobility of sentiment and action; true worth." That is Mr. Webster's first definition of "dignity." Now, then, we hold that a man at work, engaged in any kind of required labor, is in a state of being worthy, honorable. We hold that labor, work, toil, drudgery, elevates the mind and character of those who engage in it—that it is idleness that degrades mind and character, body and soul; wrecks the man physically and morally. The editor of the *Industrial World* insists upon it "that there is no such real thing as the dignity of labor," therefore and necessarily, nothing in labor that is "worthy or honorable." The idea in the editor's eye which obscures the dignity of labor is "dropping sweat," "posture," and "physical exertion, flagging strength, and a tired frame." Manifestly the editor of the *Industrial World and Iron Worker* believes there is dignity in idleness, in leisure, in laziness, sprawling in the shade, in hugging the bed. The editor of the *Industrial World and Iron Worker* would never point to the ant, to the bee, nor to the beaver as examples of work and thrift. As between the army of dudes and the dinner-bucket brigade, the dudes would have all the dignity and the toilers with "tasked muscles and smirched faces" all the degradation. The editor, in getting down to business, down to his task, pen in hand and with beaded sweat on his massive forehead, declares, "Hardship is the most conspicuous attribute of labor," that "it is the outcome of the primal curse, 'In the sweat of thy face shalt thou eat bread.'"[53] He says this when it is declared that God Himself worked six days to build His universe, and rested from His labor on the seventh day.[54] He says this in the face of the fact that Jesus, the son of God, worked at the carpenter's trade, and in face of the declaration of the Messiah that "Hitherto my Father worketh and I work."[55]

But the editor of the *Industrial World and Iron Worker* grows spiritual as he proceeds. His soul gets full of sublimating, etherializing gush, and he exclaims of labor: "It is degradation from a higher and nobler sphere of existence." Here we have it that labor is degrading, debasing, contaminating, and the lower one gets in the arbitrary classification of work, the more degrading it becomes, and with the help of a dictionary the editor of the *Industrial World and Iron Worker* classifies as follows: "Labor is hard work; toil is grievous labor; drudgery is debasing toil." In this we have the caste, the germ of aristocracy, even in labor. The common laborer is the drudge, the debased, the degraded workingman, the hewer of wood and drawer of water; the outcast, the vagabond, the man cast down "from a higher and nobler sphere of existence;" a man without "true worth," neither "worthy nor honorable;" "without elevation of mind or character," without "nobility of sentiment or action"—such are necessarily the views of the editor of a paper called the *Industrial World and Iron Worker.* It should be called the *Aristocratic World and Iron King.*

The editor of the *Industrial World and Iron Worker* represents a class of men whose education, if in any proper sense they can be said to be educated, makes asses of them in a superlative degree. In the broad field of labor the workers, by an irrevocable law, are one, and strange as it may appear, those whom the editor of the *Industrial World and Iron Worker* would assign the lowest place are of the first importance. He says:

> The engineer who operates the machinery of some steamship by opening or shutting a few valves with a very small outlay of corporeal strength occupies a higher position in the scale of labor than the fireman who sweats and toils before the furnace doors, with an incessant drain upon his physical resources; while the captain—the executive of the vessel— who examines charts, determines latitude and longitude along his course, issues orders, and bears the great burden of responsibility holds a position and exercises functions higher still. Like gradations of the skill, dexterity,

and judgment with which labor is applied exist in all occupations.

The engineer is of no more importance to the steamship than the fireman, since there would be no opening and shutting of valves were it not for the fireman; but for the man who makes the fire that makes the steam, the steamship would never move from her moorings. But behind the captain, the engineer, and the fireman, away somewhere underground, a man with "tired muscles and smirched face" is delving for the fuel. And thus it happens, nor can it ever be otherwise; it is the law as irrevocable as the law of gravitation that a condition of interdependence exists, and when the world is called upon to admire the splendid triumphs of skill, the award, whether it be gratitude or glory, belongs to all the workmen alike, and to deny this would find its vicious parallel, should the eye say to the ear, or the hand to the foot, "I have no need of thee."

The dignity of labor may be and ought to be determined by results which labor produces, and since labor produces all things, the task for those who chose to glean for facts will not be over-arduous. The monuments of labor are on every hand. Had we the space at our command it would afford us no little satisfaction to dignify labor by something more than mere mention. What the editor of the *Industrial World and Iron Worker* calls the "primal curse" is such only in the minds of cranks and visionaries who think work degrading. In work, man becomes a co-laborer with God Himself. He gives the sunshine and the rain, and the farmer sows the seed, and the world joins in the harvest home songs.

The editor of the *Industrial World and Iron Worker* closes his article as follows:

> Every step in the progress of the sciences and the arts which helps to transform drudgery into toil, toil into labor, labor into work, and work into healthful exercise is a movement in the same direction—is an advance toward what the Bible calls "the times of the restitution of all things"—is a nearer reach toward the Adamic blessedness in the Garden of Eden.

Just what the editor of the *Industrial World and Iron Worker* means by "Adamic blessedness in the Garden of Eden" can only be assumed. It is stated that God Himself came down and "planted the garden eastward in Eden," engaged in horticulture, and placed Adam in the garden to "tend it," to engage in labor, toil, drudgery, for such is the fate of all practical horticulturists. They are required to dig, remove weeds, hoe, etc., and it is not probable that Adam was exempt from such duties. This was the "Adamic blessedness" to work in a garden. The editor of the *Industrial World and Iron Worker* has visions, and dreams dreams. He sees the good time coming when costumes will be fig leaves and all will be Eden gardeners. He does not apprehend another serpent to beguile the Eves, nor another eviction on account of forbidden fruit. He is doomed to disappointment, but he will see if he lives long enough, old moss-grown, despotic ideas of an aristocracy in labor knocked higher than Gilroy's kite,[56] and possibly a time when papers bearing the titles like *Industrial World* and *Iron Worker* will cease being the organs of aristocrats, and will learn that honest toil is not debasing.

The Sunday Question[†]

September 1889

There are some propositions relating to man's moral, mental, and physical well-being, which, fortunately, have passed beyond the realm of debate, among which is the statement that man requires one day in seven for rest, rest for mind and body, and it is this fact that stamps the Sinai command, "six days shalt thou labor and do all thy work,"[57] with divine wisdom.

The seventh day was called the Sabbath—set apart for rest and for worship. Since the day when Jehovah came down upon the mountain, amidst thunder and lightning, to talk with Moses, and with His own finger wrote His commandments upon tables of stone, the world has moved forward, and as the centuries have come and gone, the movement has gained in rapidity. Empires have arisen and disappeared; powerful nations have gone forth on the pathway of conquest, and of their pomp and power only a few scattering relics remain; their language is dead, but in all their mutations, upheavals, and depressions the conquest of mind over matter, the triumphs of genius, the leveling up of the valleys and the leveling down of the mountains, there has been no change, no modification in the primal command, nor the still more primitive laws of man's mental and physical nature, requiring absolute rest from labor at least one day in seven, and those who have created circumstances making a violation of the law necessary have sinned against organic laws of man's nature—laws relating to man's moral, mental, social, and physical well-being.

When men come to investigate the subject for the purpose of determining the reason why of this violation of laws, the sad consequences of which are

† Published in *Locomotive Firemen's Magazine,* vol. 13, no. 9 (September 1889), 773–774.

physical and mental wreck and decay and social demoralization, they find in every instance it results from man's inordinate greed, his cupidity, a mercenariness that obscures all sense of justice, and conceiving that gain is the chief good and the chief end of man, proceed in their mad rush for wealth with vandal ferocity, and with as little regard for consequences as man-eating tigers.

Against this submerging tide of venality the church has offered a feeble resistance, for in spite of its protests the employments requiring constant, unremitting toil have multiplied until at last millions of men, living in lands denominated Christian, have not only no Sunday rest, nor its equivalent on any other day of the week. Their lives present only long stretches of toil without an oasis.

We need not say that the *Firemen's Magazine* is in favor of the Sunday movement. It is a righteous movement, and in consonance with man's mental and physical organism. It is an elevating and a redeeming movement. To create circumstances which deny workingmen rest will eventually kill, as certainly as to deny them of food. It is a condition that not only kills, but it demoralizes. It not only wearies the hand but it paralyzes the brain and ossifies the heart. It makes men strangers in their own homes, strangers to wife and children and to the hallowed associations which should distinguish the family circle. There is no doubt but that such is the tendency of this everlasting grind, in which of a year of 52 Sundays there is not one the toiler can call his own, when he can walk forth in his Sunday clothes to church, to the fields or woods for rest, for enjoyment, to find recuperating pleasures in a world where the Creator is, in all the circling seasons, showering benedictions upon those who have hearts and minds and souls for their appreciation.

The question arises, can we have a cessation of Sunday work for railroad employees? We answer, it is possible, but we doubt the probability of such an era. Circumstances have been created that it will be found difficult to abrogate. The world has been adopting new theories of business; old things have passed away. The present is an era of such immense activity, of such momentum, that to get back to old practices is apparently out of the question and practically impossible. Let us see what railroad officials of high authority say upon the subject. On Monday evening, February 11, 1889, President H. B. Ledyard[58] of the Michigan Central Railway, in an address delivered in the city of Detroit, said:

> The work of running Sunday trains does not simply require conductors, brakemen, engineers, and firemen, but it requires train dispatchers, operators, section men, car repairers, foremen of enginehouses, hostlers, and yardmen; in fact, I might say almost the entire force, with the exception of the clerks, to be on duty either wholly or partly. *To this army of work-*

ingmen no day comes for rest. While it is a rule with every railroad company that no man shall be allowed to go out for work if he has not had enough sleep since his last trip, I refer now to another and higher kind of rest, the rest for the mind and soul; to the day given to a man when he can pull himself together and think what there is behind him and what the future holds for him. Every merchant, every manufacturer, every banker closes his doors on Sunday, and until Monday morning rest is taken. On that day the mechanic, the laborer, has his period of rest, *but here is an army of men on whose conservatism, on whose intelligence, on whose physical and mental condition rest daily the lives of millions of people.* Why should they be denied that day of rest, the necessity for which is so imperative?

* * *

I have stated what is not a fanciful picture of the situation. You will probably ask me for the remedy; that I cannot give. I have struggled my best to decrease Sunday work, and I know that such is the desire of nearly every railroad manager in this country; but circumstances are too strong for them, and whenever anything has been done, it has proved of little avail. A railway company, leaving out its obligation to the public, is in the simplest sense a corporation, which has but one thing for sale, namely, the transportation of persons or property. It must receive its entire income from this one source, and therefore it follows that the company which has the best to sell for the least money can sell the greatest amount of transportation, or in other words, do the largest business, and earn the most money. *[Italics ours. —EVD]*

Mr. Ledyard proceeds to show the sharpness of competition between railway lines, and how completely the railroads are in the grasp of merchants and shippers and the traveling public, and adds:

You may blame the railroad companies for doing this, and probably they are not blameless, but behind them stands the stronger force of competition, backed by public opinion. The absolute cessation of Sunday work would not be practicable, or if practicable, might not, perhaps, be wise. It would in many cases entail suffering and perhaps loss. If one of you should be called tomorrow to California on account of the severe illness of some member of your family, you certainly would not feel very kindly toward the railroad company that might land you in Ogden on Saturday night and keep you there until Monday morning. These transcontinental trains between the Atlantic and the Pacific, in the interest of the public, in the prompt dispatch of the mails, ought perhaps to be run; but that the amount of Sunday work now going on would be necessary with a change of public opinion, no well-informed person believes.

We regard the foregoing remarks of President Ledyard as a fair presentation of the Sunday question from a railroader's point of observation. It is in consonance with our own observation and reflections. We deem it impracticable to stop Sunday trains. The mail trains must go. To stop them requires the action of Congress. This might be obtained eventually, but it is not in line with probabilities. Perishable freight stopped en route would entail incalculable disasters. Turn which way he will, insuperable difficulties arise which are readily suggested to every railroad employee.

We italicized this remark in President Ledyard's address, "To this army of workingmen no day comes for rest." This is the haggard statement, and for this tremendous wrong a remedy can easily be found and applied. The necessity of one day of rest in seven is admitted. The proposition is not controverted. It is axiomatic, pivotal, commanding, and convincing. There is not one good reason why it should not be had. Some Sunday trains can be stopped. To this, railroad managers assent. All cannot be stopped, hence some men must work on Sundays. Still, the one day rest in seven can be secured for all on some one day of the seven. It will involve the employment of extra men, that is all. It is simply on the part of the railroad manager a financial question. There need be no sentiment in it; there need be no discussion of the Sabbath, of worship—simply a day of rest—and whether it be Monday or Tuesday, or any other day of the week, it will be a day of rest; a day sacred to mental and physical repose, for the recuperation of mind and body, and therefore, in every essential, a Sabbath day. This is practical. The solution of the problem, so far as railroad managers are concerned, is in dollars and cents. Nor do we see in what particular the railroads would be financially inconvenienced. The pecuniary loss, if loss were to occur, would fall upon the employee, and not upon the employer. The employee would wisely sacrifice one day's wages for the vitalizing influences of rest, and if an extra hand took his place, wages would be the same, the sum total for wages would not be increased, and the rest problem would be solved.

Railroad Federation[†]

September 1889

What is the significance of federation? What is the necessity of federation? What is proposed to be accomplished by federation?

Let it be understood that federation is not amalgamation. In federation the federating orders do not surrender their autonomy, they give up no right which relates to their absolute independence in the management of their affairs, which does not involve the interests and welfare of the other orders included in the alliance.

Federation signifies unity and strength. It is "many in one." If it were required to demonstrate the axiomatic truth that "in unity there is strength," the history of the United States would supply every needed argument. Within the entire realm of illustration, nothing more convincing could be found.

Labor, a term I use in the place of workingmen, wage earners, breadwinners, etc., is weak, as compared with the power that has ceaselessly antagonized it; so weak as to be compelled to accept such terms as has been offered by those who controlled it. This being incontrovertibly true, the necessity for organization on the part of labor is universally admitted by those of its friends in any sense capable of forming a rational opinion, or of arriving at an honest conclusion. Organization is opposed not only by the enemies of labor, but by those who have controlled it in the past, and who are determined to exercise their autocratic power to debase and degrade it in the future; but also by a class of men who, having no purpose in life but to make money, would have business go forward undisturbed, totally regardless of the wrongs and injustice inflicted upon men who do the work of the world, and make progress and civilization possible. Unfortunately, there is another class opposed to the organization of workingmen, and forever in alliance with those who oppose and oppress labor interests. They are workingmen who, whatever they say to the contrary, are the slaves of the creatures who claim and assert the right to rule them and to reign over them. They are found everywhere; they have the form of men but they are not men; to use a term, they are "scabs," forever watching for opportunities to step in and accept degrading wages and conditions when a manly workingman

---

† Published as "Railroad Federation: The Question Considered by the Firemen's General Secretary" in *Commoner and Glass Worker* (Pittsburgh), September 28, 1889.

revolts. It is because of such things that labor finds it necessary to organize for its protection.

History demonstrates very conclusively that during the past 80 years, labor organizations have accomplished much in the way of resisting and overcoming the tyranny of employers. By organization, the working day has been reduced from 14 hours to 10 hours without reducing wages. By organization, in many instances, wages have been advanced, in others maintained, and in every case prevented from going to the lowest level desired. On such points volumes could be written. But the organizations, acting separately and alone, have often been overcome and disastrously defeated; and these calamities have suggested the need of federation.

This brings the question, what is proposed by federation?

In discussing the question I shall confine myself chiefly to the consideration of the federation of organizations of railroad employees.

In this discussion little need be said about the antagonistic attitudes of labor and capital. From the first, every sentence uttered in that direction has been a trick of the demagogue—mountebank fusillades in the interest of disorder. Capital is the creation of labor, and to talk of war between capital and labor finds its parallel in the assumption that the hand wars against the eyes, or vice versa.

The trouble in the past has been between *capitalists* and *workingmen;* the former seeking to crush the latter, and this proceeding necessarily results in unrest, grievances, and often in open revolt.

I am not required to say that all capitalists seek to reduce wages, or to inflict upon workingmen degrading conditions. Fortunately, such is not the case. There are many men controlling capital who recognized in workingmen their best friends. They pay liberally and promptly, and as a general proposition, they are successful in business. There are others, not animated by the American idea, who would in the briefest time possible reduce labor in the United States to the Chinese level. They would inaugurate a system of peon slavery, in many regards more odious and degrading than that of African slavery in the South, before the Sumter gun was fired that aroused a nation to arms.

To prove that there are men controlling railroad enterprises who are animated by a purpose to degrade workingmen, it is only required to mention the name of Austin Corbin.[59] He may be said to represent the entire breed of pestilential railroad magnates and the army of subordinate officials who, clothed in a "little brief authority," use it to exile peace and create pandemonium. They would introduce into the United States the caste curse of India. They employ spotters and Pinkertons; they are advocates of "blacklist" infamy; they are the implacable foes of labor organizations; they would crush out a workingman's manhood, his independence, his self-respect, all things that distinguish him from a serf, all things that make a man boastful of American citizenship, and this is done, it is claimed, in the interest of railroads, to enable them to achieve success.

Workingmen take an opposite view of the situation. They organize for the purpose of overcoming degrading conditions, to maintain their rights and prerogatives, to maintain the inalienable rights of life, liberty, and the pursuit of happiness. But organization alone does not in every case, and scarcely in any case, meet the exigencies. Workingmen favor federation, which is the climax of organization, all the organizations acting as one organization when the interests of all are involved.

It should be understood, and in the near future is likely to be comprehended, that all railroad employees have mutual interests, and particularly is this true in the transportation service. Is it worthwhile to discuss the proposition? Is it not so self-evident that argument and illustration weaken rather than strengthen the declaration?

Suppose a wrong is done switchmen, a wrong so grievous as to be unendurable, and, as a result, switchmen strike. Does it not follow that the interests of brakemen, firemen, conductors, and engineers are involved? He who does not see that the interests of all trainmen are included is incapable of distinguishing between an axiom and an ax handle. It is because of this mutual interest that federation is demanded, and it is eventually to be permanently established, and include all the organizations of railroad employees. So far, three great orders of railroad employees—firemen, brakemen, and switchmen—have federated. A Supreme Council has been established. I shall not attempt to outline the method of procedure in cases where the Supreme Council acts, further than to say that in case of trouble, a strike cannot occur without the approval of the Supreme Council, nor until every means known to a peaceful solution of the difficulties involved have been exhausted, first by the order complaining, and then by the Supreme Council. There is to be no hot-headed work. Impetuous proceedings are tabooed. The demand is reason, circumspection, and patience. If a strike is to take place, it will occur only when every expedient known to honest diplomacy is exhausted. If then a strike is authorized, every man will abandon his employment.

It will be seen by this, I think, that federation proposes peaceful measures; that its power will be exerted to prevent extreme measures, and that it does not favor violence and turbulence; and this, I believe, will eventually be the conclusion of all railroad officials.

In the discussion of federation, there is a broader field which invites the writer, and those who are giving the labor question intelligent consideration. If time permitted, I should gladly enter it to indicate, as best I might, the drift of opinion in the ranks of labor. There is going forward a mighty mustering of the mind forces of the times, and workingmen are neither supine nor silent. The labor question in all its phases is up for debate, and the labor press of the country will forever keep it in its advanced position until right, truth, and justice, one and indivisible, prevail. The labor question is in Congress, in the legislature, in the bank, and in the counting room. It is in the school and in the college. It is in the lawyer's office and the clergyman's study . . . It is everywhere a topic. And last, but not least, the labor question is being discussed wherever a plow turns a furrow, wherever an anvil rings, wherever a shuttle clicks, a spindle whirls, or an engine exerts its mighty power. It is discussed in cab and roundhouse and it will not down.

In this majestic debate, those who can read the signs of the times must, we feel satisfied, conclude that the federation of the hosts of labor will secure blessings as redeeming and exalting as were ever vouchsafed to man, since the morning stars sang together.[60]

Labor Day, 1889[†]

October 1889

September 2, 1889, Labor Day, was celebrated throughout the length and breadth of the land by multiplied thousands of workingmen. It was Labor's holiday. Picnics were in order. Men, women, and children went forth from their homes to the groves, to the sunny highlands, by babbling brooks, by silent rivers, bent upon rational enjoyments. There was music and dancing, speaking and feasting. Dull care and toil were left behind, and rest and pleasure ruled the day.

It was a new departure and dates a new regime. It means that in the future, workingmen are to have more enjoyment. It means that education and the

---

† Published as "Labor Day" in *Locomotive Firemen's Magazine,* vol. 13, no. 10 (October 1889), 874.

refining influence of education are having the effect designed. The movement is full of promise. It betokens "a good time coming" for which so many prayers have been offered up, and which is coming because workingmen have declared that it shall come.

God helps those who try to help themselves. God never helps a coward, nor did cowards ever win a battle. Labor Day presages the eight-hour day. Labor Day voices the fact that the hosts of labor are coming closer together. Imaginary partitions are being broken down, and imaginary lines of divisions are disappearing. The bond of union is growing stronger; sympathies which were but yesterday weak and narrow are today strong and broad. Labor days vitalize principles, exalt truth, and speak for an era of justice. Labor days dignify labor. There was a time when the badge of labor symbolized degradation. It is so no longer to men who are not born to wear yokes. The time is not distant when Labor Day, like the Fourth of July, will be a national holiday, by virtue of statutes. A labor Sabbath, when in honor of labor and its achievements, all the people shall cease from work and make the day notable by demonstrations of joy and gladness.

The Triumph of Federation[†]
October 1889

From the day that the *Magazine* declared for federating railroad organizations for mutual protection to the present, doubts have here and there, now and then, been expressed, first as to the feasibility of federation, as also of the benefits it would confer. At present the doubters are less vociferous and objections have degenerated to mere croakings.

Three great organizations have federated. From the start, from the word "go," federation has been a victory, a splendid triumph—not a disturbing element has appeared; harmony has reigned supreme. The feasibility, the wisdom of federation crushes every discordant note. The federated organizations are satisfied; indeed they are more than satisfied. It was an experiment. That it

---

† Published in *Locomotive Firemen's Magazine,* vol. 13, no. 10 (October 1889), 908.

should have been a success from its initial condition emphasizes not only the wisdom and the necessity of the undertaking, but the sagacity of those who had the courage to make the venture.

It was claimed by those who favored federation that it would promote arbitration and prevent strikes. The Supreme Council has been in existence six months. In this time, one grievance that threatened a strike has been amicably adjusted by the Supreme Council. Someone may say, "One swallow does not make summer." True, but one swallow tells of the coming of the vernal season, of summer, and of the harvest. One trouble has been adjusted. It shows what may be done in the future. It inspires confidence, it silences doubts, and presages "the good time coming" when strikes shall forever disappear and a reign of good feeling exist between the railroad employer and employee. What more could be asked? Federation voices strength, harmony, and victory, and those who want such things may advocate federation with the assurance that they are right.

Important Lessons[†]

November 1889

In the discussion of labor questions there is no escape from the consideration of wages, and of late many collateral propositions are forced upon the attention of investigators, as for instance agitation is going forward upon the point made by many that all work on Sundays, save that of charity, that which is absolutely required, shall be forbidden. Not because of the Sinai command solely, but because man's physical, mental, and moral well-being demands one day's rest in seven; that one-seventh of a man's life shall be dedicated and consecrated to rest—freedom from toil. Then we have the eight-hour question up for debate, not a new topic, but one which for various reasons has lately assumed more importance than has hitherto been accorded it.

As the discussions proceed, the field broadens, and new problems are brought forward for solution. We are confronted with the question of Chinese

---

[†] Published in *Locomotive Firemen's Magazine,* vol. 13, no. 11 (November 1889), 971–973.

labor, the "pauper labor" of Europe, and "foreign contract" labor, all matters of unquestioned importance and so considered by the Congress of the United States. As we proceed, we find in most of the legislatures of the states that bills are introduced designed to repeal or modify certain laws which do injustice to labor, and necessarily to laboring men, or for the enactment of laws demanded by public opinion to put a final stop to the rulings of courts which have in numerous instances made them odious.

But of all the questions fruitful of discussion and unrest, not one approximates the importance of strikes—strikes in general and great strikes in particular. When a great strike occurs, a great wrong, or a nest of wrongs, is disclosed, and when the strike is over, without reference to results, the country is invited to study "the lesson of strikes." The invitation is accepted by a steadily increasing number of students, and from time to time we are presented with reports. This thing of studying the lessons of strikes is immensely beneficial to the country at large, and it is to be hoped that the investigations will proceed, and the more assiduous the students, the better it will be for society at large. Bradstreet reports 679 strikes during the year 1888 involving 211,841 employees, a decline from 1887 of 23 percent in number of strikes and of 58 percent in strikers; against 1886 the decrease in number of strikers is 52 percent. Higher wages or fewer hours were causes of strikes by 68 percent of the strikers in 1888, against 62 in 1887. Trades union questions were behind the strikes of 17 percent of the men enrolled in 1888, against 22 percent of the year before. Sympathetic strikes almost disappeared last year. About 45 percent of those striking were in Pennsylvania in 1888, against 32 percent in 1887. Only 38 percent of the strikes in 1888, involving 50 percent of the whole number who went out, resulted in favor of the employees, against 42 percent of the strikes, and 38 percent of those involved in 1887. There were 74,837 employees locked out in 1888, against 46,000 in 1887, of whom 82 percent were successful. The number of days' labor lost by striking and locked-out employees in 1888 was 7,562,480, against 10,250,921 in 1887. If the labor be placed at $1.50 per man, the estimated loss of wages to striking and locked-out employees in 1888 would be $11,343,720, against $15,380,881 in 1887, a decline of 25 percent. In favoring the public with such valuable statistics, Bradstreet has afforded great aid to those who desire to study the lesson of strikes. And here, we inquire, what are the lessons taught?

Except in rare instances the lesson taught by a strike is that it occurred because of injustice more or less flagrant to which the strikers were subjected. It follows, logically, that those who study the lessons of strikes should be animated by a desire to learn the cause of strikes, what it is that gives rise to them, brings them into existence, and if this is not done the time devoted to study-ing the lessons of strikes is thrown away—indeed, worse than thrown away. In the absence of a full understanding of cause the discussion of effects has always been wild, and conclusions unsound and often vicious. Those who are responsible for causes which lead to strikes seek by every means in their power to obscure them. They resort to every species of subterfuge to evade exposure, not hesitating when the case is desperate to resort to mean mendacity, anything to delude investigators and lead the public to false conclusions—and while practicing their schemes of deception seek to magnify the effects of strikes, and because disaster follows a strike, their energies are concentrated upon a purpose to convince the public that strikers alone are responsible for any and all inconvenience to which it may be subjected.

It is needless to say that in the past, those who have perpetrated the wrongs that have been productive of strikes have been able, in a degree most lamen-table, to obscure their iniquitous schemes and, by the use of money, secure the influence of the press to aid them in debauching public opinion. We hear much about the "public heart," the "public conscience," the "public judgment," etc. But the powerful corporations, by the use of money, have ever been able to reach the public ear through the press and thus secure verdicts in their favor. As a general proposition, the public could study the lessons of strikes only through the press, and hence, if the press was less than just in presenting the facts, if it failed to tell the whole truth or, for any consideration, it distorted facts, the verdict of the public, based upon such perversions of truth, would convict the innocent and permit the guilty to escape merited censure. This is just what has been going on for years past, and as a consequence the conclusion has been reached that men who strike are in the wrong or that the wrong complained of did not justify the strike.

The great public studies strikes only when inconveniences to the public result—and as a consequence there are hundreds of strikes in which the great public feels no concern whatever. But a strike by railroad employees, which in-terferes with transportation, at once creates universal anxiety; but this anxiety has no reference to the rights or the wrongs of employees. The great public is selfish to the last degree. It studies the lessons of strikes only as its interests are involved. The great public wants trains to run regularly; any obstruction creates unrest, alarm, and indignation. The great public does not stop to inquire the reason why the strike occurred, by which transportation was interrupted, and confusion took the place of order, or, if it does inquire, it is told by the corpora-tion that "organized labor, again, with mob blindness and violence is attacking capital." The wires flash the news over the country, the press reproduces the falsehood, a verdict is rendered against the strikers. The redress they sought is denied. The corporation triumphs and workingmen pay the penalty of idleness and the sacrifices incident to idleness.

We have pointed out the way the lessons of strikes are studied by the great majority. But a change is coming in the methods of studying the lessons of strikes. The press is no longer the pliant tool of the corporation. A press devoted to labor interests has been established and is exerting a mighty influence, and not only the labor press proper, but the political press, without reference to party, in numerous instances when a strike occurs, seeks to give the public the correct view of the matter. This being the case, the lessons of strikes are likely, at no distant day, to be productive of many and great benefits to society.

Of the 679 strikes in 1888, 464 of them were caused by demands for higher wages or a reduction of hours constituting a day's work. In numerous instances, it is found that while wages are beggarly low, the number of hours out of 24 men are required to work is an injustice which all fair-minded men admit without controversy. Men who are studying the lessons of strikes for the purpose of finding remedies discover in low wages and excessive hours devoted to toil the fruitful cause of the mental and physical wrecks, which everywhere bear testimony that the prosperity about which some people are so boastful is productive of social misery and degradation to a degree well calculated to produce alarm. The strike is therefore simply a protest against a condition of things, which, steadily growing worse, is fraught with danger to the peace and prosperity of society. As a consequence the investigation of strikes is becoming a matter of national importance, and it is becoming clearer every day to men capable of reasoning from cause to effect that employers who insist upon the minimum of pay and the maximum of hours are the enemies of society, selfish and soulless men who, considering only their own welfare, would fill the land with idleness and crime if, thereby, they could add to their private fortunes.

If a strike never occurred, if workingmen were so abject, so debased and degenerate, as to accept wrong and insult without protest or resistance, if American workingmen could be reduced to the level of the Chinese and the lowest order of Italian and Hungarian slaves, capitalists would be serene. The work of degradation would go steadily forward and the workingman's chains would be the more securely riveted. But American workingmen will protest, they will agitate, they will strike, and it is because of this manliness that thinking men, statesmen, philanthropists, and economists are called upon to study the lessons of strikes, and the more the lessons are studied, the better it is for the strikers.

In all such investigations it is found that workingmen are not the enemies of capital or of capitalists, but that they simply resist wrongs which, if
not effectually eradicated, torn up by the roots, will be productive of consequences which no patriot can contemplate with composure. The outlook is full
of promise. Throughout the broad land the hosts of labor are coming together.
They too are studying the lessons of strikes. They are the students of labor
problems. They are measuring and weighing with scientific exactness the opposition that confronts them. The unifying process may be slow, but it is certain.
The right men for leaders may not have been found, but they will come. The
final outcome is to be federation—not for the aggrandizement of one man, or
any set of men, not for office or the emoluments of office, but for the redemption of labor from the thralldoms of unjust and discriminating laws and its
emancipation from the degrading domination of corporations. The drift is in
that direction and the immediate future is one of hopefulness.

Land[†]

November 1889

———

Mr. Henry George is of the opinion that private property in land is the prolific
cause of numberless curses to the human family and a ceaseless menace to
modern civilization. He says, "The great cause of inequality in the distribution
of wealth, is inequality in the ownership of land." To remedy the evils which
flow from such a cause, "common ownership of land must be substituted for
individual ownership." The change proposed is extreme, though within the
realm of the possible, and the author of *Progress and Poverty* is of the opinion
that "nothing else will go to the cause of the evil;" in nothing else is there the
slightest hope. This, then, is the remedy. "We must make land common property." Common property is common ownership, public ownership, or, more
properly, government ownership.

The history of individual or private ownership of land, as also the government or national ownership of land, is an interesting study, because it serves to

† Published in *Locomotive Firemen's Magazine,* vol. 13, no. 11 (November 1889), 968–970.

show the antiquity of ownership. Accepting the Bible as authentic history, it will be found that the first instance of private or individual ownership in land was a grant made by Jehovah Himself to Abraham, the patriarch, AM 2086 and BC 1918,[61] as follows:

> And the Lord said unto Abram . . . Lift up now thine eyes, and look from the place where thou art northward, and southward, and eastward, and westward: For all the land which thou seest, to thee will I give it, and to thy seed for ever. . . . Arise, walk through the land in the length of it and in the breadth of it; for I will give it unto thee.[62]

There is no mistaking this language. The grant was absolute. It was, as lawyers say, a conveyance, a cession. The title passed from God, the creator, to Abram the individual, and to his seed. A few years later, the following is recorded: "And He (the Lord) said unto him (Abram), I am the Lord that brought thee out of Ur of the Chaldees, to give thee this land to *inherit* it."[63] Here is another form of title that of inheritance, an unquestionable title—a right, a title descendable by law. But it seems that Abram had some misgivings after all about the title to the inheritance, and he investigated as follows: "And he said, Lord God, whereby shall I know that I shall inherit it?"[64] Abram was finally satisfied and later, "in the same day, the Lord made a covenant with Abram saying: 'Unto thy seed have I given this land from the river of Egypt unto the great river, the river Euphrates.'"[65] This seemed to satisfy the old patriarch. He felt that his title was good as against all other claimants. Time wore on; the name of Abram had been changed to Abraham. Rachel had died, and the husband wanted a sepulcher, a possession, a place to bury his dead wife, and he selected the "cave of Machpelah." He would not accept the land as a gift from the children of Heth nor from Ephron the son of Zobar who owned the cave, and after considerable negotiating, Ephron sold Abraham the cave for "four hundred shekels of silver, current money," equal to about $230.[66] The incident serves to show that in this faraway age, thousands of years before the advent of Christ, there was such a thing as the individual ownership of land; that land was bought and sold and titles given very much as at present, and as to the justice of such proceedings, it will be observed that Jehovah recognized the propriety of the transaction, and that Abraham, who talked with God, insisted upon paying cash down to make sure of a title to so much land as was required for a "burying place," to the field and the trees that were in the field and the cave.

There is therefore no question about the antiquity of titles to land held by individuals, and Henry George, when he proposes to wipe out individual ownership of land, antagonizes a principle of accepted right and justice at least 4,000 years old. But it should not be contended that anything in government is right because of its antiquity, and Mr. George has at least some grounds for demanding the common or national ownership of land. Those who take a lively interest in the theories of Mr. George, a sort of a modern Lycurgus,[67] will derive satisfaction, doubtless, in refreshing their minds upon the Spartan land laws as introduced by Lycurgus. He found Sparta in a sad condition. The few owned all the land, the greater part of the people were poor. Lycurgus believed by destroying private ownership in land he would banish from the country envy, fraud, luxury, extreme poverty, and excessive wealth. But he did not tax land to bring about his sweeping reform, he persuaded land owners to give up their possessions to the commonwealth that a new division might be made, and all the people live together in a perfect equality. After this Lycurgus divided all the movables, goods and chattels of the people. He then cried down all gold and silver money and introduced iron; the coins being so heavy that it required two oxen to haul $100. Lycurgus swept along in his pathway of reform like a Kansas cyclone. He required all the people to eat at public tables. The home was banished from Sparta. He believed that children belonged more to the state than to their parents; as a result, as soon as a boy was born the elders of each tribe visited him; if strong, well made, he was ordered to be brought up by the state, otherwise his doom was to perish. All of these things were in the line of reforms and the Delphian god informed Lycurgus that as long as Sparta observed his laws she would be a glorious and happy city. That Mr. George has the same ideas that influenced Lycurgus is shown when he says, as the result of destroying private ownership in land by taxation, that "there would be a great and increasing surplus revenue from the taxation of land values, for material progress, which would go on with greatly accelerated rapidity, would tend constantly to increase rent. This revenue arising from the common property could be applied·to the common benefit, as were the revenues of Sparta." He could establish "public baths, museums, libraries, gardens, lecture rooms, music and dancing halls, theaters, universities, technical schools, shooting galleries, playgrounds, gymnasiums, etc."[68]

Isn't that a beautiful picture?—a sort of a heaven on earth. Lycurgus thought he had done that for Sparta and was anxious to die when the priestess told him nothing more could be done to make his countrymen happy and prosperous. But Mr. George sees still more good to be derived from destroying private ownership in land, giving it to the government to be exclusively taxed. He says, contemplating the vast surplus revenues to be derived from land, "heat, light, and motive power, as well as water, might be conducted through our streets at public expense, our roads lined with fruit trees, discoverers and inventors rewarded, scientific investigations supported, and in a thousand ways the public revenues made to foster efforts for the public benefit;"[69] and better still, "thieves, swindlers, and other classes of criminals"[70] would soon be eliminated from society.

Manifestly, Mr. George would be a modern Lycurgus, and would make the United States another Sparta. Is he visionary? Can anyone read such fanciful, fantastic, utopian, and shadowy notions without realizing that their author is a dreamer, a castle-builder in an age of practical ideas?

But we have, in history, another instance of the overthrow of individual ownership in land—that of Egypt, during the seven years' famine. Pharaoh did not tax the land to obtain possession of it, but he got possession of it all except that portion which belonged to the priests. When the years of famine began, the King was ready for business. First, he obtained all the money of his subjects, then all the cattle was transferred to Pharaoh, and finally, all their lands. This done, Joseph, the agent of the King in this business, informed the Egyptians, "Behold I have *bought you this day and your land for Pharaoh.*"[71] Poor, famine-cursed creatures, they gave first their money, then their cattle, and finally themselves and their lands to the King, and private ownership in land in Egypt ceased, and forever afterwards the King in the way of revenue received "one-fifth" of the product of the land. Mr. George, as a panacea for a thousand or more ills which afflict society, and as a preliminary movement to the advent of the millennium, proposes to make the United States of America like Sparta under Lycurgus, or Egypt under Pharaoh, and by taxation utterly uproot all individual ownership in land, and so profoundly impressed is Mr. George in the righteousness of his reform ideas that he says:

> By the time the people of the United States are sufficiently aroused to the *injustice* and *disadvantages* of individual ownership of land, to induce them to attempt its nationalization, they will be sufficiently aroused to nationalize it in a much more direct and easy way than by purchase. They will not trouble themselves about compensating the proprietors of land.[72]

If the policy of Lycurgus is adopted, individual landowners will be persuaded to give up their titles. Pharaoh obtained possession of all the land by purchasing it with bread when a seven-year famine raged, but Mr. George anticipates when the people are "sufficiently aroused" to do away with "individual ownership," they will adopt a different method, which is neither persuasion nor purchase, and this done, all the revenues are to be derived from land, and the surplus is to be of such boundless proportions that the government will be able to adorn the earth until it shall become a paradise. There is to be neither wilderness nor waste places; even deserts will bloom like Edens. The government will be the landlord and the people, all tenants. Deeds and mortgages will be things of the past. The government will be parental, and as all will be tenants, an officeholder will claim, with some show of propriety, that he has a sort of a divine right to rule, because there is something that smacks of the divine when a government assumes to take care of the people and direct all their ways, as it could do when once the owner of all the land. With an ever-increasing revenue, "public baths, museums, libraries, gardens, lecture rooms, music and dancing halls, theaters, universities, technical schools, shooting galleries, playgrounds, gymnasiums, etc." would abound, free to all. Then we should have parks, fountains, race courses, shaded avenues, baseball grounds, and games without charge. Land would pay all with one tax, the land tax. Mr. George believes crime and criminals would disappear, and that prisons would no more be required. Necessarily, the land tax and the destruction of "individual ownership of land" would reconstruct human nature, and men and women, under the influence of the new regime, would become sublimated creatures and the songs of the "better land" would no longer excite a desire to possess it, for the earth would be good enough. The subject is inviting, and we may write of it again in the near future.

The Tyranny of Austin Corbin[†]

November 1889

Impudence, hypocrisy, chicane, knavery, and such other mental and moral defects as go to make up the modern scoundrel have no limits, and if such moral monstrosities have cash, as in the case of Corbin, they are able to push themselves to the front, and with exhibitions of effrontery that defy exaggeration or characterization, play the role of injured innocence, and demand for themselves a verdict of endorsement in the face of facts which pronounce them irredeemably vile, depraved, and capable of perpetrating deliberate crimes, richly meriting the title of villain, and which ought to subject them to penal servitude.

The times, prolific of such abnormal productions, have not brought to the surface a creature of mental and moral deformities more repulsive than Austin Corbin, who in the October number of the *North American Review,* writes of "The Tyranny of Labor Organizations."[73]

Austin Corbin has money, a boast that any successful burglar, counterfeiter, or pirate can make with equal nonchalance. Money, more than charity, is made to obscure a multitude of faults, but in Austin Corbin's case, while money paralyzes justice, thereby permitting him to practice his schemes of knavery, it has not saved him from the detestation of all honorable men. He is known to be a depraved wretch capable of concocting schemes of robbery, and this he has done with such a reckless disregard of law, with such shameless perversity, with such a piratical defiance of right, justice, and public opinion that the Congress of the United States was called upon to investigate his deep-laid schemes of wreck and robbery, and a committee of congressmen visited the "black hills," where his rule has produced poverty, degradation, and famine, and as directed, have prepared a bill which, if it becomes a law, will, in some measure at least, check the evils his rule has inflicted.

That such an abnormal combination of all that is loathsome in greed, of all that is depraved in morals, of all that is disreputable in business, of all that is false in profession, not content with a reputation for infamy which makes his name the synonym of all things despicable, should seek further conspicuousness by slandering labor organizations, can be accounted for only upon

† Published as "Austin Corbin in the *North American Review*" in *Locomotive Firemen's Magazine,* vol. 13, no. 11 (November 1889), 961–964.

the hypothesis that his inherent venom, like that of the rattlesnake at certain seasons, has so diffused itself through his mental, moral, and physical organism as to render him blind to all things decent. There is not a labor organization on the continent that does not loathe the name of Austin Corbin, and his paper published in the *Review* will serve to intensify their detestation.

Austin Corbin, more properly Austin Cobra, starts out by saying, "It is a mistake to assume that employers are always wealthy capitalists." No labor organization in the country ever made such a mistake. On the contrary they know, as well as does Cobra Corbin, "that in a vast majority of cases employers are not men of great wealth." Many stockholders in great enterprises are people of moderate means. Such was notably true in the case of the Philadelphia & Reading Railroad, in which widows and orphans and men of small means made investments and received large dividends, but when such men as Cobra Corbin got hold and dominated the affairs of the splendid property, it was wrecked and became the most corrupt corporation on the continent, but never until Cobra Corbin inserted his fangs into the corporation did it reach such a low degree of demoralization as to demand of the Congress of the United States an investigation and legislation to check, if possible, a career of unprecedented scoundrelism. The rascalities of Corbin are now as well understood as the treason of Benedict Arnold, or the colossal boodle career of Boss Tweed.

This superlative record of knavery is now known to the nation by virtue of the report made by the congressional committee. It is not given to every scamp to have a national reputation, nor is every exposed knave proud of notoriety. Corbin is an exception. He seems to glory in his infamy, and has the vanity to suppose that by denouncing labor organizations his name will go down to history after the fashion of the fool bull that tried to arrest the speed of a locomotive.

In his article on "The Tyranny of Labor Organizations," Corbin asserts "there never has been a time," and assumes "there never will be" a time the worker will not be permitted to leave "his employer's service," and upon the heels of this old chestnut remarks, "the worker in this country at least, under the law, happily, is not a slave." By all the pagan gods at once, what a discovery! Not a slave "under the law." Ho! all ye workingmen, are you not under lasting obligations to Cobra Corbin for the declaration? And yet this embodiment of hate toward labor organizations without law has compelled men on the Philadelphia & Reading Railroad, and in the mines controlled by that corporation, to play the part of slaves, to renounce their rights as men and as citizens, and yield to his dictation, the penalty of refusal being idleness. "Some employers," says Corbin, and he is of the number, "employ no new men who are members of any of the labor unions: applicants are required to promise not to join any while retaining their employment; those who prefer the unions are required to quit the service and promotions are entirely confined to those of undoubted loyalty to their employer and hit policy."

It is eminently worthwhile for the workingmen, and all others who are interested in labor problems, to compare the "tyranny of labor organizations" with the tyranny of Corbin's rule in the anthracite regions of Pennsylvania, as set forth in the paragraph we have quoted. But preliminary to such comparisons the terms "tyranny" and "tyrant" should be defined. In this country the laws recognize neither one nor the other; nevertheless, in defiance of laws men exercise tyrannical authority over the affairs of men as autocratic and despotic as characterizes the reign of a Russian tsar, and this has been done by Austin Corbin to an extent that the congressional committee which investigated his methods did not hesitate to say he had "Russianized" the anthracite coal regions of Pennsylvania. To accomplish his tyrannical purpose he found it necessary to attack labor organizations, not because such organizations were tyrannical in their methods of operation, but because they stood in the way of his despotic sway.

What are the methods he adopted to carry out his nefarious designs? It is in proof that by cruelty and oppression he drove his employees to resistance. He deliberately inaugurated a strike which had these villainous purposes in view, characterized by hypocrisy, tyranny, and robbery. He intended to advance the price of coal, and thereby rob the public. He intended to reduce wages, and thereby rob his employees. He intended to break up labor organizations, and thereby reduce the men who would accept employment under him, and the vile creatures who played the part of caitiffs in response to his orders, to the degraded condition of serfs. His schemes succeeded. He did rob the public, he did reduce wages, and he did abolish labor organizations. Nor is this all. Corbin's villainies did reach the attention of Congress, and a committee of that body passed judgment upon him, the first instance on record, and now the scoundrel is known to the nation not only as a tyrant, but a pirate as well, a brass-cheeked, bronzed-faced monstrosity who, metaphorically at least, is gibbeted before the world, and has become the target for the righteous maledictions of all men who abhor hypocrisy and depravity.

Such is the imperfect characterization of the man who stains the pages of the *North American Review* with the venom of intense hatred, but the excessive malignity of the attack, like an overdose of some poisons, defeats the purpose in view, and while labor organizations are not harmed, Corbin, by a law of retributive justice, is made more conspicuously infamous.

In what regard, we inquire, are labor organizations tyrannical? Throughout their entire history they have sought to achieve for workingmen better conditions. Not by antagonizing capital, but by defeating the impoverishing and degrading schemes of such heartless scoundrels as Austin Corbin. To defend labor organizations when attacked by such knaves as Austin Corbin, it is not required to say that they have made no mistakes, that every movement and method has been perfection, the embodiment of wisdom, and therefore deserving of approval. Labor organizations are human, and therefore fallible. This may be said with equal propriety of all human organizations, including the church; but it may be said, and should be said, because it is an eternal truth as imperishable as the pillars of God's throne, that from first to last, everywhere, in all zones that belt the earth, where there has been a labor organization, their purpose has been to resist tyranny, oppression, despotism, and degradation; to obtain fair wages for work; to elevate their membership in the scale of being; to obtain food, clothing, and shelter befitting human beings, and something more for rainy days, for sickness and old age; to advance in educational power, consideration, and influence; in moral excellence, in culture and refinement; to awaken noble aspirations, that in all things pertaining to citizenship there should be such development of mind forces, such comprehension of duties and prerogatives as would redound to the welfare of the state and be accepted as guarantees of the perpetuity of free institutions. Such are the undeniable facts of history relating to labor organizations. They have been written in tears and blood, with "an iron pen and lead in the rock forever."[74] The chronicles are filled with records of victories and defeats, but every repulse has inspired defiance, and every triumph has emphasized the conquering truth, that

> Freedom's battle, oft begun,
> Bequeath'd from bleeding sire to son,
> Tho' baffled oft is ever won.[75]

And in confirmation of the truth, there is not a breeze nor a gale that freshens and blows in all our broad land, from ocean to ocean, from gulf to inland sea, that does not touch and unfold the banner of a labor organization bearing the motto, "The final triumph of labor draweth nigh." And yet it is these labor organizations that Austin Corbin, the bloated, cash-cursed representative of ideas as hostile to American institutions and to the genius of our government as ever sent a head to the block or a neck to the halter seeks to overthrow. What are the methods employed by virtue of which he has gained a temporary victory?

1. To give employment to no man who is a member of a labor organization.

2. To require a pledge of every man employed that he will not join a labor organization.

3. Men employed who favor labor organizations are required to abandon their work.

4. Promotions are entirely confined to men of undoubted loyalty to Corbin and his policy.

Corbin has at least 35,000 men in his employ who have yielded to his enslaving program. They have renounced their rights as men and as citizens; they and their wives and children are Corbin's slaves; they are reduced to commodities; they are Corbin's chattels, and this condition of degrading servitude, of monstrous tyranny, comes at a time when the emancipated African slaves and their descendants are manfully asserting and maintaining rights which Corbin's employees, for considerations of bread and meat, throw to the winds. It is such facts that compelled the congressional committee to declare that Corbin was "Russianizing" the anthracite regions of Pennsylvania.

It must not be assumed that Corbin is the only tyrant who rashes into print with his pleas to "excuse his devilish deeds." He is not the only gold-plated giant who uses his tyrannous strength to crush labor organizations. He may be more soulless than others of his type, may have more rattles on his tail and more fangs in his mouth, he may be the representative reptile, he may take more delight than others in seeing men resign their hopes, renounce their rights, and forget their wrongs when yielding to orders from his iron lips, but there are others animated by his example of infernal despotism who, reveling in the weakness and wickedness of luxurious power, have determined to break the bonds of brotherhood which bind man to man, and this accomplished, make the very sun in the heavens blush for the degeneracy of American citizens, who resign their birthright at a time when the school and the church, press, poet and orator, the philanthropist and the statesman would have the world believe that ours is the "land of the free and the home of the brave."

The time has come for workingmen to rise superior to faction, to look facts squarely in the face and determine to unify, to federate, consolidate, and thereby successfully resist the encroachments upon their rights and liberties by such men as Austin Corbin.

Open Letter to P. M. Arthur
of the Brotherhood of Locomotive Engineers[†]

December 20, 1889

Terre Haute, December 20, 1889

P. M. Arthur, Esq.,
Grand Chief, B of LE,
Cleveland, Ohio:

Dear Sir:—

I address you this open letter from considerations which will appear as I proceed.

It is not my nature to be boastful, but in justice to myself it is becoming to say that I reverence age when it sits with becoming grace upon a man's visage, and its fruit is a generous recognition of proprieties and an experience which will not tolerate bigotry and egotism.

I make no apologies for my youth as compared with your years, since I am no more responsible for it than you are for your age, but I should hasten to apologize should I so far forget what is due under the code which regulates the conduct of gentlemen, as to attack a man, young or old, a real or supposed enemy, behind his back, or make any charge affecting his standing, in a deliberative body when he was absent, and therefore unable to meet his assailant on the spot.

If my readings arc correct, if I have any comprehension whatever of the principles which govern the conduct of gentlemen in such matters, they scorn to attack a man from behind, or to assail him, call in question acts or motives when they known his absence affords them protection and immunity from merited rebuke and exposure.

Cowardice has no defenders in the ranks of honorable men, and in the case of denouncing a man in a public meeting, knowing him to be absent and beyond call is an offense so at war with all things directly or remotely honorable that the world will not permit the plea of old age to condone it unless it be in such instances where the infirmities of years are productive of mental feebleness and decay.

[†] Published as "An Open Letter to P. M. Arthur, Esq." in *Locomotive Firemen's Magazine*, vol. 14, no. 1 (January 1890), 39–41.

At the convention of the Brotherhood of Locomotive Engineers, held in the city of Denver, on or about the 26th of October last [1889], I am credibly informed by a gentleman present that Grand Chief P. M. Arthur took the floor, and following complimentary reference to my colleagues, Brothers [Frank] Sargent and [J. J.] Hannahan, and all the members of the Firemen's brotherhood, continuing, said that "until Mr. Debs retracted statements made in the Firemen's official organ against him and the men he represented, he [Arthur] could not be his friend."

I am not informed in general nor in particular what statements have been made "in the Firemen's official organ" against Grand Chief Arthur, the penalty for which is the loss of his friendship and the gain of his enmity.

In declaring that you are no friend of mine, and as a corollary, my enemy, you vastly magnified the real or supposed offense, which you must have had in your mind, in the opinion of those who heard you.

Now, I assure you that I am not your enemy; on the contrary, I have been your friend: when, after years of obstinate arrogance toward all other labor organizations, in an extremity brought about by your ideas of "exclusiveness" and "entangling alliances," you were compelled to abandon your lofty position and recognize other organizations of laboring men, the grand officers of the firemen's order (I was no exception then), too magnanimous to humiliate you, gave you full credit for your change of heart and paid you a tribute of personal friendship in the hope of enlisting your cooperation for the good of all, and the *Firemen's Magazine* (April number, 1888, page 248) complimented you in terms that left no doubt as to its fealty to you and your interests.[76]

In this, I have the advantage of you. My friendship for you has been of that type which, while crediting you with all the virtues you possess, has, as it seemed proper, pointed out your mistakes for your own welfare, mistakes that often aroused my compassion, but which never made me your enemy, however much applause on certain occasions in your absence I might have won by declaring myself your foe until you humbly retracted any statements you might have made. I do not nurse or cherish enmities. I do not vault into any arena to designate persons by name, to tell the audience I am not their friend, or lay down a rule which they must follow to secure my friendship, my recognition, and my fellowship. In this, you will observe, I differ widely from you. But what are the statements to which you refer, that prompted you at a great meeting in Denver to make me a victim of your ill will? What is it that you want me to retract? Why does the grand chief wave his autocratic scepter and declare that "Mr. Debs" shall "retract" certain statements, and that until the decree is obeyed, his friendship will be withheld? Again, I ask, what statements?

Does the grand chief, who is the chief editor of the *Engineers' Journal,* desire that the *Firemen's Magazine* shall pursue a course of cowardly silence, when the brotherhood of which it is the organ is insulted and assaulted? Does the grand chief propose to run both publications, the *Engineers' Journal* and the *Firemen's Magazine,* in the same rut? Does the grand chief propose that when he takes snuff, I shall sneeze? That when he prays, I shall say amen? And that when his self-abasement is declined on the part of "Mr. Debs," the grand chief will forthwith inflict the penalty of withdrawing his friendship, and secure sympathy and applause by removing bandages and plasters and exhibiting his sore toes in public meetings, and proclaiming that until "Mr. Debs" "retracts, these sores shall never heal?"

Had "Mr. Debs" been present, and permitted to reply, the grand chief would have been as silent as is the *Journal,* of which he is the chief editor, upon all vital questions relating to the welfare of workingmen. Had "Mr. Debs" been present, he would have demanded of Grand Chief P. M. Arthur to name his grievances against the *Firemen's Magazine* and its editor. What statements had appeared against Grand Chief Arthur which must be retracted, that "Mr. Debs" might bask in the sunshine of his friendship? I say, had I been present at the Denver meeting when you assailed me, and had been permitted to reply to your attack upon me, I would have made you then and there tell the meeting what statements you desired retracted. I did not have that privilege, and hence I address you this open letter.

The *Locomotive Firemen's Magazine* is always careful to be right when, for the honor, dignity, and independence of the order of which it is the official organ, it arraigns anyone who is openly or covertly its enemy, whether it be Austin Corbin, John Livingston,[77] or P. M. Arthur. The *Locomotive Firemen's Magazine* has boundless contempt for hypocrisy in any and all of its guises. Pharisaism, with its entire brood of artifices, deceits, tricks, and double-dealings, finds no resting place in the *Firemen's Magazine,* and I do not hesitate to avow that in the past it has called to account P. M. Arthur, grand chief, and chief editor of the *Engineers' Journal.* The indictments of P. M. Arthur which have appeared in the *Locomotive Firemen's Magazine* were not made in the dark; not made in a meeting where P. M. Arthur could not be heard, but in a publication widely circulated, and regularly placed where P. M. Arthur could read and ponder every word, and if the allegations were not true, if they were false, why did the chief editor of the *Engineers' Journal* remain silent? Why did he wait for an opportunity when he knew he was protected from exposure to assault his man? The explanation is easy. It was because he was wanting in those essentials that scorn the semblance of foul play.

And now, let us get down to particulars. I aver that P. M. Arthur has declared that he never had, and that while he was grand chief of the Brotherhood of Locomotive Engineers, he never would, cooperate with any other labor organization.

Is that one of the statements which you, in your Denver harangue, demanded that I should retract? Would it not be better for you to first deny the averment? Will you do it?

I aver that you favored the law prohibiting a member of the Brotherhood of Locomotive Engineers, who was a member of the Brotherhood of Locomotive Firemen, from representing his division in a convention of the Brotherhood of Locomotive Engineers until he ceased to be a member of the firemen's order. Do you deny the charge? Is that one of the statements which you, in your Denver address, demanded that I should retract to gain your friendship?

You favored the enactment of the law of your order compelling engineers, members of the Brotherhood of Locomotive Firemen, to abandon their order, that they might become members of the Brotherhood of Engineers. Is that one of the statements which, in your Denver speech, you demanded I should retract if I ever expected to realize your recognition as a friend? Do you deny the statement? Is it not true? Was it not such things as I have stated that produced the "ill feelings" about which so much has been said and written, and for which you, more than any other man, more than all other men, are responsible?

You have been the uncompromising foe of federation, and as such you have done more to embarrass and postpone the federation of railroad employees than any other man—possibly more than all other men combined. Do you deny the charge? Do you plead not guilty? No, you do not. The great brotherhood of which you are the grand chief, were you to deny the charge, would render a verdict against you in one minute. You are the recognized, implacable foe of federation. There is not a railroad corporation in the country that does not know you to be unalterably hostile to federation.

Are such statements included in the number which you demanded I should retract when you assailed me and announced the withdrawal of your friendship?

Was it my criticism upon your appointment to a committee to settle the CB&Q strike which offended you? In that matter you totally ignored the Brotherhood of Locomotive Firemen, and I excoriated you for your deliberate insult to that organization. If that is the grievance for which you demand an apology, say so.

In my absence, out of danger from a reply, your courage was equal to the occasion. You could attack with impunity. Locked in and guarded, applauded to the echo, you could cut and thrust, knock down and drag out, and everlastingly annihilate an opponent a thousand miles away. A man of such courage ought to be equal to a demand in all regards fair. Engineers and firemen like fair play—all honorable men like fair play. And now, I challenge you to debate with me, anywhere you may choose, and grievance you may have against me. I prefer the meeting should be open—free to all. You shall have an opportunity to *state* your grievances and *designate* what I have written, the penalty for which you branded me as a slanderer before the convention of the Engineers' Brotherhood.

And when the discussion is ended, if you should be possessed of more magnanimity and less bigotry than now, if you should have a fuller comprehension of the rights of the Brotherhood of Locomotive Firemen and other labor organizations, their courage and independence, and power to resist degradation, no matter by whom suggested, you will be largely benefited, and you may be assured that in your enlightenment and expansion no one will rejoice more heartily than myself.

I assure you that any eulogy that may at any time suit you to pass upon any of my fellow grand officers, even though it is done to give point to your malice toward me, will meet my hearty approval, but when you were assuring Brother John J. Hannahan of your distinguished respect and consideration for him, it was well for you that at least two witnesses were not present, for in that event your words might have blistered your tongue.

While I, with such ability as I could command, have supported every measure designed to advance the interests of organized labor, you have opposed every measure of reform that has been proposed—so far as I am informed—and what advance has been made by workingmen, aside from such success as may have attended their own order, has been achieved in spite of your protests and opposition. Would you have me retract such statements, that I may receive your pardon? First, deny the statements. Do it in any way your pleasure may dictate, in a secret meeting, on the housetop, or in the *Engineers' Journal;* all I ask is that you put your denials in proper form and permit me to see them.

In closing this somewhat extended communication, permit me to urge upon your attention the propriety of pointing out the "statements" you wish me to retract to secure the boon of your friendship. After making the schedule, you should deny each allegation. In doing this you create an issue. As the case now stands, I do not know what "statements" you refer to, or whether you admit or deny their truthfulness, and in the meantime permit me to congratulate the great brotherhood over which you preside for having performed an act of justice at Denver which meets with my unqualified approval, and which I accept as an assurance that in spite of your influence other acts will follow until the Brotherhood of Locomotive Engineers shall be as renowned for the justice of its legislation and its sympathy with other labor organizations of workingmen, particularly railroad employees, as it is for its wealth in numbers and skill, and its importance in carrying forward the great enterprises of the age in which we live.

Respectfully yours,
Eugene V. Debs

Notes

1. The 1888 General Assembly of the Knights of Labor was held in Indianapolis from November 13–27.
2. From *The Giaour: A Fragment of a Turkish Tale* (1813) by George Gordon Byron (1788–1824).
3. Origin of this poem has not been determined.
4. From *An Essay on Man*, epistle 3 (1733) by Alexander Pope (1688–1744).
5. From *Two Gentlemen of Verona* (c. 1589), act 2, scene 7, by William Shakespeare.
6. The Battle of Thermoplyae was fought in the summer of 480 BC. Leading an enormous force against a vastly outnumbered band of defenders, King Xerxes of Persia (518–465 BC) managed to win the battle but was ultimately unable to take and hold Greece, suffering decisive defeat the following year.
7. An adaptation of the opening couplet of the anonymous long poem "The Age of Gold" (1839), published in the New York literary magazine the *Knickerbocker*, vol. 13, no. 6 (June 1839). The original reads: "Oh! for a scourging pen, a scorpion's lash, / To flay the backs of fools, who worship Cash!"
8. "Spotters" were undercover railroad company agents employed to spot corrupt practices by conductors, who handled cash, canceled tickets as having been used, and maintained cargo manifests, thereby having multiple opportunities for illicit personal enrichment.
9. An invented phrase apparently coined in December 1874 in published telegraphic correspondence between federal revenue agent and poet John A. Joyce (1842–1915) and General Orville E. Babcock (1835–1884), meaning "elevated." The word gained a certain vogue in slang usage during the late 1870s and 1880s.
10. Allusion to Genesis 4:1–15.
11. From "The Old Oaken Bucket" (1818), by Samuel T. Woodworth (1785–1848). Slightly misquoted by Debs, corrected to the original here.
12. Allusion to "The Old Oaken Bucket."
13. From *Twelfth Night, Or, What You Will*, act 3, scene 4, by William Shakespeare.
14. George W. Howard (born c. 1848) was a career railroader who worked a variety of jobs running the gamut from brakeman to general superintendent in the western United States. In 1888 he launched a new pro-strike dual union, the Brotherhood of Railway Conductors, an organization that he headed until its dissolution by merger with the older and larger Order of Railway Conductors in 1892. Credited by Samuel Gompers with first having the idea of the American Railway Union, Howard was elected vice president of the organization at the time of its formation in 1893 and he toured exhaustively, speaking on the union's behalf. In 1895, shortly after being jailed with Debs and other ARU leaders for contempt, Howard broke with the ARU and established a new organization, the American Industrial Union.
15. Proverbs 25:11.
16. C. M. Morse was the pastor of the Croton Methodist Episcopal Church of New

Castle, Pennsylvania, from 1886 to 1890. Formerly editor of the *Mercer Republican* before his ordination, Morse made national news in August 1888 when he defected to Grover Cleveland and the Democrats over issues of economic and social policy.

17. C. M. Morse, "The Church and the Workingman," *Forum*, vol. 6 (February 1889), 653–661.

18. Allusion to "Abou Ben Adhem and the Angel (May His Tribe Increase)" (1838), by Leigh Hunt (1784–1859).

19. Common religious expression of the nineteenth and twentieth centuries, derived from Isaiah 6:6–8.

20. Allusion to Luke 16:19–31.

21. From Matthew 23:14.

22. From *The Merchant of Venice*, by William Shakespeare.

23. From *The Merchant of Venice*, act 1, scene 3.

24. Paul Morton (1857–1911) was the general passenger agent of the Burlington system in 1888 and the company's point man during the great Burlington strike. He would briefly serve as secretary of the Navy under President Theodore Roosevelt in 1904.

25. Grand chief conductor—chief elected officer of the ORC.

26. Archaic term for a hornless cow.

27. Excerpts of Belknap's November 21, 1888, speech, including copious quotations but omitting inflammatory passages, appeared as the lead article in the February 1889 issue of the *Railway Conductors' Monthly*, 55–59.

28. From *An Essay on Man*, epistle 2 (1733), by Alexander Pope.

29. From *Old Fortunatas* (1599), by Thomas Dekker (1572–1632).

30. Reference to financial speculator Henry S. Ives (1859–1894), nicknamed "The Napoleon of Finance." Ives unsuccessfully attempted to merge the Cincinnati, Hamilton & Dayton Railroad with the Baltimore & Ohio and Vandalia Railroads. He was later the subject of a massive civil lawsuit over misappropriation of funds by disgruntled investors, who wound up receiving five cents on the dollar on their investments in a bankruptcy.

31. Guy Fawkes (1570–1606) was an English Catholic revolutionary, hung for his part in a failed assassination plot against King James I, a Protestant. November 5, the date of Fawkes's capture in 1605, was made a national holiday, marked by the burning of Fawkes in effigy and public fireworks displays.

32. Charles Francis Adams, Jr. (1835–1915) was the reform-minded head of the Massachusetts Railway Commission from 1869 to 1879. In 1884, at the suggestion of Congress, Adams was named president of the financially troubled Union Pacific Railroad. Fiscal difficulties continued, however, and Adams was later forced to turn to Jay Gould for funding, which ended in Adams's ouster in 1890. In his later years he was active in the Anti-Imperialist League.

33. The United States and Germany stood at the brink of war in early 1889, with three warships from each country facing off amid a civil war in an incident remembered by diplomatic history as the Samoan Crisis. The armed standoff was abruptly terminated

when a March 15 hurricane wrecked five of the six ships involved. The international dispute continued until the signing of a tripartite convention between Germany, Great Britain, and the United States in 1899, resulting in a partition of Samoa by the three imperialist powers.

34. David Dixon Porter (1813–1891), the son of a naval hero of the War of 1812, was promoted to the rank of admiral, top officer of the US Navy, in 1870.

35. Porter made the statement in an interview with the *Washington Evening Star* published on March 12, 1889. In his full statement he indicated that the American Revolutionary War, the War of 1812, the Mexican-American War, and the American Civil War had each been fought over matters of principle, with each armed conflict ultimately netting positive results for the American Republic.

36. "Digger," derived from "root diggers," was a pejorative for various native American peoples of California, who were the subject of a particularly brutal nineteenth-century stereotype as being filthy, malnourished dwellers in squalor.

37. Joseph Warren (1741–1775), although commissioned as a major general of the Massachusetts Militia, fought at the June 1775 Battle of Bunker Hill as·an ordinary soldier, where he was killed in combat atop Breed's Hill.

38. James Buchanan Eads (1820–1887) was an Indiana-born civil engineer who solved the problem of lack of navigability at the mouth of the Mississippi by conceiving of a wooden jetty system that would narrow the waterway, thereby increasing the speed of water and using this force to naturally carve a channel through the silt. Eads's system was installed in 1876 and proved successful by the following year.

39. Beginning in 1876, the US Army Corps of Engineers began using dynamite to blast clear a channel at Hell Gate, a dangerous reef located at the confluence of the East River and the Harlem River that impeded simple passage to the Atlantic. In October 1885, a massive blast using three hundred thousand pounds of explosive was made, effectively clearing the channel—the largest explosion during the years before World War I.

40. Allusion to the epic poem *Lalla Rookh* (1817), by Thomas Moore.

41. From "The Battle-Field" by William Cullen Bryant.

42. Debs, "Will Labor Organizations Federate?" (February 1887), this volume, 215.

43. Debs, "Federation, the Lesson of the Great Strike" (April 1888), this volume, 236.

44. Frank P. Sargent (1851–1908) was a native of East Orange, Vermont, the son of a farmer. He apprenticed and worked as a photographer in Manchester, New Hampshire, before moving to Haverhill, Massachusetts. In 1879 he joined the United States Cavalry and was stationed at Fort Apache, Arizona. He went to work for the railroad for the first time in December 1880, starting as a wiper before gaining promotion to fireman. He joined the B of LF in October 1881 at Tucson, Arizona. He was elected vice grand master by the Denver convention of 1883 and grand master in 1885, serving in that capacity until he was promoted to commissioner general of immigration by Theodore Roosevelt in 1902. Sargent was president of the Supreme Council of United Orders of Railway Employees during its brief existence.

45. John J. Hannahan (1856–1925), from Madison, Indiana, became a fireman with the Chicago, Rock Island & Pacific Railroad in August 1878 and joined the Brotherhood of Locomotive Firemen in January 1881. He continued to work at the scoop until the time of his election as vice grand master of the B of LF at the Philadelphia Convention of 1885. He continued in that role until the middle of 1902, when he took over as grand master for Frank P. Sargent, who had been appointed commissioner general of immigration. Hannahan was replaced as grand master by W. S. Carter, of Peoria, Illinois, by the B of LF convention of 1908.

46. The Johnstown Flood of May 31, 1889, was the greatest natural disaster of the nineteenth century in the United States, resulting in the loss of 2,209 lives.

47. Allusion to the apocalyptic biblical book of Revelation, which twice uses the phrase to describe the sound of God or his heavenly minions. See Revelation 14:2, 19:6.

48. Edward Everett Hale (1802–1909), grand nephew of iconic revolutionary martyr Nathan Hale, was a novelist and prominent Unitarian minister.

49. Laurence Gronlund (1846–1899) was an activist in the Socialist Labor Party of America. His popularization of socialist ideas, *The Cooperative Commonwealth*, was one of the most influential radical books of nineteenth-century America.

50. Thomas Wentworth Higginson (1823–1911) was a radical abolitionist and Unitarian minister. Higginson was active in the Boston Underground Railroad movement.

51. Edward Bellamy (1850–1898) was a novelist whose futuristic romance, *Looking Backward, 2000–1886*, proved to be the direct inspiration for the nationalist movement. Bellamy moved toward political activity during his last years, launching a periodical dedicated to nationalist activities, *New Nation*, before dying a premature death of tuberculosis.

52. Noah Webster (1758–1843) was an American lexicographer who first published his *An American Dictionary of the English Language* in 1828.

53. From Genesis 3:19.

54. Allusion to Genesis 1–2.

55. From John 5:17.

56. Archaic expression derived from a fearsome seventeenth-century Scottish robber Gilderoy (Gilroy), who was hung higher than all others from the gallows—so high that he resembled a kite in the air.

57. Exodus 34:21 and Deuteronomy 5:13.

58. Henry B. Ledyard, Jr. (1844–1921), a graduate of West Point and resident of Detroit, was general manager of the Michigan Central Railway until his promotion as president following the death of William H. Vanderbilt in 1885. He was elected chairman of the board of directors of Michigan Central in January 1905, succeeding Chauncey Depew.

59. Austin Corbin (1827–1896) was one of the great "robber barons" of the nineteenth century. Corbin made his fortune in banking, first in the Mississippi River city of Davenport, Iowa, before coming to New York City in 1865 to form Austin Corbin & Co. His role as a financier led Corbin naturally into real estate speculation, with his

principal plan being the development of Coney Island into a tony resort community for New York City denizens. Corbin set about constructing a transportation network to provide easy access of New Yorkers to Coney Island, establishing the New York & Manhattan Beach Railroad in 1876. Corbin's Coney Island properties included the gigantic Manhattan Beach and Oriental hotels. In 1880, Corbin added to his portfolio when he headed a group of Boston and London investors in buying the Long Island Railroad. In 1886 he gained control of the Philadelphia & Reading Railroad, becoming its president. Corbin pursued an aggressively anti-union policy on all his railroads, earning the enmity of Debs and other railway brotherhood officials.

60. Allusion to Job 38:7.

61. In accordance with the reckoning of time by medieval monks, the year 2086 Anno Mundi (year after creation) and 1918 Before Christ was identified as the year that Abram came to Egypt.

62. From Genesis 13:14–17.

63. From Genesis 15:7.

64. From Genesis 15:8.

65. From Genesis 15:18.

66. See Genesis 23.

67. Lycurgus (c. 900 BC–c. 800 BC) was the semi-mythical lawgiver of the Spartan state, immortalized by Plutarch in his "Life of Lycurgus" in *Lives of the Noble Greeks and Romans* (second century AD).

68. George, *Progress and Poverty*, 454.

69. George, *Progress and Poverty*, 456.

70. George, *Progress and Poverty*, 453.

71. Allusion to Genesis 47:23.

72. George, *Progress and Poverty*, 390.

73. Austin Corbin, "The Tyranny of Labor Organizations," *North American Review*, vol. 149, no. 395 (October 1889), 413–420.

74. Allusion to Job 19:24.

75. From *The Giaour*, by George Gordon Byron.

76. In his salute to Arthur at the time of the CB&Q strike, Debs declared that the B of LF grand chief had "won distinction and an enviable fame by earnestly seeking to find the right, and in standing heroically by the right when found." See Debs, "P. M. Arthur," *Locomotive Firemen's Magazine*, vol. 12, no. 4 (April 1888), 248–249.

77. John Livingston was the president of the Railway Shareholders' Association, an anti-regulation lobbying group incorporated in New York in November 1883. In 1891 Debs would charge the RSA was a "fraud" entirely conceived by Livingston: "a cunning device, well calculated to give the knave some standing in court." *Locomotive Firemen's Magazine*, vol. 14, no. 4 (April 1891), 324.

1890

The Knights of Labor and the Farmers[†]

January 1890

Never more distinctly have coming events cast their shadows athwart the pathways of thoughtful men than at present. The uprising of the toiler and the taxpayer is phenomenal. The declaration that "history repeats itself" is not more trite than true. But the unrest that now pervades the ranks of workingmen in the United States is a new departure. Men will seek in vain for its parallel in the past. We do not mean to be understood that the present is the beginning of agitation on the part of workingmen to better their condition. That is an old story. It began before the dawn of the present century. We apprehend that some seed was sown in the faraway days, when history was scarcely better than fable. It may suit some people to trace the growth and development of ideas that have led up to the present condition of things, but our purpose at this writing is to deal with current events, and point out as best we may their logical sequences.

We are called upon to witness now, as never before in the history of nations, organization of workingmen. Labor in all of its departments is organizing, and as time goes by it is noticeable that these organizations exhibit a steadily increasing intelligence. Purposes are more sharply defined; methods are characterized by more wisdom and tact. There is a more acute discernment of the end in view. There is larger intellectual grasp, and the promise of ultimately securing redress for wrongs could scarcely be more flattering.

In this work of organization for bettering conditions, the farmers of the United States have become conspicuously prominent. They have felt the oppression of trusts, syndicates, combinations, and monopolies, which acting under the sanction of law and a corrupt judiciary, promise at no distant day to wreck them and reduce them to the condition of serfs.

In the first place the farmers organized what was called the "National Grange."[1] Then came the "Farmers' Alliance."[2] Following this was the "Farmers' Union,"[3] and then came the "Agricultural Wheel."[4] At one time the "National Grange" had 32 states in line, with 20,000 subordinate granges and a membership of 800,000. It now has a membership of about 200,000. There is another farmers' organization known as the "Farmers' Mutual Benefit Association."[5]

---

† Published in *Locomotive Firemen's Magazine*, vol. 14, no. 1 (January 1890), 6–7.

These various organizations having a membership of above 1 million federated in the city of St. Louis in December last [1889]. That they should have done this was logical. Acting separately they could accomplish little; together they are strong. Federation means harmonious action. If there are bad laws, it means their repeal. If there are vicious, corrupt lawmakers it means their retiracy to private life. If there are corrupt judges, it means that in due time they shall be stripped of their ermined robes and be removed to obscurity. This farmers' movement means that a large majority of the "4.5 million farmers" of the country will become members of the "Farmers' Alliance" for the purpose of bettering their condition. It is not required that we should set forth more particularly the objects the "Farmers' Alliance" has in view, but this may be said that the supreme idea is to fight monopolies and secure for themselves their rightful share in the profits of their products, and in this, they are at once in harmony with every toiler in the land.

Taking this view of the subject it is not only not surprising, but rather in consonance with the logic of common sense that at St. Louis there should have been an alliance formed between the Farmers' Alliance and the great order of the Knights of Labor. What more natural than that the food producers and the food consumers should act in harmony? The Knights of Labor and all workingmen, regardless of name or occupation, demand honest lawmakers and righteous laws. All toilers are opposed to combinations by which labor is robbed and oppressed and degraded, and the federation of the Knights of Labor with the Farmers' Alliance has cheering significance. It means the coming together of men who seek the highest welfare of society. It means the triumph of the right. It means the furling of factional battle flags. It means the federation of all the organizations of workingmen. Federation is the shibboleth of workingmen. The signs of the times are encouraging. The trend of the mind-forces of the country is in the right direction. The demand is work, watch, and wait.

Carnegie's "Best Fields for Philanthropy"†

February 1890

In the December [1889] number of the *North American Review,* Andrew Carnegie, the millionaire, supplements his "Gospel of Wealth"⁶ *flapdoodle* with a *poppycock* article on "The Best Fields for Philanthropy."⁷ We use the italicized slang phrases purposely and understandingly, as fitting and proper when discussing the pharisaical utterances of a man who, regardless of the ills inflicted, has become a millionaire by robbery (within the law) of thousands of American toilers. This man Carnegie, like Austin Corbin, has the golden key which unlocks the covers of the *North American Review,* whose late editor and proprietor was a millionaire, every dollar of whose wealth was inherited, and Carnegie, having enjoyed the friendship and fellowship of the millionaire editor, takes occasion to beslime his name with characteristic *rot,* in saying "he had played his part in life well," meaning, we suppose, that the dead millionaire liked his "Gospel of Wealth" because it proclaimed that the laws as they exist regarding "competition, accumulation, and distribution" should be "accepted and upheld," and that "great wealth must inevitably flow into the hands of the few exceptional managers of men." And Carnegie, comprehending the value of the privilege to put his millionaire ideas in print, compliments the *Review,* saying it "shines on, a lamp still burning, to show the great army of humanity the pitfalls which it must avoid in order to retain what has been already conquered, and to light the paths which that army must tread on its way to future conquests."

It might be proper to say just here to Andrew Carnegie that the "army" of workingmen in the United States does not accept the laws of "competition, accumulation, and distribution" as just, and will change them at the earliest day practicable. The industrial army believes that the laws are vicious, and have been fruitful of conditions of unparalleled injustice, of villainies which defy exaggeration, of robberies whose sum totals are told in the colossal fortunes of men like Andrew Carnegie. Why should the wealth created by workingmen "inevitably flow into the hands of the few exceptional managers of men"? There is no honest reason why. That it is the case is an arraignment of the Christian (?) civilization of the age. When Carnegie proclaims in his

---

† Published as "Andrew Carnegie on 'Best Fields for Philanthropy,'" in *Locomotive Firemen's Magazine,* vol. 14, no. 2 (February 1890), 104–106.

"Gospel of Wealth" that the "best obtainable conditions of competition, accumulation, and distribution" have been reached, he endorses every conceivable form of robbery practiced by unscrupulous scoundrels to enrich themselves at the expense of the poor. He endorses the land pirates and their aiders and abettors; he endorses the men who organize trusts, whereby "great wealth inevitably flows" into the hands of the few; he endorses every form of corporate robbery and monopolistic greed; he endorses the inhuman scamps whom it would be a compliment to call burglars, who corner food products and make it more difficult for the poor to obtain a sufficiency of food in a land that boasts of its ability to feed the world; and this he calls the "Gospel (the glad tidings) of Wealth."

Mr. Allen Thorndike Rice,[8] the editor millionaire of the *North American Review*—according to Carnegie—was immensely pleased with Carnegie's "Gospel of Wealth." Austin Corbin, the man who has Russianized a portion of Pennsylvania, was also doubtless delighted with Carnegie's "Gospel," and we reckon the devil himself became hilarious over it, and if he has a fireproof bookcase, Carnegie's "Gospel of Wealth" is doubtless one of his textbooks. Carnegie desires to pose before the world as a pious fellow—one of the tribe of Pharisees, who not only made "long prayers," but at the same time "devoured widows' houses," and made the poor bend their backs to "burdens grievous to be borne."[9] Carnegie takes exceptions to Christ's gospel because it says "that a rich man shall hardly enter into the kingdom of heaven" and "it is easier for a camel to go through the eye of a needle than for a rich man to enter into the kingdom of God."[10] Carnegie, while asserting that the "gospel of wealth but echoes Christ's words," endeavors to wriggle out of the tight place in which Christ's words place him. He says:

> Time was when the words concerning the rich man entering heaven were regarded as a hard saying. Today, when all questions are probed to the bottom and the standards of faith receive the most liberal interpretations, the startling verse has been relegated to the rear to await the next kindly revision as one of those things which cannot be quite understood, but which, meanwhile, it is carefully to be observed, are not to be understood literally.

It will be observed that Carnegie believes that it will be easier for him to get into heaven than for "a camel to go through the eye of a needle." But Carnegie ought to remember that Christ did not take his view of beggars—he did not denounce beggars, he took pity on them; they excited his sympathy, and he wrought miracles to feed them. Carnegie, in his "Gospel," takes no stock in beggars. "Of every $1,000 spent in so-called charity," Mr. Carnegie thought "$900 was unwisely spent," and Mr. Thorndike Rice made it "$950," and Carnegie revised his figures to suit the millionaire editor's views. In this connection, as Carnegie says that his "gospel of wealth but echoes Christ's words," it may be well to give him some of "Christ's words" in which rich men and beggars are given special prominence, as follows:

> There was a certain rich man which was clothed in purple and fine linen and fared sumptuously every day: and there was a certain beggar named Lazarus, which was laid at his gate, full of sores, and desiring to be fed with the crumbs which fell from the rich man's table: moreover, the dogs came and licked his sores. And it came to pass that the beggar died and was carried by angels into Abraham's bosom. The rich man also died and was buried, and in hell he lifted up his eyes, being in torment.[11]

Does Carnegie's "gospel of wealth but echo" the foregoing words of Christ? Or, have Christ's words, in this case, as in the "camel" and the "eye of the needle," been "relegated to the rear" to give Carnegie, Corbin, et al., a chance to escape?

Carnegie may fare better than the rich man who "dressed in purple and fine linen," and who, under his changed condition, would have been delighted to have had a little cold water. We hope he will, but while he is posing as a philanthropist par excellence, he might read Christ's gospel, and the Bible generally, with great benefit.

It is not a little amusing to note Carnegie's survey of "the best fields for philanthropy." He has seven fields, as follows: first, founding universities; second, free libraries; third, founding hospitals, medical colleges, and laboratories; fourth, founding public parks; fifth, public halls for meetings and concerts of elevating music; sixth, providing swimming baths; seventh, erecting church buildings.

In maintaining that the foregoing are "the best fields for philanthropy," Carnegie spreads himself like a green bay tree—and it is well enough to comment briefly upon such subjects. Carnegie admits that great wealth, colossal fortunes, should be administered for the best good of the community *in which* and *from which* it had been acquired. Carnegie calls it "surplus wealth." In acquiring it from a "community" it had been taken from the people. What people? From workers who alone create wealth, taken by processes as infamous as ever disgraced human affairs, taken by processes of robbery, under the laws and conditions and decisions that the best thinkers of the age, not anarchists, but statesmen, say must be changed if the liberties of the people are to be preserved.

Carnegie says the present "conditions are the best that are obtainable," and therefore "that great wealth must inevitably flow into the hands of the few exceptional managers of men." Let us see. Assuming for illustration that in the present population of the country there are 15 million men dependent upon their daily wages for subsistence, and that on an average, wages, by present "conditions," are 50 cents a day below just compensation. In that case, "the few exceptional managers of men" would rob labor daily of $7.5 million, or for 300 working days in the year, of $2.25 billion. Suppose wages are 25 cents a day less than justice demands? In that case the annual robbery would amount to $1.125 billion. Suppose the robbery to amount to 10 cents a day, and even at this low figure, "the few exceptional managers of men" would lie enriched, at the expense of labor, to the amount of $450 million annually, and this stupendous infamy, Carnegie says is "inevitable;" and the toilers, having been robbed, having been subjected to poverty, hunger, and dirt, having been reduced to rags and compelled in thousands of instances to inhabit dens, Carnegie and millionaires of his ilk look around for "fields for philanthropy" in which to bestow their swag, and he thinks universities, swimming pools, and music halls, all bearing the name of the philanthropic millionaire, is the direction the boodle ought to take, and this is the outcome of Carnegie's "Gospel of Wealth." It is to fill the land with paupers by robbery, reduce workingmen to serfs, create conditions which compel men to work at such wages as "the few exceptional managers of men" decree, or starve; and then take the "surplus wealth" thus obtained and found universities, lay out public parks, decorate "swimming holes," etc., and tell the victims of the piracies to graduate, master Latin and Greek, walk in the parks, bathe, feed on wind, and shout: "Long live Carnegie!"

Such is not the order of exercises. Carnegie's program will proceed for a time, and then the audience will demand a change. It will come. "The exceptional managers of men," the "few" who have been the beneficiaries of the "inevitable flow" of wealth into their hands, will find the "flow" immensely reduced, and the rich men who rob will find themselves calling for "water." Their "Gospel of Wealth" will be "relegated to the rear," and a gospel of justice will be enthroned. It requires patience to read Carnegie's slush about the "right modes of using immense fortunes" known to be the product of cool, Christless robbery. To read his slush about using "enormous fortunes" so they "shall not have a degrading, pauperizing tendency," when it is known that the accumulation was secured by "degrading and pauperizing" the men whose skill, sweat, and toil created the wealth that made the "enormous fortunes" possible, indicates unparalleled impudence.

The program is to stop the "inevitable flow" of wealth into the hands of the "few" and introduce new methods of "distribution." It will be done. The organization of workingmen is not a meaningless movement; it is not a holiday parade. It means business. "The best field for philanthropy" just now is where men of intelligence and courage demand simple justice for workingmen, and the "Gospel of Work" will, at no distant day, supersede Carnegie's "Gospel of Wealth," and relegate it everlastingly to the rear.

Looking Backward, 2000–1887[†]
February 1890

Edward Bellamy's book, bearing the title *Looking Backward, 2000–1887*, we learn from the title page, has reached a sale of 154,000 copies. It is safe to say that up to the time of this writing the book has had a million readers; how many more it will have is a matter that belongs to the realm of conjecture. The demand is still on and must run its course.

The author was fortunate, we think, in selecting a title for his book. The title naturally suggests the idea that the author is looking backward from 1887, but such is not the case, as the reader soon learns. He finds himself with Mr. Julian West, the hero of the romance, projected into the future 113 years and looking backward from AD 2000.

The writer was fortunate in the matter of dates. The 30th day of May, 1887, was a well chosen time for Mr. West to be put to sleep by Dr. Pillsbury, the renowned mesmerist of Boston—the home of codfish aristocracy, the Hub of the Universe, the Athens of America, the center of aesthetic art, of literature, and quite as famous for the production of "Soolivan me Soolivan," the champion slugger of the world.[12]

Mr. Julian West was a rich young man of Boston who had never performed a day's work in his life. He inherited his wealth, and lived luxuriously upon his income and belonged to Boston's upper tendom.[13] He was engaged to a charming young lady, was on the eve of solving the problem, "Is marriage a failure?," and was building a palatial house for a home. Work proceeded slowly on account of labor troubles. Strikes interfered with his plans; he became nervous, was afflicted with insomnia, was mesmerized, slept 113 years, was found by Dr. Leete in his subterranean room, and was brought to life on

---

† Published in *Locomotive Firemen's Magazine*, vol. 14, no. 2 (February 1890), 101–104.

the 30th day of May, AD 2000. For a short time after his resuscitation Mr. West was dazed and bewildered, but finding himself physically and mentally as good as new, neither old nor infirm, he began investigating the new order of things and tells his story in a way well calculated to interest his readers.

Mr. West's first surprise was in taking from the housetop a bird's eye view of Boston. It was not the Boston of the nineteenth century. "Miles of broad streets, shaded by trees and lined with fine buildings, stretched away in every direction." He beheld "open squares filled with trees, among which statues glistened and fountains flashed" and "public buildings of colossal size and architectural grandeur unparalleled" in 1887 were seen on every side. Such things convinced Mr. West that Rip Van Winkle's sleep was a short nap compared with his prolonged mesmeric torpidity—in fact, the changes he observed were of such stupendous magnitude that instead of 113 years, Mr. West thought he must have slept a thousand years. Fortunately for Mr. West, he went to sleep and waked up in Boston. If it had been Chicago, the splendor of progress that would have met his eyes would have so completely overwhelmed him that he would have doubtless given up the ghost then and there.

In the year 2000, there were no chimneys in Boston, nor elsewhere in the country. The crude methods of combustion in the days before Mr. West went to sleep had been obsolete for nearly a century, and chimneys disappeared with the crude methods.

Mr. West, having been the victim of a strike at the time he was building him a house and home, desired to know "what solution, if any, had been found for the labor question?" He informed Dr. Leete that it was "the Sphinx's riddle of the nineteenth century." The reply was that "no such thing as the labor question" was known, and that there was "no way" such a question could "arise." At the time Mr. West fell asleep there existed "widespread industrial and social troubles," and "the inequalities of society and the general misery of mankind were portents of great changes of some sort." "The most prominent feature of the labor troubles of 1887, and for some years previous," Mr. West thought, were "the strikes" that occurred. These strikes, Mr. West thought, were made "formidable" by "the great labor organization," as "the workmen claimed they had to organize to get their rights from the big corporations." Dr. Leete said that was "just it" and remarked that "the organization of labor and the strikes were an effect, merely, of the concentration of capital in greater masses than had ever been known before."

At this juncture in the conversation, the condition of things at the time Mr. West went into his 113-year trance was sharply defined. Men believed that "the concentration of capital threatened society with a form of tyranny more abhorrent than it had ever endured," and "that the great corporations were preparing for them the yoke of a baser servitude than had ever been imposed on any race." It was declared that in the closing years of the nineteenth century, "railroads had gone on combining till a few great syndicates controlled every rail in the land." It was an era of syndicates, pools, and trusts. The great trusts crushed cut all rivals. Small capitalists became the tools of the larger ones. Under such circumstances the great body of the people demanded a change, and Dr. Leete tells Mr. West that:

> Early in the last century the evolution was completed by the final consolidation of the entire capital of the nation. The industry and commerce of the country, ceasing to be conducted by a set of irresponsible corporations and syndicates of private persons at their caprice and for their profit, were entrusted to a single syndicate representing the people, to be conducted in the common interest for the common profit. The nation, that is to say, organized as the one great business corporation, in which all other corporations were absorbed; it became the one capitalist in place of all other capitalists, the sole employer, the final monopoly in which all previous and lesser monopolies were swallowed up, a monopoly in the profits and economies of which all citizens shared. The epoch of trusts had ended in The Great Trust. In a word, the people of the United States concluded to assume the conduct of their own business, just as one-hundred-odd years before they had assumed the conduct of their own government, organizing now for industrial purposes on precisely the same grounds that they had then organized for political purposes.[14]

In the foregoing, the reader learns the character of the change that had taken place during the period intervening, between 1887 and the year 2000. It is not surprising that Mr. West was greatly astonished. The codfish aristocracy of Boston had disappeared—no traces of it were left. The high hills of "upper tendom" had been leveled. The millionaire and the mendicant had vanished out of sight. The nation, with a big N, had assumed control. Hunger, cold, and nakedness did not exist in the year 2000. There were no wars, no army, no navy, no militia, and the government had no war powers. Parties and politicians had gone glimmering, and "demagoguery and corruption" were "words having only an historical meaning." The nation having become the sole capitalist, became "the sole employer," and "all the citizens, by virtue of their citizenship became employees, to be distributed according to the needs of industry." In the year 2000, the citizens between certain ages constituted an industrial army and work was "rather a matter of course, than of compulsion;" however, if a man would not work, he would "be left with no possible way to provide for his existence."

Dr. Leete informed Mr. West that there were neither children nor old men in the industrial army AD 2000; that the people held "the period of youth second to education and the period of maturity, when the physical forces began to flag, equally sacred to case and agreeable relaxation." In addition, Dr. Leete said:

> The period of industrial service is twenty-four years, beginning at the close of the course of education at twenty-one and terminating at forty-five. After forty-five, while discharged from labor, the citizen still remains liable to special calls, in case of emergencies causing a sudden great increase in the demand for labor. * * * The 15th day of October of every year is what we call Muster Day, because those who have reached the age of twenty-one are then mustered into the industrial service; at the same time, those who, after twenty-four years' service, have reached the age of forty-five are honorably mustered out.[15]

In the industrial army of AD 2000, every new recruit enters the grade of a "common laborer" in which he serves "three years." During this period he is assignable to any work at the discretion of his superiors. There is no way under heaven for him to escape. He is in for three years, and must submit. After three years the man may choose his occupation, and until he does choose he remains a "common laborer." Men who want to join the liberal professions can make their choice after three years service as "common laborers," and if they can respond to the demands made upon their brains they graduate, if not they fall out and go back to the ranks of the workers. No favoritism is shown and hence there are no quack doctors, educators or preachers, scientists or philosophers.

The nation regulates wages. Every worker gets enough. More than that could be of no possible value to anyone. It should be understood that AD 2000 there was no money, no buying or selling, no banks or bankers, neither debt nor credit. No lawyers, lawsuits, nor courts as they existed when Mr. West went to sleep. Neither states nor legislatures; the occupation of lawmakers had forever disappeared, except that something in the shape of a Congress met once in five years, but no change could be made in laws until the proposition had been considered five years. After a citizen's wages had been fixed, he received a sort of a credit card which he presented at a national warehouse when he wanted anything to eat, drink, or wear. This card represents the holder's share of the annual product of the nation. With this he must be content. The only claim he had upon the nation was his "humanity," and all shared alike. Every man, said Dr. Leete, is "expected to do his best, and is therefore equal to any other man who does his best." If a man having endowments to do twice as much as another man, and didn't do it, it held that he ought to be punished rather than rewarded if he did work to the full measure of his endowments. The people of AD 2000 were determined to keep things on a dead level. They tolerated nothing like aristocracy—not even in intellect. Money, stocks, bonds, mortgages, banks, boards of trade, bucket shops, and shylocks had all disappeared. From ocean to ocean there could not be found a millionaire, a land shark, nor a cattle king. Cornering food products belonged to the infamies of the dead past. Everybody was the ward of the nation. Everybody was prosperous, happy, and contented. Everybody had to work 24 years. At 45 all became pensioners and live upon the national bounty.

It should be understood that in the year 2000 women were provided for in a way that disbanded the Woman's Rights Party effectually. All women belonged to the Industrial Army, but were assigned to such work as was most agreeable to them. They were under a discipline entirely different from that which regulated the masculine army; in fact, the women's army constituted "rather an allied force than an integral part of the army of men." Dr. Leete said to Mr. West:

> They have a woman general-in-chief and are under exclusively feminine regime. This general, as also the higher officers, is chosen by the body of women who have passed the time of service, in correspondence in the manner in which the chief of the masculine army and the president of the nation is elected. The general of the women's army sits in the cabinet of the president and has a veto on measures respecting women's work, pending appeals to Congress. I should have said in speaking of the judiciary that we have women on the bench, appointed by the general of the women, as well as men. Causes in which both parties are women are determined by women judges, and where a man and a woman are parties to a case, a judge of either sex must consent to the verdict.[16]

Things were lovely as seen by Mr. West in the year 2000. The women were not subjected to the drudgery of housework, and a girl, without impropriety, could tell her sweetheart that she loved him without being asked to do so. The nation had abundant means out of the surplus products of labor to educate the young and support the old. Music of the best was had for the asking and was telephoned to the residences of all the people. In times of storms the people of cities went about as if the skies were cloudless protected by awnings, a sort of a national umbrella. Every dining hall was a sort of Delmonico's[17] and the cooks ranked with the best in any land. Sermons were preached to audiences of 150,000 by telephone, if the people preferred their theology that way.

There were no beggars, no poor, no sick. The term "charity" was obsolete. A man demanded his own, received it, and it answered every requirement. And here it should be understood that this millennial era, this miniature heaven, was brought about by organized labor; the industrial army of the country had solved every problem.

Unfortunately, Mr. Julian West's story is a dream, and fortunately, a dream which, unlike Rory O'Moore's,[18] is not to be interpreted by assuming that things contrary to Mr. West's vision are to exist in AD 2000. Labor is organizing; a vast industrial army is in the field and is marching toward the highlands of victory. *Looking Backward* is inspiring. It outlines a possibility, or rather many possibilities, some of which are to be accomplished facts a century in advance of AD 2000. Trusts will go; syndicates and monopolies will follow. Land-grabbers will be made to relax their grasp upon lands. Unjust laws will be repealed. Corrupt courts will be purified. Labor is organizing for such work, and those who relish good reading should read *Looking Backward.*

Knights of Labor to Shape Own Destiny[†]
March 1890

The Supreme Council is blamed for not including the Knights of Labor.

The Knights of Labor is a great and growing organization, knows its business, and is moving in lines it has chose to perform such work as it has mapped out for itself.

When did the Knights of Labor ask to federate with the brotherhoods of railroad employees?

When has Master Workman [Terence] Powderly intimated that the order of which he is at the head was shown any discourtesy by the Supreme Council?

Does the idea prevail that a local or a District Assembly of the Knights of Labor can federate, independent of the action of the supreme authority of that great order?

† Published as "The Knights of Labor" in *Locomotive Firemen's Magazine,* vol. 14, no. 3 (March 1890), 236.

Let the order of Knights of Labor shape things so that its members who are railroad employees, engineers, firemen, switchmen, trainmen, etc., can federate and have the great order of which they are members to back them, and then if they are not permitted to federate, it will be in order to know the reason why.

To howl in advance of such proceedings on the part of the Knights of Labor discloses on the part of those who make the racket a purpose to embarrass and defeat federation on the part of those who hope to profit by anarchy and confusion.

They are of the same class of malcontents who in the Knights of Labor sought the destruction of the order by abusing its grand officers, and who are still barking at the heels of Mr. Powderly. They have not succeeded in destroying the Knights of Labor, and the miserable faction engaged in trying to defeat federation by denouncing the Supreme Council and the men who compose it are doomed to still more disastrous failure.

The Common Laborer[†]
April 1890

We use the term "common laborer" in no derogatory sense. There are a vast number of workingmen who are without trades: termed, not always rightfully, "unskilled" laborers. Their importance in carrying forward the great industrial enterprises of the world has not been recognized in the past, and is not appreciated now. In this fact lies the germ of discontent and danger. This magazine is the organ of a body of workingmen, of whom it has been said they are not "skilled laborers," and that they do not become such until they are promoted to the position of engineers. Manifestly, this is an error. No one at all capable of giving an opinion in the matter hesitates to say that it requires skill to properly fire a locomotive. The term "skill" is often used in a sense which does great injustice to men who do not wear the badge of some particular trade, and hence the term "skilled laborer" is never applied to men who are known as "common laborers."

The *Firemen's Magazine* is watchful of the interests of the great body of men who are members of the Brotherhood of Locomotive Firemen. It observes

---

[†] Published in *Locomotive Firemen's Magazine*, vol. 14, no. 4 (April 1890), 293–294.

with profound interest the movements of all labor organizations because in such movements it professes to behold the redemption of labor from oppression and degradation. We make no apology for asserting that the welfare of the country centers in the one fact of doing absolute justice in all matters relating to fair wages for work, by which we mean such wages as shall make the home of the American workingman exempt from the ceaseless peril of mendicancy.

The American idea is to obtain such wages for work as will make the American home comfortable, where there shall be an abundance of food, decent clothing, apartments for rest and recreation—not shanties, not tenement houses, fit only for beasts and bats—fit dwellings, fit places for American children to be born and reared, and when the wages are sufficient to secure such needs the American idea is to maintain them; and when wages fall below securing such requirements the American idea is to organize for the purpose of obtaining them. It is clear, therefore, that the American idea is the betterment of the American workingman regardless of trade. In saying this, we state the whole case.

The American workingman is an American citizen. He has the same sovereign rights and prerogatives as any other citizen. If he can secure sufficient wages, he will be in a position to appreciate his privileges and dignity, his sovereignty. If circumstances are created which deny him such wages, which compel him to live like a pagan, like a degraded Hungarian, Italian, or Pole, who have no more conception of American citizenship than savages, those who create them and profit by them are not only enemies of workingmen, but are enemies of their government, and if their purposes cannot be thwarted, they will ultimately inaugurate revolution.

We have said the hopes of the country center in the emancipation of the workingmen from conditions which compel them to accept such wages as keep them forever on the ragged edge of mendicancy, bring them in close contact with famine, make life a ceaseless burden and horror.

The organization of men of the same trade or calling has a cheering significance. It means resistance to wrong; it makes federation to secure and to maintain the right. It means fair wages, but those organizations leave out the common laborer, that vast army of workingmen who work, and whose work is necessary to enable the skilled laborer to work, and without whose work every industrial enterprise in all lands would cease.

Do we overestimate the importance of the common laborer? They perform the initial work in all enterprises. We need not particularize. No intelligent reader will be at a loss for illustration. We do not care where the reader begins. It may be the statue of Michelangelo, the painting of Raphael, or St. Peter's

[Basilica], from foundation to dome; it may be the most delicate piece of mechanism seen in the Paris Exposition[19] or the ponderous engine, whose mighty arms set in motion the wheels and spindles and lathes of the mills; all, all, everywhere, from the deep solemnity of the mine to the capstone of monuments; cottage, palace, steepled church, domed capitols and cathedrals, the steamship and the steam-car, the bridge, the tunnel, the canal, the steel highways, the telegraph, the telephone, the fruitful fields, where the bearded wheat and tasseled corn nod in the breeze, tell of the work and importance of the common laborer.

Well, what is the world doing for the common laborer? Who will answer? He has been left out in the cold. He does not organize. We have had, and we hope still to have, words of appreciation for the organization known as the Knights of Labor. We glory in its growth. We deprecate anything that hinders its advancement. The Knights of Labor organization takes in the common laborer. In doing this, it meets a requirement of incalculable importance and is deserving of the highest commendation.

In the organization of the Knights of Labor the common or the unskilled laborer finds a home, a retreat where he can do that for himself which the skilled laborer does for himself in his organization. If the labor organization confers benefits, and none doubt the fact who know anything of their operations, why should not the common laborer, the unskilled workingman, participate in such blessings? Why should not the home of the common laborer be made bright and beautiful? Why should not the wife and children of the common laborer be surrounded with the comforts of life? No good reason why such should not be the case ever was furnished, nor will it ever be supplied. And the Knights of Labor, comprehending the importance of having such men organized, take them in, and incalculable good is to result from the movement. The labor organization is in many regards a school, an educating, elevating force; and the fact that the common laborer is to enjoy the advantages of such an organization is well calculated to inspire hopefulness in the future for the common laborer of the country. The work in which the Knights of Labor are engaged is a noble one, and all friends of the toiling masses will rejoice to see the organization achieve success.

What Can We Do for Working People?[†]

April 1890

In one form or another certain persons are continually asking, "What can we do, or, what can be done for working people?" Why should such a question be asked at all in the United States? What gives rise to it? Are there circumstances and conditions warranting such an interrogatory? Who propounds it?

In old slave times there were men who counted their human chattels by the hundred, and the question was common among them, "What can we do for these people?" They said, "By virtue of the mysterious ways of providence these descendants of Ham have been committed to our care. It is a great responsibility," and some of the more pious owners of "these people" thought that they would have to give an account at the Day of Judgment for the way they treated "these people." But the slaves were kept at work raising cotton, sugar, tobacco, peanuts, hemp, etc. They went on multiplying. The slave whip, the slave pens, and the slave blocks maintained their places, and the prices of "niggers" fluctuated little. The "nigger," male or female, was a valuable piece of property, and something had to be done for him. What? Simply clothe, feed, and shelter him. Keep him at work. If he was refractory, whip him; if funds were wanted, sell him. The question, "What can we do for 'these people'?" was easily answered. The slave owner owned his labor—owned his workingmen. The slave market was the *labor market.* The "labor market" was never overstocked. A "nigger" would always sell for something.

Negro slavery has been abolished in the United States, but according to some writers on labor questions we still have the "labor market," and now the question is asked "up North" as well as "down South," continually, by certain persons, in a kind of slobbering, deprecatory way, "What can we do, or, what can be done for working people?" Is the question answered by building palatial church edifices for the display of pomp and pride and fashion? Is it answered by paying "fat salaries," and to raise the funds sell the seats to the highest bidder and institute an aristocracy of piety?

Philanthropists of a certain type ask, "What can be done for working people?" and recommend soup houses, free baths, and more stringent laws against idleness and tramping, together with improved machinery in penitentiaries.

---

† Published in *Locomotive Firemen's Magazine*, vol. 14, no. 4 (April 1890), 291–293.

Another class devote time and investigation to diet, to show if wages decline that a man can live on ten cents a day and keep his revolting soul within his wretched body.

Another class, in answering the question, "What can we do for the working people?" reply by saying, "We will organize an insurance bureau which shall insure workingmen against accident, sickness, and death. We will supply them with medicine, doctors, and hospitals, taking so much from their wages to maintain the bureau, and then, by compelling them to sign a contract which virtually reduces them to chattels, and makes them a part of our machinery, we will permit them to work for such pay as we choose to determine."

Another class answer the question, "What can we do for working people?" by telling them that unless they consent to abandon their labor organizations, absolve themselves from all obligations to such organizations, so far as they are concerned they shall have no work at all.

There are others, still, who discuss schemes for doing great and good things for working people, excepting, so far as it has come under the notice of the writer, to pay fair, honest wages.

This whole business of doing something for working people is disgusting and degrading to the last degree. It is not desirable to deny that in some quarters the question is asked honestly, but in such cases it is always in order to manifest pity for the questioner. He is not inconvenienced by a surplus of brains. The question, "What can we do for working people?" as a general proposition finds its resemblance in a question that might be asked by the owner of a sheep ranch, "What can I do for the sheep?" The reply would be, doubtless, "Shear them." The ranch man takes care of the sheep that he may shear them, and it will be found that the men who ask with so much pharisaical solicitude, "What can we do for workingmen?" are the very ones who shear them the closest when the opportunity offers—strip them of everything of value that they may the more easily subjugate them by necessities of cold and hunger and nakedness, degrade and brutalize them to a degree that they become as fixed in their servitude as the wheels, cogs, cranks, and pins in the machinery they purchase and operate.

The real question to be propounded is, "What can workingmen do for themselves?" The answer is ready. They can do all things required, if they are independent, self-respecting, self-reliant men.

Workingmen can organize. Workingmen can combine, federate, unify, cooperate, harmonize, act in concert. This done, workingmen could control governmental affairs. They could elect honest men to office. They could make wise constitutions, enact just laws, and repeal vicious laws. By acting together they could overthrow monopolies and trusts. They could squeeze the water out of stocks, and decree that dividends shall be declared only upon cash investments. They could make the cornering of food products of the country a crime, and send the scoundrels guilty of the crime to the penitentiary. Such things are not vagaries. They are not utopian dreams. They are practical. They are honest; they are things of good report.

Workingmen are in the majority. They have the most votes. In this God-favored land, where the ballot is all powerful, peaceful revolutions can be achieved. Wrongs can be crushed—sent to their native hell, and the right can be enthroned by workingmen acting together, pulling together.

What can workingmen do for themselves? They can teach capitalists that they do not want and will not accept their guardianship, that they are capable of self-management, and that they simply want fair pay for an honest day's work, and this done, "honors are easy." Fidelity to obligation is not a one-sided affair. Mutual respect is not the offspring of arrogance. There may have been a time when it was proper for the Southern slave owner to ask himself, "What can I do to better the condition of my slaves?" He owned them, they were his property; he controlled their destiny. He made them work as he did his cattle, mules, and horses, and appropriated all their earnings. Their children were his property as were the calves and colts of his cows and mares. But there never was a time beyond the dark boundary line of slavery when an employer of American workingmen could ask himself such a question without offering a degrading insult to every self-respecting workingman, and when a working-man hears it or anything like it and his cheek does not burn with righteous indignation he may know that he is on the road to subjugation, and if there exists a more humiliating spectacle within the boundaries of all the zones that belt the earth, what is it?

At every turn the question recurs, "What can workingmen do for themselves?" The question demands an answer, and unbidden a thousand are ready. We have not space for them. Let each workingman answer for himself. For one, we say the workingman can educate himself. He can read, study, and vote. He can improve his time and perfect his skill. He can see as clearly as others coming events, and prepare for their advent.

The Brotherhood of Railway Conductors and the Supreme Council of Federation†

May 1890

Federation is gaining strength continuously. From the start, there has never appeared in print a logical objection to the federation of the various organizations of railroad employees. There has never appeared anything having the semblance of an argument showing why federation should not be adopted by such organizations. The facts, the logic, the rationale, the wherefore, and the reason why have all been in favor of federation. As a result, the more federation has been discussed, the more firmly has the conclusion been established that federation is the *one thing* needful, the *one thing* desired to solve the vexatious problems forever confronting railroad employees.

In saying this we are not unmindful of the fact that, here and there, have appeared objections relating to details—minutiae—but never an argument, nor anything approximating an argument, in opposition to federation. Under such circumstances it is not surprising that federation, once begun, not only held its own but has moved forward in conquering power.

In this connection, and in demonstration of what we have said, we introduce the following circular notice of the International Brotherhood of Railway Conductors:

> The Grand Division of the International
> Brotherhood of Railway Conductors,
> Office of the Grand Chief,
> Terre Haute, Ind., March 25, 1890

To all Subordinate Lodges:
Sirs and Brothers:—

You are hereby officially notified that in pursuance of the action taken by our First Annual Convention, the Brotherhood of Railway Conductors, through its proper representatives, made application to the Supreme Council of the Federated Orders of Railway Employees [*sic*], and it gives me pleasure to announce that the said Brotherhood of Railway Conductors has been regularly admitted to said federated body, and now constitutes

---

† Published in *Locomotive Firemen's Magazine*, vol. 14, no. 5 (May 1890), 436.

an important part of said organization, which embraces the Brotherhood of Railway Trainmen, the Brotherhood of Locomotive Firemen, and the Switchmen's Mutual Aid Association, as well as our own brotherhood. Official announcement of the foregoing will be made in the official journals of the several organizations. The Brotherhood of Railway Conductors is now in perfect alliance with the best organizations of the times and its success is no longer an open question: all that is required is for each member throughout our jurisdiction to enter vigorously into the campaign that is now going forward and which will end only when the banner of the Brotherhood of Railway Conductors floats in triumph over every railroad system in the land.

Fraternally yours,
Attest: **G. W. Howard**, *G.C.C.*
D. J. Carr, *G.S.&T.*

The federated brotherhoods now stand as follows:

The Brotherhood of Railway Trainmen
The Brotherhood of Locomotive Firemen
The Switchmen's Mutual Aid Association
The International Brotherhood of Railway Conductors

These four brotherhoods now constitute the Supreme Council of the federated orders, which is animated by the *supreme* desire to remove, as far as possible, every obstruction to progress and prosperity in the pathway of the organizations of railway employees.

The International Brotherhood of Railway Conductors, under the leadership of the gallant and far-seeing Col. G. W. Howard, saw that railway conductors needed *protection,* something they had never secured, and as a result, the order has made the most flattering progress. The organization responded to a crying demand and its growth has been equal to the most sanguine expectations of its friends. From the initial movement to the present, the Brotherhood of Railway Conductors has displayed pluck and courage. Opposition has made it the more aggressive, developing staying qualities of the highest order.

Everything possible to be done by the older orders in the federated compact to help the Brotherhood of Railway Conductors should be done with a hearty goodwill, and we are satisfied will be done. The lodges of all the federated orders should lend a helping hand to build it up and extend its beneficent sway. In this way, this helping one another, this watchful solitude for each other's welfare means, when the trials come, victory for the right.

All correspondence should be addressed to G. W. Howard, Grand Chief, B of RC, 121 South 13th Street, Terre Haute, Indiana.

The Eight-Hour Movement[†]

May 1890

The decree has gone forth that on the first day of May, 1890, an effort shall be made by the wageworkers of the United States to establish eight hours as a day's work.

The agitation of the hour question in relation to a day's work dates back to the early days of the century. It is not, therefore, a new question. It is, on the contrary, somewhat antiquated, but it is nevertheless active, vital, and aggressive. It will not down. It invites discussion. It courts investigation. In the early days of the present century 14 hours, as a general proposition, constituted a day's work.

The records show that as early as 1808 the agitation for a reduction of the hours of work was entered upon by the journeymen ship carpenters and caulkers of New York.

This was continued with more or less spirit till 1832, when the ship carpenters and calkers of Boston struck for ten hours. They did not succeed. But in 1832–33 these trades in New York and Philadelphia did succeed in establishing the ten-hour day.

The agitation continued and spread. In 1840, Martin Van Buren, president of the United States, issued his proclamation making ten hours a day's work in the navy yards of the nation.

In 1841 the governor of New Jersey recommended legislation in favor of shorter hours. He said: "Constant and unremitting toil prevents intellectual improvement and leads to physical and moral debasement."

In 1841 a firm of ship builders at Bath, Maine, adopted the ten-hour system.

In 1845 a mass meeting was held at Pittsburgh to urge the adoption of the ten-hour day. A strike followed, which continued for five weeks and proved a

---

† Published in *Locomotive Firemen's Magazine,* vol. 14, no. 5 (May 1890), 385–389.

failure, but the agitation continued.

In 1848 immense mass meetings were held in New England, New York, and Pennsylvania, and many strikes followed. American workingmen were aroused and were everywhere aggressive.

In 1847 the British Parliament passed a ten-hour law, and immediately American workingmen renewed the agitation with greater energy than at any previous period. Mass meetings were held throughout the Eastern and Middle states.

In 1847 New Hampshire passed a ten-hour law. This afforded great encouragement, and agitation was spirited throughout 1848.

In 1850 an Industrial Congress was held at Chicago, and numerous resolutions were adopted designed to ameliorate the condition of working men.

In 1853, 11 hours as a day's work went into operation in many places. Three hours had been gained to thousands of working men. In many instances, four. In Massachusetts and Rhode Island, ten hours for a day's work became the rule, but in some of the states 11 and 13 hours were still demanded. Throughout the West the ten-hour system became the rule.

In 1888 Congress passed the eight-hour law for all government workingmen.

In 1887 the National Labor Congress at Chicago urged the eight-hour movement, and in 1888 many strikes occurred for the eight-hour rule. They did not succeed, but some victories were gained.

In 1889 the Boston Eight-Hour League was formed.

In 1872 it is estimated that 100,000 men struck for eight hours. Eight hours as a day's work was established for stonemasons, plasterers, painters, plumbers, bricklayers, paperhangers, plate printers, and carpenters in some localities.

The agitation proceeded, and in 1878 and 1879 the Fourth of July was selected as the day for eight-hour agitation and demonstration.

In 1888, May 1 was designated as the day to inaugurate the eight-hour system, and a general strike resulted. The movement was not a success, nor yet a total failure. Some trades succeeded while others failed.

As indicating the progress of the eight-hour movement, it can be said: The general government has passed an eight-hour law. The same is true of California, Connecticut, Illinois, New Mexico, Pennsylvania, New York, and Indiana.

It will be observed that the agitation for a reduction of the hours of labor dates back to 1808—83 years ago. It began with journeymen ship carpenters and calkers, who were required to work 14 hours a day. The movement was opposed by ship owners, who threatened to take their ships away from New York for repairs if the workingmen persisted in their demand for a reduction of the hours of labor.

It will be observed that the agitation has never ceased from the day it began to the present. The demand for a reduction of hours of labor has occasioned many strikes and has cost many sacrifices on the part of workingmen. They were always opposed by employers, who yielded only to the inevitable. The political economist, the philanthropist, the statesman, and possibly the statistician could profitably investigate the effect of the reduction of the hours of labor from 14 to ten hours, for practically such has been the result. Instances there are, doubtless, where workingmen are required to work 11, 12, 13, and, in some cases, 14 hours a day. There are also instances where eight hours meet the requirement, but, as a general rule, ten hours constitute a day's work.

The reduction, therefore, may be said to be four hours a day as a result of agitation.

The labor statistician may, we think, enquire: What has been the influence of this reduction of the hours of labor upon the workingmen of the United States? What has been its influence upon the industries of the country? Has capital suffered? Have capitalists found the reduction of working hours from 14 to 10 inimical to their interests in any proper sense?

Such questions are practical:

First: What has been the influence of the reduction of the hours of labor upon the workingmen of the United States?

Labor statisticians deal chiefly in figures, not figures of speech; still, they are required to deal with facts. Four hours a day wrested from toil, given up to leisure, must of necessity exert a potent influence. The labor statistician could say four hours a day for 300 working days equals 1,200 hours—120 days of ten hours each. Here a number of pertinent questions arise: What influence would so much leisure exert upon the man physically? Does rational rest for the body invigorate it? Capacitate it to perform as much labor in ten hours as was performed in 14 hours? Is such a theory tenable? It is so asserted and believed, not only that as much work can be done, but that better work can be done. One hundred and twenty days in a year wrested from toil and handed over to the workingman enables him not only to recuperate his physical energies, but to improve his mind. It affords opportunities for reading and education in various ways; hence, the reduction of the hours of labor exerts a beneficial influence physically and intellectually, and it is safe to say, as a general proposition, that the reduction of the hours of labor has exerted a highly beneficial influence upon the American workingman.

Second: What has been the influence of the reduction of the hours of labor upon the industries of the country?

In replying to the interrogatory, it should be stated that in every department, production has kept abreast of the demand, while in a great number of instances, production has been in excess of demand, necessitating forced idleness. This being true, it may be affirmed that in no one instance have the industries of the country been embarrassed by the reduction of the hours of labor. If, therefore, production has been equal to the demand, and in numerous instances in excess of the demand, the assertion cannot be made with any show of propriety that the reduction of the hours of labor has been prejudicial to the rights of capital. It has not suffered. If, in any case, investments in industrial enterprises have not paid fair dividends, or no dividends, or, if they have entailed losses, the cause must be sought for and determined without reference to the reduction of the hours of labor. This being true, capitalists are required to admit that, so far, no wrong has been inflicted upon their rights and interests by the reduction of the hours of labor.

Just here comes into view the workingman in association with the machine. It is always in order to extol the machine. It is called "labor-saving." The machine performs the work, which without it would be performed by men. Who is equal to the task of determining how many men would be required to perform the work now performed by the labor-saving machines in operation in the United States? The question is not practical. It is not seriously propounded. The labor-saving machine is here; it has come to stay. It is to be multiplied indefinitely. The inventive genius of the world is aroused; new machines are to come. It is held that they mark in vivid lines the progress of our civilization. Their number and their names are past finding out. They excite admiration. They are themes for orators and poets. We do not object to such things. But there is a practical view to be taken of the subject, strictly in harmony with the duties of the labor statistician. The machine has the power—first, to displace workingmen, force them into idleness; second, to create new industries, and thereby supply opportunities for employment. The question that forces itself upon the attention of all men at all capable of grasping conditions is, does labor-saving machinery, by creating new industries, afford opportunities for employment equal to the number of men it displaces?

It may not be in the power of the most industrious and methodical statistician to arrive at conclusions upon such a proposition, for the correctness of which he would be willing to stake his reputation for accuracy. But, investigation would afford a basis for statements worthy of the importance of the subject. He would find, doubtless, a large number of men in enforced idleness—men willing to work but unable to find employment—in common parlance, he would find the "labor market" overstocked with laborers. Having ascertained this fact, the statistician would be in a position to consider causes for this enforced idleness. He might prudently inquire:

First: Is it owing to labor-saving machinery?

Second: Is it owing to the natural increase of the laboring population?

Third: Is it owing to immigration?

Fourth: Is it owing to overproduction consequent upon a want of foreign markets for the surplus of products?

Such topics, we hold, are within the admitted limits of legitimate inquiry by the various bureaus of labor statistics. Indeed, we hold that they are of supreme importance.

We think the term "labor-saving machinery" is a misnomer. It does not save labor in any proper sense. We admit the difficulty of stating the proposition. For illustration: A piece of work requires the employment of 20 men one day. A machine is introduced requiring the employment of one man, which performs the work in the same time—one day. Nineteen men are, therefore, displaced. The machine is at once proclaimed as "labor-saving," and becomes immensely popular. In what direction, in what particular has it in any proper sense saved labor? It has forced 19 men into idleness. Nor has it saved the labor of the one man who operates the machine—he is required to work, as was his wont, before the machine was introduced.

The machine, instead of being "labor-saving," is a money-making and a money-saving machine, and as such it is one of the most important, if indeed it is not the most important factor in the economics of the country, and as such in its relations to labor merits special attention. As an illustration, suppose a machine that displaces 19 workingmen costs $10,000 and wears out in ten years. Suppose the wages of the men displaced was $1.50 a day; say money is worth 8 percent. In that case, the owner of the machine in ten years would be out of pocket $18,000. The wages of the 19 men displaced by the machine, in ten years would have amounted to the sum of $85,500—as a result, in ten years the owner of the machine is the gainer by $69,500. The machine has performed the labor of 20 men requiring the oversight of one man. It is in order, and the demand partakes of the imperative for statisticians to approximate, as near as practicable, to what extent machinery opens new avenues for work and thereby affords compensation for the idleness it creates.

Grouping interrogatories, it may be assumed that machinery, the natural increase of population, immigration, and overproduction all play conspicuous parts in forcing men into idleness, and here it should be said that idleness and the ills which it inflicts are the most serious menace that confronts our institutions and our civilization.

This is not croaking. In it there is no taint of cant. Such subjects are not visionary. On the contrary, men of profound erudition are concentrating upon them all their faculties in the hope of finding a remedy.

It is stated by those familiar with the condition of workingmen and deeply interested in their welfare that there are now in the United States 1 million men in forced idleness. We do not vouch for the correctness of the estimate, though it is credited to Mr. Carroll D. Wright.[20] The number may be too high or too low, but that there is a vast army of idlers is a fact which is not denied.

It is assumed by the advocates of the eight-hour law that its adoption would be in the line of solving a threatening problem. They claim that the adoption of the eight-hour system would be highly advantageous to workingmen economically, physically, and morally.

If there are in the country 6.25 million workingmen, of whom 5 million are working ten hours a day, by reducing the hours to eight, an opportunity is at once given for 1.25 million more men to find employment. We leave out the question of wages, the supreme idea being to afford an opportunity to work for men willing to toil for such wages as they can obtain. Mathematically, the proposition is invulnerable; 5 million men working ten hours a day is 50 million hours, and 8.25 million men working eight hours a day is 50 million hours. To say that all would go to work if the opportunity was offered, or to enter a denial to such a proposition, is totally foreign to legitimate discussion. It is far better for the country to be in a position to offer men opportunities to earn their living. This being done, there will be ample time to note results. If a man has an opportunity to work and will not, he at once becomes one of the class whom it were wise to watch, but until such an opportunity is offered, nothing could be more cruel than to add to his misfortune the stigma of surveillance.

It is believed by those who advocate the eight-hour system that it will furnish relief to a vast number of men who are idle because they cannot obtain employment, and if in this they are correct, the effort to reduce the hours of labor is worthy of universal approbation. It should be encouraged.

We have assumed for the sake of illustration that there are in the country 8.25 million workingmen willing to work; that of these 5 million are at work ten hours a day, and that 1.25 million are in enforced idleness. We have assumed, as a mathematical fact, if the hours of labor are reduced from ten to eight, the 1.25 million idle men would have an opportunity for employment. In this proposition the time problem is solved. So far the eight-hour movement is not complicated by the question of wages. It does not enter into the discussion anywhere. It is left to be regulated by circumstances. The commanding idea is to obtain employment for the idle the surplus labor of the country.

Suppose that workingmen are receiving an average of $1.50 a day, and that by reducing the hours of labor from ten to eight, wages are reduced in the same ratio. In that case a man receiving $1.50 a day would receive but $1.20 a day and by giving up 30 cents a day, 1.25 million idlers are employed. As a result, the same amount, $7.5 million a day would be paid out for labor. If it be assumed that a man can live on $1.20 a day, then we have the fact that employers are not out of pocket a cent. Whatever loss is sustained falls directly upon labor—the workingmen of the country.

But suppose that the result should be, as manifestly it ought to be, that the average wages, $1.50 a day, should lie maintained, what would be the result? Simply a gain to labor of $1.875 million.

It need not be said that the subject is inviting for indefinite exploration and elaboration. With employment at fair wages, the possibilities for workingmen to improve physically and morally become probabilities. Rescued from ceaseless, grinding, exhaustive toil by the reduction of the hours of labor, domestic ties are strengthened, the cottage home of the workingman is beautified and made the abode of contentment, a fit place to rear sovereign citizens who are to shape in coming years the destinies of the Republic.

With a few dollars over and above the absolute necessities of life, there is a fund for the book and the newspaper, something for the church and lecture, for rational amusement.

Under such conditions the restlessness of society, in a great measure, ceases. Employment hushes many alarms. The wealth which labor creates is more equitably distributed, and the statistics which labor bureaus are required to collect and tabulate will bear, as never before, eloquent testimony that our civilization may boast of its triumphs rather than, at present, blush for its glaring defects.

Mrs. Leonora M. Barry: General Instructor and Director of Woman's Work, Knights of Labor[†]

May 1890

Mrs. Leonora M. Barry,[21] the subject of this sketch, is a native of the Emerald Isle, and her birthplace was the city of Cork, within sound of the "Bells of Shandon," made famous by Francis Mahony ("Father Prout"), and she, doubtless, sings with him

> With deep affection
> And recollection
> I often think of
> Those Shandon bells,
> Whose sounds so wild would,
> In the days of childhood,
> Fling round my cradle
> Their magic spells.[22]

Ireland has furnished the United States of America with many noble types of manhood—orators, statesmen, soldiers, and divines, and women too, of equal worth, and it so happens that it is now the good fortune of the *Locomotive Firemen's Magazine* to speak of one of the latter who has won an enviable renown in a work as philanthropic as has ever challenged the intellectual and spiritual gifts of women since man's inhumanity, ignorance, superstition, and mercenary greed subjected women to wrongs, entailing sufferings, mental and physical, such as demand the genius of a Milton or a Dante to fitly portray.

Mrs. Barry's maiden name was Kearney, her father being John Kearney, whose ancestors were among the first who worked to redeem the "Shamrock Isle" from a wilderness. Her mother was of English ancestry and of noble lineage, and, though suffering impoverishment through the fickleness of fortune, retained those distinguishing traits of character which survive the wreck of estates and are transmitted as a priceless heritage to children.

When Leonora was but two years old, in 1853,[23] the family emigrated to America and settled in Pierrepont, St. Lawrence County, New York. Here Leonora lived until 1866. Her home was one of rural beauty. There was "the

† Published in *Locomotive Firemen's Magazine,* vol. 14, no. 5 (May 1890), 399–402.

orchard, the meadow, the deep tangled wildwood."[24] There, among the fruit trees and maple groves, the birds sang their sweetest melodies; there the wildflowers bloomed; there bees gathered their luscious store and the brooks laughed and sang and danced their way to the sea. Amidst such scenes Leonora's childhood and young girlhood were passed. In love with the beauties of nature, no sorrow shaded her pathway, and from the horizon to the zenith no storm cloud lowered betokening sorrow. Nevertheless, a great sorrow was in store for the buoyant, happy girl, and it came. It was the death of her dear mother. It was the first great sorrow. Up to March 1866, Leonora had been gay, joyous, and as happy as the daisies, the wildflowers, and the birds. But all was changed now, a mother's voice was silenced, and the lighthearted girl became a thoughtful, ambitious, self-reliant woman. Her great desire was to teach school. Still she lingered at home until in one short year another Mrs. Kearney came to the home. That settled the question, and in 11 days after the new Mrs. Kearney came, Leonora took her destiny into her own hands, and in a short time entered upon her task of teaching. She had secured a third-grade certificate, and at $5 a week and "boarding round," commenced ascending the ladder of her ambition, in District No. 4, Pierrepont. Just here it is worthwhile to say—because it illustrates a characteristic of the noble woman, who had determined alone and single-handed to support herself—Miss Kearney began teaching in March, and though not 16 till August, she achieved the distinction of having the most successful school ever taught in the district. Having taught four terms, Miss Kearney's ambition was to teach in a school of a higher grade, but her education was defective. In her younger days, she had attended the village school six weeks, all the rest of her educational equipment had been furnished by her sainted mother. Four terms in a district school at $5 a week did not furnish sufficient surplus to attend the normal school at Potsdam, and her father deemed her education sufficient to grace a farmer's home and declined to invest for her higher training as a teacher. But the farmer, with his pigs and poultry, was not the acme of her ambition, as it was of paterfamilias; as a consequence the normal schooling was not secured, nor the father's money.

Then came another departure for our heroine. From the school she sought and obtained an opportunity to learn the art of dressmaking. Here was work in earnest, and with needle and thread and scissors. Miss Kearney joined the ranks of working women. It was stitch, snip, fit, and baste—in a word, work. Work is usually unprosaic, rather than poetic, but is not sufficiently vapid and humdrum to dissuade cupid from testing the effects of his darts upon susceptible hearts, and as a result, Miss Kearney in 1870 became Mrs. Barry, having married Mr. William K. Barry, a native of the "Gem of the Sea," a musician and composer of note and

merit. With Mrs. Barry, marriage was not a failure. As wife and mother the blessings of "Love's young dream"[25] were realized—a quiet and happy married life was
vouchsafed—but for only a comparatively brief period. On April 29, 1880, the
husband, after a lingering sickness of two years, was removed by death. This great
bereavement, in a few months, was followed by the death of a daughter, the eldest
of three children. The youngest child was only 18 months old when the father was
taken, and for many weary months the baby suffered from an affliction, testing to
the fullest extent a mother's devotion. The protracted sufferings of the husband
exhausted the savings of years, and the widow found herself confronted with the
problems that have come to thousands—work, beg, or starve. Mrs. Barry was not
long in determining her course. Work was accepted with heroic fortitude. The
ordeal was severe. A lone woman with two children to support by the work of her
hands ought to be, in this high noon of our boasted civilization, something less
than a herculean task, but to the eternal discredit of cruel and exacting employers,
it becomes one of the most doubtful and difficult enterprises a brave woman ever
undertook. Mrs. Barry was equal to the emergency, and at once sought and found
work in the Pioneer Hosiery Mill, of Amsterdam, New York. In this mill she
toiled for four years and seven months, until the fall of 1886.

In preparing this sketch for the *Locomotive Firemen's Magazine* there is no
purpose to indulge in undue laudation. Hitherto, too little has been said of heroic women who, comprehending the wants of their toiling sisters, go forth on
their missions of mercy, weeping, "bearing precious seed," believing that "they
shall doubtless come again with rejoicing, bearing their sheaves with them."[26]
Their deeds should be known. Their work, their sacrifices, their noble words
of encouragement, their inspiring example, should form a much larger part of
the literature of labor than has hitherto been awarded.

Let it be understood that Mrs. Leonora M. Barry, in the Hosiery Mills of
Amsterdam, New York, discovered that women were underpaid; that young
girls working in factories were wanting in self-respect, owing to factory associations; and that all working girls were denied the respect due them by those who
did not work. Long before Mrs. Barry ever heard of the Knights of Labor, she
was devising schemes whereby those of her sex engaged in factory work might
be benefitted mentally, morally, and physically. Her plans were deemed impractical, and those from whom she sought advice and encouragement treated
her views as visionary and laughed at them. Hers was the fate of all reformers.
The laughing tribe is numerous.

At this juncture came the Knights of Labor to Amsterdam. Mrs. Barry was
cautious and stood aloof from the organization. But when she had informed

herself of its aims, she thought she saw in the order the full realization of her dreams—the fulfillment of her hopes—and on February 12, 1884, she became a Knight of Labor. Mrs. Barry became a member of the great order of the Knights of Labor because she was in sympathy with its lofty purpose to work and battle for the good of wage earners of the country—including women—and her determination to remain with the Knights was like that of Ruth when she said to Naomi: "Whither thou goest, I will go; thy people shall be my people, and thy God my God."[27]

Mrs. Barry was not a wallflower member of the order. Her membership afforded her opportunities to work, and this purpose was discovered by her sister toilers; and, as a consequence, in a few months after her initiation, she was made master workman of Local Assembly 3636, composed exclusively of women; the first woman's local organized west of New York City, having a membership of 980 strong. At the head of such an assembly Mrs. Barry sought and found opportunities to be of service to her sister associates in factory life. Her moral sensibilities revolted at the gross disregard of proper arrangements for the sexes in the factory building, and a sweeping reform was at once inaugurated. This done, a class of young girls of the assembly was formed for instruction. This movement was a success from the first and was productive of lasting benefits.

As might be expected, the brave and aggressive woman represented her local assembly in the district assembly, No. 65, and this district assembly sent her as a delegate to the general assembly of the order, which convened at Richmond, Virginia, in 1886. At this general assembly, Mrs. Barry stood forth, the thoroughly equipped champion of working women. Their condition was her theme, and her burning words aroused the delegates to a sense of its transcendent importance. There was ignorance and degradation to be overcome. The work of education and elevation demanded the largest possible measure of effort on the part of the order. Thousands of working women throughout the land were pleading for assistance. Men were cruel, heartless, and in numerous instances lustful and corrupting. She painted the picture as she had seen it: haggard and debasing, and as a result, in Richmond she was appointed to the responsible position of general instructor and director of woman's work of the order of Knights of Labor.

So far, this sketch of Mrs. Barry reads like a romance. We found her a happy, joyous, thoughtless girl, at her home in Pierrepont, St. Lawrence County, New York. We have accompanied her along her pathway of happiness, sorrow, gloom, and poverty and found her always hopeful, always self-reliant and courageous, always sympathetic, and devising plans for the improvement of the condition of workingwomen. We have seen her a mere child, taking charge of a school, leaving the home of her childhood to earn her own living. We have seen her young heart crushed with great grief when the "old armchair" lost its occupant, and a mother's voice no longer blessed her child. We have seen her a bride at the altar, and again bowed beneath a great bereavement and required to enter the ranks of toilers to support herself and children, always courageous and self-reliant, always hopeful and determined.

We have seen Mrs. Barry in recognition of her zeal and superior abilities, made general instructor and director of woman's work of Knights of Labor, an office accepted with a "pang," because it meant the "breaking up of her tenement home and separation from her treasures." But the home was broken up and the "treasures," her two boys, left to the care of others, that the heroic woman might go forth on her mission of love and redemption to the oppressed of her sex.

In her first report to the order, we hear her say:

> Within the jurisdiction of our District Assemblies, starvation and sin are knocking at, aye, and have gained entrance at the doors of thousands of the victims of underpaid labor. And the men who have pledged themselves to the assistance of humanity and the abolition of poverty are so engrossed in the pursuit of their own ambitious desires that upon their ears the wail of woe falls unheeded, and the work of misery and destruction still goes on.
>
> Men! Ye, whose earnings count from $9 to $15 a week and upward; cease, in the name of God and humanity, cease your demands and grievances, and give us your assistance for a time to bring some relief to the poor unfortunate, whose week's work of 84 hours brings but $2.50 or $3 per week.
>
> * * *
>
> Once more we appeal to you, brothers of the Knights of Labor, by your love for the sacred name of mother, by your protecting love and respect for your wives and daughters, to sustain your manly principles, to uphold the dignity of your strong, noble manhood, and assist to uproot the corrupt system that is making slaves—not alone of poverty, but slaves to sin and shame—of those who, by the right of divine parentage, we must call sisters.

Such were the ringing words of Mrs. Barry to the delegates of the order of Knights of Labor. They are brave, clarion-tongued words, worthy of a heroine, worthy of the cause she represents; they are words fitly spoken, "like apples of gold in pictures of silver."[28] It would be well if all workingmen, no matter under what banner they march, could hear them, and better if they would ponder their import.

In the same report Mrs. Barry gives the enslaving prices at which women

work to make clothing for men, and which, to gain coarse and scanty food,
subjects wee infants to toil, and says:

> To any honest man, I say, when you purchase an overcoat, see to it that
> the maker got more than 40 cents for making it; when you buy pants, do
> not touch those that were made for 50 cents per dozen, or vests for 15
> cents each, or a shirt for 3, 4, and 6 cents each. * * * An honest man's
> back is not the place for a dishonestly manufactured article.

Such words are keynotes and should inspire those who hear them with a
determination to emancipate women from the curse which men, more cruel
than a Nero,[29] a Tiberius,[30] or a Caligula[31] visit upon them. We talk glibly of
the devastation of a Timur,[32] a Nader Shah,[33] and an Alexander; there are no
bounds to imprecations heaped upon those who steal savages from the jungles
of Africa; but Mrs. Barry recites the curses of slavery heaped upon women,
productive of poverty and starvation, sin and shame, not in the land of the
crescent, not inflicted by turbaned Turks, but in the land of the cross, inflicted
by Christian men. God save the mark.

Again in 1888, Mrs. Barry, in her report, gives an account of her travels
that embraced the continent, and says:

> It has been intimated that the Woman's Department was started on
> sentiment. Well, if so, it has turned out to be one of the most thor-
> oughly practical departments in the order. * * * Ten thousand organized
> women today look to the Woman's Department for counsel, advice,
> and assistance.

There can be no higher evidence of man's civilization than is shown in his
regard for the welfare of women, and a woman's department in all the ranks of organized labor demonstrates the fact, as nothing else could demonstrate it, that the
workingmen of America stand upon a plane of moral and intellectual culture as
high as that occupied by those whose supercilious airs indicate that they are "re-
specters of persons," and therefore a little higher than Jehovah, whom Peter said
is "no respecter of persons." But it should be said of Mrs. Barry that in demanding the amelioration of the condition of women, she grasps the whole subject and
treats it with profound philosophic acumen. Speaking of reforms demanded, she
would have a reduced number of hours of work for women, because:

> Long hours, constant toil, confinement, injurious sanitary conditions,
> uncomfortable home surroundings and lack of proper nourishment are
> killing the vital, physical, and mental strength so necessary to women, the

mothers to whom a nation must look for her strength of manhood and womanhood in future generations.

As this imperfect sketch goes to the printer, the subject of it is doing the work of an evangelist, organizing, instructing, and cheering on women workers to put forth their united energies to better their condition. In every philanthropic enterprise there will be times and occasions when deferred hopes will dampen the ardor of the stoutest hearts; but battles for the right when once begun, though baffled oft, like Tennyson's brook, go on forever.

This magazine wishes Mrs. Barry the realization of her fondest hopes, and that long before her knightly voice is silenced, victory may flash along all the lines of organized labor; a victory for women as well as for men; a victory so crushing to the oppressors of workingwomen that the women, like Miriam and all the women delivered from the hands of Pharaoh, shall take their timbrels and sing, "Labor hath triumphed gloriously over a nefarious gang of oppressors, and working women, emancipated, disenthralled, and redeemed, are free."[34]

The Brotherhood of Locomotive Engineers and Federation[†]

June 1890

We pay the members of the Brotherhood of Locomotive Engineers no idle compliment when we say the great majority of its membership favor federation, as it exists with the four federated orders of railway employees, viz.: the B of LF, the B of RT, the SMAA, and the B of RC.

To make this alliance equal to any and every emergency, the B of LE is required. With the engineers in line with the conductors, trainmen, switchmen, and firemen, ample protection to the members of each is assured, and now, as from the first, we are unable to discover any well-grounded objections the B of LE can propose to such an alliance.

We do not hesitate to admit the numerical strength of the B of LE. It

---

† Published in *Locomotive Firemen's Magazine*, vol. 14, no. 6 (June 1890), 535.

would be supreme folly to equivocate upon the conquering power of the B of LE when in alliance with other orders of railway employees it demands that the right shall triumph over the wrong, and the fact that the B of LE can muster a larger force under its banners than some other orders of railway employees is an argument in favor of rather than in opposition to federation.

It should be said in this connection that notwithstanding its numerical strength of membership, the B of LE, in case of trouble with a corporation, is not strong enough under all circumstances to "go it alone," and engineers know that such exigencies do sometimes arise when the united voice and strength of all are required to secure simple justice, and that in the absence of such an alliance, defeat is almost inevitable.

We but repeat a thrice told tale, but as true as trite, that had the engineers, firemen, trainmen, conductors, and switchmen been in compact alliance, acting as one, unified for the welfare of all, the history of the CB&Q affair would have read differently. In this notable battle, had federation existed, a victory would have been won for the right, and it is universally admitted that the battle was lost because such an alliance did not exist.

It occurs to us that just here it is well to introduce figures approximating actual conditions as illustrative of cogent reasons why the strong, numerically, should federate with the weak. Stated in tabulated form, we have something like the following:

B of LE membership		20,000
B of LF membership	18,000	
B of RT membership	16,000	
SMAA membership	6,000	
B of RC membership	2,000	
TOTAL	42,000	20,000

It will be seen that as matters now stand the federated orders number 22,000 more members than the B of LE, and it is fair to presume that this percentage of difference holds good on most of the railroad systems of the country. With such figures in full view, the arguments in favor of federation are greatly strengthened.

But there is another view to take of the subject. It will doubtless be conceded that in proportion to numbers, the greater the liability to have grievances, hence the B of LE would have more grievances than firemen, trainmen, switchmen, or conductors. The idea which we desire to present is that in proportion to the numbers of the federated orders, the greater the liability for grievances and the greater the demand for the support of the orders of less numerical strength. In a word, federation is productive of a sense of security to all against wrongs. And thus it happens that the conclusion is almost universal that with federation strikes disappear.

In saying this we are fortunately in possession of facts which triumphantly demonstrate the conclusion. It was not long since demonstrated on the Erie Railroad. It was as conclusive at Pittsburgh when the employees contended with some *fourteen different* railroads. It was a notable victory on the Q&C,[35] and in many ways demonstrated its power for good on the O&M.[36] On the Erie the engineers won a victory, at Pittsburgh the yardmen, on the Q&C the conductors and trainmen, and on the O&M, the engineers and firemen. And just here let it be said that without federation, for in every instance federation was invoked, there would have been a strike.

We do not permit ourselves to believe the B of LE, in the face of all the facts, in the face of logical conclusions, the trend of the mind forces of railway employees, will *sit down* on federation. Once in the federated body, the B of LE's power and influence would be acknowledged and every problem solved.

We shall not permit ourselves to discuss any proposition calling in question the honor or integrity of the representatives of the federated orders. It is only required to state that any intimation of dishonorable acts is unworthy of consideration and that the B of LE, should it become a member of the Supreme Council, will have no cause to regret its action. It will find men and orders honest and courageous, ready when the exigency arises to maintain every obligation to win victories for the right and to stand firmly by every pledge.

The Buddhists of Burma[†]

June 1890

Accounts have it that the Buddhists of Burma spare no expense in beautifying the temples of their gods, and in proof of this a description of a new vane of a pagoda in Rangoon is given as follows:

[†] Untitled editorial in *Locomotive Firemen's Magazine,* vol. 14, no 6 (June 1890), 492.

The vane is about three by one-and-a-half feet broad, and thickly crusted with precious stones and lovely fans of Burmese gold. One ruby alone is worth 6,000 rupees, and there are several hundred rubies alone on this beautiful thing. On the tip of the iron rod on which works the vane is a richly carved and perforated gold ornament called the Semboo. It is somewhat egg-shaped and a foot in height, tipped by an enormous diamond encircled by many smaller ones, crusted on like barnacles. All over this exquisite oval object are similar clumps of diamonds, no other stones being used for this part.[37]

After all, it is difficult to define a distinction between pagan and Christian in the matter of decorating temples of worship. The pagan idea is that such things please their gods; just what the Christian idea is, when they lavish their wealth upon temples of worship, may be a little more difficult to ascertain.

ORC Overwhelmingly Endorses Protection[†]

June 1890

We have for several days held back going to press for the sole purpose of obtaining the latest possible reliable information relating to the action of the convention of the Order of Railway Conductors in session at Rochester, upon what is termed the "strike clause" of its constitution, as also to learn the name of the fortunate member who had won the position of grand chief. The wires have amply rewarded our patience and we are able to announce to our readers that the ORC, in the matter of seeking redress for wrongs done its members, is now in line with all the great orders of railroad employees. The ORC has been in existence 22 years, but in the matter of protection started out upon an error; never did an order seek more assiduously to secure justice to its members by a mistaken conception of obligation and duty. It sought to conciliate corporations by yielding to their demands and though ceaselessly refused, it still held on to the old methods, its officers did not comprehend that new ideas and

---

[†] Published as "The ORC Convention: Protection Adopted by an Overwhelming Majority" in *Locomotive Firemen's Magazine*, vol. 14, no. 6 (June 1890), 534.

new forces had come to the front, and that a new dispensation had dawned. It was because of this fact that the Brotherhood of Railway Conductors, under the leadership of Grand Chief G. W. Howard, came into existence and now has thoroughly organized more than 60 lodges, and though in its very infancy, has been instrumental in winning a number of notable victories for its members, which have given it a national reputation. The splendid triumphs of the B of RC, we doubt not, exerted a beneficial influence upon the members of the ORC, but the rapid growth of the B of RC indicates that in the ranks of the conductors of the country there was deep-seated unrest and a determination to redeem the calling from accumulating stigmas; as a consequence they enlisted under the banner of the B of RC, an organization that has demonstrated its comprehension of the needs of railroad employees, and realizing that in these times of colossal corporate power simple organization would not answer the demand, at the earliest practical day came into line under the laws of the federated orders. While we most heartily felicitate the ORC upon its emancipation from a mistake embedded in its constitution, and wish it a successful career in demonstrating to the world the wisdom of its action, and most cordially give it the right hand of fellowship, as an organization that in the future will *strike* when all other means of redress fail, we shall not abate in the least our zeal in promoting the success of the B of RC. It started right and with chivalric courage has upheld the right. It comprehended the necessity for an order of railway conductors in full accord with other orders of railway employees, and the organization now commands universal respect.

At this writing we are not advised as to the course the reconstructed ORC will pursue in regard to federation, but whatever may be its action, we do not hesitate to say that it has done a glorious work and having taken a wise step we do not doubt others will follow in the same direction. There are now two orders of railway conductors in existence. It will be for them to determine their future relations, and it may lie possible that in the not-distant future, consolidation will occur. We have faith in the wisdom of the great body of railway employees. Demonstration follows demonstration in such rapid succession that a man must be steeped in misanthropy to doubt the triumph of the right. Where there is a will there is a way, and we are satisfied the conductors will find it.

We take this occasion to congratulate E. E. Clark,[38] Esq., late grand senior conductor, upon his elevation to the chief executive office of his order. His advancement has been rapid, showing that his brother conductors have faith in his abilities to manage affairs, and to say that we wish him success in the performance of his arduous duties but feebly expresses our felicitations.

We cannot afford to close this hasty résumé of topics suggested by the action of the conductors' convention without wishing Bro. Wheaton, in his retirement, the peace and serenity which should come to all after years of hard work. There is still a demand for active, energetic men out of office, and should Bro. Wheaton desire to continue in the battle and in the storm, we shall hope his equipments may be such as to win victories, or, at any rate, to hold his own.

Eight-Hour Day a Righteous Demand[†]
July 1890

The eight-hour question is up for debate, and the discussion will proceed until the demand that eight hours shall constitute a day's work will be granted. It is a righteous demand. There is not to be found in it, however severe the analysis, an element of injustice. By making eight hours a lawful day's work, no man, woman, nor child is wronged. This cannot be said of the demand for more than eight hours for a day's work.

No greater mistake in connection with the subject could be made than to assume and assert that only the well-being of the wageworker is considered in demanding a less number of hours for a day's work. Such a view of the subject is narrow. It lacks breadth and depth. Upon investigation it will be found to be prompted by selfishness and parsimoniousness, totally destitute of generosity and that broad philanthropy which comprehends the public good—the welfare of all.

There are doubtless those who believe that the eight-hour movement is of mushroom growth; that it has come, as did Jonah's gourd, and will perish as quickly.[39] Such persons are neither students nor philosophers. They reason badly or, more properly, they do not reason at all. They assume that agitation is the work of cranks; that it is a vagary which, like many other delusions, is to have its day, disappear, and be forgotten. Such people are doomed to disappointment. The wish is father to the thought, and sire and offspring at no distant day will fill a common grave.

---

† Published as "The Eight-Hour Movement" in *Locomotive Firemen's Magazine,* vol. 14, no. 7 (July 1890), 580–582.

The question of reducing the hours of labor, if we may measure time by events, can boast of some antiquity. The seed has been germinating during the entire nineteenth century. In a recent paper, prepared by Mr. Joseph Gruen-hut[40] of Chicago, and published in *The Knights of Labor* of that city, the facts are brought into commanding prominence. It appears that prior to 1803, 14 hours constituted a day's work. At that date a movement was made by journey-men shipwrights and house carpenters to secure a reduction to ten hours, and were threatened with "blacklisting" for their temerity. As far back as 1832, the carpenters and caulkers of Boston struck to secure ten hours for a day's work. They did not succeed, but their brethren in New York and Philadelphia were more successful and did secure the boon. That was 56 years ago—more than half a century—but to secure this limited success, there had been constant agitation from 1803 to 1833—30 years.

From 1833, the demand for a reduction of the hours of labor became more and more emphatic. In 1840, Martin Van Buren, by proclamation, established the ten-hour-day system in the navy yards of the government. The governor of New Jersey recommended legislation favoring a reduction of hours. Work-ingmen took courage, and the agitation proceeded. In 1845–46 numerous strikes occurred to secure the ten-hour system. In 1847, the British Parliament passed a ten-hour law. This aroused fresh activity in the United States among workingmen. New Hampshire led off by making ten hours a legal day's work in 1847. The agitation was kept up; strikes were frequent; employers relaxed their grasp slowly, and in 1853 eleven hours were adopted in many parts of the country as the regular workday as the result of strikes.

A number of states have adopted the ten-hour law.

In 1868 Congress passed an eight-hour law for all government working-men. Then began strikes throughout the country for the eight-hour system, and eight-hour leagues were formed, and from that day to the present the agitation has been kept up and is now more active than ever before.

In 1802–1803, when the agitation began, there were two labor organiza-tions engaged in the great work of trying to reduce the hours of labor from 14 to 10 hours. Now, labor organizations are counted by scores. Then, working-men were weak; now they are strong. Then, capital was arrogant, all-powerful; it is arrogant still, but it is no longer all-powerful; organized labor confronts it defiantly and says, as did Moses to Pharaoh, "Let my people go."[41]

From 1802 to 1890—88 years—there has been ceaseless agitation for a reduction of the hours of labor, and it may be said that four hours a day have been gained to the toilers of the land—four hours a day for rest, for recreation, for study, for mind-improvement and physical recuperation. Without this agitation on the part of the workingmen, without the strikes, the sacrifices and sufferings incident to strikes, the 14-hour day would still be in force, and yet there are men who deprecate agitation, and who have a holy horror for strikes. But the edict has gone forth—working hours must still further be reduced. Does someone ask what has been gained in 88 years of agitation? We answer, four hours a day to each workingman, or for 300 working days 1,200 hours, equal to 120 days of ten hours each. Are there those who begrudge these hours of rest and relaxation to the toiler? Yes. Find them, measure them, analyze them, and when the world knows what they are, humanity will blush crimson for their degeneracy.

The eight-hour demand to thoughtful men means much more than the gain of two hours from toil—it means opportunities for the idle to obtain work and wages, to become productive and self-supporting. Suppose, in round numbers, there are in the country 6.25 million men willing to work, and that only 5 million of them can find employment at ten hours for a day's work. Five million men working ten hours a day is 50 million hours. It is seen that there are 6.25 million workingmen, or 1.25 million idle. If the hours of a day's work are reduced from ten to eight, it will be seen that the reduction affords the idle an opportunity for employment—6.25 million men working eight hours a day is 50 million hours, the same as 5 million men working ten hours a day. For every four men working ten hours a day, by reducing the hours to eight, admits an idle man. Who are benefitted? We answer, society as a whole. No greater danger can menace society than idleness. It has been said, and it is true, that "idleness is the prolific parent of crime," and not only of crime, but of pauperism. Idleness destroys the home and wrecks the family. It is a scourge which leaves in its wake effects compared with which pestilence is a benediction. The eight-hour movement will prove to be a powerful aid in doing away with idleness.

The eight-hour question is scarcely less ethical than economical. It relates to morals as well as to money. If the idle can obtain employment, they are in the line of moral, physical, and financial advancement. If idleness leads to vice, employment is promotive of virtue. If idleness wrecks homes, employment builds homes. If idleness results in poverty and degradation, employment is productive of competency and independence.

The eight-hour movement is not only designed to afford workingmen more leisure, more rest, more opportunities for intellectual culture, but it is designed to afford men, in forced idleness, opportunities for employment and all those blessings it will confer.

The triumph of the eight-hour movement will not usher in the millennium. It will not chain the devil. It will not transform the earth into a paradise, but it will be moving things in the direction of many and great improvements. It will be scoring another victory for right, truth, and justice. It will be a harbinger note of the good time coming, when labor shall enjoy more abundantly the wealth it creates.

During the next twelve months the eight-hour discussion is to be more aggressive than ever before. The press has long since begun its crusade. One paper leads off by saying that

> The division, eight hours for rest and eight hours for recreation and improvement seems not unreasonable, though in a great many occupations, and in a vast number of individual cases, such a division could not be enforced. It is claimed that a shortening of hours would furnish relief for the unemployed by giving work and wages to a greater number of persons, but this argument is more fanciful than real.

We have shown that it is not fanciful; not a vagary. Mathematics never more clearly demonstrated a proposition than that by reducing the hours of labor more room is made for more laborers. Nor is it true that "in a vast number of individual cases" the eight-hour system "could not be enforced." The ten and 11-hour system has been enforced as against the 14-hour system. But, says the paper from which we have quoted:

> In this, as in other conflicts of interest, the trouble is to find a common standing-ground for employers and employees. The latter want ten hours' wages for eight hours' work, and the former insist they cannot pay it. Generally, except in the government or public service, a reduction of hours is accompanied by a corresponding reduction of pay. No law can prevent men from making special contracts, and the most that any enactment on the subject can do is to make eight hours a legal day's work in the absence of any contract or stipulation to the contrary. The result will probably be that in most cases employers will scale down the wages two-tenths, and if the laborer or mechanic wants to earn the old wages, he will have to work the old hours.

In this we have the keynote of the opposition the eight-hour movement is to encounter from a subsidized press. The same old cry that was heard when 14 hours was a day's work is heard again in favor of ten hours and against the adoption of eight hours. The law, if laws are enacted, fixing eight hours as a day's work, is to be violated, and then we are told that employers, if the law cannot be abrogated by chicane, as a last resort, will "scale down prices." Workingmen should understand that the establishment of the eight-hour system is not to be inaugurated without a struggle.

If, the labor organizations of the country, acting as a unit, shall say, "Eight hours shall constitute a day's work," the declaration will be the eight-hour law of the country. If employers determine they will not obey it, then, in that case, let silence brood over the land from ocean to ocean. One day will suffice. Let the fires go out in forge, and furnace, and firebox. Let the machine stand still. Give the horsepower a rest. If the ring of the anvil, the click of the shuttle, the whir and buzz of spindle and wheel can't be permitted to sing in concert the triumph of justice to labor, let them remain silent. Everything depends upon the united action of workingmen. If they are discordant, there will be no inauguration of the eight-hour movement, but if united, harmonious, and determined, they will succeed. In the meantime, let the work of agitation go forward with an increasing vigor.

The Higher Education of Women vs. Marriage[†]
July 1890

In the *Popular Science Monthly* for March 1890, we find an exceedingly well-written paper captioned "The Mission of Educated Women," written by Mrs. M. F. Armstrong.[42]

In the paper prominence is given to certain propositions which to our mind are of startling significance, and well calculated to challenge the most serious reflection—and this view of the subject, as presented by Mrs. Armstrong, is all the more grave and weighty because "educated women" are specially involved.

The paper in question is in reply to an article entitled "Plain Words on the Woman Question," by a Mr. Allen, in which he classifies certain women as "deplorable accidents," and we are left to infer that these "deplorable accidents," in Mr. Allen's opinion, are "educated women," who choose single blessedness rather than run the risks of matrimonial entanglements: in other

---

† Published in *Locomotive Firemen's Magazine*, vol. 14, no. 7 (July 1890), 577–579.

words, they are educated women who are self-reliant and prefer making their own living rather than be dependent upon husbands, and this view of the matter is warranted not only by Mrs. Armstrong's averments and admissions, but by educated women themselves who, when interrogated, had the courage to respond without circumlocution.

We do not remember to have seen in print anything relating to the "Mission of Educated Women" better calculated to arouse discussion than is found in Mrs. Armstrong's dissertation—in fact, we doubt if hitherto the position has been taken that women of high educational attainments are more disposed than their sisters who have drank less deeply at the "Pierian spring" to oppose marriage.[43] To enable the reader to have a correct view of the situation as presented by Mrs. Armstrong, we quote as follows:

> I have been for years connected with a large educational institution, where young men and women are working, side by side, under identically similar influences. The officials and teachers in this school are largely women, and women who, to quote Mr. Allen, have become "traitors to their sex," in that they have taken upon their shoulders the burden of their own support. They are, with few exceptions, highly educated, many of them college-bred, three among them being regular physicians, while all of them, if I may be permitted to judge, are of at least average attractiveness. As to health, social position, and previous condition, they offer, also, I believe, a fair average, while their intellectual standard ranks them high in the scale of feminine development.

In this we observe nothing unusual. There is no extravagance of language. People at all acquainted with the educational institutions of the country will at once accept Mrs. Armstrong's description as entirely free from exaggeration. The picture of women educators is perfect so far as it goes, and is conclusive, but had the writer so desired, she could have introduced many embellishments without injustice to her subject. Manifestly, what she says of the teachers of the institution to which she refers, is to introduce a "charming cottage" where "two" of these teachers reside, and where she had the good fortune to meet a "striking assemblage of single women, well looking, well dressed, ranging from 20 to 50 years of age, every one of whom could have in the past married, or could still marry, were it her desire to do so." These women were not fanatics; on the contrary, "they were sensible, earnest, in some cases brilliant women, who had, with more or less intention, turned their backs upon marriage, and had chosen instead lives of self-supporting independence." And it is admitted that these women "turned their backs upon marriage" because of their "higher education."

These educated women did not hesitate to furnish Mrs. Armstrong reasons for their choice when confronted with the straightforward request to "tell me why, as representative individuals, you have not married, do not marry, and are endeavoring, so far as educational methods can do it, to perpetuate your type?"

Mrs. Armstrong gives the answers of these educated women to her important interrogatory, and she says, "There were no evasions."

The general reader, or the intelligent reader, will feel a lively interest in the replies, because, whether wise or otherwise, they relate to problems of immediate and far-reaching consequences. They involve the laws of the physical, intellectual, and moral organism of men and women; God's first command, "Multiply and replenish the earth;" they involve home and all domestic relations; in a word, if the "higher education" of women is to result in their "turning their backs upon marriage," then the world will be forced, inevitably, to regard this "higher education" of women as the most stupendous evil that has visited the world since the deluge.

It will not do to suggest that a comparatively few will receive this "higher education," and therefore that the number who will "turn their backs upon marriage" will be limited. That is not the question, but rather, does the education of women tend in that direction? It is confessed that such is the influence.

We confess to no little interest in the testimony of the witnesses Mrs. Armstrong introduces in justification of their "turning their backs upon marriage." In one case, a denial is made that education "unsexes" women. It is needless to say that, in one sense, that is impossible—the term relates to masculine prerogatives, not as the result of human statutes, man's ignorance or arrogance, but of the irrevocable laws of his being, and in these laws are blended the animal propensities, the moral sentiments, and the intellectual powers. It is not required to discuss "spheres," functions, vocations, and a' that; and yet, as between men and women, orbits are thought to be sharply defined, and when women stray beyond their sphere, they are said to be "masculine," just as when degenerate savages excite the contempt of the "braves," and are known as "squaw men." Educated women are quick to discern when masculines become "squaw men," and in every instance such weaklings excite their unmitigated contempt. If a man is a man, he will be at all seasons in the right place, like a planet. He will not violate the laws of his being to become feminine. There will be something masculine, robust, strong in his tenderness, in his gentlest moods; something manly, when he kneels at the shrine of love or beauty—or, if there is not, his weakness will be detected by women, and by them he will be assigned his proper place in the ranks. And what is true of men is quite as true of women, and no special pleadings will to any considerable extent change verdicts. It is proposed by highly educated women to change somewhat the program. Says one, "In the past, it is the emotional nature of women which has been cultivated, often at a heavy cost. Now her intellect is taking charge," and this thing of being "sacrificed to emotions" is to cease. The witness asks, can it be shown that the training of her intellect makes a woman any less capable of love and devotion? And yet this very witness claims for the higher education of women the triumph of the intellect over her "emotional nature," the result of which is to prompt her to "turn her back upon marriage." And that such is the outcome of this "higher education" for women is placed beyond controversy by the testimony of "a newly graduated collegian," who said "that in our college it has become a proverb, that if a girl isn't engaged before she is a sophomore, the chances are all against her marriage." And said another highly educated woman: "We become more interested in our studies, more certain of our ability to take care of ourselves, and therefore less interested in men as possible lovers, and more independent of them as a means of support."

In view of all the facts, as stated in Mrs. Armstrong's paper, the mission of educated women is to renounce marriage, home, domesticity, and, insofar as they can influence affairs, annul the command to "multiply and replenish the earth."

Allusions to the fact that husbands are "not infrequently ready to accept assistance from the hands of the women they have undertaken to support;" to "domestic drudgery;" to marrying for "the sake of a somewhat uncertain support;" and to the fact that "the moral sense is in" educated women "more highly developed" than in men; and that they "are morally upon a higher level than men;" go to prove that woman's higher education tends directly to create an antipathy to marriage, a dislike of man, and a low estimate of what is required to establish a home.

It is from such points of observation that thoughtful people are required to contemplate the higher education of women, and the influence such teachings is to have upon women whose educational advantages have been more circumscribed. The opportunities for women to obtain an academic and collegiate education are everywhere increasing. Academies and colleges are multiplying and a vast army of young women are demanding admittance. And it is in testimony—"if a girl is not engaged before she is a sophomore, the chances are all against her marriage;" she is pretty certain to "turn her back upon marriage." As a result, those who are to marry and establish homes are to be in the future the comparatively illiterate.

We are inclined to the opinion that those who have been foremost in the advocacy of the "higher education of women" never dreamed that such results would follow, and in contemplating the outcome, so far as indicated by Mrs. Armstrong's paper on "The Mission of Educated Women," they are likely to be greatly perturbed as to further developments.

It will not be denied that women, whether highly educated, moderately educated, or not educated at all, have a right to "turn their backs upon marriage." Nor has anyone a right to change their decision. They have a right to estimate men by such standards as they may select. Such propositions are not involved in this discussion. The real point at issue is, does the higher education of women militate against marriage? And if so, is it a blessing to society? It is this thing called "higher education" that is arraigned. What must be the educational influences of a college, when "if a girl is not engaged before she is a sophomore, the chances are all against her marriage"? To discuss such questions would require more time and space than we have at our command, but they are vital, and eminently worthy of the attention of professional educators.

It is, in conclusion, worthy of remark that in proportion as men become educated, as their animal propensities are restrained, their grossness subdued, and their intellectual powers and moral sentiments are brought into harmonious relations, women have been emancipated from the enthrallments of ignorance, brutality, and superstition, the home beautified and glorified steadily and hopefully; but it is in proof that as women become educated, as they advance in intellectual culture and power, they "turn their backs upon marriage," and of a consequence upon home, since there can be no home without marriage, and in this way reverse the social order and, in fact, the heaven-ordained order. If this is to be the result of "the higher education of women," their mission is not such as to command approval of this so-called "higher education."

Is a Wrong Done to One the Concern of All?[†]

July 1890

We should find it extremely difficult to formulate a more important question for the consideration of workingmen than is presented in the caption of this article.

---

† Published in *Locomotive Firemen's Magazine*, vol. 14, no. 7 (July 1890), 586–588.

If a wrong done to one is not the concern of all, it can be said that the wrong scarcely, if at all, concerns anyone but the victim of the wrong, and with such a conclusion the term "brotherhood" loses its significance, its strength, and glory—is reduced to a level with pagan gods, to be worshiped by the ignorant and deluded, that the priests, who serve the idol and formulate its oracles, may fatten and flourish upon the superstitions of their victims. If a wrong done to one is not the concern of all, then the talk about the "brotherhood of man and the fatherhood of God" is not only a miserable delusion, worse than

> Dead Sea fruits, that tempt the eye,
> But turn to ashes on the lips.[44]

but is embellished hypocrisy, robed Phariseeism, decorated delusion, unworthy of any recognition in the ranks of sane men.

If a wrong done to one is not the concern of all, why should men waste their breath in shouting:

> When the war-drums throb no longer,
> And when the battle flags are furled,
> In the parliament of man,
> The federation of the world?[45]

If the theory is "every man for himself and the devil take the hindmost," why not admit that man has been evolved from the hog, rather than contend that God made him "a little lower than Himself," which is the reading of the "new version" of the Bible? To sing of the "federation of the world" is "flim-flam," poetic nonsense, unworthy of consideration, if it be untrue that a wrong done to one is the concern of all.

All nations worthy of the name, pagan as well as Christian, admit that a wrong done to one of their humblest citizens or subjects concerns the nation. It is a fundamental principle, without which a nation, however boastful of its power or enlightenment, would sink to soundless depths of contempt—a weak nation, when one of its citizens is subject to injury, cannot redress the wrong, *vi et armis,*[46] it can only protest, plead for its rights, and appeal to other nations for sympathy and aid, but when a citizen of a great and powerful nation is subjected to wrong, the case is different. History is full of illustrations.

During the "late unpleasantness,"[47] an obscure man, a British subject, long resident in the South, being in Louisville, Kentucky, gave expression to what were regarded treasonable sentiments and was forthwith arrested and imprisoned. He was without wealth or high social standing, but he appealed to the British minister at Washington, and forthwith an order came for his release. The wrong that he claimed had been done him at once concentrated upon his case, the power of the British Empire—and acting promptly, he walked out of his prison a free man.

Not long since, an American citizen was wrongfully confined in a loathsome Mexican prison. When he appealed to his government, he challenged its power to right the wrong, and his prison doors were thrown open, and he was permitted to again tread the sod of his country. Even China appealed to the United States to redress the wrongs done to some of the subjects of the Celestial Kingdom, and though their lives could not be restored, the loss of property was made good from the federal exchequer.[48] Nor is the date remote when an adopted citizen of the United States visiting his old European home was incarcerated and held for military duty. The fact becoming known to a commander of an American warship, at the port where the citizen was deprived of his liberty, a demand was made upon the authorities for his release, and that there might be no mistake about it, the ship was brought broadside to the town, his guns shotted and run out, and decks cleared for action. The demand was "Send the American citizen on board, place him under the protection of the flag of his country, or take the consequences." The wrong done Martin Costa was an injury to the American nation, and the American nation stood pledged and ready to redress the wrong. As a result, the imprisoned man was released.[49] It would be easy to multiply illustrations, but it is not required. The principle is well settled and is vital.

How stands the account with American workingmen? In the vast army of unorganized labor in the United States, who recognizes any wrong done to one as being an injury to all? Who protests in the name of Christ, or in the name of the Christian's God? Does the state? Does the church? Does the ermined judge? Go search the chronicles, and if you find one solitary instance of the kind, in the name of all things sacred let it go forth to the world.

The fact that unorganized workingmen were the victims of wrongs, flagrant and ceaseless, suggested organization as a remedy. The organization became the parliament of workingmen. If one of the members of the organization was wronged it became the concern of all the members, and all protested. This organization of workingmen is not of recent date, and history demonstrates that protection from wrongs and oppressions was secured through the influence of the guilds, organized centuries before the discovery of America.

It was doubtless true then as now, that a wrong done to one shoemaker, AD 1157, was regarded as an injury to any other member of the guild, but there is no intimation that the wrong done to a shoemaker was an injury to the members of every other guild. Then as now, if the guild of which the wronged shoemaker was a member was strong enough to redress the grievance, it was done; if not, the wrong triumphed and the right was cloven down. The "injury to all" simply meant an injury to all the members of that particular organization.

Since the Middle Ages, however much we may boast of the progress of civilization, the brotherhood idea of all workingmen has made little progress; perhaps more in the last decade than in all the centuries past, and yet so little as to create only a glimmering hope that the declaration, as true as any that Jehovah ever inspired, that "a wrong done to one is an injury to all" is finally to triumph over ignorance, prejudice, and all other obstacles.

It is history that the guilds of the Middle Ages, organized to protect the poor from oppression, growing in numbers, in wealth and power, became at last aristocratic and oppressive, and in numerous instances, the same tendency is observable today in the United States of America.

Within the whole realm of the ridiculous and the repulsive there is nothing more revolting than to see one workingman treating another workingman with haughty disdain, caring no more for the wrong done him than if it had been inflicted upon a beast, and all because his work is in another department of the world's industries. As certainly as the fact of interdependence exists, as certainly is a wrong done to one the concern of all. Obscured it may be, ignored it may be, but still it remains immutable and eternal, nor will workingmen achieve a complete triumph over their oppressors until it is recognized, emblazoned upon their banners, and becomes their shibboleth.

The demand for federation means that a wrong done one is the concern of all. In federation there is hope. Without it, the hopes of workingmen will be deferred until every heart will be sick. In federation envy, which is the bane of organizations, will disappear, and as federation proceeds, as education goes forward, thoughts will go deeper and higher, and will eventually include the humblest toiler. Then when a wrong is inflicted upon workingmen in mine or shop, the knowledge of the fact shall be recognized as an injury to all. In this there is nothing utopian. We have furnished illustrations of the practical working of governmental power, and if the trend of workingmen's thoughts is in that direction, the world has a right to be hopeful.

Agitation and Agitators[†]
August 1890

Agitation is the order of nature. Nature abhors quiet as it does a vacuum.

Someone may object and point to the "everlasting hills" in proof of their theory, forgetful of the fact that the hills are the product of agitation.

The sea is never still. The tides forever ebb and flow. The "dead calm" presages the storm. Air in motion is the demand.

The peacefully disposed, the quiet, inert, lethargic souls, those who glory in stagnation, have never had their way. Nature prefers agitation, hence the hurricane, the tornado, the cyclone, the lightning, and the thunderbolt; hence the volcano and the earthquake. Call them evils, it matters not, they are a ceaseless protest against stagnation.

Men cry "peace," but there is no peace. The elemental war goes on. Indeed, those who clamor for peace are agitators.

The pulpit is an agitator. The wranglers over creeds and dogmas are perhaps the most persistent of all agitators, the bedrock idea being that a wrong exists which must be found and exterminated.

All explorers, pathfinders, in religion, morals, science, government, geography, in any and every department of human affairs, are agitators. They are seldom or never popular in the beginning of their labors. Their fate, as a rule, is to suffer derision, contumely, neglect, and poverty, often penalties still more severe; the exception only vindicates the rule.

Those who are inclined to investigate facts will be satisfied that our conclusions are warranted. We could easily exhaust the space at our command by giving illustrations of the rugged road agitators have traveled, and in pointing to the ultimate triumphs they have achieved for the good of mankind.

We are not unmindful of the fact that in the army of agitators there are utopians, vagarists, men of wild fancies, impracticable people, but achievements have been of such a startling character that men who claim to be exceptionally hotheaded will exercise great caution in rendering their verdicts in classing men as "cranks" who are the *avant-couriers* in proclaiming coming triumphs of mind over matter and of right over wrong.

So much as prefatory to the declaration that just now there is manifested a

---

[†] Published in *Locomotive Firemen's Magazine,* vol. 14, no. 8 (August 1890), 712–713.

purpose to treat with contempt persons known as "labor agitators."

The employer wants quiet, stagnation; wants to be let severely alone. The agitator won't have it so. At the bottom of the labor question there exists a wrong of incalculable enormity. The labor agitator seeks to unearth it—to lay it bare, to expose it to the gaze of the world and exterminate it.

The labor agitator does not disguise his purpose. He could not if he would, and would not if he could. He is compelled to be outspoken. He must be bold. Possibly someone objects, and asserts that all labor agitators are neither honest nor in earnest; that they are wolves in sheep's clothing, traitors in disguise, unworthy of confidence, and do incalculable harm. We do not hesitate to admit to some extent the impeachment. Of Christ's twelve apostles, one was a traitor. Such objections have weight, but it is as a feather compared with a mountain. The fact remains that the great body of labor agitators are honest men, working for the accomplishment of noble purposes, fraught with the highest good to men, women, and children, who are the victims of wrongs as flagrant and cruel as can be inflicted under conditions which ought not to exist in any land, and which in the United States of America are infamous to an extent which defy exaggeration.

The mission of the labor agitator in the United States is first to persuade workingmen to organize—to get together for the purpose of the interchange of ideas relating to their pecuniary welfare. Organization is the practical recognition of the maxim, "in union there is strength," and without which labor has no strength. Without organization workingmen are at the mercy of their enemies; without organization, "labor," as was said by an Indiana member of Congress, is a "commodity, as much so as the raw materials to be worked up." Without organization the so-called "labor market" is established as it was in the days of chattel slavery, when there were slave auction blocks and slave pens, and labor was a "commodity." With organization the "market," the "block," and the pen "disappear," and labor commands wages which enable the laborer to live as becomes an American citizen.

The labor agitator wars against oppression in every form, and it is this fact that calls down upon his head the maledictions of those who have grown rich by continuous robberies. The monopolistic, subsidized press launches its anathemas against the labor agitator; they seek to inoculate the public mind with the views of such asps as Austin Corbin and his tribe of venomous reptiles, creatures who inaugurate famine and live in luxury upon the boodle secured by their piracies.

Every labor organization that exists on the continent today is a monument to the triumphs of the labor agitator. Organization is the result of agitation,

466   Building Solidarity on the Tracks

not of silence and submission—not of acquiescence in the rules of wrong, but a ceaseless protest against existing evils that must be eradicated if justice is to prevail and peace be maintained.

There is now widespread agitation to secure federation of labor organizations, because federation is the culmination of the strength sought to be secured by organization.

The agitation in this direction is logical; it is natural, practicable. There is nothing associated with the agitation that has the semblance of vagary. It is not a "crank" idea. It is not visionary. No man, no set of men, no paper or periodical of character or without character assails the proposition. It stands secure in its symmetrical strength. All that is required is to continue the agitation, keep up the bombardment. It is a winning card. The enemies of labor are afraid of it. Already they stand apart as they see labor organizations coming into line under federated banners.

The scepter is falling from the hands of labor autocrats. From the untold millions of wealth which labor creates the time is coming when a just distribution will be ordered. There is to be more agitation, more education, a profounder recognition of great truths relating to the brotherhood of man, a more intense desire to lift up the lowly and the weak; but the trend is in that direction—watch and agitate, fight and go forward. The strong forts and citadels of the enemy are being taken, and the last will eventually fall, as did Ticonderoga when the grand old veteran took possession of it, as he said, by the "authority of the Great Jehovah and the Continental Congress."[50]

Labor Day[†]

August 1890

The workingmen of the United States are making preparations to appropriately celebrate "Labor Day." The purpose is to make Labor Day, the first of September of each year, a national holiday. The idea is in all regards praiseworthy.

Just why the first day of September is chosen for Labor Day, we are not

---

† Published in *Locomotive Firemen's Magazine*, vol. 14, no. 8 (August 1890), 673–674.

informed. It may be the anniversary of some notable event in labor affairs. Be this as it may, the fact that a day has been designated as a labor holiday answers the demand. It is a rallying day for the hosts of workingmen and women, who go forth from their homes and from their everyday employment for recreation of mind and body. They, having left their toils behind them, say and sing: "Begone dull cares, I prithee begone from me."[51]

Labor Day dates a new departure. One of the inspired writers, enumerating times for certain things, says there is "a time to plant."[52] We have in the United States what is called "Arbor Day," when the people go forth and plant trees. There is something very beautiful and very practical in planting trees. The purpose is always commendable, whether the tree planted be for its wood, its fruit, its flowers, or its shade. On labor days, the people do not go forth to plant trees, but in the midst of their enjoyments, they may plant thoughts which, sending their roots down into their moral, intellectual, and spiritual being, will grow, as grow the trees "planted by the rivers of water,"[53] thoughts which in their maturity shall withstand the gales and shelter them when the storms of oppression and adversity come, thoughts that shall bear the fruit of knowledge and independence, union, and strength, of which all may freely partake, which shall enable them to distinguish between good and evil and be wise in their day and generation.

We are in full accord with the Labor Day movement. It should be a day sacred to rational enjoyment, free from anxiety, a day when mind and body, relieved of the dull routine of everyday life, find health and pleasure in relaxation. On such occasions the toilers of the land have opportunities to exchange opinions. Labor Day is a time not only for *set* speech but for free speech, a day to "plant words, and reap actions; to plant actions, and reap habits; to plant habits, and reap principle; to plant principles, and reap character; to plant character, and reap a destiny."[54]

We do not doubt that Labor Days are to yield splendid harvests of blessings to the workingmen of America. During all the hours of Labor Day, Labor's emancipation day, no bell calls us to toil. The hands on the dial plate of the clock do not remind us when work begins, or when it ends. We go forth to the forests, to the green fields, to breathe the fresh air, or listen to the melody of brook and bird and bee; our minds and hearts are in harmony with nature, with the beautiful—the good, the true; it is labor's holiday, labor's jubilee; it is a benediction and a benefaction, and though unknown, we bless the man who first suggested Labor Day.

Powderly and Gompers†
August 1890

The *Journal of the Knights of Labor* of July 3 [1890] devotes 12 columns to an elucidation of the troubles existing between the order of Knights of Labor and the American Federation of Labor. Of the Knights, Mr. Powderly is grand master workman, and of the Federation, Mr. Gompers is president.[55] They are men of ability and acknowledged leaders. As Mr. Powderly has been heard through the columns of the *Journal,* it is to be presumed that Mr. Gompers will also address the public in a similar manner, and the indications all point to a rupture fraught with incalculable harm to labor, without, as we view the situation, any compensations, for let victory settle where it may, labor sustains an injury, and if it is a draw battle its influence must be of a disastrous character. The demand of the times is to harmonize and unify workingmen, but the fight between Messrs. Powderly and Gompers will not have that effect. It will breed discord, asperities, and enmities. Two great labor organizations at war will be accepted by the foes of labor as proof positive that workingmen cannot pull together. The verdict, while apparently true, is nevertheless false. The great mass of organized workingmen, regardless of name, are friends, working for the accomplishment of the same noble and righteous purpose. To estrange them, to array them in hostile attitudes is to inaugurate a calamity far reaching in its results, which will be deplored by the friends of labor everywhere.

We note particularly what is said about the numerical strength of the Federation. If the membership is less than it was thought to be, it is a matter which ought to excite regret, for if the membership is even all that is claimed, it would still be less than it ought to be. To hear that a labor organization is losing its membership is well calculated to dampen the ardor of any other organization, and certainly there is nothing in such reports to rejoice over. We hope to see the time when the Knights of Labor can boast of regaining its numerical power, and that the Federation has not been less successful. This magazine, always on record as the friend of organized labor, always glad to hear of the growth of its grand army, would, were it possible to get the ear of Messrs. Gompers and Powderly, suggest that they get together and adjust their difficulties, since the

---

† Published in *Locomotive Firemen's Magazine,* vol. 14, no. 8 (August 1890), 705.

continuance of the internecine conflict cannot possibly benefit anyone except those who pray ceaselessly for the overthrow of organized labor.

Strike[†]

August 1890

The word "strike" is the sign of an idea which most men dislike to contemplate—and none more, we opine, than those whose purpose it is to strike.

A great many people assume that those who strike do so without counting the cost; without recognizing the fact that they will be called upon to make many and grievous sacrifices; that a strike means idleness, the expenditure of money saved, and after all, involving uncertainties relating to the final outcome.

We do not doubt that there have been unnecessary strikes, just as there have been unnecessary wars; we do not doubt that strikes have sometimes resulted from the leadership of men totally disqualified to give advice in such matters, and that the penalties for such mistakes have been severe.

After making such admissions, the fact stands out in haggard prominence that sometimes a strike is demanded regardless of costs and of sacrifices—demanded by every consideration of right and justice, and under such circumstances not to strike is to tamely submit to outrages and accept degradation; to surrender liberty, independence, self-respect—to permit the wrong to triumph without protest or struggle, and tamely become a slave.

It was said by Admiral Porter, and the declaration will bear repeating, that "a pin is worth fighting for if it involves a principle."[56]

The announcement of the American admiral is eminently American, and will do for all nations and tribes of men. It is as applicable to individuals as to nations, to workingmen as to princes, to labor organizations as to states—but a miserable, subsidized, monopolistic press, and a miserable gang of politicians, who fawn about the rich men and lick the boots of millionaires, never discuss the principle which occasions strikes, but are eternally denouncing strikes and

† Published in *Locomotive Firemen's Magazine,* vol. 14, no. 8 (August 1890), 711–712.

upholding those whose tyrannies are productive of strikes, and of such publications, *Frank Leslie's Weekly* is a notable example.

Some months since, this paper, discussing "the cost of strikes," said:

> The prime lesson for all workingmen to learn is that the only true path to freedom lies through an increasing command by each individual of the capital essential to his own employment. He who does not attain this must always find himself compelled to submit to the direction of others in all the little methods of his labor, and dependent on the will of others for the opportunity to work at all.

That is to say that it is money that secures "freedom," and without this money "workingmen" will find themselves "compelled to submit to the direction of others," depending "on the will of others for the opportunity to work at all."

Such is the logic of the organ of moneybags. It places the workingman without money just where the Negro was before Sumter's guns were fired—absolutely "dependent on the will of others" to accept such terms and treatment as "others" might dictate.

It would be impossible to consign American workingmen to a lower level of degradation. It places them at the bottom. It makes them the "mudsills" of the social, political, and business fabric. It is *caste* pure and simple—aristocracy and autocracy combined. Rights, privileges, prerogatives, liberty, independence fall prostrate in the presence of "capital."

Take a body of workingmen, employed by a capitalist. Their wages compel them to wear rags, to inhabit hovels, and to subsist upon insufficient and often offensive food. They know they are systematically robbed; they know, and the world knows, that their impoverished condition is the result of the piratical greed of their employers. The outraged men demand an increase of pay, simply to better their condition; the demand relates to the mitigation of human suffering. The men would have better clothes, food, and shelter. They would get out of the mud. They appeal to their employer for a fraction more of the wealth they create, which he is appropriating. The demand is denied. The employer's ears are deaf to all appeals. His heart is adamant. He robs and increases his wealth. The picture is not overdrawn, not overcolored. The world knows it is truthful. Under such conditions the alternatives are submit or strike, and under such circumstances the press, the pulpit, the rostrum, Congress, and the legislature, the public meeting, all, all should thunder approval of a strike. But, says the monopolistic, subsidized press, of which *Frank Leslie's Weekly* is of the meanest:

Visionaries will always be rising up and earning a cheap notoriety as friends of wageworkers, by promising them some shorter road than this to individual freedom. These visionaries, however, will generally be found to be merely using their cunning advice to others as a means to make themselves capitalists, even though the nostrum by whose sale they become capitalists in their own right be a recommendation to others to become capitalists by associated hocus pocus.

The "visionaries" are the men who, receiving 75 cents or $1 a day (often less than the amount named), demand more pay. The *practical* men are, in every instance, according to the monopolistic press, the men who refuse to be just, who refuse the workingman fair wages, who denounce labor organizations as "associated hocus pocus."

It does not matter. There is now a labor press. There are labor agitators, as there were in 1770 and 1776 revolutionary agitators, as there were abolition agitators at a later date. They were called "visionaries," but they were, nevertheless, clear-sighted, and saw coming events. The labor agitators of the present would prevent strikes, just as American patriots before the American Revolution would have prevented war. They asked for justice; it was denied—then came the strike of '76. There was misery, sacrifices, death, but out of it all came liberty and independence.

Let it not be forgotten that there is something far more deplorable than strikes. It is a condition when men, subjugated and degraded, accept chains without protest. It does not matter how starry may be your flag, it does not matter how glorious may be your traditions, how boundless your country—indeed, the more highly wrought the eulogies of such things, the weaker becomes hyperbole in seeking to depict the condition of degraded men in the midst of such surroundings—men who are too degraded to strike.

The Supreme Council and the New York Central Strike:
Statement to the Press[†]
August 25, 1890

The question of rendering financial support to the striking Knights of Labor was not considered in any form.[57] That is something with which we have nothing to do. We have given them our moral support and we can go no further. If any of the separate orders composing the federation want to assist the Knights financially they are at liberty to do it. As a matter of fact, the Knights have not asked for anything of the kind, and I believe that Mr. Powderly will be satisfied with our decision, and I certainly do not believe that he expected us to order a strike on behalf of his men.

The position of the strikers who are members of the federation and also of the Knights of Labor is just this: by striking they have acknowledged their allegiances to the Knights and to that body they must look for support. Not having acted under our constitution or by our orders, we cannot help them. They violated our laws in striking, although we coincide that, having subsequently obtained the sanction of the executive board of the Knights, their actions were legalized by that body.

"Does today's action close the connection of the Federation with the [New York] Central strike?" Mr. Debs was asked.

That is a question that cannot be answered at this time. The Council has adjourned subject to the call of the chair. New developments, complications, or entanglements are likely to arise at any time. Some of our firemen, for instance, may be asked to take the places of the strikers. Should they refuse, then they may be discharged. In such an event the services of the supreme body would again be called into play.

---

† Published as "The Debate in the Supreme Council: Some Members Favor of a General Tie-Up," in *Logansport* (Indiana) *Pharos-Tribune*, vol. 15, no. 206 (August 26, 1890), 17.

Clarification of the Supreme Council's Position on the New York Central Strike: Statement to the Press[†]

August 26, 1890

I have seen statements published since the Council adjourned to the effect that the federation would vote financial assistance to the strikers.[58] I suppose these originated because there was a great deal of talk about the Council taking such an action when it became known that a strike had not been ordered by the federation, and also perhaps because of the very strong stand the Council took in endorsing the cause of the striking Knights. But, as in the case of a strike on the Central system by the federation, there is also something in the way in the matter of financial aid. Under the rules of the federation there can be no appropriation for a strike unless the federation directly engages in the strike, and that does not exist in the present case. To call upon our emergency fund, or to levy assessments for a strike, it would be necessary first that one or more of the orders represented in the federation should be engaged in a strike, and second, that the Supreme Council should sustain the strike by the holding of just such a meeting as you have just seen held here. So you will see that it is impossible for the federation as a body to vote financial aid as the case stands. This does not prohibit the members of the different orders from giving as individuals if they so desire, and no doubt many of them will. I understand the Knights of Labor are well equipped in a financial way for the present struggle with the New York Central. We are thoroughly in sympathy with Mr. Powderly and his men and think they have justice on their side in the fight. We have given them as strong an endorsement as lay in our power, and have gone as far in every particular as the laws of our federation permit.

"What is the aggregate of the protecting fund of the locomotive firemen at the present time?" asked the correspondent.

Something over $100,000. This sum lies in the hands of subordinate lodges subject to the order of the Grand Lodge, and is only used in such an emergency as a strike. I do not now recall the protection funds of the other

---

[†] Published as part of "The Question of Financial Aid" in *Chicago Inter Ocean,* whole no. 6878 (August 27, 1890), 6.

orders in the federation, but there is one thing certain, and that is that not a cent could be appropriated for a strike that has not been endorsed by the Supreme Council.

Promiscuous Striking[†]

September 1890

Tersely stated, a strike is not only a declaration of war, but is war. Here let it be understood that the various orders of railroad employees engaged in the train service of the country deprecate strikes. They hold that strikes should be the last resort. They believe that as a general proposition they can be avoided; that justice can be secured in a vast majority of cases without war—and be it said to the credit of the organizations that their laws do not contemplate strikes except as a last resort, when every means known to diplomacy has failed, and then only when rights, sharply defined and unquestionable, have been denied.

We desire to make such propositions clear, not only to the members of the various organizations, but to railroad corporations as well. It may seem to some paradoxical, but it is true, nevertheless, that while the organizations are organized to strike, as a last resort, they are also organized to exhaust every resource at their command to prevent strikes.

We are led to such reflections by an article in the *Switchmen's Journal* for August, in which an account of the "Illinois Central Strike" is given. The *Journal* points out the matter in controversy, which was the "removal of Superintendent Russell and the reinstatement of Trainmasters Berry and Pushie." In this case, the *Journal* says, "the management naturally asked for reasons which had led the men to demand the removal of Mr. Russell, and these the committee were utterly unable to furnish, and that, too, after a delay of 24 hours." This is the case in a nutshell, and the *Journal* says, "This strike was a monstrous wrong, entered into blindly by some, recklessly by others, and without regard for the laws of the organization," and, it should be added, without regard to the rights and interests of the Illinois Central. In fact, the "monstrous wrong,"

† Published in *Locomotive Firemen's Magazine,* vol. 14, no. 9 (September 1890), 808–809.

as the *Switchmen's Journal* justly characterizes the strike, relates not only to the wrong done the railroad but to the wrong done the organizations scandalously represented by some of the men engaged in the outrage.

The brotherhood men, with weak protests, deliberately violated the laws of their respective organizations, and that they did make such protests only the more clearly defines their guilt. They knew they were doing wrong, and therefore, with their eyes wide open, they permitted themselves to cast odium upon their organizations.

The organizations of which they were members have well-defined laws relating to grievances. These laws were all shamefully ignored, and the men proceeded to formulate demands which they could not substantiate, and because they were not granted proceeded to "tie up the road" and inflict incalculable losses; the odium of such transactions falls upon the organizations, notwithstanding the wrong perpetrated is in defiance of the laws of such organizations.

We desire, in what we have to say in this matter, to be severely frank. There should be no subterfuges. We stand squarely by the law—its letter and spirit—and we would have every member of our organization do the same. If there are grievances to be adjusted, the laws of the order point out the way to have them redressed. To violate the law is itself a grievance and should be punished with marked severity. Wrongs are not corrected by perpetrating wrongs and we are greatly mistaken if the brotherhood will much longer condone flagrant departures from its laws in such matters.

It frequently occurs that men who are not members of any organization approach men who are members with their grievances. They say in substance: "Here is a grievance—thus and so—if you will give us your help we can succeed," etc. Now then, what is the simple duty of the brotherhood man? Manifestly, it is to say, "If you want to discuss grievances with me, if you want to have the influence of the brotherhood, join the order; otherwise, paddle your own canoe. The order of which I am a member has laws relating to grievances, and methods of procedure, and I am bound to recognize the binding force of such laws and therefore cannot discuss grievances and strikes with you." Instead of this, the brotherhood man ignores his order, its laws, and the obligations it imposes, and permits himself to say to the non-brotherhood man, "Go ahead, we will stand by you." As a result such disgraceful strikes as that on the Illinois Central frequently occur, in which, while the organization is disgraced, the road suffers loss, all of which could have been avoided by a faithful adherence to the laws of the order.

This magazine is the advocate of justice—justice to the membership and justice to the corporation. The railroad company has rights, and the right is sacred wherever found. The Brotherhood of Locomotive Firemen has no law that is not based upon principles of right and justice; no law that countenances wrongdoing. Its entire machinery is constructed to find the right and to eliminate the wrong. It makes no war upon railroad officials until it is demonstrated beyond all cavil that they will not concede righteous demands, and up to that point the brotherhood proceeds in a way which challenges criticism.

It is easy to see if the various brotherhoods permit the membership to join in with non-brotherhood men to inaugurate strikes or to engage in strikes not sanctioned by the laws of the order, confusion, disaster, and humiliation are inevitable. The order at once, and deservedly, loses caste, forfeits confidence, and may be justly regarded as a public enemy, whereas, by an unwavering adherence to the laws its movements wins approval, and it is accounted a public blessing.

As we have intimated, we do not believe the Brotherhood of Locomotive Firemen will much longer condone illegal methods of presenting grievances or helping men to engage in such strikes as that on the Illinois Central and many others now occurring all too frequently for anybody's good. Nor should we be surprised if the laws are so changed as to visit upon those who thus engage in unlawful strikes the penalty of expulsion. The question is becoming a serious one and demands robust treatment.

The Strike on the New York Central[†]
[excerpt]
September 1890

On the night of Friday, August 7, as unexpected as it was sudden, business on the New York Central and Hudson River Railroads from the city of New York to Buffalo was suspended—trains ceased to move, except those carrying the mails. It requires an effort of the mind to grasp the situation. The New York Central and Hudson River Railroad, more properly the New York Central

---

† Published in *Locomotive Firemen's Magazine,* vol. 14, no. 9 (September 1890), 803–805.

system of railroads, owns and leases 1,441 miles of track and employs about 20,000 hands, paying out annually for wages about $10.5 million.

The New York Central is one of the richest, strongest, and best-equipped roads on the continent. It is sometimes called the "Vanderbilt road," and "Vanderbilt" is regarded as a highly expressive synonym of wealth, fabulous wealth—and it certainly does no violence to metaphor to say it means a mountain of gold.

The company has about 900 locomotives and must necessarily have 900 engineers and 900 firemen in constant employment, and it is fair to estimate the total number of engineers and firemen in the employ of the company at 2,000.

In the state of New York the B of LE has 31 divisions and the B of LF 28 lodges, a total of 59 local organizations and a large percentage of the membership of these divisions and lodges, it is presumable, are employed on the Central. It is known that besides members of the organizations named, non-brotherhood men are employed, as also a large number of Knights of Labor. The troubles which led to the strike on the night of the 7th of August seem to have been between the Knights of Labor and the officials of the road, and related . . . chiefly to the discharge of men because they were Knights of Labor, though it is asserted that the officials violated certain pledges relating to promotion and some other minor matters.

After the strike had been inaugurated, in response to the request of T. V. Powderly, general master workman of the Knights of Labor,[59] the chief executive officers of the four orders represented in the federated body visited Buffalo and New York City. While in New York, these representatives of great labor organizations became profoundly impressed with the fact that the demands of the Knights of Labor were just, and the officials of the New York Central and Hudson River Railroad should have promptly recognized Mr. Powderly as the chief executive of the Knights of Labor, and that arbitration, as proposed by Mr. Powderly for the honorable settlement of the strike, should have been conceded by the officials of the road.

This was not done, and because it was not done, and for the purpose of enabling the Supreme Council of the United Orders of Railway Employees to hear all the facts and to take such action as the situation demanded, the Supreme Council was convened . . .

                                    * * *

We have little to do with the whys and wherefores of the discharge of the Knights of Labor employees on the New York Central. The action of the officials may have been justifiable, at least from their standpoint, though the facts warrant a different conclusion. Be this as it may, the discharged men had a right to a hearing, the denial of which by H. Walter Webb[60] exhibits him in the role of a petty tyrant, and the facts are of such consequence that labor organizations should consider them as of vital importance.

But, dismissing such reflections, the Brotherhood of Locomotive Firemen is profoundly concerned in another phase of the subject, the disclosure of which more than compensates for all the trouble experienced by the members of the Supreme Council in their efforts to arrive at honest conclusions concerning the strike.

While in the city of New York, F. P. Sargent, grand master of the Brotherhood of Locomotive Firemen, in the course of an interview with H. Walter Webb, third vice president of the New York Central, said to that official: "Suppose a locomotive fireman, a member of the Brotherhood of Locomotive Firemen, was discharged by Mr. Buchanan, the superintendent of motive power, and suppose the discharged fireman should endeavor to secure reinstatement and not succeeding, a committee should take up his case in accordance with the laws of the brotherhood, and the committee should also fail to secure the man's reinstatement, after which I, as the grand master of the brotherhood, should be called upon to adjust the difficulty with Mr. Buchanan, and should also fail, do I understand you to say, that if I called upon you, you would not treat with me as the chief executive officer of the brotherhood?" To this pointed and important question, Mr. Webb replied: "These cases are all investigated by subordinate officers of the company, and no man is discharged without just cause."

The declaration of Grand Master Sargent is that "Mr. Webb evaded the question and left the impression upon my mind that he would not recognize nor treat with me as the chief executive officer of the Brotherhood of Locomotive Firemen."

Here then, we have the case in a nutshell. This H. Walter Webb, who has money which he never earned and by virtue of which he holds a petty office and plays tyrant, has given the Brotherhood of Locomotive Firemen to understand that should he or any of his underlings wreak their revenge upon members of the brotherhood, he, Webb, would not recognize its grand chief executive officers for the purpose of having justice done; in a word, H. Walter Webb, acting for the New York Central and Hudson River Railroad, places himself and his road on record in line with the policy of Austin Corbin.

There is no escape from the conclusion that on the New York Central and Hudson River Railroad the policy relating to the recognition of organizations of railroad employees for the purpose of protecting their members against outrages is sharply defined. The declaration is, "we will discharge men at will, and for any cause whatever that may be assigned, or for no cause whatever that would bear investigation, and no organization shall interfere to remedy any wrong inflicted."

Taking this view of the case, of what importance is an organization of railway employees on the New York Central and Hudson River Railroad insofar as the protection of its members from wrongs is concerned? Manifestly, the answer must be that so far as H. Walter Webb can control such matters, such organizations are shorn of their power and their mission is ended.

The facts as stated have been brought out by the strike of the Knights of Labor and warrant the full measure of denunciation contained in the declarations of the Supreme Council.

In conclusion, what of it all? This, the fight against organization of railroad employees, is on. If labor is to win it must federate, combine. In the absence of this, defeat and degradation await the workingman.

Power vs. Power[†]

September 1890

In discussing federation it should be understood that the proposition is power versus power. It presupposes antagonistic forces, the right confronted by the wrong, truth arrayed against error, etc. If there are those who believe that human nature has undergone any radical change since our first parents ate the forbidden fruit, they are, to put it mildly, the victims of a hallucination too serious in influences for jest or raillery. It is the same old human nature, with good and bad elements so intermixed that only indomitable patience, inspired by hopes that will not down at the bidding of adversity, can so mold and fashion it as to bring out its redeeming and conquering power. It was said by Washington: "In peace, prepare for war," a maxim the nations of the earth accept as the very essence of wisdom. Why? Simply because human nature, in its normal condition, is for strife. From savagery up through all the gradations to the highest

---

[†] Published as "Federation" in *United Labor* [Denver], September 28, 1890, unspecified page. Copy in *Papers of Eugene V. Debs* microfilm collection, reel 9.

civilization, we find human nature exhibiting its native characteristics: greed, war, conquest, and oppression; the strong lording it over the weak, crushing and degrading them, compelling them in numberless ways to pay tribute.

I do not antagonize the sentimental forces in operation to sublimate human nature. I have no criticisms to offer in this connection, relating to the operations of the school, the stage, the press, and the rostrum. I simply look abroad and observe, after all their agencies have been accomplished, that the strong, in defiance of their teachings, oppress the weak—rob them, degrade them, and make life a burden to them, and viewing this deplorable picture in panorama, I am as thousands of others are, persuaded that to adjust affairs upon principles of approximate justice, some other agency must be sought and introduced.

I might wish things to be different, I might wish the world could be redeemed from the consequences of vicious human nature by prayer or pulpit oratory, but such is not the order at present. The millennium is not in sight. If the lion nowadays lies down with the lamb, the lamb is inside of the lion. It is sheer folly to talk of peace. The world is in a state of war, of war feeling, and peace exists only because preparations for war restrain the war spirit. The saying is credited to Napoleon that "God is on the side of the heaviest artillery"—in other words, if the weak go against the strong, though the weak are in the right and the strong are wrong, providence does not come to the succor of the weak, they go down.

Whatever may be said of the past, the present is not an age of miracles; on the contrary, it is an age of reason, an age of investigation. There are a thousand students of human affairs today where there was one a hundred years ago. I inquire: Who are these students? And I answer: they are men of the shop as well as men of the school. They study the census reports and say: "Here are 10 million workers, and there are 100,000 capitalists; they are fabulously rich and we are miserably poor. They exact enormous tribute from our earnings, and we pay it." They ask themselves, "Why does this state of things exist?" and the answer comes, "Because we are disorganized, because we act separately when we should act together." This fact has been discussed and workingmen are aroused; organization is going forward. It is a grand beginning. It is the glory of the nineteenth century, distinguishing it from all the centuries that have gone before; with organization many victories have been achieved, but there has been defeat as well—crushing defeat, entailing numberless woes upon the defeated. With forced idleness as the result of defeat, and the poverty, hunger, rags, and dirt it entails, many a man has lost heart and sighed for old bondage. But others, whom defeat inspires with fresh courage, whose bugle-blast is worth 10,000 men, born leaders, inspire new hopes by setting forth the fact, though one organization was defeated, if all the organizations having interests at stake had federated for the fight, victory would have flashed along the lines of the workingmen and perched upon their banners.

Is it required to demonstrate self-evident propositions? Is it demanded that I should prove that the sun shines when he mounts to meridian glory in a cloudless sky? Shall I stand in the presence of Niagara and discuss the proposition that water flows downhill? I do not care to occupy space in that way. If organizations of workingmen, having interests in common, will organize and federate, I believe the day of their defeat in any contest with the common enemy is past and gone forever. I am persuaded that federation is not only the best thing, but the only thing that can solve the labor problem, when the toiler demands his fair share of the wealth he creates.

I have at this writing no desire to discuss methods of federation. Certainly any system is better than none at all, and the discussion of the best system can be postponed to the time when all organizations of laboring men have determined that federation is essential to success. And to this it is coming. Of the fact, I do not permit myself to indulge a doubt. I do not permit myself to assume there will be no setbacks, no halting, division of counsels, wranglings here and there. Human nature will get in its work. There will be kickers and croakers, but the grand army of workers will advance. The line of march is to higher elevations of thought and purpose. There will be no return to the "fleshpots of Egypt."[61]

In a matter which is serious, from alpha to omega, I, too, would be serious. I see little opportunity for sentiment. I recognize the fact that the battle is on. Without egotism I have a fair comprehension of the power of opposing forces; but on the other hand, I comprehend the power and purposes of the federated army of workers. As they achieve success I see them better paid; living in better, brighter, and happier homes; vines climb around the porch, flowers bloom in the garden, there is music in the parlor, and there are pictures on the wall. It is the American workingman's home secured to him by the omnipotent power of organization and federation. On the other hand, if federation fails, if those who advocate it overestimate its power for good, if recognition and arbitration, compromise and concession cannot be secured by federation, then what? History will repeat itself, and on American soil the Pharaohs of oppression will be taught a lesson, the contemplation of which, even at this distance, is well calculated to thrill the mind with horror, for

> Often do the spirits of great events
> Stride on before the events
> And in today already walks tomorrow[62]

The Machine and the Man[†]

October 1890

To declaim against the machine is futile. The world will not only not listen, but it will adjudge the one who protests against the machine a crank. There are those who will listen when attacks are made upon men, when they are denounced as "tramps," as "paupers" who needed to be watched and who ought to be under constant surveillance, who will look upon poverty and all the ills and woes which accompany penury and destitution with stolid indifference, but let anyone attempt to show that the machine is responsible in any degree for the privations and distress which prevails in the ranks of workingmen, and they become intensely aroused and at once go off half-cocked, and in many a rounded period of skyscraping panegyric laud and magnify the machine. They point to the triumphs of the machine and the world, agape, listens and applauds. The result of this deifying the machine, for such it is, to an alarming extent, is to depreciate the man. In this connection we introduce the following from *The Laster,* which we suggest is well worthy of consideration:

> It is questionable, says John Stuart Mill, speaking of labor-saving machines, "if all the mechanical inventions yet made have lightened the day's toil of any human being." The reason is plain: it is not because of a desire to shorten hours of labor or lighten the work of the toiler that machinery is purchased, but because so many men will not be needed, so much more can be gotten out of so much less workmen, and so much faster will the employer get rich. Machinery and invention is good considered in itself, but, like the abuse of a great many other good things, the abuse of machinery entails many evils. The workmen do not share in its advantages; they fall to the employer alone.
>
> The industrial classes should therefore insist that they receive a share of the benefits of invention and machinery, and in no other way can it be better accomplished than by a shortening of the hours of labor. It is but just to ask that the hours of labor be reduced from time to time, in the same proportion as machinery supplements manual labor in the production of wealth. The danger that threatens the industrial world of this century is that the workman may become the slave of machinery, instead of machinery becoming the servant of the workman. In other words,

† Published in *Locomotive Firemen's Magazine,* vol. 14, no. 10 (October 1890), 870–871.

labor falls under the control of a machinery monopoly, which is as much to be dreaded as a land, coal, oil, or any of the other monopolies.

In the foregoing the case is stated in a nutshell. The point is clearly made. The machine lightens no man's toil; it has not reduced the hours of toil—such is not the mission of the machine. The machine is "labor saving" because it displaces men who want to work and must work or starve.

One machine does the work of many men. Capital is in love with the machine; was it ever in love with the man? *The Laster* says, "It is not because of a desire to shorten hours of labor or lighten the work of the toiler that machinery is purchased, but because so many men will not be needed, so much more can be gotten out of so much less workmen, and so much faster will the employer get rich."

Can this statement be clearly demonstrated? Is it a fact? Can figures make it so plain that "a wayfaring man, though a fool, need not err?"[63] It will be conceded that there are machines costing, we will say, $5,000 which, with the attention of one man, will do the work of 20 men. In that case 19 men are relieved, set adrift. We will suppose the machine will last ten years; that money is worth 6 percent interest; that it costs 1 percent a year for repairs, and that wages for workingmen are $1.50 a day. We will take a period of ten years for our illustration: There stands the factory of Doe, Roe & Co. It employs 20 men at $1.50 a day—300 days a year—amount paid out for wages in ten years, $90,000. Now then, the firm introduces a machine costing $5,000, which is operated by one man at $1.50 a day. In making the calculation, we must take into consideration the interest at 6 percent on the investment, which in ten years would be $3,000; we must also allow 1 percent a year for repairs, which in ten years would amount to $500, and the work of one man at $1.50 a day, which in ten years would amount to $4,500. Tabulated the account would stand as follows:

20 men at $1.50 a day, 10 years		$90,000
Machine, original cost	$5,000	
6 percent interest, 10 years	3,000	
1 percent, repairs, 10 years	500	
Wages one man, 10 years	4,500	13,000
Clear gain to Doe, Roe & Co.		$77,000

We are not unmindful of the fact that machinery has diversified labor, and that it has created industries. We are not assailing the machine, we simply say that it has not lightened the workingman's toil nor reduced his hours of labor. So far the workingman is not the beneficiary of the machine. The time has arrived for a change, and the change must be in the reduction of the hours constituting a day's work, without any consequent reduction in wages. This done, and the workingman would share in the blessings conferred by the machine. In the first place, by enabling those in forced idleness to obtain employment—necessarily so. Suppose there is a job of work to be done requiring 1,000 hours; 100 men working ten hours a day accomplish it in one day; reduce the hours from ten to eight, and it requires 125 men one day to perform the work; as a consequence, there would be employment for 25 men, who otherwise would be idle. Suppose the 25 men had been reduced to idleness by the machine; then, in that case, the reduction in the hours of labor would compensate for the reduction of the number of men caused by the machine. As the case now stands, the machine helps the rich and not the poor. This is wrong from every possible point of view. To inaugurate idleness is a wrong of such colossal proportions that it cannot be contemplated without a shudder. And in proportion, as the machine displaces men, the wrong takes deeper root and extends its cancerous fangs in all directions. To rejoice over the triumphs of the machine without demanding righteous compensations to the workingman is madness.

Locomotive Engineers and Federation[†]

November 1890

In a recent issue of the *National Car and Locomotive Builder* there appears an article captioned "Locomotive Engineers and Federation."

The article in question was written in the interest of railroad companies. This crops out in the opening paragraph as follows:

> The Brotherhood of Locomotive Engineers will meet in convention at Pittsburgh this month, and the delegates assembled will be called upon to settle a matter that is of considerable importance to railroad companies.

---

† Published in *Locomotive Firemen's Magazine*, vol. 14, no. 11 (November 1890), 965–967.

Here we have it stated that federation is of "considerable importance to railroad companies."

The statement is true. But why is federation of "considerable importance to railroad companies?" In answer we should say that federation is of "considerable importance to railroads," just as in 1770 the federation of the colonies was of "considerable importance" to the British.

Now, it will be remembered, and we commend the historic fact to the *National Car and Locomotive Builder,* that in that dark period of the nation's history, Tories and British emissaries tried to defeat federation. They favored kingly rule. They were in league with the English aristocracy. They said federation is of "considerable importance to England," and as they were trying to visit English oppression upon the colonies, they sought to defeat federation. These Tories used arguments against the federation of the colonies in many regards similar to those put forth by the *National Car and Locomotive Builder.* In Virginia, Pennsylvania, and New York the Tories said, "Why federate with such little, weak, and unimportant colonies as Rhode Island, Delaware, and Connecticut?" In the little colonies the Tories changed their tactics and said, "If you federate with the great colonies they will destroy you; your influence will be so small as not to be recognized by them." These enemies of federation were working for England, just as the *National Car and Locomotive Builder* is working for the railroad companies. Let us see if it is not so. The *National Car and Locomotive Builder* says:

> The proposal to make the Brotherhood of Locomotive Engineers a part of a federated organization of railroad men has been for years urged upon the engineers by the weaker orders of railroad men. In the Eastern states the prevailing sentiment among engineers is to remain independent, but the federation idea is reported to have taken such firm hold of Western men that they are ready to fight the battle for change at the coming meeting. It is easy to understand the motives of the brotherhoods of firemen, conductors, brakemen, switchmen, etc., in seeking for a coalition with the engineers, for it is the weak seeking the aid of the strong, but we entirely fail to understand what equivalent the weaker orders are prepared to give to the strong to pay for the sacrifice that would be made if the engineers undertook to make the cause of all railroad men their own.

There you have the old Tory argument to defeat the federation of the colonies when fighting the battles of liberty and independence. It is an appeal to the basest passions of human nature, an effort to array one class of workingmen, with identical interests involved, against other classes, because they are "weak." It is the argument, as we have said, of the Tories in favor of British rule, used now in favor of railroad companies and against the interests of railroad employees.

Quite likely "it is easy to understand the motives of the brotherhoods of firemen, conductors, brakemen, and switchmen." What is the motive? Is it dishonorable? Is it a motive that should occasion a blush or demand an apology? Admit as a fact, or for argument, what the *National Car and Locomotive Builder* asserts. What of it? Let it be said that the firemen, conductors, brakemen, and switchmen do appeal to the engineers to federate, because the engineers are strong. What of it? Did not the little colonies appeal to the great colonies to federate in 1770 because they were strong? Did the great colonies say to the little colonies, "We will not federate with you because you are small and weak?" No, never! Their interests were mutual and it required them all to achieve emancipation, and never in all of that eight years' war, from the time he drew his sword at Cambridge till he sheathed it at Yorktown, did George Washington tell the weak colonies to "mind their own business," intimating that he could achieve victory without them.

But as a matter of fact, while the Brotherhood of Engineers is great and strong and influential, it is not as great and strong and influential as the federated orders—the firemen, the conductors, the brakemen, and the switchmen. Nor can the Brotherhood of Engineers do more for the federated orders than the federated orders can do for it.

Let us prudently examine this phase of the subject.

The Brotherhood of Engineers claim a membership of 27,000. Admit it. The federated orders claim a membership of 50,000. Admit it, and the federated orders are stronger by 23,000 men.

These figures disclose the fact that the weak are not appealing to the strong.

Can it be said that the federated orders are appealing to the engineers at all?

Unfortunately for the argument of the *National Car and Locomotive Builder,* organ of railroad companies, it has put upon record the denials of its own assertion. It says the demand for federation comes from "Western men," members of the B of LE, who "are ready to fight the battle for change."

Here we have it, that intelligent, wide awake, progressive members of the engineers' brotherhood are demanding federation, and they know "what equivalent" the federated orders "are prepared to give" to them in case of trouble.

The *National Car and Locomotive Builder* prates of the "skillful workman and the crude laborer," for the purpose of establishing antagonisms between men who move railroad trains, and without whose assistance trains would not move at all. It is an argument in favor of caste, of aristocracy in labor. It is an exhibition of servility, totally unworthy of consideration.

Again, says the *National Car and Locomotive Builder*:

> Transcendent moral sentiment calls for the strong to give their support to
> the weak on the abstract principle of common humanity; but individuals
> have not generally responded to the high requirements of sacrifice, even
> when they are united as a brotherhood. When men's interests cease to
> be identical discord is certain to ensue, and discord is the beginning of
> disruption.

It should be said, at the expense of repetition, that the "weak" are not asking
support of the engineers upon any "moral sentiment" or principle, abstract or
concrete. It is held that the interests of all railroad employees, engaged in moving trains, are mutual, reciprocal, common, interchangeable. It is true. These
mutual interests must of necessity exist and continue as long as trains require
engineers, conductors, brakemen, firemen, and switchmen. They ought to be
in the most harmonious relations. Anything less is in the interest of the corporation, which profits by their dissensions, and to create such disagreements and
strife appears to be the ambition of the *National Car and Locomotive Builder*.

Again, says the *National Car and Locomotive Builder*:

> Should a federated organization of railroad employees, by a consolidation
> with the locomotive engineers, be made sufficiently powerful to present
> unreasonable demands on railroad companies with the probability of suc-
> cess, the tendency would be to level pay upward. The engineer would be
> called upon to lift the condition of the brakeman, the switchman, and
> probably the trackman, to his own level, and take his share in paying the
> expense in any fights necessary to bring about this elevating process.

In the foregoing, the objection is made to federation that the engineers
would be called upon "to help level pay upward; to lift the condition of the
brakeman, the switchman, and probably trackman, to his own level," etc. In
this, the basest instincts that degrade human nature are appealed to.

The engineers, having reached success in any given conflict with the corporation by the united efforts of all employees engaged in the train service, are
sought to be swerved from the pathway of honor because of the part that they
might be asked to level up the pay of other men as necessary to the train service
as themselves; the assumption being that in such cases, in fact, in all cases, the
demands "on railroad companies" would be "unreasonable."

The idea is that engineers are entirely independent of all other men engaged in the train service of the country, that no mutual interests exist, and that
federation on the part of engineers with firemen, conductors, switchmen, and

brakemen would be a proceeding without one redeeming feature. "It seems natural," says the *National Car and Locomotive Builder*, "for every man to magnify the importance of his vocation. It would be difficult to find a conductor who did not consider that his duties were more important than those performed by an engineer, and that he ought to be paid accordingly. Switchmen and brakemen reflect that their occupation is more dangerous than that of an engineer and that their pay ought to be based on the extra hazard to life and limb. Those interested in leveling pay upward find no difficulty in making arguments to support that view of the case." Such stuff can influence only those who are totally devoid of sympathy for workingmen, who antagonize "leveling pay upward" and are helping those who level pay downward, and seek to degrade labor.

To level pay upward is to level up humanity, to level up home, women, and children, to enable workingmen to obtain fair wages and live as becomes citizens of a free country, and those who oppose such leveling-up processes as railroad employees have adopted, by whatever other names they may be known, are corporation parasites, fleas in the hair of the corporation dog.

In the case of the *National Car and Locomotive Builder*, its purpose seems to be, is in fact, to array the engineers against other men with whom they must forever be in the closest association. To them it says: "The engineers are now the aristocrats among labor organizations, and their members have never failed in obtaining justice from railroad companies when their demands appealed to popular support." Here is an exhibition of flunkeyism rarely equaled, and fortunate it is that ten thousand engineers, members of the B of LF, treat such declarations with becoming disdain. They are men who cannot be cajoled and imposed upon by the paid sycophants of corporations, but who know the right and dare defend it. They have faith in their fellow workmen; they know the value of conductors, firemen, brakemen, and switchmen; they throw to the winds the aristocratic ideas of vocation and regard honest, self-respecting men their equals. They know the future is full of perils to organized labor, and that the only hope is in federation.

Already, ominous clouds are gathering along the horizon of labor. In railroad affairs stockholders want larger dividends and bondholders want more interest. High officials level pay upward for themselves, and downward for employees. If the men who do the work are to receive fair pay and fair treatment, they must come into close, compact union—nothing else—nothing less will answer the demand. Federation is feasible, honest, just, and right. To approach men, as does the *National Car and Locomotive Builder*, with despicable propositions—appealing to low and vulgar prejudices—is an exhibition of sycophantic fealty to corporations which honest engineers will be quick to discover and rebuke.

Parties[†]

November 1890

———

The history of parties, factions, cabals, cliques, juntos, leagues, and alliances would doubtless be exceedingly interesting. If the historian should begin at the beginning, his researches, we conclude, would antedate the deluge. Indeed, there seems to be good reason for believing that in heaven itself, at one period remote, a party under the leadership of Satan existed, whose ambition it was to supplant God himself in controlling the affairs of the universe.

> To set himself in glory 'bove his peers,
> He trusted to have equall'd the Most High,
> If he opposed: And with ambitious aim
> Against the throne and monarchy of God
> Raised impious war in Heav'n, and battle proud
> With vain attempt—[64]

We mention such things merely to emphasize the fact that the existence of parties, whether good or bad, is not a modern invention. Manifestly there was a party largely in the majority which took no stock in Noah's declaration that a deluge was coming. He preached it for a hundred years, and during the entire period was showing his faith by his works, for he was all the time getting his ark ready for the impending storm.[65] And from the time that the tribes formed a sort of a cooperative association and attempted to build a tower which would reach to heaven, and as a result had their language so confounded that orders could no longer be given, there have been parties dividing the inhabitants of the earth.[66]

We are of the opinion, whether a man gives the subject a casual thought or devotes to it years of investigation, he will find that parties are just now more numerous than ever before since history was rescued from fable. He will find that every nation, tribe, kingdom, and tongue is a distinct party—a primal condition

———

† Published in *Locomotive Firemen's Magazine,* vol. 14, no. 11 (November 1890), 972–974.

which the centuries have neither changed nor modified. But the investigator will find that as civilization has subdued barbarism and savagery, parties have multiplied, and now, whether it be sunrise or noon, in civilization he will find more parties in existence than in any other period of the world's history. It may be interesting to inquire why? We think the answer easy enough. It is because the human mind has been in the process of emancipation, and when most enfranchised, when the semblance of a shackle no longer appears, when the disenthrallment is complete and man expands to the full stature of a free man, there will be found the greatest number of parties. It is said of creation and of the Creator that while He bound all nature fast in fate, He left free the human will. That may have been the intention, but so far the human will has not been free, and of all the slavery that an inscrutable God ever permitted to curse the earth, that of the enslavement of the mind, the will, is the most abhorrent.

The immortal Irish orator, John Philpot Curran,[67] on one occasion while pleading for the liberty of his client and speaking "in the spirit of British law," which he said, "makes liberty commensurate and inseparable from British soil," said,

> No matter in what language his doom may have been pronounced, no matter what complexion incompatible with freedom, an Indian or an African sun may have burnt upon him; no matter in what disastrous battle his liberty may have been cloven down; no matter with what solemnities he may have been devoted upon the altar of slavery; the first moment he touches the sacred soil of Britain the altar and the god sink together in the dust; his soul walks abroad in its own majesty; his body swells beyond the measure of his chains that burst from around him, and he stands redeemed, regenerated, and disenthralled by the inevitable genius of universal emancipation.

But an Irish judge and an Irish jury did not take Mr. Curran's view of the subject, and his client, because he dared be free on Irish (British) soil, was sentenced to pay a fine of $2,500 and to be imprisoned two years, and to give bond for good behavior in the sum of $10,000. Mr. Curran's client belonged to a party which advocated the liberty of the Irish people and that was his only crime.

It is one thing to break the fetters from the body, but a far different thing to emancipate the mind, the will, the soul, to establish free speech and a free press, a free Bible and a free religion, and when this mind deliverance is secured parties and sects will multiply.

There is a form of freedom which is illusive, the body, the physical man walks abroad, but the tongue is mute and the lips move not to give utterance to sentiments showing that the mind shares the freedom of the body. Poets have sung of the "eternal spirit of the chainless mind."[68]

The figure is strong and captivating. It refers to what ought to be rather than to what is. In what land, blessed with even twilight rays of civilization, can be found a healthy intellect which does not realize this existence of penalties ready to be imposed upon opinions if men dare express them, give them to the world? In one land the penalty is dungeons, in another exile, in another death, and in others social, political, and religious ostracism. Who are the world's heroes? Accepting standard theories, they are the Caesars and Bonapartes whose monuments are human bones and skulls, and whose bloody tracks, from battlefields to their palaces, are the records of their rise and fall. At their command the nations bled until

> . . . Bloodier than the torrent flow
> Of Iser, rolling rapidly,[69]

all of the rivers ran crimson to the sea. But the real heroes of the world are the men who have battled for the emancipation of the mind, who have warred for the sovereignty of the soul, who have given thought and opinion and speech the freedom of the universe. It is not required to build monuments of bronze or brass to perpetuate the name and fame of such men. We would as soon think of building a monument to bear testimony to the glories of the noonday sun. They are the pathfinders for men living and coming, who will strike down penalties for opinions and emancipate the mind—

> For Freedom's battles oft begun, s
> Bequeath'd from bleeding sire to son,
> Tho' baffled oft, is ever won,[70]

and the multiplication of parties shall bear testimony that the "thorny stem of time" has at last budded, blossomed, and borne the delicious fruit of mental emancipation.

In this connection we are led to inquire how it happens that within the past decade we have in this country what is known as a labor party. Is it not the result of mind growth and mind emancipation? Does it not betoken the dawn of a new era? There is a labor party. There is a distinct labor literature. It may be said, and it is doubtless true, that the labor party as yet is crude, somewhat discordant. To admit such things is to compliment the working-men of the country, because it is proof positive that workingmen have minds of their own and that their differences of opinion relate to methods rather than purpose, and he is a very superficial observer who does not see in this success instead of defeat. If we were required to point out a sign of the times triumphantly indicative of the success of the labor party in the United States, we should refer at once to the deliberations going forward in the ranks of labor. Propositions are exhaustively analyzed. Obstacles arise and are removed. Breaks occur, faction impedes progress, rivalry disconcerts plans, but in spite of embarrassments and barriers organization proceeds, the party grows, and victory invites to effort.

There are those in labor organizations who occasionally evince distrustfulness in ultimate triumph because of the large number of workingmen who do not come in and keep step to the music of organization. We do not share in their doubts because we believe in the triumph of right, justice, and truth over ignorance, prejudice, and superstition. We believe that old ideas are to give place to the new. We believe in the final emancipation of mind. We believe that error and the idols of error are to go down, not immediately, but ultimately, as certain as that the sunshine will dispel fogs, or that draining a marsh will decrease malaria. It should be remembered that the idea of organizing a labor party is recent. Its years can be counted on one's fingers. Everywhere is missionary ground. The press has but just begun its work. Old parties, barnacled and moss-covered, stand in its way and are jealous of its progress, but millions of men are reading today where but hundreds were reading yesterday and but tens the day before, and as they read and meditate the scales fall from their eyes and fetters from their minds. The work of emancipation goes grandly on. More drums are beating, more banners are flying, more men are coming into line. The labor party grows. Labor is organizing. Lodges are multiplying, workingmen are coming together, and now comes the battle shout of "Federation." Men whose eyes first touched by the mighty oculist abroad in the land saw "men as trees walking"[71] now see clearly that men are marching with stately strides toward the goal of triumph. Men who but yesterday complained that when the angel came down and troubled the waters they could not step in and be healed because no one was there to help them are now standing erect, cured.[72] All the pools of thought have been agitated and the commotion continues, nor is the angel to take his flight until the mind is completely unfettered and walks abroad knowing no master but reason, sanctified by conviction.

We care not how many parties exist; only those will remain which have a mission to accomplish. Labor has a mission. It is the mission of self-emancipation. For untold centuries it has appeared bareheaded and barefooted on all the highways of progress and civilization. But it is going to wear hats and shoes in the future. In the past it has fed the world; in the future it will feed itself more abundantly. In the past it has built palaces for kings, aristocrats, monopolists, and millionaires. In the future it will build pleasant homes for itself. In the past labor has woven broadcloths and silks for others and been content with rags. In the future it will wear good clothes, and will have its equitable share of the wealth it creates.

> There's a good time coming, boys,
>   A good time coming.
> The pen shall supersede the sword,
> And Right, not Might, shall be the lord.
>   In the good time coming.
> Worth, not Birth, shall rule mankind.
>   And be acknowledged stronger;
> The proper impulse has been given;
>   Wait a little longer.[73]

The Knights of Labor and the Right of Organization[†]
November 1890

I propose, in this communication to united labor, to discuss two propositions: First, the Knights of Labor, as a labor organization, and second, the New York Central Railroad Company, as a corporation.

Stated in law phrase, the case is The Organization vs. The Corporation.

Now I hold that the whole body of organized labor throughout the United States and Canada, in England, and on the continent, regardless of trade or calling, must be in the very nature of things in sympathy with the labor organization known as the Knights of Labor.

In saying this I am not unmindful of human feasibility. I have no patience with perfectionists. I am not in sympathy with optimists, nor yet with pessimists. I do not believe everything is ordered for the best, nor for the worst; in fact, I do not believe things are ordered at all by an overruling providence.

It is far better to believe, I think, that certain immutable laws exist, which as certainly relate to *meum et tuum*—"mine and thine"—as to the solar system.

---

† Published as "The Knights of Labor" in *United Labor* (Denver), November 8, 1890.

I do not care to bandy words with creed-makers and bigots. They are not lovely to my eye. They make laws and administer them. They permit neither change of venue nor appeal, and here let it be understood that I do not refer exclusively to religious bigots, and, while the term "creed" has a theological twang, I choose to use it as a matter of "belief" on the part of railroad corporations, which, like all corporations, having no souls, their worship of mammon excludes workingmen from their temples. It is the creed of the English landlords in Ireland, a creed as devoid of humanity as a hungry tiger. As well hunt for sunflowers at the poles or for ice water in Dante's Hades, as to expect corporations to make a move, so much as the fraction of an inch, toward helping men to better their conditions who work for a living—their overworked and underpaid employees. I do not say there are not exceptions, but at this writing not one occurs to my mind.

I do not propose to discuss incidents connected with the recent strike of the Knights of Labor on the New York Central. I do not write for the purpose of crimination and recrimination. I do not propose to assert that the Knights made no mistakes in ordering and in conducting the strike. I know of no war since the world began that generals in command did not make mistakes. I know of no great enterprise—and the reader is welcome to search the list—free from mistakes.

Things are right or wrong entirely independent of the mistakes men may make.

The organization of workingmen is fundamentally, inherently, an inalienable right. In the United States of America the right is conceded. It is fixed irrevocably in the constitution and statute. It follows that the employees on the New York Central had a right, unquestioned and absolute, to organize and become a part of the great order of Knights of Labor—just as other employees on the New York Central had a right to join the brotherhoods of engineers, firemen, switchmen, conductors, and trainmen.

Having a right to organize, the organization necessarily possessed certain rights. It had the right to discuss wages, the hours of work, and questions relating to honorable treatment. It had the right to protest when the corporation inaugurated a policy of injustice. In a word, the organization possessed all the rights relating to self-preservation. It will be seen at a glance if labor organizations do not possess such rights, they are of little value to their members insofar as protection against wrong is involved.

Such rights as I have imperfectly outlined, the Knights of Labor on the New York Central asserted. They discussed labor questions, increased the membership of their assemblies, protested against wrongs inflicted by the corporation, sought redress in various ways which have the approval of all honest men, and when thrust aside by a haughty, unprincipled, and soulless corporation, struck.

In the war thus inaugurated the Knights of Labor were defeated; victory was with the corporation.

There are those, I doubt not, who will rush to the conclusion that because the corporation defeated the Knights of Labor, the corporation was right and the Knights of Labor wrong. To arrive at such a conclusion is to endorse every act of tyranny and oppression that blackens the pages of history. It reverses every maxim of justice. It dethrones truth. It crowns and glorifies wrong. It makes civilization a sham and every high aspiration of humanity a miserable vagary.

I take no stock in the doctrine that might is right. It is not true. To assume it and act upon it is a crime against humanity which defies pardon.

The colonists, defeated at Bunker Hill, in no sense detracted from the righteousness of their cause, and so on through all the poverty, wretchedness, and gloom of the revolutionary war, until at last defeats, by virtue of victory, made the horrors of Valley Forge a [more] sublime picture in the revolutionary panorama than Yorktown.

The organization of Knights of Labor on the New York Central had certain rights, and because these rights were exercised the corporation decided to bring to bear upon it for the purpose of its annihilation all of its vast resources. The penalty which the corporation imposed with relentless enmity and cruelty was that the Knights of Labor, because they were Knights of Labor, should be remanded to idleness, should be driven from their homes, should be made, insofar as the corporation had the power to execute its infernal hatred, tramps and mendicants, the victims of hunger and cold, and left to drive wither mattered not.

The question just here arises: "What is the view of the subject organized labor takes?"

It may not be a matter of special concern to the corporation. Flushed with victory, it points to the sufferings and humiliations of the Knights of Labor, and by its actions tells them such will be your fate if you should dare to resent wrong and oppression, as did the Knights of Labor.

In view of such facts, what ought to be the decision of all other organizations of railroad employees on the New York Central, and every other railroad in the land? I have no hesitancy in answering the question. It should be a decision of unqualified endorsement of the rights of organized labor to oppose the tyrannies practiced by corporations—from the action of the small boss to the highest official. If this right is not asserted and maintained by every means workingmen can devise, by protest, arbitration, and strike, then the epitaph of labor organizations can be written now, as well as when the corporation has its iron-clad hoof upon its prostrate form. The individual laborer finds himself in the world with the absolute necessities upon him which nature imposes. He must have food, shelter, and clothing. Society, as it is organized, is scarcely less autocratic. It makes demands and inflicts penalties. The workingman marries, surrounds himself with dependents. His only capital is his labor, his time, his skill, his ability to work. It is not surprising, therefore, that the workingman should feel timid. His responsibilities are great and he feels their weight. The fact is one of transcendent glory. It crowns the workingman with honor and dignity worthy of American citizenship. But acting by himself, the obligations he is under to his family make him timid. To him, idleness is something in the nature of a scourge; as a consequence, the workingman remains at his task in spite of indignities. To stop working is to invite starvation. To protest against the autocratic orders of the corporation is to invite exile.

The corporation is familiar with all the facts. It has measured the horsepower of hunger pangs. It has estimated with approximate accuracy not only what a workingman will give for his life, but to what degradations he will submit, that his wife and children might not be homeless wanderers upon the face of the earth.

Taking advantage of these noble traits of character, the corporation is eternally seeking to down the organization. The organization is a ceaseless menace to the corporation, but acting by itself is almost certain of defeat. But the defeat of the organization in any battle for right does not prove that the right was with the victors—and it means the battle will be fought again. I have faith in the enlightening influence of the labor press and in the conquering power of truth.

I am of the opinion that in the march of progressive ideas a way will be found to bring all railroad employees into harmonious alliance. The obstacles in the war are ignorance, bigotry, jealousy, and the lowest order of pride that ever cursed the world.

Aerial navigators say the time is not remote when men will fly, because the principle is in nature. There is no difficulty about power; the question relates to its application. So there is no doubt of the ultimate success of federation, of all workers with an identity of interests, into one great and powerful body. In government the principle is fundamental and it will be found a conquering principle when the workingmen become wise enough to incorporate it into their organizations.

Pictures[†]

December 1890

Professor [Daniel] DeLeon, of Columbia College, in an address before a stenographers' association, said:

> At the time of the establishment of the Republic of America, it would have been a perfectly rational prophecy to have said that the Republic could not last. Madison said that a republic could not be a permanency when any large number of the people were simply cattle. But the Republic has not gone down. Neither did those of Greece and Rome go down at once. Today one man can produce as much as it took a hundred to produce 100 years ago. The same quantity of wealth can be produced in one-fifth of the time. This is through machinery. By steam power the necessary hours of labor have been reduced to one hour as compared with ten. Transportation, giving the means of exchange of commodities, has combined with these to increase the productivity of labor one thousandfold.
>
> In view of this, wealth ought to be the most plentiful thing in the world. But if statistics are approximately true the average laborer does not earn nearly $1 a day. Wealth may have increased in the hands of some, but has not in proportion among the others. There is not enough actual wealth in the United States to supply all its inhabitants for one month. Under the present system the non-productive army is enormous. The middlemen come in also in equal numbers to the producers. All the stores dealing in the same commodity in the same neighborhood are unnecessary and prejudicial to the general good. From this follows the misery of the many and the immorality of the few. This necessitates all the police and soldiers. The people of our Four Hundred, those of Fifth Avenue and Madison Avenue, do not trust one another. They smuggle detectives into their ballrooms to prevent their diamonds being stolen—by whom? By their own guests.

The professor's subject was Bellamyism, and he spoke for the new party, known as "Nationalists." There is not a wrong of which Prof. DeLeon complains that could not be exterminated in five years by the fiat of the ballot, if all honest men could be marshaled under the banner of commonsense reform—a reform

---

† Published in *Locomotive Firemen's Magazine,* vol. 14, no. 12 (December 1890), 1104.

free from vagary, crankism, and utopian follies. For instance, trusts and monopolies could be abolished. The water upon which the people pay enormous dividends could be squeezed out of stocks and bonds; the hours constituting a day's work could be fixed beyond repeal or appeal. Honest men could be elected to make honest laws, and honest officials could be elected to execute them. Why not be practical? Why not use the means at hand to usher in an era of reform? If workingmen would organize and then federate their organizations, land piracy, trust piracy, monopoly piracy, and corporation privacy would cease.

Plan of Federation[†]

December 1890

In the month of September 1888, in the city of Atlanta, the Brotherhood of Locomotive Firemen took the initiative in the great work of bringing the various orders of railway employees, engaged in the train service of railroads, into a federated compact for mutual protection.[74]

In the month of June 1889, in the city of Chicago, the alliance was perfected, and since that time has been in full operation.

The plan of federation as devised at Chicago by the three great brotherhoods—firemen, trainmen, and switchmen—acting under the laws of the Supreme Council, has had numerous opportunities to test its efficiency. So well did it work that at the expiration of the first year of its existence, the young and stalwart Brotherhood of Railway Conductors sought and obtained admission, and now four orders of railway employees, having an aggregate membership of more than 50,000, are in line under the federated flag.

During the year 1890, these four brotherhoods, viz.: the B of LF, the B of RT, the SMAA, and the B of RC, have held conventions. In every convention the plan of federation as devised by the Supreme Council at Chicago in 1889 was *unanimously* endorsed—not a dissenting vote was cast.

Since June 1889, when the Supreme Council was organized, and federation as it exists adopted, a hue and cry went forth that the "plan" was unauthorized.

---

† Published in *Locomotive Firemen's Magazine,* vol. 14, no. 12 (December 1890), 1098.

The assertion was made, and every conceivable charge that stupidity, ignorance, envy, jealousy, or bigotry could wring in was resorted to, to create dissatisfaction and defeat the plan of federation under the Supreme Council. This ungenerous and ungrateful work went steadily forward, laying, insofar as it played at all, directly into the hands of the enemies of organized labor—into the hands of the corporation and in direct and flagrant antagonism to the federated orders.

Now, what of all this opposition? As we have said, every federated order has, within the past three months, unanimously endorsed federation as it exists, and their laws relating to grievances have in every instance been harmonized with the laws of the Supreme Council.

Could the defeat of the opponents of national federation be more overwhelming and crushing? We fail to conceive in what way a more disastrous defeat could have been accomplished.

But this is not all. Under the luminous and vitalizing light of the arguments in favor of protection, which finds its culminating power in federation, the ORC, no longer able to withstand the convincing power of reason, split at Rochester,[75] and one faction reasserted its willingness to scab—to lick corporation dirt and crawl on its belly that it might be in a better condition to be kicked—while the other faction, which having knocked out the "strike clause," continues to assert that it has no power to strike and that its principles have not been changed.

Again: the B of LE finds within its jurisdiction a mighty host of chivalric men who demand federation because they know it is right, who are men of conviction and who have the courage of conviction; who do not quail nor get down into their boots in the presence of Chauncey M. Depew, Andrew Carnegie, Cornelius Vanderbilt, or H. Walter Webb; men who are neither fossils nor fools, but trained trainmen, whose promotion made them neither dizzy nor crazy; men who love their fellow man, like D. J. Brown, the engineer of California,[76] whose splendid words, clarion-toned, have the lifting power of genuine fellowship; such men are pledged to bring the B of LE under the federated flag in due time.

Viewing the situation from our standpoint, we have no grievances to present. The outlook is full of hope, and the banner of federation never floated more proudly in the breeze than now.

Notes

1. The National Grange of the Order of Patrons of Husbandry was founded in 1867 to advocate for agricultural interests, including cooperative grain warehouses and an end to predatory railway pricing policies. The group continues into the twenty-first century, largely as a rural social organization.

2. The Farmers' Alliance was actually made up of three parallel organizations emerging during the second half of the 1870s. An agricultural anti-monopoly movement springing from the Granger movement, the Farmers' Alliance expanded their agenda into the reform of credit and monetary policy. The movement is regarded as providing the organizational nexus of the People's Party of the 1890s.

3. The Louisiana Farmers' Union was a small, regional organization of the 1880s.

4. The Agricultural Wheel was a cooperative farmers' organization that emerged in 1882, in parallel with the three Farmers' Alliance groups and advancing a similar agenda.

5. The Farmers' Mutual Benefit Association was a cooperative organization established in Illinois at the end of 1882.

6. Carnegie's article "Wealth" first appeared as the lead essay in *North American Review*, vol. 148, no. 391 (June 1889), 653–664. Borrowing self-descriptive words from Carnegie's concluding paragraph, the piece was at once widely touted in the bourgeois press as a new "Gospel of Wealth." The essay was subsequently reprinted under that title, with the modified name gaining permanence in 1901 through the eponymous book, *The Gospel of Wealth and Other Timely Essays*. In his essay Carnegie dismissed the idea of "communism" as a failed theory, positing that instead "intense Individualism" had proven itself the motive power behind economic progress. He argued that accumulated wealth in a few hands constituted "a much more potent force for the elevation of our race than if it had been distributed in small sums to the people themselves," and that it was the duty of the wealthy individual to live modestly, provide moderately for those providing service, and to disburse fortunes generously. Charitable aid was to be bestowed in such a way as "to help those who will help themselves; to provide part of the means by which those who desire to improve may do so; to give those who desire to rise the aids by which they may rise; to assist but rarely or never to do all." Carnegie dismissed the poverty and squalor of the daily life of the working class as an unfortunate side effect of the inevitable workings of the labor market.

7. Andrew Carnegie, "The Best Fields of Philanthropy," *North American Review*, vol. 149, no. 397 (December 1889), 682–699.

8. C. Allen Thorndike Rice (1851–1889), the son of a prominent publishing family, purchased the venerable *North American Review* for $3,000 in 1876. A leading Republican who had been tapped as the next ambassador to Russia by President Benjamin Harrison, Rice died at the age of 37, shortly before Debs wrote this piece.

9. Allusion to Matthew 23.

10. Matthew 19:23–24; Mark 10:25; Luke 18:24–25.

11. Luke 16:19–23.

12. Reference to Irish prizefighter John L. Sullivan (1838–1918), nicknamed "The Boston Strong Boy" and crowned as heavyweight champion in 1887.

13. Archaic American slang expression originating in the 1840s and referring to the wealthiest ten thousand citizens of a city.

14. Edward Bellamy, *Looking Backward, 2000–1887* (Boston: Ticknor & Co., 1888), chapter 5.

15. Bellamy, *Looking Backward*, chapter 6. The excised words are "till he reaches the age of fifty-five, but such calls are rarely, in fact almost never, made."

16. Bellamy, *Looking Backward*, chapter 25.

17. Delmonico's of New York City was regarded as one of the nation's top fine-dining experiences during the late 1800s and the first decades of the twentieth century. The local chain maintained a six-story flagship restaurant located at the corner of Beaver and Williams Streets.

18. Rory O'Moore (c. 1600–1655) was an Irish revolutionary who was an organizer of the Rebellion of 1641.

19. The Paris Exposition was a world's fair held from May 6 to October 31, 1889.

20. Carroll Davidson Wright (1840–1909) was a Massachusetts labor statistician who was named the first commissioner of the US Department of Labor in 1885. Wright would also serve as the chairman of the three-member United States Strike Commission named by Congress in 1894 to investigate the circumstances of the American Railway Union's Pullman strike, taking extensive testimony from Gene Debs and other union and company officials.

21. The timing of this long biography of a lesser-known functionary of the Knights of Labor was not accidental, coming amid pressure to bring relevant Local Assemblies of the Knights—who had a significant presence in the ranks of employees of certain Eastern railroad lines—into the Supreme Council's ranks.

22. From "The Shandon Bells" (c. 1835), by Francis Sylvester Mahony (1804–1866).

23. Leonora M. Kearney Barry was actually born August 13, 1849. The family emigrated in 1852.

24. Allusion to "The Old Oaken Bucket," by Samuel Woodworth (1784–1842).

25. Allusion to the eponymous poem by Thomas Moore (1779–1852).

26. From Psalm 126:6.

27. From Ruth 1:16.

28. From Proverbs 25:11.

29. Nero (37–68 AD) was the fifth and final Roman emperor of the Julio-Claudian dynasty.

30. Tiberius (42 BC–37 AD) was the second Julio-Claudian emperor of Rome.

31. Caligula (12–41 AD) was the third Julio-Claudian emperor of Rome.

32. Timur, also known as Tamerlane, (1336–1405) was a Turko-Mongol conqueror.

33. Nader Shah (1698–1747) was a powerful Persian potentate, ruling the country from 1736 until his assassination in 1747.

34. Allusion to Exodus 15:20.

35. The Queen & Crescent was a railway connecting Cincinnati and New Orleans. Trouble erupted early in 1890 over a demand by management that the line's employees terminate their membership in the various railway brotherhoods as a condition of further employment.

36. The Ohio & Mississippi Railroad connected Cincinnati with East St. Louis, Illinois.

37. Debs probably found this widely reprinted snippet in the *Mechanical News* (New York), vol. 20, no. 1 (March 15, 1890), 3.

38. Edgar Erastus Clark (1859–1930) was a former brakeman who became a railroad conductor in 1884 and rapidly rose through the ranks of the Order of Railway Conductors, winning election as grand chief conductor in 1890. He would remain at that post for 16 years, leaving to become a member of the Interstate Commerce Commission (ICC), a job that he continued from 1918 until 1921.

39. Allusion to Jonah 4.

40. Joseph Gruenhut (1840–1902) was a factory and tenement house inspector for the Chicago Health Department and the city's first statistician. A self-proclaimed socialist, Gruenhut gave testimony as a prosecution witness at the 1886 Haymarket trial.

41. From Exodus 9:1.

42. Mary Frances Armstrong (d. 1903) was an instructor at the Hampton Institute in Hampton, Virginia.

43. The Pierian spring figured in Greek mythology as a sacred fountain of knowledge.

44. From *Lalla Rookh*, by Thomas Moore.

45. From "Locksley Hall" (1842), by Alfred Tennyson (1809–1892).

46. "By force of arms."

47. That is, the American Civil War.

48. As part of an 1888 treaty between the United States and China restricting immigration, a total of $276,619 was allotted to compensate Chinese citizens who had been injured by violence in the United States.

49. In July 1853 Martin Costa, a Hungarian refugee who had taken out first papers for citizenship in the United States, was arrested at the Greek city of Smyrna and held in the brig of an Austrian warship for transportation home for trial. The American warship *St. Louis* intercepted the Austrian vessel prior to its departure, heeding claims that Costa was due the protection of the American flag. A day of consular diplomatic negotiation followed, with Costa finally released to the custody of a third party, thereby avoiding deportation.

50. References the reply of General Ethan Allen (1737–1789) to Captain William Delaplace's query as to the source of Allen's authority at the surrender of Fort Ticonderoga on May 9, 1775.

51. First line of an anonymously penned eighteenth-century song, "Begone, Dull Care."

52. Allusion to Ecclesiastes 3:2.

53. Allusion to Psalms 1:3.

54. An adaptation of an inspirational quotation of indefinite origin that emerged during the decade of the 1870s and is today frequently misattributed to Ralph Waldo Emerson

(1803–1882): "Sow a thought and you reap an action; sow an act and you reap a habit; sow a habit and you reap a character; sow a character and you reap a destiny."

55. Samuel Gompers (1850–1924), a cigarmaker by trade who became a Cigarmakers' Union functionary, was one of the earliest and most dedicated adherents of trade union federationism—the alliance of various independent trade unions under a single umbrella organization for the purposes of collective action and the amelioration of jurisdictional disputes. He founded the Federation of Organized Trades and Labor Unions in 1881, reorganized in 1886 as the American Federation of Labor, and headed that organization as its president until his death, save for a one-year interval. Gompers was initially amenable to radical reformist ideas and was supportive of Debs and his agenda of federation of the railway brotherhoods through the early 1890s. Over time he became an outspoken opponent of socialism and independent labor politics, seeking instead to advance pro-labor legislation by forcing Republicans and Democrats to compete against one another as organized labor "supported friends and opposed enemies."

56. A slight misquotation of Admiral David Dixon Porter (1813–1891), who said in a March 1889 newspaper interview, "A pin is worth fighting for, if principle is involved."

57. The matter of a general sympathy strike in conjunction with the Knights of Labor's strike of the New York Central Railroad was considered at a special session of the Supreme Council, convened in Terre Haute at 9 a.m. on August 25, 1890. The motion to conduct a general railroad strike was defeated by the representatives of the constituent brotherhoods by a vote of 8–4, with a motion to change the constitution to allow a strike by a two-thirds vote defeated by the same margin. After the one-day session adjourned at 5:15 p.m., Debs made this statement to the press.

58. Following the August 25 meeting of the Supreme Council of the United Order of Railway Employees, which refused to call a strike of federated brotherhoods against the New York Central Railroads in conjunction with an ongoing action against the line by the Knights of Labor, a Knights representative was quoted as saying, "If the dispatch is true, about no strike being ordered, it means a singlehanded fight, with the Knights doing the fighting and the other organizations aiding financially." This prompted press inquiries for clarification, which led to this statement by Debs the following day.

59. The title of the chief executive officer of the Knights of Labor was changed from "grand master workman" to "general master workman" in 1883.

60. Henry Walter Webb, Sr. (1852–1900) was a lawyer and Wall Street broker before entering railroad management. His career as a vice president of the New York Central was interrupted by tuberculosis, from which he ultimately died at the age of 48.

61. Allusion to Exodus 16:3.

62. Lines by English poet and philosopher Samuel Taylor Coleridge (1772–1834).

63. Adapted from Isaiah 35:8: "And an highway shall be there, and a way, and it shall be called The way of holiness; the unclean shall not pass over it; but it shall be for those: the wayfaring men, though fools, shall not err therein."

64. From *Paradise Lost* (1667), by John Milton (1608–1674).

65. The tale of Noah and the ark appears in Genesis 7.

66. Allusion to the tower of Babel, a tale from Genesis 11.

67. John Philpot Curran (1750–1817) was a liberal Protestant barrister who defended a number of United Irish defendants in treason trials.

68. Opening line from "The Prisoner of Chillon" (1816), by George Gordon Byron.

69. From "Hohenlinden" (1803), by Thomas Campbell (1777–1844).

70. From *The Giaour*, by George Gordon Byron.

71. From Mark 8:24.

72. Allusion to John 5:4.

73. From "The Good Time Coming" (1846), by Charles Mackay (1814–1889).

74. Reference is to the Fourteenth National Convention of the B of LF, held in Atlanta from September 10 to 19, 1888, where the Ways and Means Committee sketched out initial plans for a "Board of Federation" consisting of three delegates from each of the Brotherhood of Locomotive Engineers, Brotherhood of Locomotive Firemen, Knights of Labor, Switchmen's Mutual Aid Association, Brotherhood of Railroad Brakemen, and Brotherhood of Telegraphers.

75. The ORC held its Twenty-Third National Convention in Rochester, New York, in May 1890.

76. D. J. Brown (b. 1838) was a career locomotive engineer who worked for the Southern Pacific Railroad for more than 20 years. He retired to his Sonoma Country ranch in 1893.

1891

Fair Wages[†]

January 1891

In defining the term "wages," a high authority says:

> That which is covenanted to be paid for work done; hire; reward; that which is paid or stipulated for services; price paid for labor; the return made or compensation paid to those engaged to perform any kind of labor or services by their employers; recompense; fruit; that which is given in return. The term is commonly applied to the payment of manual or mechanical labor, other than that performed by the more educated classes, to which the word *salary* bears reference.[1]

The foregoing affords the reader all the information required relating to the meaning of the term "wages."

In very many regards, "wages" is one of the most important words in our language. It is a word that has more to do with the happiness or misery of millions of people than any other word we can think of.

The discussion of the subject brings up numerous questions, each of which is of such importance that it is difficult to select those which should have preference.

Wages are compensation for work; hence, wherever work is performed, wages have precedence. It is the bedrock, the fundamental, the supreme question. We write of the rule, not exceptions. We speak for the intelligent, the self-respecting, the ambitious and courageous workingman, not for the scab.

We have no objection to the mottos of labor organizations. They read well and sound well, but they seldom if ever indicate the pivotal purpose. It may be, indeed it is, true that labor organizations are profoundly interested in promoting morality, sobriety, intelligence, and all virtues, and yet, but for the question of wages, it is doubtful if they would exist at all.

It is well enough to extol the virtues throughout the entire list. It is an easy thing to do, and some people never weary of it. The moral reformers are exceedingly felicitous in showing how easy it is to be good, notwithstanding that the "world, the flesh, and the devil" are everlastingly on the warpath.

---

† Published as "Wages" in *Locomotive Firemen's Magazine*, vol. 15, no. 1 (January 1891), 10–11.

Just here it should be said that the pulpit, which thunders its anathemas at sin, has an eye to *salary,* which stands for wages, and but for the *salary* of the pulpit would be as silent as the grave of Adam.

This is no reflection on the pulpit; it is simply the recognition of the supreme importance of wages, compensation for services, which in the case of the pulpit frequently runs up into thousands, giving the preacher a salary equal to that of a railroad or a bank president—a fact which, however much may be said about a "free gospel," makes it occasionally as high priced as any imported luxury.

The point we make is that, say what we will, the chief concern is *money,* wages, compensation for work performed. It is everywhere, and nowhere is it as important as in the ranks of workingmen. Their happiness, comfort, advancement, intelligence, and independence hinge upon, hang upon wages.

If it be the purpose of any man, or class of men, to degrade workingmen, the first move is to reduce wages, make it difficult or impossible for a workingman to live decently, force him into habitations unfit for the abode of human beings, compel him to insufficiently clothe himself, his wife, and children, and to subsist upon insufficient and unwholesome food.

This done, and the work of degradation and demoralization goes steadily and rapidly forward. It is inevitable. No law of the universe operates with greater certainty. With advancing wages, with fair and honest wages, a movement in the opposite direction occurs; workingmen have better habitations, better clothing, better food, and in abundant supply.

But this is not all. With fair, honest wages, the workingman not only has better habitation, better clothes, and better food, but he is enabled to have a few books and papers. His home becomes brighter and more joyous. There is better furniture, there may be pictures on the walls, an instrument of music may be had, and the refining, elevating influence of music felt. Nor is this all; with fair, honest wages children of the workingmen are properly clothed to attend school and church and early in life imbibe ideas of worth and moral rectitude which influence their future lives for good.

Reduce wages, deny the workingman fair wages, subject him to wrong and injustice, and the home at once exhibits the consequences, society feels the shock, and the inmates of the poorhouses, asylums, and prisons are increased.

The man who denies his employees fair wages is a public enemy, nor does any amount of slobbering over the ills incident to work condone the wrong or make him less a monster. To studiously rob men of wages, and take the money thus obtained to build gymnasiums and bathhouses for the victims of their studied piracies and ask the public to behold the exhibitions of their interest in poor men is a species of Phariseeism that it would be difficult for the devil to duplicate. And that workingmen should, anywhere, accept such duplicity for genuine interest in their welfare is a most humiliating confession of abasement.

The question arises, how can workingmen secure fair wages for work and maintain the just standard? We answer, through the influence and power of federated organizations. There is absolutely no other way to be devised in harmony with law and justice. Legislation cannot bring about such a result, nor is it desirable. Legislation can and ought to correct numerous wrongs which aid employers directly and indirectly to rob labor and degrade the workingman. Trust, syndicates, combinations of all descriptions, organized for the accumulation of wealth at the expense of workingmen, can be and ought to be abolished. Men who water stocks and seek to declare dividends on values which do not exist can and ought to be squelched, but no law can fix the standard of wages. Workingmen can do that if once they can be persuaded to act in concert.

Nothing is more common than reference to the "labor market" and the "supply and demand" of labor. When wages go down the "labor market" is referred to as being overstocked—the supply of labor being greater than the demand. Labor is referred to as a "commodity," to take its chances like hides or hair, guano or jute, or any other article of trade.

Take the labor market and supply it with Poles, Huns,[2] and Dagos,[3] and wages go down to a level which would not furnish subsistence to a millionaire's poodle or parrot. In such an event, the American workingman has one hope, and only one, and that is to organize and federate, and say to employers that the standard of wages is thus and so, and all the Huns and Poles and Dagos on top of the ground, backed by the American scab, cannot lower the standard. It is the American standard, and organization and federation is the American way to maintain the standard. Let others do as they may; American workingmen should say, "We will not be degraded nor enslaved."

Is this to be the outcome? Have organizations made up their minds to federate and resist all encroachments upon their right to live as human beings? Manifestly, the trend is in that direction.

The discussion of the eight-hour day is well enough, as also the single tax, currency, and tariff reform, but the question of wages towers above them all. It is an ever-present and vital question. It brooks no delay. With fair, honest wages the workingman advances in intelligence, power, and influence. Deny him that, and as certain as the law of gravitation, the work of degradation begins, nor ceases until the strand is lined with wrecks.

Life at Halfway Station[†]

January 1891

More than a decade of years has passed since I became a member of the Grand Lodge of the Brotherhood of Locomotive Firemen, my induction into the office of grand secretary and treasurer having occurred July 16, 1880, and at the same date I became the editor and manager of the *Locomotive Firemen's Magazine*. These honorable and responsible positions were conferred upon me by Grand Master F. W. Arnold. At Chicago in September 1880, I was elected for one year to fill an unexpired term. At Boston in 1881, I was elected grand secretary and treasurer, and editor and manager of the *Magazine* for a term of three years. At Toronto in 1884, I was elected to the same offices for a term of two years. At Minneapolis in 1886, I was again elected to the offices named for a term of two years. At Atlanta in 1888, I was again elected for a term of two years, and at San Francisco in September 1890, I was again elected grand secretary and treasurer of the Brotherhood of Locomotive Firemen, and editor and manager of the *Locomotive Firemen's Magazine;* in all, six times I have been, without an opposing candidate or the loss of a single vote, the recipient of the unwavering confidence of the brotherhood.

Such exhibitions of unflagging trust in one who had no claims upon the brotherhood, whose duties as a member of the order had been confined to the narrow limits of one lodge, have from the first burdened me with a sense of gratitude, which defies all words at my command to express.

How well I have met the obligations which such faith in my rectitude imposed is a matter for others to debate. But this may be said: that when I entered the Grand Lodge, the order was bankrupt and had about 2,000 members. It is now rich in financial resources and can boast of more than 20,000 members. When I entered the Grand Lodge, the *Magazine* had 3,500 subscribers. Since then its monthly editions have expanded to 33,000 copies.

In saying this, I am not so foolish as to intimate that it has been because of my connection with the order—and the statement is made simply to show the splendid growth of the order—and to emphasize the fact that with this growth, the duties of the grand secretary and treasurer, and the duties of the

---

[†] Published as "To the Brotherhood" in *Locomotive Firemen's Magazine*, vol. 15, no. 1 (January 1891), 43–44.

editor and manager of the *Magazine,* have even more than proportionately increased, grown to a sum total of responsibility, of mental and physical wear and tear, which leaves little, indeed, no time at all for recreation or recuperation. It is one ceaseless demand upon mental and physical energies which if discarded one day only doubles the burden for the next, and this sapping of the vital forces, like Tennyson's brook, "goes on forever."[4]

Having reached the accepted "halfway station" in the years allotted to man—"threescore and ten"[5]—and other and less exacting business pursuits offering, I have come to the unalterable conclusion during my present official term to surrender all the trusts committed to my hands to the brotherhood and retire from all official positions in the order.

It must not be understood that this conclusion has been arrived at without a mental pang of regret. Ten years of uninterrupted fellowship with thousands of brothers beloved cannot be broken off without producing in susceptible minds feelings of sadness, and in a special sense is this true when, as in my case, these associations have been fruitful of personal satisfactions of boundless proportions.

Between myself and the great Brotherhood of Locomotive Firemen not so much as one incident has occurred to dampen my ardor for its success, to abate my devotion to its principles, or to weaken my fraternal friendship and goodwill for my brothers of the scoop and throttle, and whatever fate or fortune may have in store for me, the members of the brotherhood, one and all, will have a warm place in my heart until its pulsations cease.

As I have said, during my present term I shall resign the positions I now hold, nor will I under any conceivable circumstances be a candidate for reelection *for any other office* in the gift of the order.

Having determined to go into other business, I have deemed it prudent to make this early announcement of my purpose for a variety of reasons, the more important of which is that it enables the brotherhood, without unnecessary haste, to select from the great number of competent members the one most likely to meet the onerous requirements of the positions.

I have no desire to magnify the duties of the offices which I shall resign, nor will I underestimate their importance. Closely identified with the duties they imposed for more than ten consecutive years, my conviction is that the brotherhood will esteem it a favor to have ample time for deliberation.

As through the *Magazine* or otherwise, opportunities will offer to refer to this subject again if require, I close by subscribing myself, in all that fraternity means, the brotherhood's friend and well-wisher.

Protection[†]

January 1891

It is a mistake of no little importance to suppose that the students of phenomena confine their observations to strange and unusual appearances in the heavens, the earth, or the waters under the firmament. There is a world of mind in which those who are at all attentive may discover many things well calculated to arouse reflections of intense seriousness. It goes for nothing to say that the great majority are unobservant—heedless of passing events. There are those who never heed the signs of the times and who, if their attention could be arrested, would simply stare at them with scarcely more apprehension of their significance than so many sheep. They marry, and are given in marriage; they eat, drink, and sleep. The skies may be red, or dark and lowering, it is all the same to them. Such people do not keep up with the procession. They are always too late for the train. We can afford to dismiss them. As forces and factors, they are as copper coins among doubloons. If rich, they are like misers, who clutch and count their gold and hide it away; if poor, they accept conditions without protest, and like asses bear their burdens uncomplainingly.

But there are others who are wide awake and on the alert. They read, they think, they watch. They clamber to the highlands of vision and survey with eagle eyes the surroundings. They detect phenomena whenever and wherever they appear. They see the shadows of coming events. They are the *avant couriers* of all explorers—the pathfinders in every wilderness. They are the Johns[6] crying, "make straight paths"[7] for men who have discovered at last that "God is no respecter of persons," and who have concluded to live and be clad and fed and sheltered by divine right, without asking permission of mortals.

Here in the United States of America the uprising is phenomenal. It is a phenomenon that creates continental amazement. A writer in a magazine calls it "the Labor Crisis." He says, "The point to be determined is whether capital or labor shall, in future, determine the terms upon which the invested resources of the nation are to be employed."[8] Not exactly. The point is, shall the men who perform the labor and create all the capital share in it to the extent of living like men or of living like beasts? The point is embedded in the question: Can workingmen *protect* their inalienable rights of life, liberty, and happiness? If so,

† Published in *Locomotive Firemen's Magazine*, vol. 15, no. 1 (January 1891), 8–9.

how? The answers are easy. First, by organization. The extent of organization is phenomenal. It extends to every trade. It is steadily going forward. It alarms those who deem it for their interests to degrade workingmen—to so impoverish American laborers that they shall be content to work for such wages as satisfy Italians, Poles, Hungarians, and others who, at home, have shared their huts and dens with domestic animals and vermin—who never drew a freeman's breath nor uttered a sentiment in accord with American citizenship. We accept the announcement that a "labor crisis" is at hand. Workingmen are preparing for its coming. Every sign betokens its coming.

Those who are observant will notice that workingmen are not only organizing, but are reading. They take the papers, and at last labor has a press. If, therefore, those who oppose the emancipation of labor from debasing enthrallments predicate success upon the ignorance of workingmen, they are doomed to disappointment. The propositions up for debate in the councils of workingmen are few and simple, but fundamental. They are not to any great extent discussing Bellamyism. They are not trying to determine what will be the condition of workingmen AD 2000.[9] They are not switched off to find out whether a worker in Europe receives more or less than a worker in America. The supreme purpose is to obtain such pay for their work as will support themselves and their families decently, and this, as certainly as rivers flow to the sea, they are going to have, crisis or no crisis. It is a righteous demand and will undergo no abatement.

As matters now stand, workingmen are the victims of oppression. They are overworked and underpaid, or, if in any case justice is done them, it is the result of compact organization. That is what affords them such protection as they have. The fact is recognized and acknowledged. But it has been found that organization is but the initial step in securing protection, hence the shibboleth of workingmen today is *federation*—an alliance of all organizations—and that once perfected, labor's millennium dawns.

We must not be misunderstood. We do not mean that carpenters and brick masons are to federate with men engaged in the train service of railroads. Fortunately, these are setting a noble example of federation and are securing protection. So it may be with men identified with the building trades, and thus, wherever there is an identity of interests, such alliances secure the right and protect the right, and when an organization of workingmen is formed and its chief officers fight protection and hobnob with those who oppress labor, such an organization is certain to disappear. It cannot stand. It is a treasonable organization and ought to die. All the scabs that ever existed are not equal to the malign influence exerted by a workingman's organization in alliance with the Corbins of the period.

The era of victory is dawning. The days of doubt and despondency are passing away. The spirit of protection is abroad. Its animating, vitalizing power is felt by the hosts of labor everywhere, and they are moving forward to certain triumph.

The Seventy Millionaires[†]

January 1891

Thomas G. Shearman named 70 persons who had managed to gobble $2.7 billion.[10] Here is the list:

$150 million:
J. J. Astor, fur trade and real estate; Trinity Church, real estate.

$100 million:
C. Vanderbilt, railroads; W. K. Vanderbilt, railroads; Jay Gould, railroads; Leland Stanford, railroads; J. D. Rockefeller, Standard Oil.

$70 million:
Estate of A. Packer, coal mining and railroads.

$60 million:
William Astor, real estate; W. W. Astor, real estate.

$50 million:
Russell Sage, railroads and speculation; E. A. Stevens, real estate; Estate of Moses Taylor, railroads and trade; Estate of Brown and Ives, trade, real estate, and cotton manufacturing.

$40 million:
P. D. Armour, provisions; F. L. Ames, railroads (principally); William Rockefeller, Standard Oil; H. M. Flager, Standard Oil; Powers & Weightman, chemicals; Estate of P. Goelet, real estate.

---

† Published in *Locomotive Firemen's Magazine,* vol. 15, no. 1 (January 1891), 16.

$35 million:

C. P. Huntington, railroads; D. O. Mills, railroads; Ross Winans, railroads and engineering; C. B. Cox, coal and mining; Claus Spreckles, Hawaiian sugar; A. Belmont, banking; R. J. Livingston, real estate; Fred Weyerhauser, timber and wood products; Mrs. Mark Hopkins, railroads; Mrs. Hetty Green, speculation and banking; Estate of S. V. Harkness, railroads; Estate of R. W. Coleman, manufacturing; Estate of I. M. Singer, patents.

$25 million:

A. J. Drexel, banking; J. S. Morgan, banking; J. P. Morgan, banking; Marshall Fields, dry goods trade; David Dows, flour and speculation; J. G. Fair, railroads and silver; E. T. Gerry, real estate; Estate of Governor Fairbanks, patents; Estate of A. T. Stewart, dry goods; A. Schermerhorn, real estate.

$22.5 million:

O. H. Payne, oil; Estate of F. A. Drexel, banking; Estate of I. V. Williamson, real estate and general trade; Estate of W. F. Weld, trade, commerce, and real estate.

$20 million:

F. W. Vanderbilt, railroads; Theodore Havemeyer, sugar refining; H. O. Havemeyer, sugar refining; W. G. Warden, Standard Oil; W. P. Thompson, (?); Mrs. Schenley, real estate; J. B. Haggin, speculation; H. A. Hutchins, (?); Estate of W. Sloane, retail carpet trade; E. S. Higgins, real estate, principally; Estate of C. Tower, coal land speculation; Estate of William Thaw, railroads; Dr. Hostetter, patent medicine; William Sharon, railroads and speculation; Peter Donohue, (?).

It will be noticed that of the 70, twenty have their fortunes credited to railroads, and the average is about $39 million for each of the royal 70.

Take the twenty whose fortunes are credited to railroads, and the average shows they have absorbed $780 million of the surplus earnings of their employees, or of labor, and the fact proclaims the reason why railroad men are poorly paid. The 700,000 railroad employees barely live; the owners by hook and crook appropriate their earnings.

Bellamy Launches *The New Nation*[†]

March 1891

We have on our table No. 1, Vol. 1, of *The New Nation,* published weekly by Edward Bellamy at No. 13 Winter Street, Boston, Massachusetts. In an article captioned "The New Nation," the editor pays special attention to the question, "Why will not the old nation do?" Among the reasons why the old nation will not do, and in what special particulars the new nation will be an improvement, the editor says that:

> In the old nation, the system by which the work of life is carried on is a sort of perpetual warfare, a struggle, literally, to the death, between men and men. It is a system by which the contestants are forced to waste in fighting more effort than they have left for work. The sordid and bitter nature of the struggle so hardens, for the most part, the relations of men to their fellows, that in the domestic circle alone do they find exercise for the better, tenderer, and more generous elements of their nature.

The editor further remarks that in the old nation—that is, in the present nation, "the people are divided, against nature, into classes: one very small class being the wealthy; another and much larger class being composed of those who maintain with difficulty a condition of tolerable comfort constantly shadowed by apprehension of its loss; with, finally, a vastly greater and quite preponderating class of very poor, who have no dependence even for bare existence save a wage which is uncertain from day to day." It is also pointed out that "half of the nation—the women—are dependent upon the personal favor of the other half, the men, for their means of support;" that "a million men are crying for work;" that, "not only does wealth devour poverty, but wealth devours wealth," etc. Under the "new nation," all these things will be changed. There will be "neither rich nor poor," all will be employed except the sick, the old, and infirm, and they will have every possible attention.

In the new nation it is said that "the children will be cherished as precious jewels, inestimable pledges of the divine love to men. Though mother and father forsake them, the nation will take them up," and that "education will be

---

[†] Published as "The New Nation" in *Locomotive Firemen's Magazine,* vol. 15, no. 3 (March 1891), 234.

equal and universal, and will cover the entire period of life during which it is now enjoyed by the most favored classes," and when these things are accomplished, then—"for the first time in history, the world will behold a true republic, rounded, full-orbed, complete—a republic, social, industrial, political."

The Canadian Pacific Railway
and the Supreme Council[†]
March 1891

On Wednesday, February 4 [1891], the Supreme Council was convened at Montreal, Quebec, in response to the official call of Grand Master S. E. Wilkinson of the Brotherhood of Railroad Trainmen. For some weeks the conductors and brakemen on the eastern divisions of the system had been making ineffectual efforts to have their wages increased, which in many cases were barely above the living point, while the general average was not much better. The committee was patient to the utmost limit of endurance; they sought by every honorable means to obtain what was universally conceded to be their due, but they were doomed to disappointment. The management, while ostensibly willing to receive the committee and discuss their grievances, turned a deaf ear to every appeal for justice and finally refused point blank to make any concession that would even remotely touch the grievances involved.

At this juncture the members of the B of RT sent for their grand master and the members of the ORC appealed to their grand chief, both of whom responded promptly and made renewed efforts to have the differences between the employees and the company amicably adjusted. Failing in their efforts the Supreme Council was convened and each organization was fully represented. At the opening session the grievances were discussed and every mooted point was carefully investigated. The result of the meeting was that the grievances were approved as a whole, and a committee was directed to call on the officials and request an interview on behalf of the council. This request resulted in the committee being sent for by the officials, and after a brief conference

---

† Published in *Locomotive Firemen's Magazine*, vol. 15, no. 3 (March 1891), 248–249.

an amicable adjustment was effected, which was perfectly satisfactory to the committee and the men they represented. The concessions made by the company were such as will materially increase the pay of the employees in the train service and all hands were pleased with the outcome of the meeting.

The potent and effective influence of federation was never demonstrated to better advantage. It filled the bill, it met every requirement, it was equal to the emergency. Without federation it is safe to say that no concessions would have been made by the company. Indeed, we doubt if the employees would have had the temerity to even approach their autocratic officials on the subject of grievances.

It is proper that we should give credit to the Order of Railway Conductors and its grand officers, E. E. Clark, grand chief, and C. H. Wilkins, assistant grand chief, who cooperated with the council in all things necessary to effect a settlement. The grand officers, committees, and members of the order were in hearty accord with the spirit of the occasion and gave unquestionable evidence of their "stickability," whatever the outcome of the negotiations might be.

We had the pleasure of meeting Grand Chief Clark personally for the first time, and much to our satisfaction we found him to be a gentleman of liberal and advanced views, wide comprehension, and in all regards fully abreast of the progressive spirit of the times. We believe Grand Chief Clark to be a man of principle and honor, officially as well as personally, just such a man as will by unfaltering rectitude, courageous defense of the right, and unswerving fealty to obligations, inspire confidence and achieve success.

The Farmers' Alliance[†]

March 1891

We have not studied critically the motives that have prompted the farmers of the country to organize what is called the "Farmers' Alliance." In a general way, we understand that they demand some legislation which, as they feed all, shall if possible save themselves from starvation.

---

† Published in *Locomotive Firemen's Magazine*, vol. 15, no. 3 (March 1891), 197–199.

The farmers would, if they could, do away with national banks. That is to say, they would do away with national bank bills or currency, whereby the banks can and do expand or contract the circulating medium of the country at will, thereby giving them power to inflict untold evils upon the country.

The farmers doubtless believe it to be a stupendous wrong, to use no harsher term, for corporations to have the power to levy tribute upon the American people to pay dividends on water, and we assume that the farmers believe if railroads were content to pay dividends on honest investments they could reduce their rates and make as much or more money than at present. But the *Railway Age* takes a different view of the subject, and in a recent issue says:

> The organized war against the railways of this country which has evidently been determined upon by the Farmers' Alliance in state and national gatherings, for the avowed purpose of compelling further reductions in the already low rates of transportation on farm products and merchandise, is a matter of most serious importance to railway employees, as well as to the owners of railway securities and to the manufacturers of railway supplies.

We do not suppose that the farmers ever dreamed of doing anything to injure railway employees, nor do we see in what way the free coinage of silver or the issue of government "promises to pay" to take the place of national bank bills would result in the injury of men who operate the railroads of the country, and it is to be presumed that railway employees will in the future, as in the past, vote pretty much as they please, unless their employers shall find ways and means to intimidate them and squeeze their manhood out of them. The *Railway Age,* in pursuing the subject, injects into its article the following remarkable utterances:

> Hitherto railway men, as such, have taken very little part in political campaigns. Left free by their employing companies to vote as they please, they have followed their personal preferences and selected their candidates, often without any regard to the attitude of the latter toward railway interests: not infrequently, strange to say, they have voted for legislators and other officers on avowedly anti-railway tickets.

"Hitherto," says the *Age,* "railway men" have been *"left free by their employing companies to vote as they please,"* and having been "left free to vote as they please," have voted *"anti-railway tickets."* The intimation is that in future railway employees will not be "left free to vote as they please." "Their employing companies" are to discipline them and keep them from perpetrating what the *Age* deems it proper to stigmatize as "supreme folly." We do not remember to have seen anything in print of recent date more repulsive, more insulting to the intelligence and independence of railway employees, than the intimation that since *hitherto* their employing companies have left them free to vote as they please, a change of program in this regard may be adopted when the railroad employees will *not* be left free to vote as they please. This form of intimidation has been carried quite far enough in the United States, and the *Railway Age* has only to brush away the coverts behind which it now writes and formulate its platform in honest words to learn that railway employees will vote as they please quite independent of "their employing companies."

The *Age's* form of intimidation has had its day. Railway employees are neither the livestock nor the rolling stock of railway corporations, but citizens who know their rights and are quite as capable of casting an intelligent vote as the editor of the *Railway Age*.

The fact that a railway employee writes in the interest of railway corporations is not remarkable. Such letters could be multiplied indefinitely. The old dodge of wreck and ruin has been played until it no longer frightens. This thing of tying railway employees, body and soul, to the corporation has been done, may be done again, but not to the extent the *Railway Age* evidently anticipates, or to the extent the "Railway Employee in Dakota" outlines.

The Dakota man's scheme is simply immense. Indeed, that term scarcely defines its sweep. It would be highly interesting to know in what department of railroad service the Dakota correspondent of the *Railway Age* is employed. He talks like a president, or a vice president, or a general manager; and still he may be merely a switchman or a hostler, since in these, as in other departments of the railroad service, there are men who are eminently capable, when occasion requires it, to take either side of an important question and discuss it intelligently.

This Dakota employee wants to organize what "might be called 'The National Railway Employees' Protective Association,' to which should be eligible every person employed on railroads, every stock and bondholder, all interested bankers, car, locomotive or other railway supply manufacturers, and their employees; in fact there are few, if any, who are engaged in the manufacturing or mining industries who should not be eligible to become members of this organization if they are the least interested in the success and prosperity of the railways of the country." This railroad employee of Dakota is "convinced, after a careful study of the subject, that in order to protect the capital invested in the railways of the United States and in all those industries intimately connected therewith; to prevent the further reduction of the wages of the men employed in these industries; to give capital confidence enough to push forward the development of the country; to stimulate the manufactures which have declined since the decline of railroad construction; to enable the railways to employ a sufficient force for each department; to prevent hostile or unjust legislation against the railroads; and to preserve all the railway properties at a proper standard of excellence, the most effectual remedy at the present and for all time to come would be a thorough organization of all the employees and others interested." The Dakota employee, who writes like a stockholder or a bondholder, says that "the object of such an association would be to cause its members to vote at every election only for such representatives or senatorial candidates, state or national, as would be pledged to do all in their power to promote the welfare of all concerned, and at all times to oppose with their vote and influence any legislation which proposed to reduce the income of the capitalist below a just and reasonable profit on his investment, or which would have a tendency to reduce the wages of employees below what could be considered a liberal allowance for their services."

Here we have outlined a great railroad party, all to be members of "The National Railway Employees' Protective Association," and all to *vote* straight railroad tickets at every election—vote for men opposed to the reduction of the income of capitalists. It would be sad indeed if the income of Mr. Jay Gould should be reduced a few millions, or if the Vanderbilts should be so cramped that they could not pay more than $5,000 a year for a *chef*. The Rothchilds would doubtless weep over such destitution; and the point is made that all railway employees should join in with stockholders and bondholders to maintain rates, so that wages may not be reduced, which suggests the inquiry—when did the corporation come forward and say to their employees, "Our road is now making money 'hand over fist,' and your wages are to be advanced?"

We are inclined to the opinion that the Dakota employee's scheme won't work. His plea for the capitalist is too top heavy. It is not built on the plan of the pyramids. His great solicitude for the capitalist is by far too pronounced and the "employee" dodge is "too thin." He is a master of verbal legerdemain. His word jugglery may be, as the Yankees say, "smart." Never did spider sing more sweetly to the fly; never were pussy's paws more velvety. Some flies may go into the parlor, some mice may be caught, but the great body of railway employees won't "tumble" to the Dakota idea immediately. A great many railway employees are giving all subjects relating to work and wages, earnings and dividends, careful study, and the conclusion is that a very large percentage of their earnings go to enrich capitalists, and they want a fair deal. They may not get it. They have been defeated in the past, and the future may have grievous disappointments in store for them, but to ask them to join with stockholders and bondholders and stock waterers and bankers and millionaires to increase the incomes of the rich, that the crumbs which fall from their tables may not decrease in size nor quantity, is really carrying the joke too far by half. Old things are passing away. There are hopes of a new regime, and workingmen are not going to vote against its coming.

Labor Organizations and the Labor Press[†]

March 1891

We write entirely independent of partisan influence. We propose to discuss the election of last November upon propositions which, if not new, have not been brought into deserved prominence, in fact, have not been alluded to at all as factors in the recent struggle.

It does not matter to the *Magazine* which of the two great parties of the country, considered as an aggregation of men, succeed. We are not interested as to whether *A* or *B* goes to the legislature or to Congress—nor are we tied to the fortunes of any nominee for president. Parties are of no consequence to workingmen except as they advocate principles and policies which antagonize class legislation and seek to do justice to all.

Hitherto the workingmen, by party leaders, have been regarded as a class of citizens in the keeping of bosses, to be brought into line and voted as they might decide.

The employer has regarded them as largely subject to his will—an unthinking herd of little intelligence who were deflected right or left as he might choose. He had but to indicate his pleasure and his employees obeyed without question or protest. The employer was supposed to know everything; the employee nothing, or so little as to exert no influence at all in deciding his vote.

In these regards the country has been awakened to a sweeping change of program, and it is eminently worthwhile to inquire what causes have been at work to produce the new order of things.

We shall state them briefly, and they are signs of the times of wonderful import.

---

† Published in *Locomotive Firemen's Magazine,* vol. 15, no. 3 (March 1891), 245–246.

In the first place, labor organizations are in the nature of schools. Every member of a labor organization is more or less a student of economic questions. He no longer accepts the dictum of the employer. He studies and thinks for himself. He grasps facts, he analyzes statistics, he notes investments and dividends; he estimates the constant increase of watered stocks and marks well how interested parties mix fiction and facts for the purpose of reducing wages—and in the lodge and assembly rooms discusses economic questions with earnestness and with an intelligent appreciation of cause and effect, which rivets attention and secures conviction.

This constitutes a new era in politics, a new departure in campaigns. There is not a labor organization in the country that has not put into operation mind forces hitherto dormant. It will no longer do to count upon the votes of workingmen based upon party fealty—partisan prejudice or the pride of partisan victory. Something more rational is now demanded. The boss can no longer cajole nor intimidate. Workingmen will no longer blindly follow a banner nor a transparency. Symbols must hereafter relate to something practical.

Workingmen see that money erects the palatial residences and surrounds their owners with luxury. The fact does not create envy in the minds of workingmen. They do not want to pull down the palace nor destroy the carpets, furniture, mirrors, and paintings, but knowing these riches are secured from their surplus earnings, they are resolving that they will have comfortable homes instead of shanties or dens; they are resolving that their homes shall be supplied with the necessities and comforts of life. They are resolving that they will have so much of the wealth they create as to furnish an abundance of good food and good clothes; at any rate, they are resolving that their votes and influence shall no longer be secured for their impoverishment and degradation, and in these regards the workingmen of the country are rapidly solidifying, and insofar as their votes can change the aspect of affairs, they will cast them with a purpose to better their condition.

In proof of this, it is worthy of note that labor organizations are taking a profound interest in state and national legislation and are appointing committees to look after certain measures, to urge or to prevent their adoption. What are these measures? The list is too extended to introduce here were it in our power to name them all.

Take for instance the employment of Pinkerton thugs by corporations. A blacker crime was never perpetrated in any civilized land. It is too monstrous for contemplation, and yet the corporation of which Chauncey M. Depew is president employs Pinkerton murderers, abandoned wretches scarcely fit to be sent to hell, to overawe workingmen because they dare protest against outrages which no workingman can submit to and retain a grain of independence or self-respect.

All over this broad land, workingmen should see to it that the employment of these thugs should be made a felony and the matter should be brought to the attention of every legislature in the country.

The co-employee iniquity, which has not one trait of justice in it, an infamy which makes law a farce and judicial decisions worse than jugglery, can lie knocked in the head and killed only by express statute.[11] It is an imported infamy—an antiquated monstrosity, the spawn of the divine right to rule curse, which through all the ages has made the workingman the victim of oppression, symbolized by prisons, dungeons, rack, and thumbscrew, and yet this devilish deformity of justice, hideous as a living skeleton, stalks into all the courts and chatters its decisions against the rights of workingmen.

How long, in the name of eternal justice, is this ghastly remnant of infernalism to prevail in American courts? When will workingmen, by the fiat of the ballot, banish it to its native hell? Labor organizations exist because of a right to exist by virtue of laws that antedate constitutions, statutes, or kingly decrees—while corporations and monopolies, trusts and syndicates exist, at least in the United States, only by statutes—statutes which workingmen can, if they so decide, repeal. And still the corporation, with an impudence that defies exaggeration, decrees that a man, because he exercises his inalienable right to join a labor organization, shall not work.

Governments exercise three supreme prerogatives which touch the individual at vital points. First, government can take the life of the citizen. Second, it can deprive the citizen of liberty. Third, it can take the property of the citizen, confiscate it, and send him forth a pauper to drift or to die. But the victim in every case is awarded a trial; his case is to be determined by a jury of his peers. He can be heard in his own defense. He has the right to appeal until he reaches the highest tribunal known to the law.

Let us see how the case stands between the corporation and the victim of its hate in this God-favored land:

There stands the workingman. What is his condition? Go look at his home. There it is by the wayside. There is his wife and little ones dependent upon his daily wages. Intelligent and hardworking, he would better his condition and the condition of those dependent upon him. He joins a labor organization. In doing this he becomes obnoxious to the corporation. He is a marked man. The corporation issues its decree. The workingman is discharged. At one blow everything goes down. Without work, without wages, the home is made as dark and gloomy as a tomb. Unable to pay rent, he is evicted and thrust out upon the highway. Without money, hunger comes with its pangs and fangs. The home is broken up—the father is a tramp. Now every appalling fancy becomes a frightful fact. What becomes of the family? Would you know the details in thousands of instances? Search the records of poorhouses, prisons, and brothels.

What was the workingman's crime? What was the height and depth of his offending? The answer is, he joined a labor organization, and the corporation, with more power than the government that created it, decides without a hearing, without a trial, to take from him the means of living, which in thousands of instances is taking life, liberty, and property.

We do not paint the picture too black. We challenge the record and aver that in the archives of hell there is nothing more infernally repulsive. And such transactions are of daily occurrence, not in Russia, not in Turkey or Persia—not only in autocrat-cursed lands, but here in the United States; here where we are told the government is by the people, of the people, and for the people.

We state no hypothetical case; we are not drawing upon our imagination for the facts. There is not a reader of the *Magazine,* not a reader of newspapers, not a man of intelligence in the land who does not know that every day in the round year, men are discharged from work because they are members of some labor organization.

Just here we make the point that workingmen by concert of action can change this state of affairs by their votes. There is nothing impractical in the proposition. Why should the corporation be permitted to boycott the labor organization? Why should the corporation be permitted to inflict the direst penalties upon men for exercising an inalienable right? Why may not the monstrous wrong be eternally exiled by statute? There is no good reason why such a change may not be wrought by the ballots of workingmen. They have the power, and in due time we verily believe they will exercise it.

In surveying such subjects, the labor press of the country looms up and blazes forth like a lighthouse on a rock-bound coast. It is pointing the way to the harbor. It shows workingmen the way to steer. It is a Bethlehem star leading to redeeming possibilities, a conquering force that partisan politicians have neither weighed nor measured.

The corporation is even more obtuse than the politician. They do not see that class legislation is doomed. Their greed and their arrogance blinds them to coming events. They rely upon their money.

It was Goldsmith who said:

> For just experience tells in every soil
> That those who think must govern those who toil.[12]

But it so happens that an era has dawned when those who toil are those who think—those who write and reason, those who grasp and solve problems, and those who lead. The labor press forms a grand torchlight procession. It blazes on the highlands and in the lowlands, in the shops and in the halls of legislation. It is helping on the revolution. It is the *avant courier* of a new dispensation in law and logic. There is one demand and it is being heeded. The labor press of the country, discarding party and creed as under the old regime, is blending its clarion notes and bugle calls for unity of purpose in the councils of all labor organizations. This accomplished and labor's jubilee follows.

Corporations vs. Federation[†]

April 1891

In a recent issue of the *Rights of Labor,* published at Chicago, we find the following:

> From every point of the compass we are informed that capitalists and employers of labor are uniting to fight the labor unions. A railroad combination to fight the federation of railway employees. The owners of the London docks to fight the dockers' union. The streetcar owners to fight the streetcar unions. The carpenters and builders' association to fight the carpenters' union. The mine owners headed by that delectable prince of plunderers, W. L. Scott, to fight the miners' union.[13] Poor deluded workingmen everywhere are being used as clubs to break the heads of their fellow workingmen. What do these corporation crooks and cold-blooded employers hope for? Do they imagine they can destroy the unions, the hopes and aspirations of the workingmen, by uniting against them? May they not, by their uncalled-for war against trade unionism, arouse passions that it would be better for them not to arouse? It is barely possible that these men may discover their mistake when it is too late, when they are shorn of their ill-gotten gains and compelled to work as their fellow men do. It is best not to unfetter a lion, even though you may imagine it is a tame lion.

The foregoing is highly suggestive. We do not doubt but that federated

---

† Published in *Locomotive Firemen's Magazine,* vol. 15, no. 4 (April 1891), 344.

labor is at an early day to be tried, as if by fire. We are of the opinion that the decree has gone forth. We do not believe it will be revoked. The right to organize and to federate is conceded.

That there will be railroad combinations "to fight federation" we do not doubt.

Let us state the case tersely and fairly.

Organizations of railroad employees federate to secure rights and to maintain them.

If, therefore, railroads combine to fight federation, they combine in the interest of injustice and wrong.

The crisis is approaching. The crucial test is near at hand. We say, let it come.

If labor is to be enslaved, if it is to be manacled, if Corbin ideas are to prevail, if liberty and independence are to be enjoyed only by the employer, and the badge of serfdom is to be worn by the employee, let the facts be known—let the trial come.

We know that the federated orders of railway employees make no unjust demands, tolerate no improper methods to secure their rights.

We do not underestimate the power of money. We are not unmindful of the growth of aristocratic and autocratic ideas—but we have an abiding faith in organization, in federation, in union.

We are not prepared to contemplate the unrestricted sway of the corporation.

We would have no French revolutions in America.

"Carnegie" and "carnage" sound much alike.

The American railroad ought not to symbolize despotism; better, far better that a mile of track had never been laid.

Savagery is better than serfdom. It is enough to say, we have faith in federation.

Without federation there may come desperation, and should the era of despair come, the storm god would rule.

We prefer reason and righteousness.

Dishonest Bankers†

April 1891

Some months since, one of the most scandalous bank failures, known as the Kean failure, occurred in Chicago.¹⁴ One of the peculiarities about the wretched piece of business was the distinguished piety of Kean. He was a man of much prayer and great charities. He was one of the "sweet singers in Israel." Salvation was his theme on Sundays, and at social religious meetings weekday evenings. He loved to dwell upon his "heavenly inheritance." On such occasions Brother Kean's soul "was on fire." He seemed to have electric communication with the "spirits of just men made perfect."¹⁵ He lived in full view of the "promised land." His ears were attuned to seraphic minstrelsy. He was, when not *banking,* on the summit of some sacred mountain, looking beyond Jordan's billows to the land of "milk and honey."

Brother Kean played his religious cards splendidly. He caught more gudgeons than fell to the share of other bankers. Money flowed to him in an ever-swelling tide, and as the cash came, Bro. Kean's piety took on a keener edge. He was *sharp.* He made religion pay. He speculated in amens and hallelujahs. He was not only a "pillar in the church" but was recognized as a power in the Sunday school, where the youth of Chicago are taught to be good. Brother Kean, as might be supposed, was deeply concerned in the welfare of youth. He would have them honest and virtuous—all of which helped Brother Kean in securing *deposits.*

In all of this, Brother Kean was shrewd, astute, wily. He feathered his nest. He got to himself a great name in Chicago, and then fizzled. The bank failed, the cash was gone, and with it went his piety—all of his professions and prayers came back to roost. Like ravens and owls, they took possession of the bank, and amidst the wreck, ruin, and desolation, they croaked and hooted, while experts were determining, as near as possible, just how much Brother Kean had got away with.

But we did not begin this article so much to write about Kean, as about the hot shot other Chicago bankers deemed it prudent to fire into him on the evening of January 3, 1891.

It seems that on the evening named, the Taxpayers' Association concluded to excoriate the "praying swindler," and a number of "private bankers" concluded to be present, and put themselves on record in money matters, and this they did with considerable emphasis. As for instance, one man said that "any banker who carries his religion so far into his bank as Kean did is a dangerous man," the audience loudly applauded the sentiment, as they also applauded the assertion of Herman Felzenthal[16] that "a banker who would not pay his depositors ought to be hung." The purpose of the meeting was to appoint a committee to "formulate a bill for the better regulation of banks and the protection of depositors." One speaker remarked that "the secret of an honest bank is an honest banker. If they are honest, their banks will always pay." A lawyer said, "I believe that private banking business should be forbidden unless the person doing the business should first obtain a license under strict regulations." Another man remarked, "If a man goes to prayer meeting every morning before he goes to his bank, he is a hypocrite. He missed his calling. He ought to have been a preacher. He hasn't got time to attend to the safety of other people's money. Now, I am in favor, when a banker fails to pay, to hang him. And when men fail to pay the banker, hang them. Seriously, I think the dishonesty of bankers is overrated. I do not call the men who hang a bank sign out 'bankers.' Of 68 banking firms in the directory today, only ten are really bankers."

Another speaker said:

> I have been reading a table of embezzlements in the United States; it occupies over two columns of a newspaper. The embezzlements for the year 1890 aggregated $8,882,000. Nearly $9 million, Mr. Chairman, embezzled by all kinds of people, including bankers. From 1878 to 1890, the amount embezzled in the United States aggregated nearly $63 million. One of the biggest sums was $460,000, by a banker. A banker should be compelled to put up security with the state auditor to the extent of the capital invested. [*Applause.*] Each stockholder should be made individually liable for the entire debts of the banking company up to the last dollar he owns. You would then find fewer bank presidents fail. And I want to say that any man who, like Kean, carries his religion so far into his bank as he did, is a dangerous man. If we punished dishonest bankers here as they do in Germany, it would be a long time until a bank failed in Chicago. [*Applause.*] The criminal lawyers would have had several jobs recently. The English and Scotch laws are better than ours. I read the other day that the Glasgow bank, which failed by the dishonesty of its officials, had been wound up by the payment of every dollar due the depositors. How different in the Kean bank case. Instead of the bank owing the depositors, the investigation tended to show that the depositors owed the bank.

Another speaker referred to "the postal savings-bank system of Canada, by which depositors obtained 3.5 percent interest and their deposits guaranteed by the government. It was a matter of record that the government had not lost a cent for a period of ten years. Here in Chicago there were over 60 private banks doing business, and yet Mr. Mayer had declared there were not over ten bona fide private bankers in the city."

All of this talk was brought about by the failure of Kean's bank—all the more aggravating because Kean was an arrant hypocrite. But the question arises, are not all bankers who obtain the money of unsuspecting depositors hypocrites?

It is not important, however, to discuss such questions. Honest bankers always pay depositors. Dishonest bankers do not. They are thieves and swindlers of the worst possible type, and when religion, or more properly the profession of religion, is used as a cloak of scoundrelism, as in Kean's case, the crime merits double punishment, and here comes into prominence the fact that such colossal scoundrels in a great majority of cases go free, while comparatively smaller criminals go to prison. Such things bring law, lawmakers, and courts into deserved contempt. The great mass of the people are made to conclude that back of the law, the lawmakers, and the law's administrators are corrupt forces, and the allegations are true to such an alarming extent that the courts are often regarded as helps to crime and rascality when sufficiently gold-plated.

Free Speech[†]
April 1891

The *American Spectator,* referring to an article in the *New York Herald,* says:

> The *New York Herald* has a well-considered editorial on the right of free speech, suggested by the action of the Brooklyn authorities in refusing to allow the anarchists to hold a public meeting.
>
> "The position of the authorities," says the editor of the *Herald,* "in this matter, is not well taken. The right of discussion is founded on bedrock. Our citizens, no matter what their peculiarities of belief may be, are

---

† Published in *Locomotive Firemen's Magazine,* vol.15, no. 4 (April 1891), 306–307.

guaranteed all possible liberty of speech. They can talk themselves hoarse, or even talk themselves to death, without any infringement of law.

"It is only when an overt act is committed that the rigor of the law should be applied. If they commit a breach of the peace or indulge in deeds of violence, they should be arrested, tried, and sentenced for the offense.

"But free speech, even when it gives vent to disgusting nonsense, should be tolerated. A man who is at liberty to keep his mouth open is seldom dangerous, but it is frequently hazardous to compel a man to keep his mouth shut because he doesn't agree with the views which are generally acceptable."

We are pleased to see great metropolitan journals taking this stand. It is time that all persons who value free speech, free thought, and indeed liberty, should boldly stand forth and demand that every citizen of the Republic should be protected in the orderly exercise of his rights.

We do not propose to discuss anarchism, nor anarchists—simply "free speech," particularly this proposition announced by the *Herald*. "But free speech, even when it gives vent to disgusting nonsense, should be tolerated." Is that true? It covers the entire field of speech—all topics—all questions relating to politics, religion, and morals. It imposes no restraints. Speech is not an "overt act" and therefore should be subjected to no restraint whatever. Is that true? Is it right? Is it in consonance with our best notions of civilization?

There are in the country a class of people who advocate what is called "free love." These people denounce marriage; they advocate indiscriminate sexual intercourse. They go into communities and in the exercise of "free speech," so-called, transform homes into brothels, pollute every shrine where virtue worships. Is that what the *Herald* calls "disgusting nonsense" which is to be "tolerated," which "should be tolerated?"

Again there are those who would exercise "free speech" in the advocacy of polygamy—and for a quarter of a century or more, did advocate polygamy, unmolested, until thousands and tens of thousands were debauched, and a great territory became more loathsome than a charnel house; until the air was foully infectious and every mountain stream poured its flood tide of nastiness into Great Salt Lake. Was this simply "disgusting nonsense" which "should be tolerated?" Mind, we are running no parallels between such filth and anarchism. We are simply surveying the field of "free speech," to inquire whether or not society has the right to protect itself from unrestrained liberties in that direction.

Let it be understood that free speech is not necessarily a crime, advocating speech. That which the *Herald* styles "disgusting nonsense" is all too often a deadly virus which inoculates the mind with diseases for which there is no remedy, a fact which the *Herald* understands full well.

This *Magazine* believes in free speech and a free press—but with limitations. It would have no free-speech Satans in American Eden homes, no square foot of American soil defiled by the advocates of polygamy, no brothel beasts advocating free love, no Sodoms inviting Heaven's wrath in storms of fire.[17] In a word, certain forms of free speech are crimes against humanity and should be suppressed, and will be suppressed.

Mankind in a Bad Way[†]
April 1891

Mr. Alfred Russel Wallace,[18] in the *Fortnightly Review,* refers to his latest conversation with Darwin, when the eminent naturalist "expressed himself gloomily on the future of humanity, on the ground that in our modern civilization natural selection had no play, and the fittest did not survive. Those who succeed in the race for wealth are by no means the best or the most intelligent, and it is notorious that our population is more largely renewed in each generation from the lower than from the middle and upper classes."[19] And an American writer is quoted as saying that "We behold the melancholy spectacle of the renewal of the great mass of society from the lowest classes, the highest classes to a great extent either not marrying or not having children. The floating population is always the scum, and yet the stream of life is largely renewed from this source. Such a state of affairs, sufficiently dangerous in any society, is simply suicidal in the democratic civilization of our day."[20]

Such facts must indeed be very discouraging to philanthropists who deplore the fact that the highest classes do not marry extensively, or, if they do marry, prefer lapdogs to children; as a consequence, bearing children and obeying the command to "multiply and replenish the earth" is left to what is designated the "lowest classes," the "scum," and the "American writer" is quoted as regarding that sort of increase of population as "dangerous" anywhere, and

---

† Published in *Locomotive Firemen's Magazine,* vol. 15, no. 4 (April 1891), 294–296.

"suicidal in the democratic civilization of the day."

It is such pestiferous stuff, constantly published in the magazines, that poisons the fountains of healthy thought, than which nothing could be more vicious.

In England, where Mr. Darwin lived, and where Mr. Alfred Russel Wallace lives, there are "upper classes," classes recognized by law. To say nothing of the Queen, who for a time was amazingly prolific, the "upper classes" of England do not have many children. They care little for children, their preference being, as a general proposition, for horses and hounds. The middle class, to which Mr. Darwin belonged, and which includes merchants and bankers, traders, and "well-to-do people," guard against a numerous progeny. As a consequence, the replenishment of population is left to the lower classes, but for whom England would be without either sailors or soldiers.

Mr. Wallace is of the opinion that the fact that what he calls the "lower class," the "scum," are addicted to having children, acts as a "check to progress," and he regards the problem as serious because it has "attracted the attention of some of our most thoughtful writers, and has quite recently furnished the theme for a perfect flood of articles in our best periodicals." Mr. Wallace, it will be noted, says, "the floating population is always the scum," and that the "stream of life is largely renewed from this source," and the fact is attracting "the attention of some of the most thoughtful writers," and that periodicals are flooded with articles upon the subject.

It may be well to remark just here that whatever may be true in England, where Mr. Darwin discovered that God did not create man at all, nor anything else for that matter, the "floating population" is the "scum," but it is not true in the United States. Since Noah's ark rested on Ararat, and man was permitted to touch dry land again,[21] he has been a "floater," necessarily so. Naturally a man is a nomad. When Columbus discovered America, Europeans began floating to the New World and have kept it up ever since, and after reaching its shores, they began floating across the continent. They are still floating westward. The floating population is still engaged in subduing the wilderness—in making farms, in building towns and cities, and in laying the foundations of empire states. They move on from place to place, and instead of being a "check to progress," there would be no progress without them. And it so happens that these floaters have children and rear families. To designate them as the "scum" may suit the fancy of the "upper class" and the "middle class," as such classes exist in Europe, but here in America they constitute the bone and sinew, the strength and glory of the country.

We do not doubt that there are those in the United States who regard themselves the "upper class" and the "middle class," and that these two classes fancy there is a class below them, whom they, as readily as Mr. Wallace, call the "scum."

We do not doubt that there are people in the United States who may be properly designated as the "scum" or the "dross." They are to be found in all of the large cities, and are the class from which the New York Central draws its Pinkerton thugs when it wants to quiet dissatisfied railroad employees with bullets. We do not doubt that these people have children, too many perhaps, but when it is charged that the "stream of life is largely renewed from this source," a monstrous slander is perpetrated, for which the facts furnish no excuse.

It is doubtless true that the working classes, men engaged in physical labor, rear the largest families—and it is well that such is the case—indeed it is shown that of the 13 million families in the United States, about 11 million belong to that class who must work for a living, and of these 11 million families it would be simply villainous to intimate that any considerable number should be classed as the "scum" of our population, or to state as a fact that they are "checking progress" by having children.

It has been held by men who were supposed to understand the subject that "education, hygiene, and social refinement had a cumulative action, and would of themselves lead to a steady improvement of the civilized races," and it is said by Mr. Wallace "that view rested on the belief that whatever improvement was effected in individuals was transmitted to their progeny, and that it would be thus possible to effect a continuous advance in physical, moral, and intellectual qualities without any selection of the better or elimination of the inferior types. But of late years grave doubts have been thrown on this view, owing chiefly to the researches of Galton and Weismann[22] as to the fundamental causes to which heredity is due. The balance of opinion among physiologists now seems to be against the heredity of any qualities acquired by the individual after birth, in which case the question we are discussing will be much simplified, since we shall be limited to some form of selection as the only possible means of improving (?) the race." Just here comes into prominence the conclusion of scientists: "Education, hygiene, and social influences are no longer to be trusted," and "some form of selection" is to be introduced whereby a better type of children is to be produced. Manifestly, the "upper class" will not select from the "middle class" or the "scum," hence if an "improvement" is to come by "selection," the "scum" must select from the superior classes. The "scum" must look up and demand entrance to higher social circles.

Mr. Herbert Spencer, it is said, in a remarkable essay on the theory of population, comes to the rescue and shows by the "phenomena of the whole animal kingdom" that those animals which have the shortest lives produce "the greatest number of offspring," and the "upper" class doubtless regard such phenomena as proof that the "scum" is short-lived. It will be seen at once that Mr. Herbert Spencer's idea is to compare the "lower classes" with the lowest type of animals, rabbits and rats and the like, and this is called science; and the authors of such drool are known as scientists, investigators, men who hew out new highways of progress, men who have discovered at last that education, hygiene, and social refinement will not answer the requirements of progress, and that the hope of the world centers in "selection."

As matters now stand, it is held that population is increasing too rapidly, and "hygiene," while it promotes increase, does not improve the progeny; but, says the writer, "the facts accord with the theory that highly intellectual parents do not as a rule have large families, while the most rapid occurs in those classes which are engaged in the similar kinds of manual labor." And in this we have the final conclusion that men engaged in "manual labor" are the "scum" who have "large families" and are responsible for renewing the "stream of life."

Such is the logic of so-called science, which designates the men engaged in "manual labor" as the "scum," and deplores the fact that they rear large families.

This sort of writing floods our "best periodicals," and seeks through such avenues to degrade labor. The "upper class" is the rich, the "scum" is the poor, the toiler, the wealth creator, the taxpayer, those who build everything and preserve everything from wreck and ruin.

And here, we ask, what is the labor press of the country doing to counter-act the growth of such pernicious doctrines? Much we hope. Certainly much it can do, and much it must do, if the time is ever to come when the badge of labor is to be something besides the insignia of degradation, and scientists are to be taught the truth of Burns's philosophy that

> A prince can mak a belted knight,
>   A marquis, duke, and a' that;
> But an honest man's aboon his might,
>   Guid faith, he maunna fa' that.[23]

The Almighty Dollar†

April 1891

At this writing it does not occur to us who first used the expression "the Almighty Dollar"—nor does it matter in the least who was the author of the phrase; it has long since been canonized in the literature of the times, and all admit that it would be difficult to coin an expression more vividly indicative of the animating spirit of the age in which we live.

There is, confessedly, in the term "Almighty Dollar," a large ingredient of playful irreverence which admits of no question and is shockingly apparent when the terms "Almighty God" and "Almighty Dollar" are placed in juxtaposition, but they should be placed in close proximity to enable the reader to comprehend the force of the term as applied to the dollar.

Throughout Christendom the "dollar" has more devout worshippers than the omnipotent God—indeed, it is to be doubted if there is in all recorded history more than one instance where the dollar, in a national policy, was required to take second place or a still lower rank as compared to the station of the gods—in fact, Lycurgus, some centuries before the days of St. Paul, gave the Spartans to understand that "the love of money is the root of all evil." Lycurgus is dead, and St. Paul is dead, but the dollar is not dead. The temples of Mammon are more numerous than ever before in the world's history, the god is worshiped more devoutly and his devotees are numbered by millions, and nowhere is the idolatry more repulsive and debasing than in Christian lands, and to such an extent has the debauchery proceeded in the United States that the term "the Almighty Dollar" tamely expresses the national degradation the worship has fastened upon us.

This debauchery is universal; no class, calling, or profession has escaped its contaminations. It is a national disgrace. Its defilements are seen in every community. It pollutes the national mind, poisons every fountain of thought, and humiliates, shames, and mortifies the few who, like the immortal three, would not fall down and worship the golden image the king had set up.

The worship of "the Almighty Dollar" is fruitful of all things detestable in national life. It is the prolific source of envy, jealousy, and pride. It creates its aristocracies, all along the line, from ragpickers in their dens to the millionaires in their palatial homes. The worship of "the Almighty Dollar" breeds suicides

---

† Published in *Locomotive Firemen's Magazine,* vol. 15, no. 4 (April 1891), 291–294.

and murders, and every vulgar vice known to Sodom. It is licentious and lust-ful to a degree that ten thousand homes, however beautiful their exterior, are within like whited sepulchers, full of all manner of uncleanness; and still the worship goes forward, and the soulless, heartless devotees, with blind and des-perate eagerness, crowd around the shrine of their god like wild beasts at a lick.

In the January [1891] *Magazine,* attention was called to the announcement made by Thomas G. Shearman of New York that 70 persons had succeeded in securing $2.7 billion of the wealth of the country.

In the January *Forum* the same gentleman reiterates his statement; and in further replying to the question, "Who owns the United States?" says "one half of all the national wealth is owned by 40,000 families," and that three-fourths of it is in the possession of fewer than 250,000 families.

The term "almighty" means all-powerful, omnipotent, irresistible. The wealth of the United States expressed in round numbers is $62 billion. The population of the country is 63 million—divided into families of five each, and we have 12.6 million families. Mr. Shearman says that "40,000 families" have secured one-half of the wealth of the country—$31 million, an average of $775,000 each. Again he says that "fewer than 250,000 families have in their possession three-fourths of the wealth of the country—$46.5 billion, an average of $186,000 each." As a result, if 250,000 families have secured $46.5 billion, there remains $15.5 billion for 12,350,000 families, which would give an average of $1,255 each. Tabulated, the showing is as follows:

250,000 families at	$186,000 each =	$46.5 billion
12,350,000 families at	1,255 each =	15.5 billion
12,600,000 families	**Total**	**$62.0 billion**

But it may be profitable to extend the analysis a stage further. If the wealth of the country, $62 billion, is divided by the population, the average amount per capita would be $984.12. But according to Mr. Shearman's estimate, 250,000 fam-ilies or 1,250,000 persons have secured three-fourths of the wealth of the country, $46.5 billion, or $37,200 per capita, while 12,350,000 families, or 61,750,000 persons, have the remaining one-quarter of the wealth, or $251 per capita.

Such figures suggest to Mr. Shearman the coming of a billionaire, one man who will have one thousand millions of "the almighty dollars." He says:

> The least that can be said is that there are 70 American estates that aver-age $35 million. During the year by the consolidation of two estates, one individual has become worth at least $200 million. * * *

The evolution of such enormous fortunes, absolutely inconceivable 40 years ago as an American possibility, naturally leads us to look into the future and to ask how far this concentration of wealth may go, and whether the existing hundred millionaires foreshadow the coming billionaire. Is he coming? When will he come? What effect will his coming have upon society? Unless some great change takes place in our financial or social system, the billionaire is certainly coming and at a rapid speed.

The billionaire is coming with rapid speed and will get here on time, unless some great change takes place in our financial or social system. What changes can be wrought in either the financial or social system to head off the coming of the billionaire?

Is it proposed to take the "almighty" out of the dollar? Disarm it, deprive it of its power and subject it to restraints? Is it proposed to put a stop to the worship of the dollar? Destroy its temples and its shrines, and disperse the worshipers?

If the billionaire is coming, he is coming with ten thousand millionaires in his train. He is coming in all the pomp and circumstances that wealth can bestow; and he is coming to stay and to multiply.

Mr. Shearman predicts that the billionaire will be here AD 1930, 40 years hence, and asks, "What would be the effect upon our social order of the advent of the billionaire?" Some people are so mistaken about the effect of his coming that they have drawn "lurid pictures of his tyranny," but such pictures, Mr. Shearman thinks, "have no basis in fact or common sense." Mr. Shearman is of the opinion that "the possession of such vast wealth brings a large degree of caution, and even timidity, to its owner;" and this view he seeks to support by saying that "at the present time nineteen-twentieths of those who are worth more than ten millions keep out of active public life, and three-fourths of them are anxious to avoid even the suspicion of political influence."

Here we have the declaration that men worth from $10 million to $200 million are made "cautious and even timid" by their wealth; but men worth from $500,000 to $5 million do not hesitate to exert their political influence, or the influence of the almighty dollar with ostentation, and the opinion is expressed that those of still greater fortunes are "coming to the front" in political affairs.

It would have been well if Mr. Shearman had named a few of the men worth from $10 million to $200 million who are so exceedingly prudent and fainthearted as to take no interest in public affairs and are anxious to let it be known that they are without "political influence." True, such men may not be candidates for office, they may exercise great caution in declaring their partisan predilections, but all this caution and timidity vanishes the instant any interest they represent is in peril. Then they are no longer cautious about their declarations; they are at once transformed; they are daring to rashness and bold to audacity. Then their money, in a steady stream, goes to support lobbies, to influence legislators and courts, and the influence of "the Almighty Dollar" is usually sufficient to carry the day. It is then that the millionaires everlastingly upset Mr. Shearman's declaration that they are timid, and that they seek no political influence. They are worshipers of "the Almighty Dollar" and they eternally stand guard around the temple of their god.

Mr. Shearman says, "The lurid pictures of the tyranny and cruelty of the millionaire have no basis in fact or common sense." That depends entirely upon what Mr. Shearman and others of his ilk may call tyranny and cruelty. The millionaire does not burn the objects of his vengeance alive, apply thumbscrews, or break their bones upon the wheel. Such forms of cruelty and tyranny are not tolerated in the United States just now. But the millionaire Vanderbilts, under the laws of the Empire State of New York, did employ Pinkerton thugs to murder workingmen, an instance of "tyranny and cruelty" paralleled only in lands where a tsar, a sultan, or a shah assumes the right to murder their subjects when it suits their whim.

Mr. Shearman is of the opinion that the coming "billionaire will bring an army of paupers in his train." But this is not all. "The masses, under a system which gives to one man a larger amount of wealth than can ever be attained by a million of his fellow citizens who are fully his equals in skill and merit, and far his superiors in industry," is to breed discontent which will forever increase.

What of such a picture? A train of "paupers" and universal discontent among the masses. How much further is it to scenes which the French Revolution presented, and which live in crimson vividness? "The effect of such concentration of wealth upon public and private morals," says Mr. Shearman, "may well be anticipated with concern. Already the wealthy classes," he says, "are hard pressed by the temptations of idleness, the parent of all mischief. Gambling has increased enormously, especially around New York, and a limited license for it, previously bought from local officials, has now been purchased from the legislature." Here we have it that the state of New York is completely under the sway of millionaires, and the debauchery has proceeded until the legislature of the state licenses gambling that the millionaire class may overcome some of the "temptations of idleness."

Say what we will, "the Almighty Dollar" is *on top,* and the billionaire is coming—coming not only "with paupers in his train," but coming with influences fruitful of discontent of the masses, coming with influences "which will corrupt multitudes less favored by fortune."

This picture is drawn by Thomas G. Shearman, a close student of events, and a man careful of statements. Men talk of the conflict between capital and labor, or between labor and capitalists, as if labor, disregarding all laws, human and divine, was rushing headlong to destruction; but Mr. Shearman sees in the growth of wealth in the hands of the few the direst calamities to the nation and he sees clearly the inevitable consequences of such a state of things.

The worship of "the Almighty Dollar" will proceed and the devotees of the god will increase. Aristocracy, plutocracy, and autocracy will combine their forces against democracy. It will be money against the masses.

As matters now stand, 1.25 million persons have possession of $46.5 billion of the nation's wealth, and 61.75 million persons have possession of $15.5 billion. The plutocrats have an average of $37,500, and the democrats an average of $251.

If the masses will it, a fairer divide can be secured. If they submit to present arrangements the billionaire will come and the little share of the national wealth they now possess will disappear, and then they will have surrendered their rights and will live by permission.

Foreign Pauper Immigration[†]
May 1891

There is a ceaseless clamor against "foreign pauper immigration" to the United States. Every poor person is not a pauper, though every pauper is a poor person. A pauper is so poor that he or she must be supported by charity or starve. A pauper, as a general proposition, is unable to work. Old, infirm, or feeble minded, the law exempts them from labor—the state cares for them. There are no able-bodied, sound-minded paupers. If such persons refuse to work, the law compels them to work. They are vagrants, vagabonds, tramps, idlers by choice, and generally criminals by profession. They are not paupers, and have no just claim upon charity.

† Published in *Locomotive Firemen's Magazine,* vol. 15, no. 5 (May 1891), 399–400.

That such characters are all too often found among the immigrants from foreign countries is not denied. The point we make is that the clamor of the times includes the great mass of immigrants who seek our shorts for the purpose of bettering their condition.

Associated with this outcry against "foreign pauper immigration" is the noise made about the "pauper labor" of Europe. Do those who create the hubbub desire to be understood as denouncing poor men who work in European countries—and because they are poor, class them with paupers? If so, do they not see if poverty and work in Europe degrades workingmen to paupers, it does the same thing in America?

It should be understood that paupers do not work, and that workingmen are not paupers in any land. In this matter let us be distinctly understood. We write to correct errors of expression. Words are signs of ideas, and often of exceedingly vicious ideas. As, for instance, when a member of Congress calls labor "a commodity, as much so as any *raw material,* worked up," and the talk about "pauper labor" and "pauper laborers" is equally ridiculous.

Let us take for illustration two extremes of conditions. Jay Gould, with an income of $10 million a year, and a trackman on one of his railroads whose income is 90 cents a day—or $270 a year—a difference in incomes of $9,999,730. Both of these *gentlemen* live within their incomes; neither of them are objects of charity. The trackman is no more a pauper than Mr. Gould. He wears coarse clothes, he eats coarse fare, he lives in a humbler house—but he works, he supports himself and his family. He is independent. Let him be still further oppressed and robbed, and he will wear still coarser clothes and eat still coarser food and find a still humbler dwelling. But he is not a pauper laborer. Europe is full of men who for centuries have been oppressed, robbed, and degraded, who have struggled against conditions which agonize the brain to contemplate, and yet saved enough to get out of their bondage—to find some other land where, under God's blessings, conditions are more favorable for the poor.

At an early day, we are to have a celebration of the anniversary of the discovery of America by Christopher Columbus. Why celebrate the anniversary? What good came of the discovery if it did not afford an asylum to men who would escape from tyranny, and especially those who were workers? But it is held that those who came first secured a preemption right to the land, not only where they "squatted" but to acres without limit, and now, while making no objection to the immigration of the rich, lift their hands in "holy horror" because the poor manage to land on American shores.

The time has arrived to stop the chatter about "pauper labor" and "pauper laborers." Trust barons and great corporations may be pleased with such terms because they have the significance of slaves or serfs and do not suggest citizenship. If it can be once established that the term "workingman" is synonymous with "pauper laborer," the work of degradation speeds on more rapidly, and the Corbins of the period will be able to accomplish their purpose more perfectly.

The laws as they now stand exclude criminals and paupers from our shores, as also "contract laborers." That is enough. We have room for 400 million population. There are yet empires of waste places. Cities are in a congested condition, but it is not the fault of workingmen. Men at the head of industrial enterprises seek the towns and the cities, and the workingmen follow. There are ten thousand industries in the United States that would succeed quite as well in the country as in the city, if located on any of our railroads—the railroad, the telegraph, and the telephone have completely upset the old theory that the city was best suited for industrial enterprises—and that it still holds sway is due to the vicious ambition of cities to show the largest population, regardless of the vice and poverty which are entailed upon those who must work or starve.

When the Columbus Exposition in 1893 is thrown open to the world, what will be seen? Not a thing that does not glorify labor—labor, from the humblest toiler to the most skilled artisan—and it is hoped that Europe will contribute, as well as all the civilized nations of the earth; and who, we ask, will write of these exhibits as the product of "pauper labor" or who will voice the sentiment that the men whose skill challenges the admiration of all beholders are forbidden the privilege of coming to America? Let us be done with such gabble. When from the masthead of one of the little vessels in the squadron of Columbus the cry was heard, "Land! Land!" it meant land for the world; not for those who first robbed the Indians, but for man through all time who might seek homes in the New World. At any rate, whatever else may be said in regard to a Chinese-wall policy of exclusiveness, let us be done with the "pauper labor" folly—something that never existed since Jehovah finished the world and "rested from all the work which he had made."[24]

Labor Leaders[†]

May 1891

The *Railway Service Gazette,* in its issue of March 5 [1891], contains a somewhat extended editorial article captioned, "What Shall be Done?"

It appears that a correspondent of the *Gazette* appeals to it to at once engage in some very aggressive work in the interest of the laborers of America, "because chains are being forged for their enslavement." The writer wants the *Gazette* to send forth "clarion notes" to "rouse them from their fatal slumber." The correspondent says, "The laborers of America must federate as one man, and our thunders must shake the halls of legislation so long reeking with the corruption of party dishonesty."

To this stirring appeal, the *Gazette* responds in a way indicative of an upgrade pull, with a machine sadly out of fix, poor fuel, and a scarcity of water. But, nevertheless, the *Gazette* sends forth a "warning cry" keyed up to "clarion notes," and well calculated to "rouse labor leaders" wherever they are practicing their "golden calf" idolatry.

The *Gazette* has no faith in "labor leaders" as they exist in this AD 1891. It does not refer to one within the entire range of its observation worthy of the name of a leader. It says:

> While there are hundreds of quacks, who from the street corners and the crossroads are proclaiming that the way to salvation is perfectly familiar to them, and that they are the leaders appointed by God, we honestly believe the Moses has not yet arisen who will lead the people to the promised land, and that until the people have been far more greatly tried than they are at present, he would indeed have a rocky road to travel, did he attempt to lead them in the true direction of a betterment of their conditions.

Any reference to Moses as illustrative of the condition of workingmen in America may serve to gracefully round up a period, to embellish a sentence and generally beautify rhetoric, but it is hardly just. The student of the Bible will naturally refresh his memory by re-reading the graphic account of the wonderful undertaking of Moses. The bondage, the slavery, the degradation

---

† Published in *Locomotive Firemen's Magazine,* vol. 15, no. 5 (May 1891), 445–447.

of the Jews, we conceive, was something worse than anything yet experienced by the laborers of America, with the exception, possibly, of the coke regions of Pennsylvania.

Again, the enslaved Jews never would have got beyond the Red Sea but for the direct interposition of Jehovah, who had to fight Pharaoh with plagues, the recital of which even now horrifies the mind. And after all of the mighty hosts that crossed the Red Sea dry-shod, but two were fit to enter the promised land—all had died in the wilderness; and to make matters worse still, Moses, owing to some indiscretion, never crossed the Jordan, never entered the land of milk and honey, which, to say the least, was pretty hard on a God-chosen leader.[25]

Such facts lead us to the conclusion that the workingmen of the United States need not wait for a Moses to lead them from under an imaginary bondage or from the grasp of an imaginary Pharaoh.

Certainly we are not disposed to controvert the declarations of our esteemed contemporary as to the *blue* outlook of labor in many directions. Nor are we in a position to deny that there are "hundreds of quacks proclaiming that the way of salvation is perfectly familiar to them." But what we do see is that workingmen are everywhere organizing, and organization, to our mind, is a towering evidence of education, intelligence, self-respect, and independence. What we do hear are the "clarion" notes of labor speakers and labor writers, urging men forward in the grand work of organization—and to ears attuned to the sounding notes of organized labor; it will be found that the rank and file of organized workingmen are themselves labor leaders, that they too know the way to the "promised land"—that they do not propose either to die in the wilderness or be fed on manna.[26] They are not waiting for a Moses—nor do they expect miracles to be wrought in their favor.

What, we ask, is a "labor leader?" If there are "quacks" with their cheap nostrums, how shall we know the "simon pure" article, the orthodox remedies for the ills which afflict us?

We take it that any journal devoted to the interests of labor, and edited with the boldness that distinguishes the *Railway Service Gazette,* is a labor agitator and a labor leader, both in the highest sense of the term. We do not object to the caustic criticism of the *Gazette* when referring to pseudo-leaders and reformers—the fact that there are such emphasizes the splendid truth that the genuine leader and reformer exists. If the quack finds his dupes, it is equally true that the true man will have supporters.

We read with special satisfaction the *Gazette*'s lucid exposition of difficulties which confront workingmen. The plutocracy is here. Wealth is massing its forces; legislatures and courts are debauched; the millennium looks far distant. There are clouds along the horizon—a storm is brewing. We would withhold no fact within our knowledge. A good general wants to know as much as possible about his enemy, and the *Gazette* is equal to the occasion when it says:

> Some of the very men who rail the loudest against millionaires are the very first to lick the hand of the millionaire that permits itself to be licked, though that hand is blackened with a thousand frauds, any one of which is morally worse than those which place poor men behind prison bars. Other loud reformers, when serving on juries, never fail to tilt the scales of justice in favor of the rich and against the poor. Others still will bow, and sneak, and cringe before the rich man, lacking both in honor and intelligence, while they turn in scorn from the man in rags, though he is honest, virtuous, and intelligent.
>
> How many are there, even among the labor leaders and among the labor reformers, who do not bow and worship the golden calf, who do not honor dishonest wealth and turn from honest poverty, who do not prize money above merit, who do not give their influence and patronage to the rich and withhold it from the poor, who in a word do not each day do something to add to the volume of that mighty stream which with every increasing current is bringing all the good things to the rich and away from the poor?
>
> Here in Ohio is a railroad man, who with several associates was guilty of a robbery of $4 or $5 million. The robbery was in no essential less heinous than those that place poor men behind prison bars. He does not even take the trouble to deny or palliate the offense. He escapes through a technicality of the law, which subservient juries and subservient judges can always find, with the money of other people in his pocket. This man is one of the first citizens of Ohio. Should he come up for office he would be enthusiastically supported by the employees of his own roads, and perhaps other roads. His offense would probably never be mentioned. With such a condition, what can we expect from legislation? Why talk of the reforming influence of political parties? But suppose the hearts of the people, the railroad men, the mechanics, the laborers, were all right, what then? Suppose everywhere this man went he was met with the withering scorn and contempt that is awarded the poor man who is guilty of a similar though smaller offense.

The foregoing is an ebon or a lurid picture as one may fancy. It represents labor leaders, Heaven save the mark, as the most abject and despicable creatures that walk God's green earth or pollute the air with their pestilential breath. Traitors and apostates, no language can fitly characterize them, and hyperbole sits dumb in the presence of the task.

Where are they? Who are they? What are their names? Where do they flourish and stink? We would like to know them that with whips of flame we might help to scourge the scoundrels through the world.

We see workingmen everywhere organizing. We see lodge fires blaze everywhere, in the valleys and on mountain elevations. We see the army of organized labor marching with banners flying. We see women, too, lending their approving smiles and words. We see workingmen's publications increasing in numbers, in power and influence. We see men, but yesterday tongue-tied and silent, who today, inspired by the genius of emancipation, are telling the story of their redemption with startling eloquence. We see one of a building trade unions demanding justice of employers, and then we see other "unions," in the spirit of brotherhood, gather around and proclaim the conquering battle cry, "We are with you." It is federation. There is in it all no "golden calf," no idol worship, but evidence that men's hearts are right, that they have clear perceptions of duty; that they are loyal to obligation and that the work of education with them is far advanced.

The *Gazette,* having surveyed the situation and found it anything but lovely—a desert without an oasis, about as dreary as Stanley's description of the Congo forest[27]—proceeds to point out the remedy by saying, "If there is any material change in present conditions the reform must commence in the hearts of the people."—working people, we suppose.

We surmise the reform has come. We are inclined to the opinion that it is growing in sweep and in power—organization is the shibboleth, and the hearts of the people are not beating like "muffled drums" "funeral marches to the grave"[28] of organization.

The ORC and the B of RC†

May 1891

The Order of Railway Conductors, as originally organized, was by its constitution non-protective, or in more common parlance was a non-striking order.
But in the march of events, and under circumstances which forced the thoughts
of the membership into new channels, the order, in convention at Rochester,
NY, May 1890, eliminated the non-protective or anti-strike law from its constitution, which, without further action, left the order in a somewhat anomalous
condition. There was no law opposed to strikes, nor was there any law which
under any conditions authorized strikes, and it is presumed that at the annual
convention of the order which meets in the city of St. Louis on the 12th of May
[1891], the subject will receive special consideration, and that a definite policy
will be adopted.

Prior to the Rochester convention of the ORC, another order of railway
conductors was organized, known as the Brotherhood of Railway Conductors.
This new order was brought into existence by virtue of the fact that the ORC
did not, and under its laws could not, protect its members when they were the
victims of flagrant injustice, and throughout the entire history of railroading
no one class of employees have been subjected to greater wrongs than have
been inflicted upon railway conductors.

The B of RC has sought during its brief career to remedy the wrongs complained of, and the victories it has won and the good it has accomplished bear
eloquent testimony to the fact that there was a pressing demand for it.

The B of RC has had a phenomenal growth, and is regarded as one of the
most aggressive and progressive orders of railway employees.

But the action of the ORC in convention at Rochester leads to the conclusion that at the St. Louis Convention the order will be made *protective,* in
which case the two orders of railway conductors would be in harmony in policy
and purposes.

Should the action of the ORC be such as we have intimated, the question
arises, why have two orders? Why not consolidate? Why remain apart?

The *Magazine* is unable to suggest a reason why there should be two orders
of railway conductors, having practically the same policy, any more than it

---

† Published in *Locomotive Firemen's Magazine,* vol. 15, no. 5 (May 1891), 439.

could frame an argument in favor of two orders of locomotive firemen—and with the same policy and purposes guiding than animating them, we doubt if a rational objection to their consolidation could be formulated.

The ORC, in electing a grand chief in sympathy with protection, and whose administration of the affairs of the order evinces a clear comprehension of protection, leads naturally to the conclusion that the action of the order at St. Louis will be such as to emphasize the wisdom of having but one order of railway conductors in the country.

The legislation required to bring about the unification of the two organizations is simple, and if the spirit of compromise should prevail and be permitted to exert its power, we shall look forward to the early consolidation of the two orders, a consummation which we do not doubt would be fruitful of lasting benefits.

Conditions[†]

June 1891

Our attention is called to an article in the *Christian Union*, by Rev. George Thomas Dowling, D.D.,[29] in which the learned divine brings his love to bear upon the rich and the poor, his purpose being to persuade the poor that after all they are as happy as the rich and should therefore be contented with their lot. Those who read the meditations of the pious D.D. will readily see that his anxieties circle around the rich—and his solicitude is so pronounced that it is more than probable his salary will be raised. The rich man, this ambassador of the "King of Kings" assumes, may "step up or down at will, while the poor must be content with what chance offers for bettering their condition." What the *chances* are for the poor to better their condition the Rev. Dowling, D.D., fails to point out, but he tells his readers that "nothing but his own inclination prevents the rich man from making himself a pauper," while "inclination does not solve the problem for the poor man." The poor man, manifestly, has no inclination to make himself poorer—and God knows, in thousands of instances he could not, if he had the inclination—and if he has an inclination to rise

---

† Published in *Locomotive Firemen's Magazine,* vol. 15, no. 6 (June 1891), 498.

he must wait for a chance. Inclination is of little consequence to him, and in a vast majority of cases where a *chance* arises, someone gets in ahead and the poor still languish waiting for another chance to rise.

The theory of the Rev. Dowling, D.D., suggests a scrap of divine history, where we deem it worthwhile to reproduce in this connection as it illustrates that some centuries ago, another *force* than "chance" made its appearance as follows:

> Now there is at Jerusalem by the sheep market a pool, which is called in the Hebrew tongue Bethesda, having five porches.
>
> In these lay a great multitude of impotent folk, of blind, halt, withered, waiting for the moving of the water.
>
> For an angel went down at a certain season into the pool, and troubled the water: Whosoever then first after the troubling of the water stepped in was made whole of whatever disease he had.
>
> And a certain man was there which had an infirmity thirty and eight years.
>
> When Jesus saw him lie, and knew that he had been now a long time in that case, he saith unto him, Wilt thou be made whole.
>
> The impotent man answered him. Sir, I have no man, when the water is troubled, to put me into the pool: but while I am coming another steppeth down before me.
>
> Jesus saith unto him, Rise, take up thy bed and walk.[30]

The incident discloses a new departure in human affairs—a new force—things that the Rev. Dowling, D.D., fails to see. It no longer requires that an angel should come down and trouble the waters that men may be cured of their infirmities. Everywhere the waters are troubled—and a voice says to every poor man, every workingman, "Rise," and in obedience to the command they are rising. They are not waiting for chances and opportunities, but are creating them. Every lodge room is a Bethesda—and even an infirm scab may be cured of his diseases, and be redeemed from corporation slavery.

The rich, for whom the titled fat-salaried clergy are so exceedingly solicitous, may not like the command to "rise," which workingmen are heeding and obeying, but their antagonism is losing its potency. The inclination of workingmen is finding practical means for assertion. They are no longer waiting for someone to put them into the pool; by the mighty force of organization, they go in—and confident of the righteousness of their cause, they are prepared to fight a good fight for the emancipation of labor; they are prepared to "withstand in the evil day, and having done all to stand."[31]

The platitudes of the pulpit, the degeneracy of the church, the debauchery of legislatures, the corruptions of high life, the arrogance of the rich will not swerve them from their course—animated by the declaration of the "carpenter's son," who said, "My father worketh hitherto and I work,"[32] they will work on and work ever, work if required, as do the corals who lay the foundations of continents in the depths of the sea, and build until their superstructure rises above the waves and is clothed in eternal verdure.

A Crisis of Federation Affairs[†]

June 1891

Every consideration of fealty to right and justice demands that the *Locomotive Firemen's Magazine* should now, as it has done in the past, advise its readers, especially the members of the Brotherhood of Locomotive Firemen, of such facts as may come to its knowledge, derived from unquestionable sources, calculated in any wise to promote the interests of the federated orders of railway employees, and, as certainly, and if possible with more distinctness, lay bare such other facts as the editor believes have a tendency to detract from the prosperity and power of such organizations and eventually disrupt federation.

Profoundly impressed with the fact that a crisis has come in the affairs of the federated orders imperatively demanding plain speech, and with unqualified friendship for each of the federated orders, I shall write of recent incidents, which under the most favorable presentation are well calculated to arouse feelings of despondency in the ranks of the most hopeful.

No one, I assume, has entertained the idea that any organization of men, however guarded by declarations of principles and the enactment of wise laws, could fully overcome man's fallibilities. No such claim by any sane man was ever advanced, but it has been assumed, based upon self-evident truths, that "in unity there is strength," and, therefore, that organizations of workingmen, having interests in common—mutual interests—could promote the welfare of

---

[†] Published as "To the Federated Orders of Railway Employees" in *Locomotive Firemen's Magazine*, vol. 15, no. 6 (Jun 1891), 534–38.

their members by federation; that in federation the largest possible power of human effort could be exerted; that by federation the wrong could be cloven down and the right enthroned; that by federation, principles of justice could be established and maintained; and that not only the welfare of workingmen would thereby be promoted but the prosperity and happiness of society as well.

Such propositions have never been denied. The opponents of federation have simply made objections, but have offered no arguments, because there were none at their command. The principles upon which federation is based are as eternal as any axiom in mathematics. In every arraignment they can stand any test that enmity or ignorance can devise. If, in a contest, victory comes—as come it has in the past, and is destined to come in the future to men who are capable of comprehending the power of federation—its advocates and defenders may of right be jubilant; and when defeat comes—as come it has in the past when the right has been overpowered and crushed, the eternal truth that "in unity there is strength," and that in federation that strength can be secured in the largest measure, has never lost a fraction of its claim to recognition. On the contrary, it stands as the rallying point of workingmen, and will remain as immovable as the eternal hills as long as heartless plutocrats devise methods of cruelty and injustice to labor.

Notwithstanding such things, there is serious trouble existing in the Supreme Council of the federated orders of railway employees; troubles which had their origin in matters as foreign to federation as it is possible to conceive, but the parties involved, being related to the Supreme Council by virtue of the membership of the orders, a *few* of whose members disagreeing upon a comparatively trivial matter were permitted to generate irritations and animosities until the Supreme Council was, by call, convened for the purpose of restoring amicable relations.

In laying such matters before the members of the brotherhood, I am compelled to indulge in details to enable the reader to comprehend the situation.

In the yards of the C&NW Railway[33] at Chicago there was a yardmaster by the name of McNerney,[34] and a switchman by the name of Crowe.[35]

McNerney was a member of the Brotherhood of Railroad Trainmen, and Crowe was a member of the Switchmen's Mutual Aid Association.

Between these two men feelings quite the opposite of amicable existed, and as a result, McNerney discharged Crowe.

It is not surprising that the switchmen in the yard at once rallied to the aid of their fellow member and championed his cause. They appointed a committee to visit the railroad official who had authority to reinstate Crowe, and an hour was set by that official to meet the committee and hear the grievance. When the hour arrived, Superintendent Miller, the official in question, failed to show up, notwithstanding it was his own appointment.

This treatment of the switchmen on the part of Superintendent Miller had the effect to temporarily demoralize them, and the result was a strike of short duration, continuing only a few hours and causing little embarrassment to the road, and though brought about by the neglect and improper treatment of Superintendent Miller, was not justifiable under the laws of the switchmen's organization nor the laws of the Supreme Council.

The switchmen, though Crowe had been reinstated, smarting under the action of McNerney toward Crowe, demanded and secured his discharge as yardmaster.

These incidents naturally involved the two orders—the B of RT and the SMAA, both members of the Supreme Council of the federated orders—and as a consequence, a call was made for convening that body to investigate the situation, and it convened for that purpose in the city of Chicago on April 13 [1891].

When the Supreme Council had convened, it was found that there was really no business to be brought before it of a character demanding anything more than the friendly advice of its members to heal any wounds that a mere personal conflict between two members of the body had inflicted.

The good offices of the members of the Supreme Council were promptly tendered and amicable relations it was believed had been established. At any rate the surface indications were satisfactory and the outlook promised harmony.

On May 16 another demand was made for convening the Supreme Council, and on that date it did convene again in the city of Chicago, the call growing out of the following order issued by the authorities of the Chicago & Northwestern Railway:

> The switching service of the Chicago & Northwestern Railway Company as at present performed is not satisfactory to the public nor to the management of the company, therefore all yardmasters and switchmen now in the employ of this company are discharged from its service on and after 7 a.m., May 14, 1891.
>
> In reorganizing the switching service of this company's lines preference will be given to such men previously in its employ as are, in the judgment of the company, capable and worthy.
>
> **S. Sanborn,** General Superintendent
Approved: **J. M. Whitman,** General Manager

The foregoing is probably the most extraordinary order ever issued by a railroad corporation in the world. It should be understood that on the part of the switchmen there was neither a strike nor a contemplated strike; that the men were at their posts performing all of their duties. No note of warning had been given, and yet like a thunderbolt from a clear sky came the order which in an instant remanded about 400 workingmen into idleness and shrouding hundreds of homes in gloom.

I confess that I cannot contemplate such an exhibition of corporation power for an instant without a shudder. It is an exhibition of autocratic power that ought to excite universal alarm, an exhibition of vengeance that startles like a midnight alarm bell. I do not believe that workingmen can contemplate it without realizing that it portends calamities for them in the near future of a character that defies exaggeration.

It is said that the three highest prerogatives of law are to take a man's life, to deprive him of his liberty, and to confiscate his property. In view of such powers, what must be the sensations of a workingman, or the friend of a workingman, when he reads the order I have introduced, driving 400 or more men into idleness? An order which, in depriving a man of work and wages, invites penury followed by hunger and rags, and all too often deprives the wretched victim of shelter. Nor is this all—nor the worst. Such orders recruit the ranks of criminals, people jails and penitentiaries, and provoke suicide. Nor is that all, or the worst of all. Such orders break up homes, scatter families, degrade women, make them the prey of lustful scoundrels, and cover the body social with cancerous blotches that cry ceaselessly for redress.

My readers have read the order and the order was the immediate cause of convening the Supreme Council of the federated orders of railway employees in Chicago, May 16, 1891.

What could the Supreme Council do to mitigate the woes of the crushed switchmen? There was no strike. What then? This:

The Switchmen's Mutual Aid Association, one of the members of the Supreme Council, arraigned the Brotherhood of Railroad Trainmen, another member of the Supreme Council, for having entered into a conspiracy with the officers of the Chicago & Northwestern Railway Company to deprive the members of the SMAA of employment, and that the order of the officers of the C&NW Railway was the *direct* outgrowth of that conspiracy.

The officers of the Switchmen's Mutual Aid Association boldly made the charge of conspiracy, and it was the *grievance* which they presented to the Supreme Council for its action.

The officers of the Brotherhood of Railroad Trainmen *did not deny* the charge. They virtually confessed that they had formed such an alliance, and that but for such a league the switchmen would not have been dismissed.

The reader has the case as succinctly as it is in my power to state it.

From the first day that I heard of a purpose to organize a Brotherhood of Railroad Brakemen I have been the earnest friend of the order, now the Brotherhood of Railroad Trainmen. I have sought on all occasions in its youth and in its maturer years to aid its progress. This is said without any attempt at self-laudation, and could be said by me only under such extraordinary circumstances as make it necessary for me to recite a record which that order has made, and which I deplore.

Here let me say that the charge of conspiracy made against the B of RT by the grand officers of the SMAA was fully sustained, in fact, was not denied.

It requires an effort to comprehend the depth and sweep of the enmity that could have prompted such a betrayal of trust, of confidence, and of obligation. It is probably without a parallel. I know of nothing approximating it in the affairs of brotherhoods of workingmen. To illustrate it, darker records than labor organizations furnish must be sought, and how and where to find them will readily be suggested.

I write of these transactions because I heard the testimony as it came on the heated breath of the officers of the SMAA, because I heard the admissions, the equivocations, explanations, and extenuations of the defense—each one of which made the case more wretched and added to the enormity of the wrong complained of.

I desire to have my readers fully aware of the explanations of the officers of the B of RT. This is due them. With these explanations they must go before the great brotherhood of trainmen. With these explanations and extenuations they must stand before all organized railway employees, before organized workingmen in every department of labor, and with these explanations and extenuations they must stand at the bar of public opinion.

I have, as I write, before me the utterances of the Chicago press pro and con, but I prefer to place matters on record as I saw and heard them myself.

In the first place, the officials of the B of RT charged the switchmen generally, and particularly on the C&NW Railway, as being insubordinate, fomenters of trouble, and disregardful of the laws of their own organization and of the laws of the Supreme Council.

Suppose, for the sake of argument, I admit the truth of such allegations; in what possible way does such an admission justify on the part of the B of RT officials to enter into a conspiracy with the officers of a corporation to inflict penalties upon the adjudged delinquents?

Again, I inquire, if the charges formulated by the officers of the B of RT have not been brought by corporations against members of every order represented by the Supreme Council of the federated orders of railway employees, as also against other orders not represented in that body?

It is well known that in all organizations there have been restless men, chafing under restraint, and ready to take the law into their own hands for the purpose of redressing grievances, and would it not be the height of presumption on the part of the officers of the B of RT so much as to intimate exemption for their order?

But such explanations in the case under consideration serve only to aggravate the charge the officers of the SMAA brought against the officers of the B of RT since, though it might be true that certain members of the SMAA had been premature in seeking to right certain grievances in the past, at the time the conspiracy was formed between the officers of the C&NW Railway and the officers of the B of RT, the switchmen on the system were attending to their duties with as much loyalty to the interests of the road as were the members of the B of RT, and these switchmen would now be at work instead of being idle except for a conspiracy to strike them down unwarned entered into by the B of RT.

What is offered by the officers of the B of RT as extenuating the character of the plot to *down* the switchmen on the C&NW Railway?

In this connection, I refer to the order of the railway officials. It will be noticed that *every* switchman and yardmaster in the employ of the company was at once and at the same time discharged. Look at it, probe it, analyze it, and then hunt through all the tomes of fact and fiction, and nothing like it can be found in human edicts against workingmen. Union men and non-union men alike felt the crushing blow; not one escaped. When the Creator in His wrath decreed to send a storm of fire and brimstone upon Sodom, the old patriarch, Abraham, interceded for the doomed city. He pleaded with God and put the question, "Wilt thou also destroy the righteous with the wicked?" and Jehovah said he would spare the city if there were "fifty righteous" in it. Abraham then proposed "forty-five." Then "forty" was proposed, then "thirty," then "twenty" was named as the number, and finally God said He would not destroy the city, as decreed, if ten righteous could be found in it. Sodom was the wickedest city at that time in the world, and yet, ten good men could have saved it from the storm of Jehovah's wrath.[36]

Who pleaded for the switchmen on the C&NW Railway system? What Abraham went before President Hughitt[37] and asked, if there are fifty, forty-five, forty, thirty, or even ten good switchmen on your roads, will you withhold your cruel decree? Or "will you so modify it as to retain the good men, whether union or non-union men?" In all the wide world no such sympathetic man could be found. President Hughitt kept his plans secret, except to his own officials, and the officials and committee of B of RT. Did the grand officers of the B of RT interpose on behalf of the doomed switchmen? Was there among them an Abraham whose heart could be touched by a knowledge of the impending disaster that was soon to overwhelm them? The testimony in the case supplies no fact glowing with such fraternal light. On the contrary, it was desired to have the official decree, like a Kansas cyclone in a village of haystacks, strike down all, because it could then be pleaded that the officials of the corporation and the B of RT had not *discriminated* against members of the SMAA, that the decree, like the heavenly rain, had fallen upon the just and the unjust alike.

In all the long history of duplicity, was there ever anything quite so thin as such a deception?

But the conspiracy disclosed another feature, which was designed—heaven save the mark—to enable the trainmen to remain true to the laws of their order and to the laws of the Supreme Council.

I have said that the conspiracy, like all such schemes, was concocted in secret. Had the switchmen been apprised of it, they would have struck, and would have been justifiable in so doing. If they had struck, no trainmen could have taken their places except as scabs, but it was held by the officials of the B of RT if the switchmen's places were vacated by a discharge, then they, the trainmen, could take their places without violating any law.

I ask the reader to ponder this phase of the conspiracy. I ask every large-hearted member of the B of RT to give it his unprejudiced consideration. I invite every member of the B of LF and of B of RC to bestow upon this phase of the conspiracy special attention.

The testimony is that the grand officers of an order, a member of the Supreme Council, deliberately enters into a plot to drive certain members of another organization, a member of the Supreme Council, out of employment.

The plotting officials keep the doom of hundreds of switchmen a profound secret, because upon this secrecy depends the success of the conspiracy. If known, the switchmen would strike; if they struck, though their positions would be vacated, the trainmen could not take them without violating laws, *but if they were all discharged, in accordance with the terms of the plot, then, in that case, the trainmen could take their places with impunity.* In that case, the would be *law-proof scabs—legal scabs*, recognized by the laws of their own organization and the laws of the Supreme Council, and any grievance growing out of such acts of perfidy, could not be dealt with by the Supreme Council.

I assert that every member of all of the organizations of railway employees should give this technical excuse for treason careful consideration.

Regardless of the objections to repetition, I desire to present to the reader the theory of the conspiracy entered into between the officials of the C&NW Railway and the B of RT.

Independent of any federated compact, each labor organization, standing by itself, it has been held by all honorable workingmen that for one organization to plot and scheme to down another organization was an act in all regards flagitious and deserving of condemnation, the accepted theory being that one labor organization should seek to promote the welfare of others, for, although marching under different banners, the purpose of all is the same— all seeking to lighten the burdens of labor and increase the happiness and prosperity of toilers.

Just here comes into full view the still higher obligations imposed by federation. The theory of friendship and good will supposed to animate all labor organizations in their intercourse with each other becomes, in federation, a matter of plighted faith and of obligation under the sanction of law—a solemn compact, a union of hearts, and a union of hands—a compact having for its supreme purpose, help in time of need; a compact glowing with a double share of the fraternal spirit, and pledged to every reasonable sacrifice to maintain the right when any party to the compact was attacked by the common enemy.

In this federation of organizations of railway employees the SMAA and the B of RT held honorable membership. If either of them was in trouble it behooved the other to lend every possible assistance to secure relief—to remove embarrassments and make its way smooth.

Now then, the SMAA had had some trouble with the officials of the C&NW Railway. These troubles, so far as the switchmen were concerned, had been adjusted. But the railroad officials were anxious to discharge them. Although a great and powerful corporation, in view of the power believed to exist in federation, it hesitated. It dared not strike down its switchmen. Here and there one or more could be removed, but to remove them all, when they were peacefully at work doing their duty faithfully, was a contract the C&NW Railway did not care to take.

In this dire dilemma the B of RT, a member of the federation, came to the rescue of the railroad officials, and a conspiracy was hatched. Then Benedict

Arnoldism crept in, but unfortunately for the switchmen and for federation, no Major André,[38] with the documents in his boots, was captured, and on May 14 the conspiracy triumphed—the switchmen felt its crushing power—the trainmen took the places of their federated brothers, and the grand officers of B of RT shook hands with the officials of the C&NW Railway, while the overpowered switchmen, powerless and moneyless, are permitted to stare the future in the face and accept with such stoicism as they can command whatever fate conspiracy and treason have in store for them.

The Supreme Council, convened May 16, found itself powerless either to approve or rebuke the B of RT. But a vote was taken on the merits of the grievance submitted by the SMAA against the B of RT, upon which nine votes were cast—six sustaining the grievance and three in the negative. The B of LF was deprived of its vote on account of the inability of the vice grand master [J. J. Hannahan], who was in Georgia, to reach Chicago in time for the meeting, the laws of the Council requiring a full representation. How the B of LF would have voted is not known, but how I would have voted is sufficiently indicated in the foregoing.

I do not hesitate to believe that the enemies of federation will greatly rejoice over what they will designate a collapse of federation. They will meet each other with smiles, and as they clasp hands say, "I told you so." Corporations will chuckle over the victory. But I surmise that their greatest satisfaction will be derived from the belief that they have succeeded in arraying two great orders of railway employees in open hostility to each other, and in practically wrecking the Supreme Council of the federated orders.

As was to have been expected, the *Railway Age,* the acknowledged friend of the corporation and the implacable foe of labor organizations, heartily approves the course pursued by the B of RT, and in a leading editorial glorifies the *loyalty* to the corporation displayed by that organization.

Just here the questions arise, are the two great organizations, the SMAA and the B of RT, opposed to each other? Is it to be believed that the Brotherhood of Trainmen is committed to the relentless policy of exterminating the SMAA? Has the unfortunate episode I have related wrecked the Supreme Council? I do not hesitate to answer in the negative.

I do not underestimate the gravity of the situation—nor do I underestimate the broad common sense of the rank and file of the men who constitute the membership of the federated orders. They are men who comprehend right, justice, and fair play. There is in their ranks an abiding faith in fraternity, fellowship, goodwill, in the blessings of organization and in the strength of federation.

That our good ship, federation, is in a storm, I have shown; that it is beating fiercely upon her is readily inferred; that there have been hidden reefs and treacherous currents in her pathway is now known; but she is not wrecked. Above the howlings of the storm is heard the clear voice of Frank Sweeney, pledging that the order of which he is grand master will never scab.[39]

In this supreme hour the requirement is to find the wrong and extirpate it, crush it.

I believe that passion will subside, that those who have thirsted for revenge are satiated. I believe that wrong has accomplished the largest measure of damage in its power and that now the champions of the right in the federated orders will demand, in no uncertain tones, that the fullest reparation shall be made by those who have been or may be adjudged in the wrong and that the mandate will be obeyed.

The Supreme Council meets in annual session June 15, 1891. It will be a full meeting, and its action will doubtless be decisive.

In the meantime the friends of federation, of justice, of right, of fair play, and the enemies of conspiracy, treason, and duplicity, should manfully discuss the questions growing out of the record I herewith submit.

It was a dark day for federation, for liberty and independence, when Washington, with his ragged, half-starved, and half-frozen veterans suffered at Valley Forge. It was a gloomy time, when Gen. Greene,[40] in the Carolinas, was required to uphold the flag of independence with soldiers, many of whom were as naked as when they were born, and wore upon their shoulders tufts of moss, upon which to carry their muskets, but the cause these immortal men fought and suffered for, supported by federation, finally won.

The federated orders of railway employees are pledged to principles which grow in importance as the months go by. To read the order of the railroad officials, issued May 14, by which 400 or more honest men were banished from work tells in letters as vivid as the lightning's flash what there is in store for organized labor. If the holts of corporation vengeance can be stayed, federation alone is equal to the requirement. I believe federation has come to stay, and believing that means will be devised to strengthen and perpetuate this bulwark of workingmen's rights, I close this communication.

A Plutocratic Government[†]

June 1891

Is it premature to suggest that a plutocratic government in the United States in the not-remote future is not only possible, but is well up toward the head in the list of probabilities?

Does someone inquire what is meant by a plutocratic government, or a plutocracy? We will permit Mr. Webster to explain. He says a plutocracy is "a form of government in which the supreme power is lodged in the hands of the wealthy classes; government by the rich."

At present, numerous writers, orators, statesmen, legislators, and others of less note aver that ours is a government by the people, that it is not a plutocratic nor an aristocratic government, but a democratic government. The averment, if we consult constitutions, is true; but if laws and decisions of courts are investigated it will be found that much is going on in the way of government strictly in accord with Mr. Webster's definition of plutocracy, "a government by the wealthy classes; the rich," and if the question is asked, what are the facts upon which such assertions are based, the reply may be prudently made that Mr. Thomas G. Shearman,[41] in the January [1891] *Forum,* prints a table showing how the wealth of the country is distributed at present, as follows:

Class	Number of families	Total wealth to families	Average wealth to families	Individuals per family	Average per individual
Rich	182,000	$43,300,000,000	$237,912	5	$47,582
Middle	1,200,000	7,500,000,000	6,250	5	1,250
Working	11,620,000	11,200,000,000	964	5	193
Total	13,002,000	$62,000,000,000			

Referring to Mr. Webster's definition of plutocracy, a government by the rich, the foregoing figures must impress every candid mind that the United States is approaching plutocratic conditions with fearful rapidity; indeed, Mr. Shearman says that "the evils" of "such an unequal distribution of wealth are even more serious than any here suggested, and might possibly include the *destruction of republican government, which is even now little better than a form among us.*"

---

† Published in *Locomotive Firemen's Magazine,* vol. 15, no. 6 (June 1891), 492–493.

It is now seen that of the estimated wealth of the country, $62 billion, 182,000 families out of 13,002,000 families have possession of $43.3 billion— equal to $237,912 to a family, or $47,582 to each member of the plutocratic family, allowing five individuals to a family. While this is true of the plutocratic class, the 11,620,000 families of workers have only $11.2 billion of the wealth of the country, equal to $964 to the family and $193 to the individual.

It will be borne in mind that the exhibit we supply is not furnished by an anarchist, a socialist, a "labor agitator," but by one of the clearest-headed thinkers of the times, himself a man of ample fortune—a lawyer who does not consider cases of small fees—nor is he particularly opposed to millionaires. He sees the drift of affairs and points out inevitable results, unless some means can be devised for a more equitable distribution of the wealth that labor creates, nor does he hesitate to say that the plutocrats have now such an influence upon political affairs that our republican government is "little better than a form among us."

In this connection it should be said that labor organizations have one supreme purpose in view, and that is to inaugurate a system of distribution of wealth whereby an individual worker may have more than $193 and the individual plutocrat less than $47,582, or that a family of five workers shall have more than $964 of the country's wealth, while a plutocratic family of five has $237,912 of the country's wealth.

To accomplish their patriotic purpose labor organizations would have wise laws and honest courts, and these things which must be had if a republican government is to be a fact rather than a form they would secure by argument, reason, and the ballot. If a change of program cannot be brought about by such means then a plutocracy will be, if not already established, a "government by the rich," and when such a government is in full operation in this "land of the free and home of the brave," what will follow need not here be conjectured. History repeats itself, and those who study history need not err in their conclusions. There is a time to apply remedies, the time is now—the present—and it will be well if legislatures and courts give the subject special consideration.

The Tramp[†]

June 1891

We clip the following pen picture of the "tramp" from the Chicago *Herald:*

> The time of the year for violets, and also for tramps, is drawing near. Did you ever stop and think just what it means to be a tramp? It means no work, no money, no home, no shelter, no friends. Nobody in all the world to care whether you live, or die like a dog by the roadside. It means no heaven for such rags to crawl into, no grave to hide them out of sight, no hand stretched out in all the world to feel any interest in you, and no spot in all the world to call your own, not even the mud wherein your vagrant footprint falls; no prospect ahead, and no link unbroken to bind you to the past. I tell you, when we sit down and figure out just what the term means, it will not be quite so easy next time the wretched tramp calls at our door to set the dog upon him or turn him empty-handed away. Let them work, you say. Look here, my good friend, do you know how absolutely impossible a thing it is getting to be in this overcrowded country for even a willing man to work?
>
> It used to be that "every dog had his day," but the dogs far outnumber the days in free America. I know well-educated, competent men who have been out of employment for months and years. I know brave and earnest women, with little children to support, who have worn beaten paths from place to place seeking no charity, but honest employment, and failed to find it. What chance is there for a ragged tramp when such as these fail? Remember, once in a while, if you can, that the most grizzled and wretched tramp that ever plodded his way to a pauper's grave was once a child and cradled in arms perhaps as fond as those that enfolded you and me. Remember that your mother and his were made sisters by the pangs of maternal pain, and perhaps in the heaven from which the saintly eyes of your mother are watching for you, his mother is looking out for him. Perhaps—who knows?—the footfall of the ragged and despised tramp shall gain upon yours and find the gate of deliverance first, in spite of your money and your pride. Stranger things have happened.

In the foregoing there is abundant food for reflection. From the center to

---

[†] Published in *Locomotive Firemen's Magazine,* vol. 15, no. 6 (June 1891), 487–489.

the circumference of the country, on all the highways and byways, the tramp may be seen. He is always ragged, always hungry—often filthy, often vicious—always the victim of misfortune.

The advent of the tramp is of recent date. He is the product of the war of the rebellion. He came, strange to say, when peace was declared. When the armies were disbanded and the soldiers came marching home with waving banner, shouts of victory, and bands playing national anthems in honor of a Union "one and indivisible," the tramp made his appearance. Families were broken up, children scattered, and employment almost impossible. Men started out to find work. Then the tramp was an honest, courageous man. His purpose was to find work; but all over the broad land the same conditions prevailed.

The war created intense activity in every department of industry. When peace came, the reaction was universal. The demand for army supplies ceased; shops were closed, and the army of idlers increased at a fearful rate. To add to the grimness of the situation, there came a financial, mercantile, and industrial panic, brought about by bankers, gold speculators—the men who had grown rich upon the misfortunes of others. Before the fierceness of the storm, the strong and the weak went down together. Failures were piled upon failures; bankruptcy was universal. Factory, forge, and shop were silent. Gloom enshrouded the land. The cry was gold! gold! gold! Confidence was wrecked and the workingmen of the nation were the victims of untold calamities, and tramps multiplied.

The haggard truth that "idleness is the prolific parent of crime" was brought into fearful prominence. The cry was "work!" but there was not work for all. Multiplied thousands were idle, and were steadily drifting into criminal habits. The result was inevitable—a crime committed by one tramp was charged to all the unfortunate class. Suspicion was everywhere aroused. The tramp, without home, friends, money, or work, became an outcast—a vagabond. The hand of society was against him, and his hand was against society, and now the country is confronted with the fact that it has an established vagabond class known as the "tramp." These outcasts are everywhere, and their number is steadily increasing. They are found by the wayside, in barns, under haystacks; they beg, they steal, and they are incendiaries or murderers, as suits their necessities to live. They are on all the railway trains, stealing transportation at the risk of their lives. During the inclement season they herd together in cities, and when summer comes they tramp throughout all the rural districts, and everywhere are regarded as the enemies of society.

The picture is not overdrawn. It is needless to say there are honest tramps seeking for employment, ready and willing to do an honest day's work for such wages as they can obtain, but they seldom, if ever, get credit for their good intentions, and are classed with the vicious.

It is well, just here, to inquire if the industrial system now in vogue in the United States is favorable for the increase of the tramp army.

It will not be denied that now, as never before, industries are being controlled by the few. Necessarily so, because the few have secured vastly the largest percentage of the wealth of the country. The few, so to speak, are the generals of industry, and hence the commanders of workingmen. Their authority is supreme—absolute. There is no appeal from their decision. Courts cannot interfere, as for instance, when the papers announce that certain corporations have dismissed from employment *certain hundreds* of employees, or have, for their convenience, "locked" them out. There is no appeal. Work and wages cease. Wages down to a point that barely sufficed to keep soul and body together have all been expended. Henceforth what? What of the future? Does the corporation care? Does the general commanding enquire? Does society interest itself in the matter? Do Christians contemplate the grim situation of the unfortunates with prayerful solicitude? Not a bit of it. The discharged employees are required to face the storm as best they can. There are always some heroes in such calamities who survive, strong men who can battle against adversity and live, but there are a far greater number who go down; who, disheartened and despairing, give up the struggle and join the army of tramps.

Here we ask, what force or forces are employed to counteract such disasters? We know of but one—*organization*. It is the one force that antagonizes the tramp policy of the Generals of Industry—the commanders of workingmen. It is the one thing needful in times like the present, when industries are consolidating into great trusts, and one man, by the exercise of the power born of consolidated wealth, remands men, at his will, to idleness and to all the woes which idleness inflicts.

We do not content that organization as it now exists is equal to the emergency, for, stately as it may appear to some, it still lacks the essentials of invincibility. But the movement is in the right direction. Hopes brighten as we contemplate the trend of workingmen's thought and aspiration. The one thing wanting is the unification of workingmen's organizations; not "amalgamation"— the term conveys no proper idea of requirements. To illustrate our idea: Take the carpenters' movement. Their demand is an eight-hour day, certain stipulated wages, etc. Carpenters form one class of the "building trades." There are others: the stone masons, the brick masons, the plasterers, the plumbers, the hod carriers. These all belong to the building trades. If there is a lockout of the one, let it be, by the commanding power of unification, the lockout of all. Let the hush of Pompey come upon the city when the Generals of Industry pursue a policy that remands any one of these trades into idleness, relying upon scabs to do their work. This would prove availing; this would make organization invincible; this is federation—it is organized victory.

Take a textile factory, where there are pickers, carders, spinners, and weavers, and other distinct departments. If each is organized, and all are federated, the General of Industry—the arrogant commander of wageworkers—will consider long and well before he attacks the united body, before he issues his commands to replenish and multiply the army of tramps.

It is not required to proceed further with the illustration. To use a phrase, the reader will readily "catch on."

We do not hesitate to admit that the outlook sometimes is gloomy. The resources of the Generals of Industry are so vast and so quickly applied that resistance seems, sometimes, almost vain. But the fact remains, hopes center in organization and unification—in federation. Without it, tramps will multiply as the sands of the desert. Workingmen, if they hope for security from the corporation, will not emulate the confiding lamb in the presence of the wolf, the fool fly when listening to the flattering siren song of the spider. When too late, they will say farewell to independence and join the ranks of idlers and fall into line with the army of tramps.

An American Aristocracy[†]

July 1891

The president of Harvard University is very much concerned about the establishment of an American aristocracy. In this there is nothing peculiar. We doubt if there is an institution of learning in the country the president of which does not share the anxiety of President Eliot of Harvard,[42] nor need we exclude the smaller institutions, the colleges, academies, high schools, etc., in all of which the seeds of aristocracy are diligently cultivated.

† Published in *Locomotive Firemen's Magazine*, vol. 15, no. 7 (July 1891), 586–587.

The Harvard president professes that he does not want an aristocracy of titles and privileges, such as is rotting and festering in Europe, but an aristocracy of education, intellect, refinement, and, necessarily, money, because the learned advocate of an American aristocracy sees no chance for its establishment unless there are founded ancestral homes, to be held from generation to generation, involving the idea of entailment; the ancestral estate, with its castle, to be taken by the oldest male heir, etc., all of which involves fundamental changes in the laws and institutions of the country.

Such an aristocracy, President Eliot believes, would develop an honorable pride in name and home and become an incentive to meritorious conduct, and eventually become the glory of the nation.

All of Mr. Eliot's ideas of an American aristocracy converge on an "ancestral home"—some spot to be made sacred by inheritance, by associations, by family traditions, etc., and the idea is to educate American children so that in due time we shall have an American aristocracy—an exclusive set, known and recognized as "the aristocracy."

It will occur to numerous readers that President Eliot is seeking to dwarf the fundamental ideas of American institutions—the created equality of man, and, if possible, the more explicit declaration of St. Peter that "God is no respecter of persons." The Harvard president, with all his book lore, fails to perceive the trend of human thought. He makes no note of the fact that the term "aristocracy" is everywhere becoming odious; that democracy is the shibboleth of the people in all lands where there is any desire to distinguish between right and wrong, truth and error. Learned though he be, his learning, if it has not made him "mad," has reduced him to a crank, filled his mind with vagaries, and made him the exponent not only of folly but of an impossibility.

Here in the United States it is possible for certain people to imagine themselves aristocrats. The work began long ago and has been kept up to the present. Boston has its codfish, mackerel, and herring aristocracy, dating back to the early days of fishhooks, bait, and seines, colored somewhat with rum, beads, and slave ships—traffic in human flesh. It has its factory aristocracy, built up to colossal proportions upon woman and child labor, in establishments often more loathsome than prisons; an aristocracy which is giving back to the wilderness thousands of "ancestral homes," homes where bats and owls hold high carnival, farms abandoned to wild beasts and reptiles, facts which President Eliot might contemplate with profit. In all of the great cities we have the "American aristocracy" for which the Harvard president pants and sighs, meditates and writes. New York has its "400," with Ward McAllister its historian,[43] made of

Wall Street shearers of lambs and those distinguished fakirs who, with magic art, change water into wealth, so that experts are incapable of telling "which from t'other," and all is set down as equally entitled to dividends. In all of the great cities, in fact in all the cities of the country, there is to be found an American aristocracy, minus the "ancestral home," and minus pedigree, the ancestral name, the castle, etc.

President Eliot, manifestly, has not given the subject he discusses the study its importance demands, and which it should command. Everywhere the American aristocracy in some stage of development can be seen. In Michigan, a skunkery promises such profits that within a generation an aristocratic family will be founded as notable as that of the Astors or the Vanderbilts. Why not? Skinning skunks for their fur is quite as reputable as skinning coons and muskrats, and the indications are that in the near future the skunk *rampant* or *passant* will proclaim the proprietor of the Michigan skunkery equal to the most exacting demands of President Eliot for an American aristocracy. Mr. Freeland can have his "ancestral home" near or remote from his skunkery, and in his palatial banqueting hall may entertain the aristocracy in a style equal to anything recorded under the old regime.

If President Eliot were as well informed as he ought to be, he would know that there is a budding aristocracy to be found in every mercantile establishment, from a corner grocery to the "house" which "controls the market." He has only to read the papers to learn how rapidly aristocratic families are striding to the front, giving "teas," "chocolates," "coffees," etc., always careful to have full descriptions of costumes, together with "diamond and pearl ornaments" appear in the press. The trust barons, the bonanza kings, the bucket-shop lords, and the lamb-shearing sir knights constitute a still higher grade of American aristocracy, while the railroad tsars, sultans, and shahs are on top, and have the largest army of retainers to supply them with the needful to maintain their establishments.

To help on matters, we have an aristocratic religion, aristocratic churches, and aristocratic cemeteries, and we think President Eliot need not vex his learned soul further. Like Rip Van Winkle, should he go to sleep for twenty years, upon waking he would find the American aristocracy shining like a dead mackerel at full moon, and sufficiently offensive to make a brass dog hold its nose.

The People's Party[†]

July 1891

The convention which assembled in the city of Cincinnati during the month of May to organize a "new party," the "People's Party," or a "third party," succeeded insofar as preliminaries were concerned. About 1,500 delegates responded to roll call. Committees were appointed, discussion took a wide range, and enthusiasm marked every step of the proceedings, from start to finish.

The great work of the convention was to formulate a platform. This was accomplished as follows:

Platform of the People's Party

Your Committee on Resolutions beg leave to submit the following:

That in view of the great social, industrial, and economical revolution now dawning upon our civilized world, and the new and living issues confronting the American people, we believe the time has arrived for the crystallization of the political reform forces of our country, and the formation of what should be known as the People's Party of the United States of America.

1. That we most heartily endorse the demands of the platform adopted at St. Louis in 1890; Ocala, Florida, in 1890; and Omaha, Neb., in 1891, by the industrial organizations there represented; summarized as follows: The right to make and issue money is a sovereign power to be maintained by the people for the common benefit, hence we demand the abolition of national banks as banks of issue, and as a substitute for national bank notes, we demand that legal tender treasury notes be issued in sufficient volume to transact the business of the country on a cash basis without damage or especial advantage to any class, or cause such notes to be legal tender in payment of all debts, public and private, and such notes when demanded by the people shall be loaned to them at not more than 2 percent per annum upon non-perishable products, as indicated in the sub-treasury plan, and also upon real estate, with proper limitation upon the quantity of land and amount of money.

2. We demand free and unlimited quantity (coinage) of silver.

3. We demand the passage of a law prohibiting alien ownership of land

---

† Published in *Locomotive Firemen's Magazine,* vol. 15, no. 7 (July 1891), 624–625.

and that Congress take prompt action to devise some plan to obtain all lands now owned by alien and foreign syndicates, and that all lands held by railroads and other corporations in excess of such as is actually used and needed by them be reclaimed by the government and held for actual settlers only.

4. Believing the doctrine of equal rights to all and special privileges to none, we demand that taxation, national, state, or municipal, shall not be used to build up one interest or class at the expense of another.

5. We demand that all revenues, national, state, or county, shall be limited to the necessary expenses of the government, economically and honestly administered.

6. We demand a just and equitable system of tax on income.

7. We demand a most rigid, honest, and just national control and supervision of means of public communication and transportation, and if this control and supervision does not remove the abuse now existing, we demand government ownership of such communication and transportation.

8. We demand the election of president, vice president, and United States senators by a direct vote of the people.

9. That we urge united action of all progressive organizations in attending the conference called for February 22, 1892, by six of the leading reform organizations.

10. That a national central committee be appointed by this conference to be composed of a chairman to be elected by this body, and of three members . . . from each state represented, to be named by each state delegation.

11. That this central committee shall represent this body, attend the national conference on February 22, 1892, and if possible unite with that and all other reform organizations there assembled. If no satisfactory arrangements can be affected, this committee shall call a national convention not later than June 1, 1892, for the purpose of nominating a candidate for president and vice president.

12. That the members of the central committee for each state where there is no independent political organization conduct an active system of political agitation in their representative states.

Those who will critically scan the foregoing document, the platform upon which the "People's Party" proposes to do battle, and at the same time provide themselves with the latest platform declarations of the Democratic and Republican parties, will be able to discover what new departures are proposed by the "third party."

The issue of "greenbacks" to take the place of national bank notes is not a new idea. It has often been suggested, and it would seem to be an easy matter, but practically, it would require a great deal of legislation to avoid serious financial embarrassments.

The new departure in finance proposed in the platform of the "People's Party" is for the government to put afloat all the paper money required, make it receivable for all debts both public and private, and then loan it out to anybody and everybody at 2 percent per annum upon "imperishable products, and also upon real estate, with proper limitations upon the quantity of land and amount of money." The scheme, should it be put into practice, would at once develop into startling proportions.

The demand for free and unlimited coinage of silver is a question that is now before Congress, and exhaustive arguments have been made for and against the proposition; more are to follow. It is thought by some who have examined the subject that it ought to be sufficient to coin the American product of the mines, others would limit the amount, while others would have our mints coin all that offers from the outside world.

The prohibition of the alien ownership of land in the United States is eminently a correct idea; and it is unquestionably just to require railroad corporations to dispose of their lands, reserving only so much as will enable them to transact their business.

In plank 7 we have the proposition of government control of "public communication and transportation," that is to say, if those in charge do not make rates reasonable, the government shall become the owner of all railroads and telegraph lines.

It is easy enough to formulate such a proposition, but since government ownership would require an expenditure of about $10 billion, and since labor would have to pay every dollar off the vast sum, we do not apprehend that the government will immediately take the contract.

We think it likely that the new party or People's Party will give the country a "shaking up." The indications are that party lines will undergo some radical changes and that under changed political conditions, laws will be enacted that will modify in numerous instances situations which now are fruitful of complaints and widespread unrest.

We should like to see laws passed that would either squeeze the water out of corporation stocks and bonds, upon which the people pay dividends, or compel those who control the water to pay taxes on every dollar it represents.

We should like to see laws enacted that would permit a poor man to have his case tried in the courts of the country the same as a rich man, and when it could be shown that a bribed and debauched judge ruled against the rights of the poor man, he should have his filth-bedrabbled robes torn from him and be sent to a felon's cell by the shortest and most expeditious route.

The indications are that such a party is coming which will discard and anathematize class legislation and inaugurate a reign of justice. As we view matters such is the sign of the times.

Remedies for Wrongs[†]

July 1891

One of the questions up for debate relates to the inauguration of a policy in the United States which shall establish on a permanent basis amicable relations between employers and employees.

These relations, as a general proposition, to use a common phrase, are "strained"—that is to say, instead of mutual confidence there exists mutual suspicion, the result being widespread unrest, forebodings of evil too often realized in industrial affairs.

Annually a certain amount of surplus wealth is created. Statisticians present the figures, and demonstrate that this added wealth mounts up to billions—sums so vast as to bewilder the mind.

The axiomatic truth is stated that labor, and labor alone, creates this wealth.

In looking abroad—in taking a wide survey of the situation and of conditions—the conclusion is arrived at that in the distribution of this surplus wealth labor has never been justly treated.

[†] Syndicated article published in multiple newspapers. As published in the *Wilkes-Barre Evening Leader,* whole no. 3661 (July 17, 1891), 2.

Where the Line is Drawn

It is just here that the controversy begins, and the longer it is continued the more sharply defined become the lines that separate those engaged in the discussion.

Usually, on the side of the capitalists, there is great impatience with those who seek to demonstrate that labor does not receive its just share of the wealth it creates, and, refusing to call to their aid arguments based upon facts demonstrated by figures, they at once begin to pile epithets upon those who advocate the rights of labor. They prefer defamation to logic, and their policy in the past has been to them fruitful of success.

Of late years, however, the tactics of capitalists have not been exempt from intelligent and caustic criticism, which has yielded reformatory influences extending far beyond the boundaries of labor, and have entered the domain of economics, political economy, statesmanship, and politics. Everywhere, on all sides, there is to be seen a mighty mustering of the mind forces of the country, the purpose being to find a solution of what is called the "labor problem"—such an adjustment of equities relating to the distribution of the wealth which labor creates as will satisfy just demands.

This new departure has been brought about by the organization of workingmen—not only the organization of numbers, physical force, but moral and intellectual force; and the among to this force, its discipline and power, has amazed the country and alarmed capitalists.

It is held in circles far removed from anarchists, socialists, communists, whatever such terms are supposed to mean, that something must be done to greatly modify present conditions if the country is to have industrial peace, based upon justice.

"Armed Peace"

As things exist now, industrial peace is, to use a European term, "armed peace." Where a semblance of peace is found it is patchwork, a combination of fear and force, strategy on one side and starvation on the other. The industrial class is hungry, the employer class is venal, a condition fruitful of enmities which, steadily deepening into hatred, must inevitably be productive of results which cannot be thought of with the least degree of composure.

In the discussions of the antagonisms found in industrial circles, the central, the pivotal point upon which every argument turns, radiates, and converges is that the producers of wealth are ceaselessly impoverished, while the capitalistic class is as steadily growing richer. On the one hand, the most conservative writers, the profoundest thinkers, to whom the pages of the best publications of the period are open, present the facts and support them by arguments so cogent that the public no longer hesitates to render the verdict that the complaints of producers are just, and that remedies must be sought and applied if the widespread unrest is to be abated.

The Farmers Are in It

The farmers of the country "feed all," not only the home population; but the surplus product of the farms of America is the principle item of our foreign commerce. These farmers declare the rates of transportation so high that, as a general proposition, the profits of farming are swept away, and worse still, that their capital, their investments in farms, and their equipment is steadily absorbed until bankruptcy and ruin stare them in the face. This grievance, it is shown by state and national statistics, is not trumped up, is not a vagary, but a grim fact, and the farmers are organizing for the purpose of finding a remedy. Nothing within the entire realm of prudence could be more natural.

These farmers start out upon the proposition that railroad rates of transportation are to them ruinously exorbitant. They show the figures and demonstrate that their products, their investments and toil bring no profits, but, on the contrary, plunge them further and still further into debt. They say—and they demonstrate the truth of their declarations—that the rates of transportation are too high, needlessly exorbitant, because railroad corporations, not content with collecting revenues based upon actual investments, double such investments by the addition of water, and thus compel the farmers to bear a double burden. That the farmers tell the truth in this arraignment is no longer debatable. The proof is overwhelming; it is no longer categorically denied.

The farmers say: "We have tried all the great political parties, but they have turned a deaf ear to our complaints, to our entreaties, and to the facts. We will no longer trust them." Hence, the Farmers' Alliance, the new departure in politics.[44]

On the other side are the corporations, which, in a fight at once federate, unify, consolidate; and they represent in cash and water about $9 billion, an incomprehensible sum of money.

The Corporation's Evil Influence

In the past, and even now, the corporation has dominated legislation—debauched legislatures, courts, and congresses. Its power has been autocratic. It has issued its decrees and it has been obeyed. To pay dividends on water it has not only impoverished the farmers, but it has robbed the railroad employees of

fair pay, of honest wages, and thus it happens that the farmers and the employees have practically the same grievance; the rate of transportation impoverishes
the farmers, and the rate of wages impoverishes the employees, and both are
robbed that dividends may be collected on water; and this stupendous wrong
has proceeded for years, and has been upheld by legislation and by the courts.

It is just here that the von Moltke strategy and tactics of the corporation
come prominently into view.[45] The corporation, as in the case of Iowa, says
to the farmers, "If you reduce rates we will reduce the number of trains; if
previously we charged you so much as to destroy your profits, we will now so
reduce facilities that your products will be delayed in reaching market, and
your condition will be worse instead of better; you will have jumped from the
frying pan into the fire; and since you appeal to the legislature for redress, we
will show you that we have our employees under such subjection that they
will hold meetings and protest against your plans of redress, and we will issue
our orders and have our employees vote against candidates who are pledged to
introduce bills to remedy the evils of which you complain."

This is history, true to the letter—naked, unadorned truth. It has been
written, and can be produced when required.

The play upon the employee is done so artistically that satisfactory re-
sponses are anticipated, and disappointments are few and far between.

Intimidating the Employee

The employee, metaphorically, is incited to look down into his flour barrel,
to make a survey of his smokehouse, inquire about his grocery bills, count his
surplus cash, and balance his bankbook. This done, he is told that to reduce
rates of transportation, to comply with the demands of the farmers, one of two
things is certain to happen—he will be relieved of employment entirely, or his
wages will be reduced; in either case the penalty would be crushing, and taking
alarm at the intimidating threat, the employee is bulldozed to the extent that
he arrays himself against the farmers and obeys orders; but he goes, or has his
wages reduced all the same. Nor is this the end of the humiliating business.

The railroad employee, realizing that he too ought to have some legislation
to redeem him from the serfdom imposed by "common law," which is no law
at all, goes to the legislature for redress—as, for instance, if disabled in the line
of his duty he demands the right of going into court with his claim for redress,
or if killed, that his heirs may have a hearing and a jury decide the case.

The farmer in such cases may, doubtless does, say to the railroad employees
who are battling for justice: "When our bill was up for a redress of our wrongs

you opposed us under the whip of the corporation, and now in return we mock at your solicitations. Endure your wrongs as we endure ours. Wanting in courage, you not only deserted us in time of need, but you protested against justice being done us, and petitioned to secure our defeat."

Such is the law of human nature, and having secured this antagonism between the farmers and the employees the corporation is happy, and is in a position to bring its resources to bear and maintain the practice of the "common law" iniquity, by which the infamy is perpetrated, and the crippled employee, at his leisure, may whistle for redress; or, if killed, his wife and children, enshrouded in gloom, may die of starvation.

Manifestly, there is a common ground upon which farmers and railroad employees may meet and battle for justice, side by side; not only railroad employees, but all wealth producers, for all of them have interests in common.

A Demand for Justice

It is no longer doubted that a "third party," or a new party, is to enter the field of politics. There is no mistaking the signs of the times. The shibboleth of this new party is "Justice to the producers of wealth."

In finding remedies for colossal wrongs it is quite probable some mistakes will be made, but they will be infinitesimal compared with the mistakes that have been made in establishing the wrongs complained of. It sometimes happens that a broken bone is set in such a way as to produce a deformity, and it has to be broken again as a remedy. When antiquated wrongs are torn up by the roots the operation has often been production of commotion—of revolutions, of war, and of all the evils which war entails; but the time must come, it is the verdict of history. The eternal years are pledged to the triumph of truth.

Here, in what is termed a "God-favored land," wrongs ought to be eradicated by peaceful methods; but in view of recent events, when a continent shook beneath the tramp of armed men; when all the streams ran crimson to the sea; when sulfurous clouds obscured the sun in its meridian brightness; when the thunder of the far-flashing artillery, the scream of shells, and the rattle of musketry blended with dying groans and the shouts of the living that the star-spangled banner must be what it never had been, the symbol of freedom, here, with such facts in full view, it [would be] well to be cautious in outlining the future.

It is largely within the province of prudent speech to say that many of the wrongs of which the producers of wealth complain could be removed by legislation; to say that all could be so extirpated would be folly.

Sovereign Power of the People

The sovereign people could, if they would, compel railroads to collect dividends on actual cash investments. The sovereign power of the people touches all things relating to government. It knows no bounds; from it there is no appeal. It makes and unmakes constitutions and laws. In granting a franchise it may absolutely determine the terms of its existence. To say that it creates a corporation with power to collect dividends on water, on fictitious capital, is preposterous; but admitting, for the sake of the argument, that this has been done, then it becomes the sovereign power, by legislation, to remedy the wrong and afford an overtaxed people the relief demanded. It is not required to enlarge the argument, since all wrongs the result of legislation, or non-legislation, may be cloven down or uprooted by the sovereign power of the people, and a political party with such a battle cry will not want for popular favor.

To succeed it will have to overcome the power of organized capital, organized capitalists, the plutocratic class, and every movement in that direction ought to be hailed by wealth producers, by workers in every department of industry, with loud acclamations of approval.

In some regards the outlook is cheerful; in others it is gloomy. The plutocratic class believes they can disrupt the Farmers' Alliance, and to do this they propose to use members of the Alliance, just as railroad corporations propose to defeat federation by debauching members of organizations high in official position.

The Coming Battle

It should be understood that the plutocrats and the corporations will yield only as superior power compels them to surrender their vantage ground. The coming battle is to be one of giants, not of pygmies. The new party will come forward with proof of the wrongs of which it complains, and will pile up the facts to alpine heights. Their arguments will have the power of axioms. Ten thousand eloquent tongues will plead the cause of justice to workingmen, the wealth producers of the country.

But on the other side will be the plutocrats with their cash and their decree for the people, when the day of election comes, to vote the plutocratic ticket, to fall down and worship the golden image they have set up, and they will see to it that the fiery furnace is in full view to warn the recalcitrants of their doom. How many will yield it is too early to conjecture. It will be a battle for freedom, and once begun, though defeat may attend the first engagement, the fight will be renewed. If victory by the ballot is too long postponed; if the Pharaohs of the period will not listen to just demands; if the cry of the oppressed takes on a deeper moan, a louder wail, then destiny, always pledged to the redemption of the oppressed, by pillars of cloud and pillars of fire,[46] will lead them to freedom, though it be through another Red Sea.[47]

The Expulsion of the B of RT[†]

August 1891

We have on our table the *Railway Service Gazette* of July 9 [1891], in which reference in numerous ways is made to the action of the Supreme Council expelling the Brotherhood of Railroad Trainmen.

The *Gazette* is an ardent advocate of federation, and it commends and applauds the expulsion of the B of RT.

We do not question in the least the *Gazette*'s loyalty to federation or to the welfare of railroad employees, nor are we disposed to enter upon any lengthy criticism of the *Gazette*'s position relating to the justice of the penalty visited upon the B of RT. In one place the *Gazette* says:

> Every reader of the *Gazette* should bear in mind that while the Supreme Council could, under its present laws, take no other action than that which was taken in passing sentence upon those who participated in the Chicago & Northwestern conspiracy, *it is not intended to intimate that the Trainmen's Association did anything deserving censure, those who participated in the conspiracy alone being responsible.*

The italics are ours, and are introduced to emphasize the position the *Magazine* has taken in the matter. The great body of the trainmen were absolutely *innocent* but by the penalty are made to suffer with the guilty. This could have been avoided and ought to have been avoided.

As we view the case, the *Gazette* is unfortunate in its illustrations and conclusions, as for instance, it says:

> But we are told that in expelling the grand officers of the Trainmen's Association, all the members of the association are punished. This is absurd.

† Published in *Locomotive Firemen's Magazine,* vol. 15, no. 8 (August 1891), 720–721.

> Everyone at all acquainted with the laws which govern the federation knows that no other action could have been taken. As well say that when the United States Senate expels the two senators of a certain state, who have been guilty of treason, that the people of the whole state are punished, because they are left without representation in the Senate. And so, too, they are in a certain measure, for it was their misfortune to be represented by traitors, but no one for a moment intimates that the whole people of the state are tainted by the treason of their senators.

Here we have the declaration repeated that the B of RT was innocent, and also the declaration that is "absurd" to say the "members of the association are punished." And, again, the admission is made that "in a certain measure" they are punished. But let such things pass; the misfortune of the *Gazette's* illustration and conclusion lies in the fact that the action of the Supreme Council in expelling the B of RT is as unlike the action of the Senate of the United States in the two senators of the state as it is possible to conceive.

By the action of the Senate two members are expelled—not the state they represented. By the action of the Supreme Council, assuming the B of RT to represent the state, representatives and state go out together. The B of RT is absolutely out of the federation, and can be represented in that body only by readmission. Does the *Gazette* see the point?

It is not required to pursue the subject, as the *Gazette* has supplied an illustration which upsets its conclusion.

Still, we are inclined to introduce one more of the *Gazette's* illustrations. It says:

> Benedict Arnold, previous to his treason, was a general of the Continental Army, and enjoyed confidential relations with George Washington. As well say after a court martial found him guilty, that he should continue to hold his commission, and still share the secrets of the commander-in-chief, until such time as Arnold's state had taken action in the matter.

Benedict Arnold, at the time of his treason, commanded West Point. He had troops under him. His treason was discovered, but his troops were not punished by Washington. They were not dismissed from the army.

In the case of the penalty inflicted by the Supreme Council upon the grand officers of the B of RT, the order was also expelled. The penalty fell with equal force upon officers and men. The officers, not alone were expelled, but the men who made up the rank and file of the brotherhood.

A different course could have been pursued. The verdict could have been transmitted to the Brotherhood of Railroad Trainmen, giving that organization an opportunity to seek out the guilty, those who had betrayed their trust, and impose upon them, wherever found, the penalty their treachery merited. If the Brotherhood of Trainmen declined to receive the verdict or adequately punish the offenders, such action or non-action would be equivalent to an approval of the conspiracy and the organization *as a whole* would be inculpated, and it would then be time enough to arraign and punish the entire organization.

We must not be understood as entering a plea for the traitors who plotted to secure the dismissal of the switchmen on the Northwestern. From the first we stated that expulsion from the ranks of organized labor was what they deserved, nor have we modified our opinion, so far as they are concerned, in the slightest degree. It is to be hoped that the members of the B of RT will thoroughly investigate the matter, punish the conspirators, and again join the federated forces.

From Americans to Slavs and from Independence to Slavery[†]

August 1891

The *New York World* is entitled to a vote of thanks from every labor organization in the land for its exposition of the coke curse of Pennsylvania. When the representative of the *World* visited the coke region, there were 15,000 men on strike, "of whom," says the *World*,

> it is a fair estimate to say 12,000 are Slavonians, 1,500 are Germans, and the other 1,500 are composed of Irish, Scotch, Negroes, and native white Americans. Not over 1,000 of the strikers, including the Negroes, were born on American soil, and not over 2,000 of them can speak the English language. The great mass of the strikers, and especially the Slavs, are ignorant of our manners, customs, and language, and mean to stay in this country only long enough to save a few hundred dollars, when they hope to return

† Published in *Locomotive Firemen's Magazine*, vol. 15, no. 8 (August 1891), 683–684.

whence they came, there to live in comparative ease on the money they have taken with them. They are the Chinese of the coke region.

This condition of the population of the coke region was brought about by the H. C. Frick Company,[48] a twin monstrosity of the Philadelphia & Reading Railroad Company, the history of which the *World* gives as follows:

> Years ago the mines and coke ovens were worked by native Americans, most of whom were born in the vicinity, and many of whom owned their little homes on the hillside and tilled a little plot of ground and kept a cow or two in connection with their work about the mines. As late as 1880 there were only about 3,000 coke ovens in this 400 and more square miles, which make up what is known as "The Connellsville Coke Region." Now there are nearly 16,000 ovens. But with the growth of the industry the native American has almost disappeared, and the work he used to do is now done by the imported "pauper labor of Europe."

In the foregoing, the reader has a word picture pleasing to the American ear. An artist could reproduce it on canvas and it would please the eye. The H. C. Frick Company has transformed this rural, this industrial district, where a few years since the people were contented, thrifty, and virtuous, into a hell "where blood and carnage clothes the ground in crimson"[49]—where men, women, and children are evicted from their hovels and made to take their chances with rats and reptiles, foxes and groundhogs, to live and die, not even Frick or the devil caring what calamities overtake them.

About 1880, so says the *World*'s account, there was a boom in the iron industries of the United States; an era of prosperity had dawned, but not for American workingmen; the men who should have reaped their full share of the prosperity were, instead, impoverished. From 3,000 coke ovens the number was increased to 8,000, and now to 16,000. With the demand for coke and the increase of ovens came the absorption of small concerns by the larger ones, and now of the 16,000 ovens, the Frick monstrosity owns 10,000. With the boom in the iron industry came the increased demand for coke, and it was then that the christianized H. C. Frick began the importation of European cheap labor. The *World* says:

> The Frick Company sent to various employment agencies in Baltimore and Boston for laborers, and through these agencies the first installments of Slav immigrants were secured.
> When these Slavs arrived in the coke regions they were set to work at wages which, while far below those which the company was paying to its

native employees, were still greatly in excess of the wages which the Slavs had been able to earn in their own country. The agents of the company induced many of them to send for brothers, cousins, and friends whom they knew at home to come to this greatly favored land where so much could be earned in so short a time, and where what was, to them, a fortune could be saved in a few years.

But these Slavonians, almost before the operators were aware of it, had been induced to join the labor organization, and in 1886 there came a strike—a strike which at that time proved the largest and longest that the coke region had known. The Slavs went out with the rest of the workmen and stayed out until the strike was won. The operators then as now tried every means to fill the places of the strikers. Then as now families were evicted in scores, in the hope of frightening the others back to work. Then as now this refinement of coercion failed and the operators cast about for new men to fill the vacant places. The employment agencies had helped them before, why not again? And so to the agencies they went, with the result that within a few weeks hundreds of newly imported Slavs came swarming into the region to take the places of the men who were fighting, as they said, for bread for their wives and babies.

These Slavs, or Slavonians, are, if possible, more degenerate than the Chinese. They are as distinct a class of foreigners as ever invaded American shores. Trained to work for wages upon which an American would starve, to live in dens that an American dog would bark at, and to live upon scavenger food that would make an average hog turn up its snout, they could not stand Frickism. The degradations and robberies inflicted by Frick under the laws of Pennsylvania were so infamously worse than they had ever known in Slavonia that the miserable creatures struck for their rights, struck against robbery, against further degradation, and what is the result? Some of them have been shot down like dogs, some of them are writhing in the agonies of their wounds, some are starving, and all are mad. There are at least 12,000 of these idle men in a strip of country eight miles wide and 50 miles long, and area of an ordinary sized county in a western state.

The H. C. Frick Company found cheap labor. It exiled American labor. It imported Slavs. It has secured strikes, and first and last has been damaged to the amount of about $4 million—and the miserable Slavs have doubtless lost half that amount. The *World* says that the present price of coke is $1.90 a ton; that an oven every other day will produce four tons of coke—and that the net profit is $1.00 a ton. This is equivalent to supplying the H. C. Frick Company with two tons of coke from its 10,000 ovens daily, or a net profit of $20,000 a day, for say 315 working days of the year—a yearly profit of $6.3 million.

From this work Americans are driven to make room for Slavs, and now the Slavs are driven out by Italians and Negroes—but to enable these creatures to be robbed and still further degraded, Pinkerton thugs with shotted guns must constantly stand guard. The policy is Satanic, altogether infernalism. Why talk of a future hell? Here is one right under the nation's nose.

The Unity of Labor[†]

August 1891

The *Farmers' Voice* in a recent issue says:

> Philosophic thinkers now recognize the essential unity of "the labor movement" in all civilized nations. Its pleas and manifestations may have diverse local peculiarities, but all draw their force and receive their impulse from the same deep reservoir of power, which lies far below the surface in the great substratum of humanity.

All labor is independent. If, for the sake of illustration, grades of labor are introduced, it will at once be seen that the highest is absolutely dependent upon the lowest grade—that the vital nerve extends from the foot to the head—from the lowest depths to the most exalted heights, and that this nerve, subjected to injury anywhere throughout its length, will be productive of disaster more or less serious.

Do such propositions require proof? Are they not self-evident? In the very nature of things is there not a law of union, an irrevocable law, a law as eternal as that of gravitation, binding all classes, all grades of labor into one interdependent whole? A brotherhood which, discarding signs, grips, and passwords, voices trumpet-toned a truth yet to be recognized—that labor in all of its labyrinthian ramifications, high and low, whether it is bestowed at 25 cents a day or ten dollars a day, whether rendered by slave or freeman, is united, having

---

† Published in *Locomotive Firemen's Magazine,* vol. 15, no. 8 (August 1891), 679–680.

the same end in view, to produce, to build, to preserve, to carry forward all enterprises and to bless the world?

There is not, we surmise, in the world of the mind, a broader, deeper, or a more commanding truth in all the sciences and philosophies than the one we have suggested, that labor, in all of its divisions and subdivisions, in all of its branches and classifications, constitutes a oneness, a unity, which no power in earth or heaven can change. If so, it follows logically that any attempt to change the irrevocable law must be productive of confusion and injustice.

The aristocracy, not of labor, but in labor, or more properly, in labor circles, is an exhibition of mental deformity and infirmity, explainable only upon the hypothesis that labor has copied the most repulsive characteristics of the men who debase labor—the men who rob workingmen and grow rich by the tribute money they extort.

If labor could see and comprehend the eternal truths of its mission in the world, the four-dollar or the ten-dollar-a-day man would take the profoundest interest in the one-dollar-a-day man, or his more unfortunate brother who toils for a less sum than one dollar a day.

In this highly favored land we talk much of the "sovereignty of the people," we shout in lofty periods about the "power of the majority." Occasionally, to embellish a stump speech, some demagogue injects into his "flapdoodle" the Latin phrases, *"vox populi, vox Dei"*—"the voice of the people is the voice of God," while at the same time the majority, the working people of the country, because they will not unite, are the victims of the minority, and the few who are united bead down the many, and make them hewers of wood and drawers of water—that is to say, divide them into castes, set them to wrangling, and thus crush and rob them, silence them in courts and in Congress, and impose upon them degradations and humiliations not one remove from serfdom.

If workingmen were united in sympathetic bonds; if the skilled laborer was broadened rather than dwarfed as he advanced in knowledge until he, if a bricklayer, could comprehend the fact that he is dependent upon the hod carrier; if the locomotive engineer could grasp the fact that he is dependent upon the locomotive fireman, descending to or ascending from the humblest laborer, the aristocratic idea in labor circles would disappear, the interdependence of labor would at once constitute a bond of union, a chain whose links, forged and fashioned to hold workingmen in harmonious alliance, would gird them about as a defense in every time of trouble and resist invasion, though assailed by all the plutocrats that ever cursed the earth.

This desideratum, this one thing needful, has not been secured, and because it has not been obtained, the plutocrats are treating millions of work-ingmen as "dumb driven cattle."

Will this sort of thing go on forever? Men will answer just as they have confidence in the intelligence of the people, as they have confidence in the intelligence of workingmen.

The plutocrats have confidence in the people, based upon Jay Gould's theory of their integrity. When he wants a judge or a legislature, he ascertains the price and pays it. The plutocrats pursue the same policy, though there may be less directness in their methods of subjugating workingmen, and in every instance money or its equivalent—employment—is made to talk. It can coo like a dove, or utter decrees with the fierceness of a Nero. In either case work-ingmen cower and tremble. Will it be thus forever?

Divided, estranged, quarreling, forever conducting a guerrilla warfare upon each other, building up little aristocracies based upon wages, discarding fundamental principles, they will be in the future as in the past, animals to be slaughtered. But should the time come when workingmen fraternize and, rec-ognizing the interdependence of all, rally to the standard of right and justice, determined to be heard, then the millennium of labor will dawn. The pluto-cratic Satan will be chained for at least a thousand years, and the unity of labor being recognized there will be peace in the earth.

It is a question of faith in man, or faith in money. The world is taking sides. Let the debate go forward.

Caste[†]

September 1891

If the question were seriously asked by one of such commanding intellect as would secure attention, "Is there any proof whatever that our much vaunted civilization is drifting backward?" the answer would be *no* with special empha-sis. If there were those who should be so bold as to intimate that an affirma-tive reply to the interrogatory could be supported by so much as one fact, he

---

[†] Published in *Locomotive Firemen's Magazine*, vol. 15, no. 9 (September 1891), 826–827.

would be required to produce the fact, or stand convicted of heresy, worthy of thumbscrews and faggots. Indeed, it is to be questioned if the bold, outspoken Christian would be permitted to present such facts as he might believe he had secured in support of his conclusions. He would simply be charged, arraigned, tried, and condemned without an opportunity to make a defense. The cry would at once go up and go forth, "Crucify him."

Is this sheer gammon? Is it vagary—a mere whim, a hallucination? Mr. B. O. Flower,[50] in *The Arena,* writes of "society's exiles" as follows:

> It is difficult to overestimate the gravity of the problem presented by those compelled to exist in the slums of our populous cities, even when considered from a purely economic point of view. From the midst of this commonwealth of degradation there emanates a moral contagion, scourging society in all its ramifications, coupled with an atmosphere of physical decay—an atmosphere reeking with filth, heavy with foul odors, laden with disease. In time of any contagion the social cellar becomes the hotbed of death, sending forth myriads of fatal germs which permeate the air for miles around, causing thousands to die because society is too shortsighted to understand that the interest of its humblest members is the interest of all. The slums of our cities are the reservoirs of physical and moral death, an enormous expense to the state, a constant menace to society, a reality whose shadow is at once colossal and portentous. In times of social upheavals they will prove magazines of destruction; for while revolution will not originate in them, once let a popular uprising take form and the cellars will reinforce it in a manner more terrible than words can portray.
>
> Considered ethically, the problem is even more embarrassing and deplorable; here, as nowhere else in civilized society, thousands of our fellow men are exiled from the enjoyments of civilization, forced into life's lowest strata of existence, branded with that fatal word *scum.* If they aspire to rise, society shrinks from them; they seem of another world; they are of another world; driven into the darkness of a hopeless existence, viewed much as were lepers in olden times. Over their heads perpetually rests the dread of eviction, of sickness, and of failure to obtain sufficient work to keep life in the forms of their loved ones, making existence a perpetual nightmare from which death alone brings release.
>
> Say not that they do not feel this; I have talked with them; I have seen the agony born of a fear that rests heavy on their souls stamped in their wrinkled faces and peering forth from great pathetic eyes. For them winter has real terror, for they possess neither clothes to keep comfortable the body, nor means with which to properly warm their miserable tenements.

Summer is scarcely less frightful in their quarters, with the heat at once stifling, suffocating, almost intolerable; heat which acting on the myriad germs of disease produces fever, often ending in death, or, what is still more dreaded, chronic invalidism. Starvation, misery, and vice, trinity of despair, haunt their every step. The Golden Rule—the foundation of true civilization, the keynote of human happiness—reaches not their wretched quarters. Placed by society under the ban, life is one long and terrible night.

But tragic as is the fate of the present generation, still more appalling is the picture when we contemplate the thousands of little waves of life yearly washed into the cellar of being; fragile, helpless innocents, responsible in no way for their presence or environment, yet condemned to a fate more frightful than the beasts of the field; human beings wandering in the dark, existing in the sewer, ever feeling the crushing weight of the gay world above, which thinks little and cares less for them. Infinitely pathetic is their lot.[51]

We invite the careful perusal of Mr. Flower's views. Are they true? Who so bold as to deny them? Who can disprove Mr. Flower's assertions? What is the inevitable conclusion? Is it not that a civilization, professedly based upon the precepts of Christ, is even now going backwards to Brahmanism, to caste, as taught and practiced by Hindu heathen? Is not the tendency in direct conflict with the declaration of the apostle Peter, that "God is no respecter of persons"?

What is the condition of the lower castes in Brahmanism? Are they not exiles from society? To say that the miserable exiles from society in America may, if they will, rise by a sudden bound, or by regular gradations, to the higher castes is begging the question. The exiles cannot rise; with rare exceptions they sink to lower depths of degradation. It is the law of plutocracy. The cry of "room on top" is like the mirage of flowing fountains to the thirsty traveler in Sahara. Like the victim in the grasp of quicksand, the more he struggles the deeper he sinks. He is an exile. Only money can lift him out of his thralldoms, and that is used to crush him.

What is there for the woman in the great cities, who sews with a "double stitch" a shroud or a shirt? Starvation, suicide, or a life worse than either. She is an exile. Amidst all the splendors of wealth, no hand is stretched forth to save her or her children—or, if here and there one is offered, there are ten thousand raised against her.

In the palatial churches the robed divine and jewel-bedizened audience wrangle over creeds and dogmas, fly at each other's throats with the fierceness of tigers endeavoring to make it appear that an infinite God has somewhere in this universe a place in reservation worse than New York, but the way of escape for the exiles is not via the aristocratic church.

The caste era is here already. The exiles from society are increasing. We hear of their "colonies" in cities. They are *planted* every year by thousands in the Potter's fields. They are the unknown dead, and still their number increases—and this is in "the land of the free and the home of the brave"—in the closing years of the nineteenth century.

What can be done for the exiles, for the "lower castes" in this Christian land? Mr. Flower, in what we have quoted, suggests no remedy. What forces can be applied to bring the exiles back, to lift the apparently doomed castes to a level where they may realize that American institutions have some blessings in store for them?

The last hope is in the organization of workingmen and in the federation of such organizations. The power of the working class, the working caste unified, discipline, knowing the power of the ballot and wielding it discreetly could crush the power of the plutocrats and arrest the power of the growing plutocracy.

In some way this power is to be exerted. If legitimately, the revolution will be peaceful. It will come as the springtime comes, when the ice fetters are broken and the world rejoices. But come it will. The exiles will return, the castes will revolt. If the Pharaohs are stubborn, then their doom is another Red Sea.

Facts About Federation[†]

September 1891

The *Locomotive Firemen's Magazine* has from the first, with such ability as it could command, championed federation.

The principle is axiomatic. The mere statement that "in unity there is strength," is one so self-evident that argument would, were it possible, weaken the proposition.

In all of the labor organizations there is not a man so demented as to deny the central truth that in organization, united effort, there is conquering power.

---

† Published in *Locomotive Firemen's Magazine,* vol. 15, no. 9 (September 1891), 812–813.

Federation is simply carrying the power of organization to its uttermost limit. It is organization's *ultima Thule.*

There is no longer debatable ground relating to the proposition.

The difficulties in the way are entirely separate and apart from the question of the power of federation.

In federation there must be coordination. The federated bodies must be coequal.

If this supreme requisite is not recognized, then the federation becomes a farce, which instead of conferring power breeds confusion and calamities.

But to constitute federation a success instead of failure, to give it power instead of weakness, there must be an honest recognition on the part of each constituent body of the coequality of every other constituent body, just as in colonial federation, Rhode Island and Delaware were the coequals of Virginia and Massachusetts.

Again, in federation there must be the recognition of mutual interests to be guarded, protected, and promoted. If this is not done, then *ab initio,* federation is a failure—more, it is a calamity.

Moreover federation is democratic, it is not autocratic, aristocratic, nor plutocratic.

It recognizes absolute equality based upon mutual interests and not upon numerical nor financial strength; as, for instance, in colonial federation, a colony with 50,000 population was equal in the federation to a colony with 500,000 population.

It must be assumed in federation that there is an equality of intelligence, integrity, and honor, self-respect, loyalty to obligation, and of all things of good report among men. Manifestly, this must be taken for granted, since no power can determine anything to the contrary until the facts develop the lack of such essential virtues.

Coming to the federation of railway employees, such an organization is a failure if one organization assumes that it is, from any cause whatever, superior to any other organization in the federated body. Such an assumption is necessarily fatal, since it totally ignores the prime essential of federation—the protection of mutual interests.

If, therefore, one organization assumes superiority because of its larger membership, or larger wages *per diem,* or of its greater importance to the railway service, it can never federate with other orders of railway employees which it regards as inferior; or if it were to consent to federation and should demand a controlling influence, proportionate to its assumed superiority, thus discarding coequality and mutual interests to be protected, it would be a death blow to federation.

Federation, then, to be a success must recognize the coequality of the federated bodies. Federation to be a success must have a congress or a council with delegated powers by which and through which its power may be exerted, and this congress or council must be constituted by the representatives of the federated orders, and these representatives must be equal and clothed with power to enact rules for their government.

In the Supreme Council of the United Orders of Railway Employees the principles we have outlined were carried into effect.

Coequality was established and maintained. No power was assumed not clearly delegated by the orders represented, and in the exercise of these powers great good resulted.

But, says someone, the Supreme Council got into trouble and serious calamities have befallen it. That is true. But we assume that no eye but that of omnipotence could have foreseen the trouble, no hand but that of omnipotence could have guarded against the calamity.

To censure the Supreme Council, to intimate that it could have known of the treason that invaded its ranks, is to assume that fallible man can penetrate the future and foretell coming events; more, that one man may read the thoughts and know the purposes of another man. Had this Godlike power been conferred upon George Washington, Benedict Arnold had not committed treason.

Now then, with every fact before them, we challenge the most astute foe of federation to point out wherein federation, as established under the Supreme Council, has committed an error in the organization of that body of representatives indicative of a want of caution and an honest purpose to do right.

The trouble that has come upon the Supreme Council is as foreign to federation as was the treason of Arnold. It in no regard involves federation.

The Brotherhood of Railroad Trainmen stood as high for intelligence and integrity as any order of railway employees on the continent, and only God himself, who reads the thoughts of men, could have been aware that conspiracy lurked in the hearts and minds of any of its chosen representatives.

The poor driveling comments made by feeble-minded scribblers relating to the Supreme Council are totally unworthy of consideration, and will so be regarded by men who have the capacity to comprehend honest endeavor, to map out a highway for the relief of men when wronged and oppressed.

National Prosperity
[excerpt]†

September 1891

No one pretends that the United States is not prospering to an extent almost beyond the grasp of computation. Those who study statistics arrive at conclusions which at once dispel doubts, and convince the most skeptical that in spite of every obstacle the strides of the country in the march of progress are gigantic.

Among those who have discussed the subject critically is a Mr. J. C. Reiff, who gives 21 statistical reasons why everybody, particularly "security holders," should have abounding confidence in the future of this country.

* * *

It so happens that such statistics and conclusions create unrest. Wealth accumulates while the victims of poverty and wretchedness increase. The rich multiply in number, fortunes mount up to colossal proportions, the few obtain control of the surplus wealth which labor creates, and as a consequence dictate the policy under which workingmen must toil or starve, indeed, all too often toil and starve.

No statesman of the time in which we live denies that a monstrous wrong exists, in fact, a whole brood of monstrous wrongs, and that something must be done, and that without delay, if widespread disasters are to be prevented in the near future.

The discussion of these wrongs has suggested the creation of a new political party to antagonize the old parties, which, it is held, have so legislated as to make the triumph of wrong possible. Again, workingmen are constantly organizing to protect their rights, their determination being to secure, if possible, better wages, which would in some measure at least reduce the flow of wealth to the coffers of the few and thereby establish peace and contentment, where at present unrest and feelings bordering upon enmity exist.

In all of the great centers of population where the great industrial enterprises are conducted, there are fierce contentions between employer and employee, and this unrest, this feeling of antagonism between capitalists and toilers, has spread to the agricultural districts and is being fanned to a flame. The most patient and conservative of people are the most intensely aroused because of wrongs existing which none deny.

---

† Published in *Locomotive Firemen's Magazine,* vol. 15, no. 9 (September 1891), 778–779.

Statistics demonstrate that in this land progress and poverty go hand in hand, rather than progress and prosperity. The plutocrats have secured control of every avenue to wealth and levy such tribute as suits their greed, and when they are satisfied the facts demonstrate there is little left to cheer and encourage those but for whose toil no wealth would be created.

That there is to be a change in the program at an early day is not specially cheering, and in the fact lies the danger, but that efforts are being made to modify some of the more cruel conditions under which thousands work and perish keeps hope alive that eventually the right will triumph by peaceful means, and the day when history repeats itself in violence may be indefinitely postponed.

Revolution and Rebellion vs. Stagnation[†]

September 1891

There are those who cry "peace," but there is no peace,[52] nor will there be until right triumphs. Till then, there will be wars, and rumors of wars. When right, truth, and justice in holy alliance rule the world, the reign of peace will begin—not till then.

There are those who deplore war, revolution, and rebellion. Manifestly, war is to be lamented if it is waged to enthrone or to perpetuate wrong, but it expands to superlative grandeur if it is for the purpose of establishing justice and breaking the fetters of slavery. In such cases every blow struck for the downtrodden sends thrills of joy throughout the world. The covering slave looks up and sees, however dimly, the dawn of a new era when he shall be free.

There are men in the United States who are everlastingly deprecating revolution and rebellion. They prefer stagnation. Had they lived in '76 they would have said to the patriots of the time, "Pay taxes and submit to King George—pay tribute and wear a yoke." They would have been Tories. They would have said, "Peace at any price is better than war."

Such degenerate creatures constitute the extremes. In the one case they are mercenary and mean. They would make sacrifices neither of money, time,

† Published in *Locomotive Firemen's Magazine*, vol. 15, no. 9 (September 1891), 777–778.

nor comfort; they would place neither life nor property in jeopardy, and in the other case, they are degenerate, base-born and cowardly. Liberty and independence are meaningless terms to them. In these extremes there is no martyr material, but any quantity of the Judas Iscariot stuff.[53] They never won a battle for the right since Adam was driven out of Eden, nor will they win such a battle while the pendulum of time continues to vibrate. They would as soon be the subjects of a Tiberius, a Caligula, or a Nero as sovereign citizens of a republic, and there are thousands of these burlesques of men in the United States. They are either plutocrats or poltroons, in fact, both. One is on top, the other at the bottom; one is the dog, the other is the flea. On all sides is seen the moneyed aristocrat and the degenerate sycophant—the crawling dirt-eater. Together they exert a tremendous influence. As yet, they are not in the majority; at least, such is the hope. There is a mighty host who will not cower; who will neither take off their hats, shave off their whiskers, button up their coats, nor do aught else that a slave is expected to do by the command of his master and owner. The forces are not yet in operation that can crush them. They will protest against wrong though every star in the blue vault above them falls. They will speak in spite of the "gates of hell." Prisons do not intimidate them. The storms of obloquy they meet as fearlessly as veterans meet the storms of bullets, while with the lamented Lowell[54] they sing:

> Truth forever on the scaffold, Wrong forever on the throne,
> Yet that scaffold sways the future, and behind the dim unknown,
> Standeth God within the shadow, keeping watch above His own.
>
> We see dimly in the Present what is small and what is great,
> Slow of faith how weak an arm may turn the iron helm of fate.
> But the soul is still oracular; amid the market's din,
> List the ominous stern whisper from the delphic cave within,—
> "They enslave their children's children who make compromise with sin."

* * *

> Then to side with truth is noble when we share her wretched crust,
> Ere her cause bring fame and profit, and 'tis prosperous to be just;
> Then it is the brave man chooses, while the coward stands aside,
> Doubting in his abject spirit, till his Lord is crucified,
> And the multitude make virtue of the faith they had denied.
>
> Count me o'er earth's chosen heroes,—they were souls that stood alone,
> While the men they agonized for hurled the contumelious stone,
> Stood serene, and down the future saw the golden beam incline

To the side of perfect justice, mastered by their faith divine,
By one man's plain truth to manhood and to God's supreme design.

By the light of burning heretics Christ's bleeding feet I track,
Toiling up new Calvaries ever with the cross that turns not back,
And these mounts of anguish number how each generation learned
One new word of that grand Credo which in prophet-hearts hath burned
Since the first man stood God-conquered with his face to heaven
    upturned.

For Humanity sweeps onward: where today the martyr stands,
On the morrow crouches Judas with the silver in his hands;
Far in front the cross stands ready and the crackling faggots burn,
While the hooting mob of yesterday in silent awe return
To glean up the scattered ashes in History's golden urn.

The idea of the poet is that sometime "the world, the flesh, and the devil" are to be conquered. Possibly. We treasure the hope, but the outlook is not as cheery as could be desired, nor yet is it alarmingly dubious. Plutocrats will be required to surrender their grasp upon the "iron helm of fate." When labor is fully equipped and ready, things will move with more satisfactory rapidity. Till then, patience and agitation. The revolution has begun. Rebellion is in the air. Nature abhors a vacuum, and stagnation is equally out of order. Labor, mind, and muscle are in alliance. The world moves, and it is to move at no distant day in the right direction. Let free thought and free speech have full sway and the right will triumph.

The Lessons Taught by Labor Day[†]
November 1891

September 7 was very generally celebrated throughout the country by wage-workers as Labor Day. In several states the 7th of September is made, by statute, a holiday the same as the Fourth of July, the 22nd of February, or Christmas.

† Published in *Locomotive Firemen's Magazine,* vol. 15, no. 11 (November 1891), 970–971.

The more thoughtful men of the country, regardless of membership in labor organizations, are inquiring the significance of Labor Day. What does it mean? What lessons does it teach? What great fact in the history of the times is made prominent by Labor Day celebrations? Is some truth long since "crushed to earth," rising again, proclaiming that "the eternal years of God" are pledged to its triumph over error?

All civilized nations have their holidays designed to commemorate something of great national importance.

This is true of the United States. We have our Fourth of July, "Independence Day," when in various ways, by parades, orations, picnics, pyrotechnics, and by a thousand and one other methods, the people seek to commemorate the announcement made July 4, 1776, that the American colonies had set up business for themselves, and no longer recognized the authority of a king.

We celebrate the 22nd of February, the birthday of George Washington, and as the years go by, the day grows in importance. As the nation grows in population and power, the people learn to appreciate the sublime character of the man who was "first in peace, first in war, and first in the hearts of his countrymen."[55]

Labor Day, so far, selects no one individual as illustrative of events which brought workingmen into prominence as a force and a factor in all things calculated to advance civilization and give prosperity to republican institutions.

It is well that such is the fact. Labor Day, above all things, voices a new departure in moral, social, economical, and political affairs.

Labor Day is a new Independence Day. The declaration is that "in the course of human events labor is to take commanding rank in controlling human affairs."[56]

It is an announcement that from this time forward, Labor, with form erect, comprehending its rights and prerogatives, its independence and high purposes, will walk abreast with all the armies of progress and pitch its tents on lofty elevations, and fortified by intelligence, integrity, and courage, will hold the fort against all who would seek to degrade it.

The *Chicago Post,* referring to Labor Day in that city, said:

> Those simple citizens who affect to fear the "dangerous masses" had a fine opportunity to observe the object of their dread yesterday. Some 20,000 wageworkers paraded the streets for several hours. They were not all, but a very important part of the "masses." Each belonged to that class of the community in which the fashion prevails to eat the bread that is earned by the sweat of the brow. It is a large branch—the largest by all odds—and, in the mercy of providence, it will never grow smaller. It includes,

it *is,* "the masses."

Very dangerous, too, those 20,000 intelligent, self-reliant, and cheerful philosophers of toil. Dangerous to corruption in high places; dangerous to political quackery; dangerous to sanctimonious humbug and to humbug of all kinds, especially when it masks in a thin veil of pretended sympathy, stupid distrust, or blind hatred of the working "masses."

Sympathy is not exactly the nostrum for these 20,000 specimens of robust manhood. They don't ask it, don't need it, and won't have it. They want no "protection" of hypocritical men or silly women. They want room according to their strength. And, under the benign workings of "the laws of nature and of nature's God," they manage very comfortably to get what they want.

Else they might, indeed, be "dangerous"—to somebody.

Labor Day will eventually sound the death knell of plutocracy in the United States.

The era of robbery and of degradation is drawing to a close. It will at no distant day appear that the "dangerous masses" are not workingmen, but those who use their money power to filch from labor its just rewards.

Labor Day is to grow in importance and in significance. The number of workingmen who are to parade on Labor Days in the near future will startle the country. The time is near at hand when there will be millions in line, with music and banners. The time is not remote when workingmen will exact and receive their full share of the wealth they create, and then Labor Day will be Emancipation Day.

When that auspicious time shall come, workingmen will cease to be known by "numbers," and names will be reinstated. The hut will give place to habitations such as are becoming American citizenship, and though the rich will grow richer, it will not be as now, and in the past, by a series of robberies, entailing poverty, degradation, and death upon the poor.

Persecution Because of Religious Opinions in Labor Organizations[†]

November 1891

In writing this article, while denouncing proscription and persecution on account of religious opinions, generally, we refer more particularly to organizations of railroad employees, and especially to the Brotherhood of Locomotive Firemen.

Let us, so far as the United States of America is concerned, begin at the beginning.

The Constitution of the United States provides that:

"Congress shall make no law respecting an establishment of religion, or prohibiting the free exercise thereof."

From the beginning, the great body of the people of the United States put upon record their unqualified abhorrence, their deep and unconquerable detestation, of religious proscription and persecution. In some of the New England colonies the fires of religious persecution were lighted by the men who had fled from such exhibitions of infernalism as soon as their feet touched the sod of the new world, and though centuries have elapsed since these persecutions of Quakers, Baptists, and witches were perpetrated, the lapse of years has not yet sufficed to abolish the "damned spot" from the record.

In ten thousand instances the world has been confronted by the crimes perpetrated by monsters in human shape, but of them all, scanned as they have been by the light of heaven and the fires of hell, there are none which for satanic wickedness approximate the crimes committed in the name of religion.

No imagination, however far reaching; no fancy, however fervid; no vocabulary, however rich in words; no intellect, however towering, has ever been able to paint the religious bigot, engaged in his nefarious work of persecution, and the contemplation of his deeds of death by torture stands forever as the one bleak and black and horrifying monument of infamy and crime.

Who and what is a bigot? It has been written of him that he is "a wretch whom no philosophy can harmonize, no charity soften, no religion reclaim, no miracle convert; a monster who, red with the fires of hell, and bending under the crimes of earth, erects his murderous divinity upon a throne of skulls, and

† Published in *Locomotive Firemen's Magazine*, vol. 15, no. 11 (November 1891), 1029–1030.

would gladly feed, even with a brother's blood, the cannibal appetite of his rejected altar."[57]

The bigot is the enemy of man. He has no conception of the spirit of fraternization.

Who and what are the canting crew, who so smooth and so godly, are as venomous as a hooded cobra?

> Who, arm'd at once with prayer-books and with whips,
> Blood on their hands, and scripture on their lips,
> Tyrants by creed, and torturers by text
> Make this life hell in honor of the next.[58]

The question arises, are there any of these morally deformed monstrosities, these unnatural productions in the brotherhoods of railroad employees, who are carrying about with them patent-hell tinderboxes to light the fires of religious persecution in the ranks of the brotherhoods? Are there members of the brotherhoods who are using the organizations to propagate ideas destructive of the organizations, which if not checked will blast them as certainly as the storm of fire annihilated Sodom, will shake them down as an earthquake ruins cities?

The story is whispered abroad that in certain localities the lodges of the orders are being prostituted to such nefarious purposes.

We are not talking at random. To say that we approach the subject with earnestness but feebly expresses our abhorrence of the fanatical movement, and if we do not denounce it with the severity its infamy demands, it is because of a lack of ability and not of purpose.

The Brotherhood of Locomotive Firemen was not organized that its lodges might be degraded as coverts where religious (?) fanatics might formulate schemes of proscription and persecution, because of any diversity of religious opinions.

The Brotherhood of Locomotive Firemen is not an organization of religious fanatics and bigots. It is not an organization which has a purpose of collecting faggots to burn heretics, to erect wheels to break their bones, or to obtain thumbscrews to elicit recantations.

The Brotherhood of Locomotive Firemen tolerates, without question, all religious opinions, and the locomotive fireman, a member of the brotherhood, who by word or deed introduces creed questions in the lodge, or who uses the order in any way to promote religious dissension, is a deadly enemy of the order and should be forthwith expelled.

The brotherhoods of railroad employees have a right to believe that they can overcome all outward forces; that they can remove every obstacle to progress, and by stately strides achieve anticipated success. They have a right to believe these things, because experience warrants the conviction. But no matter what the past has taught, the day that religious intolerance and proscription is introduced, their glory departs and wreck and ruin is their inevitable fate.

To introduce the schemes of fanatics and bigots is to invite decay and death—a multitude of cankers and cancers to eat into the vitals of the orders and sap their life, and to create chaos where order reigned, and fling out the banner of discord in the place of the ensign of peace and prosperity.

We call upon every loyal locomotive fireman, member of our brotherhood, to at once engage in the work of stamping out the abomination of religious intolerance in the order wherever the deformity shows its presence.

In the future, as in the past, let fraternity, goodwill, brotherly kindness be the watchwords.

The question of religious conviction must be left between each man and his God for settlement. The brotherhood cannot, ought not, and must not be the arbiter.

We are all "poor wanderers of a stormy day,"[59] and the business of the brotherhood deals only with such affairs as are conducive to smooth sailing on life's tempestuous seas, and to find those havens of repose to which fraternity in its best and broadest significance contributes.

Child Labor—a Crime Against Humanity[†]

December 1891

There are a few, a precious few, as compared with the millions, who have a correct conception of the ills which flow from child labor. If the most thoughtful in the land were required to designate a social and industrial wrong more than any other prolific of mental, physical, and moral degeneracy, we doubt not that "child labor" would be named.

[†] Published as "Child Labor" in *Locomotive Firemen's Magazine,* vol. 15, no. 12 (December 1891), 1099–1101.

Turn it which way you will, examine it as you may, the question of child labor has no bright side, nor can its contemplation afford satisfaction to anyone unless their being is shockingly debased.

It is worthwhile in the discussion of the subject to descend to particulars, to analyze with unhesitating candor and severity.

Starting out with the proposition that child labor is a crime against humanity, the question arises, who is to blame? Or, where does the blame rest? Quite likely the reply will be, "Society is to be blamed," therefore, as in criminal proceedings, since a whole community or a state cannot be indicted, the crime escapes punishment.

"Oh," says one, "our civilization is to blame, the body politic, social, industrial, religious," all are involved, and hence the verdict, "Nobody is to blame."

The discussion of the evil effects of child labor is not of recent date; it began in England more than a century ago, where employers regarded children as material to be worked up, and it was worked up to an extent that horrified civilization, and finally brought Sir Robert Peel to the front to devise ways and means by which the poor children might be redeemed from conditions compared with which savagery would have been a supreme blessing.

It is held in some quarters that our civilization is peculiarly English; admit it, and then read the reports that have been submitted to parliament upon the condition of the industrial classes, and there will be little difficulty in arriving at the conclusion that American ideas of "child labor" are eminently English.

It has been held that in the United States of America, in all things pertaining to the well-being of the people, we were in advance of all other nations. In the form of government we boast that we did not borrow European ideas, but on the contrary constructed a government especially designed to establish the sovereignty of the people; a government in which the poor have rights as sacred as the rich; and that the laws would protect the rights of all alike, and yet it is true, humiliatingly true, that even now, with all our boasting, the rights of workingmen are cloven down by decisions of English courts, made when the employer was master and the workingman a slave.

But cutting adrift from such reflections, the question arises: What is the American view of child labor? Can it be said that there is any well-defined sentiment upon the subject such as exists in England?

It is possible, but by no means certain, if an appeal were made to the whole people, as in the case of a presidential election, the national judgment would be recorded against child labor, and this uncertainty indicates to what a deplorable extent the national conscience has been warped and deformed regarding a matter which the profoundest thinkers of the period regard as of supreme importance.

Why is child labor permitted? What are the incentives which underlie this crime against humanity?

Child labor is permitted by society because society is soulless, heartless, because it is dominated by ideas which regard with apparent contempt questions which relate to labor, to the employment of children, notwithstanding the age is distinguished for the discussion of all sorts of moral questions.

As a general proposition, only poor people have large families. In the homes of the rich it is no longer fashionable to be prolific. One child is the real aristocratic idea, and beyond three is plebeian and vulgar. This being true, questions relating to the prerogatives of poor men of the future are already mooted, the idea being to relieve them of the ballot. In England, while the elective franchise is being extended, in free America the codfish aristocratic class discuss the propriety of abridging it. The argument is that the masses are degenerating and that, therefore, the institutions of the country are in peril.

It is held that the life of a generation is 33 years, hence the male infants of today in 33 years will be the men who will control the destinies of the republic. It is readily seen that with such facts in full view the child-labor question becomes one of commanding gravity.

It is held by men who have investigated the subject in its moral and physical aspects that child labor is, of all others which now confront the nation, the one that should create the most active solicitude.

Who are those who favor child labor—and why are they opposed to any movement looking to the emancipation of children from toil?

There are several classes of people who favor child labor: First, indigent families whose poverty is the result of circumstances over which they have no control. Widows whose orphan children must work to keep themselves and their mothers out of the poorhouse. Second, parents degraded by multiplied vices, who have less regard for the welfare of their children than bears have for their cubs; whose children are required and compelled to work that their degenerate parents may be idle and gratify their beastly inclinations. Third, parents whose greed of gain totally obscures all consideration of the moral, physical, and intellectual welfare of their children, who are willing to coin their young lives into dollars and cents to gratify mercenary instincts and force upon society moral and physical deformities to propagate in due time a still more degenerate generation. Fourth, there is still another class, known as employers, whose natures are so deplorably depraved that the employment of children is one of the means devised to augment their wealth.

Such employers are the monsters of the age. They are without conscience. In all the fens, swamps, jungles, and stagnant waters of the world, no animated thing is found more repulsive than the creature, having the form of man, who counts his gains secured by child labor. His palatial home, his purple and fine linen, the luxuries which surround him, the food upon which he subsists, the downy bed upon which he reposes, all, everything, is damned, irrevocably cursed by the crime of child labor, by which the "human form divine"[60] is distorted, the immortal soul shriveled, the intellect shackled, and the child slave, at last grown to manhood or womanhood, sent forth to multiply a degenerate species of humanity, to describe which the language supplies no adequate terms.

Does the pulpit take cognizance of the deplorable drift of events? Does it sound the alarm? Does it mass its anathemas and hurl them at society and seek to arouse universal hostility to conditions which the devil and his imps have foisted upon humanity? How gladly would we now and here reproduce the declarations of the pulpit against the degrading crime of child labor, but unfortunately the pulpit is silent.

Our readings enable us to say that lecture bureaus are numerous, and the intellect of the country is summoned to lecture upon "temperance, righteousness, and a judgment to come," but whoever heard of a strolling lecturer, high or low, who chose for his theme the crime of child labor?

We have great institutions of learning and educators of renown, and millions are annually expended for education, but who, of all the professional educators the country boasts, has sought to arouse the national conscience to the blighting curse of child labor?

The discussion of tariffs and currency, double standards and single standards, commerce and transportation, food and famine, etc., like Tennyson's brook, goes on forever, but who discusses the crime of child labor?[61] Does echo answer who? It does more. It declares chiefly, we might say exclusively, the crime of child labor is discussed in the ranks of labor.

If there is in the United States a growing sentiment against the crime of child labor, it is chiefly due to the influence exerted by organized workingmen.

Labor bureaus are taking up the subject and compiling facts.

We have before us, as we write, the report of the Minnesota Bureau of Labor Statistics, a book of nearly 400 pages, devoted exclusively to child labor and education. From this report we make the following extract:

> If there is one proposition of government more universally accepted by our people than any other it is that the safety and permanence of repub-

lican institutions depends upon the virtue and intelligence of the people. But, children having nothing worthy of the name of education, forced into factories at an early age to toil for ten hours each day, cannot, save in very exceptional cases, develop into intelligent men and women. Yet they are to become an integral part of our people, and the men, at least, who grow from such children are to be, by our theory and practice of government, entrusted with all the important rights and duties of citizenship equally with the most intelligent persons in the land. We have based our government and public institutions upon the intelligence and virtue of the people. Everything which tends to build up that intelligence and virtue tends to strengthen and perpetuate republican institutions. Everything which tends to destroy that intelligence and virtue tends to break down our institutions. If certain tendencies of our industrial development are found to be at war with the development of the people, is there an argument needed to convince any thoughtful man that such tendencies should be checked.

To illustrate: If it be found that great factories can best be developed, goods cheapened to the public, and the production of certain classes of commodities facilitated and multiplied by applying child labor to improved machinery, does it follow that, in the long run, the people are benefited thereby? We will admit that goods are made cheaper and more plentiful, but what is the effect upon children? Are they maimed, crippled, dwarfed, distorted, withered? Will they grow up human manikins, intellectually and physically, or full rounded men and women? Are they fitted in any degree to take part in the direction of affairs, or must their lifelong lot be meek obedience? Or can they be trusted with power only at the expense of disaster?

Some philosopher has said that "dirt is only matter out of place," and, so, the multiplication of machinery is not in itself an evil; it is simply, in many cases, a perverted good. We cannot afford to destroy our men and women in their childhood for the sake of cheapening commodities. We cannot afford to undermine republican institutions, nor profit in any way by tendencies and influences which have their issue in lowering the standard of humanity. It is well that factories should prosper; it is better that men and women should be developed. Our institutions are more valuable and sacred than the material prosperity of a few individuals.

The foregoing indicates what labor bureaus are doing to point out the essential iniquities of child labor. The appeal is made to the patriot and philanthropist, to the statesman and the political economist—and, above all, to the conscience of the nation. The employment of children of tender years in factories and shops should be declared a felony. It is a crime against humanity and the state. It contemplates generations of dwarfs, physical and mental.

In this connection it is worthwhile to state that "Dr. Snow, of Fall River, Massachusetts, testified that the laboring people of that city were largely made up of foreigners, induced to come here by the manufacturers; that they were, as a class, dwarfed physically, and that after a careful examination of their antecedents he had come to the conclusion that the character of the labor they had been performing from childhood was responsible for their inferior development." Besides, he said that these dwarfed people were lacking in vitality. Parents, thus dwarfed mentally and physically, have no higher conception of childhood than to harness it to a machine at the earliest possible day, and the factory lords of Fall River, still more debased, employ children to increase their wealth.

It is doubtless true that there is a growing hostility to child labor in the United States, but the sentiment is not sufficiently pronounced to bring about a sweeping reform. Laws are often dead letters, because there are few sufficiently courageous to note their violation and fly to the protection of the infant toilers, in which regard the working children of the United States are in a more forlorn condition than dumb animals, for whose protection there is a powerful association of philanthropic men.

We have said that the champions of the children subjected to toil are found in the ranks of organized labor, and if a public sentiment is to be created that shall emancipate those children from degradation, and make their lives something better than a curse, labor organizations will have a large share of the responsibility. Said President Gompers, of the American Federation of Labor, at Detroit:

> Of all the ills that mankind suffers from, the unjust and cruel tendencies of modern methods of wealth-producing, the one that seems to me to rise to horrible proportions is that of child labor. Our centers of industry, with their mills, factories, and workshops, are teeming with young and innocent children, bending their weary forms with long hours of daily drudgery, with pinched and wan cheeks and emaciated forms, dwarfed both physically and mentally and frequently driving them to premature decay and death. The innocent smile of youthful happiness is soon transformed into wrinkles and other evidences of early decay. The life's blood of the youth of our land is too frequently sapped at the foundation. The hope of a perpetuity of free institutions is endangered when the rising generation is robbed of the opportunity to enjoy the healthful recreation of the playgrounds or the mental improvements of the schoolhouse. The children of the workers have none to raise a voice in their defense, other

than the organized wageworkers, and I appeal to you to take such action as will protect them from the contemptible avarice of unscrupulous corporations and employers.

These are brave words; words opportune and fitly spoken, and should be heeded by every workingman in the land who would emancipate childhood from the debasing influences of labor. T. V. Powderly, general master workman of the Knights of Labor, is on record as saying, "The question of child labor and education is the most important that can come before us now or at any other time."[62]

But, after all, labor organizations are not half aroused upon the enormity of the crime of child labor. In many factories children are practically buried alive, and in others, according to the New York report of factory inspectors, "children are crippled for life by machinery, which they should not be permitted to approach, much less control." The tale is one well calculated to horrify all people not dead to sympathy.

What of it all? This. Labor organizations can, if they will, score a triumph for God and humanity by making child labor a burning question, and if they fail, generations of children, born deformed in body and in mind, will bear testimony to their incapacity to grasp a question fruitful of untold ills to humanity.

Notes

1. *Zell's Popular Encyclopedia: A Complete Dictionary of the English Language with a Pronouncing Vocabulary and a Gazetteer of the World*, vol. 4 of 5 (Philadelphia: T. Ellwood Zell, 1883), 2469.

2. Ethnic slur for Hungarians, used as a catch-all phrase for multiple Slavic nationalities that were part of the Austro-Hungarian empire, including part or all of today's Slovenia, Croatia, Serbia, Slovakia, Hungary, Romania, Moldova, and Ukraine.

3. Ethnic slur for Italians.

4. Allusion to "The Brook" (1855), by Alfred Tennyson (1809–1892).

5. Allusion to Psalm 90:10: "The days of our years are threescore years and ten; and if by reason of strength they be fourscore years, yet is their strength labour and sorrow; for it is soon cut off, and we fly away." Debs coincidentally died at age 70.

6. Reference to John the Baptist, a proselytizing Jewish religious leader of whom Jesus of Nazareth is believed to have been a follower.

7. From Hebrews 12:13.

8. Henry Clews, "The Labor Crisis," *North American Review*, vol. 142, whole no. 355 (June 1886), 598.

9. Allusion to Bellamy, *Looking Backward*.

10. From Thomas G. Shearman, "The Coming Billionaire," *Forum*, January 1891, 546–557. This list was widely reproduced in the periodical press.

11. Reference is to a contemporary ruling of the courts that held companies harmless from financial consequences of on-the-job deaths or injuries that were the result of the actions of fellow employees.

12. Couplet from *The Traveller* (1764), by Oliver Goldsmith (1728–1774).

13. William L. Scott (1828–1891), a former mayor of Erie, Pennsylvania, and a Democratic congressman, was a millionaire coal-mine owner and financial speculator.

14. The failure of S. A. Kean & Co., a Chicago bank, occurred in December 1890, and was marked by piles of worthless securities and more than $42,000 in unsecured "loans" to Kean and his wife. In total, liabilities exceeded assets by more than $800,000 at the time of the bank's closure. According to the contemporary press, Kean's bank opened each day with a prayer and featured checks imprinted with Biblical verses, which inspired confidence among pious depositors. Charges of banking fraud were brought against Kean in the wake of the collapse, for which he faced a fine and up to three years in prison.

15. From Hebrews 12:23.

16. Herman Felzenthal (1834–1899) was president of the Chicago Bank of Commerce.

17. Allusion to Genesis 18–19.

18. Alfred Russel Wallace (1823–1913) was a British naturalist and biologist credited for independently conceiving the idea of natural selection.

19. Alfred Russel Wallace, "Human Selection," *Fortnightly Review*, new series vol. 48 (September 1890), 325–337. Quotation is from page 325.

20. Hiram M. Stanley, "Our Civilization and the Marriage Problem," *Arena*, vol. 2, no. 1 (June 1890), 97. Quoted by Wallace, "Human Selection," 325.

21. Allusion to Genesis 8:4.

22. Reference to Friedrich Leopold August Weismann (1834–1914) and Francis Galton (1822–1911), two leading writers on heredity during the late nineteenth century.

23. From the hymn "A Man's a Man for A' That" (1795), by Robert Burns (1759–1796).

24. Allusion to Genesis 2:2.

25. Allusion to Deuteronomy 34:4.

26. Manna, a bread product, is introduced in Exodus 16:15, and recurs throughout the Bible.

27. Henry Morton Stanley (1841–1904) was a Welsh-born American journalist and explorer who aided the kingdom of Belgium in establishing its colonial foothold in the Congo Basin.

28. From "A Psalm of Life" (1838), by Henry Wadsworth Longfellow (1807–1882).

29. George Thomas Dowling (1849–1928) was a prominent Baptist cleric and author of several published collections of sermons, including the 1917 work *The Rich Man's Poverty and the Poor Man's Wealth: And Other Practical Talks*.

30. John 5:2–8.

31. From Ephesians 6:13.

32. From John 5:17.

33. The Chicago and Northwestern Railway (C&NW), established in 1859, ran trains throughout the Midwest.

34. Frank McNerney was yardmaster of the Chicago and Northwestern Railroad's Chicago central rail yard.

35. Crowe's first name is unknown. According to a May 15, 1891 report in the *New York Tribune,* he was the foreman of a switching crew of the C&NW's Wisconsin division. In March 1891 Crowe apparently refused an instruction by C&NW Chicago yardmaster Frank McNerney to run an extra coach onto the tracks of the Galena division, resulting in Crowe's firing. This was viewed as an actionable grievance by members of the SMAA, which threatened a strike unless McNerney was fired and Crowe returned to his job. A festering jurisdictional squabble between the two brotherhoods over employees in the Northwestern's Chicago yard was ignited in the process.

36. Reference to Genesis 18:16–33.

37. Marvin Hughitt (1837–1928), a former telegrapher, was named the general superintendent of the Chicago & Northwestern in 1872 and president of the line in 1887.

38. John André (1750–1780) was a British officer involved in Benedict Arnold's conspiracy to surrender the American fort at West Point during the American Revolutionary War. Captured with incriminating documents in his possession, André was hanged as a spy.

39. Sweeney was head of the Switchmen's Mutual Aid Association.

40. Major General Nathanael Greene (1742–1786), a former top officer under George

Washington, was named commander of the Continental Army for its southern theater of operations in December 1780.

41. Thomas Gaskell Shearman (1834–1900) was a Brooklyn lawyer, political economist, and advocate of the "single tax" ideas of Henry George.

42. Charles William Eliot (1834–1926), an academic from an elite bourgeois background, was president of Harvard University from 1869 to 1909.

43. Samuel Ward McAllister (1827–1895), the husband of an heiress, was the self-appointed gatekeeper of New York social elite during the Gilded Age. He maintained a list of the city's aristocracy, deeming at the time of the grand centennial ball of 1876 the number of significant personages to be precisely four hundred—although by some accounts his actual roster of the entitled numbered six hundred.

44. The Farmers' Alliance is a general name given to a number of agrarian reform organizations established during the decades of the 1870s and 1880s. These included the National Farmers' Alliance ("Northern Alliance"), the National Farmers' Alliance and Industrial Union ("Southern Alliance"), and the Colored Farmers' National Alliance and Cooperative Union ("Colored Alliance"). This broad agrarian movement was the forerunner of the People's Party, established in 1891.

45. Reference is to Helmuth Karl Bernhard von Moltke (1800–1891), a Prussian field marshal regarded as one of the most original and innovative military strategists of the age.

46. Allusion to Exodus 13:21–22.

47. Allusion to Exodus 14, in which the oppressive army of Egypt was slaughtered in a supernatural cataclysm while pursuing the fleeing Hebrew people.

48. Henry Clay Frick (1849–1919) was a Pennsylvania-born industrialist who became a millionaire through the manufacture of coke—a non-melting high-carbon byproduct of bituminous coal created by a process of heated distillation, essential for the production of steel. Entering the business in 1871, within a decade the H. C. Frick Company had achieved a near-monopoly position for coke production in the region, leading steel magnate Andrew Carnegie to extend a business partnership to the younger man. Together, Carnegie and Frick established the United States Steel Corporation on July 1, 1892, shortly followed by a bitter and bloody company lockout of workers at the company's Homestead, Pennsylvania, facility in an effort to break union representation.

49. Origin of the phrase is uncertain. It was used in the 1854 essay "On War" by Pat Murphy, from the *Opal*, a monthly magazine published by the patients of the New York State Lunatic Asylum in Utica, but this may well have been borrowed from an earlier poetic source.

50. Benjamin Orange Flower (1858–1918), son of a Disciples of Christ minister, was a leading public intellectual of the Progressive Era and editor of the Boston monthly the *Arena*. Flower later briefly served as coeditor of Charles H. Kerr's *The New Time* from 1897 to 1898, which was the forerunner of the *International Socialist Review*.

51. B. O. Flower, "Society's Exiles," the *Arena*, vol. 4, whole no. 19 (June 1891), 37–38.

52. Allusion to Jeremiah 6:14 and 11:8.

53. Judas Iscariot was the disciple who betrayed the dissident religious leader Jesus of Nazareth to the Romans, circa 30–33 AD. Judas Iscariot is denoted with both names in the Bible to differentiate him from a second disciple named Judas. The meaning of the word "Iscariot" is a matter of debate, the most likely theory being that it is a mangling in translation of the phrase "man of Kerioth," a place in Palestine.

54. James Russell Lowell (1819–1891) died shortly before this article went to press. The poem quoted is from his 1844 work "The Present Crisis."

55. From a eulogy delivered at Washington's funeral in 1799 by Henry Lee III (1756–1818), a revolutionary war general, governor of Virginia, congressional representative, and father of Confederate States of America military leader Robert E. Lee.

56. Apparently an adaptation of Thomas Jefferson's phrasing in the Declaration of Independence.

57. The line traces to a July 1832 essay entitled "Religious Freedom," published in the Unitarian newspaper the *Gospel Anchor* of Troy, New York.

58. From "Intolerance: A Satire" (1808), by Thomas Moore.

59. From lyrics for the song "The World Is All a Fleeting Show" (1829), by Thomas Moore.

60. From "The Divine Image" (1789), by William Blake (1757–1827).

61. Allusion to "The Brook" (1855), by Alfred Tennyson (1809–1892).

62. From Powderly's keynote address to the October 1886 annual convention of the Knights of Labor, held in Richmond, Virginia.

1892

Liberating Convicts†

January 1892

The state of Tennessee has been endeavoring to make crime self-supporting and, if possible, yield a surplus. Instead of building penitentiaries on the factory plan, as is done in several states, putting in the most approved machinery and utilizing crime, muscle, and brains behind prison walls, Tennessee adopted the plan of hiring out its able-bodied thieves and cutthroats to men engaged in the mining industries of the state.

The result was that for every able-bodied villain, burglar, murderer, incendiary, and so on through the list of convicted scoundrels, an honest, law-abiding citizen was remanded to the ranks of the idle, and himself and family were compelled to take the chances of starvation, degradation, and death.

In writing of such a policy it is not required that we should be overassiduous in the search for denunciatory expression, to convey our unmitigated hostility to the policy which impoverishes honest men that contractors may amass fortunes by operating criminals.

It is a modern economic idea, in which there is, if we are to credit the sayings of lachrymose and lacteous sentimentalists, a deal of humanitarianism. It is one of those sharp tricks so frequently played nowadays upon an effeminate and overcredulous public, by which the wool is pulled over its eyes by mountebanks in morals and knaves in politics, everywhere resulting to the detriment of honest labor. And fortunately honest labor is protesting, and in Tennessee, with a vigor and determination that has given to the subject startling prominence— taking on the characteristics of a revolution.

Boiled down, the facts are that the state of Tennessee, having harvested a large crop of criminals, concluded to hire them out to work in the mines of the state.

These criminals were confined, when not employed in the mines, in stockades, secured from escape by shackles and such other means as were required. They were fed, in some regards, like wild beasts, and at the lowest possible cost. They constituted a motley mass of depravity, but they could wield picks and under the lash could be made valuable to those who had purchased them, and their condition was infinitely worse than that of slaves in "old plantation times."

† Published in *Locomotive Firemen's Magazine,* vol. 16, no. 1 (January 1892), 7–8.

The state derived from its crime a little revenue, the contractors made money "hand over fist," and honest miners and their families suffered; for them the state took no thought nor evince the slightest concern.

Here, then, was a grave state of affairs. For, at best, a little revenue, a great and powerful state was willing to adopt and pursue a policy which forced hundreds of her law-abiding, industrious, self-supporting citizens into idleness and vagabondage. And Tennessee is not the only state that has pursued and is now pursuing the same nefarious policy. But Tennessee is the only state where honest men have taken violent measures to remedy a great wrong.

In Tennessee the miners quietly armed themselves, liberated the convicts, set fire to the stockades, destroyed the property of the employers, and in every case where they made the attack success crowned their efforts. It was out-and-out rebellion, disobedience to law, and for what? Simply for bread.

All told, fully 600 convict miners have been liberated, and the governor of Tennessee admits he is powerless to punish the men who have set at defiance the laws of the commonwealth.[1]

What is the picture? Honest men organizing in regular military style, with arms and ammunition, tearing down and burning stockades, liberating prisoners, and ready to do battle and take the chances, that they may not be robbed of employment, clothing, food, and shelter by criminals. And this we doubt not they will continue to do.

This thing of educating and employing criminals for revenue, whereby honest men and their families are made to suffer, is an outrage so inherently infamous that no reason can be urged in its support worthy of a moment's consideration.

It is often said that if convicts are kept idle they would decline in health, get sick, and die. Admit it all, for the sake of argument—what is the other side of the question? Employ these convicts at half price, or even less than half that honest labor is worth, and prison-made goods go upon the market at half price, and honest men are thereby made to suffer from idleness, sickness, and death.

Between the two, if one must suffer, by all the gods at once, let it be the thief, the burglar, the footpad, the highway robber, the murderer—and not the honest man. Hence it were better that any convict in Tennessee should go free than one honest toiler and his innocent family should suffer from nakedness and hunger and be driven forth shelterless, to perish by the wayside or join the ranks of the abandoned. When a state enacts a law which in its operation adds to the perils of honest men, that the wretches behind prison bars may have work and preserve their health, it itself perpetuates a most flagitious crime for which it should wear stripes.

Recent transactions in Tennessee stand forth as a warning. Penitentiaries, as they are now conducted, having the characteristics of an industrial college, a first-class boarding house, church, and a literary club, hospitals and homes for worn-out criminals, are not after all distinguished as reformatories in morals, but are a brilliant success as health resorts.

The present is not an age of savagery and torture. If criminals were required to sit during all their incarceration in their cells, looking through a couple of inch auger-holes with such exercise as they could obtain by walking up and down in their cells, penitentiaries would perhaps become reformatory institutions.

True, robust villains would die, and the world would be all the better for the riddance. Some would lose flesh and be the worse for wear, so attenuated that they would be unable to ply their vocation immediately, and those who did survived the kindness of the treatment would reform—they would steer clear of prisons, for they would realize the curative quality of being well fed and idle. As is now the practice, a penitentiary, to the hardened wretches who find a comfortable home, is as the shelter of a great rock in a weary land. In them they regain their health and strength and go forth on their mission of cussedness; and yet in many states they are treated with more consideration and sympathy than falls to the lot of thousands of honest toilers who would rather die than steal.

Miners in Tennessee who want to work, and protest against having their bread snatched from them by convicts, have taught the legislature of that state that its policy is infamous, its laws a menace to peace and prosperity, and that the sooner they are repealed the better it will be for society.

Letter to E. E. Clark, in Cedar Rapids, Iowa[†]

January 13, 1892

Terre Haute, Indiana, Jan. 13, 1892

E. E. Clark, Esq.
Grand Chief ORC,
Cedar Rapids, Ia.
Dear Sir and Brother:—

It affords me satisfaction to acknowledge receipt of your favor of the 5th instant. It goes without saying that I have read the communication carefully.

My respect for you, personally, prompts me to find, if possible, a platform, a policy, upon which we could stand together without compromising convictions.

This desire, on my part, is not likely to be realized while you *assume* the innocence of the grand officers of the B of RT.[2]

In your case, the question of their guilt seems to be in abeyance. Your mind is not satisfied, and yet, you do not appear to be persuaded that their plea of innocence is just. You remember the old distich:

> Convince a man against his will,
> He's of the same opinion still.

I do not particularly apply this aphorism to your reflections upon the subject, and yet, I think I see a purpose on your part to find an excuse for the conspiracy, which, had it been practiced against your order, would have made your denunciations so fierce as would have aroused the paving stones of Cedar Rapids to mutiny. Take this for instance:

> I have always maintained that I thought the proper course to have been pursued by the officers of the B of RT was to satisfy the officers of the Switchmen, that they proposed to reinstate McNerney and support him in his position *at any cost.*

---

† Letter from *The Papers of Eugene V. Debs, 1834–1945* microfilm collection, reel 1, frames 82–85. Typed letter, signed. Original at Labor-Management Documentation Center, Cornell University. Not included in J. Robert Constantine's *Letters of Eugene V. Debs.*

I underline "at any cost" because with the B of RT officials "at any cost" meant *conspiracy*.

You must permit me to doubt that you would resort to conspiracy and treason to reinstate anybody—and I submit that the *term* "at any cost," unless qualified and explained, is seriously unfortunate.

It occurs to my mind that you are unfortunate in saying what I now quote:

> To make my position entirely clear to you, I will state that in my opinion the Supreme Council made a great mistake and showed themselves wanting in ability to rise to the occasion when they failed to take this matter up between the Trainmen and the Switchmen and adjust it *before any opportunity was given for a conspiracy to be entered into.*

Here, again, I underline a sentence, the force of which you did not seem to comprehend—analyzed, it makes you say that a "grave mistake"—and "wanting in ability to rise to the occasion" "created an opportunity for a conspiracy." Would you say that because certain parties adjudged Benedict Arnold guilty of improprieties of conduct, they created an opportunity for his conspiracy and treason? And that because of the "opportunity" Arnold was entitled to *consideration* for having availed himself of the "opportunity?"

Why do you beat about for a peg upon which to hang an apology for the conspirators?

You intimate that *"at any cost"* may involve conspiracy and treason; and you assume that the Supreme Council by a "grave mistake" created an opportunity for conspiracy and treason; and when you see 400 innocent switchmen set adrift, made homeless wanderers without work, wages, or food; when you know that helpless women and children were made the victims of base machinations in which the officers of the B of RT were involved; when you see it stated that the authorities of the B of RT did go east and employ men to take the places of the bludgeoned switchmen, you are still unsatisfied that there was a conspiracy and, if there was, you assume the Supreme Council created the "opportunity" for the crime.

You must permit me to believe that you did not intend to involve yourself in such a combination of propositions; that neither your head nor your heart is capable of advising or approving of such flagitious proceedings.

For the great brotherhood of trainmen I have the profoundest respect and regard, but for the men who sought to *get even* with the switchmen "at any cost," while they assume that conspiracy and treason, with or without an "opportunity" created by a "grave mistake" or otherwise, ought to be condoned or whitewashed, I have only a righteous aversion.

It is not for me to say that you have seen the testimony in the case, which force the conviction of guilt upon *all* the members of the Supreme Council, except only those who were adjudged guilty. If you have not seen the testimony, I shall hope it may be placed in your hands because, since the dawn of light, nothing has been clearer or more convincing.

From the first, those who would have the conspirators escape the just penalties of the guilt, it seems to me, are anxious to find an excuse for it rather than affix a penalty for the crime. As a consequence we hear about the wrongs which the switchmen perpetrated and, as if that was not sufficient, the "mistakes" of the Supreme Council are introduced, as if one or the other, or both combined, constituted an excuse for the outrage.

I think I do not misapprehend the real purpose of our correspondence. There have been, so far, no "cross-purposes."

Let us see. The central idea is federation, a basis of federation—working together for the upbuilding of the interests of railroad employees. This includes the B of RT. But can there be such a basis which includes men who stand convicted of conspiracy to strike down an organization with which they were once federated?

I hold that such a federation would not only be farcical but infamous. It would be an open avowal that, should the Supreme Council of such a federation commit a "grave mistake," it would afford an "opportunity" for conspiracy, and that one member of the federated body would be justifiable in getting even with any other member of the body "at any cost."

The question therefore arises: Can a federated body be organized that admits to its councils men who, disregarding every obligation, secretly plan the ruin of innocent men who had a right to expect that their rights would be sacredly guarded?

That such an organization can be formed I do not doubt—but that it can be formed and have the respect of honest men I do not believe; nor do I believe that you, when you have conned all the testimony, would approve of such an organization. It would be born with the virus of a deadly disease in its blood which sooner or later would result in its death.

If you learned that the "verdict of guilty" was rendered against the B of RT "before the trial was entered upon," you had information that I was not in possession of. I disclaim any knowledge of an "agreement" alleged to have been "entered into" at Chicago, affixing the penalty of expulsion, or any penalty, either before or after the trial. My connection with the affair, from first to last, is an open book. Up to the time of the conspiracy the grand officers of the B of RT were my warm personal friends and I was theirs. It was anything but a pleasant duty for me to condemn their official conduct, and I only did it after mature deliberation. In this I was animated solely by an overwhelming sense of official duty, which I could have evaded only at the sacrifice of my manhood and self-respect. Disagreeable as the task has been, I have unflinchingly performed it to the best of my ability, notwithstanding the enmities I incurred, which, were they ten times as great, would not have deflected me from my purpose.

I note your answer to my question in reference to the accusation that the idea of expelling the B of RT from the Supreme Council originated with me. I do not accuse anyone of misrepresentation, but there is certainly a mistake somewhere. At the last meeting of the Council, in the presence of Brother [George W.] Howard and the other members, I made a statement of the facts in the case which completely vindicated me of any purpose, at any time, to expel or otherwise inflict penalties upon the B of RT, other than those who were proven guilty of the conspiracy.

Let me say further that in my antagonism to the grand officers of the B of RT I am influenced by no personal feeling, nor am I swayed by any motives of revenge. A sacred principle has been struck down, trampled upon, and every consideration of duty, fidelity, and honor demands, in terms I can neither disregard nor ignore, that I shall espouse the cause of the men who, whatever may be said to the contrary, were cruelly robbed of employment and remanded to idleness for no other purpose than to gratify a remorseless spirit of revenge upon a handful of their fellow men.

You gave it as your opinion that "every organization should administer their own affairs." I agree with you. And still, if reports that seem of unquestioned authority are true, that policy was not carried out at the Galesburg convention,[3] at least so far as certain outside influences could be brought to bear upon certain "affairs." And if I remember rightly, the official organ of your order, in an issue preceding the convention, found it necessary to make a plea for the reelection of the grand officers, which meant, of course, for it could mean nothing else, the endorsement of the Northwestern conspiracy.

And now, Bro. Clark, permit me to say that we ought calmly and dispassionately to examine the testimony relating to the Northwestern conspiracy.

As an individual, my interests are not involved. The order of which I am a member is not directly concerned; and yet, at no period of my life have I felt a deeper interest than now in the welfare of the men employed in the train service of the country. My loyalty to organization is unabated—and I am glad to say that while I am identified with men who fire locomotives and aspire to more remunerative positions, I feel a lively solicitude for all my fellow toilers regardless of occupation.

I do not forget that we are still in touch with the holiday season, when friendly greetings are in order. I reciprocate all your fraternal words, and most cordially do I wish you and yours a happy and prosperous '92.

How'er the winds may blow, I do not doubt that in the near future the skies of labor will be brighter.

I am sincerely and fraternally yours,
Eugene V. Debs.

The Great Northwestern Conspiracy: Speech at a Mass Meeting of Railroad Workers, Battery D, Chicago[†]

January 16, 1892

Brothers:—

Most of you know me, and some of you like me, and a good many of you don't, and I am much obliged to you both. I like every man who hates me because I don't endorse the Northwestern conspiracy. *[Applause.]* I am sorry you can't all be seated, because I propose to detain you a long time, and I don't intend that one of you shall get away before I get through. *[Applause.]*

In the matter of the Northwestern conspiracy there is a principle involved that neither you nor I nor any of us can afford to ignore. If it is right for an organization to go into partnership—and do it deliberately—with a railroad corporation, to break down an associate body of workingmen, if it is right to do that on the 14th day of May, it is right to do it on the 16th of January, and it is right to do it forever!

---

† Stenographic report first published in *Age of Labor*. Reprinted in *Locomotive Firemen's Magazine*, vol. 16, no. 2 (February 1892), 150, 154–162.

On the 14th of May, 1891, after marching side by side and shoulder to shoulder with the Brotherhood of Railroad Trainmen for a period of seven years, we parted company with each other, and from that day to this we have been marching in opposite directions. *[Applause.]* I stand today where I stood then, where I have always stood—on the side of the men who move the railroad trains of the country and who have organized the several brotherhoods for the purpose of securing those rights they are daily earning in the sweat of their honest faces. I am not one of those who believe there is an irrepressible conflict between capital and labor. I believe it is possible for one man to work for another, and the two to be friendly with each other. I believe it is possible for a railroad manager to respect a railroad brakeman. *[Laughter.]* Now, isn't that a strange proposition? *[Laughter.]* And I believe it is possible for a railroad brakeman to respect a general manager. *[Continued laughter.]* I do not believe, though, that it is possible for a general manager to respect a brakeman who will enter into a conspiracy to deprive his fellow man of employment. *[Cheers.]*

In this matter of the trouble on the Northwestern road, there is a principle involved that I would have understood. There was a switchman in the employ of the company, previous to the 14th day of May, of the name of Crowe. Now just recollect the fact, will you, because Crowe, as I will show, destroyed the equanimity of the whole Northwestern system. Crowe worked for that company up to the 14th or shortly previous to the 14th day of May, when he was discharged. On the same day, and by the same decree, every switchman in the service of the company was discharged. Not a single man escaped. The company, to punish Crowe and a few other alleged offenders, found it necessary to cut adrift nearly 400 innocent men. Did you ever hear of a Crowe raising such a row as that? *[Laughter.]*

I will take up this matter from the time that Crowe and McNerney had their trouble. The fact is that the whole affair is the outgrowth of a purely personal quarrel between those two men—one a yardmaster, the other a switchman; one a member of the Brotherhood of Railroad Trainmen, the other a member of the Switchmen's Mutual Aid Association. And if you will examine the evidence you will find that the enmity for each other grew out of the fact that they belonged to different organizations. Now then, McNerney gets discharged, and a committee of trainmen comes to his rescue. They conclude that Crowe is a bad man, that McNerney has been grossly wronged. They further conclude that McNerney must be reinstated and that Crowe must be discharged. And up to this point I don't blame them, for they doubtless thought there was a principle involved and that it was their duty to fight for it. After exhausting the remedies provided for by the laws of their own organization, they had the Supreme Council convened. The deliberations of that body occupied three days, but the outcome was evidently not satisfactory to the trainmen. The committee then said, "We are going to put this matter into the hands of three men, and deputize them to act for us, with instructions that they shall reinstate McNerney at any cost." Here is where the conspiracy begins.

These three men called on the officials of the company, and they were confronted with the proposition that if McNerney was reinstated the switchmen would strike. If, on the other hand, the company refused to reinstate him, the trainmen would strike.

The press has given out the information that for two years the switchmen had virtually controlled the Northwestern road; that the officials didn't dare to discharge one of them—if they did there would be a strike.[4] Now, it seems strange to me, in view of the fact that railway managers are men of brains and decision, that the officials of the Northwestern Railway could not control their own property—that they permitted a condition of affairs to develop that necessitated the discharge of nearly 400 faithful employees, for the alleged reason that a mere handful of them were guilty of insubordination. The committee, finding themselves unable to accomplish their purposes, telegraphed to their grand master, and Brother Wilkinson comes to Chicago and they meet the Northwestern officials at the Tremont House, according to the statement of Brother Wilkinson himself. The officials say: "Now, Mister Wilkinson, suppose we discharge every switchman we have got—will you take their places?" "No, sir." That was such a revolting proposition that all of his blood boiled with indignation. "But suppose we find it necessary to reorganize our switching service, and we create some vacancies, and we call on you to help us out. How about that?" "Ah, that is a different proposition." *[Laughter and applause.]*

Well, the two propositions represent the difference there is between Tweedledee and Tweedledum. *[Applause.]* In the first instance they say, "We have got 400 switchmen doing our work. These 400 men are all in their places. Now, if they strike, won't you take their places?"—"Oh, no, we are not scabs." "But suppose we fire them bodily?"—"Ah, that is a different thing." *[Applause.]* Now, what do you think of that? Do you think it is possible for the leader of a labor organization to commit himself to that sort of a policy?

I am now going to open the proceedings of the Galesburg Convention and introduce some of the evidence offered there. I will begin with that of Brother Wheat.[5] I don't know that he is here, but I hope he is. I would like to have him hear what I am going to say about his testimony. Brother Wheat was a member of the committee of three that had the matter of McNerney's grievance in charge. In his testimony he makes some very startling revelations. His statement alone is sufficient to condemn the whole conspiracy. In his statement there is a question by a delegate from Lodge No. 74 [Los Angeles, CA]. He asks: "In the circular they sent over the country, it was said you went over to Philadelphia and employed Brotherhood men to go to Chicago and take the places of these men. Is that a fact?" That is a direct question. Now here is the answer of Brother Wheat, one of the committee of three: "I will explain that. Brother A. E. Brown was sitting in the general grievance committee rooms all the time in Chicago previous to the convening of the council, and afterwards went to Philadelphia or east to some of the lodges and reported the circumstances to these lodges. He went on the 13th; he got east about the 15th. In regard to the 17 men, they volunteered to come. A great many more wanted to come, and were told that they had no room and didn't want them. *The 17 who came here were put to work.*"

Here is an admission that the committee in charge of the Northwestern grievance sent a man east on the 13th day of May (that was one day before all the switchmen were discharged), for the purpose of hiring men to take the places of the discharged switchmen. Here is an admission by Brother Wheat himself that they sent a man east to hire men to make sure that they had enough to fill all the places of the switchmen who were cut adrift. Now, I propose to show not only that the committee did conspire with the officials of the Northwestern system, but that they had the sanction and approval of their grand officers; and more than that, before I get through I will show by their own testimony that the Northwestern Company paid their expenses for going east to hire men to take the places of the discharged switchmen. *[Applause.]*

Note particularly this question. Here is a question in the investigation at Galesburg by a delegate from Lodge No. 205 [DeSoto, MO]. He asked, "Who paid Brother Quinn's[6] expenses for going east, the grievance committee or the Northwestern road?" Here is the answer of Brother Ogden, the chairman of the trainmen's committee: "Brother Quinn's expenses on the eastern trip were a part of the expenses of the general grievance committee."

Question by the same delegate: "You say they were a part of it?" Answer by Brother Ogden: "Yes, I will tell about that. There is one account for lost time, and there is another expense account—incidental. That was a portion of his expenses as a representative on that committee. I will state further that I presented the case to the general superintendent of the Northwestern road after the entire business was over, and presented the claim that *owing to the mismanagement of the Northwestern road*—mark that, will you?—*through the division superintendent and the general superintendent,* we were compelled to come to Chicago to adjust grievances on the Northwestern road, as they *were entirely responsible for our presence in Chicago,* it was no more than just for this organization that they would lose the time that we lost *by attending to their business." [Laughter.]*

Just listen to the rest of this: "On the claim for our time it was argued at length, and they allowed for the time of the general grievance committee while sitting at Chicago, and the lodges paid the incidental expenses."

Here we have the admission that the Northwestern Company paid the greater part of the expenses incurred by the trainmen's committee, who agreed to supply, and did supply, so far as it was necessary, the places of the discharged switchmen. That is the testimony given by the chairman of the committee. I declare that in the annals of labor there is no parallel to this infamy. I declare that no organization of workingmen ever commissioned a man to go abroad to hunt up men to take the place of union men, members of a sister organization. *[Great applause.]*

On the 13th day of May, one day before the switchmen were all discharged, Grand Master Wilkinson, of the Brotherhood of Railroad Trainmen, met Brother F. P. Sargent, grand master of the Brotherhood of Locomotive Firemen and president of the Supreme Council in the city of St. Louis, and said to him in a conversation: "Tomorrow you will hear something drop."

Here is the evidence of Brother Sargent himself, page ten of the evidence taken in the investigation. The chairman says: "Mr. Sargent, you may state what you know about this conspiracy?" Answer: "I had no knowledge of it. My first knowledge of any trouble on the Northwestern so far as the Brotherhood of Trainmen and Switchmen were concerned, was communicated to me by Grand Master Wilkinson himself, in the city of St. Louis, when he said that before tomorrow I would hear something 'drop.'" And yet, Brother Wilkinson maintains he didn't know anything about a conspiracy; never heard of a conspiracy. Still, it appears that when he left here, after meeting the officials of the Northwestern in the Tremont Hotel, he was perfectly advised that "something was going to drop." *[Applause.]* What was it that was going to "drop?" It would seem to me that if he ever thought about what was going to drop it would have disturbed his equanimity to the extent at least of an occasional regret for the fate of those poor switchmen who, unoffending, innocent, without having done the first thing to merit punishment, were sent out in the world in search of employment with the brand of insubordination upon them—sufficient cause to bar them from employment by any other railway company. *[Applause.]*

True to Brother Wilkinson's prediction, something did "drop," and it dropped on the 14th day of May, when the switchmen reported for duty and were told that they were no longer wanted. That information must have come to those men as a clap of thunder would come from a clear sky, and more especially to those who had never given their employers the slightest cause to be dissatisfied with them. I want you gentlemen to ponder this phase of the conspiracy well. I want you to think of the lot of a switchman. Most of you know that a switchman has to go to work early, that he must work until late, and that he is subject to almost everybody's abuse. For every crust of bread that a switchman eats he has got to take the risk of losing life or limb. You can imagine the feelings that must have taken possession of these men when they were deprived of work, men who never gave the company the slightest reason to be dissatisfied with them. "You are all discharged, from the city of Chicago to the city of Omaha, and all through the Northwest. There are some of you we are going to take back, but we will pick them. And there are some of you we will not take back. We will take you back, John Brown and George Jones; but we will not take you back, Sam Smith, nor you, Joe Green." These men had all been working together, you understand, side by side; had shared each other's privations and dangers and liked each other. George says: "I cannot go back and leave Joe out in the cold. I have been working with him for a long, long time. I would feel kind of guilty to go back into the service of the company and leave him out." *[Applause.]*

The Northwestern Company said: "We would have taken 80 percent of them back." Yes, but there was someone there to decide who should go back. And do you know, I have a good deal of respect for the switchmen who wouldn't go back and leave their comrades out in the cold. *[Loud applause.]*

What is more natural than for a switchman to stand by a switchman? Gentlemen, you all know something about railroads, and you all know something about switchmen; and when some of you hear the word "switchmen," there is something in the very term that seems obnoxious. Do you know that the switchman, the average switchman, although he does not wear the best clothes, nor mark a very high degree on the social thermometer, carries as much pressure of manhood to the square inch as any man in the railroad service from the car greaser to the railroad president? *[Loud applause.]* Did you ever hear—and you have heard of almost everything against the switchmen—in fact, I think the vocabulary has been strained to do the switchmen justice—have you ever heard of a switchman scabbing? *[Shouts of "Never!" Great applause.]*

One of the great troubles with the switchmen is their extreme zeal in the cause of union labor—their hearts are too big; they have done our fighting when we didn't have the nerve to do it ourselves. *[Great applause.]* I remember, in the CB&Q trouble,[7] when the engineers and firemen with all their boasted strength had gone down, when the verdict had been recorded that the corporation had triumphed, that those brave men had gone down in defeat, the switchmen threw themselves into the breach as the old guard did at Waterloo, and went down with the engineers and firemen in irretrievable disaster. *[Tremendous applause.]*

When it was asked of the Northwestern committee and Brother Wilkinson if they would fill the places of the switchmen if the company discharged them, the record shows that the committee said to the officials: "While we will not fill their places, we will keep the business of the company moving until you get things in shape." Mark that well. I want to read that from the record, so there will be no mistake about it. Here is Brother Wheat—I will confine myself to his testimony for a while. He is good authority. *[Laughter.]* He was one of the three that did the business with the sanction of the grand officers. Brother Wheat says, in answer to a question by the delegate of Lodge No. 298 [St. Louis, MO]: "I told them (the officials) that we should see to it that the business of the company was done—that the business of the company did not stop." How's that? Analyzed, that simply means this: The officials asked the trainmen if they would take the switchmen's places. They said no. "Then if we discharge them, will you help us out?" "Yes; we won't take their places, but we will keep your business moving until you get a new set of switchmen."

What does that mean? Let us be plain and honest. It means simply this: that they would take their places and do their work, whether it was for one day or forever.

Let me ask you a question: Did Henry B. Stone,[8] in 1888, ask the scabs that came to his rescue to do anything more than to keep the business of the company moving until he got permanent fixtures to take the places of his engineers and firemen? *[Applause.]* That is the politest excuse for scabbing I ever heard. *[Laughter and applause.]* I will not take your place, I will not scab on you, but I will not neglect the company's interests. Let us suppose a case: I come along, having struck, and I meet a man that I always thought was my friend, and I see that he is doing my work. I say: "Hello, Bill, you are not at work switching these cars, taking my place?" "Oh, my, no; I am simply keeping the company's business moving. *[Laughter and loud applause.]* I would not scab for the world, but the business of the company must be kept moving." *[Laughter.]*

Let us define another term so that it will be properly understood. I just found out the other day for the first time, although I had been a close student of this question, I just found out that the Chicago & Northwestern officials did not discharge their switchmen at all; that is all a mistake—they simply reorganized the service. *[Laughter.]* The matter of pay doesn't cut any figure. I am all right, you know, except that I am not in the reorganization. *[Laughter.]*

In 1888, in February, the engineers and firemen on the CB&Q road struck because they could not get their rights. They could not get the pay they were entitled to. They could not get the protection that was due them. When they stepped down and out, their places were taken by scabs. Had Henry B. Stone, the general manager, been equal to the emergency, he could have escaped the maledictions that were heaped upon him by simply explaining to the public that he was only "reorganizing the service." *[Laughter.]*

The fact is that the Northwestern affair, probed to the bottom, analyzed honestly with due reference to the rights of the officials of the company, is without question the greatest outrage ever perpetrated upon any body of workingmen anywhere under the bending skies. *[Applause.]* The officials said, as I stated a while ago, that there were a few switchmen that ran the road for about two years. Now, if that were true, isn't it strange that the officials did not at once send for Sweeney, for Hall, for Simsrott,[9] for Downey, the officials of that organization? Isn't it strange they didn't call for those men and say: "You are at the head of these switchmen. Some of them are making themselves so offensive that we cannot control our own property." Why didn't they do that? Do you suppose for an instant that the grand officers of the switchmen would not have said to the officials: "Discharge every one of them who deserve to be discharged; you will have no trouble, for as long as you are right we will stand by you."

Let it be understood that men are not made general managers of railways upon their good looks—that is one of the professions in which brains is the chief essential. Now it is strange, or seems strange to me, that with all their fertility of resources the officials of the Northwestern Company could not devise ways and means to subdue a half dozen refractory switchmen. There is not a policeman in the city of Chicago that could not have done that in a minute and a half. *[Laughter.]* But for two years, it is alleged, the switchmen were permitted to run things with a high hand. No power could control them. Now, if that is true, it is a burning disgrace to every organization of railroad employees, without exception. If it is not true, it reveals a design to allow them to run matters up to a certain point that the officials might put in a wedge between the organizations of their employees that would destroy their effectiveness, array workingman against workingman, thereby ensuring the triumph of the corporation over them all. The plea that the Northwestern officials could not control a few switchmen without discharging them all does not satisfy me.

We have thus seen that in order to punish a single switchman—they say there were more, but no one ever named them; there is not a name in the entire testimony but that of Crowe—in order, I say, to punish a single switchman, it becomes necessary to discharge 400. Let me entreat you to think of that, and think of it seriously. And think if you have ever heard of a parallel to such an atrocious act in the annals of railroad labor? Think of a businessman in the city of Chicago having to discharge 50 faithful clerks and bookkeepers in order to punish a single one of them. I am not objecting, understand, to the discharge of a single man who has made himself unduly offensive. If I were a division superintendent, or a general manager, or a president, I would be that and nothing less. I would have discipline. I would not allow any man in my service to run my business, nor all of them combined. And I would be ashamed to confess, as the Northwestern officials have done, that they tamely submitted to having a few switchmen usurp and exercise their official authority for a period of two years. These officials will pardon me if I give them credit for more courage and self-respect and better sense. They know all about the weakness of organized labor. They understand the weak points of labor organizations. That is one of the requisites of their position. They know how to keep their employees friendly enough with each other—not to like each other. So I say they will pardon me if I do not believe they were incapable of subduing a few refractory switchmen.

They said to the trainmen: "We cannot reinstate your man without having a strike," and they said the same thing to the switchmen. Here are two bodies of men, both believing they are right, trying to get a brother reinstated; the corporation is in what you would call a dilemma, not knowing what to do, conscientiously trying to serve both, and not being able to do that, saying to one of them: "If I please you, I displease the other; if I please the other, I displease you," and worrying about that until finally the happy idea comes to them—after two years, mind you—if they go into partnership with one of them they can knock out the other. Isn't it strange it took two years to evolve such a profound idea? The trainmen made the first bid. The officials would have waited two years, yes, two thousand years before the switchmen would have said: "We will go into partnership with you and knock out all your trainmen." *[Applause.]*

When the 400 switchmen were exiled I took my stand. I made up my mind that their cause was my cause and, without reference to consequences, I enlisted in the uneven struggle between the persecuted innocence and triumphant conspiracy.

One feature of this affair deserves special notice. The press of the United States teemed with execration of the Northwestern switchmen. The capitalistic papers said: "Here is a road that found it necessary to discharge all its switchmen because they defied discipline, because they would not even allow the board of directors to declare a dividend." One of the victims of this plot, a switchman who had always faithfully performed his duty, goes out and applies for work. "Where did you come from?" "I worked for the Northwestern road as a switchman." "You can't work here." He goes a little farther and again applies for work; they put the same question and he meets with the same answer; and, gentlemen, some of these switchmen are looking for work yet.

The other day I went to St. Louis. I stopped at the Laclede Hotel.[10] After I got through with my business, I was driven to the depot. When I got out of the carriage, I had about five minutes before my train left. A poor wretched-looking fellow came up to me and said: "I beg your pardon, but isn't your name Debs? I heard you speak once." I said: "Who are you?" "Why, I was discharged from the Northwestern yards on the 14th of last May," he said. "I had a wife and three children. I was getting along pretty well. I bought a little piece of property. In my whole life I never had any trouble with anybody. On the 14th day of May I was discharged. I looked for work all over Chicago. I could not find a job even on the streets. I came away from there; I would not scab; I came over here, and I am promised a job of driving a hack.[11] Maybe I will get it; if I do, I will get on my feet again. My wife got sick and I had some bills that came due, and as I could not pay them, my little property had to go. And, of course, I have got to do the best I can for my wife and children."

That is just one of them I happened to meet. I don't know how many more there are, and I don't know where they are, and I hope I will not know, because one of them is as many as I care to see. When I saw that poor fellow, when I realized his exile and sufferings, for no reason except that he was a union man and true to his fellow men, I said that those who were responsible for his woe were destitute of every redeeming trait of human nature. *[Tremendous applause.]*

Is there any justice in a policy that plots the downfall of 400 innocent men? That is the policy of the Brotherhood of Railroad Trainmen is committed to. They met in convention in October and investigated the Northwestern conspiracy, and they rendered a verdict. Now, let us see who their witnesses were. I want you to listen carefully while I call their names. The first witness is McNerney; the second is J. D. Cuttridge, a member of their committee; the third is Ed A. Ogden, chairman of their committee; the fourth is S. E. Wilkinson, grand master; the next is P. H. Morrissey, first vice grand master; the next is William A. Sheahan, grand secretary and treasurer; the next is James Fowler, another member of the committee; the next is Brother Wheat, also a member of the committee. I have named them all. *[Laughter and applause.]*

The Galesburg papers reported that the convention had made a thorough and impartial investigation of the entire affair, and yet they never had a single witness who was not charged with being a conspirator, or an avowed defender of the conspiracy. Did you ever hear of such a trial in all your life? These men were charged with entering into a conspiracy with the Northwestern officials to defeat the switchmen. I have named all their witnesses, and every one of them was under charges. *[Laughter.]* Why didn't they call one switchman—just one? Why didn't they call Sweeney, or Simsrott, or Hall, for a single one of them? They never called any one of them, because they didn't want a single ray of truth to reach the delegation. And hence the endorsement of the conspiracy. After they had investigated the matter, upon testimony given by the conspirators and the avowed friends of the conspirators, they endorsed the conspiracy with a whoop and a hurrah. Here is an extract from the *Galesburg Republican Register,* of the 12th of October. Listen:

> Saturday evening's session, when a decision was reached regarding the whole matter, was one of the momentous occasions in the history of any labor organization in the country. Some of the scenes were worthy the skill of an artist or of the genius of a word painter. The first part of the session was taken up in answering questions. The prolonged and frequent cheering, heard far beyond the courthouse, showed that the replies to the interrogatories were acceptable to the delegates and that the greatest enthusiasm prevailed. The sentiment was evidently very nearly unanimous. The desire for the calling of the roll seems to have been practically unanimous. The delegates wanted to be put on record. Probably an hour was consumed in the roll call, for it was interrupted by remarks, by cheering, by explanation. At length it was completed. The convention, as it were, drew its breath prior to one grand explosion. The secretary announced that the motion was carried by a vote of 302 to 14. The explosion resulted. Had there been a strange spectator in the gallery, he would have thought, methinks, that the inmates of a lunatic asylum were having a jubilee, or that the delegates were members of a board of trade, at the instant of great excitement in the market. McNerney, the yardmaster of the Chicago yards of the Northwestern, was picked up bodily, hoisted by scores of hands high in the air, and borne around the room in triumph. Hats were tossed aloft. Coats were hastily doffed and thrown into the air. Some of the more excitable climbed the columns of the courthouse room . . .

Just think of the courtroom festooned with brakemen—how was that for a ghost dance? *[Laughter.]*

> . . . and from their elevated positions waved their hats and handker-chiefs. The uproar was terrific. Every strong pair of lungs was exerted to its utmost, and it was moments before the hardworking vice grand could restrain this expression of pent-up feelings.

Let me read something in connection with this scene. I will leave Brother McNerney on the tips of the hands of his enthusiastic supporters while I read. In the August [1891] issue of the *Switchmen's Journal*,[12] I find this article:

Criminal Libel

> The Chicago Press has published an interview with Frank McNerney, the now notorious Northwestern scab. In this interview McNerney says he proposes immediately to enter suit against the editor of the *Journal* for criminal libel. The ground upon which he will base his suit is that the *Journal* has referred to him as a scab. The statement is correct. The *Journal* not only accused McNerney of being a scab, but stated positively that he is that thing. No warrant has yet been served upon the editor, but the *Journal* stands ready to prove, to the satisfaction of any judge and jury that can be found, all that has been charged, and more. We court investigation. If McNerney desires to clear himself in the courts, we will afford him ample opportunity. We fully appreciate the gravity of the case. If the charge cannot be sustained, it means a trip over the road for the editor. If the charge is substantiated, another and graver one can be also, and it means that the Northwestern Company will lose the services of McNerney. The *Journal* is waiting for McNerney to take hold. If he don't pray the Almighty for help to let go, we will welcome seclusion and retirement. *[Loud applause.]*

The law of Illinois provides that a "libel is a malicious defamation, ex-pressed either by printing, or by signs or pictures, or the like, tending to blacken the memory of one who is dead, or to impeach the honesty, integrity, virtue, or reputation of one who is alive, and thereby to expose him to public hatred, contempt, ridicule, or financial injury." "Every person, whether writer or publisher, convicted of libel, shall be fined not exceeding $500, or confined in the county jail not exceeding *one year.*"

Now if McNerney, who is being tossed, you understand, on the tips of the fingers of these enthusiastic delegates, if he is not a scab—I do not say he is, mark you—if he is not a scab, I suggest that he sue John Hall, the publisher of *Switch-men's Journal,* for libel, and let those poor fellows down easy—down easy—the hard-working friends who are making an electrical fan of him. *[Laughter.]*

I don't want Brother McNerney to do that for the purpose of getting even with John Hall, but I do want him to do it to relieve the delegates who are keeping him tossing, for the sake of the men who carried him on their shoulders in Galesburg. Just after they got through doing that the same enthusiastic delegates—and I have not a word to say in any unkind spirit of what they did—but just after they got through doing that they marched down to Brother Wilkinson's house and serenaded him, and Brother Wilkinson, having been endorsed, I suppose, and feeling pretty good, made them a little speech, and he said: "Well, we have got the Supreme Council up a tree, and the tree is being chopped down." I suppose that Brother Wilkinson had his ears attuned, waiting for a dull, sickening thud, or, in other words, he waited for the Supreme Council to drop. He is still waiting. It may be that the Supreme Council will fall, stabbed to death in the household of its friends. That may be its fate—I don't know and cannot tell. But if it goes down there will be more vitality and honor in its corpse, dead and cold in its winding sheet, than there will be in ten thousand organizations and federations whose foundations are laid in broken pledges and whose cornerstone is treason to organized labor. *[Great applause.]*

I have a word for the members of the Brotherhood of Railroad Trainmen. The other day a vice grand master of that order held a meeting not very far from here, and he was asked how it was that Debs, of the Firemen, was against them in the Northwestern matter, and he responded by making a personal attack on me. I suppose the poor fellow didn't know better. He didn't know what reply to make, so he thought if he could attack me that would satisfy the men, and he did. I know precisely what answer he made to the question that was put to him. I have a transcript of his answer from at least one friend I had in that audience who was a member of his own organization. If that vice grand master, in answer to the question put to him, had said the reason that Debs was against the Trainmen in the Northwestern matter was that he did not have red whiskers, there would have been just as much sense and a good deal less malice in the answer. *[Laughter and applause.]*

Just after the trouble was over there were two circulars issued in their order by the grand officers of the Brotherhood of Railroad Trainmen. In the second one appears this:

> Mr. Debs has in the past been regarded as a true friend to the Brother-hood of Railroad Trainmen. It is true that when the organization was

an infant he nourished it, and no doubt gave it life, but that life found a too-fertile soil and outgrew the organization that at first encouraged it, and then, through jealousy, no doubt, Eugene V. Debs, after doing a good thing, attempts to destroy it; and, like the cow that upset the bucket of her own milk, he moves the adoption of a resolution, the purport of which was to reduce the membership of the Brotherhood of Railroad Trainmen about one-half, and every move of the Supreme Council since our last convention was to break up our organization.

It will thus be observed that the circular of the grand officers of the Trainmen accounts for my not endorsing their conspiracy, upon the ground that I had grown jealous of the growth of their organization. I want to put on record a few facts that have never found their way in print, that may interest some of the members of that order. I should not be charged with egotism when I say that I organized the Brotherhood of Railroad Trainmen. They speak of George Washington as being the father of his country. I am the father of the Railroad Trainmen. I organized the first lodge they ever had, and it bears my name to this day. I guaranteed their bills from the time they first organized. I guaranteed the payment of their bills until they were able to pay them themselves. Their first organizer came to the city of Terre Haute, stopped with me as my guest, and I taught him all the duties of his position. I gave his organization commercial credit. I put into the secretary's hands a letter introducing him to our engraver, men who did the work for the Brotherhood of Locomotive Firemen, a letter to our banker, a letter to every man with whom we did business. I didn't ask whether they were a solvent institution. They had no credit; they had no standing, because they had no organization. I not only did that, but I wrote for them. I wrote a letter to every friend I had in the United States, Canada, and Mexico, and I said: "I want you to do me a personal favor; I want you to find a brakeman, I want you to hand him this letter, and ask him to get a few brakemen together and encourage them to organize a lodge of the Brotherhood of Railroad Brakemen, because if there is any class of men in this country who need organization, it is the brakemen." *[Applause.]* I divided my time between the organization that paid me and the one that needed my services. I sat up many and many a night, after I had eaten my supper, until the sunshine looked into my room, working to lay a foundation for the Brotherhood of Railroad Trainmen, and if that is not true, I hope my good right arm may fall palsied at my side. *[Great applause.]*

I stood by the organization as faithfully as I stood by the Firemen. I was proud of that organization. I never had an ambition that that organization and its officers did not share. I got jealous, according to this charge. Let me show you what I said as far back as 1887. I delivered an address before that organization. You will find it published on page 498 of the *Brakemen's Journal* for the month of November of that year. And here is a part of what I said:

> I have been interested in your work from the beginning; and while I have reviewed the work done by the Brotherhood of Locomotive Engineers, the Order of Railway Conductors, the Brotherhood of Locomotive Firemen, the Switchmen's Mutual Aid Association, while I have the fullest appreciation of their work, I say to them frankly that the Brotherhood of Railroad Brakemen has accomplished more in less time than all of them combined.

Is there any element of jealousy in that statement?

Now, you will understand that if a man is jealous of another's prosperity, that feeling does not develop in an instant. If a man is jealous today he is jealous forever, and in this sense jealousy means a certain narrow, contemptible hatred for another, because he is prosperous. In this sense, jealousy means dishonesty. If I am jealous of a brakeman because he is doing well, what do you think of me? If I had been of that disposition I would never have helped the brakemen to organize, because I had sense enough to know then that, properly organized, they would become a power. And I have done everything from the inception of their organization to this day to augment their power. If I was ever jealous of that organization, I must have been jealous from the beginning, and be jealous now. I want to show the utter falsity of that charge. I want to show that as late as last December, a year ago, just previous to the Northwestern conspiracy, what I said in the official organ of the Brotherhood of Locomotive Firemen, of which I am the editor. This same Brotherhood of Trainmen had met in convention at Los Angeles. I devoted nearly three pages of the *Locomotive Firemen's Magazine* to giving a report of their proceedings, and I wrote this editorial:

> The Brotherhood of Railroad Trainmen's convention has been one of the most harmonious and successful ever held. This magazine adds its hearty congratulation. The Brotherhood of Railroad Trainmen is on the high road to still greater achievements. It comprehends conditions and is equal to the most exacting demands. The grand officers of the order are the right men to put on guard, to see that no interest of the order suffers from inattention. The *Magazine* wishes the Brotherhood of Railroad Trainmen uninterrupted prosperity.

Would such an utterance as that have been made if there had been any feeling of jealousy on account of the growth and prosperity of that organization?

In his annual speech at Columbus, Ohio, in 1889, Grand Master Wilkinson, pointing to me—and you will excuse me for introducing this, because I have got to show to you I was not animated by any spirit of jealousy when I took a position against the grand officers—said: "On my left sits the founder of our brotherhood. Everyone has learned to love him for his many manly qualities. (They seem to have deserted me.) He was our friend when we most needed a friend, and you and I in all our life will never be able to repay him for what he has done for us and for the benefit of our brotherhood." *[Loud applause.]*

Now, my friends, I am unalterably committed to the proposition that there is strength in unity. That if we would secure for the men who work upon the railroads of the continent the largest benefits that organization is capable of bestowing, we must be united. We must stand together, side by side, and shoulder to shoulder, and in every hour of conflict we must be as one man. *[Applause.]* I do not believe that it is necessary for the railroad employees of this country, every now and then, to indulge in the extremely expensive experiment of a strike in order to demonstrate to the public that they have certain rights, or that they have an organization with which to maintain these rights. I believe, as we all have believed, that a strike is disastrous to the employee, disastrous to the corporation, and disastrous to the public at large. A strike is in the nature of a calamity. On the one hand, it cuts off wages; on another it stops earnings; and on another it embarrasses and inconveniences the public. Nobody is helped by a strike. How are we going to avert a strike? By simply harmonizing all along the line. By eliminating all friction; by destroying this thing of caste that is creeping into labor organizations, and making an engineer feel that because he gets four dollars a day he is four times as big as a man who gets one dollar a day; the same feeling that makes a conductor expand to the proportions of a Jumbo in comparison with the brakeman he used to associate with. Destroy caste; destroy this thing of grading men by the pay they get.

I would classify men if I could in just one way. I would make men superior to each other, and I would decorate them with badges in proportion as they were better men, not according to their pay. *[Applause.]* If an engineer or a conductor will consider this proposition a moment he will see how foolish it is to think that he is better than a car-greaser. If that is the correct standard, where does the engineer stand compared with Jay Gould? If an engineer who gets big pay is a big man compared to a poor fellow who gets small pay, how big is he that gets 400 times as much a day as he does?

If a labor organization has a mission in this world, it is to help a man who is getting a dollar a day to get a dollar and twenty-five cents. *[Applause.]* If they have any mission, it is to help the section man and the car man. The others can, to a great extent, take care of themselves. You don't have to have an organization to see that the general manager has a turkey on his table on Thanksgiving Day. He looks out for that himself. And that is why he is a general manager. The man who cannot provide himself with a turkey on Thanksgiving Day will never be a general manager. If organized labor has any mission in this world, it is to help those who cannot help themselves. But what is organized labor in a great many cases trying to do? To cater to the power that oppresses them, and resist the power that is trying to relieve them. Let me illustrate: Take some yardmaster, and I have seen some of them and know some of them. A switchman comes along and says to the yardmaster: "Good morning, Mr. Brown." The yardmaster looks disdainfully. In about five minutes the division superintendent comes along, and he is all politeness. Mr. Brown is on his knees instantly. The division superintendent scarcely looks at the yardmaster, and the yardmaster is all smiles, glad to have the recognition of the division superintendent. The division superintendent goes along the line until he meets the general superintendent, and he pays him the same courtesies that the yardmaster paid him. He kicks the yardmaster, but he smiles at the general superintendent, and the general superintendent struts all along the line until the general manager comes along, and he shows him the same courtesies. *[Laughter.]*

Don't you know, it is an unfortunate thing in human nature that we are everlastingly ready to crook the knee when we meet somebody that can wear better clothes than we can; and our social standing is measured by that standard absolutely, and by no other. I respect always the man who knows more than I do, I pay tribute to him, but I am not willing to pay tribute to a man simply because he has a larger bank account than I have. *[Loud applause.]* I am not willing to admit that because a man happens to have in his possession more money than I have, money that perhaps he never earned, that there is due from me a recognition that I would not be willing to bestow on any man I meet, as far as the social force of dollars and cents is concerned. If we can get rid of that idea of caste in labor organizations, if we are capable of appreciating men according to their necessities, according to their honesty, we can establish an organization that will not only be a protection to the employees, but will be a guarantee to the officials that as long as they mete out justice they will never have a strike.

I believe that time is coming. I believe that gradually as we grow older in experience we will become capable of mastering these questions, and that after a while we will so fully understand this matter of organization that we can meet together in the true spirit of brotherhood; that whether we be car-men or telegraphers or what not, we can all of us who earn our bread in honest work stand together to the end of the ordeal. I have faith in the future. I have faith in the intelligence of workingmen, notwithstanding the fact that temporarily they are arrayed against each other. I believe that as a body they are trying to find the right road to travel, and I believe it is only a question of time until we will so fully understand each other that such a thing as a conspiracy will be an impossibility. *[Great applause.]*

Now, my friends, I am going to speak to you on behalf of a man who was locked out of a position for the sake of principle. If ever there was a man in this world who deserved the sympathy and support of workingmen, without reference to their occupations, that man is L. W. Rogers. *[Loud applause.]* The man who, for the sake of principle, sacrificed a position; who, for the sake of his convictions, abandoned the Grand Lodge of the Brotherhood of Railroad Trainmen. Brother L. W. Rogers is as true a man as ever stood in the ranks of labor. He is a man who will fight for the right. He is a man who will do right. He is a man you can trust. He is a man who has been tried and not found wanting. If I have a friend here tonight, I ask him to do what he can to assist Rogers in the building up of the *Age of Labor*. *[Great applause.]* It is well enough to say, "I will help," but it is better to put your hands in your pockets and pull out a dollar and say: "Rogers, you stood by what you believed was right—you stood by me, you stood by my fellows, you defended a principle. I propose to subscribe for your paper. I propose to show there are few men in this country who appreciate your splendid courage on behalf of organized labor." *[Applause.]* L. W. Rogers showed by his course and by his policy that a position glittering with all the emoluments and glory that might attach to it could not for a moment deflect him from his purpose. He stood for principle. He stood for right. He stood for you. He stood for organized labor, and it is the duty of organized labor to stand by him. *[Loud applause.]*

And now, my friends, in the bonds of fellowship, without reference to the organization you belong to, but believing as you believe, that the time is coming when "truth, crushed to earth, shall rise again,"[13] when virtue will no longer be cloven down, when hypocrisy and crime will no longer be rewarded, when the everlasting truth will prevail, when right will be king, we will meet and stand together once and for aye. *[Loud and prolonged applause.]*

Is It Possible?[†]

February 1892

———

Those who take an interest in the welfare of labor regard with special satisfaction the onward march of organization.

Already in the United States the armies of organized workingmen number fully a million. Argument, discussion, and agitation are doing a mighty work, and the indications are that past success is only the initial step in a movement which promises untold benefits to toilers.

We unhesitatingly concede all that organized labor claims. It proposes better wages. It insists upon honorable treatment by employers. It demands not only a less number of hours as a day's work, but in all cases where it is practicable, a stated number of hours, so that when from any cause the hours are increased, pay may be demanded and secured for overtime.

Nor is this all. Organized labor puts into operation many practical projects having in view the improvement of wage-men morally and socially. And further still, many of the organizations are life insurance institutions in which money paid in small amounts secures the depositors more or less money in case of disability, and in case of death a comforting sum to heirs.

Organization does still more for those who rally beneath its banners. It secures fraternal relations, a deep and abiding regard for each other's welfare. It is a bond of friendship and fellowship. It recognizes mutual interests and does all that men can do to promote harmonious relations. Nevertheless, is it possible with so much that is commendable, so much that commands approval and admiration, that in numerous instances organized labor is committing fatal mistakes? Is it possible that while organized labor rightfully claims exemption from the penalties which organized capital imposes, it itself inflicts penalties upon other violative of every principle of individual liberty which constitutes the supreme glory of American citizenship? Are there not frequent occurrences transpiring throughout the country which make such interrogatories pertinent and appropriate? If so, what is their character?

"Come, now, let us reason together," is an old exhortation. When men reason together they are frank, sincere, and without disguise. They state their propositions in a way to command approval. The tricks of diplomacy are not

———

[†] Published in *Locomotive Firemen's Magazine,* vol. 16, no. 2 (Feb 1892), 103–104.

tolerated. The purpose is to arrive at honest conclusions; to deal justly. There is no word jugglery. No sophisms, only plain, straightforward argument.

Taking these things as a basis, we start out by the assertion of a fundamental proposition that a man, at any rate an American man, has an irrevocable right to "life, liberty, and the pursuit of happiness," and when pursuing such things within the limits of law, any penalty inflicted upon him has all the ineffaceable marks of the worst form of bigotry. It is a wrong so monstrous that justice hides its face and cries out, "Shame!"

It requires no stretch of fancy to say, "There are labor organizations composed of honorable men, profoundly interested in the welfare of labor—of workingmen. They work to better the condition of toilers, are ready to make sacrifices for them. They state correct principles and advocate them, and are accomplishing good."

This can be said of labor organizations. We need not repeat what we have said in commendation of organized labor. But there are labor organizations which display a zeal very much like that which animated St. Paul when he went forth to persecute Christians, a zeal that degenerates into cruelty.[14]

There are labor organizations whose members are taught that it is *right* to deny a non-union man, or a man who is not a member of a labor organization, the privilege of working at his trade for a livelihood, and this great wrong is being perpetrated constantly throughout the country. For instance, a man is erecting a house; he has employed non-union carpenters; the fact is disclosed by the "walking delegate," and forthwith the employer of these non-union men is required to dismiss them. Such a monstrous proceeding is an assumption of power on the part of organizations to do an act of unqualified injustice, a wrong so flagrant that it ought to arouse universal indignation.

It is held that the highest prerogatives of government are first, to take a man's life, second, to deprive him of his liberty, and third, to confiscate his property, but here is a labor organization, by the *one act* of depriving a man of work, which is in some measure equal to taking his life, because it deprives him of that which sustains life, it deprives him of the means of sustaining the lives of wife and children.

Here we inquire, of what offense is the man guilty that a labor organization should strike him down? This, and *only this:* that he has refused to join a labor organization. He is a non-union carpenter, bricklayer, painter, printer, or some other mechanic, who for reasons satisfactory to himself declines to join a labor organization.

In this course of action, be it remembered, he has violated no law, human or divine. On the contrary, he could appeal to constitution and statutes in support of his cause. As a man he had a right to choose, and in doing that he wronged no man, and any penalty inflicted upon him, it is seen at a glance, is well calculated to introduce irritations fruitful of disasters, because there is not a court in Christendom which if appealed to would not grant him redress.

True, it may be said, and is said, that ostracized workingmen should join a labor organization. It has been said by those who have persecuted men to death for heresy that they could escape faggots, dungeons, thumbscrews, and tortures of every kind by subscribing to the dogmas of the church in power. Gods! Has it come to this in free America, that labor organizations have concluded to advance their fortunes by persecutions?

We are not discussing scabism. We make no reference to a class of degenerate creatures who seek the dismissal of union men that they may occupy their places, but rather to men who want fair wages and obtain them, but who choose to remain outside of labor organizations. And now we make this declaration, that imposing penalties on opinions, on acts inherently right, which neither God nor man has promulgated laws to suppress, will result disastrously to those who perpetuate the wrong.

We know of workingmen's organizations, the members of which work in harmony with men who are "non-union." These union men seek to win over the non-union men by argument and convincing facts, and are meeting with success. A more liberal spirit than is displayed in certain instances would redound to the credit of labor organizations.

The present is not the time for intolerance and persecution, and above all things, workingmen who have been the groaning victims of oppression and injustice should not use power when it is secured to inflict penalties upon other workingmen. Such an outrage should not be possible.

Is Legislation Needed? How Shall It Be Obtained?[†]
March 1892

The interrogatories which form the caption of this article are addressed particularly to railroad employees.

In a broad sense, the lawmakers of the country, whether found in legislatures or in Congress, are partisans. The term, as used in this connection, is not intended to be in any sense offensive.

Where there is free speech and a free press, there will be parties. It is inevitable, and of this result we indulge in no complaints.

"In old colony times, when we lived under a king," there were parties. There was a party that favored British taxation without representation, and a party opposed to such taxation. Hence the anti-tea party that was organized in Boston, a party that boarded a ship loaded with tea and emptied the cargo into Boston Bay, which gave rise to an old battle song of which the following, as we recollect, was a stanza:

> Johnny Bull, and many more,
> Soon they way are coming o'er,
> And when they reach our shore
> They must have their tea.
> So Johnny put the kettle on,
> Be sure to blow the fire strong,
> And load your cannon, every one,
> With strong gun-powder tea.[15]

During the revolution the Whig and Tory parties existed, next to the Republicans and Federalists; after these came the Democratic and Whig parties, then the Democratic, Whig, and Abolition parties; later the Democratic and Republican parties, with here and there a prohibition party. At this writing there are three parties in the field: the Democratic, the Republican, and the People's Party, the latter sometimes being referred to as "the Farmers' Alliance," and which at the same time claims to be a labor party, or the workingmen's party.

If we were to be guided in our estimate of parties, predicated upon professions expressed immediately prior to an election, we should be compelled to aver that all political parties are deeply concerned about the welfare of labor—that

† Published in *Locomotive Firemen's Magazine*, vol. 16, no. 3 (March 1892), 195–198.

their solicitude for the happiness and prosperity of workingmen absorbs a large percentage of their thoughts, and that they are ceaselessly wrestling with the subjects, how best to promote the interests of men whose labor pays all interest, taxes, and revenues, and keeps the world from stagnation and decay.

This system of profession, chicane, duplicity, and hypocrisy has been practiced for years and has inspired many a time workingmen

> With hopes, that but allure to fly,
> With joys, that vanish while he sips
> Like Dead Sea fruits, that tempt the eye,
> But turn to ashes at the lips.[16]

Here and there, now and then, the claims of workingmen have been recognized and laws have been placed on the statute books which modified some of the outrage that had fastened itself upon our Christian-savage jurisprudence, a relic of barbarism and a legacy of the dead past, those dark and damned ages when, in judicial parlance, it was always "master and servant," or "master and slave," but never "man and man;" when no workingman, either in court or out of court, sought to have any right restored, or respected, which had been cloven down by his "master."

The world of workers took hope when the Declaration of Independence declared that "all men are created equal," and the day on which it was first read is a national holiday wherever float the stars and stripes, and he shouts—

> Forever float that standard sheet!
> Where breathes the foe but falls before us,
> With Freedom's soil beneath our feet,
> And Freedom's banner waving o'er us.[17]

But the question arises, over whom does the starry banner float nowadays? Over a nation of freemen? Nominally it does—but in fact it does not.

Workingmen declare that they are not freemen, if their employers may, with or without law, hire Pinkerton thugs, arm them with rifles, and order them to shoot down workingmen like dogs, without provocation. These infernal cutthroats, these vagabonds from the slums, these hired outcasts, constitute a military force unknown to the state, and yet workingmen have been unable, except in a few instances, to strike down the murderous policy of some railroad corporations which employ these thugs.

We confess that in all our readings of savage and barbarian methods, we have found nothing more essentially devilish, more infernal in all regards, than the employment of Pinkerton outlaws to murder workingmen at the behest of a corporation.

We talk glibly of lands cursed by autocrats and aristocrats, and exclaim—Read our Declaration of Independence! Behold our flag! Remember Bunker Hill and Yorktown! Contemplate the territorial grandeur of our republic! And in our rapture we contemplate the luminous track of glory, permanent and bright, made by our fathers, to which we love to refer; but as one beholds an armed gang of Pinkerton murderers ready to kill railroad men, under orders from a railroad corporation, does not his blood run cold in his veins? And when men who make laws are appealed to end the infamy by enacting a law forbidding its continuance, and are given to understand that it will not be done, what, if any, is the remedy?

Is it any longer wise to continue in affiliation with any party that thus rudely and contemptuously thrusts us aside? Is it not wise to form an alliance with some party that is pledged to reform abuses so glaring that the devil himself would be unable to frame an excuse for their continuance?

Is it not of the highest importance that railroad employees should give special prominence to the "co-employee" iniquity?

It is scarcely required to offer a word in outlining its measureless injustice, and that it should be incorporated into American jurisprudence staggers belief. Railroad men fully comprehend the wrongs it inflicts.

What is the demand? It is not to repeal statutes by virtue of which this wrong, scarcely less than a crime, exists, but to enact a law which shall at once and forever strike from the records of the courts the damning evidence that with all our boasting we are living under decisions based upon neither law nor testimony, but which as effectually blast the rights of workingmen as if it were written in our constitutions that railroad employees are serfs or chattel slaves, who have no rights which courts are bound to respect.

Who, of all the wise men in America, possessed of hearts and whose sensibilities are not dead beyond the reach of hope, are not horrified almost daily by the records of the maimed and killed employees of railroads?

By the rulings of the courts, based upon no law, except that nondescript thing called the "common law"—handed down from the time when the employer was *master* and the workingman a *slave*—neither a workingman nor his heirs, having a claim against a railroad corporation for damages, have any more standing in court than an African slave in "old plantation times." The courts show them no consideration whatever, provided it is shown that he was maimed or killed by the negligence or ignorance of a co-employee, though in the employment of the co-employee he had no more voice than a man who died before the flood—and the corporation is usually prepared to show that a co-employee was the cause of the injury.

In one or two states, perhaps, the infamy has been wiped out. Why not in every state? Simply because the corporation has demanded that it should stand.

The corporation is always on hand when a legislature meets. Its agents find out who are the base-born, degenerate creatures who *represent* themselves; they find out the price of those men who are known to be "for rent" or "for sale," and paying their price, own them.

Some of them sell cheap, others demand round sums, but the average is never large and the political mendicants are easily *fixed*—and in 99 cases out of 100 the railroad employee is compelled to accept defeat.

All of this leads to the inquiry: What are railroad employees going to do about it? Will they accept defeat forever and a day? Are they so wedded to their chains that they will never make a freeman's effort to break them?

The old parties, call them by what name we may, have been tried, and their promises have been broken as often as they have been made. The corporation has won a victory in nearly every instance. Is it worthwhile to trust them further? Does not every consideration of justice, right, truth, independence, and the supreme importance of the interests at stake demand a change of policy?

There has come to the front, within a recent period, a new party, as we have said—the People's Party. It proposes certain reforms, some of which, at least, are of a character that commands widespread approval.

We are not required to print the platform of the People's Party, nor to endorse all the propositions it contains. We are not required to so much as suggest that all railroad employees should become identified with and active workers in the People's Party; but the question arises: Wherein does the People's Party antagonize any demands of railroad employees? In what plank of its platform is to be found hostility to the interests of labor?

In response, it will doubtless be said, in some quarters, that the People's Party has evinced hostility to railroads, and because of this unfriendliness the interests of railroad employees are jeopardized.

The question arises: In what way is the People's Party unfriendly to railroads? In discussing such a proposition, let us be frank.

The People's Party expresses the opinion that the *water* in railroad stock should be *squeezed* out; that railroads should do business on honest investments and not upon a basis of fraud, and that they can afford to so reduce rates of transportation for persons and freight as to make them what they were designed to be, a blessing to the country.

Railroad corporations at once set about to defeat such legislation, and at this juncture comes into view strategic movements on the part of railroad corporations of astounding audacity.

In the first place, the corporations say to the states, "If you reduce rates, we will reduce the number of trains." This reduction of the number of trains is to operate in the way of a penalty upon the sovereignty of the people, the sovereignty by virtue of which the corporation exists.

In the next place, the corporation prepares petitions to be presented to legislatures, requiring their employees to sign them, under a threat, direct or implied, that their work and wages depend upon their compliance.

In addition to this, the corporation, having immense facilities at hand, sends forth their henchmen to organize their employees into clubs for the express purpose of antagonizing the farmers, the Farmers' Alliance, and the People's Party, to the extent that such legislation as the farmers demand shall not be had.

In view of these strategic movements, how stands the case with railroad employees who demand, and ought to have, certain important laws enacted for their protection?

If railroad employees antagonize the farmers, what more natural than that the farmers shall reciprocate this hostility? Throughout the Middle, Southern, and Western states the farmers, if united, will dictate legislation. That they will unite is a logical conclusion, because everywhere their interests are practically identical.

It is urged by some that the policy mapped out by the farmers is impracticable, that they are the victims of vagaries. But is it not said in certain quarters that workingmen are "the enemies of capital" and that when they strike for their rights or against wrongs that they "become the enemies of society and constitute a 'dangerous element,'" and are not corporations ceaselessly devising schemes by which they hope to disrupt and destroy labor organizations?

But such discussions are foreign to the purpose of this article, and, returning from any seeming digression, we ask: What are the advantages railroad employees expect to gain by antagonizing the farmers or the Farmers' Alliance?

Is it believed, if railroad employees succeed in defeating the farmers, that the corporation will aid them in crushing out the Pinkerton infamy? Do railroad employees, those engaged in the train service, so much as dream that the corporation will, when the farmers are defeated, demand of legislatures that the co-employee iniquity shall no longer disgrace the jurisprudence of the country? Do railroad employees have so much as a molecule of evidence that the corporation, when it has used them as tools to defeat legislation in the interest of the farmers, will, for such exhibitions of acquiescence, at once proceed to increase their wages and promote their welfare so generously that grievance committees will no longer be required to stand guard to watch our interests, ceaselessly in peril?

Our conviction is that railroad employees are in a position to determine for themselves, independent of intimidation or any form of bulldozing, what their interests require in the way of legislation, and that every consideration of prudence demands that they should place their votes and influence where they can achieve with the greatest certainty results that will be promotive of their welfare.

The old parties, prolific of professions of fealty to labor, have, as a rule, been guilty of the most shameful apostasy. Shall we forever be their dupes, so craven that we cannot muster sufficient independence of party discipline to break the fetters that have bound us, and vote as independent, self-respecting citizens?

Such questions are now up for debate, and as between serfdom and freedom, let workingmen declare their preference. If workingmen propose to sing "Hail Columbia, happy land" in earnest, then they must add,

> Let Independence be our boast,
> Ever mindful what it cost.[18]

The time has come, as in the faraway days of the Israelites, when idol worship was making sad inroads upon the spineless sons of the chosen people—when Baal had 400 prophets and God only one Elijah, who said, "How long halt ye between two opinions? If the Lord be God, follow him; but if Baal, follow him."[19] And now, if the corporation be the railroad employees' god, let them follow it and do its bidding, but if their own independence and self-respect, their liberty and citizenship combined, is preferable—then by all the gods, let them assert themselves, be true to themselves, though the furnace of their afflictions be heated by the plutocratic Nebuchadnezzars[20] seventy times hotter than when cremated martyrs of the past demonstrated that their courage was equal to their convictions.

Russia[†]

March 1892

The autocrat of Russia[21] [Alexander III] rules over half of Europe and fully one-third of Asia. His power is absolute. Russia is a semi-barbarous country, sadly benighted and greatly in need of royal funerals. The emperor believes he has a divine right to rule Russians, and a great many of his subjects believe they have a divine right to kill him.

Russia has an established church called the "Greek church,"[22] and the emperor is at the head of the establishment. The church is a splendid burlesque, carrying about as much religious pressure to the square inch of boiler surface as falls to the lot of a man-eating tiger, a cobra, or a crocodile of the Nile. It is the kind of religion that glories in darkness, ignorance, superstition, and degradation. The priesthood of the Russian church is chiefly engaged in keeping Russians in ignorance. This done, they can be ruled and enslaved.

A great many Russians, seeing the people of other nations having the right to stand up and talk, and vote, and have parliaments, congresses, etc., have concluded that such things would be good for them, but the emperor will have none of it, hence Russians want to kill the emperor, and they are going to do it.[23] But it would do no good to kill the present emperor, since the woods are full of heirs to the throne, and just as soon as the present ruler went under, another one would pop up of the same character, and the business would all have to be done all over again. Still, if two or three grand dukes were to hand in their checks suddenly, the probability is that the next occupant would give up some of his divine prerogatives and permit the people to have a say through some representative body.

The hue and cry about emancipation of the serfs is known to be a miserable sham, the serfs being *in statu quo,* and worse off, if possible, than ever. It is not the policy of an autocrat to tolerate independence, and it is because the Russian despot will not permit liberty, because he will perpetuate the bondage of Russians, that thousands of them want to blow him up.

The latest accounts from the wretched land is that a brother of the emperor had been caught in a conspiracy having for its object the removal of the reigning despot. But should Grand Duke Sergei[24] mount the throne only a

---

† Published in *Locomotive Firemen's Magazine,* vol. 16, no. 3 (March 1892), 206.

change of rulers would result, and it is more than probable the miscreant who plotted against his brother would be the more heartless villain of the two.

It is eminently Christian for the people of the United States to send food to the famine-cursed districts of Russia, but unless it is followed until delivered to those dying of hunger, the probabilities are that the nobility will steal it.[25]

It is not easy to tell the future of Russia. A far more easy task is to predict the reigning family of the wretched land unless some one of them levels down the throne. The edict has gone forth. A century may be required to execute the decree, but the present form of despotism is doomed. There will be a revolution, a general slaughter of grand dukes and heirs to the throne. This will come and Russia, like France and the Israelites, will owe its delivery to a Red Sea.

Strikes[†]

March 1892

The world has always had a non-combatant element, those who deplored war under all circumstances, and they are still doing business at the old stand. Notwithstanding this, there are wars and rumors of wars on all of the continents and many of the islands, nor is it expected that any change will immediately occur.

It is conceded that labor strikes are declarations of war, not sanguinary, but war nevertheless; war which entails sacrifices and many woes upon those who strike—the rank and file of the armies of labor. To show how the strike wars went forward in the state of New York last year, or 1890, the following summary from the report of Mr. Peck,[26] labor commissioner of that state, is interesting. He states that there were, during the year, 6,258 in 170 trades. Of these, 5,566 were successful, 169 were compromised, 565 were unsuccessful, and 58 are pending. Number of persons engaged in strikes: 93,984. Number refused work after strike: 5,048. Amount lost in wages: $1,889,164.32. Amount expended for relief of strikers: $131,518.75. Estimated gain in wages for one year: $4,122,883.10. Loss to employers from all causes: $481,524.43.

---

† Published in *Locomotive Firemen's Magazine,* vol. 16, no. 3 (March 1892), 239–240.

In the foregoing it is shown that after deducting for loss of wages $1,889,164.32 and $131,518.75—a total of $2,020,683.07—labor gained by the wars $2,102,200.03. It is furthermore shown that employers lost, in one way and another, $481,524.43. It is not to be presumed that the losses by employers in any wise detracted from the sum total of their "creature" enjoyments; they could draw on their "surplus" and proceed as usual, but in the cases where the employees did not win a victory the situation was far different.

By reference to Mr. Peck's figures it is seen that 5,048 workers, after peace had been declared, were refused work, turned adrift to face any fate that the world might have in store for them.

The question arises, why were 5,048 men refused work? Mr. Peck does not state the reason and we are, therefore, left to conjecture.

It is probable that these 5,048 men were active in bringing about the strikes, that they saw the wrongs practiced and demanded justice, and were therefore "spotted" and made to realize that men who have the courage of convictions are the ones who are marked for penalties, and as they fall thick, merciless, and crushing, those who inflict them tauntingly exclaim, "That is what you get by striking," and a heartless world chimes in, saying, "Good enough for them, the next time they will know better than to strike." And the effect, in numerous instances, is that of intimidation upon the workingmen, who accept degradation, wrong, and injustice rather than try the strike remedy. What these wrongs are, what is the character of the injustice and degradation it is not required that we should attempt to recite. They are often such that could they be shown, as Anthony exhibited the stab holes in Caesar's mantle, would move paving stones to mutiny. There is slow death by hunger, exposure, foul air, and tasks such as only galley slaves are required to endure.

We are not an advocate of strikes, except as a last resort, and that last resort comes when employers refuse to accord a full measure of justice to employees.

We do not forget the trials which men endure when the fortunes of war go against them, when they are compelled to see scabs take their places, as in the case of the Northwestern Railroad, when 400 switchmen were made to "bite the dust," and a great brotherhood of railroad employees flung out the banner, black with treason to organized labor, which advocates protection.

When pirates sail the seas they have numerous flags, indicating nationality and that they are pursuing a legitimate trade, but when their victim has "hove to," the black flag is unfurled and the captured ship's crew have to "walk the plank," but if anything more cruel, less than death, was ever visited upon innocent men than the grand officers of the Chicago & Northwestern Railway

Company visited upon 400 switchmen, the account has escaped our notice. That was a strike on the part of the Northwestern and the B of RT conspirators, and unfortunately the fallen switchmen could not strike back.

It was a case that should have aroused the indignation of every railroad employee on the continent. It was an instance of such unpardonable perfidy as should have aroused the strike spirit everywhere, but it did not, and 400 innocent men were made the victims of idleness. Is that the whole story? Oh, no. On the contrary, the conspirators were hailed with exclamations of "well done, good and faithful servants," and were encouraged to go forward and "get even" regardless of methods or consequences.

It is a case that Mr. Peck could take up and analyze, showing how many parts of virtue and how many of villainy there were in its composition.

Strikes will continue to occur while injustice prevails, but since organized treason has become a feature of protection, it will be well for honest men to be on the lookout for conspirators.

Arbitration[†]

May 1892

Railroad employees in the train service of the country engage from time to time in one form of arbitration. They formulate grievances, choose certain members of their organization to present their hardships and wrongs to the officers of the road, where they are exhaustively discussed between the parties involved, and usually an amicable settlement is secured.

This, we are aware, is not arbitration as commonly defined in the books. The employees do not choose an arbitrator; the employer does not choose an arbitrator, leaving it for the two arbitrators to choose a third arbitrator to hear and decide grievances. Feeling entirely capable to manage their own affairs, railroad employees, engineers, conductors, firemen, switchmen, and trainmen prefer to make their own settlements, and this, insofar as we are advised, is the view taken of the subject by railroad officials.

---

† Published in *Locomotive Firemen's Magazine*, vol. 15, no. 5 (May 1892), 387–389.

By a certain class of men it is assumed that arbitration would prove a panacea for ills which affect wageworkers in all of the industries of the country. These arbitration agitators do not insist so much on voluntary arbitration where the parties each choose an arbitrator, as they do upon having a state board of arbitration appointed by a governor or a legislature, constituted by law and acting under an ironclad statute, clothed with power to settle all labor troubles. A moment's reflection will suffice to convince the average railroad employee that he has no voice in the matter. Neither of the arbitrators are selected by the railroad employees, and are not likely to know much, if anything at all, about their interests, and taking the average legislature, little effort is required to satisfy workingmen that their interests would not be a disturbing element in its deliberations. Moreover, though the legislature should be composed of intelligent workingmen, the difficulties in the way of framing a law under which a state board of arbitration would be required to act would be a task not easily performed; indeed, we doubt if a reasonably just and satisfactory law could be framed.

Those who are the most pronounced in their approval of the state board of arbitration assume that they would put an end to strikes, which they claim are unmixed evils, calamities without a redeeming feature, and they urge the creation of state boards of arbitration solely to promote the welfare of workingmen. There may be organizations of workingmen who stand in need of a state board of arbitration, though our investigation of labor questions has not led us to such a conclusion. The supreme idea in arbitration ought to be to obtain justice, fair play, fair wages, proper treatment, hours of work that would leave the toiler some opportunities for mind culture, and physical recuperation from exhaustion. The tendency everywhere is to ignore such questions on the part of employers. The vexations and exasperations which they produce are numerous and lead often to open revolt. They are of a character which, though to workingmen of unquestioned importance, are usually regarded by the public as trivial and deserving of little consideration.

Suppose a railroad corporation concludes to reduce wages 10 percent, as it has an unquestioned legal right to do, what could a state board of arbitration do to modify the ills such a reduction would inflict upon a man whose wages barely sufficed to keep soul and body together? In what way could these wronged and outraged men present their grievance to a state board of arbitration? But suppose the law constituting the board should provide that a strike would be unlawful, and that those having the grievance should first notify the board of their condition, what could the board do in the case? We answer, it could do one of two things: advise the men to submit or quit work.

Suppose the board should conclude that the men were not sufficiently compensated for their work and should direct the corporation to advance their wages, is there a man on the continent reduced to such imbecility as to suppose the corporation would obey the order? In a word, would it be advisable to confer upon boards of arbitration the power to regulate wages, since it would be able to reduce as well as advance a workingman's pay?

In this line it would be an easy matter to suggest grievances which a board of arbitration could not satisfactorily adjust, and to clothe such a board with despotic power to finally determine such questions would be so palpably at war with the liberty of citizens that it could not be tolerated for one moment.

It is pertinent to inquire: What is the chief plea urged by those who favor state boards of arbitration? This: that the creation of such a board, properly equipped, would put an end to strikes. These advocates of state boards of arbitration assume that strikes do no good, that they are productive of evil, and that legislatures should confer the necessary power upon one or more persons to see that they do not occur.

Such persons know absolutely nothing of the history of organized labor in the United States, or elsewhere. They, while ostensibly pleading the cause of labor, are, in fact, the deadly foes of labor, and the ardent friends and backers of the oppressors of labor.

There are two things which the great majority of employers demand, first the *largest* number of hours possible for a day's work, and the *smallest* possible pay for a day's work. Employers claim the right to place as overseers of employees men of their own selection, regardless of the wishes of employees. Taking these things into consideration, the friction, the unrest, the exasperation and degradation of which they have been fruitful, and they account for nearly every strike that has occurred in the United States during the current century.

It is only required to consult the record to obtain the facts demonstrating that during the past 85 years, hours of labor have been reduced at least five hours a day, reduced in every instance by the power of the strike. To obtain the concessions, little by little, men were required to make sacrifices and endure suffering, and it is doubtless true that many a valiant *labor agitator,* and those dependent upon him, endured sufferings as cruel as were visited upon martyrs. They were men who, like other men in battling for emancipation, went down to death, but they achieved a glorious heritage of time—five hours a day for thousands of toilers, who, but for their courage and sacrifice, would today be working *fourteen* instead of an average *nine* hours a day, a sum total of 313 working days of the year, or 1,565 hours, or 173 days of nine hours each.

In the matter of wages, facts magnifying the power of strikes are found in rich abundance all along the luminous track of organized labor. They have advanced prices and they have maintained prices, and except in rare instances there has been neither advance nor maintenance of wages, except by the strike, or, what was its equivalent, the *fear* of a strike, and the sum total of this advance, could it be stated in round numbers, would swell far into the billions, the benefits of which are being realized today. But to accomplish such results sacrifices were required, sufferings were experienced, hunger and nakedness and death were the penalties to thousands. The benefits have been permanent, and are today luminous among the fruitions which organized labor enjoys.

It is well to remark just here that only organized labor strikes, and we admit (which may go for all that it is worth) that organized labor does not always win in battles against organized capitalists. But in summing up the results organized labor will find nothing disheartening. Napoleon is credited with saying to his troops before the battle of the pyramids, "Forty centuries look down on you," and it may be said to organized labor, "Sixty centuries look down on you." The victories of the armies occupy large space in the history of the ages, but organized labor, by its strikes, has won many a victory for workingmen, which—though no historian has recorded them, while orators in lofty periods have not eulogized them, nor the captains who led on the hosts, though poets may not have embalmed them, nor minstrels sung them—still they have been victories which good men must applaud; for when a workingman, by a strike, secures for himself two loaves of bread, when but one was before obtainable, he has won a victory, compared with which the trophies of Alexander, Caesar, and Napoleon dwindle to contempt.

The purpose of those who advocate the creation of state boards of arbitration is, they say, to put an end to strikes. The hand which they extend to organized labor is an iron hand within a velvety glove, soft as a tiger's paw. It means that organized labor, like poor old Sampson, shall, listening to wooing words, be shorn of its strength, and once captured shall have its eyes put out[27] in the hope that eventually, by the processes of degradation, now in operation, workingmen of America may be reduced to the condition of the Chinese, Huns, Poles, and Italians, prostrate in the dirt, willing to accept whatever may be offered to them.

It would be folly to say that our presentation of the case is overwrought. Conditions of wageworkers in Pennsylvania are such that a Raphael could not paint them, nor a Dante describe them, and in all of the great centers of population in America testimony is so overwhelming that the power of exaggeration fails to describe conditions.

What is a strike? The answer is war. And what is war? Resistance to wrong. Such is the history of war in the United States. To say there have been unjust, unnecessary wars, begs the question. Who is the craven that would have the Constitution of the United States so amended that Congress should never declare war? And who but an enemy of organized labor, and a friend of scabs, would advocate the enactment of a law that so much as *squints* at depriving organized labor of the only weapon it possesses of maintaining its rights against those whose policy is oppression?

Rest[†]

May 1892

This magazine is fully committed to the advocacy of rest for workingmen. To the extent of its ability and opportunities, it has advocated the demand for eight hours as a day's work. If a man is working ten hours, as the great majority of laborers are, we would reduce the number to eight, giving him a week of six days—twelve hours additional rest. In all such propositions we are on record as favoring *rest* for the weary toiler.

Again, the *Magazine* is absolutely and uncompromisingly in favor of one entire day of rest in seven. We are of the opinion that men, particularly working men, physically and mentally require one day's rest in seven.

In all of this we omit all reference to what is called "Sunday rest." We have not deemed it advisable in the discussion of the rest question to enter the domain of theology.

The idea now is that works of "necessity and charity" may and ought to be performed on the Sabbath, or on Sundays. No man in his senses now controverts such propositions. No one contends that street railroad corporations should cease the running of cars on Sundays, because such a proceeding would inconvenience thousands. No one seriously contends that the railway service of the country should be entirely suspended on Sundays, or that steamboats or sailing craft on rivers, lakes, and bays should "tie up" on Sundays, and certainly

---

† Published in *Locomotive Firemen's Magazine*, vol. 16, no. 5 (May 1892), 448–449.

no one expects craft on the ocean to "heave to" on Sundays.

Such reflections may be profitably introduced when discussions are going forward on the Sunday rest question because they demonstrate conclusively that our civilization has completely outgrown the universal Sunday rest idea. It does not matter in the least what individuals may think about it, there stand the facts and they cannot be changed.

In the discussion of the question of opening the Columbian Exposition on Sundays, we have not narrowed it down to a railroad employee question, and those who attempt it do not grasp its significance.[28]

It so happens that in this country, by common consent, shops and factories are closed on Sundays and employees do have one day's rest in seven. Of all the toiling hosts of the country, at best but a comparative few will be able to view the wonders of the Columbian Exposition, but there are multiplied thousands who live in and near Chicago who will be able to "take it in" provided its doors are open on Sunday.

Let us see: Chicago has a population of, say, 1.25 million. Divided into families of five, there would be 250,000 families, of which, to put it prudently, two-thirds, or 166,666, are working people whose only leisure day is Sunday. Here then we have 833,333 people in Chicago alone who, if the Exposition is thrown open on Sundays, would be able to profit by the exhibition of marvelous things. To say these people could visit the Exposition on working days is mere assumption; it is begging the question. And to assume that the things to be seen are even remotely immoral, irreligious, or in the nature of desecration is too preposterous to require contradiction. It is folly run mad, unadulterated ignorance that should have no consideration whatever. The things to be seen are the handiwork of men and women, the triumph of skill in ten thousand departments of human endeavor. And they are brought together at Chicago at an expenditure of about $20 million to demonstrate the astounding triumphs of labor and skill. The Columbian Exposition is not to be a bullfight, a prize ring, nor anything else that is less than an exhibition of man's capacity to advance in all things of an elevating and a refining nature.

The rich will be there with their splendid equipages. The select few who will claim the glory of the show, but who have not contributed so much as a pin in all the varied beauties for which it may be distinguished.

Such people will be on hand by thousands every day, and it will not matter to them whether the Exposition is open or closed on Sundays. Not so with the toiling masses, for on Sundays the shops and factories are closed and in their "Sunday best" they may go and enjoy the grandest sight that money and skill has ever produced since the centuries began their march, and we assume that no spectacle of more thrilling interest will be witnessed than the multitudes of workers who will on Sundays, if the Exposition is open, throng its buildings.

Let us be done with platitudes about what Europeans will think of us if we exhibit common sense relating to the Sunday question. Americans are not Pharisees, hypocrites, nor bigots. Our civilization cannot be contaminated by looking upon the triumphs of skilled labor on Sundays. On the contrary, the eye is an educator when it sees the triumphs of skill, and men, women, and children are elevated and sublimated by such exhibitions, not degraded. The high purpose of the Exposition is to do *good,* and the more who can visit it on Sundays and other days, the more good will result. Above all things, do not close it on any day when workingmen and their families, relieved from toil and drudgery, seek to view its collected wonders.

William Lloyd Garrison[†]

June 1892

Professor Goldwin Smith[29] has written and published an essay "founded on the story of Garrison's life, as told by his children."[30]

Garrison has received the title of "the Moral Crusader," and he earned it. He sought the extirpation of human slavery in the United States. He was content with nothing short of the utter extinction of the national wrong.

We have no purpose in view in referring to Prof. Smith's book, except to magnify the work of agitators, crusaders in a righteous cause.

Garrison's mission was the abolition of African slavery, chattel slavery, a wrong beginning in 1620 by the sale of a score of African savages, and continued for more than two centuries, growing into the social, political, and industrial life of the nation, until its annihilation required the bloodiest war that ever afflicted the earth.

It is a matter of little consequence whether the author of the book treats his subject in a way to command universal approval or whether it falls below

---

† Published in *Locomotive Firemen's Magazine*, vol. 16, no. 6 (June 1892), 491–493.

such a coveted standard. The real theme is Garrison as an agitator—a man who sought to overcome a wrong, which, when he began his crusade, was esteemed by millions as one of those evils that should be let "severely alone."[31] When Garrison attacked slavery the penalty was contumely in the most aggravated sense of the term.

Much is said nowadays about "public opinion." When Garrison demanded the abolition of the African—the Negro slaves—in the United States, "public opinion," to an extent defying exaggeration, was against him. He had no support from church or press, except to an extent too limited to command any respect whatever.

He was universally ostracized, denounced as a vagarist, a lunatic, a blasphemer, a creature whom to insult and assault was in the interest of good society, the peace and welfare of the country. But Garrison was not intimidated. His courage was always equal to the demand. He had that force within him that may be likened to the pulsating engine of an ocean steamer that makes steady headway to its destined port, though winds and waves and tides interpose. He believed he was right, and no matter how fierce the storm, and regardless of obstacles, he pursued undeviatingly his course.

Says a review:

> It was of immense importance that the message he felt himself called to deliver to his countrymen and to the world should be delivered by one who felt its meaning as he felt it. That message was the infinite wrong of slavery. It was to ears unconsciously or willfully deafened that his ringing voice was addressed in season and out of season, without ceasing, without modulation of the piercing note, over and over again. If the occasion were inappropriate, so much the better; the interruption would not be ignored. If the hearers were angered, again so much the better; this wrath would be made to serve the cause. If the church were shocked, still another advantage, for the church, far more then than now, was the center of social and intellectual as well as mural life, and to stir the churchgoers was to stir the community.[32]

In this we have a picture of "the Moral Crusader." Anyone can enlarge it to suit their ideas, but no man has the power now, in the light of events, to belittle it. The fame of Garrison is secure.

Following chattel slavery, the nation is called upon to contemplate another form of slavery. It is not chattel slavery, nor Negro slavery—and yet it is a form of slavery, a form of poverty and degradation, of dependence, of hunger and squalor that has brought to the front a host of agitators, crusaders who are earnestly seeking to modify conditions which are in multiplied thousands of instances worse than those in which Garrison found the Negro slaves of the South, for generally they were well fed, clothed, and sheltered.

The agitators who go forth to plead the cause of labor against oppression are meeting opposition, in many regards similar to that which confronted Garrison.

The press has maligned them and the vile work still goes forward. The church, spasmodically, here and there discusses labor topics, but in the aggregate; its endorsement is without value, chiefly because the church in the great centers of population is as much dependent upon capital as Rockefeller's Standard Oil Trust. The school and the college take no interest in labor questions, because DDs and LLDs, MAs, BAs, and PhDs are not students of labor problems upon which the welfare of society depends.

Capital now, as in the days of Garrison, exerts its mighty power to silence agitators and perpetuate bondage. But in spite of such opposing forces, labor agitators are making headway. These men are exhibiting courage and demonstrating that their appeals are arousing workingmen to a proper sense of the situation, and these are cheering evidences that in thousands of instances beyond the limits of organized labor, hearts have been touched, consciences quickened, and judgment redeemed from the shackles of prejudice, to the extent that in the halls of Congress men of national renown do not hesitate to espouse the cause of labor.

The demand is for a greater number of labor crusaders—bolder and more determined than any that have appeared, men who, though maligned and often defeated, are never discouraged, but return to the attack with increased energy and defiance. Men who, like Scott's veterans in their march from Vera Cruz, grasped

> Their muskets and their trusty blades,
> In noonday light and midnight shades,
> With steady step marched toward the clouds—
> Their war-shouts, "Victory or shrouds."[33]

The right triumphs by virtue of agitation. Moses and Joshua, the prophets and the apostles, were all moral agitators and crusaders, and that was the charge the Pharisees brought against Jesus of Nazareth, because his preaching swept away the dead past and pointed out possibilities for the poor, which startled the world, and never more than now.

Confederation Essential to Labor's Prosperity[†]
July 1892

The century in which we live, qualify it by whatever adjective fancy or fact may suggest, is confessedly the most illustrious of the Christian era. The proposition is neither novel nor startling. It is so universally admitted as to sound like an ancient aphorism. But when the inquiry is made for the purpose of ascertaining upon what foundations the declaration rests, and what facts can be grouped and marshaled in its support, the field of investigation broadens indefinitely, and the task of those who would respond is onerous, not because facts are few and far between, but rather because of the necessity of selecting from the mass the more salient incidents, movements, discoveries, and achievements which, when arranged in their order, constitute data which defy criticism.

The space is not at my command for extended illustration, nor am I inclined to enter upon such investigations as would require a volume to do the theme full justice—nevertheless, having accepted an invitation to contribute my views upon the subject of confederation in its relation to the welfare of labor, certain sharply defined postulates should be stated, because they lead unerringly to conclusions relating to the status of labor.

It has been affirmed by high authority that the present generation knows more than any preceding generation; necessarily so, since the present generation knows all that former generations knew, and has added indefinitely and immensely to the world's store of knowledge, not only in carrying forward investigations which the past suggested, but in matters and directions which the most advanced of former generations never so much as dreamed of.

It may be prudently affirmed that the Dark Ages approached the present much nearer than historians suggest; so near, indeed, that no effort is required to point to the land where their dark shadows still linger, constituting a standing rebuke to those who are overboastful of "our Christian civilization;" indeed, it may be said, if ignorance, superstition, bigotry, and many other degenerate human qualities grew abundantly during that period of the world's history, enough remains to create no little humiliation in the ranks of thoughtful men who are now engaged in the work of emancipation. But with

---

[†] Published as "Confederation of Labor Organizations Essential to Labor's Prosperity" in *American Journal of Politics,* vol. I, no. 1 (July 1892), 63–71.

such facts in view it may be maintained that the work of evolution and revolution has so far progressed as to inspire the hope of some sort of a millennium in the not-distant future.

Christ is credited with having said, "Ye have the poor always with you,"[34] and ringing down the centuries has been heard the same doleful and reverberating declaration, and the "poor" have always been found in the ranks of labor. From the day when Lazarus was perishing at the door of the rich man's palace and the vagabond dogs "licked his sores,"[35] the badge of poverty has been worn by the world's toilers; and thousands of their oppressors have not yet "lifted up their eyes in hell," and it is to be hoped, will cease their oppressions before it is too late. Be this as it may, the "signs of the times" foreshadow new departures in national thought betokening a determination to change radically ancient methods of dealing with labor, every one of which, when subjected to the severest analysis, favors the conclusion that new mind forces are in operation, devoted to the solution of what is called the "labor problem."

It is in this regard, more than in any other phase of human affairs, that the century in which we live towers above all other centuries since history was redeemed from fable. Men in Congress are talking learnedly of the evolution of money from the time when the standard was a skin, an ox, or a sheep, until the world reached the gold or the silver standard. Darwin and his disciples enter fearlessly the domain of the occult, those realms of the unknown, where the mysteries give full play to conjecture, and tell us that the ancestors of the prehistoric man were the prehistoric monkeys, and the world is all agog with the revelation, but with the nineteenth century dawns an era in which a purpose has been evolved to excavate not only buried Babylons and Troys, but buried truths and principles which, through all the centuries, since the morning stars sang together, it has been the purpose of the ruling classes to keep entombed.

No one doubts the Herculean character of the task, no one underestimates the mountainous dimensions of the obstacles to be overcome—but there are multiplied thousands who underestimate the tremendous forces in operation to achieve for labor a victory which, when it comes, as come it will, is to baptize the world with an effulgence scarcely less dazzling than if another sun were to be flung into space.

It is not required that writers who discuss the possibilities of labor shall deal in hyperbole. We live in a daring period of the world's history. The impossibilities of yesterday become possibilities today, probabilities tomorrow, and accomplished facts the day following. To investigators, nature, however reluctantly, is forever yielding up her secrets. Is it to be presumed that this evolution is to be forever confined to electricity and steam and other forces of nature? Is it to be supposed that in the practical affairs of mankind, the mind is to be forever absorbed by the machine, and man is to be neglected? Does the hallucination prevail that man, like the silkworm, is forever to "spin his task and die"—or, like the coral insect, build continents upon which other insects are to bask in eternal sunshine while he is to remain content with the prospective possession of a tomb? Such has been the destiny of labor in the past and such it is now in many autocrat-cursed lands; but it is not true, except to a limited extent, in the United States of America, and that it should exist in any degree where our "star-spangled banner" is supposed to symbolize liberty is well calculated to revive the exclamation, "Haul down the flaunting lie," uttered before the slave-pen, block, and lash forever disappeared in the smoke and carnage of war.

Fortunately for the country, and as another evidence of the distinguishing glory of the century, labor is taking high rank in the list of subjects deemed worthy of consideration in arenas where statesmen sit in council. In state legislatures and in Congress it has secured an entrance and a position from which no opposing power can dislodge it. The labor question is in politics as certainly as the silver question or the tariff question, and rightfully so, for it is a question of not one but all industries; a question inseparable from farm and mine, forge and factory, the loom, the anvil, and the shuttle, as well as transportation, whether by rail or watercraft. It is a building question, a tax and a revenue question, and it is a capital question which, in its sum total, staggers computation.

If the scope of this article permitted figures, they could be piled up upon solid foundations, well calculated to startle statisticians.

The men who create the wealth of the country—at least that portion of them known as "organized workingmen," are profoundly in earnest in discussing their welfare and prerogatives. They do not have to be told that labor has been robbed, degraded, and enslaved. The mouths of the coal mines of the country, even in the absence of tongues, are proclaiming the deep damnation of the organized methods by which the workers in Plutonian pits are robbed and degraded. Impoverished foreigners by thousands have been imported to take the places of American workingmen or to reduce them, by processes which bear the stamp of infernalism, to conditions that arouse those fierce premonitions of vengeance which create universal alarm, and against which, in the ranks of organized labor, protests are being made to which it would be prudent to listen.

The century is one of vast inventive power, and the "labor-saving machine" multiplies in every branch of industry. Labor contemplates the marvelous expansion of machine-power with a composure born of fealty to citizenship, to law and order, demonstrating intelligence and a comprehension of all the forces and factors of progress. They observe the two facts, the multiplication of the machine and the steady increase in the army of toilers, the two facts combined constituting a problem, the seriousness of which it would be difficult to overestimate. Practically, every "labor-saving machine" represents a certain number of workingmen added to the hosts of the unemployed. Immigration contributes annually its vast increase to the force, and added to these we have millions of toilers, who must be fed, clothed, and sheltered; who must live as becomes American citizens or sink to the level of the hordes of imported Chinese, Huns, and Poles; who accept degradation without protest; and between whom and the machine there is practically little difference.

Invidious comparisons are always objectionable, but I do not hesitate to say that organized labor in the United States and elsewhere represents in the highest degree the intelligence of labor. In this country it embodies the American idea of government to an extent, all things considered, that will be looked for in vain elsewhere, no matter by what high-sounding title the organization may be known. The declaration invites criticism and is worthy of investigation.

Labor organizations advocate the universal acceptation of eight hours as a legal day's work. The proposition, subjected to the severest tests, is both philanthropic and economic. It proposes employment for the idle and additional rest for mind and body of those who are employed. The proposition is not only philanthropic and economic, but is as eminently social and educational; and viewed from whatever point the investigator may select, forces the conclusion that it is essential to the welfare of labor.

The real question, or that which is the most vital to labor, relates to wages.

It is to be questioned whether, within the entire realm of problems relating to the perpetuity of our institutions, there is one which touches the welfare of the country at so many vital points as that of wages. I am not unmindful of the opinion often expressed that its triteness embarrasses those who would discuss the labor problem, but it will be noticed that those who discuss the investment of money evince no timidity in referring to interest, dividends, and rent. The fact that these terms have been employed for centuries to do duty for capitalists has won for them no furlough and they are still on guard, nor will they be dismissed until sublimating processes of which the world has now no intimation are introduced to eliminate acquisitiveness, at once a virtue and a vice, from human nature.

I am not an advocate of such a vagary, but do not hesitate to believe that it is largely within the domain of political or governmental evolution to find a basis for the distribution of the wealth which labor creates, proximately in consonance with justice. Here again the intelligence, the sense of fair dealing, science, and the statesmanship of the century stand pledged to solve the problem. And here the remark may be introduced as worthy of reflection that the stupendous wrongs which have been inflicted upon labor during the century in the distribution of wealth in defiance of justice and which are still going forward are operating, paradoxical as it may appear, as a mighty force in correcting the injustice of which labor complains.

The attention, not only of labor organizations, but of trained thinkers, men of vast erudition, political economists, statesmen who grasp continental questions, is burdened with anxieties relating to labor. They see coming events casting their shadows before; and they know that the time for dodging and trimming is nearing its end, and that there must be readjustments; that the few, the exceedingly few, must cease their methods by which, within periods so brief as to bewilder the imagination, fortunes of colossal proportions are amassed, while labor, in ever increasing numbers, is wearing the rag-badge of destitution and squalor. The eulogies of material prosperity, which constitute much of the captivating literature of the period, are to be hushed to silence by the graphic recitals, truthful as they are vivid, of the increasing degradation of thousands because wages do not meet the requirements of the victims of conditions which cannot be contemplated without experiencing the awe produced by the premonitions of earthquakes.

The inability of labor in the past to correct the wrongs to which it has been subjected need not be commented upon. The world knows the sad story by heart, nor is it required to be boastful, and to assert that even now it is able to overcome the forces in operation to beat it down and hold it in vassalage. This may be said, however, that there was never a time in the history of labor when it was so enlightened, so defiant, and so courageous as now, in these closing years of the century. It is organizing and every lodge is a school and an army post. These schools are educating and sending forth leaders and champions of labor. They are, with many sneers, denounced as agitators, and such they are. They are voices in the wilderness, and they are blazing a new pathway for the hosts of labor. These agitators do not underestimate the forces which oppose them, nor are they unmindful that in the ranks of labor are to be found degenerate creatures who, while boasting of their independence, are willing to accept stripes and fetters rather than make sacrifices for their own welfare and the advancement of their fellow workers. In such things, there is nothing new, simply incidents that have marked all great undertakings—afflictions to be borne by those who carry forward great reforms. Labor, with stoical philosophy, bears its share of such burdens, and moves forward.

Organization is the first step in the emancipation of labor, and that is going forward satisfactorily. It is a prudent estimate to say that three millions of men and women are now marching under the banners of organized labor.

The confederation of these organizations is now, more than at any previous period, enlisting the attention of the individual organizations, and the outlook for such a consummation is cheering.

That confederation is essential to the protection of labor is one of those self-evident truths which is weakened by introducing proof. The present demands it, but as yet the demonstrations of opposing forces have not been such as to convince all "leaders" of its supreme necessity. It was the "Sumter gun" that aroused the North from its lethargy, and labor is destined to listen to decrees which will sweep away objections as the wind scatters straws.

Labor is not unobservant of the fact that capitalists are constantly forming alliances to secure, as they assert, reasonable returns for their investments, and these alliances in numerous instances have been pronounced flagrantly at war with the public welfare; and laws have been enacted to put an end to some of these piratical combinations—notably the Interstate Commerce law, and still later, the law against trusts.

Was it worthwhile to enact such legislation, and also to look into the character of the men against whose methods of enrichment the laws are intended to interpose barriers? Such inquiries have placed before the country hidden facts which have aroused universal alarm. It was proved that the purpose of those who controlled vast amounts of money was to enrich themselves regardless of the rights and welfare of others, that capitalists who usually rank as the highest type of the American citizen, pillars of society and church, distinguished in finance and commerce, the aristocracy of character and those qualities of head and heart which writers and talkers delight to dignify as the hope of the country, organize alliances for the purpose of multiplying their millions by methods which the highest lawmaking power of the nation condemns by statutes with severe penalties attached. It is such things that have prompted labor to organize for its protection and to resist encroachments upon the dearest rights that ever aroused men to resistance.

Labor is conversant with all the facts relating to the character of the forces against which it is required to contend. It has seen press and pulpit enlisted in the ranks of its enemies. It has experienced in ten thousand ways the dominating power of wealth, and in its investigations for means of retrievement has decided upon organization, a movement which means vastly more than the enrollment of men in the numerous orders now conspicuously before the country. It means education, study, intellectual equipment for impending struggles to maintain independence and the dignity of American citizenship.

The more advanced members of these labor organizations believe that the *ultima Thule* of organization is confederation. The power which confederation would confer is regarded as indispensable and, as discussion proceeds, obstacles will disappear. The difficulties in the way of confederation are entirely foreign to the question of the necessity of the compact, and relate chiefly to the adjustment of the laws and regulations under which the confederated body would act. In this, I refer more particularly to the organizations of railroad employees.

In taking a broader view of the labor field, it is equally evident that confederation is steadily gaining powerful advocates. I am not disposed to be fanciful; the subject does not invite impractical theories—organization is an admitted power, and confederation multiplies that power indefinitely. In organization the victories and defeats of labor, though by no means balanced, bring to the front the fact that with confederation, labor would be invincible. The dawning of the Christian era was ushered in by the shout, "Peace on earth."[36] Peace has not come, nor can it come, while labor is robbed of its just dues. It is possible to have a peaceful revolution by the fiat of the ballot; it is possible to prevent war by being prepared for war; and it is possible to enthrone justice for labor by the confederation of labor organizations.

Labor Representatives in Legislative Bodies[†]

July 1892

As often as elections occur in the United States for members of legislative bodies—city, county, state, or national—there is a demand to have a representative of Labor on the ticket, and the cry goes us, "Let Labor be represented."

This demand is right in all regards. It means far more than appears on the surface. To understand the full measure of its significance requires patient study.

In 1880, according to the census reports, there were 12,830,000 voters. We will assume that during the ten years from 1880 to 1890 the voting population

---

† Published in *Locomotive Firemen's Magazine*, vol. 16, no. 7 (July 1892), 581–583.

increased 25 percent, giving a total population of 16,037,500 in 1890. In 1880 estimates were made as follows, relating to the division of the 12,830,000 voters:

Engaged in manufacturing and mining	1,833,442
Engaged in transportation	484,500
Engaged in personal service	1,859,223
Engaged in agriculture (laborers)	3,323,876
Otherwise engaged	5,328,959
Total	12,830,000

Adding 25 percent to each of the foregoing items, we have results as follows for 1890:

Engaged in manufacturing and mining	2,291,802
Engaged in transportation	605,625
Engaged in personal service	2,324,029
Engaged in agriculture (laborers)	4,154,845
Otherwise engaged	6,661,199
Total	16,037,500

Without official data, we assume to give only reasonable approximations, and those who feel inclined are invited to revise our figures and, if it be practical, to more sharply define the number who vote and work for wages in all of the industries of the United States.

But of what avail is this large preponderance of labor votes? Practically it has amounted to nothing in the past, and is of little importance even now. The question arises, why this inauspicious outlook for labor in legislative assemblies? A number of replies are at once suggested. If, as we have shown, in 1890 the voting population of this country reached 16,037,500, and those who are not classed as wageworkers numbered 6,661,199, then in that case the labor vote amounted to 9,376,301—or 2,714,801 more than the vote of those not recognized as laborers. Notwithstanding such astounding facts, labor is always and eternally at the bottom, never at the top, in political affairs. True, occasionally, at long intervals, a labor candidate gets into some "Common Council," but seldom if ever as a straight-out labor candidate. The same *may* be true of legislatures and Congress, but as a general proposition the labor candidate has to be *endorsed* first by organized labor, as an inducement for one or the other of the *old* parties to nominate him, and thus, when he finally takes his seat in the deliberative body, he ceases to be a "labor member," and becomes something else, a *Democratic* or a *Republican* member; to announce himself as a "labor representative" he would have about as much influence on the body as a cipher on the left-hand side of a decimal point.[37]

We have said that in 1890 there were 9,376,301 labor voters in the country. Did these voters act together anywhere in the country? Certainly not. Why? Because of the 9,376,301, 3 million were practically scabs, with no more independence and self-respect than so many prairie dogs. They are Chinese, Italians, Huns, Poles, and that degenerate riffraff (which a large percentage of Americans) who submit, in this country as in the lands that gave them birth, to degradation without protest—accept it as their normal condition. They are in alliance with such millionaire monstrosities as the Corbins and Carnegies—who, though they have positions, are the result of well-arranged methods of villainy, are yet, when weighed in the scales of eternal justice, a thousand times more dangerous than the leper hosts they control. This leaves 6,376,301 laborers who may be supposed to believe in the dignity of labor and are honestly contending for fair wages. Of these 6,376,301—we put it largely when we say that 3 million of them are identified with labor organizations and that 3,376,301 stand aloof from labor organizations and practically oppose such organizations—these men, as well as the scabs, give their influence to employers who oppose labor organizations, not always outspoken in their hostility, but either passively or actively exhibit their opposition.

Now, then, how stands the account? There are, we assume:

Laborers who have votes	9,376,301
Scabs	3,000,000
Those who stand aloof from labor organizations	3,376,301
Organized laborers	3,000,000
Total	9,376,301

It will be observed that of the entire 9,376,301 there are, after all, only 3 million who under any circumstances could be relied on to elect labor candidates to legislatures and to Congress, and these patriotic workingmen, members of labor organizations, are opposed by 6,376,301 laborers, 3 million of whom are scabs and 3,376,301 of whom are non-union men, who, with a determination and bitterness more or less pronounced, fight the advance of labor in every honorable direction. As a general proposition they are ignorant and debased. Their intellectual qualities—we speak of the *mass*—are so low as to cast doubt upon the success of the whole labor movement. Ignorance may be organized, but it will not remain organized; the base-born are forever retiring to swell the numbers of scabs and that class of non-union men whom we estimate at 3,376,301 voters.

Still, with a cheerfulness born of faith we point to the 3 million organized laborers and say: Here is a body of men who will stand firm, who have the ability to name candidates for legislatures and for Congress—a splendid body of men, true to union principles and would love to see men wearing the badge of labor in legislative halls. How does this pan out in practical politics, in electing men to legislatures and to Congress, who get there because they are representatives of labor?

It was bad enough to say there are 3 million scabs who vote; bad enough to say these 3,376,301 non-union laborers who in their opposition to organized labor are scarcely superior to scabs; now comes the humiliating confession that the 3 million voters who belong to labor organizations split up into fragments. They are divided and they are conquered. Point to results and read the humiliating verdict: there is no unity, no cohesiveness, and as a result labor representatives in legislatures and in Congress wear the tag of some old party. Those who are so inclined may write their views upon the reasons why labor does not unite at elections, and the more they study the subject the more humiliating the facts will appear.

There are a hundred centers of population in the country which are centers of great industrial enterprises where, if organized, labor would name the candidate for Congress and all union laborers would vote for him, no opposition could defeat them. But, as has been said, union laborers cannot be induced to vote for such a candidate. As a result, after much talk of no more consequence than the idle wind, the old order is resumed and labor takes its place at the bottom, and entrusts its interests to men who, as between capital and labor, are found openly or covertly as the enemies of measures designed to promote the welfare of labor, and therefore the welfare of the nation.

Manifestly the time when laboring men will appear in legislatures and in Congress without some old party tag attached to them is remote. Can the situation be changed? How?

May Day in Europe[†]

July 1892

Weeks before May Day, i.e., May 1, 1892, the wires under the ocean were freighted with forebodings of evil which it was predicted would happen in many of the large cities of Europe, not excepting London.

It was easy to see that a sense of insecurity prevailed throughout the continent, indefinitely intensified by disastrous explosions of dynamite in the city of Paris and elsewhere.[38]

The men suspected of murderous intention are called "anarchists," and an anarchist is one whose hand is supposed to be lifted against all governments and all laws. An anarchist, whether in Chicago, Paris, Berlin, Brussels, London, or St. Petersburg, imagines he can change affairs by exploding dynamite bombs, killing a few people, and wrecking a few buildings. An anarchist is a madman. He may be a student, but he studies in the wrong direction and arrives at conclusions which involve him in ruin. He becomes a monomaniac. However rational, or apparently rational, upon other subjects, as soon as the question of labor, the wrongs and degradation of labor, is suggested, he becomes a maniac—he wants to kill somebody, he desires wreck and ruin, but is often so intensely in earnest that he accepts the penalties which the law inflicts upon him, and turns upon his judges with calm defiance and accepts death with the composure of a martyr.

The scare that for several months has prevailed in Europe, and which, apparently, has come to stay, includes crowned heads and the nobility generally. Anarchists esteem all such people as creatures who exist upon the earnings of workingmen, money of which they are ruthlessly robbed and for the want of which they are deprived of proper food, shelter, and clothing. They assume that the government is their enemy, and they become, therefore, the enemies of the government. They behold royal families and a titled aristocracy living in pomp and splendor, while they are doomed to poverty which defies exaggeration; they behold vast standing armies, machines designed to suppress any movement designed as a protest against the order of things as it exists, and as a consequence, they plot revenge in darkness. As we have said, they are madmen who do not reason. Few in numbers they may be, but they keep

---

† Published in *Locomotive Firemen's Magazine*, vol. 16, no. 7 (July 1892), 584–585.

Europe, from center to circumference, in perpetual unrest. Crowns, flashing with precious stones, no longer rest easily nor gracefully upon the heads of kings and emperors, since it is the avowed purpose of anarchists to kill them when opportunity offers.

Such is the condition of Europe as we write, and the situation demands the most serious consideration by thoughtful men in the United States.

The question arises, what is the cause of the trouble in Europe? Starvation wages in the first place, for those who work, or for the great majority of workers—and in the second place, vast bodies of men who cannot secure work at any wages. Such replies ought to suffice, but another cause of discontent, as has been remarked, is the burdens imposed upon labor to support hordes of aristocrats, who toil not, and yet live in regal splendor.

Such a condition of things will produce anarchists as certainly as swamps produce malaria. True, a few anarchists will be killed or imprisoned, but others will take their places, and extermination, while the cause exists, is an impossibility—and if the signs of the times were ever indicative of coming events, they now betoken an upheaval in Europe which will change things, whether for the better or the worse, no one knows.

It was the wise saying of Abraham Lincoln that the Republic could not exist "half slave and half free,"[39] and a government cannot exist where the many are crushed and pauperized by the few. It may require centuries to solve the problem, but its solution is inevitable.

It is a truth worth heeding that pernicious ideas spread more rapidly and grow ranker than those which inculcate virtue, and why, it may be asked, should anarchists be denounced when the press teems with declarations that the government is honeycombed with fraud and corruption, and that the avowed policy is one of stupendous robbery?

View the subject as we may, the outlook is anything but assuring to those who cry "peace."

Crimes of Christless Capitalists[†]
July 1892

The Rev. Dr. DeCosta,[40] of New York, an Episcopal clergyman, writes to Mr. Byrnes,[41] superintendent of the New York police force, as follows:

> Today capital is forcing thousands of women into a life of shame. By starvation wages capital renders virtue impossible, and when once a girl has fallen, capital takes her out of the factory and shop and sends her to the brothel, which pays enormous dividends.

Dr. DeCosta, in the foregoing, makes the common mistake of substituting capital for capitalists. It is a mistake that upsets all logic, all facts, and constitutes all arguments based upon it simply jargon. Capital is inert. It does the bidding of its owners, nothing more. Capital, in the hands of philanthropists, blesses the world and gives glory and dignity to human nature; in the hands of heartless men it does what Dr. DeCosta says it does. Why this eternal denunciation of capital, when it is the monsters, the mind- and soul-deformed capitalists who should be anathematized?

The land is full of Christless capitalists who care no more for the crimes they commit against humanity than so many sheep-killing dogs. They fix rates of wages that create poverty, rags, crime, and universal cussedness, and behold their victims going to the devil without a tremor, and by stigmatizing "capital," afford a shelter for the inhuman pirates.

It would be an easy matter for Dr. DeCosta to name the capitalists of New York who are "forcing thousands of women into lives of shame" by "starvation wages." Why doesn't he name them? He lacks the courage. It is easier to say capital than capitalist. Name the capitalists who are engaged in the nefarious work, and good men everywhere will be prompted to gibbet them before the world and excoriate them with whips of flame. These infernal capitalists are in all the churches, with iron tongues and throats of brass; they praise God and then go forth, and by reducing wages, pile up fortunes and create such woes as make angels weep.

---

† Untitled editorial published in *Locomotive Firemen's Magazine,* vol. 16, no. 9 (August 1892), 689.

Final Annual Meeting of the Supreme Council†

August 1892

On June 20, 1892, the fourth and last annual meeting of the Supreme Council of the United Orders of Railway Employees was held in the city of Chicago.

The meeting was eminently harmonious. It was called according to law, called to order according to law, the deliberations were according to law, and the Supreme Council was disbanded according to law. Possibly, some facetious gentlemen may suggest, "according to the law of necessity."

The Supreme Council, during its existence, transacted business according to law. It tried members for treason according to law and inflicted the penalty according to law. It was law-abiding first, last, and all the time. It shirked no responsibility. Its courage was equal to its conviction, and though it disbanded, it is not disgraced. There is no stain upon its escutcheon. Its flag was never trailed in the dirt. It never surrendered to a foe, only to the inevitable.

The Supreme Council was the outgrowth of an idea as vital as ever announced to workingmen, practical and potential, and though the Supreme Council no longer exists, the principle upon which it was founded survives.

A principle never dies. It is more enduring than the stars. A principle like truth may be "crushed to earth," but like truth it will "rise again," because the "eternal years" are pledged to its survival.

Federation is not dead, nor can it be said that it "sleepeth."

On every hand is heard the demand for federation. The unification of labor organizations for the purpose of protection is now the motto of the armies of labor, and railroad employees are not indifferent to the call. The demand for an organization of organizations is the desideratum, the one thing wanted. That it will come is as certain as that morning follows the night.

Those who helped to organize the Supreme Council were the *avant couriers* in a new departure of labor efforts. They were the pathfinders through a wilderness of doubt and anxiety to highlands of vision and to positions of power.

No words they said require modification nor need they be solicitous about the effect their courageous words produced. They were winged words and are even now fulfilling their splendid mission.

---

† Published as "The Supreme Council" in *Locomotive Firemen's Magazine,* vol. 16, no. 8 (August 1892), 733.

A truth set forth on its mission to battle for supremacy may be embarrassed by a lie. It may be put to the torture, but it never surrenders. The world is full of lies. Treachery, duplicity, and treason to truth sometimes come forth so splendidly equipped as to appear invincible. But the day of reckoning comes, the mills of the gods grind on, and finally the truth triumphs.

We look forward to the time when a Supreme Council will be established that will accomplish the work the disbanded Supreme Council was organized to perform, and which it did perform up to a time when emergencies arose which only infinite wisdom could have foreseen, and even then the Supreme Council met the crisis, and though the penalty was disbandment, its honor and integrity survive the dispersion.

The *Firemen's Magazine* has printed many pages since it began the advocacy of federation and urged the organization of the Supreme Council, but of them all not one glows with words more fraught with devotion to the welfare of men engaged in the train service of railroads and the welfare of labor than those where we used such arguments as we could command in favor of federation.

It would not be difficult to tell in a few words why the Supreme Council has ceased to exist. But we do not care to play Mark Antony and exhibit the mantle of the Supreme Council to show where treason got in its work.

The Supreme Council was a creation of federation. Federation lives and will flourish long after those who rendered the disbandment of the Supreme Council necessary are dead and forgotten, or, if they are remembered, it will be only for their ignorance and treason to labor.

Notes

1. Democrat John P. Buchanan (1847–1930) was governor of Tennessee for a single two-year term, beginning in January 1891.

2. It is worth noting that during the era of steam locomotion, brakemen (that is, members of the Brotherhood of Railroad Trainmen) served under the direction and authority of conductors (that is, members of the Order of Railway Conductors), the two crafts having a relationship akin to the locomotive firemen who served under the authority of the locomotive engineers. The switchmen were not part of the running trades and were regarded to some extent as unkempt outsiders by the conductors and brakemen.

3. The Brotherhood of Railway Trainmen held their 1891 annual convention in Galesburg, Illinois, in October of that year. The gathering boldly endorsed the actions of their officials in the Northwestern affair and returned the officers of the order for another term.

4. The two-year interval apparently derives from an 1889 incident mentioned in a B of RT circular involving the firing of two of its members, Lindsey and Ingalls, apparently at the behest of the SMAA. The B of RT claimed this event had inaugurated a "war of extermination in the Northwestern yards" against it. The actual McNerney-Crowe incident took place early in March 1891.

5. J. E. Wheat was the financier of the Belvidere, Illinois, lodge of the B of RT.

6. Apparently Daniel Quinn, master of the Troy, New York, lodge of the B of RT.

7. The 1888 strike of the Chicago, Burlington & Quincy Railroad, which began late in February as a walkout of organized locomotive engineers and firemen, and was joined in the eleventh hour by the switchmen.

8. General manager of the Chicago, Burlington & Quincy Railroad.

9. William A. Simsrott (1861–1896) of Chicago was the grand secretary and treasurer of the SMAA. Simsrott made national news in May 1894 when he vanished without a trace in Chicago, with foul play suspected by his family. He mysteriously reemerged several weeks later and was immediately hospitalized for alcoholism. A subsequent investigation of the SMAA's finances reported $32,500 missing from the union's coffers, but due to a legal technicality the brotherhood was unable to litigate for return of its funds. Simsrott's embezzlement played a large part in the SMAA's downfall in the aftermath of the 1894 Pullman strike. Simsrott died in Chicago of tuberculosis.

10. Landmark six-story hotel located in downtown St. Louis that was constructed in 1872 and demolished in 1961.

11. A horse-drawn taxi.

12. As of this writing there are no specimens of the 1891 volume of *Switchmen's Journal* known to have survived.

13. From "The Battle-Field," by William Cullen Bryant.

14. Allusion to Acts 8:2: "As for Saul, he made havock of the church, entering into every

house, and haling men and women committed them to prison."

15. First verse of a song written in 1813 by an unknown author, sung to the tune of "Molly, Put the Kettle On."
16. From *Lalla Rookh*, by Thomas Moore.
17. Four concluding lines by Fitz-Greene Halleck (1790–1867) appended to the poem "American Flag" (1819), by Joseph Rodman Drake (1795–1820). For Halleck's claim of authorship, see *New York Musical Pioneer and Chorister's Budget*, vol. 2, no. 11 (August 1, 1857), 1.
18. Lyrics from "Hail Columbia," written in 1798 by Joseph Hopkinson (1770–1842) and set to music composed in 1789 by Philip Phile (c. 1734–1793) for the inauguration of George Washington. The song was regarded as an unofficial national anthem during the nineteenth century.
19. 1 Kings 18:21.
20. Assyrian king of the sixth century BC held responsible for the destruction of the temple of Jerusalem.
21. Alexander Alexandrovich Romanov (1845–1894), best known as Alexander III of Russia, was tsar of the Russian Empire from 1881 until his death. His reign is remembered for its particularly reactionary domestic agenda.
22. Actually, the Russian Orthodox Church.
23. While his father Alexander II was assassinated in 1881, and his son Nikolai II deposed in the spring of 1917 and executed the next year, Alexander III died without the assistance of the Russian revolutionary movement, succumbing to kidney disease on November 1, 1894, at the age of 49.
24. Sergei Alexandrovich Romanov (1857–1905), younger brother of Tsar Alexander III, was governor general of Moscow from 1891 to 1905. He was killed by a bomb thrown into his carriage by a member of the combat organization of the Socialist-Revolutionary Party (PSR).
25. The Russian famine of 1891, triggered by two successive years of bad weather and poor harvests, and exacerbated by the failure of the state to take prompt ameliorative action, killed an estimated four hundred thousand people.
26. Charles Fletcher Peck (1845–1912) was the first commissioner of the Bureau of Labor Statistics of New York, appointed by Democratic governor Grover Cleveland in 1883.
27. Allusion to Judges 16.
28. The World's Columbian Exposition, held to celebrate the four hundredth anniversary of Columbus's arrival in the Americas, was held in Chicago from May 1 to October 30, 1893. Due to political pressure wielded by religious zealots, the fair's enabling legislation in 1892 required the closure of the exhibition on Sundays; this in turn generated a political reaction by progressives seeking weekend access for the working class. The final result was a muddled compromise in which the fair was opened to the public on Sundays, although no machines could be operated and most of the exhibits nevertheless remained shuttered.

29. Goldwin Smith (1823–1910) was a prominent and prolific historian at Oxford University.
30. Goldwin Smith, *The Moral Crusader, William Lloyd Garrison* (New York: Funk and Wagnalls Co., 1892). Founded on "The Story of Garrison's Life Told by His Children."
31. Allusion to an oft-quoted phrase in an 1860 campaign speech on behalf of the Republican ticket by Salmon Chase (1808–1873), who promised a hostile audience of his party's intention to "let slavery very severely alone in all the states" in which it was already established.
32. Source unknown.
33. Source unknown.
34. From Matthew 26:11.
35. Allusion to Luke 16.
36. From Luke 2:14.
37. That is, zero.
38. Paris was swept by a bomb panic in 1892 when an anarchist bombed the Restaurant Véry on April 25 in retaliation against a waiter there having informed on François Koenigstein-Ravachol (1859–1892). Ravachol was an anarchist leader who had previously attempted to use dynamite to kill prominent judges, albeit unsuccessfully.
39. From Lincoln's "House Divided" speech, delivered in Springfield, Illinois, June 16, 1858.
40. Benjamin Franklin DeCosta (1831–1904) was a Massachusetts clergyman, magazine editor, and historian.
41. Thomas F. Byrnes (1842–1910) was head of the New York City Police Department from 1880 to 1895.

Appendix

Official Circular No. 8 (1888–89)
of the Brotherhood of Locomotive Firemen[†]
January 19, 1889

Terre Haute, Ind., January 19, 1889

To all Subordinate Lodges:

Dear Sirs and Brothers:—

It becomes imperatively necessary for us to again address the lodges of our order on matters connected with the strike on the CB&Q. And in the performance of this duty, it is of special consequence that the membership have a clear understanding of all the facts in the case, that there may be no misapprehension on their part, and that they may be fully prepared to silence any unjust criticisms, that the ignorance, prejudice, or mendacity of the enemies of our brotherhood may make.

The Situation at Atlanta

It will be remembered that the strike on the CB&Q was a joint struggle, entered upon by the B of LE and the B of LF, and this fact must be steadily kept in view because every movement of our order has been predicated upon this idea.

At the biennial convention held at Atlanta, the CB&Q strike was exhaustively discussed.[1] Nothing was overlooked. Nothing was obscured. The convention was animated by a desire to find bottom facts upon which to act.

It was no secret that the financial condition of the brotherhood was critical; how critical will appear from the following résumé. The convention was informed that to sustain the strike required of the brotherhood about $45,000 a month. That payment had been made for the month of July, but to make the July payment it had been necessary to overdraw the special fund to the amount of $22,000; the August payment was then due—$45,000, and in a few days there would be a demand for the September payment, making a grand total of $112,000. These were startling figures, and were well calculated to make the convention pause in its deliberations. There was some diversity of opinion

---

† Published as a two-page printed leaflet. Specimen in Tim Davenport collection. Included as an appendix item due to uncertainty of authorship.

relating to the policy which ought to be adopted. But it was held, as we have stated, that the strike was a joint struggle, and that to determine to withhold further payments to our men would be equivalent to declaring the strike off; it would be an abandonment of the men at a critical time, and that if in consequence of such a policy the strike should collapse, the entire responsibility would rest upon the Brotherhood of Locomotive Firemen. The convention decided not to take that responsibility. It decided to remain loyal to the men, and loyal to the B of LE. Never in the history of brotherhood trials were men animated by a loftier courage. Never was fealty to principle more splendidly illustrated—and the final determination was to assess the membership, raise the money, pay it over to the men, and take the brotherhood to Richmond,[2] and say to the Brotherhood of Locomotive Engineers, "Here is the Brotherhood of Locomotive Firemen without a stain upon its escutcheon. It has met every obligation. It has stood by you in the thickest of the fight. There are no flies on the Brotherhood of Locomotive Firemen. It is all right."

Having done this, and it could not have done more, the B of LF waited to see what course the B of LE would pursue.

Nothing within the whole realm of questions was more natural than for locomotive firemen, members of the brotherhood, to ask, will the B of LE recognize our brotherhood? Will it recognize our courage, our sacrifices, and our fidelity? Our grand officers were present at Richmond waiting to hear and to know what the B of LE would do. They did not have to wait long. The humiliation mapped out for the B of LF came in due time.

The Action of the B of LE

Completely ignoring the B of LF, treating it as of no consequence whatever, totally regardless of its services and its sacrifices, the B of LE proceeded to appoint a committee of nine to devise ways and means whereby the strike on the CB&Q might be brought to a close. In this movement no allusion was made to the B of LF. The B of LE did not so much as propose to consult the B of LF, nor was the committee of nine authorized by the Richmond convention to consult with the B of LF or with any of its officers. One of the committee of nine was to go over the CB&Q system. Having obtained such information as he could glean, he was to report to his committee, his associates, and there and then exercise supreme authority in the matter of the strike.

It is well, just here, to recall the fact that the strike was a joint affair from the first, so said, so accepted. But was it so in fact? If it was, did not the Richmond convention effectually disjoint it, dislocate the joint? Or, rather, did not the Richmond convention amputate the B of LF, something like sawing its legs off and casting it aside?

It may be said that the chairman of the engineer's committee of nine invited the B of LF to participate in the deliberations of the committee. When? Before the facts upon which the committee was to act were obtained? Not at all—and moreover the actions of the Richmond convention contemplated nothing of the sort. It was an afterthought, and served to bring into bolder prominence the earthquake *shake* to which the B of LF had been subjected. Notwithstanding this, Grand Master Sargent did appoint two members of the B of LF to proceed to Chicago and hear final results and report, but this action in no sense condones the humiliating policy pursued by the Richmond convention toward the B of LF.

Taking into consideration all the facts, it must be conceded, we think, that the B of LF would have been entirely justified in having nothing to do with the committee of nine, but the Brotherhood of Locomotive Firemen had interest at stake and it was doubtless wise to have representatives at headquarters, to take official cognizance of the last act in the CB&Q strike.

The fact is frequently stated that the B of LF owes the B of LE the sum of $26,000. This is true. The B of LE advanced this sum as a loan, voluntarily, and it was so accepted by the grand officers of our order. There is nothing improper in this, unless the purpose be to intimate that by virtue of such indebtedness the B of LE has acquired a right to domineer over the B of LF. Under peculiar circumstances the B of LF contracted the debt named, which it is amply able to pay, and which will be paid, and with interest, if demanded, at an early day, and the B of LE—which we are glad to know is rich and prosperous—will never have occasion to place the indebtedness of the B of LF on the debit side of its profit and loss account.

Financial Statement

A financial statement showing the receipts and disbursements on account of the CB&Q strike will be made and embodied in a report to all the lodges at the earliest possible moment. This report will show the payments of every lodge, as also every contribution made from all sources, so that every member may become familiar with every detail.

The Employment of CB&Q Strikers

Now that the strike on the CB&Q is off, a great many men who stood by their principles heroically and sacrificed all will be out in search of employment. We desire that in every case where a lodge knows of a vacancy, the secretary of the lodge shall at once notify the Grand Lodge, or should there be information of a probable vacancy we desire to have information relating to it, as in that case we may be of service to those who are in search of employment. And we desire to impress upon the members of all the lodges the importance of the work, as it is in the highest degree fraternal. Should one of the "Q" strikers make his appearance anywhere in search of work, we know of no more brotherly service than to take him and introduce him to the Master Mechanic, and in all other prudent ways to put him in a position to receive wages.

Yours fraternally,
F. P. Sargent,
Grand Master

Eugene V. Debs,
Grand Sec. and Treas.

Official Circular No. 1 of the Supreme Council of the United Orders of Railway Employees[†]

June 6, 1889

Chicago, Ill., June 6, 1889

To all Subordinate Lodges:

Dear Sirs and Brothers:—

You are hereby notified that at a meeting of the representatives of the three orders above named, held in the city of Chicago, Ill., beginning June 3, 1889, a plan of federation was formulated and agreed upon, the same being now in full force and effect.

The federation board, having jurisdiction of the three organizations, is known as the Supreme Council of the United Orders of Railway Employees, and its acts and decisions upon all matters of grievance are final.

† Published as a three-page printed leaflet. Specimen in Tim Davenport collection.

A constitution and common seal have been adopted, and a copy of the constitution of the Supreme Council will in due time be forwarded to each lodge of each organization, which shall be the property of the lodge and shall be kept with the secret work of the lodge, and under no circumstances shall the said constitution be taken from the lodge-room, except by authority of the lodge.

The Supreme Council takes occasion to warn all members of the several organizations placed in its jurisdiction against the so-called voluntary relief associations, which are being organized upon some of the principal railways. The purpose of such relief associations is apparent to the most casual observer. The methods employed to capture employees is like the alluring song of the spider to the fly. Of course it is made to appear that the authors of the movement are animated by a purely philanthropic spirit; that the high purpose is to provide for "our dear employees," who must be cared for on the same principle that the owners of plantations in the days of chattel slavery provided for their slaves.

Brothers, the simple purpose of such movements, stripped of their alluring embellishments, is to undermine and ultimately destroy every organization of railway employees. At first the system is voluntary, so as to make the bait more tempting, and the scheme more plausible; but as soon as a sufficient number of the employees have been taken in under the voluntary arrangements, penalties more or less direct will be attached to the non-participants, and later on it will be found that the so-called voluntary plan is compulsory, and that the men have placed themselves in a position to be the victims of the despotic sway of the corporation.

We are persuaded that the time has not come for railroad employees to abdicate their manhood, sacrifice their self-respect, and strip themselves naked of independence. We are inclined to the opinion that railroad employees have an ambition above the plane contemplated by Voluntary Relief Associations, which would reduce them to the level of serfs and constitute them a part of the rolling stock of the corporation. We take the position that a corporation is simply required to treat its employees fairly and pay them fair wages for fair work. If this is done, the employees can provide for their own relief in their own way, they can employ their own doctors and otherwise administer their own affairs without becoming the wards of the corporation or being subjected to humiliations of surveillance under the guise of solicitude for their welfare.

Brethren, we call your attention to this matter for your own good. We would warn you against what we believe to be an organized effort to destroy your organization, thereby depriving you of the protection you now enjoy, and which, if successful, will place you at the mercy of the corporation.

Now that the organizations of brakemen, switchmen, and firemen have federated, the supreme desire is unity and harmony all along the line. Let local discontent and factional feeling disappear. Let the motto be, "Each for all and all for each."

The step we have taken has far-reaching significance. It practically unites the three organizations into one body for mutual protection. We appeal to each member who is enlisted under the banner of federation to be a true soldier in the cause. Let the past with its differences and prejudices be forgotten. A new era has dawned and the future is rich with promise. Hand in hand we shall march forward together, animated with high ambitions and noble purposes. Our sympathies for each other, born of mutual peril and mutual privations, should cement us together as one brotherhood, and to be a true and devoted member of that brotherhood should be the ambition of each and all who hope for the triumph of labor over corporate oppression and injustice.

We salute you, brethren, on behalf of the Supreme Council of the United Orders of Railway Employees, and trusting that your hearts are attuned, as are our own, to the harbinger notes of victory, we are

Yours fraternally,
F. P. Sargent,
President

Frank Sweeney,
Vice President

E. F. O'Shea,
Secretary and Treasurer

S. E. Wilkinson,
W. G. Edens,
John Downey,
John A. Hall,
John J. Hannahan,
Eugene V. Debs,
Supreme Council UORE[3]

The Days of Long Ago: Letter to the Editor
of *Locomotive Firemen's Magazine*†
January 1912

On my last eastern trip I was surprised and delighted at Corning, New York, to meet Horace W. Plummer,[4] the first elected vice grand master of the Brotherhood of Locomotive Firemen. I had not met him since the Indianapolis convention of 1875, which he attended as a grand officer and I as a visitor. We were boys then, and to me now it seems to have been only the other day.

How the years have gone by! And how many of the boys of that day have vanished with the years!

There is melancholy as well as joy in that kind of a meeting. As we sat there and talked about the boyhood days that had vanished we sought to rejuvenate ourselves by reviewing the scenes of those early days.

It was at the first annual convention held at Hornellsville, New York, in December 1874, that Horace Plummer was elected vice grand master and also vice president of the "Firemen's Life Insurance Association," as the insurance department was then called. Joshua Leach presided over the convention and there William N. Sayre was elected first grand secretary and treasurer.

On the same eastern trip it was also my pleasure to meet I. H. Crossman, the old pioneer of Buffalo Lodge 12, who has been staunch and true in storm and shine through all these years. I met him also at the Indianapolis convention in 1875.

Plummer and Crossman were both charter members of Erie Lodge 2 of Hornellsville, organized, I believe, by Josh Leach in December 1873.

Few, very few, of the pioneers of that day still survive to share in its interesting reminiscences. Most of them have passed over the range and are remembered only by the few who still remain to recall their loyal devotion when it required courage indeed to share in the work of laying the foundations of the brotherhood.

Allow me to send my warmest greeting to all the surviving members of the olden day. A new generation has now appeared and there have been many changes, but the memories of the old pioneers will never be wholly forgotten.

In my travels I meet many of the members of the brotherhood, but only a

† Published in *Locomotive Firemen's Monthly Magazine*, vol. 52, no. 1 (January 1912), 117.

few of those with whom I sat in convention a third of a century ago.

On February 27, coming, it will be 37 years since I first joined the brotherhood. The vivid recollection of that day and the vent of my life associated with that day inspire some of my most happy reminiscences.

Many years have passed since I have been connected with the brotherhood, but I have not lost my interest in its members. We have not traveled the same road, nor had the same experiences, but my heart has ever been with them and always will be while it continues to beat. I have always felt a peculiar attachment for firemen and enginemen and this attachment seems to grow stronger with the passing years.

My glad greeting and the warmest wishes of my heart go out to all the members of the brotherhood in which I spent all the years of my young manhood.

Eugene V. Debs

Notes

1. The Fourteenth Annual Convention (First Biennial Convention) of the Brotherhood of Locomotive Firemen was held in Atlanta from September 10 to 19, 1888.
2. The Twenty-Fifth Annual Convention of the Brotherhood of Locomotive Engineers opened October 17, 1888, at Belvidere Hall in Richmond, Virginia.
3. Original includes large-format facsimile signatures.
4. Horace W. Plummer (1849–1917) of Hornellsville, New York, began his career as a machinist on the Erie Railroad before becoming a fireman. He was promoted to engineer in 1879 and worked in that capacity for the rest of his life.

Index

About the Editors

Tim Davenport is involved with several online radical history projects, including his Early American Marxism website, Marxists Internet Archive, and Wikipedia. He is a member of the Historians of American Communism, the Organization of American Historians, the Society for Historians of the Gilded Age and Progressive Era, and the Labor and Working-Class History Association. He is coeditor with Paul LeBlanc of *The "American Exceptionalism" of Jay Lovestone and His Comrades, 1929–1940* (Haymarket Books, 2018).

David Walters is a lifelong socialist and trade unionist. He was one of the founders of the Marxists Internet Archive and remains with the MIA as a volunteer. He is currently director of the Holt Labor Library in San Francisco.

About Haymarket Books

Haymarket Books is a radical, independent, nonprofit book publisher based in Chicago. Our mission is to publish books that contribute to struggles for social and economic justice. We strive to make our books a vibrant and organic part of social movements and the education and development of a critical, engaged, international left.

We take inspiration and courage from our namesakes, the Haymarket martyrs, who gave their lives fighting for a better world. Their 1886 struggle for the eight-hour day—which gave us May Day, the international workers' holiday—reminds workers around the world that ordinary people can organize and struggle for their own liberation. These struggles continue today across the globe—struggles against oppression, exploitation, poverty, and war.

Since our founding in 2001, Haymarket Books has published more than five hundred titles. Radically independent, we seek to drive a wedge into the risk-averse world of corporate book publishing. Our authors include Noam Chomsky, Arundhati Roy, Rebecca Solnit, Angela Y. Davis, Howard Zinn, Amy Goodman, Wallace Shawn, Mike Davis, Winona LaDuke, Ilan Pappé, Richard Wolff, Dave Zirin, Keeanga-Yamahtta Taylor, Nick Turse, Dahr Jamail, David Barsamian, Elizabeth Laird, Amira Hass, Mark Steel, Avi Lewis, Naomi Klein, and Neil Davidson. We are also the trade publishers of the acclaimed Historical Materialism Book Series and of Dispatch Books.

Also available from Haymarket Books

The American Socialist Movement, 1897–1912
Ira Kipnis

The Bending Cross: A Biography of Eugene Victor Debs
Ray Ginger, introduction by Mike Davis

Lucy Parsons: An American Revolutionary
Carolyn Ashbaugh

The Labor Wars: From the Molly Maguires to the Sit Downs
Sidney Lens

A Short History of the U.S. Working Class: From Colonial Times to the Twenty-First Century (Revolutionary Studies)
Paul Le Blanc